BEGINNING R

BEGINNING

R

THE STATISTICAL PROGRAMMING LANGUAGE

BEGINNING R

THE STATISTICAL PROGRAMMING LANGUAGE

Mark Gardener

John Wiley & Sons, Inc.

Beginning R: The Statistical Programming Language

Published by
John Wiley & Sons, Inc.
10475 Crosspoint Boulevard
Indianapolis, IN 46256
www.wiley.com

Published simultaneously in Canada

ISBN: 978-1-118-16430-3

ISBN: 978-1-118-22616-2 (ebk)

ISBN: 978-1-118-23937-7 (ebk)

ISBN: 978-1-118-26412-6 (ebk)

Manufactured in the United States of America

10 9 8 7 6 5 4 3 2 1

For general information on our other products and services please contact our Customer Care Department within the United States at (877) 762-2974, outside the United States at (317) 572-3993 or fax (317) 572-4002.

Wiley publishes in a variety of print and electronic formats and by print-on-demand. Some material included with standard print versions of this book may not be included in e-books or in print-on-demand. If this book refers to media such as a CD or DVD that is not included in the version you purchased, you may download this material at http://booksupport.wiley.com. For more information about Wiley products, visit www.wiley.com.

Library of Congress Control Number: 2012937909

It is much easier to be critical than to be correct.

— Benjamin Disraeli

CREDITS

EXECUTIVE EDITOR
Carol Long

PROJECT EDITOR
Victoria Swider

TECHNICAL EDITOR
Richard Rowe

PRODUCTION EDITOR
Kathleen Wisor

COPY EDITOR
Kim Cofer

EDITORIAL MANAGER
Mary Beth Wakefield

FREELANCER EDITORIAL MANAGER
Rosemarie Graham

ASSOCIATE DIRECTOR OF MARKETING
David Mayhew

MARKETING MANAGER
Ashley Zurcher

BUSINESS MANAGER
Amy Knies

PRODUCTION MANAGER
Tim Tate

VICE PRESIDENT AND EXECUTIVE GROUP PUBLISHER
Richard Swadley

VICE PRESIDENT AND EXECUTIVE PUBLISHER
Neil Edde

ASSOCIATE PUBLISHER
Jim Minatel

PROJECT COORDINATOR, COVER
Katie Crocker

COMPOSITOR
Craig Woods, Happenstance Type-O-Rama

PROOFREADER
James Saturnio, Word One

INDEXER
John Sleeva

COVER DESIGNER
LeAndra Young

COVER IMAGE
© iStock / Mark Wragg

ABOUT THE AUTHOR

MARK GARDENER (`http://www.gardenersown.co.uk`) is an ecologist, lecturer, and writer working in the UK. He has a passion for the natural world and for learning new things. Originally he worked in optics, but returned to education in 1996 and eventually gained his doctorate in ecology and evolutionary biology. This work involved a lot of data analysis, and he became interested in R as a tool to help in research. He is currently self-employed and runs courses in ecology, data analysis, and R for a variety of organizations. Mark lives in rural Devon with his wife Christine (a biochemist), and still enjoys the natural world and learning new things.

ACKNOWLEDGMENTS

FIRST OF ALL MY THANKS GO OUT TO the R project team and the many authors and programmers who work tirelessly to make this a peerless program. I would also like to thank my wife, Christine, who has had to put up with me during this entire process, and in many senses became an R-widow! Thanks to Wiley, for asking me to do this book, including Paul Reese, Carol Long, and Victoria Swider. I couldn't have done it without you. Thanks also to Richard Rowe, the technical reviewer, who first brought my attention to R and its compelling (and rather addictive) power.

Last but not least, thanks to the R community in general. I learned to use R largely by trial and error, and using the vast wealth of knowledge that is in this community. I hope that I have managed to distill this knowledge into a worthy package for future devotees of R.

— Mark Gardener

CONTENTS

INTRODUCTION

THIS BOOK IS ABOUT DATA ANALYSIS and the programming language called R. This is rapidly becoming the *de facto* standard among professionals, and is used in every conceivable discipline from science and medicine to business and engineering.

R is more than just a computer program; it is a statistical programming environment and language. R is free and open source and is therefore available to everyone with a computer. It is very powerful and flexible, but it is also unlike most of the computer programs you are likely used to. You have to type commands directly into the program to make it work for you. Because of this, and its complexity, R can be hard to get a grip on.

This book delves into the language of R and makes it accessible using simple data examples to explore its power and versatility. In learning how to "speak R," you will unlock its potential and gain better insights into tackling even the most complex of data analysis tasks.

WHO THIS BOOK IS FOR

This book is for anyone who needs to analyze any data, whatever their discipline or line of work. Whether you are in science, business, medicine, or engineering, you will have data to analyze and results to present. R is powerful and flexible and completely cross-platform. This means you can share data and results with anyone. R is backed by a huge project team, so being free does not mean being inferior!

If you are completely new to R, this book will enable you to get it and start to become familiar with it. There is no assumption that you know anything about the program to begin with. If you are already familiar with R, you will find this book a useful reference that you can call upon time and time again; the first chapter is largely concerned with installing R, so you may want to skip to Chapter 2.

This book is not about statistical analyses, so some familiarity with basic analytical methods is helpful (but not obligatory). The book deals with the means to make R work for you; this means learning the language of R rather than learning statistics. Once you are familiar with R you will be empowered to use it to undertake a huge variety of analytical tasks, more than can be conveniently packaged into a single book. R also produces presentation-quality graphics and this book leads you through the complexities of that.

WHAT THIS BOOK COVERS

R is a computer program and statistical programming language/environment. It allows a wide range of analytical methods to be used and produces presentation-quality graphics. This book covers the language of R, and leads you toward a better understanding of how to get R to do the things you need. There is less emphasis on the actual statistical tests; indeed, R is so flexible that the list of tests it can perform is far too large to be covered in an introductory book such as this. Rather, the aim is to become familiar with the language of R and to carry out some of the more commonly used statistical methods. In this way, you can strike out on your own and explore the full potential of R for yourself.

So, the focus is on the operation of R itself. Along the way you learn how to carry out a range of commonly used statistical methods, including analysis of variance (ANOVA) and linear regression, which are widely used in many fields and, therefore, important to know. You also learn a range of ways to produce a wide variety of graphics that should suit your needs.

This book covers most recent versions of R. The R program does change from time to time as new versions are released. However, most of the commands you will need to know have not changed, and even older (in computer terms) versions will work quite happily.

HOW THIS BOOK IS STRUCTURED

The book has a general progressive character, and later chapters tend to build on skills you learned earlier. Therefore if you are a beginner, you will probably find it most useful to start at the beginning and work your way through in a progressive manner. If you are a more seasoned user, you may want to use selected chapters as reference material, to refresh your skills.

No approach to learning R is universally adequate, but I have tried to provide the most logical path possible. For example, learning to produce graphics is very important, but unless you know what kinds of analyses you are likely to need to represent, making these graphs might seem a bit prosaic. Therefore, the main graphics chapter appears after some of the chapters on analysis.

In general terms, the book begins with notes on how to get and install R, and how to access the help system. Next you are introduced to the basics of data—how to get data into R, for example. After this you find out how to manipulate data, carry out some basic statistical analyses, and begin to tackle graphics. Later you learn some more advanced analytical methods and return to graphics. Finally, you look at ways to use R to create your own programs.

Each chapter begins with an overview of the topics you will learn. The text contains many examples and is written in a "copy me" style. Throughout the text, all the concepts are illustrated with simple examples. You can download the data from the companion website and follow along as you read (details on this are discussed shortly). The book contains a variety of activities that you are urged to follow; each is designed to help you with an important topic. The chapters all end with a series of exercises that help you to consolidate your learning (the solutions are in the appendix). Finally, the chapters end with a brief summary of what you learned and a table illustrating the topics and some key points, which are useful as reference material. Following is a brief description of each chapter.

Chapter 1: Introducing R: What It Is and How to Get It—In this chapter you see how to get R and install it on your computer. You also learn how to access the built-in help system and find out about additional packages of useful analytical routines that you can add to R.

Chapter 2: Starting Out: Becoming Familiar with R—This chapter builds some familiarity with working with R, beginning with some simple math and culminating in importing and making data objects that you can work with (and saving data to disk for later use).

Chapter 3: Starting Out: Working With Objects—This chapter deals with manipulating the data that you have created or imported. These are important tasks that underpin many of the later exercises. The skills you learn here will be put to use over and over again.

Chapter 4: Data: Descriptive Statistics and Tabulation—This chapter is all about summarizing data. Here you learn about basic summary methods, including cumulative statistics. You also learn how about cross-tabulation and how to create summary tables.

Chapter 5: Data: Distribution—In this chapter you look at visualizing data using graphical methods—for example, histograms—as well as mathematical ones. This chapter also includes some notes about random numbers and different types of distribution (for example, normal and Poisson).

Chapter 6: Simple Hypothesis Testing—In this chapter you learn how to carry out some basic statistical methods such as the t-test, correlation, and tests of association. Learning how to do these is helpful for when you have to carry out more complex analyses and also illustrates a range of techniques for using R.

Chapter 7: Introduction to Graphical Analysis—In this chapter you learn how to produce a range of graphs including bar charts, scatter plots, and pie charts. This is a "first look" at making graphs, but you return to this subject in Chapter 11, where you learn how to turn your graphs from merely adequate to stunning.

Chapter 8: Formula Notation and Complex Statistics—As your analyses become more complex, you need a more complex way to tell R what you want to do. This chapter is concerned with an important element of R: how to define complex situations. The chapter has two main parts. The first part shows how the formula notation can be used with simple situations. The second part uses an important analytical method, analysis of variance, as an illustration. The rest of the chapter is devoted to ANOVA. This is an important chapter because the ability to define complex analytical situations is something you will inevitably require at some point.

Chapter 9: Manipulating Data and Extracting Components—This chapter builds on the previous one. Now that you have seen how to define more complex analytical situations, you learn how to make and rearrange your data so that it can be analyzed more easily. This also builds on knowledge gained in Chapter 3. In many cases, when you have carried out an analysis you will need to extract data for certain groups; this chapter also deals with that, giving you more tools that you will need to carry out complex analyses easily.

Chapter 10: Regression (Linear Modeling)—This chapter is all about regression. It builds on earlier chapters and covers various aspects of this important analytical method. You learn how to carry out basic regression, as well as complex model building and curvilinear regression. It is also important because it illustrates some useful aspects of R (for example, how to dissect results). The later parts of the chapter deal with graphical aspects of regression, such as how to add lines of best fit and confidence intervals.

Chapter 11: More About Graphs—This chapter builds on the earlier chapter on graphics (Chapter 7) and also from the previous chapter on regression. It shows you how to produce more customized graphs from your data. For example, you learn how to add text to plots and axes, and how to make superscript and subscript text and mathematical symbols. You learn how to add legends to plots, and how to add error bars to bar charts or scatter plots. Finally, you learn how to export graphs to disk as high-quality graphics files, suitable for publication.

Chapter 12: Writing Your Own Scripts: Beginning to Program—In this chapter you learn how to start producing customized functions and simple scripts that can automate your workflow, and make complex and repetitive tasks a lot easier.

WHAT YOU NEED TO USE THIS BOOK

The only things you need to use this book are a computer and enthusiasm! The R program works on any operating system, so you can use Windows, Macintosh, or Linux (any version). R even works quite adequately on ancient (in computer terms) computers, so you do not need anything particularly hi-spec. An Internet connection is required at some point because you need to get R from the R-project website. However, it is perfectly possible to download the installation files onto a separate computer and transfer them to your working machine.

If you already have a version of R, it is not necessary to get the latest version. R is continually changing and improving, but the older versions of R will most likely work with this book because the basic command set has changed relatively little. Having said that, I suggest you update your version of R if it is older than 2009.

CONVENTIONS

To help you get the most from the text and keep track of what's happening, we've used a number of conventions throughout the book.

The commands you need to type into R and the output you get from R are shown in a monospace font. Each example that shows lines that are typed by the user begins with the > symbol, which mimics the R cursor like so:

```
> help()
```

Lines that begin with something other than the > symbol represent the output from R (but look out for typed lines that are long and spread over more than one line), so in the following example the first line was typed by the user and the second line is the result:

```
> data1
 [1] 3 5 7 5 3 2 6 8 5 6 9
```

TRY IT OUT

The *Try It Out* is an exercise you should work through, following the text in the book.

1. They usually consist of a set of steps.
2. Each step has a number.
3. Follow the steps through with your copy of the database.

How It Works

After each *Try It Out*, the code you've typed is explained in detail.

WARNING *Boxes with a warning icon like this one hold important, not-to-be forgotten information that is directly relevant to the surrounding text.*

NOTE *The pencil icon indicates notes, tips, hints, tricks, and asides to the current discussion.*

As for styles in the text:

- We *highlight* new terms and important words when we introduce them.
- We show keyboard strokes like this: Ctrl+A.
- We show filenames, URLs, and code within the text like so: `persistence.properties`.
- We present code in two different ways:

```
We use a monofont type with no highlighting for most code examples.
We use bold to emphasize code that's particularly important in the present context.
```

SOURCE CODE

As you work through the examples in this book, you may choose either to type in all the data and code manually or to use the source code and data object files that accompany the book. All of the data and source code used in this book is available for download at `http://www.wrox.com`. You will find the data sets that you need for each example activity are accompanied by a download icon and note indicating the name of the data file so you know it's available for download and can easily locate it in the download file. Once at the site, simply locate the book's title (either by using the Search box or by using one of the title lists) and click the Download Code link on the book's detail page to obtain all the source code for the book.

There will only be one file to download and it is called `Beginning.RData`. This one file contains all the example datasets and scripts you need for the whole book. Once you have the file on your computer you can load it into R by one of several methods:

- For Windows or Mac you can drag the `Beginning.RData` file icon onto the R program icon; this will open R if it is not already running and load the data. If R is already open, the data will be appended to anything you already have in R; otherwise only the data in the file will be loaded.
- If you have Windows or Macintosh you can also load the file using menu commands or use a command typed into R:
  - For Windows use File ➪ Load Workspace, or type the following command in R:

    ```
    > load(file.choose())
    ```

  - For Mac use Workspace ➪ Load Workspace File, or type the following command in R (same as in Windows):

    ```
    > load(file.choose())
    ```

- If you have Linux then you can use the `load()` command but must specify the filename (in quotes) exactly, for example:

  ```
  > load("Beginning.RData")
  ```

The `Beginning.RData` file must be in your default working directory and if it is not you must specify the location as part of the filename.

***NOTE** Because many books have similar titles, you may find it easiest to search by ISBN; this book's ISBN is 978-1-118-164303.*

Alternatively, you can go to the main Wrox code download page at `http://www.wrox.com/dynamic/books/download.aspx` to see the code available for this book and all other Wrox books.

ERRATA

We make every effort to ensure that there are no errors in the text or in the code. However, no one is perfect, and mistakes do occur. If you find an error in one of our books, like a spelling mistake or faulty piece of code, we would be very grateful for your feedback. By sending in errata you may save another reader hours of frustration and at the same time you will be helping us provide even higher quality information.

To find the errata page for this book, go to `http://www.wrox.com` and locate the title using the Search box or one of the title lists. Then, on the book details page, click the Book Errata link. On this page you can view all errata that has been submitted for this book and posted by Wrox editors.

***NOTE** A complete book list including links to each book's errata is also available at* `www.wrox.com/misc-pages/booklist.shtml`.

If you don't spot "your" error on the Book Errata page, go to `www.wrox.com/contact/techsupport.shtml` and complete the form there to send us the error you have found. We'll check the information and, if appropriate, post a message to the book's errata page and fix the problem in subsequent editions of the book.

P2P.WROX.COM

For author and peer discussion, join the P2P forums at `p2p.wrox.com`. The forums are a web-based system for you to post messages relating to Wrox books and related technologies and interact with other readers and technology users. The forums offer a subscription feature to e-mail you topics of interest of your choosing when new posts are made to the forums. Wrox authors, editors, other industry experts, and your fellow readers are present on these forums.

At `http://p2p.wrox.com` you will find a number of different forums that will help you not only as you read this book, but also as you develop your own applications. To join the forums, just follow these steps:

1. Go to `p2p.wrox.com` and click the Register link.
2. Read the terms of use and click Agree.
3. Complete the required information to join as well as any optional information you wish to provide and click Submit.
4. You will receive an e-mail with information describing how to verify your account and complete the joining process.

***NOTE** You can read messages in the forums without joining P2P but in order to post your own messages, you must join.*

Once you join, you can post new messages and respond to messages other users post. You can read messages at any time on the web. If you would like to have new messages from a particular forum e-mailed to you, click the Subscribe to this Forum icon by the forum name in the forum listing.

For more information about how to use the Wrox P2P, be sure to read the P2P FAQs for answers to questions about how the forum software works as well as many common questions specific to P2P and Wrox books. To read the FAQs, click the FAQ link on any P2P page.

1

Introducing R: What It Is and How to Get It

WHAT YOU WILL LEARN IN THIS CHAPTER:

- Discovering what R is
- How to get the R program
- How to install R on your computer
- How to start running the R program
- How to use the help system and find help from other sources
- How to get additional libraries of commands

R is more than just a program that does statistics. It is a sophisticated computer language and environment for statistical computing and graphics. R is available from the R-Project for Statistical Computing website (`www.r-project.org`), and following is some of its introductory material:

> *R is an open-source (GPL) statistical environment modeled after S and S-Plus. The S language was developed in the late 1980s at AT&T labs. The R project was started by Robert Gentleman and Ross Ihaka (hence the name, R) of the Statistics Department of the University of Auckland in 1995. It has quickly gained a widespread audience. It is currently maintained by the R core-development team, a hard-working, international team of volunteer developers. The R project webpage is the main site for information on R. At this site are directions for obtaining the software, accompanying packages, and other sources of documentation.*

R is a powerful statistical program but it is first and foremost a programming language. Many routines have been written for R by people all over the world and made freely available from the R project website as "packages." However, the basic installation (for Linux, Windows or Mac) contains a powerful set of tools for most purposes.

Because R is a computer language, it functions slightly differently from most of the programs that users are familiar with. You have to type in commands, which are evaluated by the program and then executed. This sounds a bit daunting to many users, but the R language is easy to pick up and a lot of help is available. It is possible to copy and paste in commands from other applications (for example: word processors, spreadsheets, or web browsers) and this facility is very useful, especially if you keep notes as you learn. Additionally, the Windows and Macintosh versions of R have a graphical user interface (GUI) that can help with some of the basic tasks.

WARNING *Beware when copying and pasting commands into R from other applications; R can't handle certain auto formatting characters such as en-dashes or smart quotes.*

R can deal with a huge variety of mathematical and statistical tasks, and many users find that the basic installation of the program does everything they need. However, many specialized routines have been written by other users and these libraries of additional tools are available from the R website. If you need to undertake a particular type of analysis, there is a very good chance that someone before you also wanted to do that very thing and has written a package that you can download to allow you to do it.

R is open source, which means that it is continually being reviewed and improved. R runs on most computers—installations are available for Windows, Macintosh, and Linux. It also has good interoperability, so if you work on one computer and switch to another you can take your work with you.

R handles complex statistical approaches as easily as more simple ones. Therefore once you know the basics of the R language, you can tackle complex analyses as easily as simple ones (as usual it is the interpretation of results that can be the really hard bit).

GETTING THE HANG OF R

R is unlike most current computer programs in that you must type commands into the console window to carry out most tasks you require. Throughout the text, the use of these commands is illustrated, which is indeed the point of the book.

Where a command is illustrated in its basic form, you will see a fixed width font to mimic the R display like so:

```
help.start()
```

When the use of a particular command is illustrated, you will see the user-typed input illustrated by beginning the lines with the > character, which mimics the cursor line in the R console window like so:

```
> data1 = c(3, 5, 7, 5, 3, 2, 6, 8, 5, 6, 9)
```

Lines of text resulting from your actions are shown without the cursor character, once again mimicking the output that you would see from R itself:

```
> data1
 [1] 3 5 7 5 3 2 6 8 5 6 9
```

So, in the preceding example the first line was typed by the user and resulted in the output shown in the second line. Keep these conventions in mind as you are reading this chapter and they will come into play as soon as you have R installed and are ready to begin using it!

The R Website

The R website at `www.r-project.org` is a good place to visit to obtain the R program. It is also a good place to look for help items and general documentation as well as additional libraries of routines. If you use Windows or a Mac, you will need to visit the site to download the R program and install it. You can also find installation files for many Linux versions on the R website.

The R website is split into several parts; links to each section are on the main page of the site. The two most useful for beginners are the Documentation and Download sections.

In the Documentation section (see Figure 1-1) a Manuals link takes you to many documents contributed to the site by various users. Most of these are in HTML and PDF format. You can access these and a variety of help guides under Manuals ➪ Contributed Documentation. These are especially useful for helping the new user to get started. Additionally, a large FAQ section takes you to a list that can help you find answers to many question you might have. There is also a Wiki, and although this is still a work in progress, it is a good place to look for information on installing R on Linux systems.

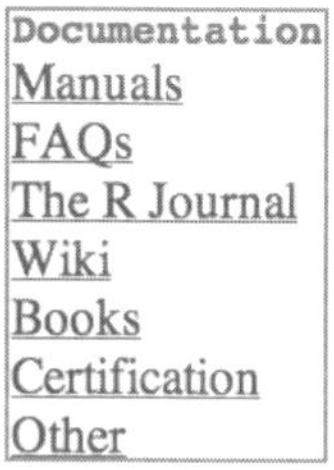

Documentation
Manuals
FAQs
The R Journal
Wiki
Books
Certification
Other

FIGURE 1-1

In the Downloads section you will find the links from which you can download R. The following section goes into more detail on how to do this.

Downloading and Installing R from CRAN

The Comprehensive R Archive Network (CRAN) is a network of websites that host the R program and that mirror the original R website. The benefit of having this network of websites is improved download speeds. For all intents and purposes, CRAN is the R website and holds downloads (including old versions of software) and documentation (e.g. manuals, FAQs). When you perform searches for R-related topics on the internet, adding CRAN (or R) to your search terms increases your results. To get started downloading R, you'll want to perform the following steps:

1. Visit the main R web page (`www.r-project.org`); you see a Getting Started box with a link to download R (see Figure 1-2). Click that link and you are directed to select a local CRAN mirror site from which to download R.

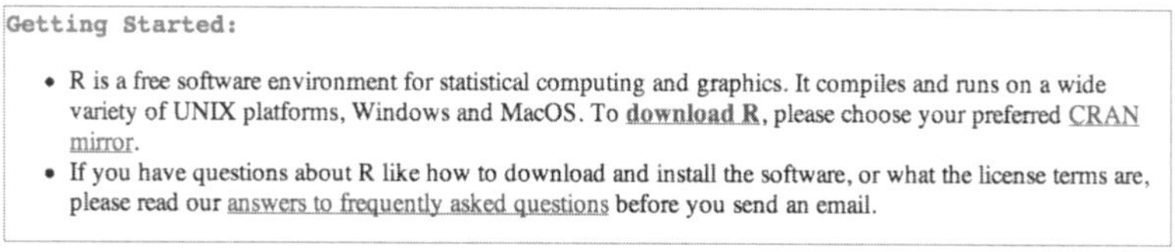

Getting Started:

- R is a free software environment for statistical computing and graphics. It compiles and runs on a wide variety of UNIX platforms, Windows and MacOS. To **download R**, please choose your preferred CRAN mirror.
- If you have questions about R like how to download and install the software, or what the license terms are, please read our answers to frequently asked questions before you send an email.

FIGURE 1-2

2. The starting page of the CRAN website appears once you have selected your preferred mirror site. This page has a Software section on the left with several links. Choose the R Binaries link to install R on your computer (see Figure 1-3). You can also click the link to Packages, which contains libraries of additional routines. However, you can install these from within R so you can just ignore the Packages link for now. The Other link goes to a page that lists software available on CRAN other than the R base distribution and regular contributed extension packages. This link is also unnecessary for right now and can be ignored as well.

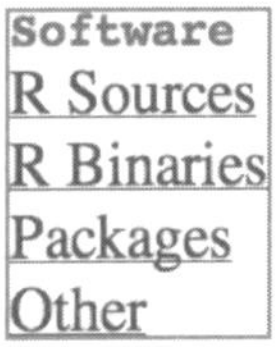

Software
R Sources
R Binaries
Packages
Other

FIGURE 1-3

3. Once you click the R Binaries link you move to a simple directory containing folders for a variety of operating system (see Figure 1-4). Select the appropriate operating system on which you will be downloading R and follow the link to a page containing more information and the installation files that you require.

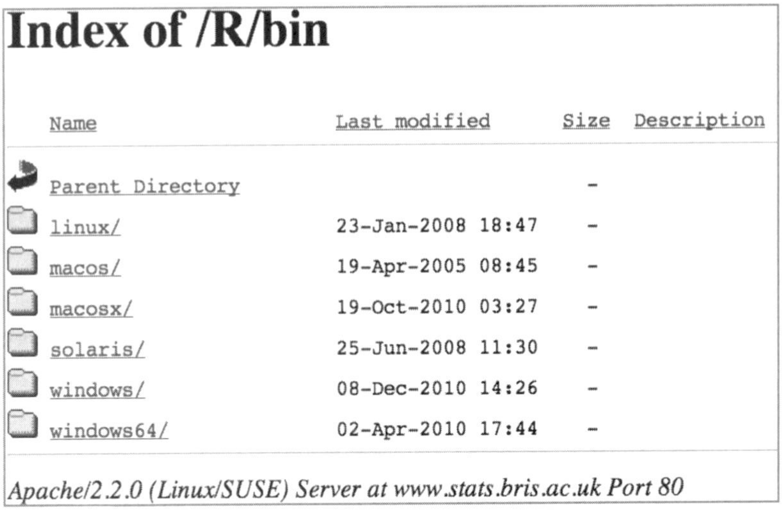

Index of /R/bin

Name	Last modified	Size	Description
Parent Directory		-	
linux/	23-Jan-2008 18:47	-	
macos/	19-Apr-2005 08:45	-	
macosx/	19-Oct-2010 03:27	-	
solaris/	25-Jun-2008 11:30	-	
windows/	08-Dec-2010 14:26	-	
windows64/	02-Apr-2010 17:44	-	

Apache/2.2.0 (Linux/SUSE) Server at www.stats.bris.ac.uk Port 80

FIGURE 1-4

The details for individual operating systems vary, so the following sections are split into instructions for each of Windows, Macintosh, and Linux.

Installing R on Your Windows Computer

The install files for Windows come bundled in an `.exe` file, which you can download from the `windows` folder (refer to Figure 1-4). Downloading the `.exe` file is straightforward (see Figure 1-5), and you can install R simply by double-clicking the file once it is on your computer.

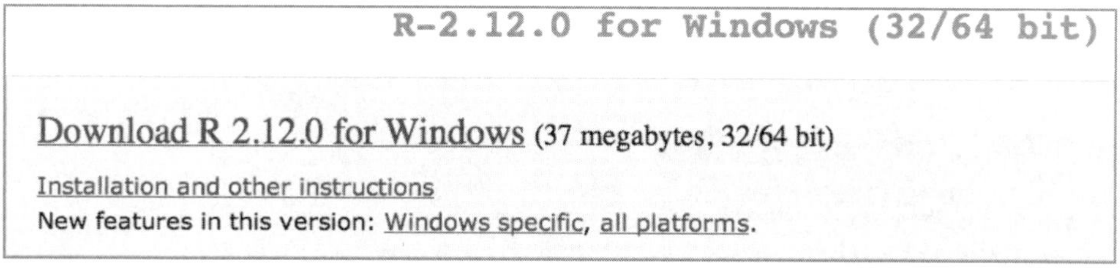

R-2.12.0 for Windows (32/64 bit)

Download R 2.12.0 for Windows (37 megabytes, 32/64 bit)

Installation and other instructions

New features in this version: Windows specific, all platforms.

FIGURE 1-5

Run the installer with all the default settings and when it is done you will have R installed.

Versions of Windows post XP require some of additional steps to make R work properly. For Vista or later you need to alter the properties of the R program so that it runs with Administrator privileges. To do so, follow these steps:

1. Click the Windows button (this used to be labeled Start).
2. Select Programs.
3. Choose the R folder.
4. Right-click the R program icon to see an options menu (see Figure 1-6).

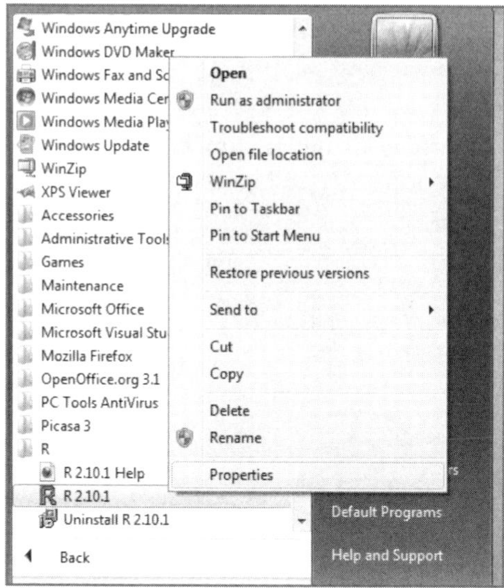

FIGURE 1-6

5. Select Properties from the menu. You will then see a new options window.

6. Under the Compatibility tab, tick the box in the Privilege Level section (see Figure 1-7) and click OK.

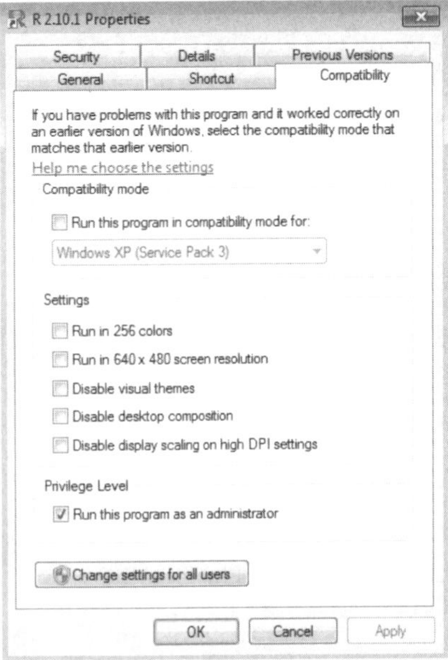

FIGURE 1-7

7. Run R by clicking the Programs menu, shortcut, or quick-launch icon like any other program. If the User Account Control window appears (see Figure 1-8), select Yes and R runs as normal.

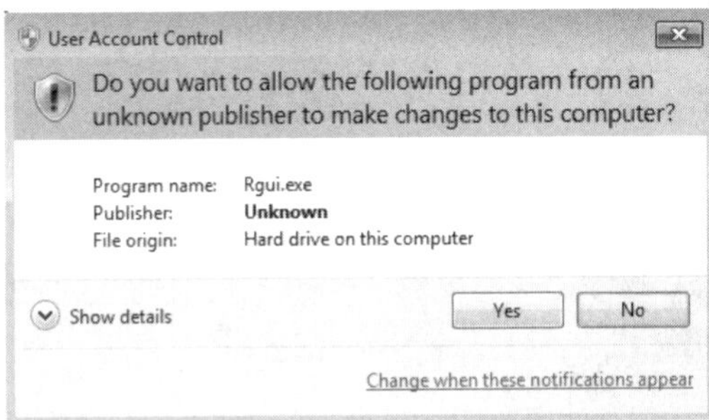

FIGURE 1-8

Now R is set to run with administrator access and will function correctly. This is important, as you see later. R will save your data items and a history of the commands you used to the disk and it cannot do this without the appropriate access level.

Installing R on Your Macintosh Computer

The install files for OS X come bundled in a DMG file, which you can download from the `macosx` folder (refer to Figure 1-4).

Once the file has downloaded it may open as a disk image or not (depending how your system is set up). Once the DMG file opens you can double-click the installer file and installation will proceed (see Figure 1-9). Installation is fairly simple and no special options are required. Once installed, you can run R from Applications and place it in the dock like any other program.

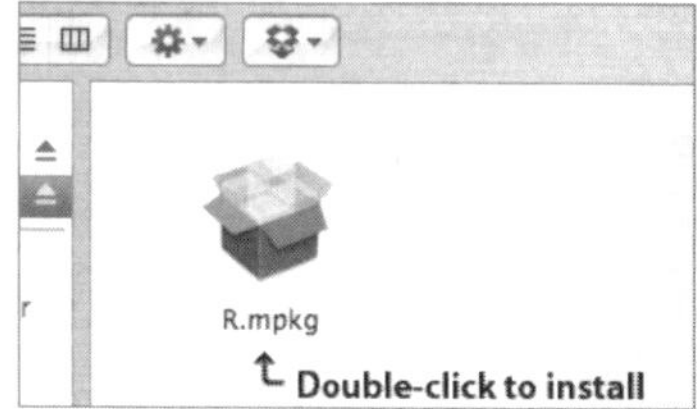

FIGURE 1-9

Installing R on Your Linux Computer

If you are using a Linux OS, R runs through the Terminal program. Downloadable install files are available for many Linux systems on the R website (see Figure 1-10). The website also contains instructions for installation on several versions of Linux. Many Linux systems also support a direct installation via the Terminal.

Index of /R/bin/linux

Name	Last modified	Size	Description
Parent Directory		-	
debian/	18-Oct-2010 17:16	-	
redhat/	25-Nov-2009 17:01	-	
suse/	18-Dec-2009 10:11	-	
ubuntu/	11-Oct-2010 06:06	-	

Apache/2.2.0 (Linux/SUSE) Server at www.stats.bris.ac.uk Port 80

FIGURE 1-10

The major Linux systems allow you to install the R program directly from the Terminal, and R files are kept as part of their software repositories. These repositories are not always very up-to-date however, so if you want to install the very latest version of R, look on the CRAN website for instructions and an appropriate install file. The exact command to install direct from the Terminal varies slightly from system to system, but you will not go far wrong if you open the Terminal and type **R** into it. If R is not installed (the most likely scenario), the Terminal may well give you the command you need to get it (see Figure 1-11)!

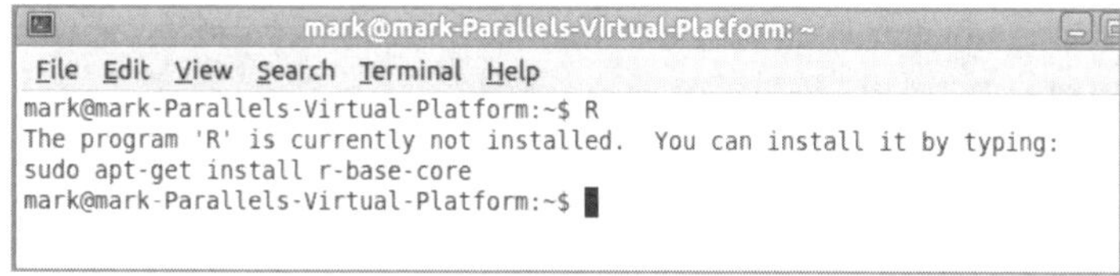

FIGURE 1-11

In general, a command along the following lines will usually do the trick:

```
sudo apt-get install r-base-core
```

In Ubuntu 10.10, for example, this installs everything you need to get started. In other systems you may need two elements to install, like so:

```
sudo apt-get install r-base r-base-dev
```

The basic R program and its components are built from the `r-base` part. For many purposes this is enough, but to gain access to additional libraries of routines the `r-base-dev` part is needed. Once you run these commands you will connect to the Internet and the appropriate files will be downloaded and installed.

Once R is installed it can be run through the Terminal program, which is found in the Accessories part of the Applications menu. In Linux there is no GUI, so all the commands must be typed into the Terminal window.

RUNNING THE R PROGRAM

Once R is installed you can run it in a variety of ways:

- In Windows the program works like any other—you may have a desktop shortcut, a quick launch icon, or simply get to it via the Start button and the regular program list.
- On a Macintosh the program is located in the Applications folder and you can drag this to the dock to create a launcher or create an alias in the usual manner.
- On Linux the program is launched via the Terminal program, which is located in the Accessories section of the Applications menu.

Once the R program starts up you are presented with the main input window and a short introductory message that appears a little different on each OS:

- In Windows a few menus are available at the top as shown in Figure 1-12.

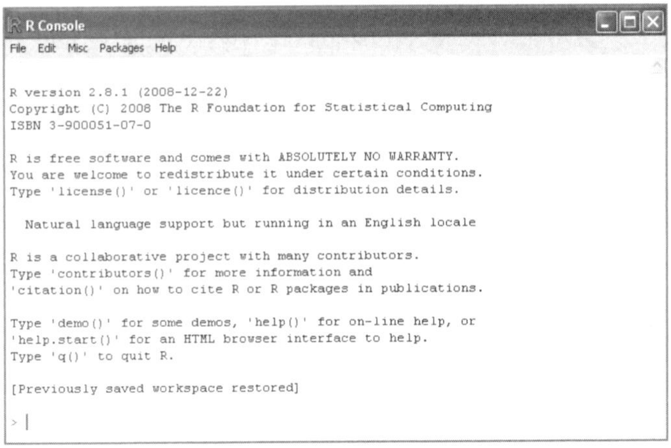

```
R Console
File Edit Misc Packages Help

R version 2.8.1 (2008-12-22)
Copyright (C) 2008 The R Foundation for Statistical Computing
ISBN 3-900051-07-0

R is free software and comes with ABSOLUTELY NO WARRANTY.
You are welcome to redistribute it under certain conditions.
Type 'license()' or 'licence()' for distribution details.

  Natural language support but running in an English locale

R is a collaborative project with many contributors.
Type 'contributors()' for more information and
'citation()' on how to cite R or R packages in publications.

Type 'demo()' for some demos, 'help()' for on-line help, or
'help.start()' for an HTML browser interface to help.
Type 'q()' to quit R.

[Previously saved workspace restored]

> |
```

FIGURE 1-12

➤ On the Macintosh OS X, the welcome message is the same (see Figure 1-13). In this case you also have some menus available and they are broadly similar to those in the Windows version. You also see a few icons; these enable you to perform a few tasks but are not especially useful. Under these icons is a search box, which is useful as an alternative to typing in help commands (you look at getting help shortly).

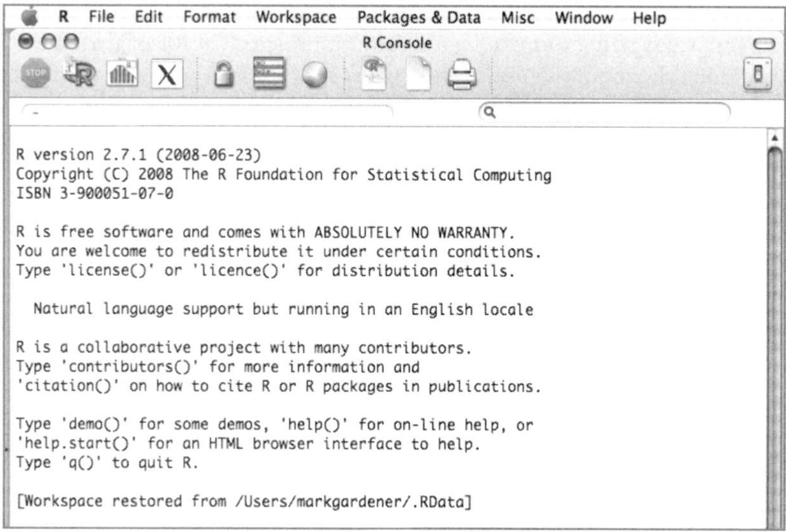

FIGURE 1-13

➤ In Linux systems there are no icons and the menu items you see relate to the Terminal program rather than R itself (see Figure 1-14).

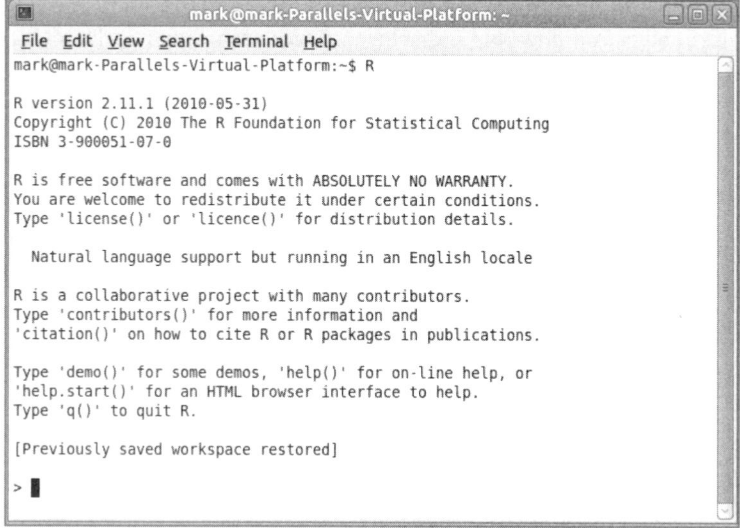

FIGURE 1-14

R is a computer language, and like any other language you must learn the vocabulary and the grammar to make yourself understood and to carry out the tasks you want. Getting to know where help is available is a good starting point, and that is the subject of the next section.

FINDING YOUR WAY WITH R

Finding help when you are starting out can be a daunting prospect. A lot of material is available for help with R and tracking down the useful information can take a while. (Of course, this book is a good starting point!) In the following sections you see the most efficient ways to access some of the help that is available, including how to access additional libraries that you can use to deal with the tasks you have.

Getting Help via the CRAN Website and the Internet

The R website is a good place to find material that supports your learning of R. Under the Manuals link are several manuals available in HTML or as PDF. You'll also find some useful beginner's guides in the Contributed Documentation section. Different authors take different approaches, and you may find one suits you better than another. Try a few and see how you get on. Additionally, preferences will change as your command of the system develops. There is also a Wiki on the R website that is a good reference forum, which is continually updated.

NOTE *Remember that if you are searching for a few ideas on the internet, you can add the word CRAN to your search terms in your favorite search engine (adding R is also useful). This will generally come up with plenty of options.*

The Help Command in R

R contains a lot of built-in help, and how this is displayed varies according to which OS you are using and the options (if any) that you set. The basic command to bring up help is:

```
help(topic)
```

Simply replace `topic` with the name of the item you want help on. You can also save a bit of typing by prefacing the `topic` with a question mark, like so:

```
?topic
```

You can also access the help system via your web browser by typing:

```
help.start()
```

This brings up the top-level index page where you can use the Search Engine & Keywords hyperlink to find what you need. This works for all the different operating systems. Of course, you need to know what command you are looking for to begin with. If you are not quite sure, you can use the following command:

```
apropos('partword')
```

This searches through the help files for matches to the word you typed, you replace `'partword'` with the text you want to search for. Note that unlike the previous `help()` command you do need the quotes (single or double quotes are fine as long as they match).

Help for Windows Users

The Windows default help generally works fine (see Figure 1-15), but the Index and Search tabs only work within the section you are in, and it is not possible to get to the top level in the search hierarchy. If you return to the main command window and type in another help command, a new window opens so it is not possible to scroll back through entries unless they are in the same section.

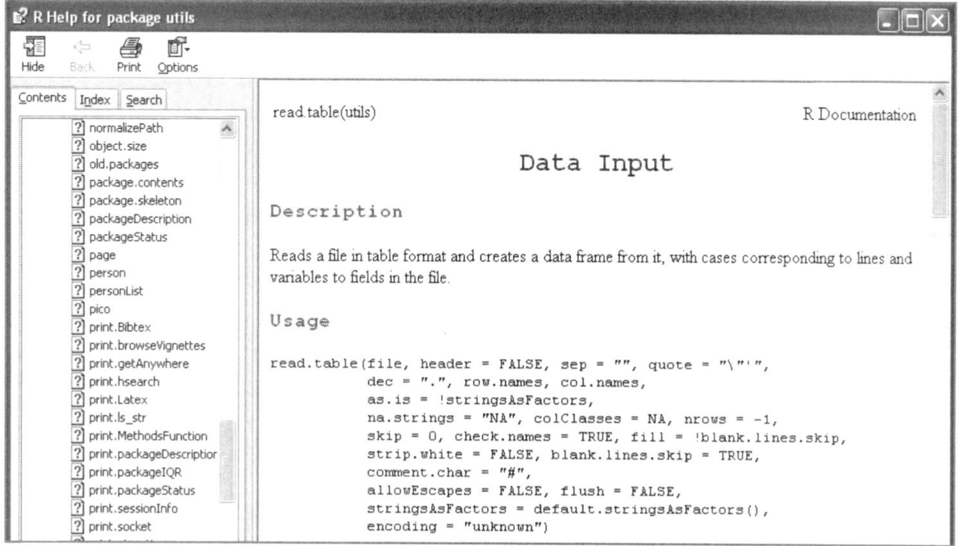

FIGURE 1-15

Once you are done with your help window, you can close it by clicking the red X button.

Help for Macintosh Users

In OS X the default help appears in a separate window as HTML text (see Figure 1-16). The help window acts like a browser and you can use the arrow buttons to return to previous topics if you follow hyperlinks. You can also type search terms into the search box.

Scrolling to the foot of the help entry enables you to jump to the index for that section (Figure 1-17). Once at the index you can jump further up the hierarchy to reach other items.

The top level you can reach is identical to the HTML version of the help that you get if you type the `help.start()` command (see Figure 1-18), except that it is in a dedicated help window rather than your browser.

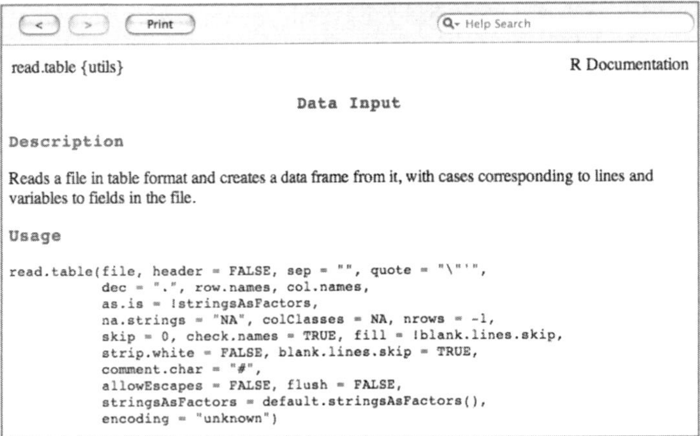

read.table {utils} R Documentation

Data Input

Description

Reads a file in table format and creates a data frame from it, with cases corresponding to lines and variables to fields in the file.

Usage

```
read.table(file, header = FALSE, sep = "", quote = "\"'",
           dec = ".", row.names, col.names,
           as.is = !stringsAsFactors,
           na.strings = "NA", colClasses = NA, nrows = -1,
           skip = 0, check.names = TRUE, fill = !blank.lines.skip,
           strip.white = FALSE, blank.lines.skip = TRUE,
           comment.char = "#",
           allowEscapes = FALSE, flush = FALSE,
           stringsAsFactors = default.stringsAsFactors(),
           encoding = "unknown")
```

FIGURE 1-16

See Also

The *R Data Import/Export* manual.

scan, type.convert, read.fwf for reading *fixed width formatted* input; write.table; data.frame.

count.fields can be useful to determine problems with reading files which result in reports of incorrect record lengths.

[Package *utils* version 2.7.1 Index]

FIGURE 1-17

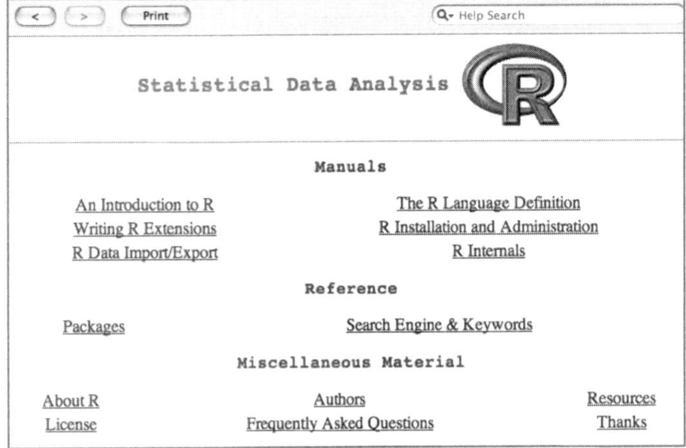

FIGURE 1-18

Once you are finished you can close the window in the usual manner by clicking the red button. If you return to the main command window and type another help item, the original window alters to display the new help. You can return to the previous entries using the arrow buttons at the top of the help window.

Help for Linux Users

Help in Linux is displayed by default as plain text and appears in the Terminal window, temporarily blotting out what was displayed previously (see Figure 1-19).

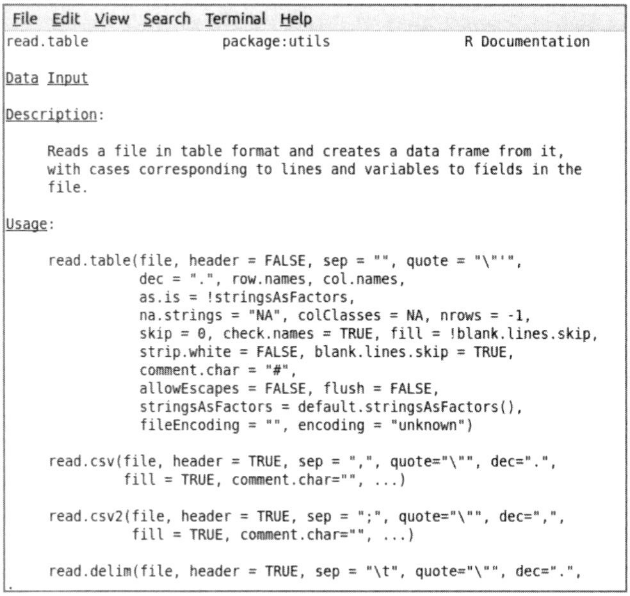

```
File Edit View Search Terminal Help
read.table               package:utils               R Documentation

Data Input

Description:

     Reads a file in table format and creates a data frame from it,
     with cases corresponding to lines and variables to fields in the
     file.

Usage:

     read.table(file, header = FALSE, sep = "", quote = "\"'",
                dec = ".", row.names, col.names,
                as.is = !stringsAsFactors,
                na.strings = "NA", colClasses = NA, nrows = -1,
                skip = 0, check.names = TRUE, fill = !blank.lines.skip,
                strip.white = FALSE, blank.lines.skip = TRUE,
                comment.char = "#",
                allowEscapes = FALSE, flush = FALSE,
                stringsAsFactors = default.stringsAsFactors(),
                fileEncoding = "", encoding = "unknown")

     read.csv(file, header = TRUE, sep = ",", quote="\"", dec=".",
              fill = TRUE, comment.char="", ...)

     read.csv2(file, header = TRUE, sep = ";", quote="\"", dec=",",
               fill = TRUE, comment.char="", ...)

     read.delim(file, header = TRUE, sep = "\t", quote="\"", dec=".",
```

FIGURE 1-19

Once the topic is displayed you can scroll down (and back up) using the down and up arrows. When you are finished, hit the Q key and return to the Terminal window.

Help For All Users

A good way to explore the help features of R however, and the way that is universal to all OS is to use the HTML version of the system. Although at this point you will not really know any R commands, it is a useful time to look at a specific command to illustrate the help feature. In this example you look at the `mean()` command. As you may guess, this determines the arithmetic mean of a set of numbers. Try the following:

1. First, type in the following command:

   ```
   help.start()
   ```

2. This brings up the main help pages in your default browser. Click the `Packages` link and then click the `base` link. Navigate your way down to the `mean()` command and look at the entry there.
3. Navigate back to the first page and use the `Search Engine` link to search for the `mean` command. You will see several entries, depending on which additional packages are installed.
4. Select the `base::mean` entry in this case, which brings up help for the command to determine the arithmetic mean.

Anatomy of a Help Item in R

Knowing how to get the most out of the help files is very handy and a good way to learn more about R and how it works. Take a look at a specific example of a help window here using the `mean()` command again. You start by bringing up the help item for this command. You can type one of the following:

```
help(mean)
?mean
```

Alternatively, you might have used the HTML help and put this into the search box. In any event you will get a help entry that looks like Figure 1-20. The entry begins with the name of the command, followed by the name of the package in curly brackets where the command is found.

mean {base} R Documentation

Arithmetic Mean

Description

Generic function for the (trimmed) arithmetic mean.

FIGURE 1-20

In Figure 1-20 you see `mean{base}`. This tells you that the `mean()` command is found in the `base` package. This entry becomes more useful when you come to use commands and routines that are not part of the standard installation of R, which you will look at shortly.

At the top of your help entry you also see a title and a brief description of what the command does. The next part tells you how to use the command in detail (see Figure 1-21) and the syntax (that is, how to write out the command). The syntax is important because you need to ensure that when you type something, R "knows" exactly what you want to do.

Usage

```
mean(x, ...)

## Default S3 method:
mean(x, trim = 0, na.rm = FALSE, ...)
```

Arguments

`x`	An R object. Currently there are methods for numeric data frames, numeric vectors and dates. A complex vector is allowed for `trim = 0`, only.
`trim`	the fraction (0 to 0.5) of observations to be trimmed from each end of `x` before the mean is computed. Values of trim outside that range are taken as the nearest endpoint.
`na.rm`	a logical value indicating whether `NA` values should be stripped before the computation proceeds.
`...`	further arguments passed to or from other methods.

Value

For a data frame, a named vector with the appropriate method being applied column by column.
If `trim` is zero (the default), the arithmetic mean of the values in `x` is computed, as a numeric or complex vector of length one. If `x` is not logical (coerced to numeric), integer, numeric or complex, `NA` is returned, with a warning.
If `trim` is non-zero, a symmetrically trimmed mean is computed with a fraction of `trim` observations deleted from each end before the mean is computed.

FIGURE 1-21

The help entry shows what arguments are required as part of the command (think of them as additional instructions) and gives a bit of explanation. The bottom part of a help entry typically gives some references (see Figure 1-22) and some other related commands. In Windows or Macintosh, these are hyperlinks so you can click them and jump to their help entries. In Linux the help is plain text so there are no hyperlinks. If, however, you used `help.start()` and brought up the HTML help system in your web browser, the hyperlinks do appear.

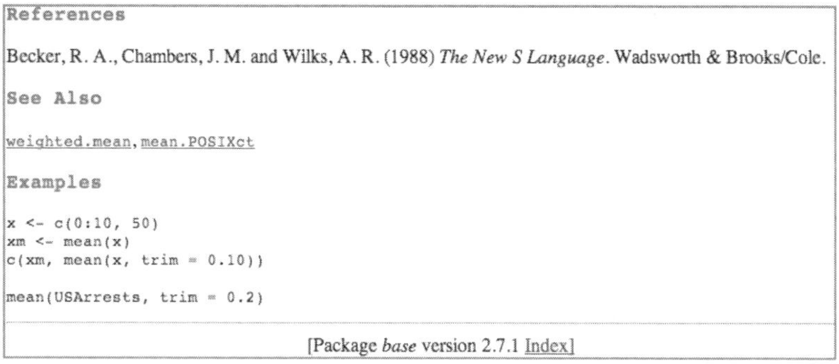

References

Becker, R. A., Chambers, J. M. and Wilks, A. R. (1988) *The New S Language*. Wadsworth & Brooks/Cole.

See Also

weighted.mean, mean.POSIXct

Examples

```
x <- c(0:10, 50)
xm <- mean(x)
c(xm, mean(x, trim = 0.10))

mean(USArrests, trim = 0.2)
```

[Package *base* version 2.7.1 Index]

FIGURE 1-22

At the very end you see some examples of how to use the command "in action." These examples can be copied to the clipboard and pasted into the main command console so you can see what they do. Sometimes these examples can be a bit tricky to interpret, but as you learn more about R you will be able to decipher how they work and what they do more easily. The example of the `mean()` command is simple, but even this might seem a bit daunting at this stage!

The first line of the examples in Figure 1-22 is creating a series of numbers so that you have something to make a mean of. Here R makes an item called `x`, which comprises the values 0 to 10 with a 50 at the end. The next line uses the `mean` command in its simplest form and generates a standard mean from the `x` item. The result is called `xm`. The third line takes the result of your mean (`xm`) and also makes a new mean using the `trim` argument. Try typing the commands from the example in the help entry yourself or copy and paste from R. The commands look like this:

```
> x <- c(0:10, 50)
> xm <- mean(x)
> c(xm, mean(x, trim = 0.10))
```

You should see two values as the result:

```
[1] 8.75 5.50
```

The first (8.75) is the mean of the series of values and the second (5.50) is the trimmed mean, a way of knocking off extreme values.

The final example line takes a trimmed mean (a bit more trim, using a larger trim value of 0.2 rather than the 0.1 used before) of an example data set called `USArrests`. R contains a lot of built-in example data; these data are often used for examples and you can access them yourself quite easily. To see what the `USArrests` data looks like type:

```
USArrests
```

Note that R is case sensitive and that you need to type the name exactly as it appears here. By opening a simple help entry, reading through it carefully, and looking at the examples, you can learn a lot about how R works and what you are able to do with it.

COMMAND PACKAGES

The R program is built from a series of modules, called *packages*. These packages are libraries of commands that undertake various functions. When you first start R several packages are loaded on your computer and become ready for use. You can see what is available by using the `search()` command like so:

```
> search()
 [1] ".GlobalEnv"        "tools:RGUI"         "package:stats"      "package:graphics"
 [5] "package:grDevices" "package:utils"      "package:datasets"   "package:methods"
 [9] "Autoloads"         "package:base"
```

Here you can see, for example, no less than seven packages; these are loaded and start to carry out the most basic and important functions in R. Learning how to deal with these packages is useful, because you may want to add extra analytical routines to your installation of R to extend its capabilities.

Standard Command Packages

When you use the `search()` command you can see what packages are loaded and ready for use. You can see, for example, the `graphics` package, which carries out many of the routines required to create graphs.

Several other packages are ready-installed but not automatically loaded and immediately available. For example, the `splines` package contains routines for smoothing curves, but is not automatically loaded. To see what packages are available you can type:

```
installed.packages()
```

The output can be quite long, especially if you have downloaded additional packages to your version of R. Running and manipulating packages is examined shortly, but first you should read the next section where you will consider additional packages and what they might do for you.

What Extra Packages Can Do for You

The basic installation of R provides a wealth of commands that carry out many of the tasks that you might need. However, it cannot do everything—there may well be occasions when you need to run a particular type of analysis and the commands you need are not available. Because of the way R is put together it is possible to create specialist libraries of commands that can be bolted on whenever required. Many such packages are available from the CRAN website.

If you need to conduct a particular analysis and find that the basic installation of R does not have appropriate commands available, there is every chance that someone before you has come across the same problem. The CRAN website contains more than 2,600 additional packages that are available to carry out many extra "things" that were not included in the basic installation of R.

You can see an entire list of these additional packages by going to the CRAN website and clicking the Packages hyperlink. There are a lot, so browsing by name is going to take quite a while. One way to see what types of thing are available is to use the CRAN Task Views link. This enables you to browse by topic and highlights the sorts of thing that you may want to do and shows the specific packages that are available. In this way you can target the types of package most relevant to your needs.

At time of writing 28 Task Views were available. The subjects are listed in Table 1-1.

TABLE 1-1: Task Views and Their Uses

TITLE	USES
Bayesian	Bayesian Inference
ChemPhys	Chemometrics and Computational Physics
ClinicalTrials	Clinical Trial Design, Monitoring, and Analysis
Cluster	Cluster Analysis & Finite Mixture Models
Distributions	Probability Distributions
Econometrics	Computational Econometrics
Environmetrics	Analysis of Ecological and Environmental Data
ExperimentalDesign	Design of Experiments (DoE) & Analysis of Experimental Data
Finance	Empirical Finance
Genetics	Statistical Genetics
Graphics	Graphic Displays & Dynamic Graphics & Graphic Devices & Visualization
gR	gRaphical Models in R
HighPerformanceComputing	High-Performance and Parallel Computing with R
MachineLearning	Machine Learning & Statistical Learning
MedicalImaging	Medical Image Analysis
Multivariate	Multivariate Statistics
NaturalLanguageProcessing	Natural Language Processing
OfficialStatistics	Official Statistics & Survey Methodology
Optimization	Optimization and Mathematical Programming
Pharmacokinetics	Analysis of Pharmacokinetic Data
Phylogenetics	Phylogenetics, Especially Comparative Methods

continues

TABLE 1-1 *(continued)*

TITLE	USES
Psychometrics	Psychometric Models and Methods
ReproducibleResearch	Reproducible Research
Robust	Robust Statistical Methods
SocialSciences	Statistics for the Social Sciences
Spatial	Analysis of Spatial Data
Survival	Survival Analysis
TimeSeries	Time Series Analysis

Alternatively, you can search the Internet for your topic and you will likely find quite a few hits that mention appropriate R packages.

How to Get Extra Packages of R Commands

The easiest way to get these packages installed is to do it from within R itself. Windows and Macintosh have menu items that will assist this process. In Linux you must type in a command directly. You can also use this command in Windows or Macintosh. The next few sections look at each OS in turn.

How to Install Extra Packages for Windows Users

In Windows you can use the Packages menu. You have several options, but Install Package(s) is the one you will want most often. After you have selected a local mirror site you are presented with a list of available binary packages from which you can choose the ones you require (see Figure 1-23).

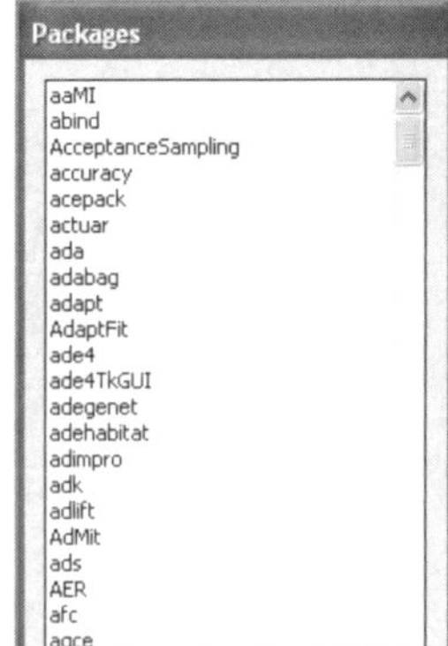

FIGURE 1-23

Once you have selected the packages you require, click OK at the bottom and the packages will be downloaded and installed directly into R.

If you have acquired package files directly from the Internet (usually as `.zip`), you can use the Install Package(s) from Local Zip Files option in the Packages menu. This allows you to select the files you want, and once again the packages are unzipped and installed right into R.

How to Install Extra Packages for Macintosh Users

In OS X navigate to the Packages & Data menu and select the Package Installer option. This brings up a window where you can select the package(s) that you want to install (see Figure 1-24). The window initially appears blank and you can click the Get List button to acquire the list from your selected source, which by default is the CRAN list of binary packages (those compiled and ready to go).

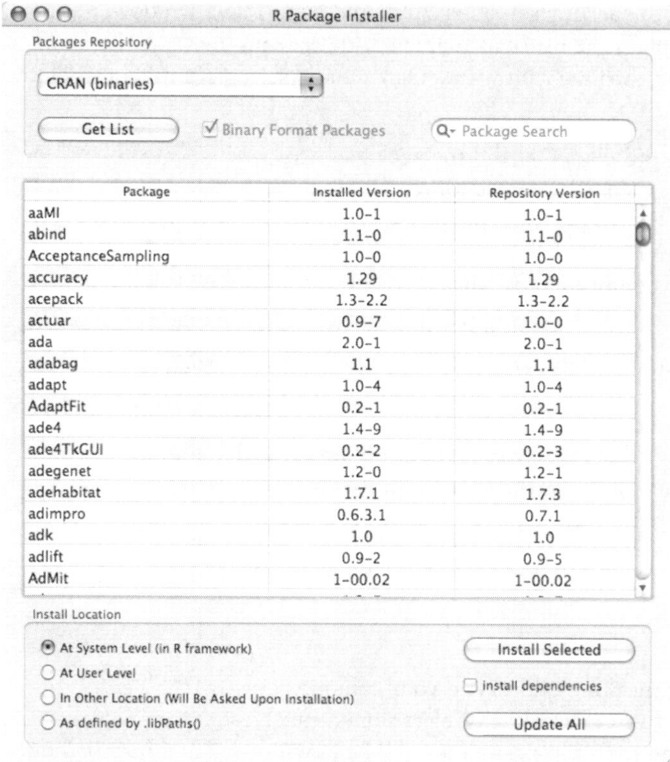

FIGURE 1-24

The next task is to select the package(s) you require and click the Install Selected button. (You can select multiple items using Cmd+click, Shift+click, and so on). It is simplest to locate the new packages in the default location (at the system level), where they are then available for all users. Once you click the Install Selected button, the selected packages are downloaded and installed into R.

It is also possible to download packages using your web browser and install the archive files. Usually the CRAN packages come as `.tgz` files. To manage the installation of these files, use the same window as before (refer to Figure 1-24) but this time alter the Packages Repository so that it reads Local Binary Package rather than the current CRAN (binaries). The page will remain blank because R will not know where to look for the file(s), so you need to click the Install button and then select the file(s) you require.

How to Install Extra Packages for Linux Users

In Linux systems there is no GUI and therefore no ready menu for you to use. You need to type a command into the console window to install any packages that you want. These commands will also work in Windows or Macintosh versions. You can view a list of available packages quite easily using the following command:

```
install.packages()
```

Note that you end the command with parentheses. This command brings up a window allowing you to select your location and then displays the list of available packages from the CRAN system. You can select these packages by clicking each one you want. They remain selected until you click them again, as shown in Figure 1-25.

Once you have selected what you want, click OK and the packages are retrieved. Unlike Windows or OS X the packages are source files and are "built" once they are downloaded. For all practical purposes, when you click OK the packages are installed for you and are ready to use (you just have to wait while the packages are compiled and built).

If you know the name of a package you can install it directly by adding its name into the parentheses of the command like so:

```
install.packages('ade4')
```

This gets the `ade4` package from the CRAN repository and downloads and installs it for you. Note that the name of the package you require must be in quotes; single or double quotes are fine as long as they are not mixed.

You can install many possible packages of commands. For example, try the following command:

```
install.packages("gdata")
```

FIGURE 1-25

This starts the process of installing the `gdata` library to your computer. First you will be asked to select the local mirror site—select something near to your geographic location and the appropriate files will be downloaded and installed into your system. The `gdata` package provides various programming tools for data manipulation, you can find out more by typing `help(gdata)`.

NOTE *In the text you will see references to library and package. These terms are interchangeable. Think of a package as being the bundle of code that you download and a library as being what you get when you make the code available for use in R.*

Running and Manipulating Packages

Once you have some packages installed you need to be able to access the new commands available in these packages. The packages are not automatically ready for use and you must load them to make the library of code routines available for use.

You can see which packages are loaded and running using the following command:

```
search()
```

If you do this before you load any additional packages, you will see the core form of the R basic distribution. The following resulted from the `search()` command on a Mac OS X with R version 2.7.1 installed:

```
> search()
 [1] ".GlobalEnv"        "tools:RGUI"        "package:stats"
```

```
 [4] "package:graphics"  "package:grDevices" "package:utils"
 [7] "package:datasets"  "package:methods"   "Autoloads"
[10] "package:base"
```

You can see that the basic R program is actually comprised of several smaller units, no less than seven packages in this case. By default the new packages are not automatically ready for use but need to be loaded.

Loading Packages

It is simple to load packages as required. Start by issuing the following command:

```
library(package)
```

The `library()` command retrieves the appropriate package and makes its contents available for you (think of it as adding to your library of available commands). Note that you do not need to put the package name in quotes. Most authors try hard to avoid using names for commands that exist in other packages. However, some duplication is unavoidable. If you load a library that contains a command with a duplicate name, you are given a brief message to this effect. The new command is the one that works and the older version is temporarily unavailable.

You can see what packages are installed using the following command:

```
installed.packages()
```

If you have downloaded a lot of packages, this display can be quite extensive. As well as additional packages, the display lists the basic parts of the R distribution.

Windows-Specific Package Commands

In Windows you can see what packages are available to be used by selecting Load Package from the Packages menu. This brings up a simple list, from which you can select a package to load (see Figure 1-26).

If you want to load a package, select one (or more) and click OK, otherwise you can simply use the list to view items you have downloaded and then click the Cancel button.

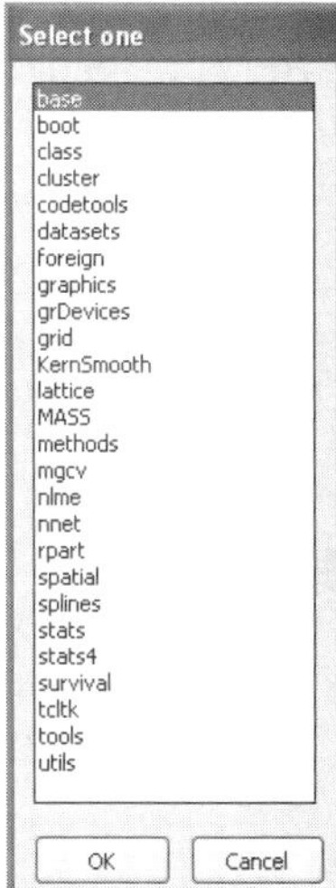

FIGURE 1-26

Macintosh-Specific Package Commands

In Macintosh OS you can use the Package Manager option in the Packages & Data menu (see Figure 1-27). This brings up a window that lists all the packages downloaded and available for use.

If you click a package name you gain access to the help for that package, so you are able to explore the commands without loading the library. If you decide to load a particular package (or more than one), you can check the box in the Status column. You can also unload a package which is discussed in the next section.

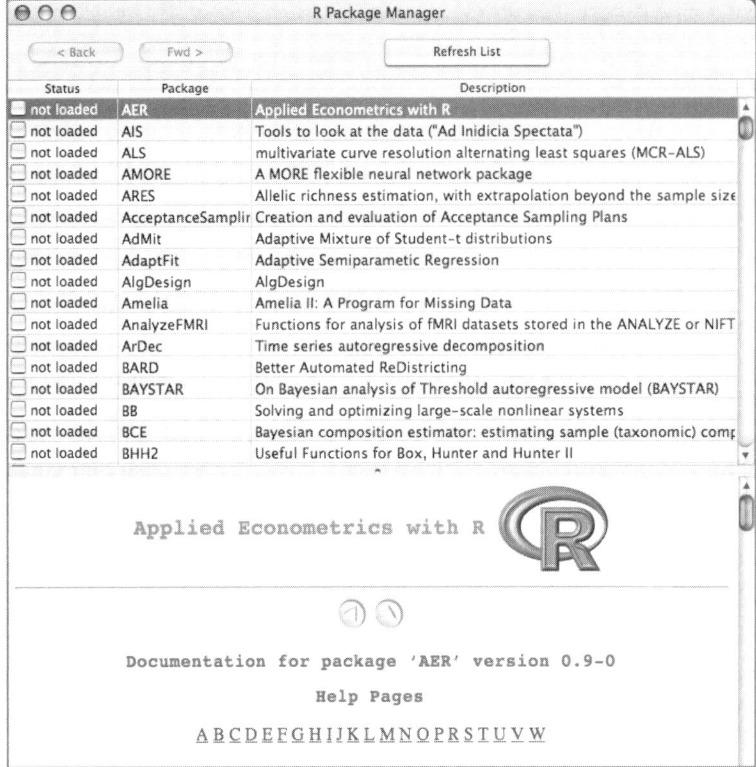

FIGURE 1-27

Removing or Unloading Packages

If you have loaded some packages and want to remove one, perhaps to free up an overwritten command, you can use the `detach()` command like so:

```
detach(package:name)
```

You simply replace the `name` part with the name of the package that you want to remove. Once removed, a package is not totally gone; you can still use the `library()` command to get it back when required.

SUMMARY

- The Comprehensive R Archive Network (CRAN) is available via `www.r-project.org`. This is the place to get software and related documentation.
- You use R by typing commands into the console window.
- In Windows and Macintosh the GUI provides some additional menu items.

- R has an extensive help system, which you can access via the `help()` command. The `help.start()` command opens the help system in a web browser.
- Adding CRAN to a web search often brings up useful entries when searching for information.
- You can obtain many additional packages of commands and you can install these additional packages using the `install.packages()` command.

EXERCISES

You can find answers to these exercises in Appendix A.

1. Try installing the `coin` library from within R—note that this will load some additional libraries too.
2. Load the `coin` library of commands and check to see what commands are available in this library.
3. Load the `MASS` library (it is already installed) and find help about the `bcv` command.
4. Check to see which libraries of commands are loaded and ready for use.
5. Clear out the `coin` library that you loaded earlier.

▶ WHAT YOU LEARNED IN THIS CHAPTER

TOPIC	KEY POINTS
Obtaining R	The website `www.r-project.org` is the home of the Comprehensive R Archive Network (CRAN) and is the source of software and documentation.
Installing R	The R website contains specific installers for the main operating systems. In Linux, R can often be installed from the command line in the Terminal.
Running R	R is driven by typing commands into the console window. Windows and Macintosh operating systems have additional menus. In Linux, R is driven via the Terminal and there are no menus.
THE HELP SYSTEM	**R CONTAINS EXTENSIVE DOCUMENTATION, WHICH CAN BE ACCESSED BY VARIOUS COMMANDS.**
`help(command)` `?command`	Brings up a help entry for the specified command.
`help.start()`	Opens the help system in the system default browser.
`apropos("partword")`	Shows all the commands that contain the `"partword"`.
ADDITIONAL PACKAGES OF R COMMANDS	**R IS BUILT FROM VARIOUS MODULES CALLED PACKAGES. ADDITIONAL PACKAGES PROVIDE EXTRA COMMANDS FOR SPECIFIC PURPOSES. THESE PACKAGES ARE FOUND ON THE WEBSITE AND CAN BE MANAGED USING VARIOUS COMMANDS. IN WINDOWS AND MACINTOSH THE GUI ALSO HAS MENUS THAT HELP WITH PACKAGE MANAGEMENT.**
`install.packages("pkg")`	Installs a library (package) of commands from the CRAN website.
`installed.packages()`	Shows a list of the packages that are installed.
`library(pkg)`	Loads a package of commands, making them available for use (the package must already be installed).
`search()`	Shows a list of packages (and other objects) that are loaded and available for use.
`detach(package:name)`	Makes a package unavailable for use. Replace `name` with the package name to be detached. The named package will now not show up when the `search()` command is used.

2

Starting Out: Becoming Familiar with R

WHAT YOU WILL LEARN IN THIS CHAPTER:

- How to use R for simple math
- How to store results of calculations for future use
- How to create data objects from the keyboard, clipboard, or external data files
- How to see the objects that are ready for use
- How to look at the different types of data objects
- How to make different types of data objects
- How to save your work
- How to use previous commands in the history

So far you have learned how to obtain and install R, and how to bring up elements of the help system. As you have seen, R is a language and the majority of tasks require you to type commands directly into the input window. Like any language you need to learn a vocabulary of terms as well as the grammar that joins the words and makes sense of them. In this chapter you learn some of the basics that underpin the R language. You begin by using R as a simple calculator. Then you learn how to store the results of calculations for future use. In most cases, you will want to create and use complex data items, and you learn about the different kinds of data objects that R recognizes.

SOME SIMPLE MATH

R can be used like a calculator and indeed one of its principal uses is to undertake complex mathematical and statistical calculations. R can perform simple calculations as well as more complex ones. This section deals with some of R's commonly used mathematical functions. Learning how to carry out some of these simple operations will give you practice at using R and typing simple commands.

Use R Like a Calculator

You can think of R as a big calculator; it will perform many complicated calculations but generally, these are made up of smaller elements. To see how you can use R in this way, start by typing in some simple math:

```
> 3 + 9 + 12 -7
[1] 17
```

The first line shows what you typed: a few numbers with some simple addition and subtraction. The next line shows you the result (17). You also see that this line begins with [1] rather than the > cursor. R is telling you that the first element of the answer is 17. At the moment this does not seem very useful, but the usefulness becomes clearer later when the answers become longer. For the remainder of this book, the text will mimic R and display examples using the > cursor to indicate which lines are typed by the user; lines beginning with anything else are produced by R.

Now make the math a bit more complicated:

```
> 12 + 17/2 -3/4 * 2.5
[1] 18.625
```

To make sense of what was typed, R uses the standard rules and takes the multiplication and division parts first, and then does the additions and subtractions. If parentheses are used you can get a quite different result:

```
> (12 + 17/2 -3/4) * 2.5
[1] 49.375
```

Here R evaluates the part(s) in the parentheses first, taking the divisions before the addition and subtraction. Lastly, the result from the brackets is been multiplied by 2.5 to give the final result. It is important to remember this simple order when doing long calculations!

NOTE *R ignores spaces, so when you type your math expressions there is no need to include them. In practice however, it is helpful use them because it makes the commands easier to read and you are less likely to make a mistake.*

Many mathematical operations can be performed in R. In Table 2-1 you can see a few of the more useful mathematical operators.

TABLE 2-1: Some of the Mathematical Operations Available in R

COMMAND/OPERATION	EXPLANATION
`+ - / * ( )`	Standard math characters to add, subtract, divide, and multiply, as well as parentheses.
`pi`	The value of pi (π), which is approximately 3.142.
`x^y`	The value of x is raised to the power of y, that is, xy.
`sqrt(x)`	The square root of x.
`abs(x)`	The absolute value of x.
`factorial(x)`	The factorial of x.
`log(x, base = n)`	The logarithm of x using base = n (natural log if none specified).
`log10(x)` `log2(x)`	Logarithms of x to the base of 10 or 2.
`exp(x)`	The exponent of x.

`cos(x)`
`sin(x)`
`tan(x)`
`acos(x)`
`asin(x)`
`atan(x)`
	Trigonometric functions for cosine, sine, tangent, arccosine, arcsine, and arctangent, respectively. In radians.

Some of the mathematical operators can be typed in by themselves—for example, `+ - * ^` but others require one or more additional instructions. The `log()` command, for example, requires one or two instructions, the first being the number you want to evaluate and the second being the base of the log you require. If you type in only a single instruction, R assumes that you require the natural log of the value you specified. In the following activity you have the opportunity to try out some of the math and gain a feel for typing commands into the R console window.

TRY IT OUT Type Some Math

Perform the following steps to practice using some math in R.

1. Type in the following math command using the value of π:

```
> pi * 2^3 - sqrt(4)
```

2. Now try using the `abs()` command with some math:

```
> abs(12-17*2/3-9)
```

3. Now type a simple factorial:

```
> factorial(4)
```

4. Next, try typing the following logarithms (all give the same answer because they are different forms of the same thing):

```
> log(2, 10)
> log(2, base = 10)
> log10(2)
```

5. Now type in a natural log:

```
> log(2)
```

6. Follow up by typing the exponent:

```
> exp(0.6931472)
```

7. Type in a logarithm again:

```
> log10(2)
```

8. Reverse the logarithm like so:

```
> 10^0.30103
```

9. Now try some trigonometry:

```
> sin(45 * pi / 180)
```

10. Finally, try reversing the trigonometry from step 9:

```
asin(0.7071068) * 180 / pi
```

How It Works

The first three examples are fairly simple math. The pi part is simply a standard variable ($\pi \approx 3.142$), and the `sqrt()` part is a command that determines the square root of whatever is in the following parentheses. The 2^3 part is equivalent to 2^3, which you cannot type directly because R uses plain text. Similarly, the `abs()` and `factorial()` commands perform their brand of math on the contents of the parentheses.

The `log()` command gives you the natural log as default unless you specify the base required as an additional instruction. For convenience, R provides two alternative commands, `log10()` and `log2()`, which allow you to specify base 10 or 2 more simply. Here you used three versions of the `log()` command to achieve the same results (0.30103). The next logarithm commands you used illustrated how to "reverse" natural and regular bases.

Finally, you evaluated the sine of 45°. However, because R uses radians rather than degrees you had to multiply the angle in degrees by π divided by 180 to obtain the correct result. You determined the arcsine of 0.707, essentially reversing the process from before. However, R works in radians so you multiplied the result by 180 divided by π to get an answer in degrees.

Now that you have the idea about using some simple math you need to look at how you can store the results of calculations for later use.

Storing the Results of Calculations

Once you have performed a calculation you can save the result for use in some later calculation. The way to do this is to give the result a name. R uses named objects extensively and understanding these objects is vital to working with R. To make a result object you simply type a name followed by an equals sign, and then anything after the = will be evaluated and stored as your result. The formula should look like this:

```
object.name = mathematical.expression
```

The following example makes a simple result object from some mathematical expressions; the result can be recalled later:

```
> ans1 = 23 + 14/2 - 18 + (7 * pi/2)
```

Here R is instructed to create an item called `ans1` and to make this from the result of the calculation that follows the = sign. Note that if you carry out this command you will not see a result. You are telling R to create the item from the calculation but not to display it. To get the result you simply type the name of the item you just created:

```
> ans1
[1] 22.99557
```

You can create as many items as you like (although eventually you would fill up the memory of your computer); here is another example:

```
> ans2 = 13 + 11 + (17 - 4/7)
```

Now you have two results, `ans1` and `ans2`. You can use these like any other value in further calculations. For example:

```
> ans1 + ans2 / 2
[1] 43.20986
> ans3 = ans2 + 9 - 2 + pi
```

In these examples the = sign is used. This is perfectly logical but R allows you an alternative. In older versions of R and in most of the help examples you will see that the = sign is rarely used and a sort of arrow is used instead. For example:

```
> ans4 <- 3 + 5
> ans5 <- ans1 * ans2
```

Here two new result objects are created (`ans4` and `ans5`) from the expressions to the right of the "arrow." This is more flexible than the = sign because you can reverse the direction of the arrow:

```
> ans3 + pi / ans4 -> ans6
```

If the regular = sign was used instead in this example, you would get an error.

The results you have created so far are simple values that have resulted from various mathematical operations. These result objects are revisited later in the chapter. The "Making Named Objects" section provides a look at listing the objects created as well as some rules for object names. Most often you will have sets of data to examine; these will comprise more complicated sets of numbers. Being able to create more complex data is covered in the next section.

READING AND GETTING DATA INTO R

So far you have looked at some simple math. More often you will have sets of data to examine (that is, samples) and will want to create more complex series of numbers to work on. You cannot perform any analyses if you do not have any data so getting data into R is a very important task. This next section focuses on ways to create these complex samples and get data into R, where you are able to undertake further analyses.

Using the combine Command for Making Data

The simplest way to create a sample is to use the `c()` command. You can think of this as short for `combine` or `concatenate`, which is essentially what it does. The command takes the following form:

```
c(item.1, item.2, item.3, item.n)
```

Everything in the parentheses is joined up to make a single item. More usually you will assign the joined-up items to a named object:

```
sample.name = c(item.1, item.2, item.3, item.n)
```

This is much like you did when making simple result objects, except now your sample objects consist of several bits rather than a single value.

Entering Numerical Items as Data

Numerical data do not need any special treatment; you simply type the values, separated by commas, into the `c()` command.

In the following example, imagine that you have collected some data (a sample) and now want to get the values into R:

```
>data1 = c(3, 5, 7, 5, 3, 2, 6, 8, 5, 6, 9)
```

Now just create a new object to hold your data and then type the values into the parentheses. The values are separated using commas.

The "result" is not automatically displayed; to see the data you must type its name:

```
> data1
 [1] 3 5 7 5 3 2 6 8 5 6 9
```

Previously the named objects contained single values (the result of some mathematical calculation). Here the named object `data1` contains several values, forming a sample. The `[1]` at the beginning shows you that the line begins with the first item (the number 3). When you get larger samples and more values, the display may well take up more than one line of the display, and R provides a number at the beginning of each row so you can see "how far along" you are. In the following example you can see that there are 41 values in the sample:

```
 [1]  582  132  716  515  158   80  757  529  335  497 3369  746  201  277  593
[16]  361  905 1513  744  507  622  347  244  116  463  453  751  540 1950  520
[31]  179  624  448  844 1233  176  308  299  531   71  717
```

The second row starts with `[16]`, which tells you that the first value in that row is the 16th in the sample. This simple index system makes it a bit easier to pick out specific items.

You can incorporate existing data objects with values to make new ones simply by incorporating them as if they were values themselves (which of course they are). In this example you take the numerical sample that you made earlier and incorporate it into a larger sample:

```
> data1
 [1] 3 5 7 5 3 2 6 8 5 6 9
> data2 = c(data1, 4, 5, 7, 3, 4)
> data2
 [1] 3 5 7 5 3 2 6 8 5 6 9 4 5 7 3 4
```

Here you take your first `data1` object and add some extra values to create a new (larger) sample. In this case you create a new item called `data2`, but you can overwrite the original as part of the process:

```
> data1 = c(6, 7, 6, 4, 8, data1)
> data1
 [1] 6 7 6 4 8 3 5 7 5 3 2 6 8 5 6 9
```

Now adding extra values at the beginning has modified the original sample.

Entering Text Items as Data

If the data you require are not numerical, you simply use quotes to differentiate them from numbers. There is no difference between using single and double quotes; R converts them all to double. You can use either or both as long as the surrounding quotes for any single item match, as shown in the following:

```
our.text = c("item1", "item2", 'item3')
```

In practice though, it is a good habit to stick to one sort of quote; single quote marks are easier to type.

The following example shows a simple text sample comprising of days of the week:

```
> day1 = c('Mon', 'Tue', 'Wed', 'Thu')
> day1
[1] "Mon" "Tue" "Wed" "Thu"
```

You can combine other text objects in the same way as you did for the numeric objects previously, like so:

```
> day1 = c(day1, 'Fri')
> day1
[1] "Mon" "Tue" "Wed" "Thu" "Fri"
```

If you mix text and numbers, the entire data object becomes a text variable and the numbers are converted to text, shown in the following. You can see that the items are text because R encloses each item in quotes:

```
> mix = c(data1, day1)
> mix
 [1] "3"   "5"   "7"   "5"   "3"   "2"   "6"   "8"   "5"   "6"   "9"   "Mon"
[13] "Tue" "Wed" "Thu" "Fri"
```

The `c()` command used in the previous example is a quick way of getting a series of values stored in a data object. This command is useful when you don't have very large samples, but it can be a bit tedious when a lot of typing is involved. Other methods of getting data into R exist, which are examined in the next section.

Using the scan Command for Making Data

When using the `c()` command, typing all those commas to separate the values can be a bit tedious. You can use another command, `scan()`, to do a similar job. Unlike the `c()` command you do not insert the values in the parentheses but use empty parentheses. The command then prompts you to enter your data. You generally begin by assigning a name to hold the resulting data like so:

```
our.data = scan()
```

Once you press the Enter key you will be prompted to enter your data. The following activity illustrates this process.

TRY IT OUT Use scan() to Make Numerical Data

Perform the following steps to practice storing data using the scan() command.

1. Begin the data entry process with the `scan()` command:

```
> data3 = scan()
```

2. Now type some numerical values, separated by spaces, as follows:

```
1: 6 7 8 7 6 3 8 9 10 7
```

3. Now press the Enter key and type some more numbers on the fresh line:

```
11: 6 9
```

4. Press the Enter key once again to create a new line:

```
13:
```

5. Press the Enter key once more to finish the data entry:

```
13:
Read 12 items
```

6. Type the name of the object:

```
> data3
 [1]  6  7  8  7  6  3  8  9 10  7  6  9
```

How It Works

The initial command creates a new data object (called `data3` in this case) and initiates the data entry process. You do not type any data at this stage but you do need the parentheses; in this way R knows that the word `scan` is a command and not a data item. Once you press the Enter key R shows a `1:` and waits for you to enter data. The data can now be typed in with only spaces to separate them.

When you press the Enter key R displays `11:`, indicating that the next item you type is the eleventh. You can now type more values on the new line. Once the Enter key is pressed the cursor moves to a new line once more. This time the row begins with `13:`, which indicates that you have typed in twelve values so far and that the next one would be the thirteenth. The data entry process is finished by pressing Enter on the blank line; R then reminds you how many data items were typed in as part of this `scan()` command, in this case twelve. The data that were entered are not displayed, so to see what data you have entered, simply type the data object's name (`data3` in this case).

Entering Text as Data

You can enter text using the `scan()` command, but if you simply enter your items in quotes you will get an error message. You need to modify the command slightly like so:

```
scan(what = 'character')
```

You must tell R to expect that the items typed in are characters, not numbers; to do this you add the `what = 'character'` part in the parentheses. Note that `character` is in quotes. Once the command runs it operates in an identical manner as before.

In the following example a simple data item is created containing text stating the days of the week:

```
> day2 = scan(what = 'character')
1: Mon Tue Wed
4: Thu
5:
Read 4 items
```

Note that quotes are not needed for the entered data. R is expecting the entered data to be text so the quotes can be left out. Typing the name of the object you just created displays the data, and you can see that they are indeed text items and the quotes are there:

```
> day2
[1] "Mon" "Tue" "Wed" "Thu"
```

Using the Clipboard to Make Data

The `scan()` command is easier to use than the `c()` command because it does not require commas. The command can also be used in conjunction with the clipboard, which is quite useful for entering data from other programs (for example, a spreadsheet). To use these commands, perform the following steps:

1. If the data are numbers in a spreadsheet, simply type the command in R as usual before switching to the spreadsheet containing the data.
2. Highlight the necessary cells in the spreadsheet and copy them to the clipboard.
3. Return to R and paste the data from the clipboard into R. As usual, R waits until a blank line is entered before ending the data entry so you can continue to copy and paste more data as required.
4. Once you are finished, enter a blank line to complete data entry.

If the data are text, you add the `what = 'character'` instruction to the `scan()` command as before.

At this point, if you can open the file in a spreadsheet, proceed with the aforementioned four steps. If the file opens in a text editor or word processor, you must look to see how the data items are separated before continuing.

If the data are separated with simple spaces, you can simply copy and paste. If the data are separated with some other character, you need to tell R which character is used as the separator. For example, a common file type is CSV (comma-separated values), which uses commas to separate the data items. To tell R you are using this separator, simply add an extra part to your command like so:

```
scan(sep = ',')
```

In this example R is told to expect a comma; note that you need to enclose the separator in quotes. Here are some comma-separated numerical data:

```
23,17,12.5,11,17,12,14.5,9
11,9,12.5,14.5,17,8,21
```

To get these into R, use the `scan()` command like so:

```
> data4 = scan(sep = ',')
1: 23,17,12.5,11,17,12,14.5,9
9: 11,9,12.5,14.5,17,8,21
16:
Read 15 items
> data4
 [1] 23.0 17.0 12.5 11.0 17.0 12.0 14.5  9.0 11.0  9.0 12.5 14.5 17.0  8.0 21.0
```

Note that you have to press the Enter key to finish the data entry. Note also that some of the original data had decimal points (for example, 14.5); R appends decimals to all the data so that they all have the same level of precision. If your data are separated by tab stops you can use `"\t"` to tell R that this is the case.

If the data are text, you simply add `what = 'character'` and proceed as before. Here are some text data contained in a CSV text file:

```
"Jan","Feb","Mar","Apr","May","Jun"
"Jul","Aug","Sep","Oct","Nov","Dec"
```

To get these data entered into R, perform the following steps:

1. Open the data file; in this case it has opened in a text editor and we see the quotes and the comma separators.
2. Highlight the data required.
3. Copy to the clipboard.
4. Switch to R and type in the `scan()` command.
5. Paste the contents of the clipboard.
6. Press Enter on a blank line to end the data entry (this means that you have to press Enter twice, once after the paste operation and once on the blank line).
7. Type the name of the data object created to view the entered data.

The set of operations appears as follows:

```
> data5 = scan(sep = ',', what = 'char')
1: "Jan","Feb","Mar","Apr","May","Jun"
7: "Jul","Aug","Sep","Oct","Nov","Dec"
13:
Read 12 items
> data5
 [1] "Jan" "Feb" "Mar" "Apr" "May" "Jun" "Jul" "Aug" "Sep" "Oct" "Nov" "Dec"
```

NOTE *Note that* `char` *is typed rather than* `character`. *Many R commands will accept abbreviations. In general as long as an instruction is unambiguous then R will work out what you want.*

In this example both `sep =` and `what =` instructions are used. Additionally, the `scan()` command allows you to create data items from the keyboard or from clipboard entries, thus enabling you to move data from other applications quite easily. It is also possible to get the `scan()` command to read a file directly as described in the following section.

Reading a File of Data from a Disk

To read a file with the `scan()` command you simply add `file = 'filename'` to the command. For example:

```
> data6 = scan(file = 'test data.txt')
Read 15 items
> data6
 [1] 23.0 17.0 12.5 11.0 17.0 12.0 14.5  9.0 11.0  9.0 12.5 14.5 17.0  8.0 21.0
```

In this example the data file is called `test data.txt`, which is plain text, and the numerical values are separated by spaces. Note that the filename must be enclosed in quotes (single or double). Of course you can use the `what =` and `sep =` instructions as appropriate.

R looks for your data file in the default directory. You can find the default directory by using the `getwd()` command like so:

```
> getwd()
[1] "C:/Documents and Settings/Administrator/My Documents"

> getwd()
[1] "/Users/markgardener"

> getwd()
[1] "/home/mark"
```

The first example shows the default for a Windows XP machine, the second example is for a Macintosh OS X system, and the final example is for Linux (Ubuntu 10.10).

NOTE *The directories listed are separated by forward slashes; the backslash character is not used.*

If your file is somewhere else you must type its name and location in full. The location is relative to the default directory; in the preceding example the file was on the desktop so the command ought to have been:

```
> data6 = scan(file = 'Desktop/test data.txt')
```

The filename and directories are all case sensitive. You can also type in a URL and link to a file over the Internet directly; once again the full URL is required.

It may be easier to point permanently at a directory so that the files can be loaded simply by typing their names. You can alter the working directory using the `setwd()` command:

```
setwd('pathname')
```

When using this command, replace the `pathname` part with the location of your target directory. The location is always relative to the current working directory, so to set to my `Desktop` I used the following:

```
> setwd('Desktop')
> getwd()
[1] "/Users/markgardener/Desktop"
```

To step up one level you can type the following:

```
setwd('..')
```

You can look at a directory and see which files/folders are within it using the `dir()` or `list.files()` command:

```
dir()
list.files()
```

The default is to show the files and folders in the current working directory, but you can type in a path (in single quote marks) to list files in any directory. For example:

```
dir('Desktop')
dir('Documents')
dir('Documents/Excel files')
```

Note that the listing is in alphabetical order; files are shown with their extensions and folders simply display the name. If you have files that do not have extensions (for example: `.txt`, `.doc`), it is harder to work out which are folders and which are files. Invisible files are not shown by default, but you can choose to see them by adding an extra instruction to the command like so:

```
dir(all.files = TRUE)
```

In Windows and Macintosh OS there is an alternative method that enables you to select a file. You can include the instruction `file.choose()` as part of your `scan()` command. This opens a browser-type window where you can navigate to and select the file you want to read:

```
> data7 = scan(file.choose())
Read 15 items
> data7
 [1] 23.0 17.0 12.5 11.0 17.0 12.0 14.5  9.0 11.0  9.0 12.5 14.5 17.0  8.0 21.0
```

In the preceding example the target file was a plain text file with numerical data separated by spaces. If you have text or the items are separated by other characters, you use the `what =` and `sep =` instructions as appropriate, like so:

```
> data8 = scan(file.choose(), what = 'char', sep = ',')
Read 12 items
> data8
 [1] "Jan" "Feb" "Mar" "Apr" "May" "Jun" "Jul" "Aug" "Sep" "Oct" "Nov" "Dec"
```

In this example, the target file contained the month data that you met previously; the file was a CSV file where the names of the months (text labels) were separated with commas.

NOTE *Using the* `file.choose()` *instruction does not work on Linux operating systems.*

The `file.choose()` instruction is useful because you can select files from different directories without having to alter the working directory or type the names in full.

So far the data items that you have created are simple; they contain either a single value (the result of a mathematical calculation) or several items. A list of data items is called a *vector*. If you only have a single value, your vector contains only one item, that is, it has a length of 1. If you have multiple values, your vector is longer. When you display the list R provides an index to help you see how many items there are and how far along any particular item is. Think of a vector as a one-dimensional data object; most of the time you will deal with larger datasets than single vectors of values.

Reading Bigger Data Files

The `scan()` command is helpful to read a simple vector. More often though, you will have complicated data files that contain multiple items (in other words two-dimensional items containing both rows and columns). Although it is possible to enter large amounts of data directly into R, it is more likely that you will have your data stored in a spreadsheet. When you are sent data items, the spreadsheet is also the most likely format you will receive. R provides the means to read data that is stored in a range of text formats, all of which the spreadsheet is able to create.

The read.csv() Command

In most cases you will have prepared data in a spreadsheet. Your dataset could be quite large and it would be tedious to use the clipboard. When you have more complex data it is better to use a new command—`read.csv()`:

```
read.csv()
```

As you might expect, this looks for a CSV file and reads the enclosed data into R. You can add a variety of additional instructions to the command. For example:

```
read.csv(file, sep = ',', header = TRUE, row.names)
```

You can replace the `file` with any filename as before. By default the separator is set to a comma but you can alter this if you need to. This command expects the data to be in columns, and for each column to have a helpful name. The instruction `header = TRUE`, the default, reads the first row of the CSV file and sets this as a name for each column. You can override this with `header = FALSE`. The `row.names` part allows you to specify row names for the data; generally this will be a column in the dataset (the first one is most usual and sensible). You can set the row names to be one of the columns by setting `row.names = n`, where `n` is the column number.

NOTE *In Windows or Macintosh you can replace the filename with a command,* `file.choose()`*; you do not need to type anything into the parentheses. This will open a browser-like window and allow you to select the file you require.*

Some simple example data are shown in Table 2-2. Here you can see two columns; each one is a variable. The first column is labeled `abund`; this is the abundance of some water-living organism. The second column is labeled `flow` and represents the flow of water where the organism was found.

TABLE 2-2: Simple Data From a Two Column Spreadsheet

ABUND	FLOW
9	2
25	3
15	5
2	9
14	14
25	24
24	29
47	34

In this case there are only two columns and it would not take too long to use the `scan()` command to transfer the data into R. However, it makes sense to keep the two columns together and import them to R as a single entity. To do so, perform the following steps:

1. If you have a file saved in a proprietary format (for example, XLS), save the data as a CSV file instead.
2. Now assign the file a sensible name and use the `read.csv()` command as follows:

```
> fw = read.csv(file.choose())
```

3. Select the file from the browser window. If you are using Linux, the filename must be typed in full. Because the `read.csv()` command is expecting the data to be separated with commas, you do not need to specify that. The data has headings and because this is also the default, you do not need to tell R anything else.
4. To see the data, type its name like so:

```
> fw
  abund flow
1     9    2
2    25    3
3    15    5
4     2    9
5    14   14
6    25   24
7    24   29
8    47   34
```

You can see that each row is labeled with a simple index number; these have no great relevance but can be useful when there are a lot of data.

In the general, the `read.csv()` command is pretty useful because the CSV format is most easily produced by a wide variety of computer programs, spreadsheets, and is eminently portable. Using CSV means that you have fewer options to type into R and consequently less typing.

Alternative Commands for Reading Data in R

There are many other formats besides CSV in which data can exist and in which other characters, including spaces and tabs, can separate data. Consequently, the `read.table()` command is actually the basic R command for reading data. It enables you to read most formats of plain-text data. However, R provides variants of the command with certain defaults to make it easier when specifying some common data formats, like `read.csv()` for CSV files. Since most data is CSV though, the `read.csv()` is the most useful of these variants. But you may run into alternative formats, and the following list outlines the basic `read.table()` as well as other commands you can use to read various types of data:

- In the following example the data are separated by simple spaces. The `read.table()` command is a more generalized command and you could use this at any time to read your data. In this case you have to specify the additional instructions explicitly. The defaults are set to `header = FALSE`, `sep = " "` (a single space), and `dec = "."`, for example.

```
data1 data2 data3
1 2 4
4 5 3
3 4 5
3 6 6
4 5 9

> my.ssv = read.table(file.choose(), header = TRUE)
> my.ssv = read.csv(file.choose(), sep = ' ')
```

- The next example shows data separated by tabs. If you have tab-separated values you can use the `read.delim()` command. In this command R assumes that you still have column heading names but this time the separator instruction is set to `sep = "\t"` (a tab character) by default:

```
data1 data2 data3
1     2     4
4     5     3
3     4     5
3     6     6
4     5     9

> my.tsv = read.delim(file.choose())
> my.tsv = read.csv(file.choose(), sep = '\t')
> my.tsv = read.table(file.choose(), header = TRUE, sep = '\t')
```

- The next example also shows data separated by tabs. In some countries the decimal point character is not a period but a comma, and a semicolon often separates data values. If you have a file like this you can use another variant, `read.csv2()`. Here the defaults are set to `sep = ";"`, `header = TRUE`, and `dec = ","`.

```
day   data1 data2 data3
mon   1     2     4
tue   4     5     3
wed   3     4     5
thu   3     6     6
fri   4     5     9
```

```
> my.list = read.delim(file.choose(), row.names = 1)
> my.list = read.csv(file.choose(), row.names = 1, sep = '\t')
> my.list = read.table(file.choose(), row.names = 1, header = TRUE,
 sep = '\t')
```

NOTE *It is best to keep data names brief. R will accept the letters a–z and A–Z as well as the numbers 0–9, but the only other characters allowed are the period and the underscore. Names are case sensitive and must not begin with a number.*

NOTE *If you want to use the* `read.csv()` *command to read in a tab-separated file this is fine, but you need to remember to tell R the separator character* (`'\t'`) *explicitly.*

These commands essentially all perform the same function; the differences lie in the defaults. Regardless of which method you choose, getting data into R is a fundamental operation; you cannot do anything without having the data first. Bear the following checklist in mind when looking to get data from disk:

1. Check the format of the data file and note the separator character.
2. Look to see if columns are labeled.
3. Use the appropriate `read.xxx()` command to get your data into R. The `read.csv()` command is the most useful and has the fewest additional instructions to type.
4. You can use the `file.choose()` instruction to save typing the filename in full unless you are using a Linux computer.
5. Make sure the name you select for your data is short but meaningful; this cuts down on typing and helps you to find it later.
6. If your data has row names use the `row.names =` instruction to point to the column in the file that contains them.

Missing Values in Data Files

In the examples you have seen so far the samples in the data files have all been the same length. In the real world samples are often of unequal size. The following example contains two samples, one called `mow` and one called `unmow`. The `mow` sample contains five values, whereas the `unmow` sample contains only four values. When these data are read into R from a spreadsheet or text file, the program recognizes that you have multiple columns of data and sets them out accordingly. R makes your data into a neat rectangular item and fills in any gaps with `NA`.

NOTE *IThe* `NA` *item is a special object in its own right and you can think of this as "Not Applicable" or "Not Available."*

In the following example the data were stored in a CSV file and were read into R with the `read.csv()` command:

```
> grass = read.csv(file.choose())
> grass
  mow unmow
1  12     8
2  15     9
3  17     7
4  11     9
5  15    NA
```

Here the data have been called `grass` and you can see that R has filled in the gap using `NA`. R always pads out the shorter samples using `NA` to produce a rectangular object. This is called a *data frame*. The data frame is an important kind of R object because it is used so often in statistical data manipulation and is how you generally have data in spreadsheets.

Although the `NA` can be dealt with fairly easily you should strive to create data frames that do not contain them if at all possible. In the following example the data have been rearranged. There are still two columns, but the first contains all the values and the second contains a name that relates to one of the previous column headings:

```
  species   cut
1      12   mow
2      15   mow
3      17   mow
4      11   mow
5      15   mow
6       8 unmow
7       9 unmow
8       7 unmow
9       9 unmow
```

You can see that the label in the second column corresponds to a value in the first column. The first five items relate to the previous `mow` sample and the next four belong to the `unmow` sample. In statistical parlance the `species` column is called the *response variable* and the `cut` column is the *predictor variable* (or *predictor factor*).

R recognizes `NA` as a special kind of data object. It is important to know when your data contains `NA` items and what to do when you encounter them.

VIEWING NAMED OBJECTS

So far you have seen examples of creating data objects from some simple math and from reading in data files. In a general way you "make" new items by providing a name followed by the instruction that creates it. R is object oriented, which means that it expects to find named things to deal with in some way. For example, if you are conducting an experiment and collecting data from several samples, you want to create several named data objects in R in order to work on them and do your analyses later on.

As a reminder, the following examples show a few of the different ways you have seen thus far to create named items:

```
answer1 = 23 + 17/2 + pi/4
my.data = read.csv(file.choose())
sample1 = c(2, 5, 7, 3, 9, 4, 5)
```

Now it is time to learn how to view these items in R and remove them as necessary. The following sections cover these topics.

Viewing Previously Loaded Named-Objects

Once you have made a few objects and have them stored in R, you might forget what you have previously loaded as time goes on. You need a way to see what R objects are available; to do this you use the `ls()` command like so:

```
ls()
```

Viewing All Objects

The `ls()` command lists all the named items that you have available. You can also use the `objects()` command; (this is identical in function but slightly longer to type!) The result of either command is to list the objects stored in R at the current moment:

```
> ls()
[1] "answer1" "my.data" "sample1"
```

This example contains three objects. The objects are listed in alphabetical order (with all the uppercase before the lowercase); if you have a lot of objects, the display will run to more lines like so:

```
 [1] "A"          "A.r"          "B"          "CI"
 [5] "CI.1"       "CI.dn"        "CI.up"      "Ell.F"
 [9] "F"          "F1"           "area"       "az"
[13] "bare"       "beetle.cca"   "beta"       "bf"
[17] "bf.beta"    "bf.lm"        "biol"       "biol.cca"
[21] "biomass"    "bird"         "bp"         "bs"
[25] "bss"        "but"          "but.lm"     "c3"
```

Here there are 28 objects. At the beginning of each new row the display shows you an index number relating to "how far along" the list of items you are. For example the `bare` data object is the 13th item along (alphabetically). If you do not have any named objects at all, you get the following "result":

```
> ls()
character(0)
```

Viewing Only Matching Names

You may want to limit the display to objects with certain names; this is especially helpful if you have a lot of data already in R. You can limit the display by giving R a search pattern to match. For example:

```
> ls(pattern = 'b')
 [1] "bare"       "beetle.cca" "beta"       "bf"         "bf.beta"
 [6] "bf.lm"      "biol"       "biol.cca"   "biomass"    "bird"
```

```
[11] "bp"          "bs"          "bss"         "but"         "but.lm"
[16] "cbh"         "cbh.glm"     "cbh.sf"      "food.b"      "nectar.b"
[21] "pred.prob"   "prob2odd"    "tab.est"     "tab1"        "tab2"
```

Here the pattern looks for everything containing a "b". This is pretty broad so you can refine it by adding more characters:

```
> ls(pattern = 'be')
[1] "beetle.cca" "beta"       "bf.beta"
```

Now the pattern picks up objects with "be" in the name. If you want to search for objects beginning with a certain letter you use the ^ character like so:

```
> ls(pattern = '^b')
 [1] "bare"        "beetle.cca" "beta"        "bf"          "bf.beta"
 [6] "bf.lm"       "biol"        "biol.cca"    "biomass"     "bird"
[11] "bp"          "bs"          "bss"         "but"         "but.lm"
```

Compare the following search listings. In the first case the pattern matches objects beginning with "be" but in the second case the letters are enclosed in square brackets:

```
> ls(pattern = '^be')
[1] "beetle.cca" "beta"

> ls(pattern = '^[be]')
 [1] "bare"        "beetle.cca" "beta"        "bf"          "bf.beta"
 [6] "bf.lm"       "biol"        "biol.cca"    "biomass"     "bird"
[11] "bp"          "bs"          "bss"         "but"         "but.lm"
[16] "eF"          "eF2"         "env"
```

The effect of the square brackets is to isolate the letters; each is treated as a separate item, hence objects beginning with "b" or "e" are matched. You can receive the same result using a slightly different approach as well:

```
ls(pattern = '^b|^e')
```

The vertical brace (sometimes called a *pipe*) character stands for `or`, that is, you want to search for objects beginning with "b" or beginning with "e".

To find objects ending with a specific character you use a dollar sign at the end like so:

```
> ls(pattern = 'm$')
 [1] "bf.lm"          "but.lm"          "cbh.glm"          "dep.pm"
 [5] "dm"             "frit.glm"        "frit.lm"          "frit.sum"
 [9] "hlm"            "mf.lm"           "mr.lm"            "n.glm"
[13] "newt.glm"       "newt.test.glm" "sales.lm"         "sm"
[17] "t.glm"          "test.glm"        "test.lm"          "test1.glm"
[21] "tt.glm"         "worm.pm"
```

You can use the period as a wildcard and R will match any character:

```
> ls(pattern = 'a.e')
[1] "area"        "bare"         "date"         "sales"        "sales.frame"
[6] "sales.lm"    "sales.ts"     "water"

> ls(pattern = 'a..e')
[1] "tab.est"    "treatment"
```

In the first example a single wildcard was used but in the second there are two. This pattern matching uses more or less the same conventions as standard Regular Expressions, which are found in many programs. The ones demonstrated here are only a few of the array of options available. You can use `help(regex)` in R to see much more detail.

Removing Objects from R

You can remove objects from memory and therefore permanently delete them using the `rm()` or `remove()` commands. To remove objects you can simply list them in the parentheses of the command:

```
rm(list)
remove(list)
```

You can type the names of the objects separated by commas. For example:

```
>rm(answer1, my.data, sample1)
```

This removes the objects `answer1`, `my.data`, and `sample1` from the workspace. You can use the `ls()` command to produce a list, which will then be deleted. You need to include the instruction `list` in the command like so:

```
>rm(list = ls(pattern  = '^b'))
```

Here the `ls()` command is used to search for objects beginning with "b" and remove them.

WARNING *Use the* `rm()` *command with caution; R doesn't give you a warning before it removes the data you indicate, it simply removes it after receiving the command.*

SPRING CLEANING WITH RM()

At times it's important to do some spring cleaning and remove everything. You can use the `rm()` command like so:

```
rm(list = ls())
```

In Windows or Macintosh OS you can use one of the menu commands to achieve the same result.

In Windows, select the Misc menu and then Remove All Objects. In OS X, use the Workspace menu and select Clear Workspace. In both cases you do get a warning and a chance to change your mind.

TYPES OF DATA ITEMS

So far you have seen how to create some simple mathematical results, how to create simple samples, and how to read in more complex data containing multiple columns. Now is a good time to look at the types of data items that you may come across. Your data items can exist in one of two forms: numbers or text values. R regards these as `numeric` or `character`.

Number Data

Plain values that are whole numbers are `integer` values, whereas values that contain decimals are `numeric`. The distinction is fairly minor, but if you have a list of values that contain both integers and decimals, R will regard the entire sample as `numeric`.

```
> data3
 [1]  6  7  8  7  6  3  8  9 10  7  6  9
> data7
 [1] 23.0 17.0 12.5 11.0 17.0 12.0 14.5  9.0 11.0  9.0 12.5 14.5 17.0  8.0 21.0
```

In the first example the values are all whole numbers. In the second example some of them have decimal places, but R appends decimals to all of the data to achieve an equal level of precision; in this case they all have at least one decimal place.

Text Items

If you do not have numbers, you must have text. R recognizes two sorts of text data items. You can think of the first kind as plain text labels; R calls these `character` values.

```
> data8
 [1] "Jan" "Feb" "Mar" "Apr" "May" "Jun" "Jul" "Aug" "Sep" "Oct" "Nov" "Dec"
```

These items display as plain text and have the quote marks to remind you. However, another type of non-numeric data is called a `factor`:

```
> cut
[1] mow    mow    mow    mow    mow    unmow unmow unmow unmow
Levels: mow unmow
```

Here the data are text but they are not in quotes. When they are displayed the text appears plain without quote marks, but with an additional line showing you how many different things there are in this list. Recall the data that you met previously:

```
> grass
  species   cut
1      12   mow
2      15   mow
3      17   mow
4      11   mow
5      15   mow
6       8 unmow
7       9 unmow
8       7 unmow
9       9 unmow
```

When R reads the data from the data file it assumes that the text column corresponds to the numeric column and sets the text to a `factor` rather than as a `character`. In most instances this is what you want for statistical analyses. However, you can elect to read any column as plain text using the `as.is =` instruction. To do this for the previous mowing data, for example, you would type:

```
grass2 = read.csv(file.choose(), as.is = 2)
```

Here you tell R that the second column in your data file is to be regarded as plain text rather than a `factor`.

Converting Between Number and Text Data

You can shift between the two kinds of text quite easily. The following example begins with data that is a factor. The `as.character()` command is used to convert to plain text. Then the plain text is converted back to a factor using the `as.factor()` command:

```
> cut
[1] mow    mow    mow    mow    mow    unmow unmow unmow unmow
Levels: mow unmow
> cut2 = as.character(cut)
> cut2
[1] "mow"   "mow"   "mow"   "mow"   "mow"   "unmow" "unmow" "unmow" "unmow"
> cut3 = as.factor(cut2)
> cut3
[1] mow    mow    mow    mow    mow    unmow unmow unmow unmow
Levels: mow unmow
```

In this case new data objects were created but the original object could be overwritten with the new one.

You can do a similar thing with numbers. If you begin with data that contain decimals, that is, `numeric`, you can convert to integers using the `as.integer()` command. You can convert integer values to `numeric` using the `as.numeric()` command:

```
> data7
[1] 23.0 17.0 12.5 11.0 17.0 12.0 14.5  9.0 11.0 9.0 12.5 14.5 17.0 8.0 21.0
> data7i = as.integer(data7)
> data7i
 [1] 23 17 12 11 17 12 14  9 11  9 12 14 17  8 21
> data7n = as.numeric(data7i)
> data7n
 [1] 23 17 12 11 17 12 14  9 11  9 12 14 17  8 21
```

WARNING *Once the decimal places have been lost you cannot re-create them so the information is lost.*

You can also convert numbers to text using `as.character()`:

```
> data7c = as.character(data7)
> data7c
 [1] "23"   "17"   "12.5" "11"   "17"   "12"   "14.5" "9"    "11"   "9"    "12.5"
[12] "14.5" "17"   "8"    "21"
```

You can also try converting text into numbers like so:

```
> data7nt = as.numeric(data7c)
> data7nt
 [1] 23.0 17.0 12.5 11.0 17.0 12.0 14.5  9.0 11.0  9.0 12.5 14.5 17.0  8.0 21.0
```

This works out fine if the text is sensible; in the preceding example the text values were originally numbers. Now see what happens if you try this on a factor:

```
> cut
[1] mow   mow   mow   mow   mow   unmow unmow unmow unmow

> cut.n = as.numeric(cut)
> cut.n
[1] 1 1 1 1 1 2 2 2 2
```

Here you get a surprising (but potentially useful) result; the numbers relate directly to the different factors that you have. If you try to convert something that really is not going to work, R gives a warning like so:

```
> data8
 [1] "Jan" "Feb" "Mar" "Apr" "May" "Jun" "Jul" "Aug" "Sep" "Oct" "Nov" "Dec"
> data8n = as.numeric(data8)
Warning message:
NAs introduced by coercion
> data8n
 [1] NA NA NA NA NA NA NA NA NA NA NA NA
```

In this case the data is plain text and cannot be forced into any sensible number, so you end up with a string of `NA`s. If you were to convert the plain text to a factor first and then to a number, that would be a different story:

```
> data8c = as.numeric(as.factor(data8))
> data8c
 [1]  5  4  8  1  9  7  6  2 12 11 10  3
```

Here one command is nested inside the other. R evaluated the `as.factor()` part first and then converted that into numbers. You started with twelve months and can see that they have been assigned numbers; notice how R has indexed them alphabetically.

THE STRUCTURE OF DATA ITEMS

The data that you have can exist in a variety of forms (or structures). For example, you may have many individual samples, each item being a separate entity. On the other hand, you may have complicated data—the results of surveys, for example—that each contain several columns of values. R recognizes several forms of data and these forms each have their own particular uses. This section focuses on these different forms of data.

Your data can exist as numerical or character data as you saw in the previous section. However, these data items can also be constructed and put together in a variety of ways. This section looks at these different structures: vector, matrix, data frame, and list.

Vector Items

So far you have met two kinds of data: vectors and data frames. A vector can be thought of as a one-dimensional object. You created vectors containing a single item from some mathematical operations; you also created vectors by making simple samples of values and text. Here are two simple vectors:

```
> data8
 [1] "Jan" "Feb" "Mar" "Apr" "May" "Jun" "Jul" "Aug" "Sep" "Oct" "Nov" "Dec"
> data7
 [1] 23.0 17.0 12.5 11.0 17.0 12.0 14.5  9.0 11.0  9.0 12.5 14.5 17.0  8.0 21.0
```

The first one is a vector of text values; the second is a vector of numeric values. You could also have a vector of factors—the `cut` object from earlier is an example of a `factor` vector:

```
> cut
[1] mow   mow   mow   mow   mow   unmow unmow unmow unmow
Levels: mow unmow
```

Data Frames

You have also already met the data frame. A data frame is a two-dimensional object, that is, it has rows and columns. R treats the columns as separate samples or variables, and the rows represent the replicates or observations. All data frames are rectangular and R will pad out any "short" columns using `NA`.

Here is a simple example that you met previously. There are two columns; one represents a sample called `mow` and contains five replicates/observations. The second column is called `unmow` and contains four observations:

```
> grass
  mow unmow
1  12     8
2  15     9
3  17     7
4  11     9
5  15    NA
```

Each column can be a separate type of data; in the following example the data are reorganized so that the first is numeric and the second is a factor:

```
> grass
  species   cut
1      12   mow
2      15   mow
3      17   mow
4      11   mow
5      15   mow
6       8 unmow
7       9 unmow
8       7 unmow
9       9 unmow
```

The second form of the data frame is most useful, especially for statistical analyses. This is because there are no `NA` items.

Matrix Objects

A *matrix* is a two-dimensional data object. At first glance a matrix looks just like a data frame:

```
> bird
               Garden Hedgerow Parkland Pasture Woodland
Blackbird          47       10       40       2        2
Chaffinch          19        3        5       0        2
Great Tit          50        0       10       7        0
House Sparrow      46       16        8       4        0
Robin               9        3        0       0        2
Song Thrush         4        0        6       0        0
```

In this example you can see some observations of a variety of common birds and the habitat in which they were observed. The matrix has rows and columns just like a data frame but the object is handled differently, and some commands require a matrix to operate on rather than a data frame. Unlike a data frame, a matrix cannot contain mixed data; all the columns must be the same type, that is, all numeric or all character. A matrix can consist of a single row or a single column and so can also appear just like a vector object. You learn how to tell which is which shortly.

List Objects

A *list* is a series of items bundled together to form a single object. In the following example the `grass` data you met previously has been made into a list:

```
> grass.l
$mow
[1] 12 15 17 11 15

$unmow
[1] 8 9 7 9
```

When you look at it you see each vector listed separately along with its name, which is prefixed with a dollar sign. This example list is very simple and contains only two vectors. A list could be constructed from objects of various sorts, and you might have, for example, a matrix, a data frame, and several vectors containing a mixture of numbers and characters. The list is a flexible object but also harder to deal with, as you will find out in due course.

EXAMINING DATA STRUCTURE

As you collect and work on new data you will inevitably build a collection of items. Different kinds of analysis will require different approaches, and you will need to examine a data object in order to work out what kind it is so that you can determine the best strategy for dealing with it.

The vector is the smallest unit in the data structure. When you start to bundle vectors together you make more complex items. The complex item you make can be a data frame, a matrix, or a list.

You need a way to tell which form your data are in. If you look at a particular object, you can get a clue; a simple vector will be a one-dimensional set of characters or numbers. A data frame or a matrix will have a rectangular two-dimensional structure. A list will appear as a series of separately named vectors; each name starts with a dollar sign ($). The difficulty is differentiating between the matrix and the data frame. You can use the `str()` command to examine the structure of an object like so:

```
> str(grass)
'data.frame': 9 obs. of  2 variables:
 $ species: int  12 15 17 11 15 8 9 7 9
 $ cut    : Factor w/ 2 levels "mow","unmow": 1 1 1 1 1 2 2 2 2
```

In this example you see that the data object (`grass`) is a data frame with two columns. The first is named `species` and is an integer, whilst the second is named `cut` and is a factor. If the object were a list, the `str()` command would produce something like the following:

```
> str(grass.l)
List of 2
 $ mow  : int [1:5] 12 15 17 11 15
 $ unmow: int [1:4] 8 9 7 9
```

Here you can see that your object is a list comprising two vectors of numbers. The list is helpful for occasions where you have objects of varying length that you want to tie together. The data frame requires objects to be of the same length and pads out to a rectangular shape using `NA`. The data frame is a powerful object because it can hold mixed items, so you can have a column of numbers followed by a column of factors. The matrix, on the other hand, is comprised of a rectangular (two-dimensional) block of one kind of object. So, you can have a numerical matrix or a character matrix, but not a mixture.

Now let's examine the `bird` matrix that you met previously. If you apply the `str()` command to the matrix you get something like the following:

```
> str(bird)
 int [1:6, 1:5] 47 19 50 46 9 4 10 3 0 16 ...
 - attr(*, "dimnames")=List of 2
  ..$ : chr [1:6] "Blackbird" "Chaffinch " "Great Tit" "House Sparrow " ...
  ..$ : chr [1:5] "Garden" "Hedgerow" "Parkland" "Pasture" ...
```

The result of the command does not say that the item is a matrix explicitly. You can see that the type of data contained in the matrix is listed first; in this case the data are integer numbers. Then you see the row and column names listed.

You can also look at all the named objects you have at once using the `ls.str()` command. However, this can lead to quite lengthy output if you have many objects. You can use the `pattern =` instruction to narrow down your focus in the same way you met previously using the `ls()` command. For example:

```
ls.str(pattern = 'data')
```

This lists all the objects with "data" in their name and shows you the structure of each.

You can obtain information about the type of object by using the `class()` command. This gives you the class of object, so, for example, if you examined some of the data from the current examples you get the following:

```
> class(grass.l)
[1] "list"

> class(grass)
[1] "data.frame"

> class(bird)
[1] "matrix"
```

These examples show that you are dealing with a list, a data frame, and a matrix, respectively. If you examine a simple vector object, you get the class of data. For example:

```
> class(month)
[1] "character"

> class(mow)
[1] "integer"
```

Here you can see that the `month` data are text (that is, characters) and the `mow` data are integers (that is, numbers).

Later in section "Constructing Data Objects" you learn how to create each particular type of object and how to convert from one to the other. Before you get there you will discover more about the R interface next.

WORKING WITH HISTORY COMMANDS

When using R you have to be prepared to undertake a bit of typing. However, you can save yourself a lot of time by using the built-in history. Everything you type from the keyboard is potentially stored in a history file. You can access the previous command history by using the arrows on the keyboard. The up arrow scrolls back through the list of previous lines of the history. The down arrow moves forward. Once you reach a line that you want to repeat you can simply hit the Enter key. Alternatively, you can use the left and right arrows to move into the line; you can then edit the command. You can also click on the line you have reached and edit from there.

NOTE *You can copy and paste text to and from any application. This means that you could copy commands from R into a word processor where you can keep them for another time. You could copy text from a previous command and paste it into the current line. This allows you great flexibility; you might use this facility to build up a library of useful commands that you can call on when needed to save you typing. You might also use this to create your own help file by keeping notes alongside each command.*

Using History Files

The history of previous commands is saved to disk each time you quit R (provided you say "yes" when asked if you want to save the workspace). You can access this list of commands in one of several ways according to which computer OS you are using. These access methods are outlined in the following sections.

Viewing the Previous Command History

You can view the current list of history items using the `history()` command like so:

```
> history(max.show = 25)
```

In Windows or Macintosh this opens up a new window that displays the contents of the current history. The text can be copied to the clipboard.

On Linux you get a list of the items in the main console window. The list can be scrolled using the arrow keys and text can be copied to the clipboard. When you are done, press the Q key to return to the main console window.

The `max.show` part of the command instructs R to display up to a certain number of items; the default is set to 25.

```
> history()
```

Saving and Recalling Lists of Commands

You can save the current history set to a disk file using the `savehistory()` command. Conversely, you can load a list of instructions from a file using `loadhistory()`. The basic forms of the commands are like so:

```
savehistory(file = '.Rhistory')
loadhistory(file = '.Rhistory')
```

You must specify the filename in quotes; the default name is blank followed by the `.Rhistory` extension. The file location is relative to the working directory (remember the `getwd()` command). In Windows you can also use the File menu to bring up Load History or Save History options.

Alternative History Commands in Macintosh OS

In Macintosh OS X the history items can be accessed and manipulated in an additional alternative fashion. The toolbar contains an icon that opens out a sidebar. This sidebar contains a list of the history items as shown in Figure 2-1.

At the foot of the sidebar are buttons that allow the loading or saving of history files. Any item can be pasted into the R console window by double clicking it.

You can still use the `loadhistory()`, `savehistory()`, and `history()` commands as described previously.

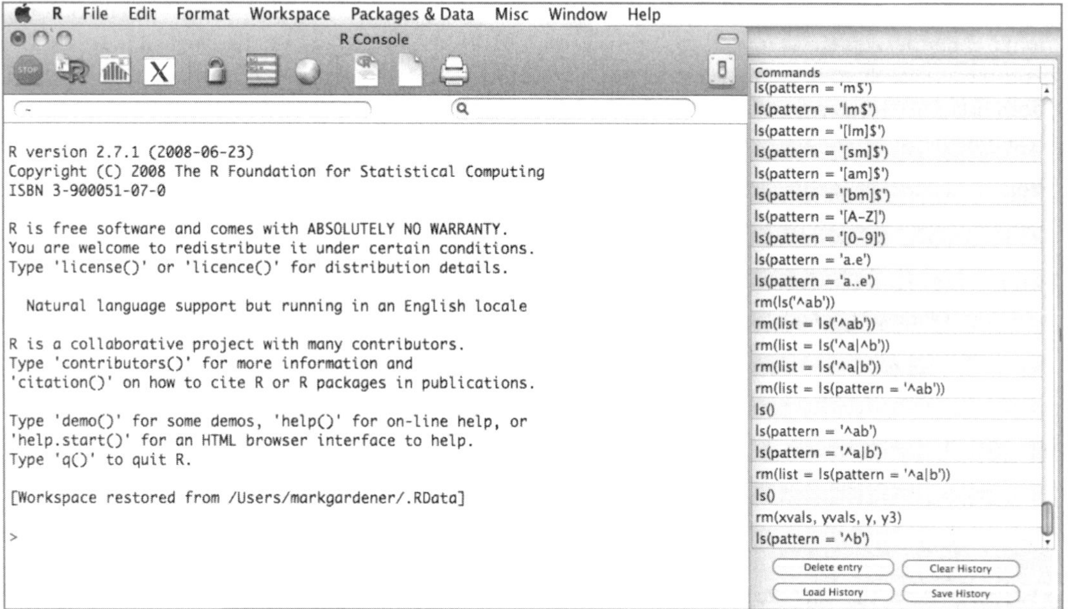

FIGURE 2-1

Editing History Files

The history files are saved on disk as plain text. This means that you can open them in any word processor and edit/manipulate them how you like. The history files saved by default have the `.Rhistory` extension. The files are stored in the default working directory unless you specified otherwise during the save operation. You can find out what the default directory is using the `getwd()` command described earlier.

When you save a history file and give it a name it becomes visible to the OS and to you in the file browser. The default history file has a name starting with a period and this makes it invisible in normal circumstances. The method you use to view these invisible files depends on the OS you are using.

In Macintosh you can check/alter the default history file by going to the Preferences menu. In Windows and Linux you must use a command like the following:

```
Sys.setenv('R_HISTFILE' = 'myhistory.Rhistory')
```

You place the filename you require in quotes, remembering that the file will be saved in the default directory.

The history file does not grow infinitely; the number of entries is capped. You can set the limit from the preferences in Macintosh OS X, but in Windows or Linux you must use something along the following lines:

```
Sys.setenv('R_HISTSIZE' = 512)
```

Unfortunately these commands only work while R is running and are "forgotten" when you quit. To make them permanent you need to get these commands to run automatically each time R is started. To do this search your home directory for a file called `.Rprofile`; it will be a hidden file. If this file does not exist, you can create one in a text editor and add the lines you require. These will be run when R opens.

You can check what the defaults for the history file and its size are by using the following commands, which work for all operating systems:

```
> Sys.getenv('R_HISTFILE')
          R_HISTFILE
"myhistory.Rhistory"
> Sys.getenv('R_HISTSIZE')
R_HISTSIZE
     "512"
```

If the default has not altered from the original, you will see a pair of quote marks. In practice there is little point altering the default history file. It is, however, useful to be able to save or load a set of commands as was described earlier (in the section "Saving and Recalling Lists of Commands").

SAVING YOUR WORK IN R

Once you begin working with R and creating named objects you will have a mixture of data items and results. You will want to save these to disk in order to work on them later or perhaps to share with others. You can use several methods to save your work. This section describes the most popular ones, including saving upon exit, saving to a disk, and saving to a text file.

Saving the Workspace on Exit

When you quit R, a message appears asking if you want to save the `workspace image`; it is a good habit to say yes. When you do, R saves all the objects currently in memory to the default workspace file (in your default working directory). The history items are also saved to their separate file.

This is a good way to keep all that you have been working on together so you can pick up where you left off. However, you can also save various objects to disk, either individually or in groups. This is especially useful if you are working on several projects and want to send data to a colleague or simply to keep items in separate places.

Saving Data Files to Disk

It is not really convenient to quit R every time you want to save your work to disk. Sometimes, if you are working on several items or projects at a time you may even want to save these separately. Fortunately, R provides a solution; you can save individual objects, or indeed all the objects, to disk at any time using the `save()` command.

Save Named Objects

The `save()` command operates like so:

```
save(list, file = 'filename')
```

You need to specify a filename and it must be in quotes. The file will be saved to the current working directory by default. The `list` instruction can be in one of two forms: you can simply type the names of the objects you want to save separated with commas or you can link to a list of names created by some other means. Look at the examples that follow:

```
> save(bf, bf.lm, bf.beta, file = 'Desktop/butterfly.RData')
> save(list = ls(pattern = '^bf'), file = 'Desktop/butterfly.RData')
```

In the first case three objects were specified (`bf`, `bf.lm`, and `bf.beta`), and in the second example the `ls()` command was used to create a list of objects beginning with `bf`. In both cases, the output file was saved to the `Desktop` folder rather than the default.

Note that if you link to a list you must put the `list` instruction in the command explicitly, like so:

```
> mylist = c('bf', 'bf.beta', 'bf.lm')
> save(list = mylist, file = 'Desktop/butterfly.RData')
```

In this case the first command makes a simple list called `mylist`, which contains the names of the objects. The second command saves the objects to disk. Note also that the filename is completed by giving it an `.RData` extension; this is the preferred extension for saved data.

If you try to read an `.RData` file with a word processor, you will see a load of gibberish; data saved using the `save()` command is encoded. You are able to write files in a more generalized format using the `write()` command, as you see shortly.

Save Everything

If you want to save all the objects in memory, but there are a lot of them, it would be quite tedious to type all their names. R provides you with two alternative options:

```
save(list = ls(all=TRUE), file = 'filename')
save.image(file = 'filename')
```

In the first case everything is specified using the `ls()` command. The second example is a special command that allows you to save everything with a bit less typing. This is essentially what happens when you are asked to save the workspace when you quit R. If you do not specify a filename, the default is used; the filename defaults to `".RData"`.

In both Windows and Macintosh OS X you can manipulate the workspace using the menu options. In Windows these are found under the File menu; in OS X they are in the Workspace menu.

NOTE *In Windows and Macintosh operating systems when you double-click on an* `.Rdata` *file, R will open and load the data. If R was not open already, the only data in its memory when it does open will be the data you clicked. If R was already open, the data will be added to those items already in memory. When you exit R the workspace will be saved to the same file you opened (assuming you say "yes" when prompted), so it is easy to keep projects separate.*

Reading Data Files from Disk

When you save a file to disk, R saves the data in a binary format. This means that the file cannot be read by a regular word processor or text editor. You can read one of these binary files from within R using the `load()` command:

```
load(file = 'filename.Rdata')
```

You need to put the filename in quotes (single or double, as long as the pair match) and remember to include the extension. The usual extension to use is `.Rdata`. If the file is not in your working directory the full path must be entered (all in the quotes). Alternatively, you can use the `file.choose()` instruction and select your file if you are using Windows or Macintosh operating systems.

```
load(file = file.choose())
```

Once the file is read, any data objects that were saved in it are available and can be seen by using the `ls()` command.

It is also possible to load binary data items directly from your operating system by double-clicking the file you want. In Windows and Macintosh systems the `.Rdata` file extension should automatically become associated with R when you install the program. This is a useful way to open R because the only data that is loaded will be the data within the `.Rdata` file.

NOTE *Keeping track of your data objects is an important discipline, and you should check regularly what data objects you have in R and ensure that important items are saved to disk.*

Creating data objects and transferring them to and from disk are really important activities. You will need to save data to disk in order to share with colleagues or simply to archive the data and keep your projects separate. In the following activity you get a chance to practice creating a simple data item, save it to disk, and reload it.

TRY IT OUT Save and Read a Binary Data File to and from Disk

In this activity you create a simple data object and save it to disk. Then you remove it and load the saved version from the disk.

1. To start with you should look to see what data objects you already have:

   ```
   > ls()
   ```

2. Now you can create a simple data object; anything will do, but follow the example to create a simple numerical vector:

   ```
   > savedata = c(9, 2, 4, 6, 5, 7, 9, 2, 1, 1, 7)
   ```

3. You can see that your new data object exists by typing its name or by using the `ls()` command:

   ```
   > savedata
    [1] 9 2 4 6 5 7 9 2 1 1 7
   ```

4. Now save your new data object to a file:

```
> save(savedata, file = 'savedata test.Rdata')
```

5. Next, remove it from R using the `rm()` command:

```
> rm(savedata)
```

6. You can check that the object is gone by typing its name or using the `ls()` command. Once you are convinced that the data is really gone you can use the `load()` command to read the file from disk:

```
> load(file = 'savedata test.Rdata')
```

7. Alternatively you can use `file.choose()` as the filename and select the file from the browser (this does not work in Linux):

```
> load(file = file.choose())
```

8. Check that the data has been loaded by typing its name or using the `ls()` command once again:

```
> savedata
[1] 9 2 4 6 5 7 9 2 1 1 7
```

How It Works

You started by checking to see what named objects you already have using the `ls()` command, because you do not want to overwrite an existing object. The `c()` command is a simple way to construct a short numerical vector. The `save()` command writes objects to disk while the `load()` command reads them in. In this case you removed the original data object using the `rm()` command so that you could check that your `load()` command worked correctly.

WARNING *If you create a new object that has the same name as an existing object, the new one will overwrite the old and you will not get a warning. So, it is a good idea to check what object names exist with an* `ls()` *command.*

Saving Data to Disk as Text Files

Saving your data in "R format" is extremely useful, especially if you are working on multiple projects; you are able to keep things separate. R maintains everything in memory though so if you have a very large amount of data, performance could suffer. In addition, there may well be times when you want to be able to save data items in a more universal format: for example, CSV or tab-delimited text. This can be useful to share data with colleagues who do not have R or to use for other purposes. For these reasons, it is available to save your data to disk as a text file instead of saving it to disk as a binary (R format) coded file.

Previously you met the `read.table()` and `read.csv()` commands (refer to the section "Reading Bigger Data Files"), which were used to transfer data into R. You can transfer data out of R using the `write.table()`, `write.csv()`, and `cat()` commands.

The command you use depends on what it is you want to save to disk. If you have a single vector of values you use `write()` or `cat()`; if you have a multiple column item containing several variables, you use `write.table()` or `write.csv()`.

Writing Vector Objects to Disk

If you have a vector, you can use the `write()` command. The basic form of the command is the following:

```
write(x, file = "data", ncolumns = if(is.character(x)) 1 else 5, sep = " ")
```

This looks a bit complicated because the `ncolumns =` part contains a conditional statement. This is because the `if()` statement creates a file with multiple columns according to the type of data. If the data are text, a single column is created. If the data are numeric, five columns are created (you can alter the number of columns). The items are separated by a space by default; you can change this by altering the `sep =` instruction. For example, the following code snippet contains a list of numbers. The `write()` command sees that these are numeric and creates five columns by default. The data are separated with commas.

```
> data7
 [1] 23.0 17.0 12.5 11.0 17.0 12.0 14.5  9.0 11.0  9.0 12.5 14.5 17.0  8.0 21.0
> write(data7, file = 'Desktop/data7.txt', sep = ',')
```

The resulting file looks like the following if viewed in a basic text editor:

```
23,17,12.5,11,17
12,14.5,9,11,9
12.5,14.5,17,8,21
```

If you want to create a single column you set the `ncolumns =` instruction to 1. If you want to create a single row you need to know how many items there are and set the number of columns to this value. You can do this automatically like so:

```
> write(data7, file = 'Desktop/data7.txt', sep = ',', ncolumns = length(data7))
```

Here a command called `length()` was used, which determines how "long" the vector of data is. The resulting file looks like the following:

```
23,17,12.5,11,17,12,14.5,9,11,9,12.5,14.5,17,8,21
```

A quicker way to achieve this result is to use the `cat()` command. Think of this as short for catalogue; just "print" the object and send it to a file.

```
> cat(data7, file = 'Desktop/data7.txt')
```

In this instance the separator is left as a space (the default) and the data values are written as a simple row of numbers.

Writing Matrix and Data Frame Objects to Disk

If you have a matrix object or a data frame, you need to use the `write.table()` command. The basic command has various instructions that can be set as follows:

```
write.table(mydata, file = 'filename', row.names = TRUE, sep = ' ', col.names =
TRUE)
```

You replace the `mydata` part with the data item you want to write to disk. The filename needs to be in quotes and its location is relative to the current working directory. Each row of data is given an index number; most of the time you do not want to save this index to a file, so you need to alter the instruction to `row.names = FALSE`. If you want to make a file with columns separated by tabs, you put `'\t'` in the `sep =` instruction. You can also specify the decimal point character using the `dec =` instruction.

If you want to make a CSV file, you could use the alternative `write.csv()` command. This is essentially the same but the default settings are slightly different:

```
write.csv(mydata, file = 'filename', row.names = TRUE, sep = ',', col.names =
TRUE)
```

The `write.table()` and `write.csv()` commands are most useful to save complex data items that contain multiple columns, such as you would expect to see in a spreadsheet. If you have a complex item like a matrix or a data frame object, this is the command you should use. List objects are also complex items, but they require special handling, as you see next.

Writing List Objects to Disk

Lists can be quite untidy and contain multiple items of varying sorts. Running an analytical command and storing the "result" generally creates a list, but you can also make a list as a way to tie together data items.

You can produce a text representation of the list using the `dput()` command and you can recall it using the `dget()` command. The two commands are simple:

```
dput(object, file = "")
dget(file)
```

The following example shows a simple list. Here it is simply two numerical vectors but it could be a lot more complex:

```
> grass.l
$mow
[1] 12 15 17 11 15

$unmow
[1] 8 9 7 9

> dput(grass.l, file = 'Desktop/grass.txt')
```

The resulting file looks like this:

```
structure(list(mow = c(12L, 15L, 17L, 11L, 15L), unmow = c(8L,
9L, 7L, 9L)), .Names = c("mow", "unmow"))
```

This is not exactly what you would want in a spreadsheet, but it is the best you can do without pulling out the bits you want and re-arranging them. You can recall the list using `dget()`; in the following example a new object is created from the file using this command:

```
grass.list = dget(file = 'Desktop/grass.txt')
```

The `dput()` command attempts to write an ASCII representation of your object to disk so that it can be recalled using the `dget()` command. The process does not always work smoothly. In general, data objects that are lists are recalled successfully but results of analyses are not. What generally happens is that the list object is reconstructed successfully, but certain attributes are lost. If your object is data this is not a problem, but if your result is a linear regression, for example, you may not be able to carry out some of the further commands that you may have wanted.

If you have complex results it is better to save them as `.Rdata` objects. If you want to use the text of a result you can easily copy it from the R console window and paste it into another program.

Converting List Objects to Data Frames

If you have a fairly simple list, perhaps containing several numerical samples, you can manipulate the list to produce a data frame and then save that to a text file.

Here is a simple list comprising of four numerical samples; you have met them all before:

```
> my.list
$mow
[1] 12 15 17 11 15

$unmow
[1] 8 9 7 9

$data3
 [1]  6  7  8  7  6  3  8  9 10  7  6  9

$data7
 [1] 23.0 17.0 12.5 11.0 17.0 12.0 14.5  9.0 11.0  9.0 12.5 14.5 17.0  8.0 21.0
```

Remember that you can check the structure of your object using the `str()` command like so:

```
> str(my.list)
List of 4
 $ mow  : int [1:5] 12 15 17 11 15
 $ unmow: int [1:4] 8 9 7 9
 $ data3: num [1:12] 6 7 8 7 6 3 8 9 10 7 ...
 $ data7: num [1:15] 23 17 12.5 11 17 12 14.5 9 11 9 ...
```

Because they are all numbers you could create a data frame that contained two columns, one for the actual numbers and one for the name of the sample each value relates to. To do this, you can use the `stack()` command like so:

```
> my.stack = stack(my.list)
```

This creates a two-column data frame:

```
   values   ind
1      12   mow
2      15   mow
3      17   mow
4      11   mow
5      15   mow
6       8 unmow
7       9 unmow
8       7 unmow
9       9 unmow
10      6 data3
11      7 data3
12      8 data3
...
```

Not all of the data are shown here for brevity (try it out on your own and you will see the entire display). Notice that the column headings are `values` and `ind`. You can easily rename them to anything you like using the `names()` command:

```
> names(my.stack) = c('numbers', 'sample')
```

Here the first column is changed to `numbers` and the second column is now called `sample`. You simply use the `c()` command to give the names you require.

To get back to the list from this new two-column data frame, you use the `unstack()` command like so:

```
> unstack(my.stack)
$data3
[1]  6  7  8  7  6  3  8  9 10  7  6  9

$data7
[1] 23.0 17.0 12.5 11.0 17.0 12.0 14.5 9.0 11.0 9.0 12.5 14.5 17.0 8.0 21.0

$mow
[1] 12 15 17 11 15

$unmow
[1] 8 9 7 9
```

This pulls the data apart back to its component samples, but you still need to create the list that "ties" the objects together. You do this like so:

```
> my.new.list = as.list(unstack(my.stack))
```

In other words, you use the `as.list()` command to make the list from the unstacked data frame!

If you have several data vectors and want to create a list from them (rather than from a data frame like the preceding example), you use the `as.list()` command and give the object names that you want to include in the list:

```
> my.list = as.list(mow, unmow, data3, data7)
```

However, this does not name the individual parts of the list (unlike the previous example where you had a data frame), so you need to add names afterwards like so:

```
> names(my.list) = c('mow', 'unmow', 'data3', 'data7')
```

You can also use the `list()` command to do the same job, and in most ways they are identical.

SUMMARY

- R can function as a simple calculator and the basic mathematical operators (for example, `+ - / *`) can be used to perform math.
- You can store results of calculations for later use simply by typing a name to hold the result; the calculation then follows an `=` sign.
- You can create data objects from the keyboard, clipboard, or external data files using `c()`, `scan()`, and `read.csv()` commands.

- You can list objects that are ready for use using the `ls()` command and you can remove (delete) objects using the `rm()` command.
- There are different types of data, numerical and character. Data can exist in one of several forms; vectors are one-dimensional: matrixes and data frames are two-dimensional. List objects are loose collections of other objects.
- You can cycle through previous commands in the history using the up and down arrows. You can also save lists of commands to a file.
- You can write data from R to disk and save your work using the `save()` command. Other commands allow all items to be saved at once or for CSV files to be written.

EXERCISES

You can find answers to these exercises in Appendix A.

1. You have the results of a simple experiment to look at the visitation of various bee species to different plants. The number of bees observed was as follows:

```
Buff tail: 10 1 37 5 12
Garden bee: 8 3 19 6 4
Red tail: 18 9 1 2 4
Honeybee: 12 13 16 9 10
Carder bee: 8 27 6 32 23
```

Make five simple numeric vectors of these data.

2. You created five vectors of data in Exercise 1. Look at the list of objects that you have in R right now and try to generate a listing that includes only the items you created from the previous example.

A. Save all the items you just created to a disk file in your working directory.

B. Now remove all the vectors that you just made.

C. Now recall the vectors from disk.

▶ WHAT YOU LEARNED IN THIS CHAPTER

TOPIC	KEY POINTS

Simple math:
`+ - / * ^ log() cos() acos() abs()`
`sqrt() pi() factorial()`
	R can perform like a regular calculator and there are a range of mathematical operators and functions that can be used. Use `help(Arithmetic)` in R to get more information.

Assigning object names:
`Object.name = calculation`
`Object.name <- calculation`
`calculation -> Object.name`
	Results of calculations can be stored as named objects. The `=` and `<-` symbols enable you to create an object from the result of the following calculation (in other words, you assign from right to left). The `->` symbol enables you to assign the results of a calculation to a named object (that is, you assign from left to right).

Object names for example:
`data1`
`Data1`
`data.1`
	Objects are allowed names using all the letters a–z and uppercase A–Z as well as the numbers 0–9. A name must begin with a letter. The only punctuation mark allowed is a period. Names are case sensitive.

Making data: `object.name = c(x, y, z)`	The `c()` command allows the concatenation of several items. It can be used to create data samples, for example.
Making data: `object.name = scan()`	The `scan()` command allows data items to be entered from the keyboard, clipboard, or a simple text file.
Making data: `object.name = read.table(file = )`	The `read.table()` command allows a text file to be read from disk. The resulting object is a data frame with columns of equal length; short columns are padded out with `NA`. The `read.csv()` command is a special case of the command with defaults set for CSV files.

Listing objects:
`ls(pattern = regex)`
`rm(item1, item2, …)`
	The `ls()` command lists all the objects currently in memory. The `rm()` command removes objects (thereby deleting them). The list can use a regular expression and refine the result by listing only certain names.

continues

...AT YOU LEARNED IN THIS CHAPTER *(continued)*

TOPIC	KEY POINTS
Data type: numerical (numeric, integer) character (factor, character)	Data can be in one of two major types, numerical for numbers or character for text. Number data can be integer or numeric. Text data can be classed as factor or character. The latter is a general type and items are shown enclosed in quotes. Factor data are text but not quoted.
Data form: vector data frame matrixlist	Data can be in one of several forms. A one-dimensional structure is a vector. Data in 2D form can be a data frame or a matrix. In a matrix all the data of the same type. A data frame can contain mixtures of data (for example, numeric and factor). Missing values and "short" columns are padded with `NA`. A list object is a collection of other objects and can contain items of different lengths and types.

History commands:
`history()`
`loadhistory()`
`savehistory()`
	Previously executed commands can be viewed using the up and down arrow keys. The entire history can be viewed using the `history()` command and files of commands can be loaded from or saved to disk.

Saving and loading data:
`save(x, y, z, …, file =)`
`save.image(file =)`
`write(x, file =)`
`write.csv(data, file =)`
`load(file =)`
	When closing R all data can be saved to the default `.RData` file. The `save()` command can be used to save one or more objects to a file. The `save.image()` command can be used to save all objects to a file. The resulting files can be recalled using the `load()` command.
	A plain text representation of a data object can be saved to disk using the `write()` or `write.csv()` commands.

Finding data on disk:
`dir()`
`getwd() setwd()`
`file.choose()`
	The `dir()` command allows the listing of files stored on disk. The working directory is where files are looked for and stored to by default. The location of the current working directory can be ascertained using `getwd()`. The working directory can be set to a new location using the `setwd()` command. Filenames must be specified explicitly but on Windows and Mac systems `file.choose()` can be used in place of a name, allowing a file to be selected by the user.

3

Starting Out: Working With Objects

WHAT YOU WILL LEARN IN THIS CHAPTER:

- How to manipulate data objects
- How to select and display parts of data objects
- How to sort and rearrange data objects
- How to construct data objects
- How to determine what form a data object is
- How to convert a data object from one form to another

Data objects are the fundamental items that you work with in R. Carrying out analyses on your data and making sense of the results are the primary reasons you are using R. In this chapter you learn more about data objects and how to work with them. You learn how to recognize the different forms of data objects that R uses, and how to convert one form into another. You also learn how to sort and rearrange data, and how to extract parts of data that match criteria that you set. All of these tasks are essential in the path towards understanding R as well as being able to understand your data and analyze it effectively.

MANIPULATING OBJECTS

Now that you have a few data objects to deal with it is time to think about examining these objects and getting to grips with the actual data they contain. When you collect data the first step is to get the data into R. After this you will want to look at your data, and perform summary statistics and other analyses on them. Although many analytical operations can be conducted on the data "as is," there will be many occasions when you will want to manipulate the data you have; you may want to reorder the data into a new and more informative manner, or you may want to extract certain parts of a complex data object for some further purpose.

There are many ways to manipulate your data, and understanding how to do this is important in learning about R because the more you know about the way R handles objects, the better use you can make of R as an analytical tool.

Manipulating Vectors

Vectors are essentially the building blocks of more complicated items and you can use them to construct such objects or as data items in their own right. Being able to manipulate vectors is important because they are such fundamental objects. You can manipulate vectors in several ways, all of which can be important in data analysis. The main ways you can manipulate vectors are the following:

- Selecting and displaying certain parts
- Sorting and rearranging
- Returning logical values

Later in this chapter you will also see how to combine vectors to make more complicated data objects like a matrix, a list and data frames, which all have their own uses.

Selecting and Displaying Parts of a Vector

Being able to select and display parts of a vector can be important for many reasons. For example, if you have a large sample of data you may want to see which items are larger than a certain value. Alternatively you may want to extract a series of values as a subsample in an analysis. Being able to select parts of a vector is a basic skill that underpins many more complicated operations in R.

Here is a simple vector of numbers that form a sample:

```
> data1
 [1] 3 5 7 5 3 2 6 8 5 6 9
```

These values were the `data1` object that you created a while back. To see the entire vector you simply type its name. You can also display part of the vector using an additional part to your command as shown in Table 3-1.

TABLE 3-1: Various Ways to Select Part of a Vector Object

COMMAND	RESULT
`data1[1]`	Shows the first item in the vector.
`data1[3]`	Shows the third item.
`data1[1:3]`	Shows the first to the third items.
`data1[-1]`	Shows all except the first item.
`data1[c(1, 3, 4, 8)]`	Shows the items listed in the `c()` part.
`data1[data1 > 3]`	Shows all items greater than 3.
`data1[data1 < 5 | data1 > 7]`	Shows items less than 5 or greater than 7.

In Table 3-1 you can see how to use the square brackets after the name to select out parts of the object named.

You can use other commands on your object to help you extract various parts including the following:

```
length(data1)
```

This tells you how many elements there are in the vector, including `NA` items. You can incorporate this in the square brackets like so:

```
data1[(length(data1)-5):length(data1)]
```

This shows the last five elements of the vector.

You can use other operations. In the following example the `max()` command is used to get the largest value in the vector:

```
> data1
 [1] 3 5 7 5 3 2 6 8 5 6 9

> max(data1)
[1] 9

> which(data1 == max(data1))
[1] 11
```

The first command, `max()`, gives the actual value that is the largest numerical value in the vector (in this case 9). The second command asks which of the elements is the largest. The value obtained is 11, meaning that the eleventh item in the vector is the largest. Notice that double equal signs are used here.

NOTE *A single = usually means that you want to set something to a particular value; double == signs ensures that R knows you want to look for something equal to a value rather than setting it.*

Another useful command is one that generates sequences, `seq()`. You can use this to extract values from a vector at regular intervals. For example:

```
> data1[seq(1, length(data1), 2)]
[1] 3 7 3 6 5 9
```

This would pick out a sequence beginning with the first and ending with the last and with an interval of two. In other words, you select the first, third, fifth, and so on. You use the `length()` part to ensure that you stop once you get to the end. The general form of the `seq()` command is like so:

```
seq(start, end, interval)
```

You have to specify how far along you want to start from, where you want to end up, and how big the interval is.

These commands will work on character vectors as well as numeric, so for example:

```
> data5
 [1] "Jan" "Feb" "Mar" "Apr" "May" "Jun" "Jul" "Aug" "Sep" "Oct" "Nov" "Dec"
> data5[-1:-6]
[1] "Jul" "Aug" "Sep" "Oct" "Nov" "Dec"
```

Here the last six months in your vector of months are picked out. In the following example the biggest value is selected:

```
> which(data5 == max(data5))
[1] 9
```

In this example R has selected the ninth item, which is `"Sep"`. The items are sorted alphabetically, so the biggest is determined by that order as opposed to a numerical value.

Sorting and Rearranging a Vector

You can rearrange the items in a vector to be in one order or another using the `sort()` command. The default is to use ascending order and to leave out any `NA` items, like so:

```
> unmow
[1]  8  9  7  9 NA

> sort(unmow)
[1] 7 8 9 9
```

In the preceding example, you can see that the numbers have been re-ordered and the `NA` item has been stripped out. You can alter the sort order by using `decreasing = TRUE` as an additional instruction in the command:

```
> sort(unmow, decreasing = TRUE)
[1] 9 9 8 7
```

You can change the way `NA` items are dealt with using the `na.last =` instruction. You have three options: the default is `NA`, meaning they are dropped. If you use `TRUE` the `NA` items are placed last and if you use `FALSE` they are placed first:

```
> sort(unmow, na.last = NA)
[1] 7 8 9 9

> sort(unmow, na.last = TRUE)
[1]  7  8  9  9 NA

> sort(unmow, na.last = FALSE)
[1] NA  7  8  9  9
```

You can get an index using the `order()` command. This uses the same instructions as the `sort()` command, but tells you the position of each item along the vector:

```
> unmow
[1]  8  9  7  9 NA

> order(unmow)
[1] 3 1 2 4 5

> order(unmow, na.last = NA)
[1] 3 1 2 4

> order(unmow, na.last = FALSE)
[1] 5 3 1 2 4
```

The default instructions in the preceding example set `na.last = TRUE`, which is slightly different than the `sort()` command. You can also see here that the `order()` command reported that the third item in the vector is the first value when ordered numerically.

The `rank()` command sorts your data in a slightly different way than the `order()` command: it handles tied values. Compare the two commands in the following example:

```
> unmow
[1]  8  9  7  9 NA

> order(unmow)
[1] 3 1 2 4 5

> rank(unmow)
[1] 2.0 3.5 1.0 3.5 5.0
```

When using the `order()` command you see that the two values of 9 in the original vector are given a different value (2 and 4). There is no reason why they could not have been ordered the other way around (that is, 4 and 2); the default is to take them as they come. When you use the `rank()` command you get a different result; the two 9 values are the third and fourth largest and by default they get a shared rank of 3.5. The `NA` item is placed at the end because by default the `na.last = TRUE` is the default setting.

You can alter the way tied values are handled using the `ties.method = "method"` instruction; by default this is set to `"average"` and this is the method used in all non-parametric statistical routines. You have other options and can set `"first"`, `"random"`, `"max"`, or `"min"` as alternatives to the default `"average"`:

```
> unmow
[1]  8  9  7  9 NA

> rank(unmow, ties.method = 'first')
[1] 2 3 1 4 5

> rank(unmow, ties.method = 'average')
[1] 2.0 3.5 1.0 3.5 5.0

> rank(unmow, ties.method = 'max')
[1] 2 4 1 4 5

> rank(unmow, ties.method = 'random', na.last = 'keep')
[1]  2  3  1  4 NA
```

In the last example you can see a different option for the `na.last =` instruction; you can choose to keep any `NA` items intact. The following example also shows this:

```
> dat.na
[1]  2  5  4 NA  7  3  9 NA 12

> rank(dat.na, na.last = 'keep')
[1]  1  4  3 NA  5  2  6 NA  7
```

The `rank()` command is especially useful for non-parametric statistical testing, which relies heavily on the original data being converted to ranks.

Returning Logical Values from a Vector

Previously you saw how the `which()` command was used to tell which items in a vector met some criterion. See the following code snippet for a reminder:

```
> data1
 [1] 3 5 7 5 3 2 6 8 5 6 9

> which(data1 == 6)
[1]  7 10
```

Here it has been determined that the seventh and tenth items are equal to 6; note that two = signs are used like so ==.

If you omit the `which()` command and use the == directly you get a different sort of answer:

```
> data1 == 6
 [1] FALSE FALSE FALSE FALSE FALSE FALSE  TRUE FALSE FALSE  TRUE FALSE
```

Now you have logical answers; each item is looked at in turn to see if it is equal to 6; you get a `TRUE` or `FALSE` result for each item in the vector. You can use other mathematical operators, especially the greater than or less than symbols, like the following examples:

```
> data2 >5
 [1] FALSE FALSE  TRUE FALSE FALSE FALSE  TRUE  TRUE FALSE  TRUE  TRUE FALSE FALSE
[14]  TRUE FALSE FALSE

> data2 <5
 [1]  TRUE FALSE FALSE FALSE  TRUE  TRUE FALSE FALSE FALSE FALSE FALSE  TRUE FALSE
[14] FALSE  TRUE  TRUE
```

You can also combine items using various logical operators:

```
> data2 >5 & data2 <8
 [1] FALSE FALSE  TRUE FALSE FALSE FALSE  TRUE FALSE FALSE  TRUE FALSE FALSE FALSE
[14]  TRUE FALSE FALSE

> data8
 [1] "Jan" "Feb" "Mar" "Apr" "May" "Jun" "Jul" "Aug" "Sep" "Oct" "Nov" "Dec"

> data8 == 'Feb'| data8 == 'Apr'
 [1] FALSE  TRUE FALSE  TRUE FALSE FALSE FALSE FALSE FALSE FALSE FALSE FALSE
```

In the first example the `&` symbol was used to look for items greater than 5 AND less than 8. In the second example the pipe symbol (|) was used to match "`Feb`" OR "`Apr`".

Manipulating Matrix and Data Frames

Where you have a matrix or a data frame you have a two-dimensional object rather than the one dimension of a vector. Complex objects tend to be used for many statistical operations simply because that is the nature of statistics—you rarely have anything as simple as a single column of figures! Because most of the data you encounter will be in this more complex form it is essential to be able to manipulate and deal with the data frame and matrix objects.

Selecting and Displaying Parts of a Matrix or Data Frame

Like a vector, you can still use the square brackets when displaying a matrix or data frame, but now you need to specify two dimensions: `object[row, column]`. In the following activity you explore a data frame object, using the square brackets to select out various parts of a data frame object.

TRY IT OUT Select Parts of a Data Frame Object

Available for download on Wrox.com

Use the `mf` data from the `Beginning.RData` file for this activity, which you explore here by selecting out various parts using the square bracket syntax.

1. Look at the data frame called `mf` that contains five columns of data. To view it simply type its name:

```
> mf
  Length Speed Algae  NO3 BOD
1     20    12    40 2.25 200
2     21    14    45 2.15 180
3     22    12    45 1.75 135
4     23    16    80 1.95 120
5     21    20    75 1.95 110
6     20    21    65 2.75 120
...
```

2. Pick out the item from the third row and the third column:

```
> mf[3,3]
[1] 45
```

3. Now select the third row and display columns one to four:

```
> mf[3,1:4]
  Length Speed Algae  NO3
3     22    12    45 1.75
```

4. Display all the rows by leaving out the first value; select the first column alone:

```
> mf[,1]
 [1] 20 21 22 23 21 20 19 16 15 14 21 21 21 20 19 18 17 19 21 13 16 25 24 23 22
```

5. Specify several rows but leave out a value at the end to display all columns:

```
> mf[c(1,3,5,7),]
  Length Speed Algae  NO3 BOD
1     20    12    40 2.25 200
3     22    12    45 1.75 135
5     21    20    75 1.95 110
7     19    17    65 1.85  95
```

6. Now specify several rows but use a `-4` to indicate that you want to display all columns except the fourth:

```
> mf[c(1,3,5,7),-4]
```

```
  Length Speed Algae BOD
1     20    12    40 200
3     22    12    45 135
5     21    20    75 110
7     19    17    65  95
```

7. Because the columns are named you can select one by using its name rather than a simple value:

```
> mf[c(1,3,5,7), 'Algae']
[1] 40 45 75 65
```

8. Try giving a single value in the square brackets:

```
> mf[3]
   Algae
1     40
2     45
3     45
4     80
5     75
6     65
7     65
...
```

How It Works

The square brackets indicate that you want to subset the data object. The first value indicates the rows required and the second value, after a comma, indicates the columns required. If you leave out a value, all rows (or columns) are chosen. Within each part of the brackets you can use a variety of methods to select the items you require, `seq()` or `c()` commands, for example. If you use `-ve` values, then these are deleted from the display. Named columns (or rows) can be displayed by giving the names (in quotes) instead of a plain number.

If you specify a single value in the square brackets (rather than two), R will interpret this as a column and displays the column appropriate to the value you typed.

When you have a matrix you use the square brackets much like you did for the data frame. In the following activity you get a chance to look at a matrix object and select parts of it using the square bracket syntax.

TRY IT OUT Select Parts of a Matrix Data Object

Available for download on Wrox.com

Use the `bird` data from the `Beginning.RData` file for this activity, which you explore here by selecting out various parts using the square bracket syntax.

1. Look at the matrix object called `bird`; simply type its name:

```
> bird
                Garden Hedgerow Parkland Pasture Woodland
Blackbird           47       10       40       2        2
Chaffinch           19        3        5       0        2
Great Tit           50        0       10       7        0
```

```
House Sparrow      46        16        8       4       0
Robin               9         3        0       0       2
Song Thrush         4         0        6       0       0
```

2. You can see that there are five columns and six rows; the rows are labeled rather than having a numeric index. At first glance this appears like a data frame, so use the `str()` command to look more closely:

```
> str(bird)
 int [1:6, 1:5] 47 19 50 46 9 4 10 3 0 16 ...
 - attr(*, "dimnames")=List of 2
  ..$ : chr [1:6] "Blackbird" "Chaffinch " "Great Tit" "House Sparrow " ...
  ..$ : chr [1:5] "Garden" "Hedgerow" "Parkland" "Pasture" ...
```

3. Use the `class()` command to see that this is a matrix:

```
> class(bird)
[1] "matrix"
```

4. Select the second row and all the columns:

```
> bird[2,]
  Garden Hedgerow Parkland  Pasture Woodland
      19        3        5        0        2
```

5. Now select all rows but only the fourth column:

```
> bird[,4]
     Blackbird      Chaffinch      Great Tit      House Sparrow      Robin      Song Thrush
             2              0              7                  4          0                0
```

6. Use named rows rather than a simple number and choose all columns:

```
> bird[c('Robin', 'Blackbird'),]
          Garden Hedgerow Parkland Pasture Woodland
Robin          9        3        0       0        2
Blackbird     47       10       40       2        2
```

7. Now select a single row and column:

```
> bird[3,1]
[1] 50
```

8. Now specify a single value:

```
> bird[4]
[1] 46
```

How It Works

The `str()` command shows you details of the structure of an object. The `class()` command is a useful tool because it shows you what kind of object you are dealing with.

The `[row, column]` syntax works just like it did for the data frame with one minor difference. Typing a single value into the square brackets gives a single value rather than the column that you got with the data frame. You can type in a named row or column as long as you make sure the name is in quotes. Notice that the items are displayed in the order you typed them, so this is also a way to rearrange an object. You can also use `-ve` values to indicate rows or columns that you do not want, but note that this only works if you use numbers and not names in quotes.

In a matrix the data items are indexed starting from column one and row one, then reading down each column. Look at the following example, which shows a matrix that has been constructed in "order":

```
> test.matrix
     [,1] [,2] [,3] [,4]
[1,]    1    5    9   13
[2,]    2    6   10   14
[3,]    3    7   11   15
[4,]    4    8   12   16
```

Here you can see the data in order of their "index." You read down the first column and then carry on at the top of the next and so on. This order becomes important when you want to create a brand new matrix, as you see later in the section "Making Matrix Objects").

Sorting and Rearranging a Matrix or Data Frame

You can use the `sort()`, `order()`, and `rank()` commands on your matrix. If you specify simply the matrix object you get results along the following lines:

```
> sort(bird)
 [1]  0  0  0  0  0  0  0  0  0  2  2  2  2  3  3  4  4  5  6  7  8  9 10 10 16 19
[27] 40 46 47 50

> order(bird)
 [1]  9 12 17 20 23 24 27 28 30 19 25 26 29  8 11  6 22 14 18 21 16  5  7 15 10  2
[27] 13  4  1  3

> rank(bird)
 [1] 29.0 26.0 30.0 28.0 22.0 16.5 23.5 14.5  5.0 25.0 14.5  5.0 27.0 18.0 23.5
[16] 21.0  5.0 19.0 11.5  5.0 20.0 16.5  5.0  5.0 11.5 11.5  5.0  5.0 11.5  5.0
```

Remember that your matrix is essentially a single vector of data that contains information about how to split it up into rows and columns. If you want to sort, order, or rank rows or columns, you must specify them explicitly:

```
> sort(bird[,1])
 Song Thrush       Robin      Chaffinch    House Sparrow      Blackbird      Great Tit
           4           9             19               46             47             50

> order(bird[,1])
[1] 6 5 2 4 1 3
```

In this example the first column is used as the target to sort or order. The `order()` command allows you to give additional vectors; these are used as tie-breakers to help resolve the order of items in the first vector. Compare the following commands:

```
> order(bird[,5])
[1] 3 4 6 1 2 5

> order(bird[,5], bird[,1])
[1] 6 4 3 5 2 1
```

In the first case the result obtained is the order of the fifth column. There are a number of tied values and the result takes these in the order it finds them. In the second case the first column is used to influence the order and the final result changes. Here a second column was added to the command but more could be used.

If you have a data frame, you need a slightly different approach. You cannot perform a `sort()` command on an entire data frame, even if it is composed entirely of the same kind of data (that is, all numeric or all character). Take the following instance:

```
> grass2
  mow unmow
1  12     8
2  15     9
3  17     7
4  11     9
5  15    NA

> sort(grass2)
Error in `[.data.frame`(x, order(x, na.last = na.last, decreasing = decreasing)) :
  undefined columns selected
```

You simply get an error; the command needs to operate on a single vector. You can pick out a part of your data frame to run the `sort()` command when using the standard syntax in one of the following ways:

```
> sort(grass2[1,])
  unmow mow
[1]     8  12

> sort(grass2[,1])
[1] 11 12 15 15 17

> sort(grass2[,'mow'])
[1] 11 12 15 15 17

> sort(grass2$mow)
[1] 11 12 15 15 17
```

In the first example the first row of the data frame is sorted; the subsequent examples all sort the first column but use differing syntax. The `$`, for example, is used to obtain a single vector from a list or a data frame. This syntax can also be used in the order() command, which works pretty much the same way as it did for the matrix object:

```
> order(grass2)
 [1]  8  6  7  9  4  1  2  5  3 10

> order(grass2$mow, grass2[,2])
[1] 4 1 2 5 3

> with(grass2, order(mow,unmow))
[1] 4 1 2 5 3
```

In the first case the order() command takes the entire data frame, because the command did not specify any explicit columns (or rows) to order. The next two cases illustrate two ways to use the syntax to order the first column, using the second column as a tie-breaker. You can sometimes use the $ to extract a particular part of a data item (most often a list or a data frame). In the case of the data frame you can add the name of a column after the $ to use it as an item in its own right. In the last example you can see a new command, with(). This temporarily "opens up" the data frame and allows you to utilize the contents of the specified object. You look at this in a bit more detail shortly in the section "Viewing Objects within Objects").

Manipulating Lists

When you have a list the square brackets give a different result compared to other data objects you have met. The following example shows a list item; you can check its structure using the str() command:

```
> str(my.list)
List of 4
 $ mow  : int [1:5] 12 15 17 11 15
 $ unmow: int [1:4] 8 9 7 9
 $ data3: num [1:12] 6 7 8 7 6 3 8 9 10 7 ...
 $ data7: num [1:15] 23 17 12.5 11 17 12 14.5 9 11 9 ...
```

Here there are four elements in the list; each has a name preceded by a dollar sign. The list is a one-dimensional object, so you can use only a single value in the square brackets. In other words, you can only get out one entire part of the list. For example:

```
> my.list[1]
$mow
[1] 12 15 17 11 15
```

You will need to use a slightly different convention to extract the elements; you must use the $ in the name. This is the only way you can utilize the sort(), order(), or rank() commands on list items.

```
> sort(my.list$mow)
[1] 11 12 15 15 17

> order(my.list$mow, my.list$unmow)
Error in order(my.list$mow, my.list$unmow) : argument lengths differ
```

In the first case the `mow` vector is extracted from the list and a `sort()` command is performed. In the next case the `order()` command is used. This fails because the two items are of different lengths; you therefore cannot use the second item as a tie-breaker. You can, however, use the `order()` command on any of the separate items in the list:

```
> order(my.list$unmow)
[1] 3 1 2 4
```

So, each `$` element of the list can be thought of as a vector (as you see in the next section). The elements of a list need not all be vectors, so you should examine the structure of a list object carefully (use the `str()` command) before carrying out manipulations.

VIEWING OBJECTS WITHIN OBJECTS

When you create a list, matrix, or data frame you are bundling together several items. In matrix and data frame objects the items are all the same length (resulting in the rectangular object), but in a list object the items can be different lengths. Each of these objects can contain several items, but you may have noticed that these do not appear when you use the `ls()` command.

Looking Inside Complicated Data Objects

Previously you looked at some data called `fw`. The data were presented as a data frame with two columns like so:

```
> fw
  abund flow
1     9    2
2    25    3
3    15    5
4     2    9
5    14   14
6    25   24
7    24   29
8    47   34
```

If you use the `ls()` command you will see `fw` listed as one of the objects but you will not see `abund` or `flow`. If you type the name of one of these you will get an error:

```
> abund
Error: object 'abund' not found
```

The problem is that the `abund` and `flow` data are contained within the `fw` object and R cannot "see" them. You can use the `$` to help penetrate the data and extract parts you want to view. For example, if you append `$` and then the name of the required column you will view that column of data:

```
> fw$abund
[1]  9 25 15  2 14 25 24 47
```

Here the entire `abund` data column has been selected. It does not matter if you put spaces before or after the `$`, but it is probably a good habit to leave them out because it reinforces the idea that `fw$abund` is an object in its own right.

You can now use the square brackets as before to select out parts of the item:

```
> fw$abund[1:4]
[1]  9 25 15  2
```

When the target object is a list you can use the `$` to extract each part. In the following example, the `mow` component of the list is extracted:

```
> my.list$mow
[1] 12 15 17 11 15
```

You can now subset this using the square brackets:

```
> my.list$mow[1:4]
[1] 12 15 17 11
```

If you try this with a matrix, however, you get a quite different result:

```
> bird$Garden
Error in bird$Garden : $ operator is invalid for atomic vectors
```

This is because a matrix is essentially a single data item that has been displayed in rows and columns; recall what you saw when you tried a single value in the square brackets for a matrix. You can still extract parts of a matrix using the names of the columns, but you need a slightly different approach. You can use the column name in the square brackets like so:

```
> bird[,'Garden']
     Blackbird     Chaffinch      Great Tit    House Sparrow     Robin     Song Thrush
            47            19             50               46         9               4
```

Notice that the column name is placed in quotes. Notice also that R cannot display the result neatly on a single row and presents the results as best as it can, given the constraints of the display.

Because there are also row names in your matrix you can use these names:

```
> bird['Robin',]
  Garden Hedgerow Parkland  Pasture Woodland
       9        3        0        0        2
```

You can also use the names of data frames. In the following example, the `NO3` column of the `mf` data frame is picked out:

```
> mf[,'NO3']
 [1] 2.25 2.15 1.75 1.95 1.95 2.75 1.85 1.75 1.95 2.35 2.35 2.35 2.05 1.85 1.75
[16] 1.45 1.35 2.05 1.25 1.05 2.55 2.85 2.95 2.85 1.75
```

If your data frame has named rows rather than plain index numbers, you can use them in the same manner as you did for the matrix.

Opening Complicated Data Objects

Using the `$` to retrieve a column from a data frame is sometimes a tedious process. You can temporarily make the items within a data object available for R to "see" using the `attach()` command.

This allows the columns of a data frame and the elements of a list to be viewed without the need to use the $ sign. For example:

```
attach(my.list)
attach(mf)
```

If you try to do this for a matrix you get an error like so:

```
> attach(bird)
Error in attach(bird) :
  'attach' only works for lists, data frames and environments
```

The `attach()` command is useful because it can help reduce typing. Occasionally you may have a data object with the same name as one that you retrieve using `attach()`. If that happens you see a message similar to the following:

```
> attach(mf)
The following object(s) are masked from 'package:datasets':

     BOD
```

The `mf` data contains a column headed `BOD`. It so happens that there is a data item called `BOD` already in the `datasets` package (R provides many data examples that are used mainly in the help examples). For the time that you use `attach()` the older item is unavailable. When you are finished it is therefore a good idea to `detach()` the data. This will permit the older item to become available once more.

The items that are attached do not appear when you do an `ls()` command. You can see which items are attached using the `search()` command:

```
> search()
 [1] ".GlobalEnv"        "package:MASS"      "mf"
 [4] "tools:RGUI"        "package:stats"     "package:graphics"
 [7] "package:grDevices" "package:utils"     "package:datasets"
[10] "package:methods"   "Autoloads"         "package:base"
```

Here you can see the packages that are loaded, and also the `mf` object. Items within any of these objects are available and "seen" by R.

NOTE *Once you are done with the data object you should* `detach()` *it.*

You can also use a command that attaches the data only transiently while you perform a single command; this is the `with()` command. The basic form of the command is:

```
with(object, ...)
```

In place of the `...` you can type more or less any regular command such as the following:

```
> Algae
Error: object 'Algae' not found
```

```
> with(mf, Algae)
 [1] 40 45 45 80 75 65 65 65 35 30 65 70 85 70 35 30 50 60 70 25 35 85 80 80 75

> with(mf, sum(Algae))
[1] 1460
```

In the first example you see that the `Algae` object is not found. In the second example the `with()` command is used to view the vector of data. In this case it was a bit long-winded, because you could have typed `mf$Algae` to achieve the same result. In the final example the `sum()` command is used, which simply adds up the values and gives a final total. For fairly short commands the `$` is generally useful, but when you encounter long and more complicated commands, using `with()` can save quite a bit of typing.

Quick Looks at Complicated Data Objects

It is useful to see what a data object consists of so that you can decide which columns or rows to utilize. You can simply type the name of an object, of course. However, this might produce a lot of output. You have already met the `str()` command; this is one way to see what an object is comprised of. You might elect to show just the first few lines of a data object; which you can do using the `head()` command. This shows the top of your data object and by default shows the first six rows. For example:

```
> head(mf)
  Length Speed Algae  NO3 BOD
1     20    12    40 2.25 200
2     21    14    45 2.15 180
3     22    12    45 1.75 135
4     23    16    80 1.95 120
5     21    20    75 1.95 110
6     20    21    65 2.75 120
```

This can be helpful because it shows you what the columns are called and gives you an idea of what the data look like. You can also display the bottom of the data using the `tail()` command:

```
> tail(mf)
   Length Speed Algae  NO3 BOD
20     13    21    25 1.05 235
21     16    22    35 2.55 200
22     25     9    85 2.85  55
23     24    11    80 2.95  87
24     23    16    80 2.85  97
25     22    15    75 1.75  95
```

This is potentially more useful because you can also see how many rows there are in total (assuming there are no set row names). You can elect to show a different number of rows using the `n =` instruction like so:

```
> head(bird, n = 3)
          Garden Hedgerow Parkland Pasture Woodland
Blackbird     47       10       40       2        2
Chaffinch     19        3        5       0        2
Great Tit     50        0       10       7        0
```

In this case the data are in a matrix. The command works on list objects too:

```
> head(my.list, n= 2)
$mow
[1] 12 15 17 11 15

$unmow
[1] 8 9 7 9
```

There is another way to get information about an object; you can use the `summary()` command. The output you get depends on the type of object you have. If you have a data frame, you can see some summary statistics like so:

```
> summary(grass)
    species          cut
 Min.   : 7.00   mow  :5
 1st Qu.: 9.00   unmow:4
 Median :11.00
 Mean   :11.44
 3rd Qu.:15.00
 Max.   :17.00
```

Here the `summary()` command gives some simple statistics about the numeric data called `species`. The `cut` variable is a factor and the command shows the different levels as well as the number of observations in each.

If the object you are examining is a list, you are presented with a slightly simpler summary output:

```
> summary(my.list)
      Length Class  Mode
mow    5     -none- numeric
unmow  4     -none- numeric
data3 12     -none- numeric
data7 15     -none- numeric
```

In this case you can see that there are four items of varying length. The final column shows you that they are all numbers.

The summary command also works on a matrix. In the following example the matrix contains numerical values:

```
> summary(bird.m)
     Garden          Hedgerow           Parkland          Pasture          Woodland
 Min.   : 4.00   Min.   : 0.000   Min.   : 0.00   Min.   :0.000   Min.   :0
 1st Qu.:11.50   1st Qu.: 0.750   1st Qu.: 5.25   1st Qu.:0.000   1st Qu.:0
 Median :32.50   Median : 3.000   Median : 7.00   Median :1.000   Median :1
 Mean   :29.17   Mean   : 5.333   Mean   :11.50   Mean   :2.167   Mean   :1
 3rd Qu.:46.75   3rd Qu.: 8.250   3rd Qu.: 9.50   3rd Qu.:3.500   3rd Qu.:2
 Max.   :50.00   Max.   :16.000   Max.   :40.00   Max.   :7.000   Max.   :2
```

Each of the named columns is summarized using basic statistics. If the matrix contains non-numerical data you get a different summary. In the following example, the matrix contains months of the year (that is, it contains character data):

```
> yr.matrix
     Qtr1  Qtr2  Qtr3  Qtr4
row1 "Jan" "Apr" "Jul" "Oct"
```

```
row2 "Feb" "May" "Aug" "Nov"
row3 "Mar" "Jun" "Sep" "Dec"
```

When you use the `summary()` command you see each element listed along with how many there were in each "category"; in this case the values are all 1 because there is only one of each month:

```
> summary(yr.matrix)
  Qtr1     Qtr2     Qtr3     Qtr4
 Feb:1    Apr:1    Aug:1    Dec:1
 Jan:1    Jun:1    Jul:1    Nov:1
 Mar:1    May:1    Sep:1    Oct:1
```

If the data are a simple vector, the output you get depends on the type of item. The following examples show the results for numeric data followed by character data:

```
> summary(data4)
   Min. 1st Qu.  Median    Mean 3rd Qu.    Max.
   8.00   11.00   12.50   13.93   17.00   23.00

> summary(data5)
   Length     Class      Mode
       12 character character
```

The `summary()` command is designed to be used to produce specialized output as the result of other commands. So, programmers who have produced a statistical routine, for example, can create a customized layout to display the result.

It is often useful to see the column names of a complex data object, perhaps as a reminder of the variables in a complex multiple regression. R provides several ways to view and set names, as you find out in the following section.

Viewing and Setting Names

You may want to see just the column (or row) names contained within an object. This is often a useful means of reminding yourself of the contents of a complex data object. You may also want to alter or create row or column names. Several similar commands can do this; the following list provides examples of each:

- The most basic command that enables the viewing of column or row is `names()`. The result you get depends on the object you are looking at:

  ```
  > names(my.list)
  [1] "mow"    "unmow" "data3" "data7"

  > names(fw)
  [1] "abund" "flow"

  > names(mf)
  [1] "Length" "Speed"  "Algae"  "NO3"    "BOD"

  > names(bird)
  NULL
  ```

  The first example shows the result from looking at a list. The second and third examples are both data frames, and the last is a matrix. Notice how you do not get names for a matrix.

➤ You can look at row names in a similar fashion using the `row.names()` command:

```
> row.names(my.list)

> row.names(fw)
[1] "1" "2" "3" "4" "5" "6" "7" "8"

> row.names(mf)
 [1] "1"  "2"  "3"  "4"  "5"  "6"  "7"  "8"  "9"  "10" "11" "12" "13" "14" "15"
[16] "16" "17" "18" "19" "20" "21" "22" "23" "24" "25"

> row.names(bird)
[1] "Blackbird"      "Chaffinch "     "Great Tit"      "House Sparrow "
[5] "Robin"          "Song Thrush "
```

This time the command has worked for the matrix but not for the list object. You do not even get a result with the list object.

➤ To amend the results from the previous example, you can modify the command and use a subtly different command, `rownames()`:

```
> rownames(my.list)
NULL
```

You still do not get anything apparently useful, but you do at least get a result.

➤ You can also use `colnames()` in a similar way:

```
> colnames(mf)
[1] "Length" "Speed"  "Algae"  "NO3"    "BOD"

> colnames(my.list)
NULL

> colnames(bird)
[1] "Garden"    "Hedgerow" "Parkland" "Pasture"   "Woodland"
```

You still do not get any names for the list, but the data frame and matrix names display okay.

➤ There is yet another command, `dimnames()`; this looks at both the row and column names at the same time:

```
> dimnames(my.list)
NULL

> dimnames(mf)
[[1]]
 [1] "1"  "2"  "3"  "4"  "5"  "6"  "7"  "8"  "9"  "10" "11" "12" "13" "14"
"15"
[16] "16" "17" "18" "19" "20" "21" "22" "23" "24" "25"

[[2]]
[1] "Length" "Speed"  "Algae"  "NO3"    "BOD"
```

```
> dimnames(bird)
[[1]]
[1] "Blackbird"       "Chaffinch"      "Great Tit"       "House Sparrow"
[5] "Robin"           "Song Thrush"

[[2]]
[1] "Garden"    "Hedgerow" "Parkland" "Pasture"   "Woodland"
```

NOTE *Sometimes R will display double square brackets like so [[1]]. This helps you to differentiate between displayed elements on the screen.*

The command shows the row names first and then the column names, much like the `[row, col]` instruction you used when extracting parts of objects. The command does not work on a list; rows and columns are not really appropriate for lists, which contain items of differing lengths.

You can use these commands to create names as well as seeing what the current names are set to, like so:

```
> names(mf)
[1] "Length" "Speed"  "Algae"  "NO3"    "BOD"

names(mf) = c('len','sp', 'alg', 'no3', 'bod')

> names(mf)
[1] "len" "sp"  "alg" "no3" "bod"
```

In this example the names of the columns in the `mf` data object (a data frame) are examined/displayed. Here new names are created using the `c()` command, although any object that was a vector of characters could be used. Finally the names just set are reviewed. Remember that if you can get the names using the `names()` command, you can also set them.

You can do the same thing using the `colnames()` or `rownames()` commands:

```
> sites = c('Taw', 'Torridge', 'Ouse', 'Exe', 'Lyn', 'Brook', 'Ditch', 'Fal')
> rownames(fw) = sites
> fw
         abund flow
Taw          9    2
Torridge    25    3
Ouse        15    5
Exe          2    9
Lyn         14   14
Brook       25   24
Ditch       24   29
Fal         47   34
```

In this example a separate vector was created to contain the names (the names may be useful for other data). If you can use the command to read the names, you can use it to set the names too; so `colnames()` and `rownames()` will work on a matrix.

You can also use the `dimnames()` command to set both row and column names simultaneously; the general form of the command is like so:

```
dimnames(our.object) = list(rows, columns)
```

In the following example a character vector object is created for each of the rows and names; these are then used to create the names:

```
> species = c('Bbird', 'C.Finch', 'Gt.Tit', 'Sparrow', 'Robin', 'Thrush')
> habitats = c('Gdn', 'Hedge', 'Park', 'Field', 'Wood')
> dimnames(bird) = list(species, habitats)
> bird
        Gdn Hedge Park Field Wood
Bbird    47    10   40     2    2
C.Finch  19     3    5     0    2
Gt.Tit   50     0   10     7    0
Sparrow  46    16    8     4    0
Robin     9     3    0     0    2
Thrush    4     0    6     0    0
```

It would, of course, be possible to type the names in one single command by specifying them explicitly like so.

```
> dimnames(bird) = list(c('Bbird', 'C.Finch', 'Gt.Tit', 'Sparrow', 'Robin',
'Thrush'), c('Gdn', 'Hedge', 'Park', 'Field', 'Wood'))
```

You can reset names using `NULL`. You simply use this instead of a named object or a `c()` list of labels:

```
>dimnames(bird) = list(NULL, habitats)
>colnames(bird) = NULL
>names(fw) = NULL
```

The `dimnames()` command will work perfectly well with `NULL` for a matrix, but it will not work with a data frame. In practice it is best to keep `dimnames()` exclusively for matrix objects and to use an alternative for other object types.

The various commands associated with names are summarized in Table 3-2.

TABLE 3-2: Commands to View and Set Names for Data Objects

COMMAND	APPROPRIATE OBJECTS
`names()`	Works on list, matrix, and data frame
`row.names()`	Works on matrix and data frame
`rownames()`	Works on matrix and data frame
`colnames()`	Works on matrix and data frame
`dimnames(row, col)`	Will get and set names for matrix and data frame but `NULL` only works for matrix

Rotating Data Tables

Thus far it has been assumed that the columns of data frames and matrix objects are fixed. However, you can easily rotate a frame or a matrix so that the rows become the columns and the columns become the rows. To do this you use the `t()` command; think of it as short for transpose. The following example begins with a data frame that contains two columns of numeric data; the rows are also named:

```
> fw
         count speed
Taw          9     2
Torridge    25     3
Ouse        15     5
Exe          2     9
Lyn         14    14
Brook       25    24
Ditch       24    29
Fal         47    34

> fw.t = t(fw)
> fw.t
      Taw Torridge Ouse Exe Lyn Brook Ditch Fal
count   9       25   15   2  14    25    24  47
speed   2        3    5   9  14    24    29  34
```

The final object is transposed so that there now are two rows rather than two columns. In addition the new object is in fact a matrix rather than a data frame. You can see this more clearly if you try the same `t()` command on a simple vector:

```
> mow
[1] 12 15 17 11 15
> t(mow)
     [,1] [,2] [,3] [,4] [,5]
[1,]   12   15   17   11   15
```

Vectors are treated like columns, although when displayed they look like rows (this is a bit confusing). In any event, when you apply a `t()` command you get a matrix object as a result. You can easily convert your object to a data frame, if that is what you want, using the `as.data.frame()` command. You see in more detail how to switch an object from one kind to another in an upcoming section, "Converting from One Object Type to Another."

CONSTRUCTING DATA OBJECTS

You have seen how to make simple vectors using the `c()` and `scan()` commands. You also used `read.table()` and `read.csv()` to import from other programs; these tend to become data frames. In the previous section you looked at ways of manipulating data objects, but now it is time turn to methods of constructing them.

You have already looked at ways to create vector objects using the `c()` and `scan()` commands (in the section "Reading and Getting Data into R"). These objects are the simplest to construct. This section introduces you to constructing other objects, including lists, data frames, and matrix objects.

Making Lists

You will usually start making a list by having several vector objects that you would like to combine in some fashion to make a complicated object (that is, something other than a simple vector). The simplest complicated object is perhaps the list and this allows you to link together several vector items of varying type or size. Lists are useful because you can tie together more or less anything to make a single object that can be used to keep project items together, for example. It is also the only way to tie together very disparate objects.

To join several vector object together you use the `list()` command. In the following example there are five vectors; the first four are numeric and the last one is comprised of characters:

```
> mow; unmow; data3; data7; data8
[1] 12 15 17 11 15
[1] 8 9 7 9
[1]  6  7  8  7  6  3  8  9 10  7  6  9
[1] 23.0 17.0 12.5 11.0 17.0 12.0 14.5  9.0 11.0  9.0 12.5 14.5 17.0  8.0 21.0
[1] "Jan" "Feb" "Mar" "Apr" "May" "Jun" "Jul" "Aug" "Sep" "Oct" "Nov" "Dec"
```

Notice that you can type several commands on a single line; each one is separated using a semicolon. To make these objects into a simple list, you should do something like the following:

```
> grass.list = list(mow, unmow, data3, data7, data8)
> grass.list
[[1]]
[1] 12 15 17 11 15

[[2]]
[1] 8 9 7 9

[[3]]
 [1]  6  7  8  7  6  3  8  9 10  7  6  9

[[4]]
 [1] 23.0 17.0 12.5 11.0 17.0 12.0 14.5  9.0 11.0  9.0 12.5 14.5 17.0  8.0 21.0

[[5]]
 [1] "Jan" "Feb" "Mar" "Apr" "May" "Jun" "Jul" "Aug" "Sep" "Oct" "Nov" "Dec"
```

You simply give the names of the objects as part of a `list()` command. The list contains no names so you should use one of the commands you learned previously to make some, because you will surely forget what the data are without them:

```
> names(grass.list) = c('mow', 'unmow', 'data3', 'data7', 'months')
```

In this case the names are typed in using a `c()` command, but you might already have a character vector of names somewhere that you could use instead like so:

```
> my.names = c('mow', 'unmow', 'data3', 'data7', 'months')
> names(grass.list) = my.names
```

Lists are the simplest of the complicated objects that you can make and are useful to allow you to keep together disparate objects as one.

Making Data Frames

A data frame is a collection of columns of data. The various columns can be different sorts so you might have several columns of numbers and several of characters. The important thing is that all the columns are the same length; in other words, the vectors that go in to make up the frame are of the same length. Any "short" vectors are padded out using NA. To make a data frame you use the `data.frame()` command:

```
my.frame = data.frame(item1, item2, item3)
```

In the parentheses you give the names of the objects that you want to use as the columns, separated with commas. If you have vectors of unequal size, you must pad out the short ones yourself. In the following example, a simple data frame is created from two samples of numbers:

```
> sample1 = c(5,6,9,12,8)
> sample2 = c(7,9,13,10,NA)
> sample1 ; sample2
[1]  5  6  9 12  8
[1]  7  9 13 10 NA
> my.frame = data.frame(sample1, sample2)
> my.frame
  sample1 sample2
1       5       7
2       6       9
3       9      13
4      12      10
5       8      NA
```

In this case only a single NA item had to be typed in; notice that it does not require quotes, because it is a special object in its own right. If you had more than a few NA items, the typing could become quite tedious. You can use a command called `rep()` to repeat items multiple times. The general form of the command is:

```
rep(item, times)
```

If you required four NAs, for example, you would type `rep(NA, 4)`. In the following example the same values are used but data are created using a column for all the values (the response variable) and one for the grouping variable (the predictor variable):

```
> response = c(5,6,9,12,8,7,9,13,10)
> predictor = c(rep('open',5), rep('closed', 4))
> response ; predictor
[1]  5  6  9 12  8  7  9 13 10
[1] "open"   "open"   "open"   "open"   "open"   "closed" "closed" "closed"
[9] "closed"
> my.frame2 = data.frame(response, predictor)
> my.frame2
  response predictor
1        5      open
2        6      open
3        9      open
4       12      open
5        8      open
6        7    closed
7        9    closed
8       13    closed
9       10    closed
```

In this example the first five values are from one sample (which is called `open`), and the next four values are from another sample (called `closed`). The resulting data frame does not contain any `NA` values at all and the result is a neat rectangular data frame.

You can also use the `length()` command to extend or trim a vector. The following example contains two numerical vectors. If you want to make them into a data frame, they need to be the same length.

```
> mow;unmow
[1] 12 15 17 11 15
[1] 8 9 7 9

> length(unmow) = 5
> mow;unmow
[1] 12 15 17 11 15
[1]  8  9  7  9 NA

> length(unmow) = 4
> mow;unmow
[1] 12 15 17 11 15
[1] 8 9 7 9

> length(unmow) = length(mow)
> mow;unmow
[1] 12 15 17 11 15
[1]  8  9  7  9 NA
```

If you set the `length()` of the vector to a value greater than its current length, `NA` items are added at the end. If you set the `length()` to a value smaller than its current length, values at the end are lost.

If you want to create a data frame from vectors of different lengths, the shorter vectors will need to be lengthened using `NA` so that all the vectors are the same length. In the preceding example the length of the longest vector was used to set the length of the shorter ones like so:

```
length(short.vector) = length(long.vector)
```

This saves time, typing, and errors. You can easily check which the longest vector is; once you know this you can use the preceding command. You can also use the up arrow to recall the last command, which you can then edit.

Making Matrix Objects

A matrix is also a rectangular object, and the columns of a matrix are also of equal length. You can create a matrix using one of several commands, depending what objects you have to begin with.

If you have vectors of data that you want to form the columns of your matrix, you can combine them using the `cbind()` command. The following example uses the same two numeric vectors created earlier:

```
> sample1 ; sample2
[1]  5  6  9 12  8
[1]  7  9 13 10 NA
> cmat = cbind(sample1, sample2)
> cmat
     sample1 sample2
[1,]       5       7
```

```
[2,]      6       9
[3,]      9      13
[4,]     12      10
[5,]      8      NA
```

NOTE *Matrix and data frame objects are two-dimensional and rectangular. This means that the columns must all be the same length. Any short items must be padded out with* `NA` *items.*

In this example you can see that the columns are named; the names are taken from the names of the vector objects that were combined. You may also want to use the samples as rows, and to do that you use the `rbind()` command in a similar fashion:

```
> rmat = rbind(sample1, sample2)
> rmat
        [,1] [,2] [,3] [,4] [,5]
sample1    5    6    9   12    8
sample2    7    9   13   10   NA
```

Now the rows are named from the names of the vectors that were used to create the rows of the matrix. A matrix is designed to hold items all of one sort; in other words, the data must be all numbers or all characters and cannot be a mixture of both. If you try to create a matrix using a mixture, the result is that all the items are converted to characters. The following example shows a vector of simple characters, which will be used to make a new matrix along with the numeric vectors from before:

```
> sample3
[1] "a" "b" "c" "d" "e"
> mix.mat = cbind(sample1, sample2, sample3)
> mix.mat
     sample1 sample2 sample3
[1,] "5"     "7"     "a"
[2,] "6"     "9"     "b"
[3,] "9"     "13"    "c"
[4,] "12"    "10"    "d"
[5,] "8"     NA      "e"
```

You can see that all the data items are "converted" to characters; you can also see this using the `str()` command:

```
> str(mix.mat)
 chr [1:5, 1:3] "5" "6" "9" "12" "8" "7" "9" "13" "10" NA ...
 - attr(*, "dimnames")=List of 2
  ..$ : NULL
  ..$ : chr [1:3] "sample1" "sample2" "sample3"
```

This is not an insurmountable problem but it does highlight one major difference between a matrix and a data frame. If you want to extract numbers from a "mixed" matrix, you must force the items to be numeric like so:

```
> as.numeric(mix.mat[,1])
[1]  5  6  9 12  8
```

Note that the contents of the matrix have not been altered but merely extracted from the data matrix as numbers. You might attempt to overwrite a column and try to force the matrix to assume a numerical value:

```
> mix.mat[,1] = as.numeric(mix.mat[,1])
> mix.mat
     sample1 sample2 sample3
[1,] "5"     "7"     "a"
[2,] "6"     "9"     "b"
[3,] "9"     "13"    "c"
[4,] "12"    "10"    "d"
[5,] "8"     NA      "e"
```

Here is an attempt to rewrite the first column with the values "forced" as numbers. You can see that it simply does not work! The only exception is the `NA` item. This is a special R object; the `NA` always remains as it is (note that it does not appear in quotation marks).

You have yet another method to create a matrix from scratch: the `matrix()` command. You use this for occasions where your data are in a single vector of values (either numbers or characters). Mixed items will all end up as characters. In the following example the two sample vectors you just met are made into a new object by joining them together:

```
> sample1 ; sample2
[1]  5  6  9 12  8
[1]  7  9 13 10 NA
> all.samples = c(sample1, sample2)
> all.samples
 [1]  5  6  9 12  8  7  9 13 10 NA
```

Now the `matrix()` command can be used to make a new matrix. When you do this you can choose how many rows or columns you want to make; in this case there are two samples so you would want either two rows or two columns:

```
> mat = matrix(all.samples, nrow = 2)
> mat
     [,1] [,2] [,3] [,4] [,5]
[1,]    5    9    8    9   10
[2,]    6   12    7   13   NA
```

In this example the matrix was created with two rows using the `nrow = 2` instruction. However, when you look at the original data you see that the rows created do not match with the original samples. This is because the `matrix()` command places the items in order starting at the first row and column, but fills the data column by column. You asked for rows and when you did, R worked out how many columns were required. To get the data set out in appropriate fashion, you must specify the matrix with an appropriate number of columns like so:

```
> mat = matrix(all.samples, ncol = 2)
> mat
     [,1] [,2]
[1,]    5    7
[2,]    6    9
[3,]    9   13
[4,]   12   10
[5,]    8   NA
```

NOTE *When you create a matrix from a single vector of data you must bear in mind that the items will be placed in order to fill up each column in turn. You can alter this by using the* `byrow = TRUE` *instruction in the* `matrix()` *command.*

Once a matrix is created you can use the `rownames()` or `colnames()` commands to create names for the rows or columns. You can also use the `dimnames()` command to make labels for both rows and columns at the same time. The `dimnames()` command can also be used as an instruction within the `matrix()` command like so:

```
> cnam = c('Sample1', 'Sample2')
> rnam = c('Site1', 'Site2', 'Site3', 'Site4', 'Site5')
> mat = matrix(all.samples, ncol = 2, dimnames = list(rnam, cnam))
> mat
      Sample1 Sample2
Site1       5       7
Site2       6       9
Site3       9      13
Site4      12      10
Site5       8      NA
```

In this example names are created for the rows and columns as separate character vectors. This required slightly more typing but it gives greater flexibility because you might want to use the character vectors for some other purpose. You might easily have specified the names all in one command like so:

```
> mat = matrix(all.samples, ncol = 2, dimnames = list(c('Site1', 'Site2',
'Site3', 'Site4', 'Site5'), c('Sample1', 'Sample2')))
```

The longer command is fine but more complicated, and therefore you are more likely to make a mistake. In general it is better to use shorter commands to make a longer one, to avoid errors.

Re-ordering Data Frames and Matrix Objects

Earlier you met the `order()` command, which was used to get an index relating to the order of items in a vector (in the section “Manipulating Objects”). You also saw this `order()` command applied to data frame and matrix objects. Additionally, you can use the `order()` command to help you take apart a matrix or data frame and rebuild it in a new order; in other words, you can re-sort the entire frame or matrix. You can also create a new frame with only some of the original columns. In either event you begin by creating an index to sort the data. In the following activity you get a chance to reorder a data frame.

Re-order a Data Frame and Add Additional Columns

Available for download on Wrox.com

Use the `grass2` data from the `Beginning.RData` file for this activity, which you use to reorder and add to.

1. Look at the data frame called `grass2` simply by typing its name:

```
> grass2
```

```
  mow unmow
1  12     8
2  15     9
3  17     7
4  11     9
5  15    NA
```

2. Create an index using the values in the `mow` column, with ties resolved by the `unmow` column:

```
> ii = with(grass2, order(mow, unmow))
```

3. Look at the index you just created:

```
> ii
[1] 4 1 2 5 3
```

4. Now create a new data frame using the sort index you just made:

```
> grass2.resort = grass2[ii,]
> grass2.resort
  mow unmow
4  11     9
1  12     8
2  15     9
5  15    NA
3  17     7
```

5. Select a different order for the columns by specifying them in the square brackets in a new order:

```
> grass2.resort = grass2[ii, c(2, 1)]

> grass2.resort
  unmow mow
4     9  11
1     8  12
2     9  15
5    NA  15
3     7  17
```

6. Now create a new vector of values:

```
> sheep = c(12, 14, 17, 21, 17)
> sheep
[1] 12 14 17 21 17
```

7. Finally, create a data frame that includes the original data plus the new vector you just created. Use the sort index from before:

```
> grass2.resort = with(grass2, data.frame(mow, unmow, sheep)[ii,])
> grass2.resort
  mow unmow sheep
4  11     9    21
1  12     8    12
2  15     9    14
5  15    NA    17
3  17     7    17
```

To start off you used the `with()` command because the `mow` and `unmow` objects were inside the `grass2` data frame. You re-ordered the `mow` column and used the `unmow` column to help resolve tied values. The result of the `order()` command was saved as a result object (called `ii`) to be used in the rebuilding process. After this process note how the row names show their old values.

Of course you can also omit columns or indeed add them, as long as any new vectors are of the same length as the ones in the data frame. You created a new vector of values called `sheep`. The sort index was used to create a new data frame from the two existing columns in the `grass2` data frame plus the new `sheep` vector. In this instance the `data.frame()` command is required because the `sheep` vector was not part of the original data frame being modified.

Matrix objects can be re-ordered in a similar fashion to data frames, but you cannot use quite the same syntax to get the columns you require. The following example shows the `bird` data you met earlier. A new sort index is created:

```
> bird
              Garden Hedgerow Parkland Pasture Woodland
Blackbird         47       10       40       2        2
Chaffinch         19        3        5       0        2
Great Tit         50        0       10       7        0
House Sparrow     46       16        8       4        0
Robin              9        3        0       0        2
Song Thrush        4        0        6       0        0
> ii = order(bird[,1], bird[,2], bird[,4])
> ii
[1] 6 5 2 4 1 3
```

The first column is selected as the main re-sorted column and the second and fourth columns are used as tie-breakers. A new matrix can now be created using the sort index; if you do not need to add any extra columns, you can simply specify what you want using the square brackets:

```
> bird[ii,c(5:1)]
              Woodland Pasture Parkland Hedgerow Garden
Song Thrush          0       0        6        0      4
Robin                2       0        0        3      9
Chaffinch            2       0        5        3     19
House Sparrow        0       4        8       16     46
Blackbird            2       2       40       10     47
Great Tit            0       7       10        0     50
```

In this instance the sort index is used to re-order the rows; the columns are specified in reverse order. If you want to add a new column of data you must incorporate it using either the `matrix()` or the `cbind()` commands as you have seen earlier. The new data you want to add can be in the form of a simple vector or a matrix. In the following example there are extra samples in both forms; the `Urban` item is a vector whereas the `bird.extra` item is a matrix:

```
> Urban
[1] 11  8  9 28  9  1
> bird.extra
```

```
                Urban
Blackbird          11
Chaffinch           8
Great Tit           9
House Sparrow      28
Robin               9
Song Thrush         1
```

The `cbind()` command can be used to make the new matrix because there are columns of data; either of the following commands will create the same result:

```
> cbind(bird, Urban)[ii,]
> cbind(bird, bird.extra)[ii,]

              Garden Hedgerow Parkland Pasture Woodland Urban
Song Thrush        4        0        6       0        0     1
Robin              9        3        0       0        2     9
Chaffinch         19        3        5       0        2     8
House Sparrow     46       16        8       4        0    28
Blackbird         47       10       40       2        2    11
Great Tit         50        0       10       7        0     9
```

In the first case the simple vector is used to form the extra column; the row names are already in place from the original `bird` matrix. In the second example the matrix object is used as the source of the additional column, and once again the row names are transferred. If the additional data were in the form of a simple data frame, the result would be the same. You can also re-order the columns as you create the new matrix simply by typing the order you want them to appear in the square brackets. For example, if you wanted to reverse their order you would type the following:

```
> cbind(bird, bird.extra)[ii,6:1]
```

Using `cbind()` is easier than the `matrix()` command because you retain the row and column names in the newly created matrix. It is possible to use the `matrix()` command, but you would then have to re-establish the names. In the following example a new matrix is created using the existing data and the new `Urban` data:

```
> matrix(c(bird, Urban), ncol = 6)[ii,]

     [,1] [,2] [,3] [,4] [,5] [,6]
[1,]    4    0    6    0    0    1
[2,]    9    3    0    0    2    9
[3,]   19    3    5    0    2    8
[4,]   46   16    8    4    0   28
[5,]   47   10   40    2    2   11
[6,]   50    0   10    7    0    9
```

The sort index is applied to re-order the rows. You see that the names are lost; you can add them afterwards using the `rownames()` and `colnames()` commands or you might add the `dimnames =` instruction to the `matrix()` command much as you saw previously.

You can use the `order()` command to alter the order of the columns as well as the rows. In the following example, the sort index is created using the information in the third row (relating to the Great Tit) and using the fourth and first rows as tie-breakers. This time the `rbind()` command is used to reassemble the matrix into a new order based on the sort index:

```
> ii = order(bird[3,], bird[4,], bird[1,])
> ii
```

```
[1] 5 2 4 3 1
> rbind(bird[,ii])
              Woodland Hedgerow Pasture Parkland Garden
Blackbird            2       10       2       40     47
Chaffinch            2        3       0        5     19
Great Tit            0        0       7       10     50
House Sparrow        0       16       4        8     46
Robin                2        3       0        0      9
Song Thrush          0        0       0        6      4
```

The result is that your columns have been re-ordered based on the data in the third row.

NOTE *If you want to re-order both rows and columns you must do one operation and then the other; you simply cannot do it on both at the same time.*

FORMS OF DATA OBJECTS: TESTING AND CONVERTING

R utilizes different forms of data objects. The main forms, which you have met, are vector, data frame, list, and matrix. The various forms of data objects have slightly different properties and some commands require the data to be in one particular form (the help entry for each command specifies if a certain form of object is required). You can determine the form of object you have using the `class()` command. You can convert an object from one form to another using a variety of commands that you will meet shortly. It is important to be able to determine the form of object you are dealing with and be able to convert it to another form so that you can explore the full potential of R.

Testing to See What Type of Object You Have

You can get an idea of what sort of object something is by looking at it; you met the `str()` command previously (in the section "Examining Data Structure") which does just that. You can also use the `class()` command to get a result which gives the form of object (also introduced in the section "Examining Data Structure"). It is important to know what form of object you are dealing with in order to know how to handle it. In this section you will learn how to create tests for object form using the `class()` command.

The `class()` command gives you direct information in a single category about an object form. The following command can be used as a *class test*:

```
if(any(class(test.subject) == 'test.type') == TRUE) TRUE else FALSE
```

You simply replace the `test.subject` part with the name of the object you want to test and replace the `test.type` part with the class type you want to return as `TRUE`. Note that the `test.type` must be in quotes.

Some objects can be of more than one class-type and the `any()` command takes care of this. It looks at the entire result of the `class()` command and if any of them give a `TRUE` result, then you get a `TRUE` result. If all of them are `FALSE`, the final result is also `FALSE`.

Once you have an idea about the forms of objects you are dealing with you may want to switch an object from one form to another. This is the subject of the next section.

Converting from One Object Form to Another

You now know how to see what sort of object you are dealing with. You can inspect objects and work out what they are, and you can also test them with explicit commands. For day-to-day operations you can simply use the `class()` command to inspect an object, but if you are writing a script to run automatically you must get more in depth and use the programming method (the class-test). When working with programming in R, once you know what form of object you are dealing with you may want to alter it into a different form. This can be useful because some operations require your data to be in one specific form. For example, the `barplot()` command, which you will encounter later in Chapter 7, "Introduction to Graphical Analysis," requires data to be in a matrix format before the graph can be produced. Therefore, it is important to know how to convert an object into another form.

Convert a Matrix to a Data Frame

The matrix and data frame objects are similar in that they are both rectangular, two-dimensional objects. You can convert a matrix into a data frame using the `as.data.frame()` command. The following example shows a numeric matrix:

```
> mat
      Sample1 Sample2
Site1       5       7
Site2       6       9
Site3       9      13
Site4      12      10
Site5       8      NA

> mat2frame = as.data.frame(mat)
> mat2frame
      Sample1 Sample2
Site1       5       7
Site2       6       9
Site3       9      13
Site4      12      10
Site5       8      NA
```

After you have converted the object you can see that it looks exactly the same as before; row and column names have been preserved. Of course you can use `str()` or `class()` commands to confirm that the object is in a new form. You can do the same thing for a character matrix. The following example shows a matrix of months of the year converted into a data frame:

```
> yr.matrix
     Qtr1  Qtr2  Qtr3  Qtr4
row1 "Jan" "Apr" "Jul" "Oct"
row2 "Feb" "May" "Aug" "Nov"
row3 "Mar" "Jun" "Sep" "Dec"

> yr.frame = as.data.frame(yr.matrix)
> yr.frame
     Qtr1 Qtr2 Qtr3 Qtr4
row1  Jan  Apr  Jul  Oct
```

```
row2  Feb  May  Aug  Nov
row3  Mar  Jun  Sep  Dec
```

After the conversion you see that you have converted the character items into a data frame. Each column is composed of three items that are character variables. The frame treats these as factors, which makes little practical difference. The factor data can be treated like regular character data and is easily converted using the `as.character()` command.

Convert a Data Frame into a Matrix

Similarly, you can switch a data frame into a matrix using the `as.matrix()` command. In this case, of course, if you have a data frame with mixed number and character variables the result will be a character matrix. If the data frame is all numeric, the matrix will be numeric. The following example begins with an all-numeric data frame:

```
> grass2
  mow unmow
1  12     8
2  15     9
3  17     7
4  11     9
5  15    NA
> grass2.mat = as.matrix(grass2)
> grass2.mat
     mow unmow
[1,]  12     8
[2,]  15     9
[3,]  17     7
[4,]  11     9
[5,]  15    NA
```

The final matrix is all numeric; remember that any `NA` items are kept as they are.

The next example begins with a data frame that has two columns, one is numeric and the other is a character (in this instance actually a factor):

```
> grass
  rich graze
1   12   mow
2   15   mow
3   17   mow
4   11   mow
5   15   mow
6    8 unmow
7    9 unmow
8    7 unmow
9    9 unmow
> grass.mat = as.matrix(grass)
> grass.mat
  rich graze
1 "12" "mow"
2 "15" "mow"
3 "17" "mow"
4 "11" "mow"
5 "15" "mow"
6 " 8" "unmow"
7 " 9" "unmow"
```

```
8 " 7" "unmow"
9 " 9" "unmow"
```

Here you can tell that the results are all characters because they show the quotation marks. If your data frame contains row names like the following example, you can see an important difference between the frame and the matrix. The starting point is a simple data frame. This contains two columns of numeric data and each row is named:

```
> fw
         count speed
Taw          9     2
Torridge    25     3
Ouse        15     5
Exe          2     9
Lyn         14    14
Brook       25    24
Ditch       24    29
Fal         47    34

> fw.mat = as.matrix(fw)
> fw[,1]
[1]  9 25 15  2 14 25 24 47

> fw.mat[,1]
     Taw Torridge     Ouse      Exe      Lyn    Brook    Ditch      Fal
       9       25       15        2       14       25       24       47
```

A new matrix is made from the existing data frame, and if you display each object they appear identical. However, if you display only the first column you see a difference. In the data frame you get to see just the values. If you display the matrix you see the row names as well as the data. At present this seems like a fairly trivial difference, but you need to remember that the matrix and the data frame have slightly different properties. In general, the matrix is better at dealing with named rows and columns.

Convert a Data Frame into a List

You can make a list object from a data frame very easily by using the `as.list()` command. The following example starts with a data frame that contains several columns of numeric data:

```
> frame.list = as.list(mf)
> frame.list
$len
 [1] 20 21 22 23 21 20 19 16 15 14 21 21 21 20 19 18 17 19 21 13 16 25 24 23 22

$sp
 [1] 12 14 12 16 20 21 17 14 16 21 21 26 11  9  9 11 17 15 19 21 22  9 11 16 15

$alg
 [1] 40 45 45 80 75 65 65 65 35 30 65 70 85 70 35 30 50 60 70 25 35 85 80 80 75

$no3
 [1] 2.25 2.15 1.75 1.95 1.95 2.75 1.85 1.75 1.95 2.35 2.35 2.35 2.05 1.85 1.75
[16] 1.45 1.35 2.05 1.25 1.05 2.55 2.85 2.95 2.85 1.75

$bod
 [1] 200 180 135 120 110 120  95 168 180 195 158 145 140 145 165 187 190 157  90
[20] 235 200  55  87  97  95
```

The resulting list contains elements that match up to the columns of the original data frame. In this example they were all numeric, but the process also works well on data frames that contain both numeric and character columns. A data frame is by definition a rectangular object; so all the columns are the same length. This results in lists with equally sized elements; any NA items are transferred to the list.

Convert a Matrix into a List

If you try to convert a matrix to a list you end up with a horrendous mess! This is because a matrix is essentially a single list of data that the matrix displays in rows and columns for your convenience. If you want to make a list from a matrix, the answer is to convert the matrix to a data frame first and then convert this data frame into a list object. In the following example the matrix is converted into a frame and then a list all in one command:

```
> yr.list = as.list(as.data.frame(yr.matrix))
```

Convert a List to Something Else

If you start with a list it is generally a bit more difficult to convert it to another type of object. The main reasons are that the list can contain items of differing length, and these can be of differing sorts (numeric, character, and so on). This is of course why the list object is useful.

If all the items in the list happen to be the same length, it is easy to convert into a data frame using the `data.frame()` command. It does not matter if the individual items are numeric or character vectors, because the data frame can handle mixed items. The following example shows a list composed of several numeric vectors:

```
> a.list
$len
 [1] 20 21 22 23 21 20 19 16 15 14 21 21 21 20 19 18 17 19 21 13 16 25 24 23 22

$sp
 [1] 12 14 12 16 20 21 17 14 16 21 21 26 11  9  9 11 17 15 19 21 22  9 11 16 15

$alg
 [1] 40 45 45 80 75 65 65 65 35 30 65 70 85 70 35 30 50 60 70 25 35 85 80 80 75

$no3
 [1] 2.25 2.15 1.75 1.95 1.95 2.75 1.85 1.75 1.95 2.35 2.35 2.35 2.05 1.85 1.75
[16] 1.45 1.35 2.05 1.25 1.05 2.55 2.85 2.95 2.85 1.75

$bod
 [1] 200 180 135 120 110 120  95 168 180 195 158 145 140 145 165 187 190 157  90
[20] 235 200  55  87  97  95

> a.frame = data.frame(a.list)
> str(a.frame)
'data.frame': 25 obs. of  5 variables:
$ len: int  20 21 22 23 21 20 19 16 15 14 ...
 $ sp : int  12 14 12 16 20 21 17 14 16 21 ...
 $ alg: int  40 45 45 80 75 65 65 65 35 30 ...
 $ no3: num  2.25 2.15 1.75 1.95 1.95 2.75 1.85 1.75 1.95 2.35 ...
 $ bod: int  200 180 135 120 110 120 95 168 180 195 ...
```

You can see by using the `str()` command that the new object is indeed a data frame. If you wanted your list to be a matrix, the simplest option is to convert to a data frame first and then make that into a matrix using the `as.matrix()` command; you could do this in a single command by nesting like so:

```
> a.matrix = as.matrix(data.frame(a.list))
```

WARNING *If you try to make a matrix object from a list in one operation you get an unusual result. It is more desirable to convert the list to a data frame first and then make the matrix from this.*

If your list object contains items that are of differing lengths, it is a little trickier to get them into a different form. The simplest way is to extract the components of the list to separate vectors, pad them with `NA` items as required, and then re-assemble into a data frame.

You can easily extract the individual parts by appending the `$` to the list name. In the following example one of the vectors is extracted and assigned a new name:

```
> algae = a.list$alg
> algae
 [1] 40 45 45 80 75 65 65 65 35 30 65 70 85 70 35 30 50 60 70 25 35 85 80 80 75
```

You may try to combine the list data into a two-column data frame where one column contained the values and the other related to the group the value belonged to. In the following example there is a simple list composed of two samples. They are both numeric and are of unequal length. Use the `stack()` command to combine the values into a data frame:

```
> grass.l
$mow
[1] 12 15 17 11 15

$unmow
[1] 8 9 7 9

> grass.stak = stack(grass.l)
> grass.stak
  values   ind
1     12   mow
2     15   mow
3     17   mow
4     11   mow
5     15   mow
6      8 unmow
7      9 unmow
8      7 unmow
9      9 unmow
```

The command has taken each vector in the list and joined them together to make a column in the data frame. The second column relates to the name of the list item. Here there were two items, `mow` and `unmow`. You can see how the names of these have transferred to the data frame. The column headings are `values` and `ind`. The `values` column always contains the contents of the individual vectors from the list. The ind column contains the name of the vector that relates to each corresponding value. Think of this as the independent variable; this is indeed the main reason for the stack() command, to create a column of values (dependent variable) and a grouping column (independent variable). You can change the names to something more meaningful using the names() command:

```
> names(grass.stak) = c('species', 'cut')
> grass.stak
  species    cut
1      12    mow
2      15    mow
3      17    mow
4      11    mow
5      15    mow
6       8 unmow
7       9 unmow
8       7 unmow
9       9 unmow
```

You can reverse the process using the unstack() command. When you have a simple two-column data frame, you use the command like so:

```
> unstack(grass.stak)
$mow
[1] 12 15 17 11 15

$unmow
[1] 8 9 7 9
```

When you have a more complicated situation you need to modify the command. In the following example there is a data frame with three columns; the first column holds numeric data and relates to the height of plants grown under various conditions. The second column is a character variable, a factor relating to the species grown. The final column relates to the watering treatment; in this case there are three levels of watering. Here are the data:

```
> pw
   height    plant water
1       9 vulgaris    lo
2      11 vulgaris    lo
3       6 vulgaris    lo
4      14 vulgaris   mid
5      17 vulgaris   mid
6      19 vulgaris   mid
7      28 vulgaris    hi
8      31 vulgaris    hi
9      32 vulgaris    hi
10      7   sativa    lo
11      6   sativa    lo
12      5   sativa    lo
13     14   sativa   mid
14     17   sativa   mid
15     15   sativa   mid
16     44   sativa    hi
17     38   sativa    hi
18     37   sativa    hi
```

You can use an additional instruction in the `unstack()` command to create the new two-column object. The more general form of the `unstack()` command is like so:

```
unstack(object, form = response ~ grouping)
```

The `form =` part tells the `unstack()` command which columns of data to select from the original data frame. In the plant and watering example the `response` is the height, but there are two choices regarding the `grouping` part:

```
> unstack(pw, form = height ~ plant)

  sativa vulgaris
1      7        9
2      6       11
3      5        6
4     14       14
5     17       17
6     15       19
7     44       28
8     38       31
9     37       32

> unstack(pw, form = height ~ water)

  hi lo mid
1 28  9  14
2 31 11  17
3 32  6  19
4 44  7  14
5 38  6  17
6 37  5  15
```

In the first case the `plant` variable was chosen and this results in two columns of data, one for each of the two species. In the second example the `water` variable was chosen and this results in three columns that correspond to each of the three original watering treatments.

You can choose which columns to stack up by adding the `select =` instruction to the `stack()` command. The preceding example ended up with three columns; you can re-stack these data and list the columns you require in one of two ways:

```
> pw.us = unstack(pw, form = height ~ water)
> pw.us

  hi lo mid
1 28  9  14
2 31 11  17
3 32  6  19
4 44  7  14
5 38  6  17
6 37  5  15

> stack(pw.us, select = c(hi, lo))

   values ind
1      28  hi
2      31  hi
3      32  hi
```

```
4       44  hi
5       38  hi
6       37  hi
7        9  lo
8       11  lo
9        6  lo
10       7  lo
11       6  lo
12       5  lo
```

In this case the required columns were given in a `c()` command as part of the `select =` instruction. In the following example the columns you do *not* want are given by prefacing the name with a minus sign (-):

```
> stack(pw.us, select = -lo)
   values ind
1      28  hi
2      31  hi
3      32  hi
4      44  hi
5      38  hi
6      37  hi
7      14 mid
8      17 mid
9      19 mid
10     14 mid
11     17 mid
12     15 mid
```

So, list objects are tricky beasts! They are very useful though because they can "tie together" objects of different sorts.

SUMMARY

- You can extract parts of an object using `$` or `[]` syntax.
- Objects can be reordered and sorted using `order()` and `sort()` commands.
- The `rank()` command can also sort data and is used in many statistical routines.
- Data objects can be in a variety of forms, for example, vector, data frame, matrix, or list.
- You can use the `class()` command to determine what form of item a data object is.
- Objects can be converted from one form to another.

EXERCISES

You can find answers to these exercises in Appendix A.

1. You have the results of a simple experiment to look at the visitation of various bee species to different plants. The number of bees observed was as follows:

   - **Buff tail**: 10 1 37 5 12
   - **Garden bee**: 8 3 19 6 4
   - **Red tail**: 18 9 1 2 4
   - **Honeybee**: 12 13 16 9 10
   - **Carder bee**: 8 27 6 32 23

   Make five simple numeric vectors of these data. Now join the bee vectors together to make a data frame. Each row of the resulting frame relates to a specific plant so you could assign names to the rows.

   The plant names are Thistle, Vipers bugloss, Golden rain, Yellow alfalfa, and Blackberry. Use these names to create row labels for the data.

2. Make a matrix object from the original data that you used in Exercise 1. You could do this two ways; try both.

   A. Convert the matrix into a data frame.

   B. Take the original data frame from Exercise 1 and convert that into a matrix.

   C. Try making a list. Use the plant names from above as an object to include in the list along with the original bee data as individual vectors or as a frame or matrix. You might also include a vector of bee names with your list.

3. First of all tidy up by removing all the vectors you created as part of the other exercises. Keep the bee data frame and the bee list that you made but remove the rest.

   A. Display the data for the Blackberry only.

   B. Now display the data for Golden rain and Yellow alfalfa.

   C. Display the data for the Red tail bee only.

4. Look at the bee data you created in Exercise 1. Re-order the data so that the Buff tail column is sorted in decreasing abundance (you can use the Red tail column as a tie-breaker).

   Now re-order the columns so that the top row (Golden rain) is in decreasing abundance from left to right.

▶ WHAT YOU LEARNED IN THIS CHAPTER

TOPIC	KEY POINTS

Constructing data objects:
`data.frame()`
`matrix()`
`cbind() rbind()`
`list()`
	Complex data objects can be created using various commands. The `data.frame()` command takes 1D vectors of equal length and creates a data frame. The `matrix()` command creates a 2D matrix object from a single 1D vector. The `cbind()` and `rbind()` commands assemble a matrix, by columns or rows, from several other objects. The `list()` command creates a list from several other objects.

Summarizing data objects:
`summary()`
`str()`
`class()`
`length()`
`max()`
`min()`
`head()`
`tail()`
	Objects can be summarized and viewed in a variety of ways. The `summary()` command gives a broad overview, while the `str()` command is useful to see the object structure. The type of object can be ascertained using the `class()` command. The `length()` command can be used to determine the number of items in an object. The `max()` and `min()` commands display the largest and smallest values in a numeric object. The `head()` and `tail()` commands are used to display the first or last few rows of an object.

Extracting parts and manipulating objects:
`attach()`
`detach()`
`with()`
`$ [row, col]`
`names()`
`rownames()`
`sort()`
`order()`
`rank()`
`stack()`
	The contents of complicated data objects are not directly visible to R. To access the columns of a data frame, for example, you can use the `attach()` command. You can "close" the object using `detach()`. The `with()` command enables the contents of a complicated object to be accessed temporarily. You can access elements of data objects using the `$` and `[row, col]` syntax. You can set or view the names of columns or rows using the `names()`, `rownames()` or `colnames()` commands. Objects can be rearranged using `sort()` or `order()` commands. The `rank()` command shows the relative size of numeric vectors. The `stack()` command is used to recombine objects, for example to join two vectors into one and create a second (factor) vector that shows the origin of each observation.

Converting objects between forms:
`as.data.frame()`
`as.matrix()`
`as.list()`
	Objects can be converted from one form to another using a variety of commands. For example, the `as.data.frame()` command converts an object to a data frame.

4 Data: Descriptive Statistics and Tabulation

WHAT YOU WILL LEARN IN THIS CHAPTER:

- How to summarize data samples
- How to use cumulative statistics
- How to create summary tables
- How to cross-tabulate
- How to test for different object types

Important elements in data analysis include summary and descriptive statistics. These provide a shorthand way of describing and summarizing your data, which is important in pointing you towards the correct analytical procedure and helping you understand your data. There are three main ways you can describe or summarize your data:

- Summary statistics
- Tabulation
- Graphical

In this chapter you will learn about using summary statistics to provide a shorthand way of describing your data as opposed to merely listing the contents. You will also look at tabulation as a method to create summaries. Tables can split your data into manageable chunks that show you patterns that you would otherwise miss. Producing a graphical summary of your data is also important because a visual impression can convey more to a reader than numerical values; these are the subjects of Chapter 5.

SUMMARY COMMANDS

An essential starting point with any set of data is to get an overview of what you are dealing with. There are a few ways to go about doing this. You might start by using the `ls()` command to see what named objects you have. You can then type the name of one of the objects to view its contents. However, if the object contains a lot of data, the display may be quite long (and somewhat overwhelming); you will want a more concise method to examine objects. You could use the `str()` command, which shows you something about the structure of the data. Take, for instance, the following data frame called `grass`. This contains two columns: one is titled `rich` and relates to the number of plant species found in quadrats and the other is titled `graze` and relates to the mowing treatment of the site:

```
> grass
  rich graze
1   12   mow
2   15   mow
3   17   mow
4   11   mow
5   15   mow
6    8 unmow
7    9 unmow
8    7 unmow
9    9 unmow
```

In this case, there are not too many observations so you can easily see all the data. If you use the `str()` command like so, you see a more concise summary of the `grass` object:

```
> str(grass)
'data.frame': 9 obs. of  2 variables:
 $ rich : int  12 15 17 11 15 8 9 7 9
 $ graze: Factor w/ 2 levels "mow","unmow": 1 1 1 1 1 2 2 2 2
```

However, the `str()` command is designed to help you examine the structure of a data object rather than providing a statistical summary. By contrast, the `summary()` command is designed to give a quick statistical summary of data objects. The output you get depends on the object you are looking at. In this case there is a data frame so each column is summarized:

```
> summary(grass)
      rich          graze
 Min.   : 7.00   mow  :5
 1st Qu.: 9.00   unmow:4
 Median :11.00
 Mean   :11.44
 3rd Qu.:15.00
 Max.   :17.00
```

Here you see some basic statistics for the numeric column; you can see the largest and smallest values as well as central (median and mean) measures. The second column does not contain numbers, so you see a list of the different factors along with a count for each. Here you see five observations for the `mow` treatment but only four replicates for the `unmow` treatment.

If your data contain character items that are in quotes, they are treated as standard characters rather than as factors. When you attempt a `summary()` you get slightly different results. In the following example, you can see a simple vector in two forms:

```
> graze
[1] "mow"    "mow"    "mow"    "mow"    "mow"    "unmow" "unmow" "unmow" "unmow"
> summary(graze)
   Length     Class      Mode
        9 character character
```

Here, the data are true characters (notice the quotes) and the summary merely tells you that there are nine of them. Earlier, you created a data frame using these data alongside a vector of numbers (the `rich` data). The resulting data frame converted the character items into factors. They are still characters (as opposed to numbers), but are handled differently. In most statistical analysis you want your character data as factors. If you extract the data from the data frame and run a `summary()`, you get a different result:

```
> grass$graze
[1] mow   mow   mow   mow   mow   unmow unmow unmow unmow
Levels: mow unmow
> summary(grass$graze)
  mow unmow
    5     4
```

The `summary()` command is therefore more useful; you can see two factors and the number of observations (replicates) for each.

The `summary()` command works for both matrix and data frame objects by summarizing the columns rather than the rows. You can think of vectors as individual columns, and the `summary()` command works on vectors in this fashion. When it comes to list objects though, things are not so simple. In the following example there is a list that comprises two numeric vectors of unequal length:

```
> grass.l
$mow
[1] 12 15 17 11 15

$unmow
[1] 8 9 7 9

> summary(grass.l)
      Length Class  Mode
mow   5      -none- numeric
unmow 4      -none- numeric
```

The `summary()` command looks at the object as a series of columns, but because a list does not have any columns, you get a simpler result. You can get the "proper" summary by applying the command to each item in the list. However, you do need to specify the name exactly:

```
> grass.l$mow
[1] 12 15 17 11 15
> summary(grass.l$mow)
   Min. 1st Qu.  Median    Mean 3rd Qu.    Max.
     11      12      15      14      15      17
```

In the preceding example you see that by adding the `$` you can extract an item from the list and the `summary()` command works as you expect.

It is sometimes useful to see what the columns are called, especially when the data are in a large data frame. Similarly, on some occasions you need a reminder of the row names. You can use the `names()` command and its variants, which you met previously. Table 4-1 is a reminder of these options.

TABLE 4-1: Summary of Commands to Find or Add Names to Rows and Columns of Data Objects

COMMAND	EXPLANATION
`names()`	Works on list or data frame objects. Gets or sets names for columns of a data frame or the elements of a list.
`row.names()`	Works on matrix or data frame objects.
`rownames()`	Works on matrix or data frame objects.
`colnames()`	Works on matrix or data frame objects.
`dimnames()`	Gets row and column names for matrix or data frame objects.

SUMMARIZING SAMPLES

In Chapter 2, you looked at some simple math. In general you were operating on simple numbers; that is, you looked at single values as opposed to a set of numbers that formed a sample. When you have repeated measurements (that is, a sample) you usually want to summarize the data by showing things like the average. In R you have a variety of commands that operate on samples; these samples of data might be individual vectors, or they may be columns in a data frame or part of a matrix or list.

Summary Statistics for Vectors

The simplest data object you will encounter is the vector. A vector is a single column of values—a one-dimensional object. There are a variety of simple summary statistics that can be applied to a vector of numbers, some of which you will meet shortly. In general there are two kinds of summary commands:

- Commands that produce a single value as a result
- Commands that produce multiple values as a result

The following sections deal with each of these kinds of summary commands.

Summary Commands With Single Value Results

You can use several commands to help you summarize simple numeric data. Table 4-2 shows some of the commands that produce a single value as their result.

TABLE 4-2: Commands that Produce a Single Value as a Summary Statistic

COMMAND	EXPLANATION
`max(x, na.rm = FALSE)`	Shows the maximum value. By default `NA` values are not removed. A value of `NA` is considered the largest unless `na.rm = TRUE` is used.
`min(x, na.rm = FALSE)`	Shows the minimum value in a vector. If there are `NA` values, this returns a value of `NA` unless `na.rm = TRUE` is used.
`length(x)`	Gives the length of the vector and includes any `NA` values. The `na.rm =` instruction does not work with this command.
`sum(x, na.rm = FALSE)`	Shows the sum of the vector elements.
`mean(x, na.rm = FALSE)`	Shows the arithmetic mean.
`median( x, na.rm = FALSE)`	Shows the median value of the vector.
`sd(x, na.rm = FALSE)`	Shows the standard deviation.
`var(x, na.rm = FALSE)`	Shows the variance.
`mad(x, na.rm = FALSE)`	Shows the median absolute deviation.

In the following activity you will examine some of the simple summary statistics on some numerical vectors.

TRY IT OUT Using Summarizing Commands on a Sample

Available for download on Wrox.com

Use the `data2` and `unmow` data objects from the `Beginning.RData` file for this activity. You will be using some simple summarizing commands on these data.

1. Type the name of the object you will be examining, in this case `data2`:

```
> data2
 [1] 3 5 7 5 3 2 6 8 5 6 9 4 5 7 3 4
```

2. Display the average of the sample as a mean value:

```
> mean(data2)
[1] 5.125
```

3. Now determine the largest value in the sample:

```
> max(data2)
[1] 9
```

4. Next determine the smallest value in the sample:

```
> min(data2)
[1] 2
```

5. Look now at how many items are in the sample:

```
> length(data2)
[1] 16
```

6. Now look at a different data sample, the `unmow` object:

```
> unmow
[1]  8  9  7  9 NA
```

7. Work out the standard deviation of the complete `unmow` sample:

```
> sd(unmow)
[1] NA
```

8. Calculate the standard deviation but remove `NA` items with an additional instruction:

```
> sd(unmow, na.rm = TRUE)
[1] 0.9574271
```

How It Works

The various commands operate on the vector of values to return a simple result. However, if `NA` items are present the final value will also be `NA`. For most commands you can ensure that any `NA` items are ignored by adding the `na.rm = TRUE` instruction to the command. Now you get a "proper" result.

NOTE *Many summarizing commands use the* `na.rm` *instruction to eliminate* `NA` *items from the summary. However, this is not universal, the* `length()` *command does not use* `na.rm` *for example.*

Omitting NA Items

The `length()` command does not use the `na.rm` instruction so you need a way to overcome this; fortunately there is a solution. You can use the `na.omit()` command to strip out `NA` items. Essentially, you use this to temporarily remove `NA` items like so:

```
> length(na.omit(unmow))
[1] 4
```

Altering Sample Length

You can use the `length()` command to alter the length of a vector by setting it to a numeric value. The vector is shortened if your value is less than the current setting. If the setting is longer than the current setting, `NA` items are added to make it the required length. This can be useful if you want to make a data frame from vectors of unequal length; you can set the length of all vectors to be the same as the longest one:

```
> unmow
[1]  8  9  7  9 NA
> length(unmow)
[1] 5
```

```
> length(unmow) = 4
> unmow
[1] 8 9 7 9
> length(unmow) = 6
> unmow
[1]  8  9  7  9 NA NA
```

In the preceding example, the original vector contained five elements but one was NA, producing a length of five. When you set the length to four, the last element (NA in the preceding example) is stripped off. When you reset the length to six, you get an additional two NA items at the end.

Summary Commands With Multiple Results

So far the commands you have used have produced a single value as a result. However, many commands produce several values. When you looked at some of the mathematical operations in Chapter 2, you applied your math to simple numbers. If you apply a math function to a vector, you get an answer back for each element of the vector like so:

```
> data2
 [1] 3 5 7 5 3 2 6 8 5 6 9 4 5 7 3 4
> log(data2)
 [1] 1.0986123 1.6094379 1.9459101 1.6094379 1.0986123 0.6931472 1.7917595
 [8] 2.0794415 1.6094379 1.7917595 2.1972246 1.3862944 1.6094379 1.9459101
[15] 1.0986123 1.3862944
```

Of course, the log() command is not one you would normally think of as a summary command. Summary commands that do produce multiple results are illustrated here:

```
> summary(data2)
   Min. 1st Qu.  Median    Mean 3rd Qu.    Max.
  2.000   3.750   5.000   5.125   6.250   9.000

> quantile(data2)
  0%  25%  50%  75% 100%
2.00 3.75 5.00 6.25 9.00

> fivenum(data2)
[1] 2.0 3.5 5.0 6.5 9.0
```

You have already met the basic summary() command. For this simple numeric vector you get two measures of centrality: the mean and median. You also get the extremes as well as the inter-quartile values. The quantile() command shows the quartiles by default; that is, the 0%, 25%, 50%, 75% and 100% quantiles. However, you can select other quantiles. The command allows other instructions as follows:

```
quantile(x, probs = seq(0, 1, 0.25), na.rm = FALSE, names = TRUE)
```

The x part is the data object you wish to examine. The probs = instruction enables you to select one or several quantiles to display, defaulting to 0, 0.25, and so on as you saw in the preceding example. This is what the seq(0, 1, 0.25) command is doing; setting a start of 0, an end of 1, and a step of 0.25. This is the same as c(0, 0.25, 0.5, 0.75, 1). The names = instruction tells R if it should display the name of the quantiles produced. In the following activity you examine some of the options for the quantile() command for yourself.

TRY IT OUT Using the quantile() Command

Available for download on Wrox.com

Use the `data2` and `unmow` data objects from the `Beginning.RData` file for this activity. You will use the `quantile()` command on these data.

1. Start by looking at the sample vector, `data2`.

```
> data2
 [1] 3 5 7 5 3 2 6 8 5 6 9 4 5 7 3 4
```

2. Now look at the 20% quantile:

```
> quantile(data2, 0.2)
20%
  3
```

3. Next pick out three quantiles, 20%, 50%, and 80%:

```
> quantile(data2, c(0.2, 0.5, 0.8))
20% 50% 80%
  3   5   7
```

4. Now try some quantiles in non-numeric order:

```
> quantile(data2, c(0.5, 0.75, 0.25))
 50%  75%  25%
5.00 6.25 3.75
```

5. Select some quantiles but suppress the headings:

```
> quantile(data2, c(0.2, 0.5, 0.8), names = F)
[1] 3 5 7
```

6. Look at a new data object that contains `NA` items:

```
> unmow
[1]  8  9  7  9 NA NA
```

7. Display the basic quantiles for the new sample:

```
> quantile(unmow)
Error in quantile.default(unmow) :
  missing values and NaN's not allowed if 'na.rm' is FALSE
```

8. Remove the effect of the `NA` items using the `na.rm` instruction:

```
> quantile(unmow, na.rm = T)
  0%  25%  50%  75% 100%
7.00 7.75 8.50 9.00 9.00
```

How It Works

The `quantile()` command produces multiple results but you can alter the default to produce quantiles for a single probability or several (in any order). The names of the quantiles selected are displayed as percentage labels but you can suppress this using the `names = FALSE` instruction. If the data contain `NA` items, you must remove them using the `na.rm = TRUE` instruction, otherwise you get an error message.

The `fivenum()` command produces a similar result to `quantile()`, but in this case 25% and 75% quantiles (the inter-quartiles) are replaced by the lower and upper hinge values. These are similar to the quantiles and for samples with odd-number lengths they are the same:

```
> dat
[1] 1 2 3 4 5 6
> quantile(dat)
  0%  25%  50%  75% 100%
1.00 2.25 3.50 4.75 6.00

> fivenum(dat)
[1] 1.0 2.0 3.5 5.0 6.0
```

By default `NA` items are removed, but you could include the `NA` using `na.rm = FALSE` as an instruction in the command if you want to keep them in (in which case all the quantiles would be `NA`).

Cumulative Statistics

Cumulative statistics are those that are applied sequentially to a series of values. For example, you may want to track the interest received on an investment. If your data are the interest payments received then the cumulative sum would give you a running total. You can think of the commands that calculate cumulative statistics as being in one of two forms:

- Simple cumulative commands
- Complex cumulative commands

You will look at both types in this section. Simple commands require only the name of the data object. For complex commands you have to create more complicated instructions to produce the desired result.

Simple Cumulative Commands

Table 4-3 shows several simple commands that you can use that return cumulative values.

TABLE 4-3: Commands that Produce Cumulative Values

COMMAND	EXPLANATION
`cumsum(x)`	The cumulative sum of a vector
`cummax(x)`	The cumulative maximum value
`cummin(x)`	The cumulative minimum value
`cumprod(x)`	The cumulative product

In the following activity you try out some cumulative statistics for yourself.

TRY IT OUT Cumulative Statistics

Available for download on Wrox.com

Use the data2 and data5 data objects from the Beginning.RData file for this activity; this contains the data objects that you will need to produce cumulative statistics.

1. Start by looking at a simple numerical vector, data2.

```
> data2
 [1] 3 5 7 5 3 2 6 8 5 6 9 4 5 7 3 4
```

2. Determine the cumulative sum of these data:

```
> cumsum(data2)
 [1]  3  8 15 20 23 25 31 39 44 50 59 63 68 75 78 82
```

3. Now look at the cumulative maximum value of the sample:

```
> cummax(data2)
 [1] 3 5 7 7 7 7 7 8 8 8 9 9 9 9 9 9
```

4. Try looking at the cumulative minimum:

```
> cummin(data2)
 [1] 3 3 3 3 3 2 2 2 2 2 2 2 2 2 2 2
```

5. Now look at the cumulative product of the sample:

```
> cumprod(data2)
 [1]           3          15         105         525        1575        3150
 [7]       18900      151200      756000     4536000    40824000   163296000
[13]   816480000  5715360000 17146080000 68584320000
```

6. Try a cumulative command on a vector of character data (for example, data5):

```
> data5
 [1] "Jan" "Feb" "Mar" "Apr" "May" "Jun" "Jul" "Aug" "Sep" "Oct" "Nov" "Dec"
> cummax(data5)
 [1] NA NA NA NA NA NA NA NA NA NA NA NA
Warning message:
NAs introduced by coercion
```

7. Now look at a data sample that includes NA items:

```
> dat.na
[1]  2  5  4 NA  7  3  9 NA 12
```

8. Try a cumulative command on these data:

```
> cumprod(dat.na)
[1]  2 10 40 NA NA NA NA NA NA
```

How It Works

The cumulative commands produce the expected result until you try them on a vector of character data. If you try these on character data you get an error, and your "result" is a list of NA items. If your numeric vector contains any NA items, the commands will "work" up to the first NA item, and subsequently you get NA.

Complex Cumulative Commands

You can use cumulative commands in combination with others to produce additional useful measures; for example, the running mean. The basic arithmetic mean is the sum divided by the number of observations. You can get the cumulative sum, but you also need the cumulative number of observations; you can use the `seq()` command to help. If you have a sample of numeric values you can create an index like so:

```
> data2
 [1] 3 5 7 5 3 2 6 8 5 6 9 4 5 7 3 4
> seq(along = data2)
 [1]  1  2  3  4  5  6  7  8  9 10 11 12 13 14 15 16
```

In this case you have created a simple index for your sample; you have 16 items. You can also use a "quick" version like so:

```
> seq_along(data2)
 [1]  1  2  3  4  5  6  7  8  9 10 11 12 13 14 15 16
```

USING THE SEQ() COMMAND

The `seq()` command can be used in more than one way. The main purpose of the command is to generate sequences of values. You can specify the start point, end point, and interval for the sequence you require like so:

```
> seq(from = 1, to = 10, by = 2)
[1] 1 3 5 7 9
```

The command can be abbreviated, and the following produces the same result:

```
> seq(1, 10, 2)
[1] 1 3 5 7 9
```

If you use the `along =` instruction you can create an index for a vector:

```
> seq(along = data2)
  [1]  1  2  3  4  5  6  7  8  9 10 11 12 13 14 15 16
```

However, if you omit the `along =` part and specify the vector name you get the same result:

```
> seq(data2)
  [1]  1  2  3  4  5  6  7  8  9 10 11 12 13 14 15 16
```

The `seq_along()` command is thus the equivalent of using the `along =` instruction in the regular `seq()` command.

If you now combine the cumulative sum and "how far along" you are, you can make a running mean like so:

```
> cumsum(data2) / seq(along = data2)
 [1] 3.000000 4.000000 5.000000 5.000000 4.600000 4.166667 4.428571 4.875000
 [9] 4.888889 5.000000 5.363636 5.250000 5.230769 5.357143 5.200000 5.125000
```

For other cumulative statistics you may have to be a bit more creative. For example, you might want to use a running median. None of the cumulative commands can really help you here. The answer is to use the `seq_along()` command as an index and container and determine your median as you step along. The following example and subsequent steps illustrate the process:

```
> data2
 [1] 3 5 7 5 3 2 6 8 5 6 9 4 5 7 3 4
> md = seq_along(data2)
> md
 [1]  1  2  3  4  5  6  7  8  9 10 11 12 13 14 15 16
> for(i in 1:length(md)) md[i] = median(data2[1:i])
> md
 [1] 3 4 5 5 5 4 5 5 5 5 5 5 5 5 5 5
```

1. Begin by creating an item called `md`, which acts as the repository for your final result. In the meantime you can also use this as an index to help you generate the median.
2. Use the `for()` command to make your `median()` work 16 times (in this case). The first part of the command tells R how many times to set the temporary item `i`.
3. Now use the `median()` command to place a value into your result object (called `md`); do this 16 times and you end up with a final vector of 16 values, which represents the running median.
4. The `for()` command has two main parts: the first part (in the parentheses) is where you set the number of times you want to repeat your `expression` (the second part). It is common to use `i` as a variable name in `for()` commands (think of it as `i` for index), but there is no reason not to use anything you like!
5. Separate the variable from the sequence you want to use with the word `in`. Finally, create an `expression` that uses your repeating variable. The following shows the general form of the `for()` command:

   ```
   for(var in seq) expression
   ```

You could easily replace the `median` part in the example to another command and produce a running *something*. In the following example the `sd()` command is used rather than `median()` to determine the running standard deviation:

```
> md = seq_along(data2)
> for(i in 1:length(md)) md[i] = sd(data2[1:i])
> md
 [1]       NA 1.414214 2.000000 1.632993 1.673320 1.834848 1.812654 2.100170
 [9] 1.964971 1.885618 2.157440 2.094365 2.006400 1.984833 2.007130 1.962142
```

In this example the first item in the result is `NA` because you cannot calculate a standard deviation of a single value. You look at the `for()` command again in Chapter 10, where you learn a bit more about customizing functions and creating simple scripts and programming.

Summary Statistics for Data Frames

So far you have looked to summarize a single vector of data, but there may be times when you want to summarize a more complicated object. Some of the commands you have used already will work on more complex objects, and some need a bit of persuading.

Generic Summary Commands for Data Frames

Table 4-4 gives a quick guide to the results expected for some of the generic summary commands you met previously; it is not complete but it covers the more useful summary commands.

TABLE 4-4: Summary Commands that Can be Applied to Data Frames

COMMAND	EXPLANATION
`max(frame)`	The largest value in the entire data frame
`min(frame)`	The smallest value in the entire data frame
`sum(frame)`	The sum of the entire data frame
`fivenum(frame)`	The Tukey summary values for the entire data frame
`length(frame)`	The number of columns in the data frame
`summary(frame)`	Gives summary for each column

The list of summary commands that will work on a data frame is quite short. You can always extract a single vector from your data frame and perform a summary of some sort on that. This approach will not work for the rows of a data frame though. In general it is better to use more specialized commands when dealing with the rows and columns of data frames. You will meet these commands in the following sections.

Special Row and Column Summary Commands

Two summary commands are designed especially for row data—`rowMeans()` and `rowSums()`:

```
> rowMeans(fw)
    Taw Torridge      Ouse       Exe       Lyn     Brook     Ditch       Fal
    5.5     14.0      10.0       5.5      14.0      24.5      26.5      40.5
> rowSums(fw)
    Taw Torridge      Ouse       Exe       Lyn     Brook     Ditch       Fal
     11       28        20        11        28        49        53        81
```

In the example here each row has a row name so these are displayed. If you did not have the row names the values for the various rows would appear as a simple vector of values like so:

```
> rowSums(mf)
 [1] 274.25 262.15 215.75 240.95 227.95 228.75 197.85 264.75 247.95 262.35 267.35
[12] 264.35 259.05 245.85 229.75 247.45 275.35 253.05 201.25 295.05 275.55 176.85
[23] 204.95 218.85 208.75
```

Corresponding `colSums()` and `colMeans()` commands function in the same manner. In the following example you see the `mean()` and `colMeans()` commands compared:

```
> colMeans(mf)
    len      sp     alg     no3     bod
 19.640  15.800  58.400   2.046 145.960
> mean(mf)
    len      sp     alg     no3     bod
 19.640  15.800  58.400   2.046 145.960
```

see that essentially you get the same display/result. These commands also use the na.rm instruction, and by default this is set to FALSE. If you want to ensure that NA items are removed, you add na.rm = TRUE as an instruction in the command.

The apply() Command for Summaries on Rows or Columns

The colMeans() and rowSums() commands are designed as quick alternatives to a more general command, apply(). The apply() command enables you to apply a function to rows or columns of a matrix or data frame. The general form of the command is like so:

```
apply(X, MARGIN, FUN, ...)
```

In this command the MARGIN is either 1 or 2, where 1 is for rows and 2 is for columns. You replace the FUN part with your command (the function you want to apply) and you can also add additional instructions if they are appropriate to the command/function you are applying. For example, you might add the na.rm = TRUE instruction:

```
> apply(fw, 1, mean, na.rm = TRUE)
     Taw Torridge     Ouse      Exe      Lyn    Brook    Ditch      Fal
     5.5     14.0     10.0      5.5     14.0     24.5     26.5     40.5
```

In this case you see that the row names of the original data frame are displayed. If your data frame had no set row names, you would simply see your result as a vector of values like so:

```
> apply(mf, 1, median, na.rm = TRUE)
 [1] 20 21 22 23 21 21 19 16 16 21 21 26 21 20 19 18 17 19 21 21 22 25 24 23 22
```

Summary Statistics for Matrix Objects

A matrix looks like a frame but is not; in effect, the data are a single vector that happens to be split into rows and columns. In the following example you see a matrix comprised of some numeric values relating to observations of some common British birds in various habitats:

```
> bird
              Garden Hedgerow Parkland Pasture Woodland
Blackbird         47       10       40       2        2
Chaffinch         19        3        5       0        2
Great Tit         50        0       10       7        0
House Sparrow     46       16        8       4        0
Robin              9        3        0       0        2
Song Thrush        4        0        6       0        0
```

You cannot extract parts of a matrix using $ like you could with a data frame, but you can use the square brackets to retrieve information about any row or column:

```
> mean(bird[,2])
[1] 5.333333
> mean(bird[2,])
[1] 5.8
```

The first example returns the mean for the second column, whilst the next example returns the mean for the second row. You can also use the colMeans() and rowSums() commands like you used before:

```
> colSums(bird)
  Garden Hedgerow Parkland  Pasture Woodland
     175       32       69       13        6
```

```
> rowMeans(bird)
    Blackbird     Chaffinch     Great Tit House Sparrow         Robin
         20.2           5.8          13.4          14.8           2.8
  Song Thrush
          2.0
```

The `apply()` command also works equally well for a matrix as it does for data frame objects, like so:

```
>apply(bird, 2, median)
  Garden Hedgerow Parkland  Pasture Woodland
    32.5      3.0      7.0      1.0      1.0
```

In this case you extract the median values for the columns of the matrix. You can also choose certain elements of the result to display by appending square brackets after the command, as shown in the following example:

```
> apply(bird,1,median)[1:2]
Blackbird Chaffinch
       10         3

> apply(bird,1,median)[c(1,2,4)]
    Blackbird     Chaffinch House Sparrow
           10             3             8

> apply(bird,1,median)[c(1,2,'Robin')]
 <NA>  <NA> Robin
   NA    NA     2

> apply(bird,1,median)[c('Blackbird','Robin')]
Blackbird     Robin
       10         2
```

In the first example you display only the first and second items. In the next example you select the first, second, and fourth items. The third example shows that you cannot mix numbers and text. In the final example you select the column results you want using their column names (in quotes).

Summary Statistics for Lists

List objects do not work in quite the same manner as matrix or data frame objects. As with most of the summary commands that you have met, many will simply fail to work, so a different approach is needed. In the following example you have a simple list that is comprised of two vectors of numbers that are unequal in length:

```
> grass.l
$mow
[1] 12 15 17 11 15

$unmow
[1] 8 9 7 9

> summary(grass.l)
      Length Class  Mode
mow   5      -none- numeric
unmow 4      -none- numeric
```

```
> mean(grass.l)
[1] NA
Warning message:
In mean.default(grass.l) : argument is not numeric or logical: returning NA
> sum(grass.l)
Error in sum(grass.l) : invalid 'type' (list) of argument
> length(grass.l)
[1] 2
```

The only useful result you get here is the `length()` command, which confirms that you have two elements in your list. You could examine each element of the list in turn by using the `$` syntax like so:

```
> mean(grass.l$mow)
[1] 14
> max(grass.l$unmow)
[1] 9
```

Using `$` is fine, but it's quite tedious if you have more than one or two elements to consider. It is also not generalized enough; it would be better to have a method that did not rely on individual items being named (other than the list object). Instead, you can use a special version of the `apply()` command that works specifically on list objects. The command is `lapply()`; think of it as short for "list apply." This is easy enough to use—you simply name the list and the function you want to apply to each list element like so:

```
> lapply(grass.l, mean, na.rm = TRUE)
$mow
[1] 14
$unmow
[1] 8.25
```

You are still able to add extra instructions to the command; in this example you ensure that `NA` items are removed before the `mean()` command is applied. The result you get back is in the form of a list pretty much like the original object. You can change this to produce a "nicer" output using a variant of the command `sapply()` like so.

```
> sapply(grass.l, mean, na.rm = TRUE)
  mow unmow
14.00  8.25
```

The resulting output is in fact a matrix. This enables you to undertake other manipulations because a matrix object is a bit easier to deal with than a list. If you want to carry out further manipulations on the result, make an object to hold the result:

```
> grass.mn = sapply(grass.l, mean, na.rm = TRUE)
```

Now you have a new object that can be used later.

SUMMARY TABLES

Just as you did with the vector, matrix, list, and data frame objects in Chapter 3, you can manipulate, alter, and produce table objects using the `table()` command to summarize a data sample. Using this command you can create a few special kinds of table objects, including contingency tables and complex (flat) contingency tables. A contingency table is particularly useful when you have a large number of observations and you want to condense the data into a smaller format. A complex (flat) table is a type of contingency table that is useful when creating just one single table as opposed to multiple ones. Additionally, you can use cross-tabulation to reassemble data into a tabular format as necessary. This section covers how to work with table objects in all of these capacities.

Making Contingency Tables

A contingency table is a way to redraw data and assemble it into a table that shows the layout of the original data in a manner that allows the reader to gain an overall summary of the original data. You can create contingency tables using the `table()` command. The command can handle data in simple vectors or more complex matrix and data frame objects, as you see shortly. The more complex the original data, the more complex the resulting contingency table will be.

Creating Contingency Tables from Vectors

The simplest data object from which you can create a contingency table is a vector. In the following example you have a simple numeric vector of values:

```
> data2
 [1] 3 5 7 5 3 2 6 8 5 6 9 4 5 7 3 4
> table(data2)
data2
2 3 4 5 6 7 8 9
1 3 2 4 2 2 1 1
```

Here you use the `table()` command to organize the data into a simple contingency table. This table shows you how many items in the data match up to the various integer values; you can see that there are three 3s, for example, but only a single 8. You can visualize this better, perhaps, if you rewrite the data in numerical order:

```
> sort(data2)
 [1] 2 3 3 3 4 4 5 5 5 5 6 6 7 7 8 9
```

Here the `sort()` command is used to reorder the data values; if you compare this to the table you just created you can see more clearly what the `table()` command has done. You can use the `table()` command on character data too; in the following example you have a simple vector of labels:

```
> graze
[1] "mow"    "mow"    "mow"    "mow"    "mow"    "unmow" "unmow" "unmow" "unmow"
> table(graze)
graze
  mow unmow
    5     4
```

You can see from the table that there are five items in the `mow` treatment and four in the `unmow` treatment.

Creating Contingency Tables from Complicated Data

The numeric data that go with the labels from the preceding section's example are assembled into a data frame like so:

```
> grass
```

```
  rich graze
1   12   mow
2   15   mow
3   17   mow
4   11   mow
5   15   mow
6    8 unmow
7    9 unmow
8    7 unmow
9    9 unmow
```

If you use the `table()` command on these data you get a contingency table like the following:

```
> table(grass)
    graze
rich mow unmow
  7    0     1
  8    0     1
  9    0     2
  11   1     0
  12   1     0
  15   2     0
  17   1     0
```

You see the numerical data in the first column, followed by a column for each of the `graze` treatments. The table shows you how many times a particular numerical value cropped up in each of the `graze` treatments.

When your data are all numeric you get a more complex table as a result, because each numeric value in the second column is treated as a separate "level" and compared to each value in the first column. In the following example you have a simple data frame that contains two columns of numeric data:

```
> fw
         count speed
Taw          9     2
Torridge    25     3
Ouse        15     5
Exe          2     9
Lyn         14    14
Brook       25    24
Ditch       24    29
Fal         47    34

> table(fw)
     speed
count 2 3 5 9 14 24 29 34
   2  0 0 0 1  0  0  0  0
   9  1 0 0 0  0  0  0  0
   14 0 0 0 0  1  0  0  0
   15 0 0 1 0  0  0  0  0
   24 0 0 0 0  0  0  1  0
   25 0 1 0 0  0  1  0  0
   47 0 0 0 0  0  0  0  1
```

If you have more complex data frames (that is, with more than two columns), you get a more complex result; you end up with multiple tables. Each of the individual tables shows the first two columns in the data frame, but the values in the other columns are picked out one by one with all the various combinations. This can get complicated to say the least. Here is a simple example where you have a data frame containing a column of numeric values and two columns of factors (character variables):

```
> pw
   height    plant water
1       9 vulgaris    lo
2      11 vulgaris    lo
3       6 vulgaris    lo
4      14 vulgaris   mid
5      17 vulgaris   mid
6      19 vulgaris   mid
7      28 vulgaris    hi
8      31 vulgaris    hi
9      32 vulgaris    hi
10      7   sativa    lo
11      6   sativa    lo
12      5   sativa    lo
13     14   sativa   mid
14     17   sativa   mid
15     15   sativa   mid
16     44   sativa    hi
17     38   sativa    hi
18     37   sativa    hi
```

If you use a `table()` command on these data you get three tables produced as a result. The command produces a table for each of the `water` treatments. Here only the first one is shown:

```
> table(pw)
, , water = hi

      plant
height sativa vulgaris
    5       0        0
    6       0        0
    7       0        0
    9       0        0
    11      0        0
    14      0        0
    15      0        0
    17      0        0
    19      0        0
    28      0        1
    31      0        1
    32      0        1
    37      1        0
    38      1        0
    44      1        0
```

The first table shown examines the situation for the first treatment; the factors are considered in order so the hi treatment comes first (because of alphabetical sorting). The other factors are shown in separate tables; the next one being for the lo treatment:

```
, , water = lo

      plant
height sativa vulgaris
     5      1        0
     6      1        1
     7      1        0
     9      0        1
...
```

Here just the first few lines are shown of the next table in the set. The final table in the example shows the situation when the water treatment is set to mid:

```
, , water = mid

      plant
height sativa vulgaris
     5      0        0
     6      0        0
     7      0        0
     9      0        0
...
```

If you have more than a couple of columns of data, things can rapidly get out of hand, and you may end up with a lot more output than you bargained for. You need a way to control which columns are summarized by the table. You can do this with a bit of tweaking to the table() command.

Creating Custom Contingency Tables

Rather than use all the columns (or rows) of a data frame, you could create a contingency table that uses only part of the data. In this situation you can actually select each separate row and column to use, as detailed in the following sections.

Selecting Columns to Use in a Contingency Table

The table() command enables you to specify which columns of data you want to use to create your contingency table; simply provide the names of the vector objects in the command instruction:

```
> table(height, water)
Error in table(height, water) : object 'height' not found
```

In this example though the command cannot find the objects you want because they are part of the pw data frame. You can get around this in one of several ways. You could use $ and specify the full name or you could use the attach() command to "open up" the data frame. In the following example the $ syntax is used:

```
> table(pw$height, pw$water)

    hi lo mid
  5  0  1   0
```

```
6   0 2  0
7   0 1  0
9   0 1  0
11  0 1  0
14  0 0  2
15  0 0  1
17  0 0  2
19  0 0  1
28  1 0  0
31  1 0  0
32  1 0  0
37  1 0  0
38  1 0  0
44  1 0  0
```

The result is a table that shows you a column for each of the three `water` treatments. Notice that the names of the items are not given; the `height` and `water` labels are gone and you only get the names of the three `water` treatments. If you had used the `attach()` command the names would be shown. Of course, there is a way around this; you can use your own labels. To do so, specify the names you require as labels as an instruction in the `table()` command like so:

```
> table(pw$height, pw$water, dnn = c('Ht', 'H2O'))
    H2O
Ht   hi lo mid
  5   0  1   0
  6   0  2   0
  7   0  1   0
...
```

Here you have used a slightly different label than the name of the original vectors; you see the first few lines of the table and can see your customized labels at the top. There is yet another way to get the names of the vectors within the data frame recognized: you can use the `with()` command. This is like using the `attach()` command but you do not have to remember to `detach()` the data afterwards.

The `with()` command works in a general manner. To use it you simply put in the name of the data you want to access and then carry on with the command you wanted to use all in the same line, like so:

```
> with(pw, table(height, water))
```

Now the names of the data columns are available to the `table()` command and the labels reappear:

```
      water
height hi lo mid
     5  0  1   0
     6  0  2   0
     7  0  1   0
...
```

Selecting Rows to Use in a Contingency Table

If you want to use only certain rows of a data frame to form the basis for a contingency table, you need to use a slightly different approach. Essentially this involves creating a matrix object and making a contingency table from that. This topic is discussed in the next section.

Creating Contingency Tables from Matrix Objects

So far you have looked at using the `table()` command on vectors and data frames. You can use the command on matrix objects too, but you need to remember that they have a slightly different structure. Here is a matrix that you have met before; bird observation data:

```
> bird
              Garden Hedgerow Parkland Pasture Woodland
Blackbird         47       10       40       2        2
Chaffinch         19        3        5       0        2
Great Tit         50        0       10       7        0
House Sparrow     46       16        8       4        0
Robin              9        3        0       0        2
Song Thrush        4        0        6       0        0
```

When you use the `table()` command you get the following result:

```
> table(bird)
bird
 0  2  3  4  5  6  7  8  9 10 16 19 40 46 47 50
 9  4  2  2  1  1  1  1  1  2  1  1  1  1  1  1
```

The data in the matrix are treated like a single vector, so your resulting table displays accordingly. The `$` convention does not work with a matrix, so you are therefore also unable to use the `attach()` command. You can, however, use the square brackets to pick out rows and columns to make into your table:

```
> table(bird[,1], bird[,2], dnn = c('Gdn', 'Hedge'))
    Hedge
Gdn  0 3 10 16
  4  1 0  0  0
  9  0 1  0  0
  19 0 1  0  0
  46 0 0  0  1
  47 0 0  1  0
  50 1 0  0  0
```

In this (preceding) example you used the first and second columns and created your contingency table; you need to specify the names for display using the `dnn =` instruction. You can do something similar for row data:

```
> table(bird[3,], bird[1,], dnn = c('Gt. Tit', 'BlackBrd'))
       BlackBrd
Gt. Tit 2 10 40 47
     0  1  1  0  0
     7  1  0  0  0
     10 0  0  1  0
     50 0  0  0  1
```

Here you chose the third and first rows to compare and make up into a contingency table. Once again you must include explicit names for your table display.

With a bit of manipulation you can make your matrix into a data frame and read the column names using the `with()` command:

```
> with(as.data.frame(bird), table(Garden, Pasture))
      Pasture
Garden 0 2 4 7
```

```
4  1 0 0 0
9  1 0 0 0
19 1 0 0 0
46 0 0 1 0
47 0 1 0 0
50 0 0 0 1
```

In this example you use the `as.data.frame()` command to temporarily convert the object to a data frame.

Using Rows of a Data Frame in a Contingency Table

Using a matrix means that you are able to look at the rows to construct your contingency table. If you have a data frame, perhaps you could use the same square bracket convention to do the same thing? Try it in the following example:

```
> fw
         count speed
Taw          9     2
Torridge    25     3
Ouse        15     5
Exe          2     9
Lyn         14    14
Brook       25    24
Ditch       24    29
Fal         47    34

> table(fw[1,], fw[2,])
Error in sort.list(y) :
  'x' must be atomic for 'sort.list'
Have you called 'sort' on a list?
```

The short answer is no, you cannot! You could try the same trick as before and convert the object to a matrix though:

```
> with(as.matrix(fw), table(fw[1,], fw[2,]))
Error in eval(substitute(expr), data, enclos = parent.frame()) :
  numeric 'envir' arg not of length one
```

However, this also fails. The only way to get this to work is to force each item in the table as a matrix like so:

```
> table(as.matrix(fw)[1,], as.matrix(fw)[2,], dnn = c('Taw', 'Torridge'))
   Torridge
Taw 3 25
  2 1  0
  9 0  1
```

You could also make a new matrix and then apply the `table()` command to the new object:

```
> fw.mat = as.matrix(fw)
> table(fw.mat[1,], fw.mat[4,], dnn = c('Taw', 'Exe'))
   Exe
Taw 2 9
  2 0 1
  9 1 0
> rm(fw.mat)
```

Rotating Data Frames

You can rotate the data so that the rows become the columns and vice versa. You can use the `t()` command to transpose a data frame like so:

```
> t(fw)
      Taw Torridge Ouse Exe Lyn Brook Ditch Fal
count   9       25   15   2  14    25    24  47
speed   2        3    5   9  14    24    29  34
```

Now the result is a matrix, so you need to use the square brackets to select the columns (that is, the original rows) that you require:

```
> table(t(fw)[,1], t(fw)[,2], dnn = c('Taw', 'Torridge'))
   Torridge
Taw 3 25
  2 1  0
  9 0  1
```

This approach will also work on a matrix. You can use the `t()` command to rotate a matrix in exactly the same way as for a data frame.

Selecting Parts of a Table Object

A table is a special sort of matrix, and you deal with tables in similar ways to matrix objects. You can extract various elements of a table object exactly as you would for a matrix object. In the following activity you create a contingency table and select out various components of it.

TRY IT OUT Selecting and Displaying Parts of a Contingency Table

Available for download on Wrox.com Use the `pw` data object from the `Beginning.RData` file for this activity; you will use this to create and examine a custom contingency table.

1. Use the `pw` data frame as the starting point for a custom contingency table:

```
> pw.tab = with(pw, table(height, water))
```

2. View the resulting contingency table:

```
> pw.tab
      water
height hi lo mid
    5   0  1   0
    6   0  2   0
    7   0  1   0
    9   0  1   0
    11  0  1   0
    14  0  0   2
    15  0  0   1
    17  0  0   2
    19  0  0   1
    28  1  0   0
    31  1  0   0
    32  1  0   0
```

```
37  1  0   0
38  1  0   0
44  1  0   0
```

3. Examine the table object structure using the `str()` command:

```
> str(pw.tab)
 'table' int [1:15, 1:3] 0 0 0 0 0 0 0 0 0 1 ...
 - attr(*, "dimnames")=List of 2
  ..$ height: chr [1:15] "5" "6" "7" "9" ...
  ..$ water : chr [1:3] "hi" "lo" "mid"
```

4. Now display only the first three rows of the contingency table:

```
> pw.tab[1:3,]
      water
height hi lo mid
     5  0  1   0
     6  0  2   0
     7  0  1   0
```

5. Next display the first three rows of the first column:

```
> pw.tab[1:3,1]
5 6 7
0 0 0
```

6. Now display the first three rows of the first and second columns:

```
> pw.tab[1:3,1:2]
      water
height hi lo
     5  0  1
     6  0  2
     7  0  1
```

7. Display the column labeled `hi`:

```
> pw.tab[,'hi']
 5  6  7  9 11 14 15 17 19 28 31 32 37 38 44
 0  0  0  0  0  0  0  0  0  1  1  1  1  1  1
```

8. Now display the first three rows of two of the columns:

```
> pw.tab[1:3, c('hi', 'mid')]
      water
height hi mid
     5  0   0
     6  0   0
     7  0   0
```

9. Display some of the columns in a new order:

```
> pw.tab[1:3, c('mid', 'hi')]
      water
height mid hi
     5   0  0
     6   0  0
     7   0  0
```

10. Try displaying two columns using a mix of name and number:

```
> pw.tab[,c('hi',3)]
Error: subscript out of bounds
```

11. Look at the length of the table object:

```
> length(pw.tab)
[1] 45
```

12. Finally, display some consecutive items:

```
> pw.tab[16:30]
 [1] 1 2 1 1 1 0 0 0 0 0 0 0 0 0 0
```

How It Works

The first step is to create the table object using two of the columns to produce a simple contingency table. The `str()` command shows that the resulting object is a table. The table can be displayed much like a matrix by using the square brackets to define the rows and columns required. The rows and columns can be specified as numbers or names (if appropriate), but you cannot mix names and numbers in the same command.

The `length()` command produces a result that reflects the number of items in the table; this is similar to a matrix but different from a data frame (where the command produced the number of columns).

A table object is a special kind of object in its own right, but it also has certain properties of a matrix. This will become important to remember when you begin to develop logical tests, as you will see shortly in the section, "Testing for Table Objects."

Converting an Object into a Table

You can convert an object into a table by using the `as.table()` command if it is already a matrix because they are very similar objects. If you have a data frame, however, you must convert it to a matrix first and then convert that into a table. You can do this in one go as follows (however, if you have no row names you may end up with character labels rather than numbers):

```
> as.table(as.matrix(mf))
    len     sp    alg     no3    bod
A 20.00  12.00  40.00   2.25 200.00
B 21.00  14.00  45.00   2.15 180.00
C 22.00  12.00  45.00   1.75 135.00
D 23.00  16.00  80.00   1.95 120.00
E 21.00  20.00  75.00   1.95 110.00
F 20.00  21.00  65.00   2.75 120.00
G 19.00  17.00  65.00   1.85  95.00
...
```

In this case your row names have ended up as uppercase characters; here you can see only the first seven rows of the result. If you try to convert a table directly into an object you get an error, like so:

```
> as.table(mf)
Error in as.table.default(mf) : cannot coerce into a table
```

If you have a list object you have to do a few contortions to get the data in the right form. First, you must use the `stack()` command to get the individual elements out in a frame-like form. Then you can convert to a matrix and finally a table; quite a performance!

In the following example you begin with a simple list containing only two items:

```
> grass.l
$mow
[1] 12 15 17 11 15

$unmow
[1] 8 9 7 9

> gr.tab = as.table(as.matrix(stack(grass.l)))

> colnames(gr.tab) = c('spp', 'graze')

> gr.tab
  spp graze
A 12  mow
B 15  mow
C 17  mow
D 11  mow
E 15  mow
F  8  unmow
G  9  unmow
H  7  unmow
I  9  unmow
```

You have to set the names for the columns separately because the `stack()` command produces default names of `values` and `ind`. Note that you use the `colnames()` command to alter the names.

Testing for Table Objects

You can test to see if an object is a table using the `is.table()` command. This produces a `TRUE` result if you do have a table and a `FALSE` result if you do not:

```
> is.table(bird)
[1] FALSE
> is.table(gr.tab)
[1] TRUE
```

You can also use the `class()` command to see if an object is a table directly:

```
> class(gr.tab)
[1] "table"
```

The `class()` command can form the basis of a logical test by using the `if()` command in the following manner:

```
> if(class(gr.tab) =='table') TRUE else FALSE
[1] TRUE
```

NOTE *The* `if()` *command is useful in enabling options. The basic form of the command is as follows:*

```
if(condition) what.to.do.if.TRUE else what.to.do.if.FALSE
```

You set the `condition` *to test in the main brackets. After this you put what to do if the result of the* `condition` *is* `TRUE`. *The* `else` *part allows you to specify what to do if the result of the condition is* `FALSE`.

Complex (Flat) Tables

You can use an alternative version of the `table()` command to make "flat" tables; that is, rather than make several tables, the rows or columns are subdivided to make a single table. The command is `ftable()` and you can use it in several ways.

Making "Flat" Contingency Tables

In the following example you see the plant watering data frame that you met earlier. This has a column of numerical `height` data and two columns of factors, `plant` and `water`. When you create the "flat" contingency table you get something like the following:

```
> ftable(pw)
                 water hi lo mid
height plant
5      sativa           0  1   0
       vulgaris         0  0   0
6      sativa           0  1   0
       vulgaris         0  1   0
7      sativa           0  1   0
       vulgaris         0  0   0
9      sativa           0  0   0
       vulgaris         0  1   0
11     sativa           0  0   0
       vulgaris         0  1   0
14     sativa           0  0   1
       vulgaris         0  0   1
15     sativa           0  0   1
       vulgaris         0  0   0
17     sativa           0  0   1
       vulgaris         0  0   1
19     sativa           0  0   0
       vulgaris         0  0   1
28     sativa           0  0   0
       vulgaris         1  0   0
31     sativa           0  0   0
       vulgaris         1  0   0
32     sativa           0  0   0
       vulgaris         1  0   0
37     sativa           1  0   0
       vulgaris         0  0   0
38     sativa           1  0   0
```

```
        vulgaris       0  0   0
44      sativa         1  0   0
        vulgaris       0  0   0
```

Here you can see that the rows are subdivided between the two levels of the `plant` factor.

You can use the command much like the `table()` command and specify two or more columns of the data to use in the table. The order of the columns you specify are used to construct the contingency table. You can also use a slightly different syntax to tell R what sort of output you require; the general form of the command is as follows:

```
ftable(column.items ~ row.items, data = data.object)
```

You use the tilde (~) character to create a formula where the left side contains the variables you want to use as the row headings (in other words, stuff that forms the columns), separated by commas. After the tilde you put the names of the vectors that you want to form the row items.

These commands give you great flexibility in creating contingency tables. In the following activity you practice creating some "flat" contingency tables.

TRY IT OUT Create "Flat" Contingency Tables from Complex Data

Available for download on Wrox.com

Use the `pw` data from the `Beginning.RData` file for this activity, which you will use to create a "flat" contingency table.

1. Start by creating a contingency table from the `pw` data object. Use the columns in the order in which they appear in the original data:

```
> with(pw, ftable(height, plant, water))
                  water hi lo mid
height plant
5      sativa            0  1   0
       vulgaris          0  0   0
6      sativa            0  1   0
       vulgaris          0  1   0
7      sativa            0  1   0
       vulgaris          0  0   0
9      sativa            0  0   0
       vulgaris          0  1   0
...
```

2. Now create another contingency table but specify the columns in a new order:

```
> with(pw, ftable(height,water,plant))
                plant sativa vulgaris
height water
5      hi                0        0
       lo                1        0
       mid               0        0
6      hi                0        0
       lo                1        1
       mid               0        0
...
```

3. Next try creating a flat table using the ~ syntax. Keep the same column order as the first table you created:

```
> ftable(plant ~ height + water, data = pw)
                   plant sativa vulgaris
height water
5      hi                0        0
       lo                1        0
       mid               0        0
6      hi                0        0
       lo                1        1
       mid               0        0
...
```

4. Now try to create the same table as the first but using the new ~ syntax:

```
> ftable(water ~ height + plant, data = pw)
                      water hi lo mid
height plant
5      sativa               0  1   0
       vulgaris             0  0   0
6      sativa               0  1   0
       vulgaris             0  1   0
...
```

5. Now specify the main response variable as the main grouping variable in your flat table:

```
> ftable(height ~ water + plant, data = pw)
                     height 5 6 7 9 11 14 15 17 19 28 31 32 37 38 44
water plant
hi    sativa                0 0 0 0  0  0  0  0  0  0  0  0  1  1  1
      vulgaris              0 0 0 0  0  0  0  0  0  1  1  1  0  0  0
lo    sativa                1 1 1 0  0  0  0  0  0  0  0  0  0  0  0
      vulgaris              0 1 0 1  1  0  0  0  0  0  0  0  0  0  0
mid   sativa                0 0 0 0  0  1  1  1  0  0  0  0  0  0  0
      vulgaris              0 0 0 0  0  1  0  1  1  0  0  0  0  0  0
```

6. Finally, re-create the last table without the ~ syntax:

```
> with(pw, ftable(water, plant, height))
```

How It Works

To start with you had to use the `with()` command so that the names of the columns in the original data could be "read" by R. The order in which you enter the columns is very important; in this case `height` was specified first and this forms the column margin of the table. The next item inserted was `plant` followed by `water`; is the order in which they appear. If you change the order, obviously the appearance of the table is different and your data are summarized in a different way that may make more (or less) sense. In the next table `height` was kept as the main column, but the order of the factor variables was swapped.

The ~ syntax allows great flexibility and enables you to create contingency tables relatively easily. The column specified before the ~ forms the main body of the table, whereas those to the right of the ~ form the groupings of the table in the order they were specified. The final example shows that the most compact table uses the main response variable as the main body.

You can extract parts of your table exactly using the square brackets, like you did in an earlier activity. In the next example the contingency table contains two data columns; these relate to the different levels in the `plant` column:

```
> gr.t = ftable(plant ~ height + water, data = pw)

> gr.t
              plant sativa vulgaris
height water
5      hi                0        0
       lo                1        0
       mid               0        0
6      hi                0        0
       lo                1        1
       mid               0        0
...
```

You can now use the square brackets to extract rows and columns of the resulting contingency table object.

```
> gr.t[1:3,]
     [,1] [,2]
[1,]    0    0
[2,]    1    0
[3,]    0    0
```

Here only the first three rows are selected. Notice that the names are not displayed. The simplest way to extract a part of the object is to make a logical unit of some sort and to create a separate matrix from it and name that. For example, you can use the first three rows from the preceding example; these relate to the `height` of 5. Make a matrix and give it sensible names before displaying the full result:

```
> gr.sub = gr.t[1:3,]
> gr.sub
     [,1] [,2]
[1,]    0    0
[2,]    1    0
[3,]    0    0

> colnames(gr.sub) = c('sativa', 'vulgaris')
> rownames(gr.sub) = c('hi','lo','mid')

> gr.sub
    sativa vulgaris
hi       0        0
lo       1        0
mid      0        0
```

You could also do this in one go by specifying the names as part of the command like so:

```
> gr.sub = matrix(gr.t[1:3,],ncol =2, dimnames = list(c('hi','lo','mid'),
c('sativa','vulgaris')))
```

This time you have to use the `matrix()` command to set the row and column names (using the `dimnames` instruction).

Making Selective "Flat" Contingency Tables

A contingency table is best kept as a complete item. As you saw earlier, you can subset a "flat" table using the square brackets syntax. However, this is not a straightforward process. It would be better if you could create a contingency table right at the outset that matched certain conditions. The following activity shows how you can do this.

TRY IT OUT Creating Selective "Flat" Contingency Tables

Available for download on Wrox.com

Use the `pw` data object from the `Beginning.RData` file for this activity, which you will use to create a "flat" contingency table.

1. Start by creating a "flat" contingency table with a conditional column:

```
> with(pw, ftable(height==14, water, plant))
            plant sativa vulgaris

      water
FALSE hi              3        3
      lo              3        3
      mid             2        2
TRUE  hi              0        0
      lo              0        0
      mid             1        1
```

2. Now add an additional condition to another column:

```
> with(pw, ftable(height==14, water=='hi', plant))
            plant sativa vulgaris

FALSE FALSE           5        5
      TRUE            3        3
TRUE  FALSE           1        1
      TRUE            0        0
```

3. Make a new data object as a subset of the original data:

```
> pw.t = pw[which(pw$height==14),]

> pw.t
   height    plant water
4      14 vulgaris   mid
13     14   sativa   mid
```

4. Finally, create a "flat" table from the new (subsetted) data:

```
> with(pw.t, ftable(height, plant, water))
                water hi lo mid
height plant
14     sativa          0  0   1
       vulgaris        0  0   1
```

How It Works

When you insert a conditional column into the `ftable()` command, the resulting contingency table includes the data for both `TRUE` and `FALSE` results of the condition. You can add conditional statements for other columns (and also more complex conditional statements for the single column) and produce more `TRUE` and `FALSE` results.

To make a selective `ftable` object you must create a new data frame that contains only the data you require. Now you can use the `ftable()` command on the new data to produce a result that contains no `TRUE` or `FALSE` results, only "real" data.

Now you have seen how to create "flat" contingency tables and how to be selective when doing so, using only certain data and even including conditional statements to create a selective table. You now need to be able to tell if an object is a "flat" table; that is the subject of the next section.

Testing "Flat" Table Objects

You can use the `class()`, command to see what kind of object you are dealing with. The `class()` command gives you a label for each kind of object. The class of an object is used to determine how R handles it; you can find out what an object is and also set the class of an object. The bottom line is that you can use the class to test if your object is an `ftable` object by looking at its `class` like so:

```
> if(class(gr.t) == 'ftable') TRUE else FALSE
[1] TRUE
```

Here you look to see if the class is `"ftable"`; if it is, you give a `TRUE` result, otherwise you get a `FALSE` result.

Summary Commands for Tables

A table is usually a way of summarizing some data and is often the end point of an operation (for example, making a contingency table). At times, however, you may want to perform certain actions on a table itself. You have already met some commands that could be useful, for example `rowMeans()`, `colSums()`, and `apply()`. These will work equally well on a table as they will on a matrix. However, you can use some additional commands, which are summarized in Table 4-5.

TABLE 4-5: Table Summary Commands

SUMMARY COMMAND	EXPLANATION
`rowSums()` `colSums()`	Determines the sum of rows or columns for a data frame, matrix, or table object.
`rowMeans()` `colMeans()`	Determines the mean of rows or columns for a data frame, matrix, or table object.
`apply(x, MARGIN, FUN)`	Applies a function to rows or columns of a data frame, matrix, or table. If `MARGIN = 1` the rows are used, if `2` the columns are used.
`prop.table(x,` `margin = NULL, FUN)`	Returns the contents of a data frame, matrix, or table as a proportion of the total specified margin. The default uses the grand total, `margin = 1` uses row totals, and `margin = 2` uses column totals.

`addmargins(A,`
`margin = c(1, 2),`
`FUN = sum)`
	Returns a function applied to rows and/or columns of a matrix or table.

In the following activity you try out some of these summary commands to get a feeling for what they can do for you. You use a table of bird observation data that you have met before. The object in question is actually a matrix object but, as you have seen, a matrix acts very much like a table. In this case the way the data are arranged forms a contingency table. Each cell in the table is a unique combination of two factors.

TRY IT OUT Carrying Out Summary Commands on a Contingency Table

Available for download on Wrox.com

Use the `bird` data from the `Beginning.RData` file for this activity, which you will use as the contingency table to explore.

1. Start by looking at the `bird` data object:

```
> bird
              Garden Hedgerow Parkland Pasture Woodland
Blackbird         47       10       40       2        2
Chaffinch         19        3        5       0        2
Great Tit         50        0       10       7        0
House Sparrow     46       16        8       4        0
Robin              9        3        0       0        2
Song Thrush        4        0        6       0        0
```

2. Use the `rowSums()` command to look at sums of rows:

```
> rowSums(bird)
    Blackbird     Chaffinch     Great Tit House Sparrow         Robin   Song Thrush
          101            29            67            74            14            10
```

3. Now try the `apply()` command to look at column sums:

```
> apply(bird, MARGIN = 2, FUN = sum)
  Garden Hedgerow Parkland  Pasture Woodland
     175       32       69       13        6
```

4. Use the `margin.table()` command to get an overall total:

```
> margin.table(bird)
[1] 295
```

5. Use the `margin.table()` command to determine row sums:

```
> margin.table(bird, 1)
    Blackbird     Chaffinch     Great Tit House Sparrow         Robin   Song Thrush
          101            29            67            74            14            10
```

6. Now use the `margin.table()` command to determine column sums:

```
> margin.table(bird, margin = 2)
  Garden Hedgerow Parkland  Pasture Woodland
     175       32       69       13        6
```

7. Use the `prop.table()` command to display the table data as proportions of the total sum:

```
> prop.table(bird)
                  Garden   Hedgerow   Parkland     Pasture    Woodland
Blackbird     0.15932203 0.03389831 0.13559322 0.006779661 0.006779661
Chaffinch     0.06440678 0.01016949 0.01694915 0.000000000 0.006779661
```

```
Great Tit     0.16949153 0.00000000 0.03389831 0.023728814 0.000000000
House Sparrow 0.15593220 0.05423729 0.02711864 0.013559322 0.000000000
Robin         0.03050847 0.01016949 0.00000000 0.000000000 0.006779661
Song Thrush   0.01355932 0.00000000 0.02033898 0.000000000 0.000000000
```

8. Add a margin instruction to the `prop.table()` command to display the table as proportions of the row totals:

```
> prop.table(bird, margin = 1)
                 Garden  Hedgerow  Parkland    Pasture   Woodland
Blackbird     0.4653465 0.0990099 0.3960396 0.01980198 0.01980198
Chaffinch     0.6551724 0.1034483 0.1724138 0.00000000 0.06896552
Great Tit     0.7462687 0.0000000 0.1492537 0.10447761 0.00000000
House Sparrow 0.6216216 0.2162162 0.1081081 0.05405405 0.00000000
Robin         0.6428571 0.2142857 0.0000000 0.00000000 0.14285714
Song Thrush   0.4000000 0.0000000 0.6000000 0.00000000 0.00000000
```

9. Now use the `addmargins()` command to determine a row of mean values for the table:

```
> addmargins(bird, 1, mean)
                Garden  Hedgerow Parkland  Pasture Woodland
Blackbird     47.00000 10.000000     40.0 2.000000        2
Chaffinch     19.00000  3.000000      5.0 0.000000        2
Great Tit     50.00000  0.000000     10.0 7.000000        0
House Sparrow 46.00000 16.000000      8.0 4.000000        0
Robin          9.00000  3.000000      0.0 0.000000        2
Song Thrush    4.00000  0.000000      6.0 0.000000        0
mean          29.16667  5.333333     11.5 2.166667        1
```

10. Use the `addmargins()` command to work out a column median for the table:

```
> addmargins(bird, 2, median)
              Garden Hedgerow Parkland Pasture Woodland median
Blackbird         47       10       40       2        2     10
Chaffinch         19        3        5       0        2      3
Great Tit         50        0       10       7        0      7
House Sparrow     46       16        8       4        0      8
Robin              9        3        0       0        2      2
Song Thrush        4        0        6       0        0      0
```

How It Works

The `rowSums()` and `colMeans()` commands are general; you have used these before to work out sums and means for rows and columns. The `apply()` command is more flexible; you use it to apply a function to rows (`MARGIN = 1`) or columns (`MARGIN = 2`).

The `margin.table()` command is essentially the same as `apply()` when used with `FUN = sum`. If you leave out the `margin` instruction you get the complete total. Using `margin = 1` gives the row sums and `margin = 2` returns the column sums.

You can use the `prop.table()` command to display the table data as proportions of the total sum. You can add an index for the rows or columns in the same way as for the `margin.table()` command; in this way you can express the data in your table as proportions of the various row or column sums.

The `addmargins()` command enables you to use any function on rows or columns. The margin part defaults to both rows and columns, whereas the function applied defaults to the sum. In this case, the row/column index works like so: A value of 1 refers to rows, but the function is applied to the row items. Essentially, you get a row of results. In most situations you are going to use the function to produce summaries for both rows and columns.

You can see that you have several ways to achieve the same result. In some cases one command is a simpler version of something more complex but in others subtle differences exist.

Cross Tabulation

The table-creating commands that you have looked at so far build up frequencies of observations across categories. However, you may already have the frequency data, and in this case you need to reassemble the data into a tabular format. You met one table that had already been created when you looked at the bird observation data. If you look at the raw data file, you see that there are three columns: one for the species, one for the habitats, and one for the quantity (that is, the frequency of observations):

```
> birds
          Species  Habitat Qty
1       Blackbird   Garden  47
2       Chaffinch   Garden  19
3       Great Tit   Garden  50
4   House Sparrow   Garden  46
5           Robin   Garden   9
6     Song Thrush   Garden   4
7       Blackbird Parkland  40
8       Chaffinch Parkland   5
9       Great Tit Parkland  10
10  House Sparrow Parkland   8
11    Song Thrush Parkland   6
12      Blackbird Hedgerow  10
13      Chaffinch Hedgerow   3
14  House Sparrow Hedgerow  16
15          Robin Hedgerow   3
16      Blackbird Woodland   2
17      Chaffinch Woodland   2
18          Robin Woodland   2
19      Blackbird Pasture    2
20      Great Tit Pasture    7
21  House Sparrow Pasture    4
```

These data are in data frame format and were read into R using the `read.csv()` command. Your task is to reorganize the data into a contingency table; if you try this using the `table()` command you end up with a simple table like so:

```
> with(birds, table(Species, Habitat))
               Habitat
Species          Garden Hedgerow Parkland Pasture Woodland
  Blackbird           1        1        1       1        1
  Chaffinch           1        1        1       0        1
  Great Tit           1        0        1       1        0
  House Sparrow       1        1        1       1        0
  Robin               1        1        0       0        1
  Song Thrush         1        0        1       0        0
```

This is not really what you want because this shows you only which categories have observations (your data are reduced to ones and zeros). If you add the `Qty` column into the mix you end up with multiple tables, one for each `Qty`:

```
> with(birds, table(Species,Habitat,Qty))
, , Qty = 2

                Habitat
Species          Garden Hedgerow Parkland Pasture Woodland
  Blackbird           0        0        0       1        1
  Chaffinch           0        0        0       0        1
  Great Tit           0        0        0       0        0
  House Sparrow       0        0        0       0        0
  Robin               0        0        0       0        1
  Song Thrush         0        0        0       0        0

, , Qty = 3

                Habitat
Species          Garden Hedgerow Parkland Pasture Woodland
  Blackbird           0        0        0       0        0
  Chaffinch           0        1        0       0        0
  Great Tit           0        0        0       0        0
  House Sparrow       0        0        0       0        0
  Robin               0        1        0       0        0
  Song Thrush         0        0        0       0        0
...
```

Here just the first couple of tables produced are shown. The `ftable()` command gives you a single table, but you still end up with 1s and 0s:

```
> with(birds, ftable(Species,Habitat, Qty))
                        Qty 2 3 4 5 6 7 8 9 10 16 19 40 46 47 50
Species       Habitat
Blackbird     Garden        0 0 0 0 0 0 0 0  0  0  0  0  0  1  0
              Hedgerow      0 0 0 0 0 0 0 0  1  0  0  0  0  0  0
              Parkland      0 0 0 0 0 0 0 0  0  0  0  1  0  0  0
              Pasture       1 0 0 0 0 0 0 0  0  0  0  0  0  0  0
              Woodland      1 0 0 0 0 0 0 0  0  0  0  0  0  0  0
Chaffinch     Garden        0 0 0 0 0 0 0 0  0  0  1  0  0  0  0
              Hedgerow      0 1 0 0 0 0 0 0  0  0  0  0  0  0  0
              Parkland      0 0 0 1 0 0 0 0  0  0  0  0  0  0  0
              Pasture       0 0 0 0 0 0 0 0  0  0  0  0  0  0  0
              Woodland      1 0 0 0 0 0 0 0  0  0  0  0  0  0  0
...
```

The first few lines of the resulting table are shown here. You want to end up with the original frequency data (titled `Qty` in the data frame). To do that you use a cross-tabulation command called `xtabs()`. The basic form of the command is as follows:

```
xtabs(freq.data ~ categories.list, data)
```

Notice that you have the tilde (~) symbol like you met when using the `ftable()` command. On the left of the ~ you put the name of the frequency data; on the right you put the categories you want to cross-tabulate separated by the plus sign. The first variable after the ~ forms the row categories and the next variable you type forms the columns categories. At the end you type the name of the data object (so that R can "find" the variables). For the bird observation data you would type something like the following:

```
> birds.t = xtabs(Qty ~ Species + Habitat, data = birds)
> birds.t
                Habitat
Species          Garden Hedgerow Parkland Pasture Woodland
  Blackbird          47       10       40       2        2
  Chaffinch          19        3        5       0        2
  Great Tit          50        0       10       7        0
  House Sparrow      46       16        8       4        0
  Robin               9        3        0       0        2
  Song Thrush         4        0        6       0        0
```

This does the job nicely and now you see the data rearranged as required.

Testing Cross-Table (xtabs) Objects

When you use the `xtabs()` command, the object you create is a kind of table and gives a `TRUE` result using the `is.table()` command. It also gives a `TRUE` result if you use the `as.matrix()` command. As far as R is concerned it holds two sorts of `class`. You can see this using the `class()` command:

```
> class(birds.t)
[1] "xtabs" "table"
```

If you want to test for the object being an `xtabs` object you have a problem, because now the class result has two elements, shown in the following:

```
> if(class(birds.t) == 'xtabs') TRUE else FALSE
[1] TRUE
Warning message:
In if (class(birds.t) == "xtabs") TRUE else FALSE :
  the condition has length > 1 and only the first element will be used
```

When you try it you get a result of sorts but you also get an error message. You are lucky to get a result simply because the `"xtabs"` result was the first. In reality, you need a way of scanning the entire "result" and picking out the bit you want, wherever it may be. You can do that with the following:

```
> if(any(class(birds.t) == 'xtabs')) TRUE else FALSE
[1] TRUE
```

The `any()` command enables you to match any of the elements in a vector. In this case the upshot is that you will pick out the `xtabs` item even if it is not the first in the bunch.

A Better Class Test

The commands for testing for object types that you have seen so far are not the only ones at your disposal. Two other commands are especially useful:

- `is(object, "type")`
- `inherits(object, "type")`

Both these commands return a `TRUE` result if the `class()` of an object matches the "type" you specify in the instruction. These are especially powerful and useful because they mean that you do not need to use complicated `if()` and `any()` commands!

Recreating Original Data from a Contingency Table

If you have an `xtabs` object, you can reassemble it into a data frame using the `as.data.frame()` command:

```
> as.data.frame(birds.t)
         Species  Habitat Freq
1      Blackbird   Garden   47
2      Chaffinch   Garden   19
3      Great Tit   Garden   50
4  House Sparrow   Garden   46
5          Robin   Garden    9
6    Song Thrush   Garden    4
7      Blackbird Hedgerow   10
8      Chaffinch Hedgerow    3
9      Great Tit Hedgerow    0
10 House Sparrow Hedgerow   16
11         Robin Hedgerow    3
12   Song Thrush Hedgerow    0
13     Blackbird Parkland   40
14     Chaffinch Parkland    5
15     Great Tit Parkland   10
16 House Sparrow Parkland    8
17         Robin Parkland    0
18   Song Thrush Parkland    6
19     Blackbird Pasture     2
20     Chaffinch Pasture     0
21     Great Tit Pasture     7
22 House Sparrow Pasture     4
23         Robin Pasture     0
24   Song Thrush Pasture     0
25     Blackbird Woodland    2
26     Chaffinch Woodland    2
27     Great Tit Woodland    0
28 House Sparrow Woodland    0
29         Robin Woodland    2
30   Song Thrush Woodland    0
```

Now you have re-created the original data with one or two minor differences. The `Qty` column has been renamed `Freq` and the rows with zero frequency are included. Neither of these are significant issues; you can alter the name of the `Freq` column by amending the command like so:

```
> as.data.frame(birds.t, responseName = 'Qty')
```

If you want to remove the zero data you need to take your new data frame and select those rows with a `Freq` greater than zero, like so:

```
> birds.td = as.data.frame(birds.t)
> birds.td = birds.td[which(birds.td$Freq > 0),]
```

You begin by creating a new object to accept the data frame; the object is called `birds.td` in this example. Then you select all rows that have `Freq` greater than `0`. Notice that you have overwritten the original data frame with the amended one in this example. This is not essential but it is done here so that you do not have to delete a temporary object later. If you make a mistake you can easily recall the previous command and start over again.

If you have a contingency table that is not a table object but something like a matrix, then you need to alter the class of the object before you convert the object to a data frame. This is the subject of the next section.

Switching Class

You can use the `class()` command to alter which class an object is as well as see what class the object currently is. This can be useful for occasions where an object needs to be in a certain class for a command to operate. In the following example you can see the `bird` object queried and then reset using the `class()` command:

```
> class(bird)
[1] "matrix"
> class(bird) = 'table'
```

The matrix of bird observations is now classed as a table. You can now proceed to create a data frame from the table using the `as.data.frame()` command:

```
> bird.df = as.data.frame(bird)
           Var1     Var2 Freq
1     Blackbird   Garden   47
2     Chaffinch   Garden   19
3     Great Tit   Garden   50
4 House Sparrow   Garden   46
5         Robin   Garden    9
6   Song Thrush   Garden    4
7     Blackbird Hedgerow   10
8     Chaffinch Hedgerow    3
9     Great Tit Hedgerow    0
10 House Sparrow Hedgerow   16
...
```

Notice that the columns are not labeled appropriately and that the zero data are still intact. You can alter the names of the columns using the `names()` command and reconstruct the data omitting the zero rows as you saw in the preceding section. Here is the entire process:

```
> bird.tt = bird
> class(bird.tt) = 'table'
> bird.tt = as.data.frame(bird.tt)
> names(bird.tt) = c('Species', 'Habitat', 'Qty')
> bird.tt = bird.tt[which(bird.tt$Qty > 0),]
> rownames(bird.tt) = as.numeric(1:length(rownames(bird.tt)))
```

In the first command you simply create a duplicate matrix to work on, keeping your original intact. The second command changes the class to "table". The third command creates the data frame of original values. The fourth command alters the names of the columns. The penultimate command selects out the data that are greater than zero, effectively deleting 0 observations. The final command reinstates the row index labels to a continuous sequence.

SUMMARY

- You can summarize data items using the `summary()` command, which may give a specific result or a general summary.
- Specific summary commands include `mean()`, `median()`, `max()`, `min()`, `sd()`, `quantile()`, and `length()`.
- Cumulative statistics can be obtained via the `cumsum()` and `cummax()` commands. These can form the basis of simple custom functions to calculate for (for example, the running mean).
- Data frame and matrix objects can have summary functions applied to the rows and columns (for example, `colSums()`, `colMeans()`, `rowSums()`, and `rowMeans()` commands). The `apply()` command allows any function to be applied to rows or columns. The `lapply()` and `sapply()` commands are special variants designed to work on list objects.
- Contingency tables can be made using the `table()` command; the `ftable()` command creates "flat" tables for use with more complex data.
- You can convert raw data into a contingency table using the `xtabs()` command. This cross tabulation is similar to the PivotTable of Excel.
- The `class()` command can be used to tell what kind of object you are dealing with and can form the basis of a logical test.

EXERCISES

Available for download on Wrox.com

You can find answers to the exercises in Appendix A.

Use the `Beginning.RData` file for these exercises; the file contains the required data objects.

1. Have a look at the `mf` data object. Determine what kind of object this is and carry out some simple statistical summaries on these data.

2. Look at the `bfs` data object. Construct contingency tables using both the `table()` and `ftable()` commands. How can you get one command to produce the same layout of table as the other and what is the key difference between these results?

3. Look at the `invert` data object. Here you can see a data frame with three columns. Use cross tabulation to construct a contingency table showing the relationship between `Taxa` and `Habitat`. Save the resulting table as an object. What kind of object do you have and how can you reconstruct the original data?

▶ WHAT YOU LEARNED IN THIS CHAPTER

TOPIC	KEY POINTS
Summarizing objects: summary()	The summary() command is a general command that provides a summary of an object. If you have numerical data, then you get a numerical summary (for example, mean, max, min) but if the data are text, you get a note of how many different items you have. Using the summary() command on the result of many analytical routines produces a special summary suited to the kind of analysis performed.
Summarizing samples: mean() median() max() min() sd() var() length() sum() quantile() fivenum()	Numerical samples can be summarized by many commands. Simple commands like mean() produce a single result (the mean), whereas others produce several. The quantile() command, for example, produces five values as its result (the five basic quartiles).
Cumulative statistics: cumsum() cummax() cummin() cumproduct() seq_along()	Some commands produce cumulative values, for example the cumsum() command results in the cumulative sum of a numeric sample. The seq_along() command creates a simple index. These commands can be combined and used to create a range of cumulative statistics. For example the running mean: cumsum(my.data) / seq(along = my.data)
Summarizing rows and columns: colSums() colMeans() rowSums() rowMeans() apply() lapply() sapply()	The rows and columns of two-dimensional data objects can be summarized in various ways. The colSums() and rowMeans() commands, for example, produce the sum and mean values for columns and rows, respectively. The apply() command is more flexible in that any function can be applied to the columns (default) or rows of a data frame or matrix. The lapply() and sapply() commands are similar but are designed to work with list objects.

TOPIC	KEY POINTS

Contingency tables and cross tabulation:
`table()`
`ftable()`
`xtabs()`
	Contingency tables can be created using the `table()` command. When the data contains several columns, a "flat" table can be produced using the `ftable()` command.
	Data can be cross-tabulated to form contingency tables using the `xtabs()` command.
	Contingency tables can be reorganized into a data frame using the `as.data.frame()` command.

Table summaries:
`margin.table()`
`prop.table()`
`addmargins()`
	Tables can be summarized in exactly the same way as data frames and matrix objects by using `apply()`, for example. In addition, several commands are aimed explicitly at contingency tables. The `margin.table()` command gives sums for rows/columns. The `prop.table()` command determines the proportion that table entries make toward the total. The `addmargins()` command applies any function to rows/columns of a table.

Testing table objects:
`is.table()`
`is.matrix()`
`class()`
`any()`
`is(object, "type")`
`inherits(object, "type")`
	You can test to see if an object is of a certain type; using `is.table()` and `is.matrix()` commands, for example, will test for a table and a matrix, respectively. These commands produce a `TRUE` or `FALSE` result.
	The `class()` command can be used to view or set the current type of an object. Objects can have more than one class so if a test is required the `any()` command can be used to match any of the classes that may be present.
	The `is()` and `inherits()` commands can extract the class of an object directly and return a `TRUE` result if the class matches the `"type"`.

Logic and testing:
`for()`
`if() else`
`any()`
	The `for()` command can be used to create loops (for example, in creating cumulative statistics like a running median).
	The `if()` command is used to test some condition and carry out a command if the result is `TRUE`. It can add the command `else` to the end to carry out a command when the result is `FALSE`.
	The `any()` command can be used in testing conditions to match any item in a list.

continues

▶ WHAT YOU LEARNED IN THIS CHAPTER *(continued)*

TOPIC	KEY POINTS

Programming/custom functions:
`any()`
`for()`
`if() else`
`function()`
	The `any()` command enables the matching of any element in a list containing several items.
	The `for()` command is used to create programming loops.
	The `if()` command is used in logical testing of some condition and can be paired with `else` to provide an alternative.
	Customized commands can be created using the `function()` command.

Creating sequences: `seq()`	The `seq()` command produces sequences of values.

Reading data objects:
`attach()`
`detach()`
`with()`
	Variables contained within other data objects, such as the columns of a data frame, are usually inaccessible to R. They can be accessed using the `$` syntax (for example, `my.data$column`).
	Alternatively, the enclosing object can be "opened" using the `attach()` command. The `detach()` command closes the enclosing object.
	The `with()` command enables temporary access to an enclosing object.

5

Data: Distribution

WHAT YOU WILL LEARN IN THIS CHAPTER:

- How to create histograms and other graphics of sample distribution
- How to examine various distributions
- How to test for the normal distribution
- How to generate random numbers

Whenever you have data you should strive to find a shorthand way of expressing it. In the previous chapter you looked at summary statistics and tabulation. Visualizing your data is also important, as it is often easier to interpret a graph than a series of numbers. Whenever you have a set of numerical values you should also look to see what the distribution of the data is. The classic normal distribution for example, is only one kind of distribution that your data may appear in. The distribution is important because most statistical approaches require the data to be in one form. Knowing the distribution of your data will help you towards the correct analytical procedure. This chapter looks at ways to display the distribution of your data in graphical form and at different data distributions. You will also look at ways to test if your data conform to the normal distribution, which is most important for statistical testing. You will also look at random numbers and ways of sampling randomly from within a dataset.

LOOKING AT THE DISTRIBUTION OF DATA

When doing statistical analysis it is important to get a "picture" of the data. You usually want to know if the observations are clustered around some middle point (the average) and if there are observations way out on their own (outliers). This is all related to the *distribution* of the data. There are many distributions, but common ones are the *normal* distribution, *Poisson*, and *binomial*. There are also distributions relating directly to statistical tests; for example, *chi-squared* and *Student's t*.

It is necessary to look at your data and be able to determine what kind of distribution is most adequately represented by them. It is also useful to be able to compare the distribution you have with one of the standard distributions to see how your sample matches up.

You already met the `table()` command, which was a step toward gaining an insight into the distribution of a sample. It enables you to see how many observations there are in a range of categories. This section covers other general methods of looking at data and distributions.

Stem and Leaf Plot

The `table()` command gives you a quick look at a vector of data, but the result is still largely numeric. A graphical summary might be more useful because a picture is often easier to interpret. You could draw a frequency histogram, and indeed you do this in the following section, but you can also use a stem and leaf plot as a kind of halfway house. The `stem()` command produces the stem and leaf plot.

In the following activity you will use the `stem()` command and compare it to the `table()` command that you used in Chapter 4.

TRY IT OUT Make a Stem and Leaf Plot

Available for download on Wrox.com

Use the `data2`, `data4`, and `grass` data objects from the `Beginning.RData` file for this activity.

1. Start by looking at a simple vector of numerical values:

```
> data2
 [1] 3 5 7 5 3 2 6 8 5 6 9 4 5 7 3 4
```

2. Now create a contingency table using the `table()` command:

```
> table(data2)
data2
2 3 4 5 6 7 8 9
1 3 2 4 2 2 1 1
```

3. Create a basic stem and leaf plot using the `stem()` command:

```
> stem(data2)

  The decimal point is at the |

  2 | 0000
  4 | 000000
  6 | 0000
  8 | 00
```

4. Now increase the number of bins used by adding a `scale = 2` instruction:

```
> stem(data2, scale = 2)

  The decimal point is at the |

  2 | 0
  3 | 000
```

```
  4 | 00
  5 | 0000
  6 | 00
  7 | 00
  8 | 0
  9 | 0
```

5. Look at a sample vector with decimal values (that is, not integers):

```
> data4
 [1] 23.0 17.0 12.5 11.0 17.0 12.0 14.5  9.0 11.0  9.0 12.5 14.5 17.0  8.0 21.0
> stem(data4)

  The decimal point is 1 digit(s) to the right of the |

  0 | 899
  1 | 11233
  1 | 55777
  2 | 13
```

6. Make the scale wider to show the data differently:

```
> stem(data4, scale = 2)

  The decimal point is at the |

   8 | 000
  10 | 00
  12 | 055
  14 | 55
  16 | 000
  18 |
  20 | 0
  22 | 0
```

7. Look at a more complicated data object, a data frame:

```
> grass
  rich graze
1   12    mow
2   15    mow
3   17    mow
4   11    mow
5   15    mow
6    8 unmow
7    9 unmow
8    7 unmow
9    9 unmow
```

8. Create a stem and leaf plot from the numerical vector in the data frame using the `$` syntax:

```
> stem(grass$rich)

  The decimal point is 1 digit(s) to the right of the |

  0 | 7899
  1 | 12
  1 | 557
```

9. Now select a single treatment from the data with a conditional statement:

```
> with(grass, stem(rich[graze == 'mow']))

  The decimal point is at the |

  10 | 0
  12 | 0
  14 | 00
  16 | 0
```

How It Works

The `stem()` command redraws the data in such a way that you can see the range of numeric categories on the left and a representation of the frequency on the right. The picture is drawn using the original values so that you can see the numbers as well as a visual representation of the distribution. You need to read the title of the plot, which tells you where the decimal place is located.

In the first plot you can see four categories (or bins); the top bin is labeled "2" and the next one is "4." You can see that there are four 0s in the first bin. This indicates that there are four items in the range 2 to 4. You can alter the way the bins are represented and make the scale of the axis wider using the `scale =` instruction in the command.

Sometimes decimal places are rounded up, and altering the `scale` instruction can provide a better picture of the data. In general, the default `stem()` command tries to provide a clear picture of the distribution, which sometimes leads to loss of decimal places.

The `stem()` command is a quick way of assessing the distribution of a sample and is also useful because the original values are shown, allowing the sample to be reconstructed from the result. However, when you have a large sample you end up with a lot of values and the command cannot display the data very well; in such cases a histogram is more useful.

Histograms

The histogram is the classic way of viewing the distribution of a sample. You can create histograms using the graphical command `hist()`, which operates on numerical vectors of data like so:

```
> data2
 [1] 3 5 7 5 3 2 6 8 5 6 9 4 5 7 3 4
> hist(data2)
```

In this example you used a simple vector of numerical values (these are integer data) and the resulting histogram looks like Figure 5-1: the frequencies are represented on the y-axis and the x-axis shows the values separated into various bins. If you use the `table()` command you can see how the histogram is constructed:

```
> table(data2)
data2
2 3 4 5 6 7 8 9
1 3 2 4 2 2 1 1
```

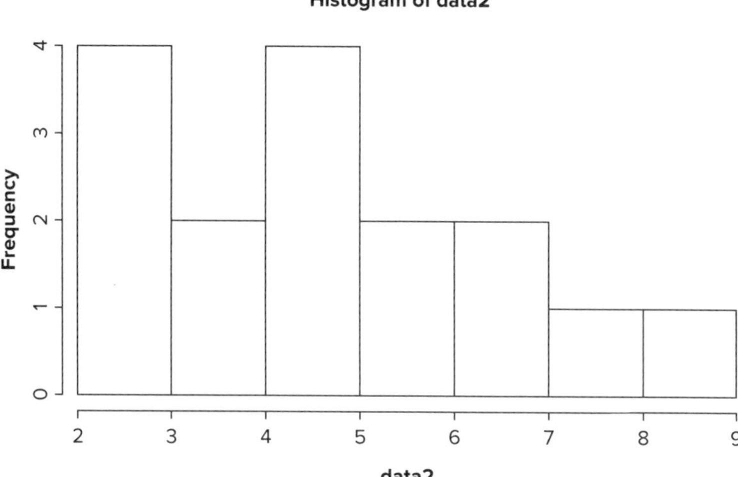

FIGURE 5-1

The first bar straddles the range 2 to 3 (that is, greater than 2 but less than 3), and therefore you should expect four items in this bin. The next bar straddles the 3 to 4 range, and if you look at the table you see there are two items bigger than 3 but not bigger than 4. You can alter the number of columns that are displayed using the `breaks =` instruction as part of the command. This instruction will accept several sorts of input; you can use a standard algorithm for calculating the breakpoints, for example. The default is `breaks = "Sturges"`, which uses the range of the data to split into bins. Two other standard algorithms are used: `"Scott"` and `"Freedman-Diaconis"`. You can use lowercase and unambiguous abbreviation; additionally you can use `"FD"` for the last of these three options:

```
> hist(data2, breaks = 'Sturges')
> hist(data2, breaks = 'Scott')
> hist(data2, breaks = 'FD')
```

Thus you might also use the following:

```
> hist(data2, breaks = 'st')
> hist(data2, breaks = 'sc')
> hist(data2, breaks = 'fr')
```

You can also specify the number of breaks as a simple number or range of numbers; the following commands all produce the same result, which for these data is the same as the default (`Sturges`):

```
> hist(data2, breaks = 7)
> hist(data2, breaks = 2:9)
> hist(data2, breaks = c(2,3,4,5,6,7,8,9))
```

Being able to specify the breaks exactly means that you can produce a histogram with unequal bin ranges:

```
> hist(data2, breaks = c(2,4,5,6,9))
```

The resulting histogram appears like Figure 5-2.

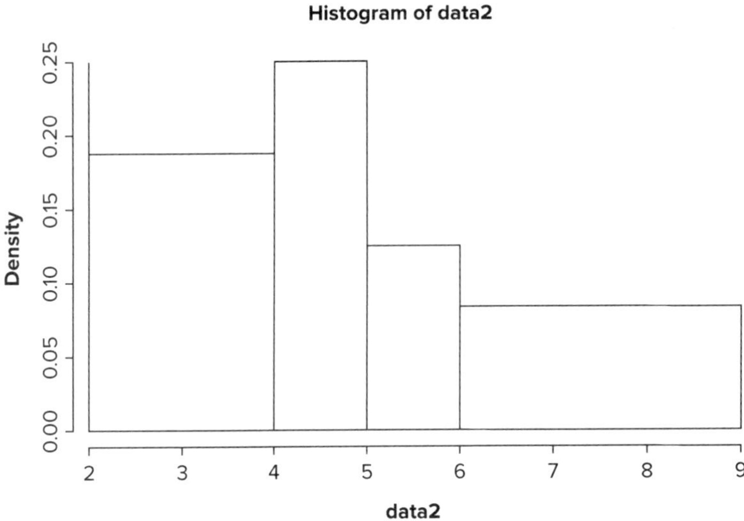

FIGURE 5-2

Notice in Figure 5-2 that the y-axis does not show the frequency but instead shows the density. The command has attempted to keep the areas of the bars correct and in proportion (in other words, the total area sums to 1). You can use the `freq =` instruction to produce either frequency data (`TRUE` is the default) or density data (`FALSE`).

You can apply a variety of additional instructions to the `hist()` command. Many of these extra instructions apply to other graphical commands in R (see Table 5-1 for a summary).

TABLE 5-1: A Summary of Graphical Commands Useful with Histograms

GRAPHICAL COMMAND	EXPLANATION
`col = 'color'`	The color of the bars; a color name in quotes (use `colors()` to see the range available).
`main = 'main.title'`	A main title for the histogram; use `NULL` to suppress this.
`xlab = 'x.title'`	A title for the x-axis.
`ylab = 'y.title'`	A title for the y-axis.
`xlim = c(start, end)`	The range for the x-axis; put numerical values for the start and end points.
`ylim = c(start, end)`	The range for the y-axis.

These commands are available for many of the other graphs that you meet using R. The color of the bars is set using the `col =` instruction. A lot of colors are available, and you can see the standard options by using the `colors()` command:

```
colors()
```

You can also use an alternative spelling.

```
colours()
```

Note that this command does not have any additional instructions and you simply type the brackets. There are more than 650 colors to choose from!

As an example, here is a histogram created with a few additional instructions (see Figure 5-3):

```
> hist(data2, col='gray75', main=NULL, xlab = 'Size class for data2',
ylim=c(0, 0.3), freq = FALSE)
```

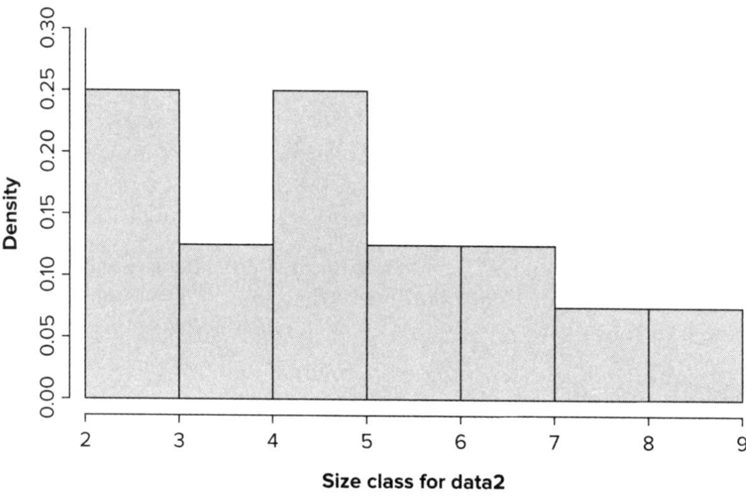

FIGURE 5-3

To create the histogram in Figure 5-3, perform the following steps:

1. Begin by specifying the vector of values you require.
2. Next you use a new light gray color, `gray75`, before moving on to suppress the main title (you can add a title as a caption using your word processor).
3. Next, specify a title for the x-axis. The default scale of the y-axis in this case runs from 0 up to 0.25, but to give the axis a bit more room, alter the range from 0 to 0.3; you must always specify both the start and end points in the instruction.
4. Lastly, change the plot from one of frequency to density by using `freq = FALSE`. You could specify these instructions in any order; the name of the vector of data usually goes first but you could put this later if you used `x = data.name` to specify it explicitly.

You can even avoid a fair bit of typing if you omit the spaces and use a few abbreviations like so:

```
> hist(co='gray75',ma=NULL,xla='Size class for data2',yli=c(0,0.3),fr=F,x=data2)
```

However, if you show the command to anyone else they may not be able to recognize the abbreviations. There is another (more sensible) reason to demonstrate the reordering of the command. If you want to create histograms for several vectors of data you can use the up arrow to recall the previous command. If the name of the data vector is at the end, it is quicker to edit it and to type the name of the new vector you want to plot.

***NOTE** Every command has a set of possible instructions that it will accept. You can abbreviate the instructions you give as long as they are unique and unambiguous.*

Density Function

You have seen in drawing a histogram with the `hist()` command that you can use `freq = FALSE` to force the y-axis to display the density rather than the frequency of the data. You can also call on the density function directly via the `density()` command. This enables you to draw your sample distribution as a line rather than a histogram. Many statisticians prefer the density plot to a regular histogram. You can also combine the two and draw a density line over the top of a regular histogram.

You use the `density()` command on a vector of numbers to obtain the kernel density estimate for the vector in question. The result is a series of `x` and `y` coordinates that you can use to plot a graph. The basic form of the command is as follows:

```
density(x, bw = 'nrd0', kernel = 'gaussian', na.rm = FALSE)
```

You specify your data, which must be a numerical vector, followed by the bandwidth. The bandwidth defaults to the `nrd0` algorithm, but you have several others to choose from or you can specify a value. The `kernel =` instruction enables you to select one of several smoothing options, the default being the `"gaussian"` smoother. You can see the various options from the help entry for this command. By default, `NA` items are not removed and an error will result if they are present; you can add `na.rm = TRUE` to ensure that you strip out any `NA` items.

If you use the command on a vector of numeric data you get a summary as a result like so:

```
> dens = density(data2)
> dens

Call:
 density.default(x = data2)

Data: data2 (16 obs.);     Bandwidth 'bw' = 0.9644

       x                 y
 Min.   :-0.8932   Min.   :0.0002982
 1st Qu.: 2.3034   1st Qu.:0.0134042
 Median : 5.5000   Median :0.0694574
 Mean   : 5.5000   Mean   :0.0781187
 3rd Qu.: 8.6966   3rd Qu.:0.1396352
 Max.   :11.8932   Max.   :0.1798531
```

The result actually comprises several items that are bundled together in a list object. You can see these items using the `names()` or `str()` commands:

```
> names(dens)
[1] "x"          "y"          "bw"         "n"          "call"       "data.name"
[7] "has.na"

> str(dens)
List of 7
 $ x        : num [1:512] -0.893 -0.868 -0.843 -0.818 -0.793 ...
 $ y        : num [1:512] 0.000313 0.000339 0.000367 0.000397 0.000429 ...
 $ bw       : num 0.964
 $ n        : int 16
 $ call     : language density.default(x = data2)
 $ data.name: chr "data2"
 $ has.na   : logi FALSE
 - attr(*, "class")= chr "density"
```

You can extract the parts you want using `$` as you have seen with other lists. You might, for example, use the `$x` and `$y` parts to form the basis for a plot.

Using the Density Function to Draw a Graph

If you have a density result you can create a basic plot by extracting the `$x` and `$y` components and using them in a `plot()` command like so:

```
> plot(dens$x, dens$y)
```

However, for all practical purposes you do not need to go through any of this to produce a graph; you can use the `density()` command directly as part of a graphing command like so:

```
> plot(density(data2))
```

This produces a graph like Figure 5-4.

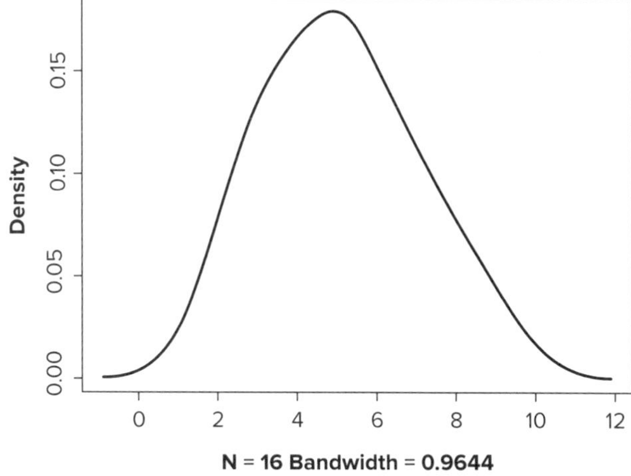

FIGURE 5-4

The `plot()` command is a very general one in R and it can be used to produce a wide variety of graph types. In this case you see that the axes have been labeled and that there is also a main title. You can change these titles using the `xlab`, `ylab`, and `main` instructions as you saw previously. However, there is a slight difference if you want to remove a title completely. Previously you set `main = NULL` as your instruction, but this does not work here and you get the default title. You must use a pair of quotation marks so set the titles to be empty:

```
> plot(density(data2), main = "", xlab = 'Size bin classes')
```

The preceding command removes the main title and alters the title of the x-axis. You can change other aspects of the graph as well; for instance, you already met the `xlim` and `ylim` instructions to resize the `x` and `y` axes, respectively.

Adding Density Lines to Existing Graphs

One use you might make for the density command is to add a density line to an existing histogram. Perhaps you want to compare the two methods of representation or you may want to compare two different samples; commonly one sample would be from an idealized distribution, like the normal distribution. You can add lines to an existing graph using the `lines()` command. This takes a series of `x` and `y` coordinates and plots them on an existing graph. Recall earlier when you used the `density()` command to make an object called `dens`. The result was a list of several items including one called `x` and one called `y`. The `lines()` command can read these to make the plot.

In the following example you produce a simple histogram and then draw two density lines over the top:

```
> hist(data2, freq = F, col = 'gray85')
> lines(density(data2), lty = 2)
> lines(density(data2, k = 'rectangular'))
```

In the first of the three preceding commands you produce the histogram; you must set the `freq = FALSE` to ensure the axis becomes density rather than frequency. The next two commands draw lines using two different density commands. The resulting graph looks like Figure 5-5.

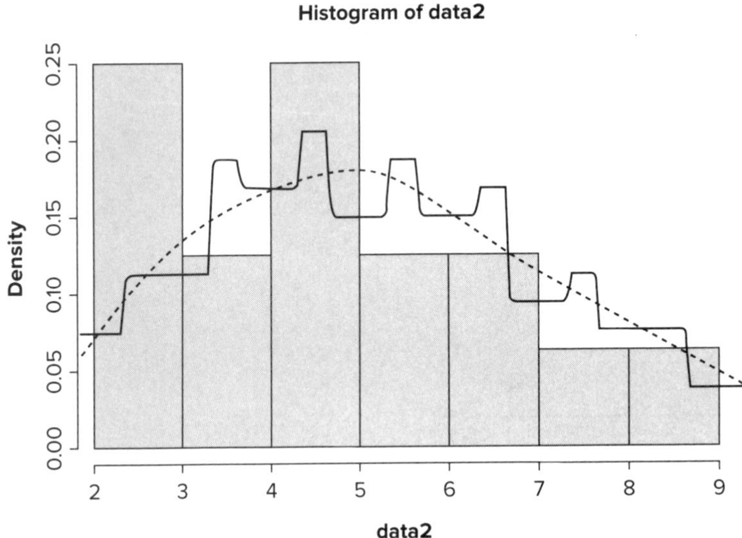

FIGURE 5-5

Here you made the rectangular line using all the default options. The gaussian line has been drawn using a dashed line and this is done via the `lty =` instruction; you can use a numerical value where 1 is a solid line (the default), 2 is dashed, and 3 is dotted. Other options are shown in Table 5-2.

TABLE 5-2: Options for Line Style in the lty Instruction

VALUE	LABEL	RESULT
0	blank	Blank
1	solid	Solid (default)
2	dashed	Dashed
3	dotted	Dotted
4	dotdash	Dot-Dash
5	longdash	Long dash
6	twodash	Two dash

You can use either a numerical value or one of the text strings (in quotes) to produce the required effect; for example, `lty = "dotted"`. Notice that there is an option to have blank lines. It is also possible to alter the color of the lines drawn using the `col =` instruction. You can make the lines wider by specifying a magnification factor via the `lwd =` instruction.

Some additional useful commands include the `hist()` and `lines(density())` commands with which you can draw an idealized distribution and see how your sample matches up. However, first you need to learn how to create idealized distributions.

Types of Data Distribution

You have access to a variety of distributions when using R. These distributions enable you to perform a multitude of tasks, ranging from creating random numbers based upon a particular distribution, to discovering the probability of a value lying within a certain distribution, or determining the density of a value for a given distribution. The following sections explain the many uses of distributions.

The Normal Distribution

Table 5-3 shows the commands you can use in relation to the normal distribution.

TABLE 5-3: Commands Related to the Normal Distribution

COMMAND	EXPLANATION
`rnorm(n, mean = 0, sd = 1)`	Generates *n* random numbers from the normal distribution with mean of 0 and standard deviation of 1
`pnorm(q, mean = 0, sd = 1)`	Returns the probability for the quantile `q`

continues

TABLE 5-3 *(continued)*

COMMAND	EXPLANATION
`qnorm(p, mean = 0, sd = 1)`	Returns the quantile for a given probability `p`
`dnorm(x, mean = 0, sd = 1)`	Gives the density function for values `x`

You can generate random numbers based on the normal distribution using the `rnorm()` command; if you do not specify the mean or standard deviation the defaults of 0 and 1 are used. The following example generates 20 numbers with a mean of 5 and a standard deviation of 1:

```
> rnorm(20, mean = 5, sd = 1)
 [1] 5.610090 5.042731 5.120978 4.582450 5.015839 3.577376 5.159308 6.496983
 [9] 3.071729 6.187525 5.027074 3.517274 4.393562 3.866088 4.533490 6.021554
[17] 5.359491 5.265780 3.817124 5.855315
```

You can work out probability using the `pnorm()` command. If you use the same mean and standard deviation as in the preceding code, for example, you might use the following:

```
> pnorm(5, mean = 5, sd = 1)
[1] 0.5
```

In other words, you would expect a value of 5 to be halfway along the x-axis (your result is the cumulative proportion). By performing the following command you can turn this around and work out a value along the x-axis for any quantile; that is, how far along the axis you are as a proportion of its length:

```
> qnorm(0.5, 5, 1)
[1] 5
```

You can see here that if you go 50 percent of the way along the x-axis you expect a value of 5, which is the mean of this distribution. You can also determine the density given a value. If you use the same parameters as the previous example did, you get the following:

```
> dnorm(c(4,5,6), mean = 5, sd = 1)
[1] 0.2419707 0.3989423 0.2419707
```

Here you work out the density for a mean of 5 and a standard deviation of 1. This time you calculate the density for three values: 4, 5, and 6.

Additionally, you can use the `pnorm()` and `qnorm()` commands to determine one- and two-tailed probabilities and confidence intervals. For example:

```
> qnorm(c(0.05, 0.95), mean = 5, sd = 1)
[1] 3.355146 6.644854
```

Here is a situation in which it would be useful to compare the distribution of a sample of data against a particular distribution. You already looked at a sample of data and drew its distribution using the `hist()` command. You also used the `density()` command to draw the distribution in a different way, and to add the density lines over the original histogram. If you create a series of random numbers with the same mean and standard deviation as your sample, you can compare the "ideal" normal distribution with the actual observed distribution.

You can start by using rnorm() to create an ideal normal distribution using the mean and standard deviation of your data like so:

```
> data2.norm = rnorm(1000, mean(data2), sd(data2))
```

The more values in your distribution the smoother the final graph will appear, so here you create 1000 random numbers, taking the mean and standard deviation from the original data (called data2). You can display the two distributions in one of two ways; you might have the original data as the histogram and the idealized normal distribution as a line over the top, or you could draw the ideal normal distribution as a histogram and have your sample as the line. The following shows the two options:

```
> hist(data2, freq = FALSE)
> lines(density(data2.norm))

> hist(data2.norm, freq = F)
> lines(density(data2))
```

In the first case you draw the histogram using your sample data and add the lines from the ideal normal distribution. In the second case you do it the other way around. With a bit of tweaking you can make a quite acceptable comparison plot. In the following example you make the ideal distribution a bit fainter by using the border = instruction. You also modify the x-axis and main titles. The lines representing the actual data are drawn and made a bit bolder using the lwd = instruction. The resulting graph looks like Figure 5-6.

```
> hist(data2.norm, freq = F, border = 'gray50', main = 'Comparing two
distributions', xlab = 'Data2 size classes')
> lines(density(data2), lwd = 2)
```

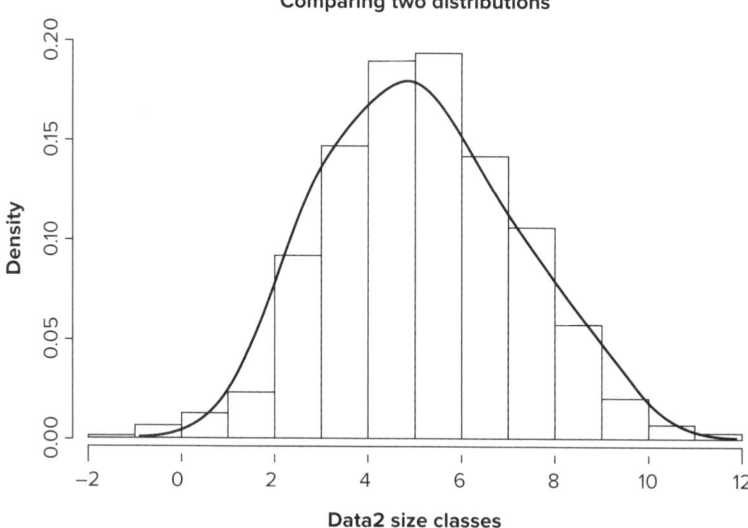

FIGURE 5-6

You can see that you get a seemingly good fit to a normal distribution. Mathematical ways to compare the fit also exist, which you look at later in the chapter.

Other Distributions

You can use a variety of other distributions in a similar fashion; for full details look at the help entries by typing `help(Distributions)`. Look at a few examples now to get a flavor of the possibilities. In the following example, you start the Poisson distribution by generating 50 random values:

```
> rpois(50, lambda = 10)
 [1] 10 12 10 13 10 11  8 17 14  7 12  9 16  8 15  5  6  7 10 11 15 15 10  6 10 12
[27] 14 11  7 12 14 10  8 12  7 13  8  7  8  6  8 10  9 12 12  5 11 12 11 12
```

The Poisson distribution has only a single parameter, `lambda`, equivalent to the mean. The next example uses the binomial distribution to assess probabilities:

```
> pbinom(c(3, 6, 9, 12), size = 17, prob = 0.5)
[1] 0.006363 0.166153 0.685471 0.975479
```

In this case you use `pbinom()` to calculate the cumulative probabilities in a binomial distribution. You have two additional parameters: `size` is the number of trials and `prob` is the probability of each trial being a success.

You can use the Student's t-test to compare two normally distributed samples. In this following example you use the `qt()` command to determine critical values for the `t-test` for a range of degrees of freedom. You then go on to work out two-sided p-values for a range of t-values:

```
> qt(0.975, df = c(5, 10, 100, Inf))
[1] 2.571 2.228 1.984 1.960

> (1-pt(c(1.6, 1.9, 2.2), df = Inf))*2
[1] 0.10960 0.05743 0.02781
```

In the first case you set the cumulative probability to 0.975; this will give you a 5 percent critical value, because effectively you want 2.5 percent of each end of the distribution (because this is a symmetrical distribution you can take 2.5 percent from each end to make your 5 percent). You put in several values for the *degrees of freedom* (related to the sample size). Notice that you can use `Inf` to represent infinity. The result shows you the value of `t` you would have to get for the differences in your samples (their means) to be significantly different at the 5 percent level; in other words, you have determined the critical values.

In the second case you want to determine the two-sided p-value for various values of `t` when the degrees of freedom are infinity. The `pt()` command would determine the cumulative probability if left to its own devices. So, you must subtract each one from 1 and then multiply by 2 (because you are taking a bit from each end of the distribution). You can get the same result using a modification of the command using the `lower.tail =` instruction. By default this is set to `TRUE`; this effectively means that you are reading the x-axis from left to right. If you set the instruction to `FALSE`, you switch around and read the x-axis from right to left. The upshot is that you do not need to subtract from one, which involves remembering where to place the brackets. The following example shows the results of the various options:

```
> pt(c(1.6, 1.9, 2.2), Inf)
[1] 0.9452 0.9713 0.9861
```

```
> pt(c(1.6, 1.9, 2.2), Inf, lower.tail = FALSE)
[1] 0.05480 0.02872 0.01390

> pt(c(1.6, 1.9, 2.2), Inf, lower.tail = FALSE)*2
[1] 0.10960 0.05743 0.02781
```

In the first result you do not modify the command at all and you get the standard cumulative probabilities. In the second case you use the `lower.tail = FALSE` instruction to get probabilities from "the other end." These probabilities are one-tailed (that is, from only one end of the distribution), so you double them to get the required (two-tailed) values (as in the third case).

In the next example you look at the F distribution using the `pf()` command. The F statistic requires two degrees of freedom values, one for the numerator and one for the denominator:

```
> pf(seq(3, 5, 0.5), df1 = 2, df2 = 12, lower.tail = F)
[1] 0.08779150 0.06346962 0.04665600 0.03481543 0.02633610
```

In this example you create a short sequence of values, starting from 3 and ending at 5 with an interval of 0.5; in other words, 3, 3.5, 4, 4.5, 5. You set the numerator `df` to 2 and the denominator to 12, and the result gives the cumulative probability. In this case it is perhaps easier to use the "other end" of the axis, so you set `lower.tail = FALSE` and get the p-values expressed as the "remainder" (that is, that part of the distribution that lies outside your cut-off point[s]).

The four basic commands `dxxx()`, `pxxx()`, `qxxx()`, and `rxxx()` provide you access to a range of distributions. They have common elements; the `lower.tail =` instruction is pretty universal, but each has its own particular instruction set. Table 5-4 gives a sample of the distributions available; using `help(Distributions)` brings up the appropriate help entry.

TABLE 5-4: The Principal Distributions Available in R

COMMAND	DISTRIBUTION
dbeta	beta
dbinom	binomial (including Bernoulli)
dcauchy	Cauchy
dchisq	chi-squared
dexp	exponential
df	F distribution
dgamma	gamma
dgeom	geometric (special case of negative binomial)
dhyper	hypergeometric
dlnorm	log-normal
dmultinom	multinomial

continues

TABLE 5-4 *(continued)*

COMMAND	DISTRIBUTION
dnbinom	negative binomial
dnorm	normal
dpois	Poisson
dt	Student's t
dunif	uniform distribution
dweibull	Weibull
dwilcox	Wilcoxon rank sum
ptukey	Studentized range
dsignrank	Wilcoxon signed rank

The final distribution considered is the uniform distribution; essentially "ordinary" numbers. If you want to generate a series of random numbers, perhaps as part of a sampling exercise, use the `runif()` command:

```
> runif(10)
 [1] 0.65664996 0.58738275 0.07514039 0.34420863 0.30101891 0.58277238 0.24750941
 [8] 0.09282271 0.65748986 0.10004270
```

In this example `runif()` creates ten random numbers; by default the command uses minimum values of 0 and maximum values of 1, so the basic command produces random numbers between 0 and 1. You can set the `min` and `max` values with explicit instructions like so:

```
> runif(10, min = 0, max = 10)
 [1] 8.6480966 6.4076579 1.0365540 9.8101588 5.4944734 8.2056503 4.2407627
 [8] 0.2206528 4.9709090 9.1819653
```

Now you have produced random values that range from 0 to 10. You can also use the density, probability, or quantile commands; use the following command to determine the cumulative probability of a value in a range of 0 to 10 (although you hardly needed the computer to work that one out).

```
> punif(6, min = 0, max = 10)
[1] 0.6
```

Random Number Generation and Control

R has the ability to use a variety of random number-generating algorithms (for more details, look at `help(RNG)` to bring up the appropriate help entry). You can alter the algorithm by using the `RNGkind()` command. You can use the command in two ways: you can see what the current settings are and you can also alter these settings. If you type the command without any instructions (that is, just a pair of parentheses) you see the current settings:

```
> RNGkind()
[1] "Mersenne-Twister" "Inversion"
```

Two items are listed. The first is the standard number generator and the second is the one used for normal distribution generation. To alter these, use the `kind =` and `normal.kind =` instructions along with a text string giving the algorithm you require; this can be abbreviated. The following example alters the algorithms and then resets them:

```
> RNGkind(kind = 'Super', normal.kind = 'Box')
> RNGkind()
[1] "Super-Duper" "Box-Muller"

> RNGkind('default')
> RNGkind()
[1] "Mersenne-Twister" "Box-Muller"

> RNGkind('default', 'default')
> RNGkind()
[1] "Mersenne-Twister" "Inversion"
```

Here you first alter both kinds of algorithm. Then you query the type set by running the command without instructions. If you use `default` as an instruction, you reset the algorithms to their default condition. However, notice that you have to do this for each kind, so to restore the random generator fully you need two `default` instructions, one for each kind.

There may be occasions when you are using random numbers but want to get the same random numbers every time you run a particular command. Common examples include when you are demonstrating something or testing and want to get the same thing time and time again. You can use the `set.seed()` command to do this:

```
> set.seed(1)
> runif(1)
[1] 0.2655087

> runif(1)
[1] 0.3721239

> runif(1)
[1] 0.5728534

> set.seed(1)
> runif(3)
[1] 0.2655087 0.3721239 0.5728534
```

You use a single integer as the instruction, which sets the starting point for random number generation. The upshot is that you get the same result every time. In the preceding example you set the seed to 1 and then use three separate commands to create three random numbers. If you reset the seed to 1 and generate three more random numbers (using only a single command this time) you get the same values!

You can also use the `set.seed()` command to alter the kind of algorithm using the `kind =` and `normal.kind =` instructions in the same way you did when using the `RNGkind()` command:

```
> set.seed(1, kind = 'Super')
> runif(3)
[1] 0.3714075 0.4789723 0.9636913

> RNGkind()
[1] "Super-Duper" "Inversion"
```

```
> set.seed(1, kind = 'default')
> runif(3)
[1] 0.2655087 0.3721239 0.5728534

> RNGkind()
[1] "Mersenne-Twister" "Inversion"
```

In this example you set the seed using a value of 1 (you can also use negative values) and altered the algorithm to the Super-Duper version. After you use this to make three random numbers you look to see what you have before setting the seed to 1 again but also resetting the algorithm to its default, the Mersenne-Twister.

Random Numbers and Sampling

Another example where you may require randomness is in sampling. For instance, if you have a series of items you may want to produce a random smaller sample from these items. See the following example in which you have a simple vector of numbers and want to choose four of these to use for some other purpose:

```
> data2
 [1] 3 5 7 5 3 2 6 8 5 6 9 4 5 7 3 4
> sample(data2, size = 4)
[1] 3 8 9 6
```

In this example you extract four of your values as a separate sample from the `data2` vector of values. You can do this for character vectors as well; in the following example you have a character vector that comprises 12 months. You use the `replace =` instruction to decide if you want replacement or not like so:

```
> sample(data8, size = 4, replace = TRUE)
[1] "Apr" "Jan" "Feb" "Oct"

> sample(data8, size = 4, replace = TRUE)
[1] "Feb" "Feb" "Jun" "May"
```

Here you set `replace = TRUE` and the effect is to allow an item to be selected more than once. In the first example all four items are different, but in the second case you get the `Feb` result twice. The default is to set `replace = FALSE`, resulting in items not being selected more than once; think of this as not replacing an item in the result vector once it has been selected (placed).

You can extend this and select certain conditions to be met from your sampled data. In the following example you pick out three items from your original data but ensure that they are all greater than 5:

```
> data2
 [1] 3 5 7 5 3 2 6 8 5 6 9 4 5 7 3 4
> sample(data2[data2 > 5], size = 3)
[1] 7 9 8
```

If you leave the `size =` part out, you get a sample of everything that meets any conditions you have set:

```
> sample(data2[data2 > 5])
[1] 9 8 7 6 6 7

> data2[data2 > 5]
[1] 7 6 8 6 9 7
```

In the first case you randomly select items that are greater than 5. In the second case you display all the items that are greater than 5. When you merely display the items they appear in the order they are in the vector, but when you use the `sample()` command they appear in random order. You can see this clearly by using the same command several times:

```
> sample(data2[data2 > 5])
[1] 8 6 7 9 7 6
> sample(data2[data2 > 5])
[1] 6 9 7 8 7 6
> sample(data2[data2 > 5])
[1] 7 7 9 6 8 6
```

Because of the way the command is programmed you can get an unusual result:

```
> data2
 [1] 3 5 7 5 3 2 6 8 5 6 9 4 5 7 3 4
> sample(data2[data2 > 8])
[1] 7 6 4 2 3 5 9 1 8
```

You might have expected to get a single result (of 9) but you do not. Instead, your condition has resulted in 1 (there is only 1 item greater than 8). You are essentially picking out items that range from 1 to > 8. Because there is only one item > 8 you get a sample from 1 to 9, and if you look you see nine items in your result. In the following example, you look for items > 9:

```
> data3
 [1]  6  7  8  7  6  3  8  9 10  7  6  9
> sample(data3[data3 > 9])
 [1]  1  5  4  7  6 10  3  8  9  2
```

Because there is only one of them (a 10) you get ten items in your result sample. This is slightly unfortunate but there is a way around it, which is demonstrated in the help entry for the `sample()` command. You can create a simple function to alter the way the `sample()` command operates; first type the following like so:

```
> resample <- function(x, ...) x[sample(length(x), ...)]
```

This creates a new command called `resample()`, which you use exactly like you would the old `sample()` command. Your new command, however, gives the "correct" result; the following example shows the comparison between the two:

```
> data2
 [1] 3 5 7 5 3 2 6 8 5 6 9 4 5 7 3 4

> set.seed(4)
> sample(data2, size = 3)
[1] 2 6 7

> set.seed(4)
> resample(data2, size = 3)
[1] 2 6 7

> set.seed(4)
> sample(data2[data2 > 8])
[1] 3 5 2 8 4 7 1 9 6
```

```
> set.seed(4)
> resample(data2[data2 > 8])
[1] 9
```

In this example you use the `set.seed()` command to ensure that your random numbers come out the same; you use a value of 4 but this is merely a whim, any integer will suffice. At the top you can see that you get exactly the same result when you extract three random items as a sample from your original vector. When you use the `sample()` command to extract values > 8 you see the error. However, you see at the bottom that the `resample()` command has given the expected result.

Creating simple functions is quite straightforward; in the following case the function is named `resample` and this appears as an object when you type an `ls()` command:

```
> ls(pattern = '^resa')
[1] "resample" "response"
> str(resample)
function (x, ...)
 - attr(*, "source")= chr "function(x, ...) x[sample(length(x), ...)]"
```

In this example you choose to list objects beginning with "res" and see two objects. If you use the `str()` command you can see that the `resample` object is a function. If you type the name of the object you get to see more clearly what it does—you get the code used to create it:

```
> resample
function(x, ...) x[sample(length(x), ...)]

> class(resample)
[1] "function"
```

The left part shows the instructions expected; here you have `x` and three dots. The `x` simply means a name, the vector you want to sample, and the three dots mean that you can use extra instructions that are appropriate. The right part shows the workings of the function; you see your object represented as `x`, and the `sample()` and `length()` commands perform the actual work of the command. The final three dots get replaced by whatever you type in the command as an extra instruction; you used the `size =` instruction in one of the previous examples. In the following examples you use another appropriate instruction and one inappropriate one:

```
> resample(data2[data2 > 8], size = 2, replace = T)
[1] 9 9

> resample(data2[data2 > 8], size = 2, replace = T, na.rm = T)
Error in sample(length(x), ...) : unused argument(s) (na.rm = TRUE)
```

In the first case the `replace = TRUE` instruction is valid because it is used by `sample()`. In the second case, however, you get an error because the `na.rm =` instruction is not used by either `sample()` or `length()`.

Creating functions is a useful way to unlock the power of R and enables you to create templates to carry out tedious or involved commands over and over again with minimal effort. You look at the creation of custom functions in more detail in Chapter 10.

The Shapiro-Wilk Test for Normality

You commonly need to compare a sample with the normal distribution. You saw previously how you could do this graphically using a histogram and a density plot. There are other graphical methods, which you will return to shortly, but there are also statistical methods. One such method is the Shapiro-Wilk test, which is available via the `shapiro.test()` command. Using it is very simple; just provide the command with a numerical vector to work on:

```
> data2
 [1] 3 5 7 5 3 2 6 8 5 6 9 4 5 7 3 4

> shapiro.test(data2)

        Shapiro-Wilk normality test

data:  data2
W = 0.9633, p-value = 0.7223
```

The result shows that the sample you have is not significantly different from a normal distribution. If you create a sample using random numbers from another (not normal) distribution, you would expect a significant departure. In the following example you use the `rpois()` command to create 100 random values from a Poisson distribution with `lambda` set to 5:

```
> shapiro.test(rpois(100, lambda = 5))

        Shapiro-Wilk normality test

data:  rpois(100, lambda = 5)
W = 0.9437, p-value = 0.0003256
```

You see that you do get a significant departure from normality in this case. If you have your data contained within another item, you must extract it in some way. In the following example you have a data frame containing three columns, two of numeric data and one of characters:

```
> grass3
  rich graze poa
1   12   mow   4
2   15   mow   5
3   17   mow   6
4   11   mow   5
5   15   mow   4
6    8 unmow   5
7    9 unmow   6
8    7 unmow   8
9    9 unmow   7
> shapiro.test(grass3$rich)

        Shapiro-Wilk normality test

data:  grass3$rich
W = 0.9255, p-value = 0.4396
```

In this case you use the $ to get the rich sample as your vector to compare to normality. You probably ought to test each grazing treatment separately, so you have to subset a little further like so:

```
> with(grass3, shapiro.test(rich[graze == 'mow']))

        Shapiro-Wilk normality test

data:  rich[graze == "mow"]
W = 0.9251, p-value = 0.5633
```

In this example you select the mow treatment; the with() command has saved you a little bit of typing by enabling you to read inside the grass data frame temporarily. When you have only a couple of treatment levels this is not too tedious, but when you have several it can become a chore to repeat the test for every level, even if you can use the up arrow to recall the previous command. There is a way around this; you will see the command in more detail in Chapter 9, but for now an example will suffice:

```
> tapply(grass3$rich, grass3$graze, shapiro.test)
$mow

        Shapiro-Wilk normality test

data:  X[[1L]]
W = 0.9251, p-value = 0.5633


$unmow

        Shapiro-Wilk normality test

data:  X[[2L]]
W = 0.8634, p-value = 0.2725
```

In this example you use the command tapply(), which enables you to cross-tabulate a data frame and apply a function to each result. The command starts with the column you want to apply the function to. Then you provide an index to carry out the cross tabulation; here you use the graze column. You get two results because there were two levels in the graze column. At the end you specify the command/function you want to use and you can also add extra instructions if they are applicable. The result is that the shapiro.test() is applied to each combination of graze for your rich data.

The Kolmogorov-Smirnov Test

The Kolmogorov-Smirnov test enables you to compare two distributions. This means that you can either compare a sample to a "known" distribution or you can compare two unknown distributions to see if they are the same; effectively you are comparing the shape.

The command that allows you access to the Kolmogorov-Smirnov test is ks.test(), which fortunately is shorter than the actual name. You furnish the command with at least two instructions; the first being the vector of data you want to test and the second being the one you want to compare it to. This second instruction can be in various forms; you can provide a vector of numeric values or you can use a function, for example, `pnorm()`, in some way. In the following example you look to compare a sample to the normal distribution:

```
> ks.test(data2, 'pnorm', mean = 5, sd = 2)

        One-sample Kolmogorov-Smirnov test

data:  data2
D = 0.125, p-value = 0.964
alternative hypothesis: two-sided

Warning message:
In ks.test(data2, "pnorm", mean = 5, sd = 2) :
  cannot compute correct p-values with ties
```

In this case you specify the cumulative distribution function you want as a text string (that is, in quotes) and also give the required parameters for the normal distribution; in this case the mean and standard deviation. This carries out a one-sample test because you are comparing to a standard distribution. Note, too, that you get an error message because you have tied values in your sample. You could create a normal distributed sample "on the fly" and compare this to your sample like so:

```
> ks.test(data2, pnorm(20, 5, 2))

        Two-sample Kolmogorov-Smirnov test

data:  data2 and pnorm(20, 5, 2)
D = 1, p-value = 0.3034
alternative hypothesis: two-sided

Warning message:
In ks.test(data2, pnorm(20, 5, 2)) :
  cannot compute correct p-values with ties
```

Now in this example you have run a two-sample test because you have effectively created a new sample using the `pnorm()` command. In this case the parameters of the normal distribution are contained in the `pnorm()` command itself. You can also test to see if the distribution is less than or greater than your comparison distribution by adding the `alternative =` instruction; you use `less` or `greater` because the default is `two.sided`.

You can, of course, use other distributions; the following example compares a data sample to a Poisson distribution (with `lambda = 5`):

```
> ks.test(data2, 'ppois', 5)

        One-sample Kolmogorov-Smirnov test

data:  data2
D = 0.241, p-value = 0.3108
alternative hypothesis: two-sided

Warning message:
In ks.test(data2, "ppois", 5) : cannot compute correct p-values with ties
```

Quantile-Quantile Plots

Earlier you looked at histograms and density plots to visualize a distribution; you can perhaps estimate the appearance of a normal distribution by its bell-shaped appearance. However, it is easier to judge if you can get your distribution to lie in a straight line. To do that you can use quantile-quantile plots (QQ plots). Many statisticians prefer QQ plots over strictly mathematical methods like the Shapiro-Wilk test for example.

A Basic Normal Quantile-Quantile Plot

You have several commands available relating to QQ plots; the first of these is `qqnorm()`, which takes a vector of numeric values and plots them against a set of theoretical quantiles from a normal distribution. The upshot is that you produce a series of points that appear in a perfectly straight line if your original data are normally distributed. Run the following command to create a simple QQ plot (the graph is shown in Figure 5-7):

```
> data2
 [1] 3 5 7 5 3 2 6 8 5 6 9 4 5 7 3 4
> qqnorm(data2)
```

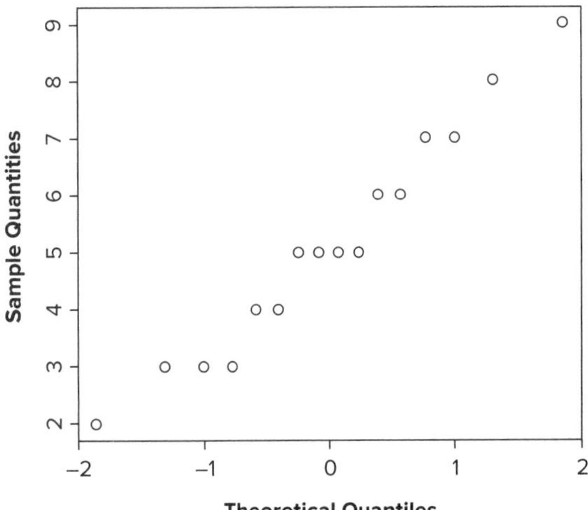

FIGURE 5-7

The main title and the axis labels have default settings, which you can alter by using the `main`, `xlab`, and `ylab` instructions that you met previously.

Adding a Straight Line to a QQ Plot

The normal QQ plot is useful for visualizing the distribution because it is easier to check alignment along a straight line than to check for a bell-shaped curve. However, you do not currently have a straight line to check! You can add one using the `qqline()` command. This adds a straight line to an existing graph. You can alter the appearance of the line using various instructions; you can change the color, width, and style using `col`, `lwd`, and `lty` instructions (which you have met previously). If you combine the `qqnorm()` and `qqlines()` commands you can make a customized plot; the following example produces a plot that looks like Figure 5-8:

```
> qqnorm(data2, main = 'QQ plot of example data', xlab = 'Theoretical',
ylab = 'Quantiles for data2')
> qqline(data2, lwd = 2, lty = 2)
```

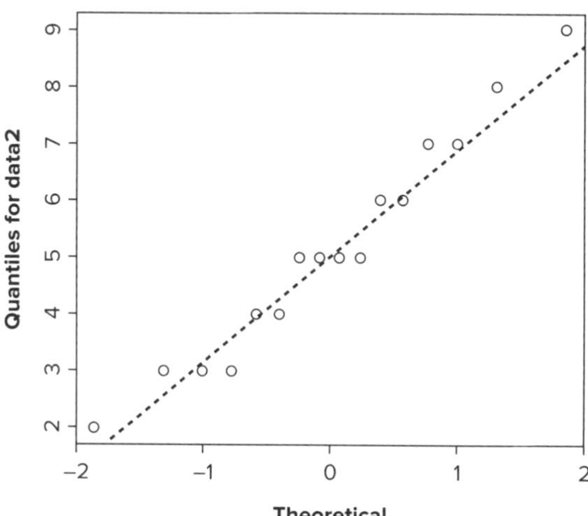

FIGURE 5-8

In Figure 5-8 you produce a plot with a slightly thicker line that is dashed. You can now judge more easily the fit of your data to a normal distribution.

Plotting the Distribution of One Sample Against Another

You can also plot one distribution against another as a quantile-quantile plot using the `qqplot()` command. To use it you simply provide the command with the names of the two distributions you want to compare:

```
> qqplot(rpois(50,5), rnorm(50,5,1))
> qqplot(data2, data1)
```

In the top example you compare two distributions that you create "on the fly" from random numbers. The bottom example compares two samples of numeric data; note that this is *not* simply one sample plotted against the other (because they have different lengths you could not do that anyhow). It would be useful to draw a straight line on your `qqplot()` and you can do that using the `abline()` command. This command uses the properties of a straight line (that is, `y = a + bx`) to produce a line on an existing plot. The general form of the command is:

```
abline(a = intercept, b = slope)
```

You supply the intercept and slope to produce the straight line. The problem here is that you do not know what the intercept or slope values should be! You need to determine these first; fortunately the `abline()` command can also use results from other calculations. In the following example you take the `data2` sample and compare this to a randomly-generated normal distribution with 50 values; you set the mean to 5 and the standard deviation to 2:

```
> qqp = qqplot(data2, rnorm(50,5,2))
```

This makes a basic plot; your sample is on the x-axis and the sample you compare to, the random one, is on the y-axis. Notice that you do not just make the plot but assign it to an object; here called `qqp`. You do this because you want to see the values used to create the plot. If you type the name of your plot (`qqp`) you see that you have a series of x-values (your original `data2`) and a series of y-values:

```
> qqp
$x
 [1] 2 3 3 3 4 4 5 5 5 5 6 6 7 7 8 9

$y
 [1] 1.405236 2.625890 3.429247 4.037570 4.433178 4.648895 4.983500 5.292363
 [9] 5.372463 6.154243 6.424723 6.817186 7.360115 7.580486 7.976507 8.793080
```

The `qqplot()` command has used the distribution you created (using the `rnorm()` command) as the basis to generate quantiles for the y-axis. Now the `x` and `y` values match up. You can use these values to determine the intercept and slope and then draw your straight line:

```
> abline(lm(qqp$y ~ qqp$x))
```

Another new command must be introduced at this point: `lm()`, which carries out linear modeling. This command determines the line of best fit between the `x` and `y` values in your `qqp` object. The `abline()` command is able to read the result directly so you do not have to specify the `a =` and `b =` instructions explicitly. The final result is a straight line added to your QQ plot.

***NOTE** If two samples are drawn from the same distribution then the* `abline(0,1)` *command will demonstrate the fit between these samples. If you calculate and draw the actual best-fit line you can visualize any differences in distribution between the samples.*

So, the final set of commands appears like this:

```
> qqp = qqplot(data2, rnorm(50, 5, 2))
> abline(lm(qqp$y ~ qqp$x))
```

This produces the plot shown in Figure 5-9.

You can alter the titles of the plot and the appearance of the line using the same commands that you met previously (`main`, `xlab`, `ylab`, `lwd`, `lty`, and `col`).

You look at graphical commands in more detail in Chapter 7 and also Chapter 11. You also look more carefully at the `lm()` command (in Chapter 10), which is used in a wide range of statistical analyses.

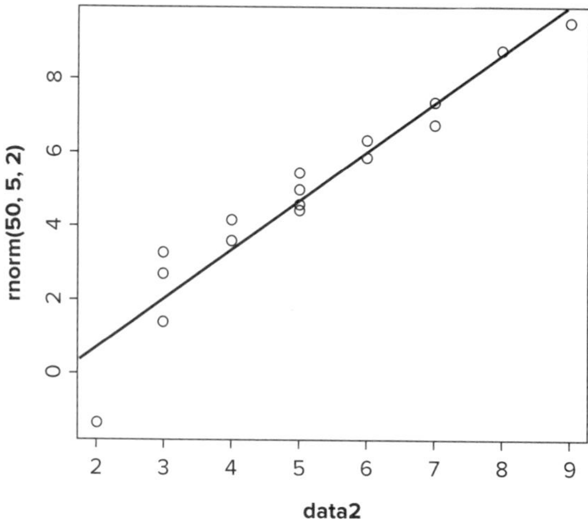

FIGURE 5-9

SUMMARY

- You can visualize the distribution of a numeric sample using the `stem()` command to make a stem-leaf plot or the `hist()` command to draw a histogram.
- A variety of distributions can be examined with R; these include the normal, Poisson, and binomial distributions. The distributions can be examined with a variety of commands (for example, `rfoo()`, `pfoo()`, `qfoo()`, and `dfoo()`, where `foo` is the distribution).
- You can test the distribution of a sample using the Shapiro-Wilk test for normality via the `Shapiro.test()` command. The Kolmogorov-Smirnov test can compare two distributions and is accessed via the `ks.test()` command.
- Quantile-Quantile plots can be produced using `qqnorm()` and `qqplot()` commands. The `qqlines()` command can add a straight line to a normal QQ plot.

EXERCISES

Available for download on Wrox.com

You can find the answers to these exercises in Appendix A.

Use the `Beginning.RData` file for these exercises; the file contains the data objects you require.

1. Examine the `orchis2` data object. Here you see a two-column data frame with a response variable (`flower`) and a predictor variable (`site`). Produce a histogram for the `sprayed` site. Now overlay a density plot.

2. Determine the critical value (at 5% and 1% two-tailed) of the Wilcoxon statistic for a two-sample test where n = 8 for both samples. If you carried out a Wilcoxon two-sample test, where each sample contained ten replicates, and got a result of 77, how could you determine the statistical significance?

▶ WHAT YOU LEARNED IN THIS CHAPTER

TOPIC	KEY POINTS

Numerical distribution (for example, norm, pois, binom, chisq, Wilcox, unif, t, F):
`rfoo()`
`pfoo()`
`qfoo()`
`dfoo()`
	Many distributions are available for analysis in R. These include the normal distribution as well as Poisson, binomial, and gamma. Other statistical distributions include chi-squared, Wilcox, F, and t.
	Four main commands handle distributions. The `rfoo()` command generates random numbers (where `foo` is the distribution), `pfoo()` determines probability, `dfoo()` determines density function, and `qfoo()` calculates quantiles.

Random numbers:
`RNGkind()`
`set.seed()`
`sample()`
	Random numbers can be generated for many distributions. The `runif()` command, for example, creates random numbers from the uniform distribution.
	A variety of algorithms to generate random numbers can be used and set via the `RNGkind()` command. The `set.seed()` command determines the "start point" for random number generation.
	The `sample()` command selects random elements from a larger data sample.

Drawing distribution:
`stem()` `hist()`
`density()` `lines()`
`qqnorm()` `qqline()`
`qqplot()`
	The distribution of a numerical sample can be drawn and visualized using several commands: the `stem()` command creates a simple stem and leaf plot, for example. The `hist()` command draws classic histograms, and the `density()` command allows the density to be drawn onto a graph via the `lines()` command.
	Quantile-quantile plots can be dealt with using `qqnorm()`, which plots a distribution against a theoretical normal. A line can be added using `qqline()`. The `qqplot()` command enables two distributions to be plotted against one another.

Testing distribution:
`shapiro.test()`
`ks.test()`
	The normality of a distribution can be tested using the Shapiro-Wilk test via the `shapiro.test()` command. The Kolmogorov-Smirnov test can be used via the `ks.test()` command. This can test one distribution against a known "standard" or can test to see if two distributions are the same.

TOPIC	KEY POINTS
Graphics: plot() abline() lines() lty lwd col xlim xlab ylim ylab main colors() lm()	The plot() command is a very general graphical command and is often called in the background as the result of some other command (for example, qqplot()). The abline() command adds straight lines to existing graphs and can use the result of previous commands to determine the coordinates to use (for example, the lm() command, which determines slope and intercept in the relationship between two variables). The lines() command adds sections of line to an existing graph and can be used to add a density plot to an existing histogram. Many additional parameters can be added to plot() and other graphical commands to provide customization. For example, col alters the color of plotted elements, and xlim alters the limits of the x-axis. A comprehensive list can be found by using help(par). The colors() command gives a simple list of the colors available.

Simple Hypothesis Testing

WHAT YOU WILL LEARN IN THIS CHAPTER:

- How to carry out some basic hypothesis tests
- How to carry out the Student's t-test
- How to conduct the U-test for non-parametric data
- How to carry out paired tests for parametric and non-parametric data
- How to produce correlation and covariance matrices
- How to carry out a range of correlations tests
- How to test for association using chi-squared
- How to carry out goodness of fit tests

Many statistical analyses are concerned with testing hypotheses. In this chapter you look at methods of testing some simple hypotheses using standard and classic tests. You start by comparing differences between two samples. Then you look at the correlation between two samples, and finally look at tests for association and goodness of fit. Other tests are available in R, but the ones illustrated here will form a good foundation and give you an idea of how R works. Should you require a different test, you will be able to work out how to carry it out for yourself.

USING THE STUDENT'S T-TEST

The Student's t-test is a method for comparing two samples; looking at the means to determine if the samples are different. This is a parametric test and the data should be normally distributed. You looked at the distribution of data previously in Chapter 5.

Several versions of the t-test exist, and R can handle these using the `t.test()` command, which has a variety of options (see Table 6-1), and the test can be pressed into service to deal with two- and one-sample tests as well as paired tests. The latter option is discussed in the later section "Paired T- and U-Tests"; in this section you look at some more basic options.

TABLE 6-1: The t.test() Command and Some of the Options Available.

COMMAND	EXPLANATION
`t.test(data.1, data.2)`	The basic method of applying a t-test is to compare two vectors of numeric data.
`var.equal = FALSE`	If the `var.equal` instruction is set to `TRUE`, the variance is considered to be equal and the standard test is carried out. If the instruction is set to `FALSE` (the default), the variance is considered unequal and the Welch two-sample test is carried out.
`mu = 0`	If a one-sample test is carried out, `mu` indicates the mean against which the sample should be tested.
`alternative = "two.sided"`	Sets the alternative hypothesis. The default is `"two.sided"` but you can specify `"greater"` or `"less"`. You can abbreviate the instruction (but you still need quotes).
`conf.level = 0.95`	Sets the confidence level of the interval (default = 0.95).
`paired = FALSE`	If set to `TRUE`, a matched pair t-test is carried out.
`t.test(y ~ x, data, subset)`	The required data can be specified as a formula of the form `response ~ predictor`. In this case, the data should be named and a subset of the predictor variable can be specified.
`subset = predictor %in% c("sample.1", "sample.2")`	If the data is in the form `response ~ predictor`, the subset instruction can specify which two samples to select from the predictor column of the data.

Two-Sample t-Test with Unequal Variance

The general way to use the `t.test()` command is to compare two vectors of numeric values. You can specify the vectors in a variety of ways, depending how your data objects are set out. The default form of the `t.test()` does not assume that the samples have equal variance, so the Welch two-sample test is carried out unless you specify otherwise:

```
> t.test(data2, data3)

     Welch Two Sample t-test

data:  data2 and data3
```

```
t = -2.8151, df = 24.564, p-value = 0.009462
alternative hypothesis: true difference in means is not equal to 0
95 percent confidence interval:
 -3.5366789 -0.5466544
sample estimates:
mean of x mean of y
 5.125000  7.166667
```

Two-Sample t-Test with Equal Variance

You can override the default and use the classic t-test by adding the `var.equal = TRUE` instruction, which forces the command to assume that the variance of the two samples is equal. The calculation of the t-value uses pooled variance and the degrees of freedom are unmodified; as a result, the p-value is slightly different from the Welch version:

```
> t.test(data2, data3, var.equal = TRUE)

	Two Sample t-test

data:  data2 and data3
t = -2.7908, df = 26, p-value = 0.009718
alternative hypothesis: true difference in means is not equal to 0
95 percent confidence interval:
 -3.5454233 -0.5379101
sample estimates:
mean of x mean of y
 5.125000  7.166667
```

One-Sample t-Testing

You can also carry out a one-sample t-test. In this version you supply the name of a single vector and the mean to compare it to (this defaults to 0):

```
> t.test(data2, mu = 5)

	One Sample t-test

data:  data2
t = 0.2548, df = 15, p-value = 0.8023
alternative hypothesis: true mean is not equal to 5
95 percent confidence interval:
 4.079448 6.170552
sample estimates:
mean of x
    5.125
```

Using Directional Hypotheses

You can also specify a "direction" to your hypothesis. In many cases you are simply testing to see if the means of two samples are different, but you may want to know if a sample mean is lower than another sample mean (or greater). You can use the `alternative =` instruction to switch the emphasis from a two-sided test (the default) to a one-sided test. The choices you have are between "two.sided", "less", or "greater", and your choice can be abbreviated.

```
> t.test(data2, mu = 5, alternative = 'greater')

        One Sample t-test

data:  data2
t = 0.2548, df = 15, p-value = 0.4012
alternative hypothesis: true mean is greater than 5
95 percent confidence interval:
 4.265067      Inf
sample estimates:
mean of x
    5.125
```

Formula Syntax and Subsetting Samples in the t-Test

The t-test is designed to compare two samples (or one sample with a "standard"). So far you have seen how to carry out the t-test on separate vectors of values. However, your data may well be in a more structured form with a column for the response variable and a column for the predictor variable. The following data are set out in this manner:

```
> grass
  rich graze
1   12   mow
2   15   mow
3   17   mow
4   11   mow
5   15   mow
6    8 unmow
7    9 unmow
8    7 unmow
9    9 unmow
```

This way of setting out data is more sensible and flexible, but you need a new way to deal with the layout. R deals with this by having a "formula syntax." You create a formula using the tilde (~) symbol. Essentially your response variable goes on the left of the ~ and the predictor goes on the right like so:

```
> t.test(rich ~ graze, data = grass)

        Welch Two Sample t-test

data:  rich by graze
t = 4.8098, df = 5.411, p-value = 0.003927
alternative hypothesis: true difference in means is not equal to 0
95 percent confidence interval:
 2.745758 8.754242
sample estimates:
  mean in group mow mean in group unmow
              14.00                8.25
```

If your predictor column contains more than two items, the t-test cannot be used. However, you can still carry out a test by subsetting this predictor column and specifying which two samples you want to compare. You must use the `subset =` instruction as part of the `t.test()` command. The following example illustrates how to do this using the same data as in the previous example.

```
> t.test(rich ~ graze, data = grass, subset = graze %in% c('mow', 'unmow'))
```

You first specify which column you want to take your subset from (`graze` in this case) and then type `%in%`; this tells the command that the list that follows is contained in the `graze` column. Note that you have to put the levels in quotes; here you compare `"mow"` and `"unmow"` and your result (not shown) is identical to that you obtained before.

TRY IT OUT Carry Out Student's t-Tests on Some Data

Available for download on Wrox.com

Use the data on orchids (`orchid`, `orchid2`, `orchis`, and `orchis2`) from the `Beginning.RData` file for this activity, on which you will be carrying out a range of t-tests.

1. Use the `ls()` command to see the data you require; they all begin with "orchi":

```
> ls(pattern='^orc')
[1] "orchid"  "orchid2" "orchis"  "orchis2"
```

2. Look first at the `orchid` data. This comprises two columns relating to two samples:

```
> orchid
   closed open
1       7    3
2       8    5
3       6    6
4       9    7
5      10    6
6      11    8
7       7    8
8       8    4
9      10    7
10      9    6
```

3. Carry out a t-test on these data without making any assumptions about the variance, like so:

```
> attach(orchid)
> t.test(open, closed)

   Welch Two Sample t-test

data:  open and closed
t = -3.478, df = 17.981, p-value = 0.002688
alternative hypothesis: true difference in means is not equal to 0
95 percent confidence interval:
 -4.0102455 -0.9897545
sample estimates:
mean of x mean of y
      6.0       8.5

> detach(orchid)
```

4. Now carry out another two-sample t-test but use the "classic" version and assume the variance of the two samples is equal:

```
> with(orchid, t.test(open, closed, var.equal = TRUE))
    Two Sample t-test

data:  open and closed
t = -3.478, df = 18, p-value = 0.002684
alternative hypothesis: true difference in means is not equal to 0
95 percent confidence interval:
 -4.0101329 -0.9898671
sample estimates:
mean of x mean of y
      6.0       8.5
```

5. This time look at the `open` sample only and carry out a one-sample test to compare the data to a mean of 5:

```
> t.test(orchid$open, mu = 5)

    One Sample t-test

data:  orchid$open
t = 1.9365, df = 9, p-value = 0.08479
alternative hypothesis: true mean is not equal to 5
95 percent confidence interval:
 4.831827 7.168173
sample estimates:
mean of x
        6
```

6. Now look at the `orchis` data object. It has two columns, `flower` and `site`. Use the `str()` or `summary()` command to confirm that there are two samples in the `site` column:

```
> str(orchis)
'data.frame':      20 obs. of  2 variables:
 $ flower: num  7 8 6 9 10 11 7 8 10 9 ...
 $ site  : Factor w/ 2 levels "closed","open": 1 1 1 1 1 1 1 1 1 1 ...
```

7. Carry out a t-test using the formula syntax; you do not need to make assumptions about the variance:

```
> t.test(flower ~ site, data = orchis)
```

8. Now look at the `orchis2` data object. It has two columns, `flower` and `site`. Use the `str()` or `summary()` command to confirm that there are three samples in the `site` column:

```
> str(orchis2)
'data.frame':      30 obs. of  2 variables:
 $ flower: num  7 8 6 9 10 11 7 8 10 9 ...
 $ site  : Factor w/ 3 levels "closed","open",..: 1 1 1 1 1 1 1 1 1 1 ...
```

9. Use a `subset` instruction to carry out a t-test on the `open` and `closed` sites:

```
> t.test(flower ~ site, data = orchis2, subset = site %in% c('open', 'closed'))
```

10. Now return to the orchid data. Carry out a one-sample test on the open sample to see if it has a mean of less than 7:

```
> t.test(orchid$open, alternative = 'less', mu = 7)

	One Sample t-test

data:  orchid$open
t = -1.9365, df = 9, p-value = 0.04239
alternative hypothesis: true mean is less than 7
95 percent confidence interval:
     -Inf 6.946615
sample estimates:
mean of x
        6
```

11. Look again at the orchis2 data, which has three samples in the site column. Carry out a t-test on the sprayed sample to see if its mean is greater than 3. You can use either of the following commands:

```
> t.test(orchis2$flower[orchis2$site=='sprayed'], mu = 3, alt = 'greater')
> with(orchis2, t.test(flower[site=='sprayed'], mu = 3, alt = 'g'))

	One Sample t-test

data:  orchis2$flower[orchis2$site == "sprayed"]
t = 1.9412, df = 9, p-value = 0.04208
alternative hypothesis: true mean is greater than 3
95 percent confidence interval:
 3.061236      Inf
sample estimates:
mean of x
      4.1
```

How It Works

The first part is simply a way to list the data objects by matching items that begin with the text "orc". In the first t-test you had to use the attach() command to enable you to specify the column names. Notice that the result begins by telling you that you have carried out the Welch Two-Sample t-test.

In the next case you used the with() command to allow R to access the columns in the orchid data. By adding var.equal = TRUE you carry out the "classic" t-test and treat the variances of the samples as equal. Note that in step 11 you used an abbreviation.

The formula syntax is a convenient way to describe your data; the formula is of the form response ~ predictor. The subset instruction enables you to select two samples from a column variable; the form of the instruction is subset = predictor %in% c("item.1", "item.2").

The subset instruction works only in conjunction with the formula syntax.

The t-test is a powerful and flexible tool, as you have seen. You can also carry out paired tests using the t.test() command, but before that you look at the U-test, which you can think of as the non-parametric equivalent to the t-test.

THE WILCOXON U-TEST (MANN-WHITNEY)

When you have two samples to compare and your data are non-parametric, you can use the U-test. This goes by various names and may be known as the Mann-Whitney U-test or Wilcoxon sign rank test. You use the `wilcox.test()` command to carry out the analysis. You operate this very much like you did when performing the `t.test()` previously.

The `wilcox.test()` command can conduct two-sample or one-sample tests, and you can add a variety of instructions to carry out the test you want. The main options are shown in Table 6-2.

TABLE 6-2: The wilcox.test() Command and Some of the Options Available.

COMMAND	EXPLANATION
`wilcox.test(sample.1, sample.2)`	Carries out a basic two-sample U-test on the numerical vectors specified.
`mu = 0`	If a one-sample test is carried out, `mu` indicates the value against which the sample should be tested.
`alternative = "two.sided"`	Sets the alternative hypothesis. The default is `"two.sided"` but you can specify `"greater"` or `"less"`. You can abbreviate the instruction (but you still need quotes).
`conf.int = FALSE`	Sets whether confidence intervals should be reported.
`conf.level = 0.95`	Sets the confidence level of the interval (default = 0.95).
`correct = TRUE`	By default the continuity correction is applied. You can turn this off by setting it to `FALSE`.
`paired = FALSE`	If set to `TRUE`, a matched pair U-test is carried out.
`exact = NULL`	Sets whether an exact p-value should be computed. The default is to do so for < 50 items.
`wilcox.test(y ~ x, data, subset)`	The required data can be specified as a formula of the form `response ~ predictor`. In this case the data should be named and a subset of the predictor variable can be specified.
`subset = predictor %in% c("sample.1", "sample.2")`	If the data is in the form `response ~ predictor`, the subset instruction can specify which two samples to select from the predictor column of the data.

Two-Sample U-Test

The basic way of using the `wilcox.test()` is to specify the two samples you want to compare as separate vectors, as the following example shows:

```
> data1 ; data2
 [1] 3 5 7 5 3 2 6 8 5 6 9
 [1] 3 5 7 5 3 2 6 8 5 6 9 4 5 7 3 4
> wilcox.test(data1, data2)

	Wilcoxon rank sum test with continuity correction

data:  data1 and data2
W = 94.5, p-value = 0.7639
alternative hypothesis: true location shift is not equal to 0

Warning message:
In wilcox.test.default(data1, data2) :
  cannot compute exact p-value with ties
```

By default the confidence intervals are not calculated and the p-value is adjusted using the "continuity correction"; a message tells you that the latter has been used. In this case you see a warning message because you have tied values in the data. If you set `exact = FALSE`, this message would not be displayed because the p-value would be determined from a normal approximation method.

One-Sample U-Test

If you specify a single numerical vector, a one-sample U-test is carried out; the default is to set `mu = 0`, as in the following example:

```
> wilcox.test(data3, exact = FALSE)

	Wilcoxon signed rank test with continuity correction

data:  data3
V = 78, p-value = 0.002430
alternative hypothesis: true location is not equal to 0
```

In this case the p-value is taken from a normal approximation because the `exact = FALSE` instruction is used. The command has assumed `mu = 0` because it is not specified explicitly.

Using Directional Hypotheses

Both one- and two-sample tests use an alternative hypothesis that the location shift is not equal to 0 as their default. This is essentially a two-sided hypothesis. You can change this by using the `alternative =` instruction, where you can select `"two.sided"`, `"less"`, or `"greater"` as your alternative hypothesis (an abbreviation is acceptable but you still need quotes, single or double).

You can also specify `mu`, the location shift. By default `mu = 0`. In the following example the hypothesis is set to something other than 0:

```
> data3
 [1]  6  7  8  7  6  3  8  9 10  7  6  9
> summary(data3)
   Min. 1st Qu.  Median    Mean 3rd Qu.    Max.
  3.000   6.000   7.000   7.167   8.250  10.000

> wilcox.test(data3, mu = 8, exact = FALSE, conf.int = TRUE, alt = 'less')

        Wilcoxon signed rank test with continuity correction

data:  data3
V = 13.5, p-value = 0.08021
alternative hypothesis: true location is less than 8
95 percent confidence interval:
     -Inf 8.000002
sample estimates:
(pseudo)median
      6.999956
```

In this example a one-sample test is carried out on the `data3` sample vector. The test looks to see if the sample median is less than 8. The instructions also specify to display the confidence interval and not to use an exact p-value.

Formula Syntax and Subsetting Samples in the U-test

It is generally a good idea to have your data arranged into a data frame where one column represents the response variable and another represents the predictor variable. In this case you can use the formula syntax to describe the situation and carry out the `wilcox.test()` on your data. This is much the same method you used for the t-test previously. The basic form of the command becomes:

```
wilcox.test(response ~ predictor, data = my.data)
```

You can also use additional instructions as you could with the other syntax. If your predictor variable contains more than two samples, you cannot conduct a U-test and must use a `subset` that contains exactly two samples. The `subset` instruction works like so:

```
wilcox.test(response ~ predictor, data = my.data, subset = predictor %in%
c("sample1", "sample2"))
```

Notice that you use a `c()` command to group the samples together, and their names must be in quotes.

The U-test is one of the most widely used statistical methods, so it is important to be comfortable using the `wilcox.test()` command. In the following activity you try conducting a range of U-tests for yourself.

TRY IT OUT Carry Out U-Tests on Some Data

Available for download on Wrox.com

Use the butterfly abundance data called `bfc`, `bf2`, and `bfs`, which are all contained in the `Beginning.RData` file. Use the `ls()` command to remind you of the names:

```
> ls(pattern='^bf')
```

1. Look at the `bfc` data object; there are two columns in this data frame, one for each sample:

```
> bfc
   grass heath
1      3     6
2      4     7
3      3     8
4      5     8
5      6     9
6     12    11
7     21    12
8      4    11
9      5    NA
10     4    NA
11     7    NA
12     8    NA
```

2. Carry out a two-sample U-test on the two samples in the `bfc` data object. There is no need to use any additional instructions:

```
> wilcox.test(bfc$grass, bfc$heath)

    Wilcoxon rank sum test with continuity correction

data:  bfc$grass and bfc$heath
W = 20.5, p-value = 0.03625
alternative hypothesis: true location shift is not equal to 0

Warning message:
In wilcox.test.default(bfc$grass, bfc$heath) :
  cannot compute exact p-value with ties
```

3. Now look at the `grass` sample of the `bfc` data using the `summary()` command:

```
> summary(bfc$grass)
   Min. 1st Qu.  Median    Mean 3rd Qu.    Max.
  3.000   4.000   5.000   6.833   7.250  21.000
```

4. Carry out a one-sample test on the `grass` sample of the `bfc` data. Set a hypothesis that the location shift is less than 7.5:

```
> with(bfc, wilcox.test(grass, mu = 7.5, exact = F, alt = 'less'))

    Wilcoxon signed rank test with continuity correction

data:  grass
```

```
V = 23.5, p-value = 0.1188
alternative hypothesis: true location is less than 7.5
```

5. Look at the `bf2` data object. It comprises two columns, with a response variable `count` and a predictor variable `site`.

```
> str(bf2)
'data.frame':       20 obs. of  2 variables:
 $ count: int  3 4 3 5 6 12 21 4 5 4 ...
 $ site : Factor w/ 2 levels "Grass","Heath": 1 1 1 1 1 1 1 1 1 1 ...
```

6. Conduct a two-sample U-test on the `bf2` data. This time you will need to use the formula syntax:

```
> wilcox.test(count ~ site, data = bf2, exact = FALSE)

    Wilcoxon rank sum test with continuity correction

data:  count by site
W = 20.5, p-value = 0.03625
alternative hypothesis: true location shift is not equal to 0
```

7. Look at the `bf2` data object again. This time look at the `Heath` sample and carry out a one-sided U-test. Set an alternative hypothesis that the location shift is greater than the first quartile:

```
> with(bf2, summary(count[which(site=='Heath')]))
   Min. 1st Qu.  Median    Mean 3rd Qu.    Max.
   6.00    7.75    8.50    9.00   11.00   12.00

> with(bf2, wilcox.test(count[which(site=='Heath')], exact = F,
alt = 'greater', mu = 7.75))


    Wilcoxon signed rank test with continuity correction

data:  count[which(site == "Heath")]
V = 28, p-value = 0.09118
alternative hypothesis: true location is greater than 7.75
```

8. Now look at the `bfs` data object. This time you have a predictor variable with three samples. Carry out a two-sample U-test between the `Grass` and `Arable` samples:

```
> wilcox.test(count ~ site, data = bfs, subset = site %in% c('Grass', 'Arable'),
exact = F)

    Wilcoxon rank sum test with continuity correction

data:  count by site
W = 81.5, p-value = 0.05375
alternative hypothesis: true location shift is not equal to 0
```

How It Works

The basic form of the command requires the numerical vectors to be specified. If the data are inside a data frame you must use `attach()`, `with()`, or the `$` syntax to enable R to "read" them.

If a single vector is specified, a one-sample test is carried out. The `mu =` instruction gives the location shift to test and the `alternative =` instruction sets the direction of the alternative hypothesis, with `"two.sided"` being the default.

The formula syntax enables you to specify `response ~ predictor` for when you have data in that format. This also allows you to specify the data so that you do not need to use `attach()` or `with()` commands or the `$` syntax.

If you have a response variable column you have to use a more complex method to extract the sample you require. Here you used a conditional statement to select the sample and used the `summary()` command to determine the first quartile. This value was used as the `mu =` instruction along with an `alternative = "greater"` instruction to make a one-sided test.

When you have more than two samples in a predictor variable the `subset` instruction enables you to select two samples to compare; the `subset` instruction works only with the formula syntax and you specify the samples to compare in the following way: `subset = response %in% c("sample1", "sample2")`.

The U-test is a useful tool for comparing two samples and is one of the most widely used of all simple statistical tests. Both the `t.test()` and `wilcox.test()` commands can also deal with matched pair data, which you have not seen yet. This is the subject of the next section.

NOTE *The results of the* `t.test()` *and* `wilcox.test()` *commands are displayed when you run the command. However, not all of the results are displayed. If you create a new object to "hold" the result of a test, you can view the elements of the result by using the* `names()` *command. You can then access the various elements using the* `$` *syntax.*

PAIRED T- AND U-TESTS

If you have a situation in which you have paired data, you can use matched pair versions of the t-test and the U-test with a simple extra instruction. You simply add `paired = TRUE` as an instruction to your command. It does not matter if the data are in two separate sample columns or are represented as response and predictor as long as you indicate what is required using the appropriate syntax. In fact, R will carry out a paired test even if the data do not really match up as pairs. It is up to you to carry out something sensible. You can use all the regular syntax and instructions, so you can use subsetting and directional hypotheses as you like. In the following activity you try a few paired tests for yourself.

TRY IT OUT Conduct Paired t and U Tests on Some Data

Available for download on Wrox.com

You will need to get the `Beginning.RData` file for this activity: You will require several data objects, which you will use to carry out some paired tests. The file contains all the data you need.

1. Look at the `mpd` data; you can see two samples, `white` and `yellow`. These data are matched pair data and each row represents a bi-colored target. The values are for numbers of whitefly attracted to each half of the target.

```
> mpd
  white yellow
1     4      4
2     3      7
3     4      2
4     1      2
5     6      7
6     4     10
7     6      5
8     4      8
```

2. Use a paired U-test (Wilcoxon matched pair test) on these data like so:

```
> wilcox.test(mpd$white, mpd$yellow, exact = FALSE, paired = TRUE)

   Wilcoxon signed rank test with continuity correction

data:  mpd$white and mpd$yellow
V = 6, p-value = 0.2008
alternative hypothesis: true location shift is not equal to 0
```

3. Look at the means for the two samples in the `mpd` data. Round the difference up and then carry out a paired t-test, but set an alternative hypothesis that the difference in these means is less than this difference:

```
> mean(mpd)
 white yellow
 4.000  5.625
> with(mpd, t.test(white, yellow, paired = TRUE, mu = 2, alt = 'less'))

    Paired t-test

data:  white and yellow
t = -3.6958, df = 7, p-value = 0.003849
alternative hypothesis: true difference in means is less than 2
95 percent confidence interval:
      -Inf 0.2332847
sample estimates:
mean of the differences
                 -1.625
```

4. Look at the `mpd.s` data object. This comprises two columns. One is the response variable `count` and the other is the predictor variable `trap`. These are the same data as the `mpd` and are paired (the only difference is the form of the data object). Carry out a pared t-test on these data:

```
> wilcox.test(count ~ trap, data = mpd.s, paired = TRUE, exact = F)
```

```
    Wilcoxon signed rank test with continuity correction

data:  count by trap
V = 6, p-value = 0.2008
alternative hypothesis: true location shift is not equal to 0
```

5. Carry out a two-sided and paired t-test on the `mpd.s` data. Set the alternative hypothesis that the difference in means is 1 and show the 99 percent confidence intervals:

```
> t.test(count ~ trap, data = mpd.s, paired = TRUE, mu = 1, conf.level = 0.99)

    Paired t-test

data:  count by trap
t = -2.6763, df = 7, p-value = 0.03171
alternative hypothesis: true difference in means is not equal to 1
99 percent confidence interval:
 -5.057445  1.807445
sample estimates:
mean of the differences
                 -1.625
```

6. Look at the `orchis2` data. Here you have a response variable `flower` and a predictor variable `site`. The predictor variable has three samples (`open`, `closed`, and `sprayed`). Carry out a paired t-test on the `open` and `sprayed` samples:

```
> t.test(flower ~ site, data = orchis2, subset = site %in% c('open', 'sprayed'),
paired = TRUE)

    Paired t-test

data:  flower by site
t = 4.1461, df = 9, p-value = 0.002499
alternative hypothesis: true difference in means is not equal to 0
95 percent confidence interval:
 0.8633494 2.9366506
sample estimates:
mean of the differences
                    1.9
```

How It Works

Simply adding `paired = TRUE` as an instruction to a `t.test()` or `wilcox.test()` command will carry out a paired version of the test. If the sample vectors are inside a data frame you must use `attach()`, `with()`, or use the `$` syntax to allow R to read the variables.

All the regular instructions can be used, so you can carry out a directional hypothesis, for example, using `alternative = "less"` (or `"greater"`).

If the predictor variable has more than two levels (samples), you can use the `subset` instruction exactly as you did for the unpaired version.

WARNING *Paired tests are useful and more sensitive than their unpaired cousins. However, you must be careful when using them to make sure it is appropriate since all data in a data frame will appear paired. R will look to see if the length of the vectors used is the same, but if you have* `NA` *items, by default they will be removed and your result may not be what you expect.*

CORRELATION AND COVARIANCE

When you have two continuous variables you can look for a link between them; this link is called a correlation. You can go about finding this several ways using R. The `cor()` command determines correlations between two vectors, all the columns of a data frame (or matrix), or two data frames (or matrix objects). The `cov()` command examines covariance. By default the Pearson product moment (that is regular parametric correlation) is used but Spearman (rho) and Kendall (tau) methods (both non-parametric correlation) can be specified instead. The `cor.test()` command carries out a test of significance of the correlation.

You can add a variety of additional instructions to these commands. Table 6-3 gives a brief summary of them.

TABLE 6-3: Correlation Commands and Main Options.

COMMAND	EXPLANATION
`cor(x, y = NULL)`	Carries out a basic correlation between x and y. If x is a matrix or data frame, y can be omitted.
`cov(x, y = NULL)`	Determines covariance between x and y. If x is a matrix or data frame, y can be omitted.
`cov2cor(V)`	Takes a covariance matrix V and calculates the correlations.
`method =`	The default is `"pearson"`, but `"spearman"` or `"kendall"` can be specified as the methods for correlation or covariance. These can be abbreviated but you still need the quotes, and note that they are lowercase.
`var(x, y = NULL)`	Determines the variance of x. If x is a matrix or data frame or y is specified, the covariance is also determined.
`cor.test(x, y)`	Carries out a significance test of the correlation between x and y.

COMMAND	EXPLANATION
`alternative = "two.sided"`	The default is for a two-sided test but the alternative hypothesis can be given as `"two.sided"`, `"greater"`, or `"less"` and abbreviations are permitted.
`conf.level = 0.95`	If the `method = "pearson"` and n > 3, the confidence intervals will be shown. This instruction sets the confidence level and defaults to 0.95.
`exact = NULL`	For Kendall or Spearman, should an exact p-value be determined? Set this to `TRUE` or `FALSE` (the default `NULL` is equivalent to `FALSE`).
`continuity = FALSE`	For Spearman or Kendall tests setting this to `TRUE` carries out a continuity correction.
`cor.test( ~ x + y, data)`	If the data are in a data frame, a formula syntax can be used. This is of the form `~ x + y` where x and y are two variables. The data frame can be specified. All other instructions can be used including `subset`.
`subset = group %in% "sample"`	If the data includes a grouping variable, the `subset` instruction can be used to select one or more samples from this grouping.

The commands summarized in Table 6-3 enable you to carry out a range of correlation tasks. In the following sections you see a few of these options illustrated, and you can then try some correlations yourself in the activity that follows.

Simple Correlation

Simple correlations are between two continuous variables and you can use the `cor()` command to obtain a correlation coefficient like so:

```
> count = c(9, 25, 15, 2, 14, 25, 24, 47)
> speed = c(2, 3, 5, 9, 14, 24, 29, 34)

> cor(count, speed)
[1] 0.7237206
```

The default for R is to carry out the Pearson product moment, but you can specify other correlations using the `method =` instruction, like so:

```
> cor(count, speed, method = 'spearman')
[1] 0.5269556
```

This example used the Spearman rho correlation but you can also apply Kendall's tau by specifying `method = "kendall"`. Note that you can abbreviate this but you still need the quotes. You also have to use lowercase.

If your vectors are contained within a data frame or some other object, you need to extract them in a different fashion. Look at the women data frame. This comes as example data with your distribution of R.

```
> data(women)
> str(women)
'data.frame':    15 obs. of  2 variables:
$ height: num  58 59 60 61 62 63 64 65 66 67 ...
 $ weight: num  115 117 120 123 126 129 132 135 139 142 ...
```

You need to use `attach()` or `with()` commands to allow R to "read inside" the data frame and access the variables within. You could also use the `$` syntax so that the command can access the variables as the following example shows:

```
> cor(women$height, women$weight)
[1] 0.9954948
```

In this example the `cor()` command has calculated the Pearson correlation coefficient between the `height` and `weight` variables contained in the `women` data frame.

You can also use the `cor()` command directly on a data frame (or matrix). If you use the data frame `women` that you just looked at, for example, you get the following:

```
> cor(women)
          height    weight
height 1.0000000 0.9954948
weight 0.9954948 1.0000000
```

Now you have a correlation matrix that shows you all combinations of the variables in the data frame. When you have more columns the matrix can be much more complex. The following example contains five columns of data:

```
> head(mf)
  Length Speed Algae  NO3 BOD
1     20    12    40 2.25 200
2     21    14    45 2.15 180
3     22    12    45 1.75 135
4     23    16    80 1.95 120
5     21    20    75 1.95 110
6     20    21    65 2.75 120

> cor(mf)
           Length       Speed     Algae         NO3        BOD
Length  1.0000000 -0.34322968  0.7650757  0.45476093 -0.8055507
Speed  -0.3432297  1.00000000 -0.1134416  0.02257931  0.1983412
Algae   0.7650757 -0.11344163  1.0000000  0.37706463 -0.8365705
NO3     0.4547609  0.02257931  0.3770646  1.00000000 -0.3751308
BOD    -0.8055507  0.19834122 -0.8365705 -0.37513077  1.0000000
```

The correlation matrix can be helpful but you may not always want to see all the possible combinations; indeed, the first column is the response variable and the others are predictor variables. If you choose the `Length` variable and compare it to all the others in the `mf` data frame using the default Pearson coefficient, you can select a single variable and compare it to all the others like so:

```
> cor(mf$Length, mf)
     Length      Speed     Algae       NO3        BOD
[1,]      1 -0.3432297 0.7650757 0.4547609 -0.8055507
```

Covariance

The `cov()` command uses syntax similar to the `cor()` command to examine covariance. The `women` data are used with the `cov()` command in the following example:

```
> cov(women$height, women$weight)
[1] 69
> cov(women)
       height   weight
height     20  69.0000
weight     69 240.2095
```

The `cov2cor()` command is used to determine the correlation from a matrix of covariance in the following example:

```
> women.cv = cov(women)
> cov2cor(women.cv)
          height    weight
height 1.0000000 0.9954948
weight 0.9954948 1.0000000
```

Significance Testing in Correlation Tests

You can apply a significance test to your correlations using the `cor.test()` command. In this case you can compare only two vectors at a time as the following example shows:

```
> cor.test(women$height, women$weight)

        Pearson's product-moment correlation

data:  women$height and women$weight
t = 37.8553, df = 13, p-value = 1.088e-14
alternative hypothesis: true correlation is not equal to 0
95 percent confidence interval:
 0.9860970 0.9985447
sample estimates:
      cor
0.9954948
```

In the previous example you can see that the Pearson correlation has been carried out between `height` and `weight` in the `women` data and the result also shows the statistical significance of the correlation.

Formula Syntax

If your data are contained in a data frame, using the `attach()` or `with()` commands is tedious, as is using the `$` syntax. A formula syntax is available as an alternative, which provides a neater representation of your data:

```
> data(cars)
> cor.test(~ speed + dist, data = cars, method = 'spearman', exact = F)

        Spearman's rank correlation rho

data:  speed and dist
S = 3532.819, p-value = 8.825e-14
alternative hypothesis: true rho is not equal to 0
sample estimates:
      rho
0.8303568
```

Here you examine the `cars` data, which comes built into R. The formula is slightly different from the one that you met previously. Here you specify both variables to the right of the ~. You also give the name of the data as a separate instruction.

All the additional instructions are available when using the formula syntax as well as the `subset` instruction. If your data contain a separate grouping column, you can specify the samples to use from it using an instruction along the following lines:

```
subset = grouping %in% "sample"
```

Correlation is a common method used widely in many areas of study. In the following activity you will be able to practice carrying out correlation and covariance of some data.

TRY IT OUT Carry Out Correlation and Covariance

Available for download on Wrox.com

Use the `fw`, `fw2`, and `fw3` data from the `Beginning.RData` file for this activity. The other data items are built into R.

1. Look at the `fw` data object; this contains two columns, `count` and `speed`. Conduct a Pearson correlation on these two variables:

```
> cor(fw$count, fw$speed)
[1] 0.7237206
```

2. Now look at the `swiss` data object; this is built into R. Use Kendall's tau correlation to create a matrix of correlations:

```
> cor(swiss, method = 'kendall')
```

3. The `swiss` data produced a sizeable matrix. Simplify this by looking at the `Fertility` variable and correlating that to the others in the dataset. This time use the Spearman rho correlation.

```
> cor(swiss$Fertility, swiss, method = 'spearman')
     Fertility Agriculture Examination  Education  Catholic Infant.Mortality
[1,]         1   0.2426643   -0.660903 -0.4432577 0.4136456        0.4371367
```

4. Now look at the `fw` data object. It has two variables, `count` and `speed`. Create a covariance matrix:

```
> (fw.cov = cov(fw))
         count    speed
count 185.8393 123.0000
speed 123.0000 155.4286
```

5. Convert the covariance matrix into a correlation:

```
> cov2cor(fw.cov)
          count     speed
count 1.0000000 0.7237206
speed 0.7237206 1.0000000
```

6. Look at the `fw2` data object. This has the same number of rows as the `fw` object. It also has two columns, `abund` and `flow`. Carry out a correlation between the columns of one data frame and the other:

```
> cor(fw, fw2)
          abund      flow
count 0.9905759 0.7066437
speed 0.6527244 0.9889997
```

7. Carry out a Spearman rho test of significance on the `count` and `speed` variables from the `fw` data:

```
> with(fw, cor.test(count, speed, method = 'spearman'))

    Spearman's rank correlation rho

data:  count and speed
S = 39.7357, p-value = 0.1796
alternative hypothesis: true rho is not equal to 0
sample estimates:
      rho
0.5269556

Warning message:
In cor.test.default(count, speed, method = "spearman") :
  Cannot compute exact p-values with ties
```

8. Now look at the `fw2` data again. Conduct a Pearson correlation between the `abund` and `flow` variables. Set the confidence intervals to the 99 percent level and use an alternative hypothesis that the correlation is greater than 0:

```
> cor.test(fw2$abund, fw2$flow, conf = 0.99, alt = 'greater')

      Pearson's product-moment correlation

data:  fw2$abund and fw2$flow
t = 2.0738, df = 6, p-value = 0.04173
alternative hypothesis: true correlation is greater than 0
99 percent confidence interval:
 -0.265223  1.000000
sample estimates:
      cor
0.6461473
```

9. Use the formula syntax to carry out a Kendall tau correlation significance test between the `Length` and `NO3` variables from the `mf` data object:

```
> cor.test(~ Length + NO3, data = mf, method = 'k', exact = F)

    Kendall's rank correlation tau

data:  Length and NO3
z = 1.969, p-value = 0.04895
alternative hypothesis: true tau is not equal to 0
sample estimates:
      tau
0.2959383
```

10. Look at the `fw3` data object. This is the same as `fw`, except that there is an additional grouping variable called `cover`. Use a subset of the data that corresponds to the `open` group and carry out a Pearson correlation significance test:

```
> cor.test(~ count + speed, data = fw3, subset = cover %in% 'open')

    Pearson's product-moment correlation

data:  count and speed
t = -1.1225, df = 2, p-value = 0.3783
alternative hypothesis: true correlation is not equal to 0
95 percent confidence interval:
 -0.9907848  0.8432203
sample estimates:
       cor
-0.6216869
```

How It Works

The basic form of the `cor()` command requires two vectors, but if you have a data frame or numeric matrix all the columns will be used to form a correlation matrix. Any object can be correlated against any other object as long as the length of the individual vectors matches up. This works for the `cov()` command too, which determines covariance.

The `cor.test()` command enables you to carry out a significance test on the correlation. In this case you can now specify only two data vectors, but you can use a formula syntax, which makes it easier when the variables are contained within a data frame or matrix. The Pearson product moment is the default, but Spearman's rho or Kendall's tau tests can also be used. You can use the `subset` command to select data based on a grouping variable.

NOTE *Often you will create a new object to "hold" the result of a command. This will not be displayed until you type its name. However, if you enclose the entire command in brackets you can force R to display your result immediately. Compare the following examples:*

```
> fw.cor = cor(fw, fw2)
> fw.cor
          abund      flow
count 0.9905759 0.7066437
speed 0.6527244 0.9889997

> (fw.cor = cor(fw, fw2))
          abund      flow
count 0.9905759 0.7066437
speed 0.6527244 0.9889997
```

In the first example you have to type the name of the result to display it but in the second example the result is displayed immediately as well as stored (to `fw.cor`*).*

TESTS FOR ASSOCIATION

When you have categorical data you can look for associations between categories by using the chi-squared test. Routines to achieve this are accessed using the `chisq.test()` command. You can add various additional instructions to the basic command to suit your requirements. These are summarized in Table 6-4.

TABLE 6-4: The Chi-Squared Test and its Various Options.

COMMAND	EXPLANATION
`chisq.test(x, y = NULL)`	A basic chi-squared test is carried out on a matrix or data frame. If x is provided as a vector, a second vector can be supplied. If x is a single vector and y is not given, a goodness of fit test is carried out.
`correct = TRUE`	If the data form a 2 × 2 contingency table the Yates' correction is applied.
`p =`	A vector of probabilities for use with a goodness of fit test. If `p` is not given, the goodness of fit tests that the probabilities are all equal.
`rescale.p = FALSE`	If `TRUE`, `p` is rescaled to sum to 1. For use with goodness of fit tests.
`simulate.p.value = FALSE`	If set to `TRUE`, a Monte Carlo simulation is used to calculate p-values.
`B = 2000`	The number of replicates to use in the Monte Carlo simulation.

Multiple Categories: Chi-Squared Tests

The most common use for a chi-squared test is where you have multiple categories and want to see if associations exist between them. In the following example you can see some categorical data set out in a data frame. You have seen these data before:

```
> bird.df
              Garden Hedgerow Parkland Pasture Woodland
Blackbird         47       10       40       2        2
Chaffinch         19        3        5       0        2
Great Tit         50        0       10       7        0
House Sparrow     46       16        8       4        0
Robin              9        3        0       0        2
Song Thrush        4        0        6       0        0
```

The data here are already in a contingency table and each cell represents a unique combination of the two categories; here you have several habitats and several species. You run the `chisq.test()` command simply by giving the name of the data to the command like so:

```
> bird.cs = chisq.test(bird.df)
Warning message:
In chisq.test(bird.df) : Chi-squared approximation may be incorrect
> bird.cs

       Pearson's Chi-squared test

data:  bird.df
X-squared = 78.2736, df = 20, p-value = 7.694e-09
```

In this case you give the result a name and set it up as a new object, which you examine in more detail in a moment. You get an error message in this example; this is because you have some small values for your observed data and the expected values will probably include some that are smaller than 5. When you issue the name of the result object you see a very brief result that contains the salient points.

Your original data were in the form of a data frame but you might also have used a matrix. If that were so, the result is exactly the same. You can also use a table result; perhaps the result of using the `xtabs()` command on the raw data. In any event you end up with a result object, which you can examine in more detail. You might start by trying a `summary()` command:

```
> summary(bird.cs)
          Length Class  Mode
statistic  1     -none- numeric
parameter  1     -none- numeric
p.value    1     -none- numeric
method     1     -none- character
data.name  1     -none- character
observed  30     -none- numeric
expected  30     -none- numeric
residuals 30     -none- numeric
```

This does not produce the result that you may have expected. However, it does show that the result object you created contains several parts. A simpler way to see what you are dealing with is to use the `names()` command:

```
> names(bird.cs)
[1] "statistic" "parameter" "p.value"   "method"    "data.name" "observed"
[7] "expected"  "residuals"
```

You can access the various parts of your result object by using the $ syntax and adding the part you want to examine. For example:

```
> bird.cs$stat
X-squared
 78.27364
> bird.cs$p.val
[1] 7.693581e-09
```

Here you select the statistic (the X^2 value) and the p-value; notice that you do not need to use the full name here, an abbreviation is fine as long as it is unambiguous. You can see the calculated expected values as well as the Pearson residuals by using the appropriate abbreviation. In the following example you look at the expected values:

```
> bird.cs$exp
                 Garden  Hedgerow  Parkland   Pasture  Woodland
Blackbird     59.915254 10.955932 23.623729 4.4508475 2.0542373
Chaffinch     17.203390  3.145763  6.783051 1.2779661 0.5898305
Great Tit     39.745763  7.267797 15.671186 2.9525424 1.3627119
House Sparrow 43.898305  8.027119 17.308475 3.2610169 1.5050847
Robin          8.305085  1.518644  3.274576 0.6169492 0.2847458
Song Thrush    5.932203  1.084746  2.338983 0.4406780 0.2033898
```

You can see in this example that you have some expected values < 5 and this is the reason for the warning message. You might prefer to display the values as whole numbers and you can adjust the output "on the fly" by using the `round()` command to choose how many decimal points to display the values like so:

```
> round(bird.cs$exp, 0)
              Garden Hedgerow Parkland Pasture Woodland
Blackbird         60       11       24       4        2
Chaffinch         17        3        7       1        1
Great Tit         40        7       16       3        1
House Sparrow     44        8       17       3        2
Robin              8        2        3       1        0
Song Thrush        6        1        2       0        0
```

In this instance you chose to use no decimals at all and so use 0 as an instruction in the `round()` command.

Monte Carlo Simulation

You can decide to determine the p-value by a slightly different method and can use a Monte Carlo simulation to do this. You add an extra instruction to the `chisq.test()` command, `simulate.p.value = TRUE`, like so:

```
> chisq.test(bird.df, simulate.p.value = TRUE, B = 2500)

        Pearson's Chi-squared test with simulated p-value (based on 2500
        replicates)

data:  bird.df
X-squared = 78.2736, df = NA, p-value = 0.0003998
```

The default is that `simulate.p.value = FALSE` and that `B = 2000`. The latter is the number of replicates to use in the Monte Carlo test, which is set to 2500 for this example.

Yates' Correction for 2 × 2 Tables

When you have a 2 × 2 contingency table it is common to apply the Yates' correction. By default this is used if the contingency table has two rows and two columns. You can turn off the correction using the `correct = FALSE` instruction in the command. In the following example you can see a 2 × 2 table:

```
> nd
          Urt.dio.y Urt.dio.n
Rum.obt.y        96        41
Rum.obt.n        26        57

> chisq.test(nd)

	Pearson's Chi-squared test with Yates' continuity correction

data:  nd
X-squared = 29.8653, df = 1, p-value = 4.631e-08

> chisq.test(nd, correct = FALSE)

	Pearson's Chi-squared test

data:  nd
X-squared = 31.4143, df = 1, p-value = 2.084e-08
```

At the top you see the data and when you run the `chisq.test()` command you see that Yates' correction is applied automatically. In the second example you force the command not to apply the correction by setting `correct = FALSE`. Yates' correction is applied only when the matrix is 2 × 2, and even if you tell R to apply the correction explicitly it will do so only if the table is 2 × 2.

Single Category: Goodness of Fit Tests

You can use the `chisq.test()` command to carry out a goodness of fit test. In this case you must have two vectors of numerical values, one representing the observed values and the other representing the expected ratio of values. The goodness of fit tests the data against the ratios (probabilities) you specified. If you do not specify any, the data are tested against equal probability.

In the following example you have a simple data frame containing two columns; the first column contains values relating to an old survey. The second column contains values relating to a new survey. You want to see if the proportions of the new survey match the old one, so you perform a goodness of fit test:

```
> survey
        old new
woody    23  19
shrubby  34  30
tall    132 111
short    98 101
grassy   45  52
mossy    53  26
```

To run the test you use the `chisq.test()` command, but this time you must specify the test data as a single vector and also point to the vector that contains the probabilities:

```
> survey.cs = chisq.test(survey$new, p = survey$old, rescale.p = TRUE)
> survey.cs

	Chi-squared test for given probabilities

data:  survey$new
X-squared = 15.8389, df = 5, p-value = 0.00732
```

In this example you did not have the probabilities as true probabilities but as frequencies; you use the `rescale.p = TRUE` instruction to make sure that these are converted to probabilities (this instruction is set to `FALSE` by default).

The result contains all the usual items for a chi-squared result object, but if you display the expected values, for example, you do not automatically get to see the row names, even though they are present in the data:

```
> survey.cs$exp
[1]  20.25195  29.93766 116.22857  86.29091  39.62338  46.66753
```

You can get the row names from the original data using the `row.names()` command. You could set the names of the expected values in the following way:

```
names(survey.cs$expected) = row.names(survey)
> survey.cs$exp
    woody   shrubby      tall     short    grassy     mossy
 20.25195  29.93766 116.22857  86.29091  39.62338  46.66753
```

You could do something similar for the residuals and then when you inspected your result it would be easier to keep track of which value was related to which category.

In the following activity you can get a chance to practice the chi-squared test for association as well as goodness of fit by using a simple data example.

TRY IT OUT Carry Out Chi-Squared Tests on Some Data

Available for download on Wrox.com

Use the `bees` data object from the `Beginning.RData` file for this activity, which you will use to carry out a range of association and goodness of fit tests. The data are in a data frame and represent visits by various bee species to different plant species.

1. Carry out a basic chi-squared test on these data and save the result as a named object:

```
> bees
                Buff.tail Garden.bee Red.tail Honey.bee Carder.bee
Thistle                10          8       18        12          8
Vipers.bugloss          1          3        9        13         27
Golden.rain            37         19        1        16          6
Yellow.alfalfa          5          6        2         9         32
Blackberry             12          4        4        10         23
```

```
> (bees.cs = chisq.test(bees))

    Pearson's Chi-squared test

data:  bees
X-squared = 120.6531, df = 16, p-value < 2.2e-16
```

2. Look at the result you just obtained—it contains several parts. Display the Pearson residuals for the result:

```
> names(bees.cs)
[1] "statistic" "parameter" "p.value"   "method"    "data.name" "observed"
"expected"
[8] "residuals"
> bees.cs$resid
                 Buff.tail Garden.bee  Red.tail  Honey.bee Carder.bee
Thistle        -0.66586684  0.1476203  4.544647  0.18079727  -2.394918
Vipers.bugloss -3.12467558 -1.5616655  1.169932  0.67626472   2.348309
Golden.rain     4.69620024  2.5323534 -2.686059 -0.01691336  -3.887003
Yellow.alfalfa -1.99986117 -0.4885699 -1.693054 -0.59837350   3.441582
Blackberry      0.09423625 -1.1886361 -0.853104 -0.23746700   1.385152
```

3. Now run the chi-squared test again but this time use a Monte Carlo simulation with 3000 replicates to determine the p-value:

```
> (bees.cs = chisq.test(bees, simulate.p.value = TRUE, B = 3000))

    Pearson's Chi-squared test with simulated p-value (based on 3000 replicates)

data:  bees
X-squared = 120.6531, df = NA, p-value = 0.0003332
```

4. Look at a portion of the data as a 2 × 2 contingency table. Examine the effect of Yates' correction on this subset:

```
> bees[1:2, 4:5]
               Honey.bee Carder.bee
Thistle               12          8
Vipers.bugloss        13         27

> chisq.test(bees[1:2, 4:5], correct = FALSE)

    Pearson's Chi-squared test

data:  bees[1:2, 4:5]
X-squared = 4.1486, df = 1, p-value = 0.04167

> chisq.test(bees[1:2, 4:5], correct = TRUE)

    Pearson's Chi-squared test with Yates' continuity correction

data:  bees[1:2, 4:5]
X-squared = 3.0943, df = 1, p-value = 0.07857
```

5. Look at the last two columns, representing two bee species. Carry out a goodness of fit test to determine if the proportions of visits are the same:

```
> with(bees, chisq.test(Honey.bee, p = Carder.bee, rescale = T))

    Chi-squared test for given probabilities

data:  Honey.bee
X-squared = 58.088, df = 4, p-value = 7.313e-12

Warning message:
In chisq.test(Honey.bee, p = Carder.bee, rescale = T) :
  Chi-squared approximation may be incorrect
```

6. Carry out the same goodness of fit test but use a simulation to determine the p-value (you can abbreviate the command):

```
> with(bees, chisq.test(Honey.bee, p = Carder.bee, rescale = T, sim = T))

    Chi-squared test for given probabilities with simulated p-value (based on
2000
    replicates)

data:  Honey.bee
X-squared = 58.088, df = NA, p-value = 0.0004998
```

7. Now look at a single column and carry out a goodness of fit test. This time omit the `p =` instruction to test the fit to equal probabilities:

```
> chisq.test(bees$Honey.bee)

    Chi-squared test for given probabilities

data:  bees$Honey.bee
X-squared = 2.5, df = 4, p-value = 0.6446
```

How It Works

The basic form of the `chisq.test()` command will operate on a matrix or data frame. By enclosing the entire command in parentheses you can get the result object to display immediately. The results of many commands are stored as a list containing several elements, and you can see what is available using the `names()` command and view them using the `$` syntax.

The p-value can be determined using a Monte Carlo simulation by using the `simulate.p.value` and `B` instructions. If the data form a 2 × 2 contingency, then Yates' correction is automatically applied but only if the Monte Carlo simulation is *not* used.

To conduct a goodness of fit test you must specify `p`, the vector of probabilities; if this does not sum to 1 you will get an error unless you use `rescale.p = TRUE`. You can use a Monte Carlo simulation on a goodness of fit test. If a single vector is specified, a goodness of fit test is carried out but the probabilities are assumed to be equal.

SUMMARY

- A variety of simple statistical tests are built into R.
- The t-test can be carried out using the `t.test()` command. This can conduct one- or two-sample tests and a range of options allow one-tailed and two-tailed tests.
- The U-test is accessed via the `wilcox.test()` command. This non-parametric test of differences can be applied as one-sample or two-sample versions.
- Matched paired data can be analyzed using t-test or U-test by the simple addition of the `paired = TRUE` instruction in the `t.test()` or `wilcox.test()` commands.
- The `subset` instruction can be used to select one or more samples from a variable containing several groups.
- Correlation and covariance can be carried out on pairs of vectors, or on entire data frames or matrix objects using the `cor()` and `cov()` commands. A single variable can be specified to produce a targeted correlation or covariance matrix.
- Three types of correlation can be used; Pearson's Product Moment, Spearman's rho or Kendall's tau.
- Correlation hypothesis tests can be carried out using Pearson, Spearman, or Kendall methods via the `cor.test()` command. Two variables can be specified as separate vectors or using the formula syntax.
- Tests using categorical data can be carried out via the `chisq.test()` command. This can conduct standard tests of association (chi-squared tests) or goodness of fit tests. Monte Carlo simulation can be used to produce the p-value.

EXERCISES

Available for download on Wrox.com

You can find answers to these exercises in Appendix A.

Use the `hogl` and `bv` data objects in the `Beginning.RData` file for these exercises. The `sleep`, `InsectSprays`, and `mtcars` data objects are part of the regular distribution of R.

1. Look at the `InsectSprays` data. Compare the effectiveness of spray types A and B using a t-test.
2. Look at the `hogl` data. This data frame contains two columns, representing the abundance of a freshwater invertebrate (`hoglouse`) at two habitats (`slow` and `fast`). Use a U-test to compare the abundance.
3. Look at the `sleep` data; you will see that it has three columns. The `extra` column represents time of additional sleep induced by a drug. The `group` column gives a numeric value; this is the drug (1 or 2). The final column, `ID`, is simply the patient identification. Each patient was given both drugs (on different occasions) and the time of additional sleep recorded. Carry out a paired t-test on the additional sleep times and the different drugs.

4. Look at the `mtcars` data that gives data on the fuel consumption and other features of some automobiles from the 1970s. First look at a correlation matrix of these data, then focus on the correlation between `mpg` and the other variables. Finally, carry out a correlation test on the `mpg` and `qsec` (time taken to travel a quarter mile) variables.

5. Look at the `bv` data. Here you can see a column, `visit`, which relates to numbers of bees visiting various colors of flowers. The `ratio` column refers to the relative numbers of visits from a previous experiment. Carry out a goodness of fit test to see if the two experiments have given the same results.

▶ WHAT YOU LEARNED IN THIS CHAPTER

TOPIC	KEY POINTS

T-test:
`t.test(data1, data2 = NULL)`
`t.test(y ~ x, data)`
	Student's t-test can be carried out using the `t.test()` command. You must specify two vectors if you want a two-sample test; otherwise a one-sample test is conducted. A formula can be specified if the data are in the appropriate layout.
	You can use various additional instructions to specify the test you require.

U-test:
`wilcox.test(data1, data2 = NULL)`
`wilcox.test(y ~ x, data)`
	The U-test (Mann-Whitney or Wilcoxon test) can be carried out using the `wilcox.test()` command. One-sample or two-sample tests can be executed and a formula can be used if the data are in an appropriate layout.
	You can use various additional instructions to specify the test you require.

Paired tests:
`t.test(x, y, paired = TRUE)`
`wilcox.test(x, y, paired = TRUE)`
	Paired versions of the t-test and the U-test can be carried out by adding the `paired = TRUE` instruction to the command. Pairs containing `NA` items are dropped. You get an error if you try to run a paired test on two vectors of unequal length.

Subsetting: `subset = group %in% c("grp1", "grp2")`	If your data are in a form where you have a response variable and a predictor variable you can select a subset of the data using the `subset` instruction.

Covariance:
`cov(x, y)`
Pearson, Spearman, Kendall
`cov2cor(matrix)`
	Covariance can be examined using the `cov()` command. You can specify two objects, which can be vector, data frame, or matrix. All objects must be of equal length. You can specify one of `"pearson"` (default), `"spearman"`, or `"kendall"` (can be abbreviated).
	A covariance matrix can be converted to a correlation matrix using the `cov2cor()` command.

Correlation: `cor(x, y)` Pearson, Spearman, Kendall	Correlation can be carried out using the `cor()` command. You can specify two objects, which can be vector, data frame, or matrix. All objects must be of equal length. You can specify one of `"pearson"` (default), `"spearman"`, or `"kendall"` (can be abbreviated).

TOPIC	KEY POINTS

Correlation hypothesis tests:
`cor.test(x, y)`
`cor.test(~ y + x, data)`
	Correlation hypothesis tests can be carried out using the `cor.test()` command. You can specify two vectors or use the formula syntax. Unlike `cov()` or `cor()` commands you can compare only two variables at a time. You can specify one of `"pearson"` (default), `"spearman"`, or `"kendall"` (can be abbreviated) as the method to use.

Association tests: `chisq.test(x, y = NULL)`	Chi-squared tests of association can be carried out using the `chisq.test()` command. If `x` is a data frame or matrix, `y` is ignored. Yates' correction is applied by default to 2 × 2 contingency tables.
Goodness of fit tests: `chisq.test(x, p = , rescale.p = FALSE)`	Chi-squared goodness of fit tests can be carried out using the `chisq.test()` command. A single vector must be given for the test data and the probabilities to test against are given as p. If they do not sum to 1, you can use the `rescale.p` instruction. If p is not supplied the probabilities are taken as equal.

Monte Carlo simulation:
`simulate.p.value = FALSE`
`B = 2000`
	For chi-squared tests of association or goodness of fit you can determine the p-value by Monte Carlo simulation using the `simulate.p.value` instruction. The number of trials is set at 2000, which you can alter.

Rounding values: `round(object, digits = 6)`	The level of precision of displayed results can be altered using the `round()` command. You specify the numerical results to use and the number of digits to use, which defaults to 6.

7

Introduction to Graphical Analysis

WHAT YOU WILL LEARN IN THIS CHAPTER:

- How to create a range of graphs to summarize your data and results
- How to create box-whisker plots
- How to create scatter plots, including multiple correlation plots
- How to create line graphs
- How to create pie charts
- How to create bar charts
- How to move graphs from R to other programs and save graphs as files on disk

Graphs are a powerful way to present your data and results in a concise manner. Whatever kind of data you have, there is a way to illustrate it graphically. A graph is more readily understandable than words and numbers, and producing good graphs is a vital skill. Some graphs are also useful in examining data so that you can gain some idea of patterns that may exist; this can direct you toward the correct statistical analysis.

R has powerful and flexible graphical capabilities. In general terms, R has two kinds of graphical commands: some commands generate a basic plot of some sort, and other commands are used to tweak the output and to produce a more customized finish.

You have already encountered some graphical commands in previous chapters. This chapter focuses on some of the basic graph types that you may typically need to create. In Chapter 11, you will revisit the graphical commands and add a variety of extras to lift your graphs from the merely adequate, to fully polished publication quality material.

BOX-WHISKER PLOTS

The box-whisker plot (often abbreviated to boxplot) is a useful way to visualize complex data where you have multiple samples. In general, you are looking to display differences between samples. The basic form of the box-whisker plot shows the median value, the quartiles (or hinges), and the max/min values. This means that you get a lot of information in a compact manner. The box-whisker plot is also useful to visualize a single sample because you can show outliers if you choose. You can use the `boxplot()` command to create box-whisker plots. The command can work in a variety of ways to visualize simple or quite complex data.

Basic Boxplots

The following example shows a simple data frame composed of two columns:

```
> fw
         count speed
Taw          9     2
Torridge    25     3
Ouse        15     5
Exe          2     9
Lyn         14    14
Brook       25    24
Ditch       24    29
Fal         47    34
```

You have seen these data before. You can use the `boxplot()` command to visualize one of the variables here:

```
> boxplot(fw$speed)
```

This produces a simple graph like Figure 7-1. This graph shows the typical layout of a box-whisker plot. The stripe shows the median, the box represents the upper and lower hinges, and the whiskers show the maximum and minimum values.

If you have several items to plot, you can simply give the vector names in the `boxplot()` command:

```
> boxplot(fw$count, fw$speed)
```

The resulting graph appears like Figure 7-2. In this case you specify vectors that correspond to the two columns in the data frame, but they could be completely separate.

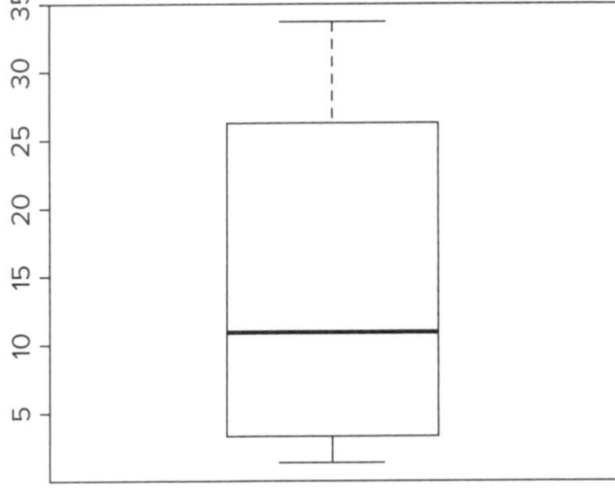

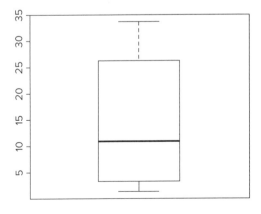

FIGURE 7-1

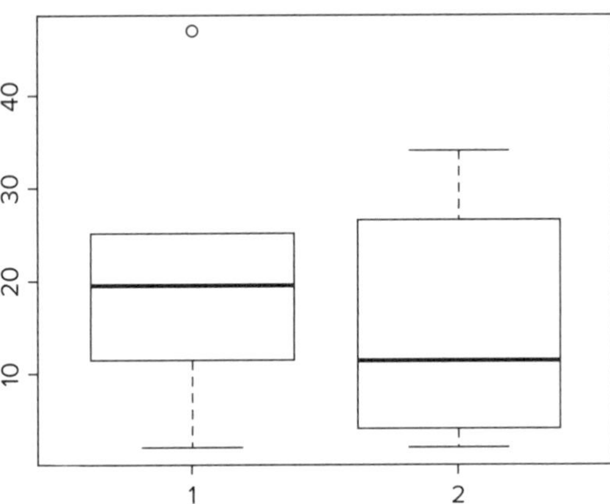

FIGURE 7-2

Customizing Boxplots

A plot without labels is useless; the plot needs labels. You can use the `xlab` and `ylab` instructions to label the axes. You can use the `names` instruction to set the labels (currently displayed as 1 and 2) for the two samples, like so:

```
> boxplot(fw$count, fw$speed, names = c('count', 'speed'))
> title(xlab = 'Variable', ylab = 'Value')
```

The resulting plot looks like Figure 7-3. In this case you used the `title()` command to add the axis labels, but you could have specified `xlab` and `ylab` within the `boxplot()` command.

Now you have names for each of the samples as well as axis labels. Notice that the whiskers of the `count` sample do not extend to the top, and that you appear to have a separate point displayed. You can determine how far out the whiskers extend, but by default this is 1.5 times the interquartile range. You can alter this by using the `range =` instruction; if you specify `range = 0` as shown in the following example, the whiskers extend to the maximum and minimum values:

```
> boxplot(fw$count, fw$speed, names = c('count', 'speed'), range = 0,
xlab = 'Variable', ylab = 'Value', col = 'gray90')
```

The final graph appears like Figure 7-4. Here you not only force the whiskers to extend to the full max and min values, but you also set the box colors to a light gray. You can see which colors are available using the `colors()` command.

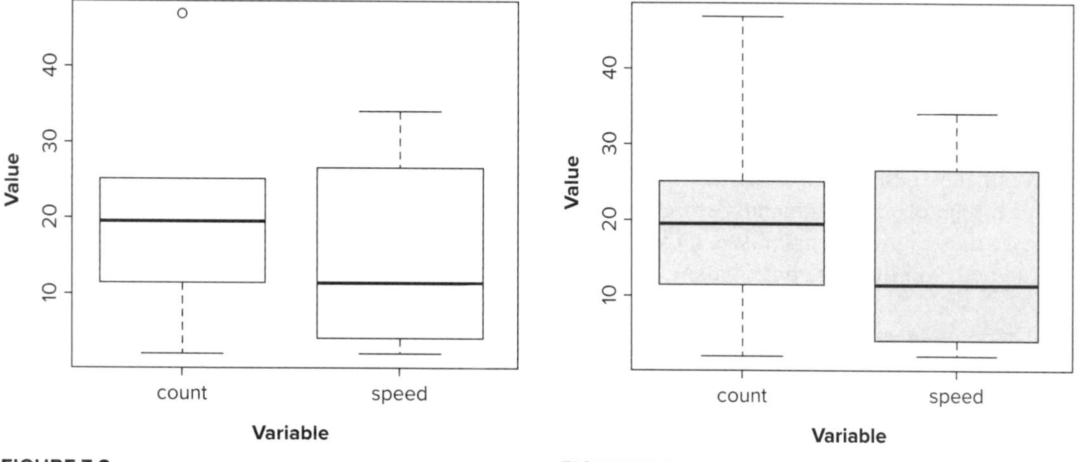

FIGURE 7-3

FIGURE 7-4

In the examples you have seen so far the data samples being plotted are separate numerical vectors. You will often have your data in a different arrangement; commonly you have a data frame with one column representing the response variable and another representing a predictor (or grouping) variable. In practice this means you have one vector containing all the numerical data and another vector containing the grouping information as text. Look at the following example:

```
> grass
```

```
  rich graze
1   12   mow
2   15   mow
3   17   mow
4   11   mow
5   15   mow
6    8 unmow
7    9 unmow
8    7 unmow
9    9 unmow
```

With data in this format, it is best to use the same formula notation you used with `t.test()`. When doing so, you use the ~ symbol to separate the response variable to the left and the predictor (grouping) variable to the right. You can also instruct the command where to find the data and set `range = 0` to force the whiskers to the maximum and minimum as before. See the following example for details:

```
> boxplot(rich ~ graze, data = grass, range = 0)
> title(xlab = 'cutting treatment', ylab = 'species richness')
```

Here you also chose to add the axis labels separately with the `title()` command. Notice this time that the samples are automatically labeled; the command takes the names of the samples from the levels of the factor, presented in alphabetical order. The resulting graph looks like Figure 7-5.

You can give additional instructions to the command; these are listed in the help entry for the `boxplot()` command. Before you learn those, however, first take a look at one additional option: horizontal bars.

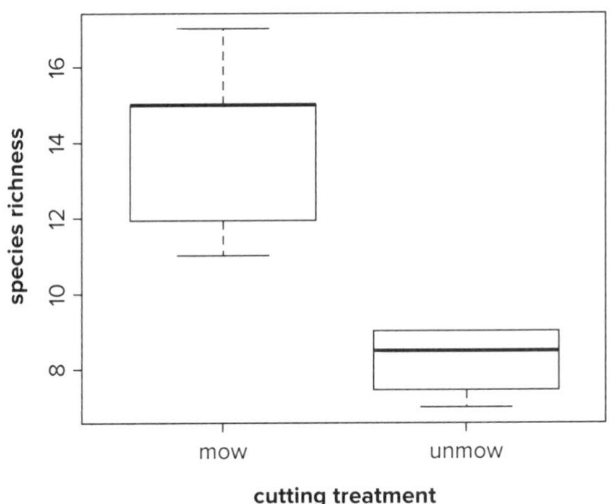

FIGURE 7-5

Horizontal Boxplots

With a simple additional instruction you can display the bars horizontally rather than vertically (which is the default):

```
> boxplot(rich ~ graze, data = grass, range = 0, horizontal = TRUE)
> title(ylab = 'cutting treatment', xlab = 'species richness')
```

When you use the `horizontal = TRUE` instruction, your graph is displayed with horizontal bars (see Figure 7-6). Notice how with the `title()` command you had to switch the `x` and `y` labels. The `xlab` instruction refers to the horizontal axis and the `ylab` instruction refers to the vertical.

In the following activity you can practice creating box-whisker plots using some data in various forms.

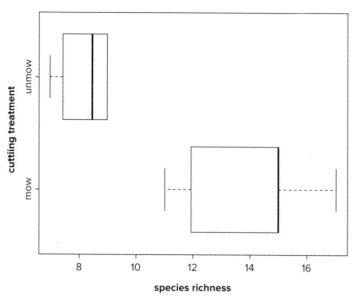

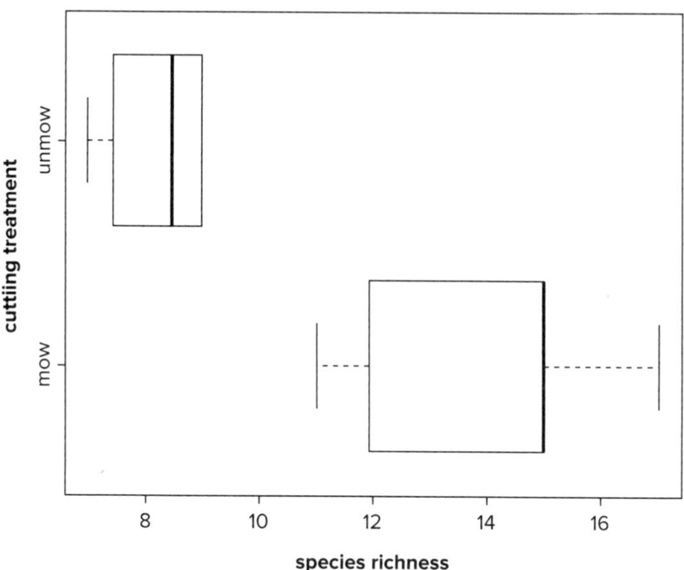

FIGURE 7-6

TRY IT OUT Creating Box-Whisker Plots

Available for download on Wrox.com

Use the `bf` and `bfs` data objects from the `Beginning.RData` file for this activity, which you will be working with to produce box-whisker plots.

1. Look at the `bf` data. The data contain three samples: `Grass`, `Heath`, and `Arable`. Draw a box-whisker plot of the `Grass` sample using the `boxplot()` command:

```
>boxplot(bf$Grass)
```

2. Now create a basic box-whisker plot comparing all three samples in the `bf` data object:

```
> with(bf, boxplot(Grass, Heath, Arable))
```

3. Add the names of the samples to the plot by specifying them explicitly:

```
> boxplot(bf$Grass, bf$Heath, bf$Arable, names = c('Grass', 'Heath', 'Arable'))
```

4. Complete the plot by adding titles to the `x` and `y` axes:

```
> title(xlab = 'Habitat', ylab = 'Butterfly Count')
```

5. Now redraw the graph but make the whiskers extend over the full range of the data. Make the bars a light blue color and add axis titles, all in a single command (your final graph should look like Figure 7-7):

```
> boxplot(bf$Grass, bf$Heath, bf$Arable, names = c('Grass', 'Heath', 'Arable'),
range = 0, xlab = 'Habitat', ylab = 'Butterfly Count', col = 'lightblue')
```

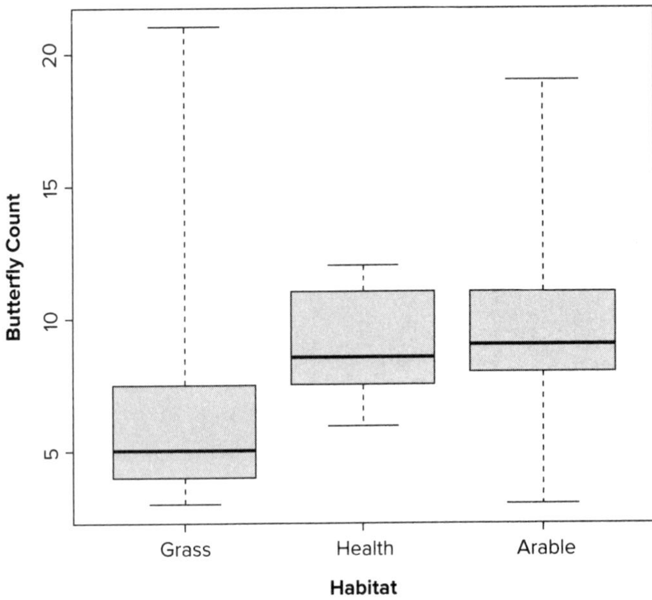

FIGURE 7-7

6. Because the data contain separate samples, you can save some typing. Redraw the graph but specify the data simply as the data frame:

```
> boxplot(bf, range = 0, col = 'lightblue')
> title(xlab = 'Habitat', ylab = 'Butterfly Count')
```

7. Look at the `bfs` data. This contains the same data as the `bf` object but in a different layout. Now you have a response variable, `count`, and a predictor variable, `site`. Use the formula syntax to draw a box-whisker plot:

```
> boxplot(count ~ site, data = bfs, range = 0, col = 'lightblue')
> title(xlab = 'Habitat', ylab = 'Butterfly Count')
```

8. Redraw the box-whisker plot using horizontal bars. Add axis titles (your final graph should look like Figure 7-8):

```
> boxplot(count ~ site, data = bfs, range = 0, col = 'lightblue', horizontal = TRUE)
> title(ylab = 'Habitat', xlab = 'Butterfly Count')
```

How It Works

Because the sample data you want to graph are contained in a data frame, you need to use the `$` syntax to get the vector to be read by R. Using the `with()` command is a useful alternative. When reading individual vectors, the `boxplot()` command does not display the sample names; you must specify them explicitly using the `names` instruction. If your data are individual samples in a data frame (or matrix), the names are taken from the column names.

You can add titles for axes separately using the `title()` command or as `xlab` and `ylab` instructions.

You can use the formula syntax when your data are in an appropriate format. The general form is to specify `response ~ grouping`, and to give the name of the data object that holds the variables. Note that the order in which the boxes appear on the graph is alphabetical when the formula syntax is used.

Remember that the `xlab` and `ylab` instructions refer to the horizontal and vertical axes, respectively. When you draw the bars horizontally, you must switch `x` and `y` axes titles.

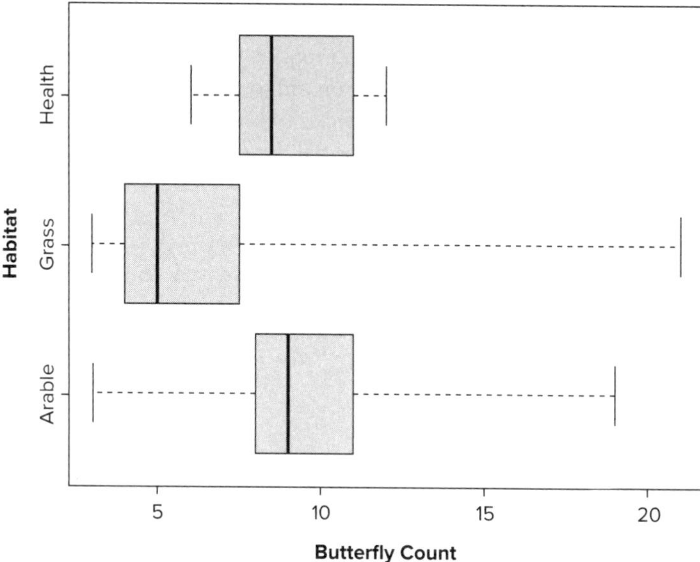

FIGURE 7-8

The order in which samples appear in your plots depends on the command that you used to create the graphic. If you use a command that reads the columns of a data frame (or matrix), the samples appear in the order in which the columns are in the data object.

If your data are in the form of a response variable and a predictor (grouping) variable, the samples will be in alphabetical order.

You can reorder the samples in a simple data frame by specifying them explicitly. For example:

```
> names(bf)
[1] "Grass"  "Heath"  "Arable"
> boxplot(bf[c(2,3,1)])
> boxplot(bf[c('Heath', 'Arable', 'Grass')])
```

The two `boxplot()` commands produce the graph with the samples in a new order.

If your data are in a `response ~ grouping` layout, it is harder to reorder the graph. The following example shows how you might achieve a reordering:

```
> with(bfs, boxplot(count[site=='Heath'], count[site=='Arable'],
count[site=='Grass'], names = c('Heath', 'Arable', 'Grass'))) # data frame
```

The box-whisker plot is very useful because it conveys a lot of information in a compact manner. R is able to produce this type of plot easily. In the rest of this chapter you see some of the other graphs that R is able to produce.

SCATTER PLOTS

The basic `plot()` command is an example of a generic function that can be pressed into service for a variety of uses. Many specialized statistical routines include a plotting routine to produce a specialized graph. For the time being, however, you will use the `plot()` command to produce `xy` scatter plots. The scatter plot is used especially to show the relationship between two variables. You met a version of this in Chapter 5 when you looked at QQ plots and the normal distribution.

Basic Scatter Plots

The following data frame contains two columns of numeric values, and because they contain the same number of observations, they could form the basis for a scatter plot:

```
> fw
         count speed
Taw          9     2
Torridge    25     3
Ouse        15     5
Exe          2     9
Lyn         14    14
Brook       25    24
Ditch       24    29
Fal         47    34
```

The basic form of the `plot()` command requires you to specify the `x` and `y` data, each being a numeric vector. You use it like so:

```
plot(x, y, ...)
```

If you have your data contained in a data frame as in the following example, you must use the `$` syntax to get at the variables; you might also use the `with()` or `attach()` commands. For the example data here, the following commands all produce a similar result:

```
> plot(fw$speed, fw$count)

> with(fw, plot(speed, count))

> attach(fw)
> plot(speed, count)
> detach(fw)
```

The resulting graph looks like Figure 7-9. Notice that the names of the axis labels match up with what you typed into the command. In this case you used the `$` syntax to extract the variables; these are reflected in the labels.

Adding Axis Labels

You can produce your own axis labels easily using the xlab and ylab instructions. For example, to create labels for these data you might use something like the following:

```
> plot(fw$speed, fw$count, xlab = 'Speed m/s', ylab = 'Count of Mayfly')
```

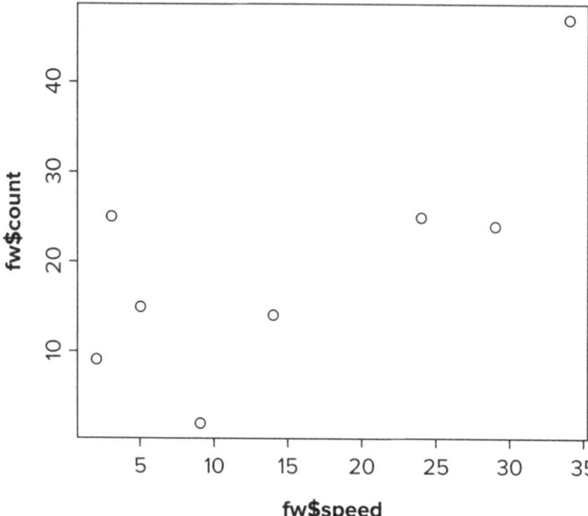

FIGURE 7-9

Previously you used the title() command to add axis titles. If you try this here you end up writing text over the top of the existing title. You can still use the title() command to add axis titles later, but you need to produce blank titles to start with. You must set each title in the plot() command to blank using a pair of quotes as shown in the following:

```
> plot(fw$speed, fw$count, xlab = "", ylab = "")
```

This is quite convoluted so most of the time it's better to set the titles as part of the plot() command at the outset.

Plotting Symbols

You can use many other graphical parameters to modify your basic scatter plot. You might want to alter the plotting symbol, for example. This is useful if you want to add more points to your graph later. The pch = instruction refers to the *plotting character*, and can be specified in one of several ways. You can type an integer value and this code will be reflected in the symbol/character produced. For values from 0 to 25, you get symbols that look like the ones depicted in Figure 7-10.

FIGURE 7-10

These were produced on a scatter plot using the following lines of command:

```
> plot(0:25, rep(1, 26), pch = 0:25, cex = 2)
> text(0:25, 0.95, as.character(0:25))
```

The first part produces a series of points, and sets the x values to range from 0 to 25 (to correspond to the pch values). The y values are set at 1 so that you get a horizontal line of points; the rep() command is used to repeat the value 1 for 26 times. In other words, you get 26 1s to correspond to your various x values. You now set the plotting character to vary from 0 to 25 using pch = 0:25. Finally, you make the points a bit bigger using a character expansion factor (cex = 2). The text() command is used to add text to a current plot. You give the x and y coordinates of the text and the actual text you want to produce. In this instance, the x values were set to vary from 0 to 25 (corresponding to the plotted symbols). The y value was set to be 0.95 because this positions the text just under each symbol. Finally, you state the text you require; you want to produce a number here so you state the numbers you want (0 to 25) and make sure they are forced to be text using the as.character instruction.

The values 26 to 31 are not used, but values from 32 upward are; these are ASCII code. The value 32 produces a space, so it is not very useful as a plotting character, but other values are fine up to about 127. You can also specify a character from the keyboard directly by enclosing it in quotes; to produce + symbols, for example, you type the following:

```
> plot(fw$speed, fw$count, pch = "+")
```

The + symbol is also obtained via pch = 3. You can alter the size of the plotted characters using the cex = instruction; this is a character expansion factor. So setting cex = 2 makes points twice as large as normal and cex = 0.5 makes them half normal size.

If you want to alter the color of the points, use the col = instruction and put the color as a name in quotes. You can see the colors available using the colors() command (it is quite a long list).

Setting Axis Limits

The plot() command works out the best size and scale of each axis to fit the plotting area. You can set the limits of each axis quite easily using xlim = and ylim = instructions. The basic form of these instructions requires two values—a start and an end:

```
xlim = c(start, end)
ylim = c(start, end)
```

You can use these to force a plot to be square, for example, or perhaps to "zoom in" to a particular part of a plot or to emphasize one axis.

You can add all of these elements together to produce a plot that matches your particular requirements. In the current example, you might type the following plot() command:

```
> plot(fw$speed, fw$count, xlab = 'Speed m/s', ylab = 'Count of Mayfly',
pch = 18, cex = 2, col = 'gray50', xlim = c(0, 50), ylim = c(0, 50))
```

This is quite long, but you can break it down into its component parts. You always start with the x and then y values, but the other instructions can be in any order because they are named explicitly. The resulting scatter plot looks like Figure 7-11.

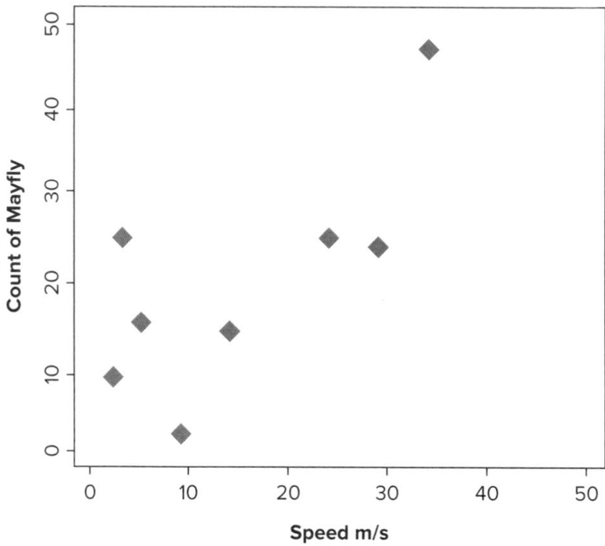

FIGURE 7-11

Using Formula Syntax

There is another way that you can specify what you want to plot; rather than giving the x and y values as separate components, you produce a formula to describe the situation:

```
> plot(count ~ speed, data = fw)
```

You use the tilde character (~) to symbolize your formula. On the left you place the response variable (that is, the dependent variable) and on the right you place the predictor (independent) variable. At the end you tell the command where to find these data. This is useful because it means you do not need to use the $ syntax or use the `attach()` command to allow R to read the variables inside the data frame. This is the same formula you saw previously when looking at simple hypothesis tests in Chapter 6.

NOTE *The formula syntax requires your variables to be in an order* `response ~ predictor`*, that is* `y ~ x`*. This is the opposite of the standard syntax where, for example, you would have* `plot(x, y)`.

Adding Lines of Best-Fit to Scatter Plots

In Chapter 5 you used the `abline()` command to add a straight line matching the slope and the intercept of a series of points when you produced a QQ plot. You can do the same thing here; first you need to determine the slope and intercept. You will look at the `lm()` command in more detail later (Chapter 10), but for now all you need to know is that it will work out the slope and intercept for you and pass it on to the `abline()` command.

```
> abline(lm(count ~ speed, data = fw))
```

Now you can see another advantage of using the formula notation: the command is very similar to the original `plot()` command. The default line produced is a thin solid black line, but you can alter its appearance in various ways. You can alter the color using the `col =` instruction, you can alter the line width using the `lwd =` instruction; and you can alter the line type using the `lty =` instruction.

The `lwd` instruction requires a simple numeric value—the bigger the number, the fatter the line! The `col` instruction is the same as you have met before and requires a color name in quotes. The `lty` instruction allows you to specify the line type in two ways: you can give a numeric value or a name in quotes. Table 7-1 shows the various options.

TABLE 7-1: Line Types that Can be Specified Using the lty Instruction in a Graphical Command

VALUE	LABEL	RESULT
0	`blank`	Blank
1	`solid`	Solid (default)
2	`dashed`	Dashed
3	`dotted`	Dotted
4	`dotdash`	Dot-Dash
5	`longdash`	Long dash
6	`twodash`	Two dash

Notice that you can draw a blank line! The number values here are recycled, so if you use `lty = 7` you get a solid line (and then again with 13).

You can use these commands to customize your fitted line like so:

```
> abline(lm(count ~ speed, data = fw), lty = 'dotted', lwd = 2, col = 'gray50')
```

If you combine the previous `plot()` command with the preceding `abline()` command like so, you get something like Figure 7-12:

```
> plot(count ~ speed, data = fw, xlab = 'Speed m/s', ylab = 'Count of Mayfly',
pch = 18, cex = 2, col = 'gray50', xlim = c(0, 50), ylim = c(0, 50))
> abline(lm(count ~ speed, data = fw), lty = 'dotted', lwd = 2, col = 'gray50')
```

The `plot()` command is very general and can be used by programmers to create customized graphs. You will mostly use it to create scatter plots, and in that regard it is still a flexible and powerful command. You can add additional graphical parameters to the `plot()` command. You see more of these additional instructions in Chapter 11, but for the time being the following activity gives you the opportunity to try making some scatter plots for yourself.

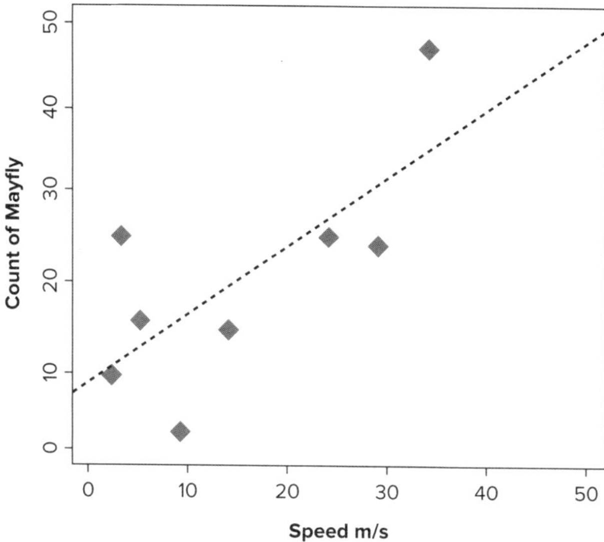

FIGURE 7-12

TRY IT OUT Make Some Scatter Plots

Available for download on Wrox.com

Use the bf data object from the Beginning.RData file for this activity. The other data, women and cars, are built in to R. You will use these data to create some scatter plots and lines of best-fit.

1. Look at the women data that come as part of R. Draw a scatter plot of these data—make the points slightly larger than standard and use a solid plotting character:

```
> plot(women, pch = 19, cex = 1.5)
```

2. Now add a line of best-fit to the women scatter plot. Make this a dashed line.

```
> abline(lm(weight ~ height, data = women), lty = 2)
```

3. Look at the cars data that come with R. Create a scatter plot of stopping distance against speed by specifying the vectors from the data. Create customized axis labels for this plot.

```
> names(cars)
[1] "speed" "dist"
> plot(cars$speed, cars$dist, xlab = 'Car speed (mph)',
 ylab = 'Stopping distance (ft)')
```

4. Add a line of best-fit to the speed-dist plot. Make this line a bit bolder than normal.

```
> abline(lm(dist ~ speed, data = cars), lwd = 2)
```

5. Look at the mf data that are part of the Beginning.RData file. Create a scatter plot of Length against BOD. Use colored plotting characters of some solid type.

```
> plot(Length ~ BOD, data = mf, col = 'blue', pch = 18)
```

6. Add a line of best-fit to the Length-BOD plot. Make the line alternate dots and dashes.

```
> abline(lm(Length ~ BOD, data = mf), lty = 'dotdash')
```

7. Now draw a scatter plot of Length against Algae from the `mf` data. Add a line of best-fit.

```
> plot(Length ~ Algae, data = mf)
> abline(lm(Length ~ Algae, data = mf), lty = 2)
```

8. In the preceding plot you can see that the line of best-fit does not cross the y-axis at the "correct" point because of the scaling of the axes. Redraw the plot and rescale the axes to show the best-fit line crossing the y-axis more effectively:

```
> plot(Length ~ Algae, data = mf, xlim = c(0,80), ylim = c(12,24))
> abline(lm(Length ~ Algae, data = mf), lty = 2)
```

How It Works

If you specify an entire data frame that contains exactly two columns, the first is taken as the `x` data and the second column is taken as the `y` data. To get the line of best-fit you need to specify the response and predictor variables from the data explicitly, using the `lm()` command and `abline()`.

You can specify the columns to plot explicitly using the `$` syntax. You can also use the `attach()` or `with()` commands.

The formula syntax is useful because you can easily work out the line of best-fit and apply this to the `abline()` and `lm()` commands that produce the line itself. The line can be altered in color, width, and style by adding the appropriate instructions. The `lty` instruction can accept a number or text: for example, `4` is the same as "`dotdash`."

The axes are scaled automatically to fit the data points into the plot area as fully as possible. To show a line of best-fit and its crossing point more effectively, you can alter the axis limits using `xlim` and `ylim` instructions.

The scatter plot is a useful tool for presentation of results and also in exploring your data. It can be useful, for example, to see a range of scatter plots for a data set all in one go as part of your data exploration. This is the focus of the next section.

***NOTE** You will probably have noticed that the axes of most plots do not "meet" in the corner. By default, R adds a bit to the end of each axis. If you draw a scatter plot with both x and y axes starting at 0, there would be a small gap. You can force the gap to disappear using the* `xaxs` *and* `yaxs` *instructions:*

```
xaxs = 'r'
yaxs = 'i'
```

If you set the instruction to `"r"` *(the default), a "regular" axis is drawn with the extra space. If you set the instruction to* `"i"` *(short for "internal"), the additional space is not added. You need to specify both* `xaxs` *and* `yaxs` *instructions as* `"i"` *for the gap to disappear around the plot origin.*

PAIRS PLOTS (MULTIPLE CORRELATION PLOTS)

In the previous section you looked at the `plot()` command as a way to produce a scatter plot. If you use the same data as before—two columns of numerical data—but do not specify the columns explicitly, you still get a plot of sorts:

```
> fw
         count speed
Taw          9     2
Torridge    25     3
Ouse        15     5
Exe          2     9
Lyn         14    14
Brook       25    24
Ditch       24    29
Fal         47    34
> plot(fw)
```

This produces a graph like Figure 7-13.

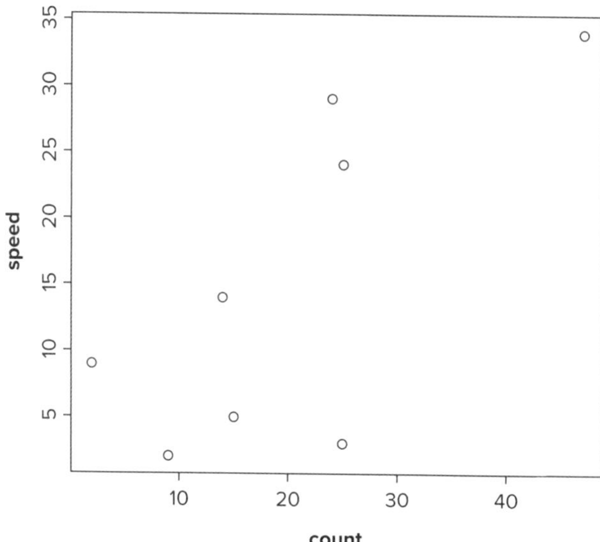

FIGURE 7-13

The data have been plotted, but if you look carefully you see that the axes are in a different order than the one you used before. The command has taken the first column as the x values, and the second column as the y values. If you try this on a data frame with more than two columns (as follows), you get something new, shown in the Figure 7-14:

```
> head(mf)
  Length Speed Algae  NO3 BOD
1     20    12    40 2.25 200
2     21    14    45 2.15 180
3     22    12    45 1.75 135
4     23    16    80 1.95 120
```

```
5      21     20     75 1.95 110
6      20     21     65 2.75 120
> plot(mf)
```

You end up with a scatterplot matrix where each pairwise combination is plotted (refer to Figure 7-14). This has created a *pairs plot*—you can use a special command `pairs()` to create customized pairs plots.

By default, the `pairs()` command takes all the columns in a data frame and creates a matrix of scatter plots. This is useful but messy if you have a lot of columns. You can choose which columns you want to display by using the formula notation along the following lines:

```
pairs(~ x + y + z, data = our.data)
```

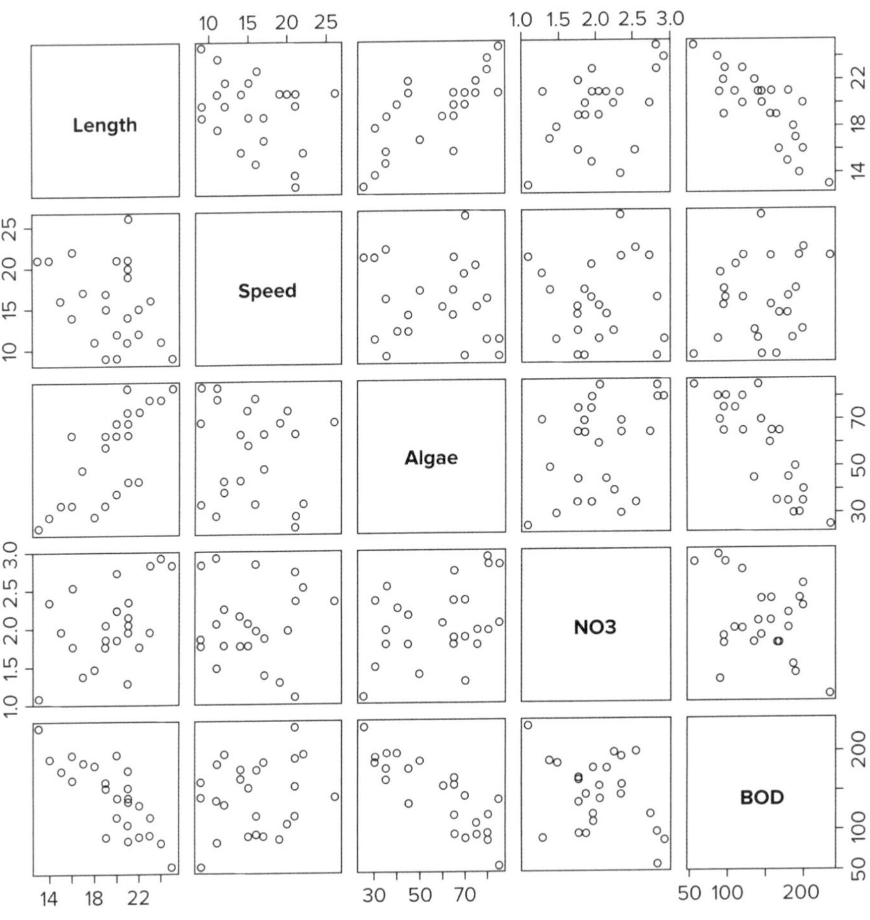

FIGURE 7-14

Your formula does not need anything on the left of the ~ because a response variable is somewhat meaningless in this context (this is like the `cor()` command you used in Chapter 6). You simply provide the required variables and separate them with + signs. If you are using a data frame, you also give the name of the data frame. In the current example you can select some of the columns like so:

```
> pairs(~ Length + Speed + NO3, data = mf)
```

This produces a graph like Figure 7-15.

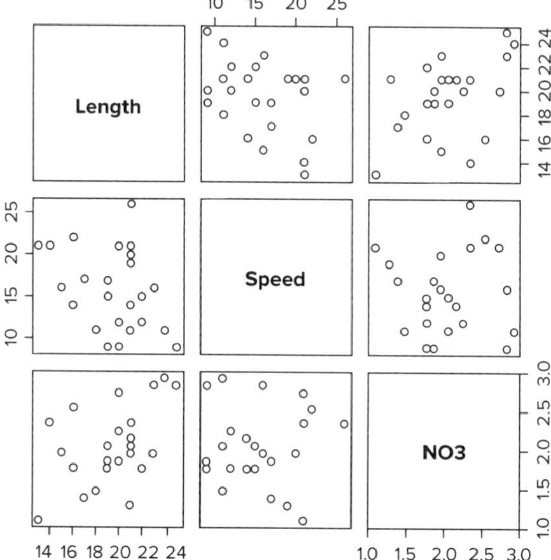

FIGURE 7-15

You can alter the plotting characters, their size, and color using the `pch`, `cex`, and `col` instructions like you saw previously. The following command produces large red crosses but otherwise is essentially the same graph:

```
> pairs(~ Length + Speed + NO3, data = mf, col ='red', cex = 2, pch = 'X')
```

It is possible to specify other parameters, but it is fiendishly difficult without a great deal of experience; the only parameters you can alter easily are the size of the labels on the diagonal, and the font style. To alter either of these you can use the following instructions:

```
cex.labels = 2
font.labels = 1
```

The default magnification for the diagonal labels is 2; you can alter this by specifying a new value. You can also alter the font style: 1 = normal, 2 = bold, 3 = italic, and 4 = bold and italic.

Pairs plots are particularly useful for exploring your data. You can see several graphs in one window and can spot patterns that you would like to explore further. In the next section you look at another use for the `plot()` command: line charts.

LINE CHARTS

So far you have looked at the `plot()` command as a way to produce scatter plots, either as a single pair of variables or a multiple-pairs plot. There may be many occasions when you have data that is time-dependent, that is, data that is collected over a period of time. You would want to display these data as a scatter plot where the y-axis reflects the magnitude of the data you recorded and the x-axis reflects the time. It would seem sensible to be able to join the data together with lines in order to highlight the changes over time.

Line Charts Using Numeric Data

If the time variable you recorded is in the form of a numeric variable, you can use a regular `plot()` command. You can specify different ways to present the data using the `type` instruction. Table 7-2 lists the main options you can set using the `type` instruction.

TABLE 7-2: The type = Instruction Can Alter the Way Data is Drawn on the Plot Area

INSTRUCTION	EXPLANATION
`type = 'p'`	Points only.
`type = 'b'`	Points with line segments between.
`type = 'l'`	Lines segments alone with no points.
`type = 'o'`	Lines overplotted with points, that is, no gap between the line segments.
`type = 'c'`	Line segments only with small gaps where the points would be.
`type = 'n'`	Nothing is plotted! The graph is produced, setting axis scales but the data are not actually drawn in.

Therefore, if you want to highlight the pattern, you can specify `type = "l"` and draw a line, leaving the points out entirely. Notice that you can use `type = "n"` to produce nothing at all! This can be useful because it enables you to define the limits of a plot window, which you can add to later.

Look at the `Nile` data that comes with R (simply type its name: `Nile`). This is stored as a special kind of object called a *time series*. Essentially, this enables you to specify the time in a more space-efficient manner than using a separate column of data. In the `Nile` data you have measurements of the flow of the Nile river from 1871 to 1970. If you plot these data you see something that resembles Figure 7-16.

```
> plot(Nile, type = 'l')
```

Here you specified `type = "l"`, which is the default for time series objects but not for regular objects.

If your data are not in numerical order, you can end up with some odd-looking line charts. You can use the `sort()` command (recall Chapter 3) to reorder the data using the x-axis data, which usually *sorts* out the problem (pardon the pun). Look at the following examples:

```
> with(mf, plot(Length, NO3, type = 'l'))
> with(mf[order(mf$Length),], plot(sort(Length), NO3, type = 'l'))
```

In the first case the data are not sorted, and the result is a bit of a mess (the result is not shown here, but you can try it for yourself). In the second case the data are sorted, and the result is a lot better.

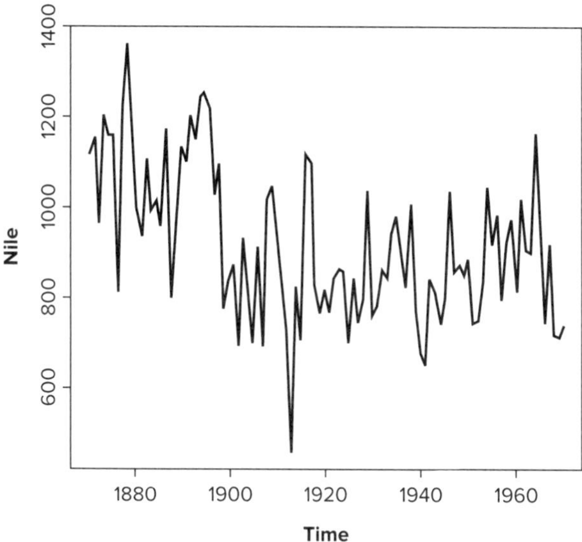

FIGURE 7-16

Line Charts Using Categorical Data

If the data you have is a sequence but doesn't have a numerical value, you have a trickier situation. For example, your time interval might be recorded as month of the year. In this case you can think of a line plot as a special case of a scatter plot, but where one axis (the dependent/x-axis) is not a numeric scale but a categorical one. The following data provides an example; in this case you have numeric data with labels that are categorical (each being a month of the year):

```
> rain
Jan Feb Mar Apr May Jun Jul Aug Sep Oct Nov Dec
  3   5   7   5   3   2   6   8   5   6   9   8
```

Alternatively, you might have data in the form of a data frame; the following example shows the same data but this time the labels are in a second column:

```
> rainfall
   rain month
1     3   Jan
2     5   Feb
3     7   Mar
4     5   Apr
5     3   May
6     2   Jun
7     6   Jul
8     8   Aug
9     5   Sep
10    6   Oct
11    9   Nov
12    8   Dec
```

In either case, you could try plotting the data using the `plot()` command like so:

```
plot(rain, type = 'b')
plot(rainfall$rain, type = 'b')
```

In the first instance of the command you simply type the name of the data vector; in the second case you have to use the `$` syntax to get the data from within the data frame. As part of the `plot()` command you add the instruction `type = 'b'`; this creates both points and lines. You do get a plot of sorts (see Figure 7-17), but you do not have the months displayed; the x-axis remains as a simple numeric index.

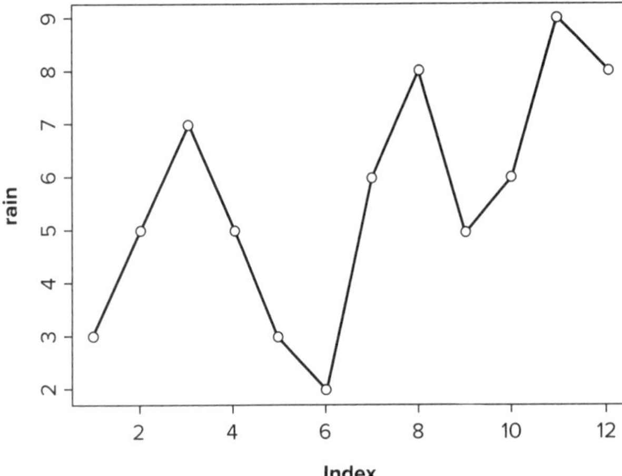

FIGURE 7-17

To alter the x-axis as desired you need to remove the existing x-axis, and create your own using the character vector as the labels. Perform the following steps to do so:

1. Start by turning off the axes using the `axes = FALSE` instruction. You can still label the axes using the `xlab` and `ylab` instructions as you have seen before. If you want to produce blank labels and add them later using the `title()` command, set them using a pair of quotes; for example, `xlab = ""`:

   ```
   > plot(rain, type = 'b', axes = FALSE, xlab = 'Month', ylab = 'Rainfall cm')
   ```

   This makes a line plot with appropriately labeled axes, but no actual axes!

2. Now construct your x-axis using the character labels you already have (or you could make new labels). The `axis()` command creates an axis for a plot. The basic layout of the command is like so:

   ```
   axis(side, at = NULL, labels = TRUE)
   ```

   The first part is where you set which side you want the axis to be created on; 1 is the bottom, 2 is the left, 3 is the top, and 4 is the right side of the plot. The `at =` part is where you determine how many tick marks are to be shown; you show this as a range from 1: n where n = how many tick marks you require, (12 in this case).

3. Finally, you get to point to the labels. In this example you use a separate character vector for the labels:

```
> month = c('Jan', 'Feb', 'Mar', 'Apr', 'May', 'Jun', 'Jul', 'Aug',
'Sep', 'Oct', 'Nov', 'Dec')
> axis(side = 1, at = 1: length(rain), labels = month)
```

   This creates an axis at the bottom of the plot (the x-axis) and sets the tick marks from 1 to 12; you use the `length()` command to make sure you get the correct number, but you could have typed `1:12` instead. Finally, you point to the month vector to get the labels; if these were contained as row names or column names you could use the appropriate command to get them: `row.names()` or `names()`, for example. If they were in a separate column, you point to them using the `$` syntax: for example, `rainfall$month`.

4. To finish off your plot, make the y-axis. You can make the y-axis using:

```
> axis(side = 2)
```

   This creates an axis for you and takes the scale from the existing plot.

5. Finally, you can enclose the whole lot in a neat bounding box. Use the `box()` command to make an enclosing bounding box for the entire plot.

The entire exercise takes the following five lines of commands:

```
> plot(rain, type = 'b', axes = FALSE, xlab = 'Month', ylab = 'Rainfall cm')
> month = c('Jan', 'Feb', 'Mar', 'Apr', 'May', 'Jun', 'Jul', 'Aug', 'Sep',
'Oct', 'Nov', 'Dec')
> axis(side = 1, at = 1: length(rain), labels = month)
> axis(side = 2)
> box()
```

The final plot looks like Figure 7-18.

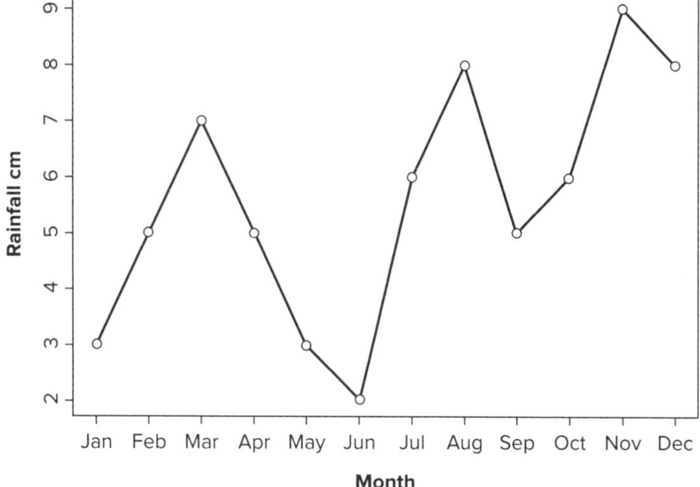

FIGURE 7-18

NOTE *R contains some inbuilt data constants that are useful for labels. For example* `month.abb` *contains the abbreviated months of the year. The full month names are contained in* `month.name`*. You can get lowercase letters (a-z) or uppercase (A-Z) using* `letters` *and* `LETTERS` *respectively.*

You can alter the plotting characters and the characteristics of the line using instructions that you have seen before: `pch` alters the plotting symbol, `cex` alters the symbol size, `lty` sets the line type, and `lwd` makes the line wider or thinner. You can use the `col =` instruction to specify a color for the line and points (both set via the same instruction).

PIE CHARTS

If you have data that represents how something is divided up between various categories, the pie chart is a common graphic choice to illustrate your data. For example, you might have data that shows sales for various items for a whole year. The pie chart enables you to show how each item contributed to total sales. Each item is represented by a slice of pie—the bigger the slice, the bigger the contribution to the total sales. In simple terms, the pie chart takes a series of data, determines the proportion of each item toward the total, and then represents these as different slices of the pie.

NOTE *The human eye is not really that good at converting angular measurements (slices of pie) into "real" values, and in many disciplines the pie chart is falling out of favor. However, the pie chart is still an attractive proposition for plenty of occasions.*

The pie chart is commonly used to display proportional data. You can create pie charts using the `pie()` command. In its simplest form, you can use a vector of numeric values to create your plot like so:

```
> data11
 [1] 3 5 7 5 3 2 6 8 5 6 9 8
```

When you use the `pie()` command, these values are converted to proportions of the total and then the angle of the pie slices is determined. If possible, the slices are labeled with the names of the data. In the current example you have a simple vector of values with no names, so you must supply them separately. You can do this in a variety of ways; in this instance you have a vector of character labels:

```
> data8
 [1] "Jan" "Feb" "Mar" "Apr" "May" "Jun" "Jul" "Aug" "Sep" "Oct" "Nov" "Dec"
```

To create a pie chart with labels you use the `pie()` command in the following manner:

```
> pie(data11, labels = data8)
```

This produces a plot that looks like Figure 7-19.

You can alter the direction and starting point of the slices using the `clockwise =` and `init.angle =` instructions. By default the slices are drawn counter-clockwise, so `clockwise = FALSE`; you can set this to `TRUE` to produce clockwise slices. The starting angle is set to 0° (this is 3 o'clock) by default when you have `clockwise = FALSE`. The starting angle is set to 90° (12 o'clock) when you have clockwise = TRUE. To start the slices from a different point, you simply give the starting angle in degrees; these may also be negative with -90 being equivalent to 270°.

The default colors used are a range of six pastel colors; these are recycled as necessary. You can specify a range of colors to use with the col = instruction. One way to do this is to make a list of color names. In the following example you make a list of gray colors and then use these for your charted colors:

```
> pc = c('gray40', 'gray50', 'gray60', 'gray70', 'gray80', 'gray90')
> pie(data11, labels = data8, col = pc, clockwise = TRUE, init.angle = 180)
```

You can also set the slices to be drawn clockwise and set the starting point to 180°, which is 9 o'clock. The resulting plot looks like Figure 7-20.

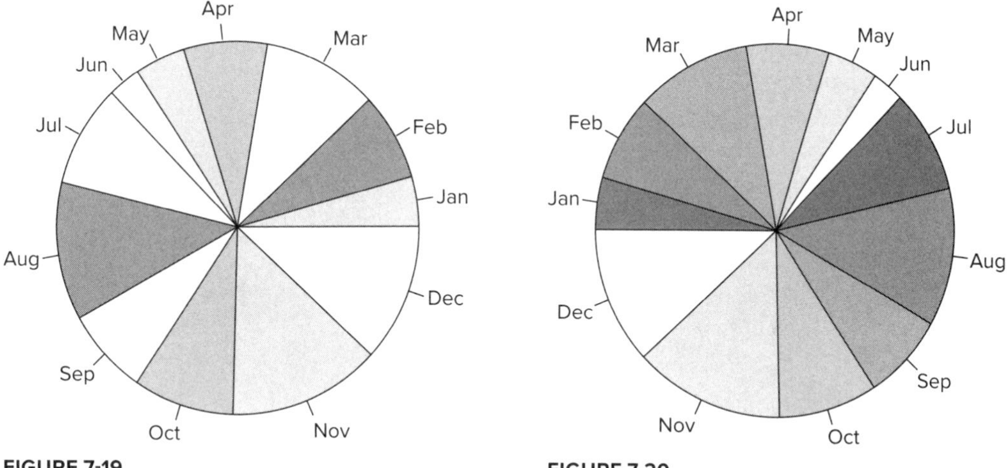

FIGURE 7-19

FIGURE 7-20

When your data are part of a data frame, you must use the $ syntax to access the column you require or use the with() or attach() commands. In the following example, the data frame contains row names you can use to label your pie slices:

```
> fw
         count speed
Taw          9     2
Torridge    25     3
Ouse        15     5
Exe          2     9
Lyn         14    14
Brook       25    24
Ditch       24    29
Fal         47    34

> pc = c('gray65', 'gray70', 'gray75', 'gray80', 'gray85', 'gray90')
> pie(fw$count, labels = row.names(fw), col = pc, cex = 1.2)
```

In this case you set the colors to six shades of gray and also use the cex = instruction to make the slice labels a little bigger. The labels = instruction points to the row names of the data frame. The final graph looks like Figure 7-21.

When your data are in matrix form, you have a few additional options: you can produce pie charts of the rows or the columns. The following data example shows a matrix of bird observation data; the rows and the columns are named:

```
> bird
             Garden Hedgerow Parkland Pasture Woodland
Blackbird        47       10       40       2        2
Chaffinch        19        3        5       0        2
Great Tit        50        0       10       7        0
House Sparrow    46       16        8       4        0
Robin             9        3        0       0        2
Song Thrush       4        0        6       0        0
```

You can use the `[row, column]` syntax with the `pie()` command; here you examine the first row:

```
> pie(bird[,1], col = pc)
```

This produces a graph like Figure 7-22; note that you use the same gray colors that you created earlier as your color palette:

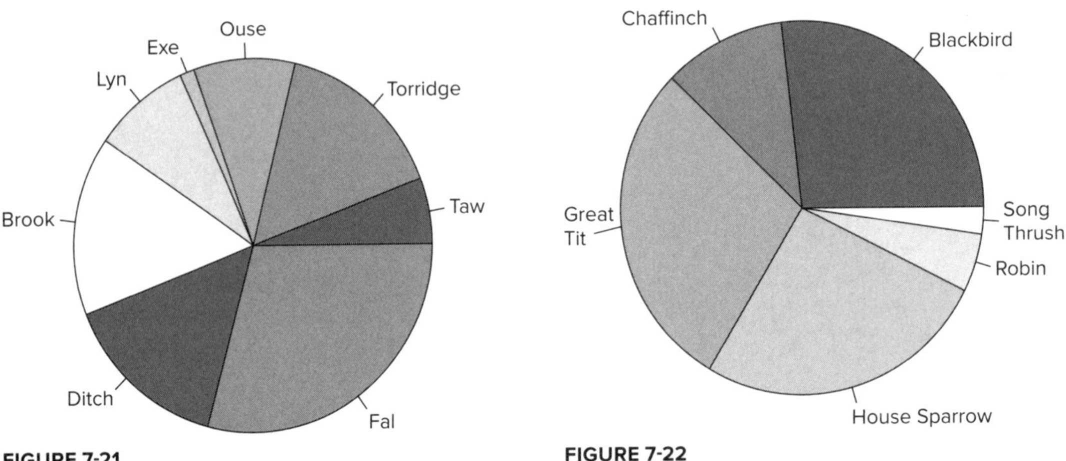

FIGURE 7-21

FIGURE 7-22

If you have your data in a data frame rather than a matrix, you get an error message like the following when you try to pie chart a row:

```
> mf[1,]
  Length Speed Algae  NO3 BOD
1     20    12    40 2.25 200

> pie(mf[1,])
Error in pie(mf[1, ]) : 'x' values must be positive.
```

When you look at the row in question, it looks as though it ought to be fine but it is not. You can make it work by converting the data into a matrix. You can do this transiently using the `as.matrix()` command. In the following example you see a data frame and the command used to make a pie chart from the first row:

```
> head(mf)
```

```
  Length Speed Algae  NO3 BOD
1     20    12    40 2.25 200
2     21    14    45 2.15 180
3     22    12    45 1.75 135
4     23    16    80 1.95 120
5     21    20    75 1.95 110
6     20    21    65 2.75 120

> pie(as.matrix(mf[1,]), labels = names(mf), col = pc)
```

You can, of course, make pie charts from the columns, in which case you specify the column you require using the `[row, column]` syntax. The following command examples both produce a pie chart of the `Hedgerow` column in the `bird` data you saw previously:

```
> pie(bird[,2])
> pie(bird[,'Hedgerow'])
```

You can add other instructions to the `pie()` command that will give you more control over the final graph. You learn some of these later in Chapter 11. Next you look at the Cleveland dot plot.

CLEVELAND DOT CHARTS

An alternative to the pie chart is a Cleveland dot plot. All data that might be presented as a pie chart could also be presented as a bar chart or a dot plot. You can create Cleveland dot plots using the `dotchart()` command. If your data are a simple vector of values then like the `pie()` command, you simply give the vector name. To create labels you need to specify them. In the following example you have a vector of numeric values and a vector of character labels; you met these earlier when making a pie chart:

```
> data11; data8
 [1] 3 5 7 5 3 2 6 8 5 6 9 8
 [1] "Jan" "Feb" "Mar" "Apr" "May" "Jun" "Jul" "Aug" "Sep" "Oct" "Nov" "Dec"

> dotchart(data11, labels = data8)
```

The resulting dot plot looks like Figure 7-23.

You can alter various parameters, but first you look at a more complex data example. Your data are best used if they are in the form of a matrix; the following data are bird observations that you used in previous examples:

```
> bird
              Garden Hedgerow Parkland Pasture Woodland
Blackbird         47       10       40       2        2
Chaffinch         19        3        5       0        2
Great Tit         50        0       10       7        0
House Sparrow     46       16        8       4        0
Robin              9        3        0       0        2
Song Thrush        4        0        6       0        0
```

With a pie chart you must create a pie for the rows or the columns separately; with the dot plot you can do both at once. You can create a basic dot plot grouped by columns simply by specifying the matrix name like so:

```
> dotchart(bird)
```

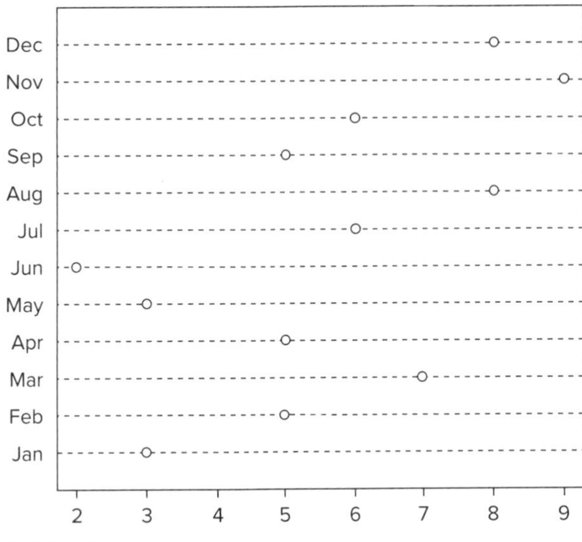

FIGURE 7-23

This produces a dot plot that looks like Figure 7-24.

Here you see the data shown column by column; in other words, you see the data for each column broken down by rows. You might choose to view the data in a different order; by transposing the matrix you could display the rows as groups, broken down by column:

```
> dotchart(t(bird))
```

You use the `t()` command to transpose the matrix and produce your dot plot, which looks like Figure 7-25.

You can alter a variety of parameters on your plot. Table 7-3 illustrates a few of the options.

TABLE 7-3: Some of the Additional Graphical Instructions for the dotchart() Command

INSTRUCTION	EXPLANATION
`color = 'color.name'`	Specifies the color to use for the plotted points and the main labels.
`gcolor = 'color.name'`	Specifies the color to use for the group labels and group data points (if specified).
`gdata = group.data`	You can specify a value to show for each group. This will typically be a mean.
`lcolor = 'gray'`	Specifies the color to use for the lines across the chart.
`cex = 1`	Sets the character expansion factor for points and all the labels on the axes.

INSTRUCTION	EXPLANATION
`xlab = 'text.label'`	You can specify a label/title for the x-axis. You can also specify one for the y-axis, but this will usually overlap the labels from the data. Use the `title()` command afterwards to place an axis label/title.
`xlim = c(start, end)`	Sets the limits of the x-axis. You specify the start and end points.
`bg = 'color.name'`	Sets the background color for the plotting symbols. This works only with an open style of symbol.
`pch = 21`	Sets the plotting character. Use a numerical value or a character from the keyboard in quotes.

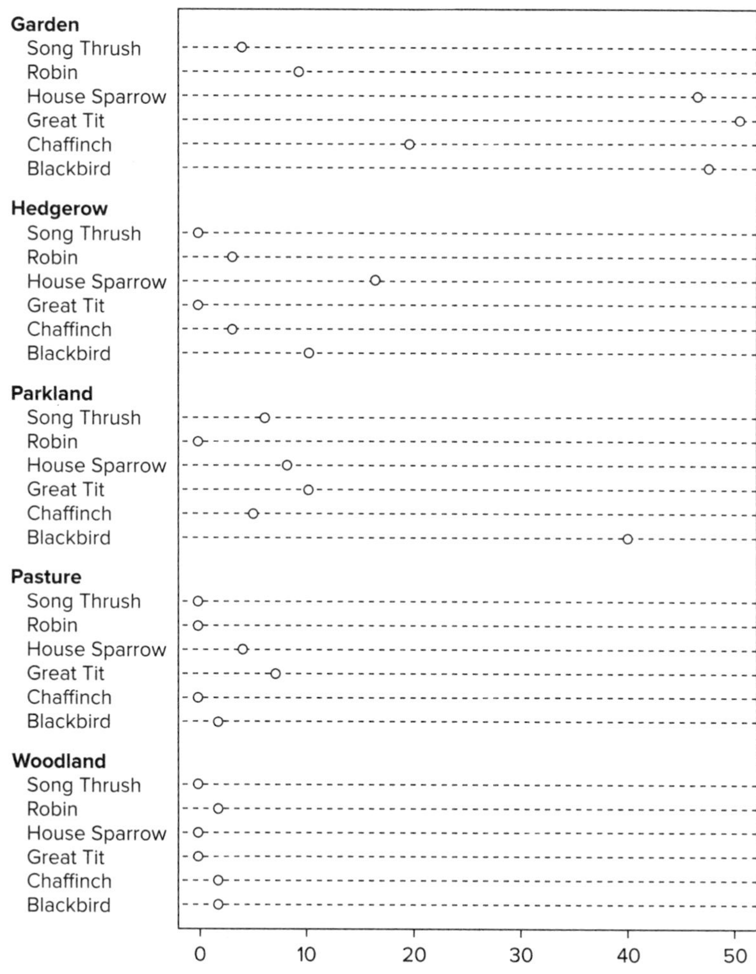

FIGURE 7-24

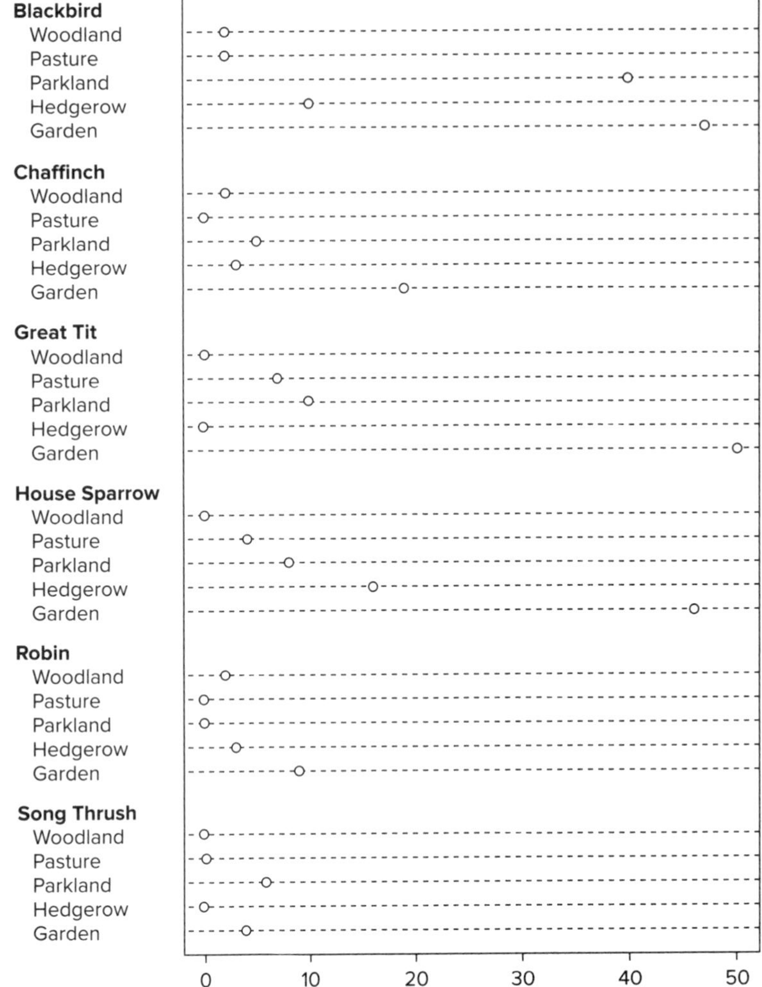

FIGURE 7-25

The following command utilizes some of these instructions to produce the graph shown in Figure 7-26:

```
> dotchart(bird, color = 'gray30', gcolor = 'black', lcolor = 'gray30',
cex = 0.8, xlab = 'Bird Counts', bg = 'gray90', pch = 21)
```

If you try to add a y-axis label using the `ylab` instruction you find it overlaps the labels you already have. So, if you want an overall y-axis title you can specify it later using the `title()` command, when it will be pushed a bit wider and not overlap.

You can also specify a mathematical function to apply to each of the groups using the `gdata =` instruction. It makes the most sense to use an average of some kind—mean or median— to do so. In the following example the mean is used as a grouping function:

```
> dotchart(bird, gdata = colMeans(bird), gpch = 16, gcolor = 'blue')
> mtext('Grouping = mean', side =3, adj = 1)
```

```
> title(main = 'Bird species and Habitat')
> title(xlab = 'Bird abundance')
```

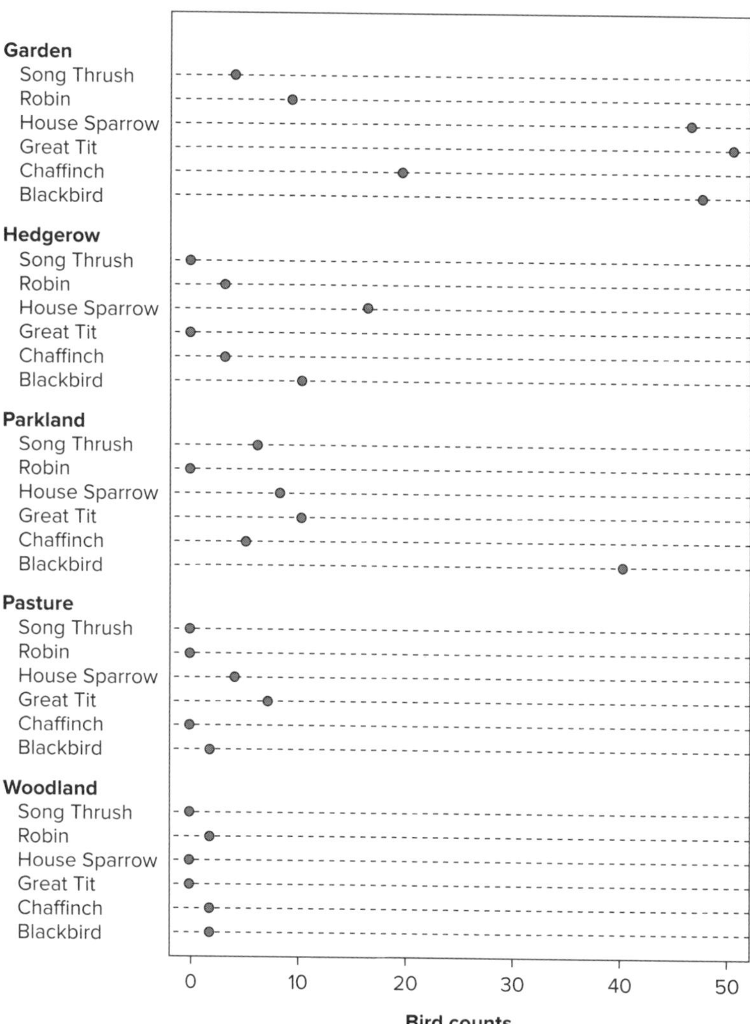

FIGURE 7-26

The first line of command draws the main plot; the mean is taken by using the `colMeans()` command and applying it to the plot via the `gdata =` instruction. You can specify this function in any way that produces the values you require, and you can simply specify the values explicitly using the `c()` command.

The plotting character of the grouping function is set using the `gpch =` instruction; here, a filled circle is used to make it stand out from the main points. The `gcolor =` instruction sets a color for the grouping points (and labels).

The second line adds some text to the margin of the plot; here you use the top axis (`side = 1` is the bottom, `2` is the left) and adjust the text to be at the extreme end (`adj = 0` would be at the other end of the axis). The final two lines add titles to the main plot and the value axis (the x-axis); the resulting plot looks like Figure 7-27.

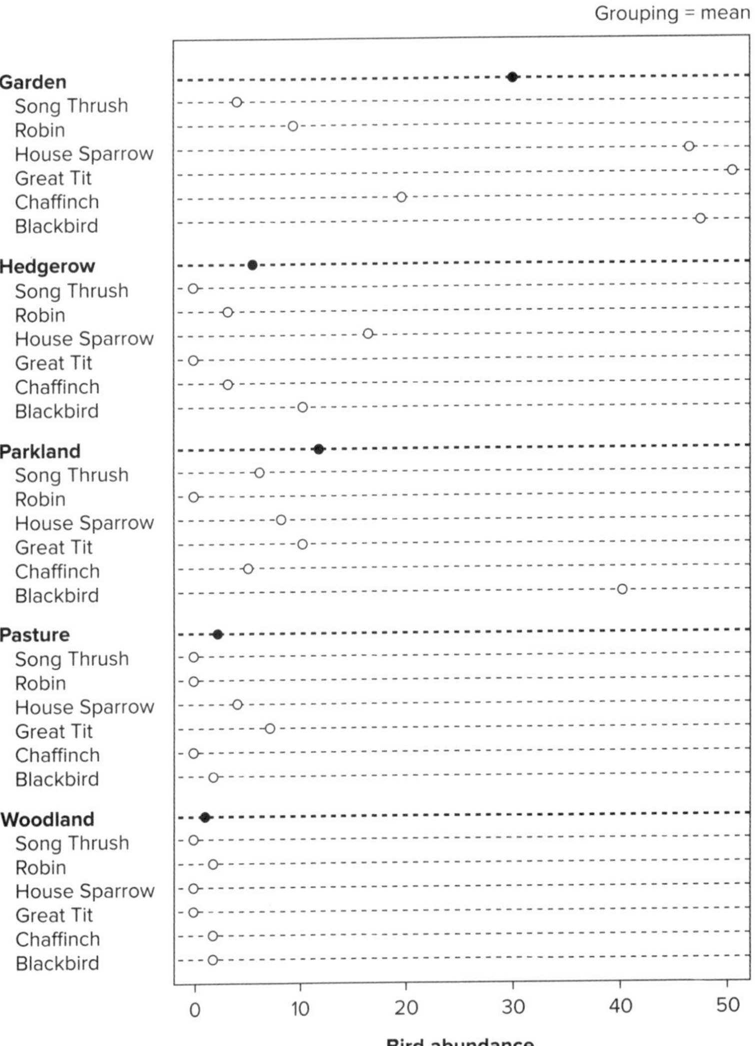

FIGURE 7-27

The `mtext()` command is explored more thoroughly in Chapter 11, where you learn more about customizing and tweaking your graphs.

The Cleveland dot chart is a powerful and useful tool that is generally regarded as a better alternative to a pie chart. Data that can be presented as a pie chart can also be shown as a bar chart, and this type of graph is one of the most commonly used graphs for many purposes. Bar charts are the subject of the next section.

BAR CHARTS

The bar chart is suitable for showing data that fall into discrete categories. In Chapter 3, "Starting Out: Working with Objects," you met the histogram, which is a form of bar chart. In that example each bar of the graph showed the number of items in a certain range of data values. Bar charts are widely used because they convey information in a readily understood fashion. They are also flexible and can show items in various groupings.

You use the `barplot()` command to produce bar charts. In this section you see how to create a range of bar charts, and also have a go at making some for yourself by following the activity at the end.

Single-Category Bar Charts

The simplest plot can be made from a single vector of numeric values. In the following example you have such an item:

```
> rain
 [1] 3 5 7 5 3 2 6 8 5 6 9 8
```

To make a bar chart you use the `barplot()` command and specify the vector name in the instruction like so:

```
barplot(rain)
```

This makes a primitive plot that looks like Figure 7-28.

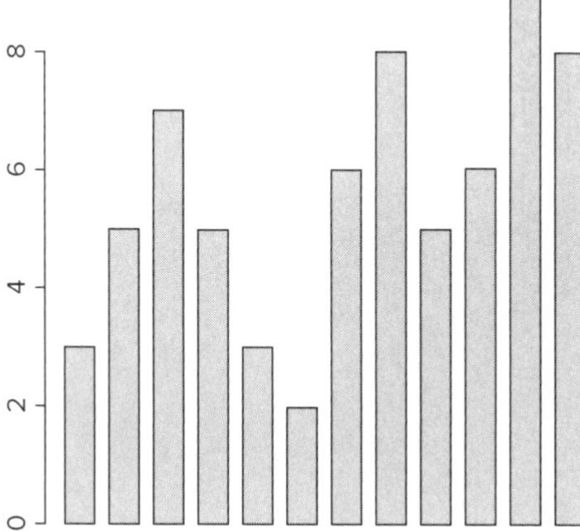

FIGURE 7-28

The chart has no axis labels of any kind, but you can add them quite simply. To start with, you can make names for the bars; you can use the `names =` instruction to point to a vector of names. The following example shows one way to do this:

```
> rain
 [1] 3 5 7 5 3 2 6 8 5 6 9 8
> month
 [1] "Jan" "Feb" "Mar" "Apr" "May" "Jun" "Jul" "Aug" "Sep" "Oct" "Nov" "Dec"
> barplot(rain, names = month)
```

In this case you already had a vector of names; if you did not, you could make one or simply specify the names using a `c()` command like so:

```
> barplot(rain, names = c('Jan', 'Feb', 'Mar', 'Apr', 'May', 'Jun', 'Jul',
'Aug', 'Sep', 'Oct', 'Nov', 'Dec'))
```

If your vector has a `names` attribute, the `barplot()` command can read the names directly. In the following example you set the `names()` of the `rain` vector and then use the `barplot()` command:

```
> rain ; month
 [1] 3 5 7 5 3 2 6 8 5 6 9 8
 [1] "Jan" "Feb" "Mar" "Apr" "May" "Jun" "Jul" "Aug" "Sep" "Oct" "Nov" "Dec"
> names(rain) = month
> rain
Jan Feb Mar Apr May Jun Jul Aug Sep Oct Nov Dec
  3   5   7   5   3   2   6   8   5   6   9   8
> barplot(rain)
```

Now the bars are neatly labeled with the names taken from the data itself (see Figure 7-29).

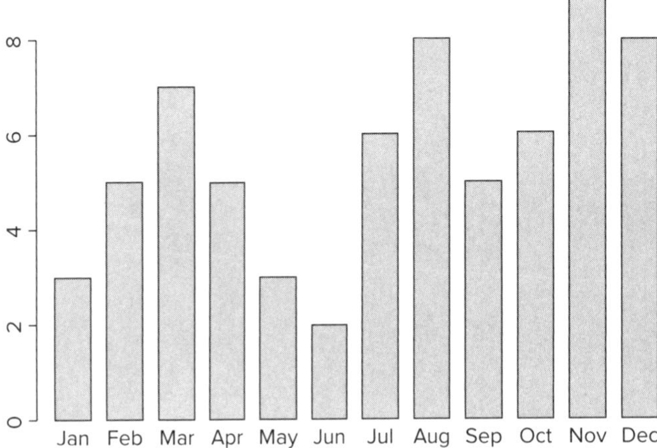

FIGURE 7-29

To add axis labels you can use the `xlab` and `ylab` instructions. You can use these as part of the command itself or add the titles later using the `title()` command. In the following example you create axis titles afterwards:

```
> barplot(rain)
> title(xlab = 'Month', ylab = 'Rainfall cm')
```

The y-axis is a bit short in Figure 7-29. You can alter the y-axis scale using the `ylim` instruction as shown in the following example:

```
> barplot(rain, xlab = 'Month', ylab = 'Rainfall cm', ylim = c(0,10))
```

Recall that you need two parts to set the y-axis limit: a starting point and an ending point. Once you implement these two parts your plot looks more reasonable (see Figure 7-30).

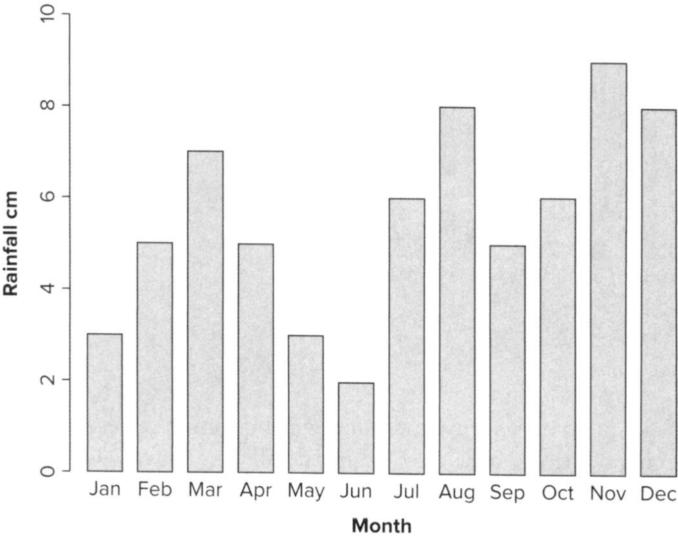

FIGURE 7-30

You can alter the color of the bars using the `col =` instruction. If you want to "ground" the plot, you could add a line under the bars using the `abline()` command:

```
> abline(h = 0)
```

In other words, you add a horizontal line at 0 on the y-axis. If you would rather have the whole plot enclosed in a box, you could use the `box()` command. You can also use the `abline()` command to add gridlines:

```
> abline(h = seq(1, 9, 2), lty = 2, lwd = 0.5, col = 'gray70')
```

In this example you create horizontal lines using a sequence, the `seq()` command. With this command you specify the starting value, the ending value, and the interval. The `lty =` instruction sets the line to be dashed, and the `lwd =` instruction makes the lines a bit thinner than usual. Finally, you set the gridline colors to be a light gray using the `col =` instruction. When you put the commands together, you end up with something like this:

```
> barplot(rain, xlab = 'Month', ylab = 'Rainfall cm', ylim = c(0,10),
col = 'lightblue')
> abline(h = seq(1,9,2), lty = 2, lwd = 0.5, col = 'gray40')
> box()
```

The final graph looks like Figure 7-31.

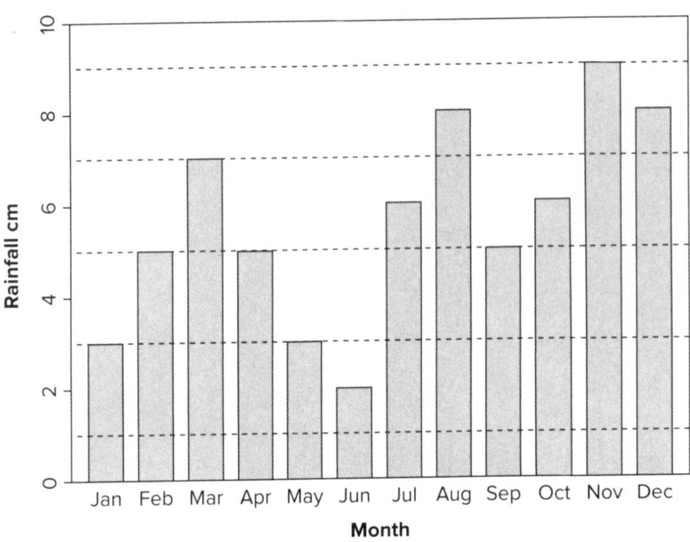

FIGURE 7-31

Previously you looked at the `hist()` command as a way to produce a histogram of a vector of numeric data. You can create a bar chart of frequencies that is superficially similar to a histogram by using the `table()` command:

```
> table(rain)
rain
2 3 5 6 7 8 9
1 2 3 2 1 2 1
```

Here you see the result of using the `table()` command on your data; they are split into a simple frequency table. The first row shows the categories (each relating to an actual numeric value), and the second row shows the frequencies in each of these categories. If you create a `barplot()` using these data, you get something like Figure 7-32, which is produced using the following commands:

```
> barplot(table(rain), ylab = 'Frequency', xlab = 'Numeric category')
> abline(h = 0)
```

In Figure 7-32 you also added axis labels and drew a line under the bars with the `abline()` command.

When your data are part of a data frame, you must extract the vector you require using the `$` syntax or the `attach()` or `with()` commands. In the following example you see a data frame with two columns. In this case you also have row names, and you can use these to create name labels for the bars:

```
> fw
         count speed
Taw          9     2
Torridge    25     3
Ouse        15     5
Exe          2     9
Lyn         14    14
Brook       25    24
```

```
Ditch        24    29
Fal          47    34

> barplot(fw$count, names = row.names(fw), ylab = 'Invertebrate Count' ,
col = 'tan')
> abline(h = 0)
```

This produces the plot shown in Figure 7-33.

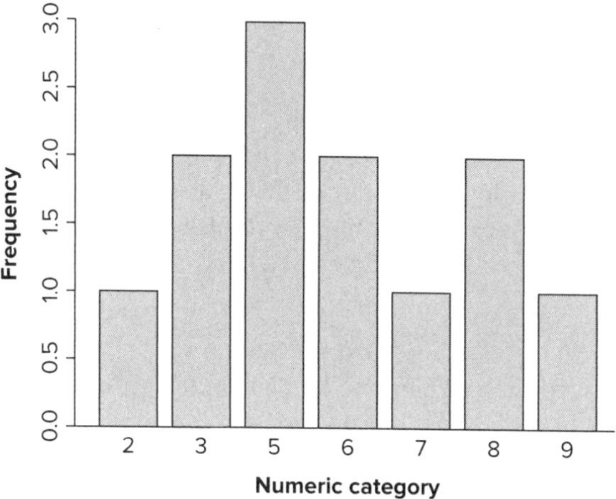

FIGURE 7-32

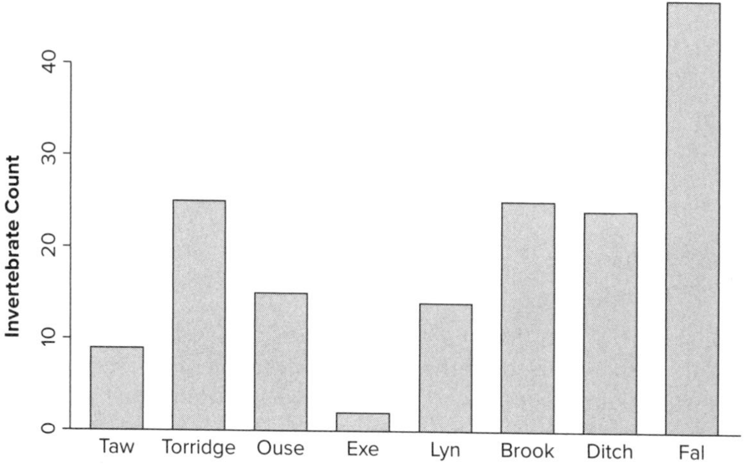

FIGURE 7-33

If you try to plot the entire data frame, you get an error message:

```
> barplot(fw)
Error in barplot.default(fw) : 'height' must be a vector or a matrix
```

This fails because you need a matrix and you only have a data frame. You need to convert the data into a matrix in some way; you can use the `as.matrix()` command to do this "on the fly" and leave the original data unchanged like so:

```
> barplot(as.matrix(fw))
```

This is not a particularly sensible plot. If you try it you see that you get two bars, one for each column in the data. Each of these bars is a stack of several sections, each relating to a row in the data. This kind of bar chart is called a *stacked bar chart*, and you look at this in the next section.

Multiple Category Bar Charts

The examples of bar charts you have seen so far have all involved a single "row" of data, that is, all the data relate to categories in one group. It is also quite common to have several groups of categories. You can display these groups in several ways, the most primitive being a separate graph for each group. However, you can also arrange your bar chart so that these multiple categories are displayed on one single plot. You have two options: stacked bars and grouped bars.

Stacked Bar Charts

If your data contains several groups of categories, you can display the data in a bar chart in one of two ways. You can decide to show the bars in blocks (or groups) or you can choose to have them stacked.

The following example makes this clearer and shows a matrix data object that you have used in previous examples:

```
> bird
              Garden Hedgerow Parkland Pasture Woodland
Blackbird         47       10       40       2        2
Chaffinch         19        3        5       0        2
Great Tit         50        0       10       7        0
House Sparrow     46       16        8       4        0
Robin              9        3        0       0        2
Song Thrush        4        0        6       0        0

> barplot(bird)
```

The plot that results is a stacked bar chart (see Figure 7-34) and each column has been split into its row components.

You can use any of the additional instructions that you have seen so far to modify the plot. For example, you could alter the scale of the y-axis using the `ylim =` instruction or add axis labels using the `xlab =` and `ylab =` instructions (the `title()` command can also do this). The colors shown are shades of gray, and at present there is no indication of which color belongs to which row category. You can alter this with some simple instructions, as you see in the next section.

Grouped Bar Charts

When your data are in a matrix with several rows, the default bar chart is a stacked chart as you saw in the previous section. You can force the elements of each column to be unstacked by using the `beside = TRUE` instruction as shown in the following code (the default is set to `FALSE`):

```
> barplot(bird, beside = TRUE, ylab = 'Total birds counted', xlab = 'Habitat')
```

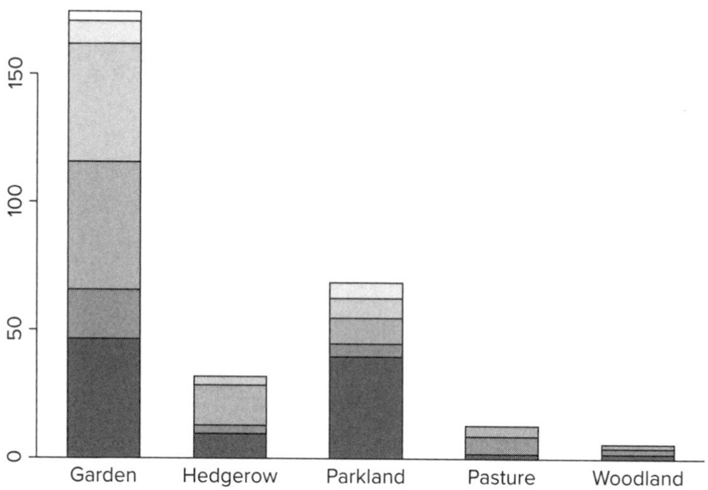

FIGURE 7-34

The resulting graph now shows as a series of bars in each of the column categories (Figure 7-35).

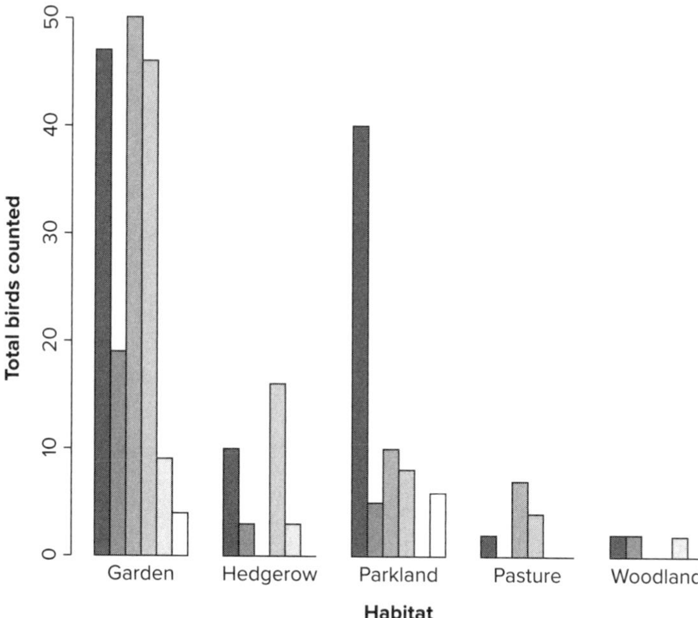

FIGURE 7-35

This is useful, but it is even better to see which bar relates to which row category; for this you need a legend. You can add one automatically using the `legend =` instruction, which creates a default legend that takes the colors and text from the plot itself:

```
> barplot(bird, beside = TRUE, legend = TRUE)
> title(ylab = 'Total birds counted', xlab = 'Habitat')
```

The legend appears at the top right of the plot window, so if necessary you must alter the y-axis scale using the `ylim =` instruction to get it to fit. In this case, the legend fits comfortably without any additional tweaking (see Figure 7-36).

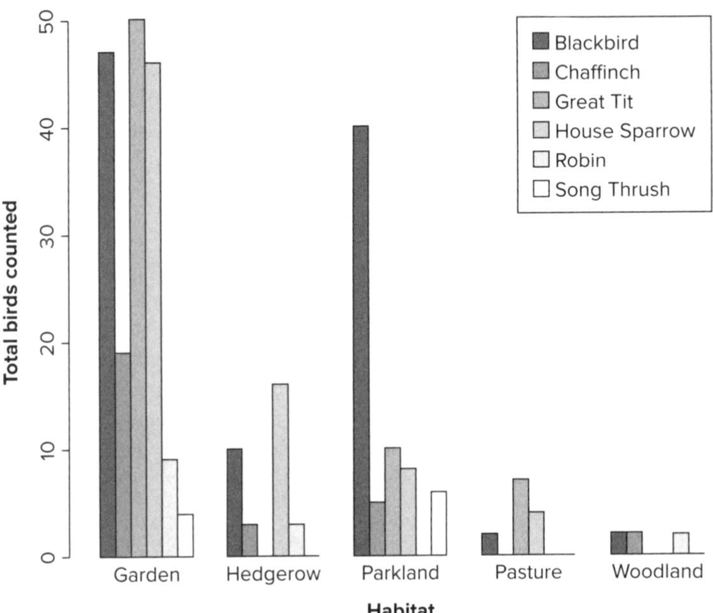

FIGURE 7-36

You can alter the colors of the bars by supplying a vector of names in some way; you might create a separate vector or simply type the names into a `col =` instruction:

```
> barplot(bird, beside = TRUE, legend = TRUE, col = c('black', 'pink',
'lightblue', 'tan', 'red', 'brown'))
```

If you would rather have the row categories as the main bars, split by column, you need to rotate or transpose the matrix of data. You can use the `t()` command to do this like so:

```
> barplot(t(bird), beside = TRUE, legend = TRUE, cex.names = 0.8,
col = c('black', 'pink', 'lightblue', 'tan', 'red', 'brown'))
> title(ylab = 'Bird Count', xlab = 'Bird Species')
```

Notice this time that another instruction has been used; `cex.names = 0.8` makes the bar name labels a bit smaller so that they display neatly (see Figure 7-37). The character expansion of the names uses a numerical value like you used previously with the `cex =` instruction; a value >1 makes text larger and <1 makes it smaller.

So far you have seen how to create simple bar charts, and also how to make multiple category charts. It is also possible to display the bars horizontally rather than vertically, which is the subject of the next section.

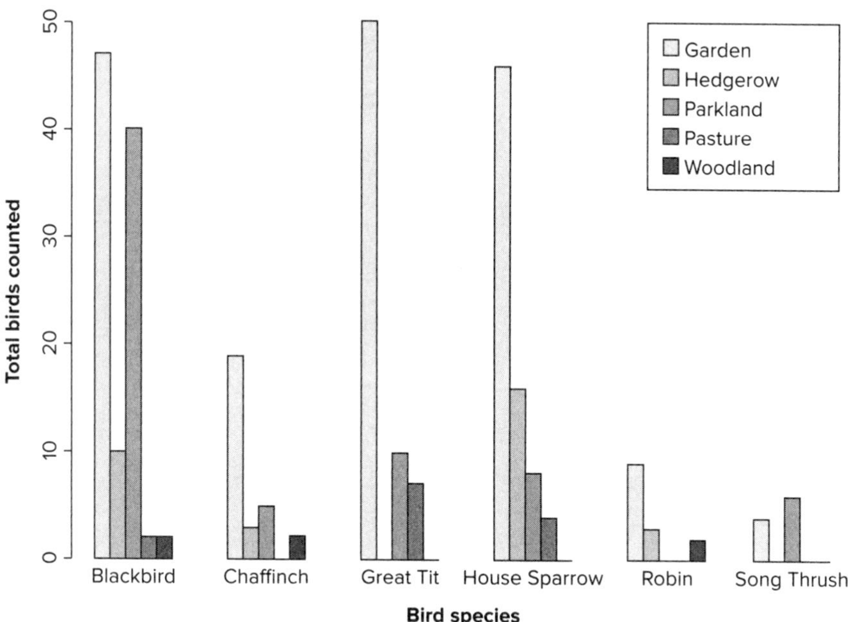

FIGURE 7-37

Horizontal Bars

You can make the bars horizontal rather than the default vertical using the `horiz = TRUE` instruction (this is slightly different from the instruction in the `boxplot()` command):

```
> barplot(bird, beside = TRUE, horiz = TRUE)
```

You can use all the regular instructions that you have met previously on horizontal bar charts as well, for example:

```
> bccol = c('black', 'pink', 'lightblue', 'tan', 'red', 'brown')
> barplot(bird, beside = TRUE, legend = TRUE, horiz = TRUE,
xlim = c(0, 60), col = bccol)
> title(ylab = 'Habitat', xlab = 'Bird count')
```

The bars now point horizontally (see Figure 7-38). The y-axis and x-axis are the original orientation as far as the commands are concerned; here the x-axis is rescaled to make it a bit longer.

The `title()` command was used here, but you could have specified the axis labels using `xlab =` and `ylab =` instructions as part of the `barplot()` command. In either case, you need to remember that the `xlab` instruction refers to the bottom axis and the `ylab` to the side (left) axis.

Bar Charts from Summary Data

In the examples of bar charts that you have seen so far the data were already in their final format. However, in many cases you will have raw data that you want to summarize and plot in one go. You will most often want to calculate and present average values of various columns of a data object. You already encountered some of the commands that can produce summary results in Chapter 3; these include `colMeans()`, `apply()`, and `tapply()`.

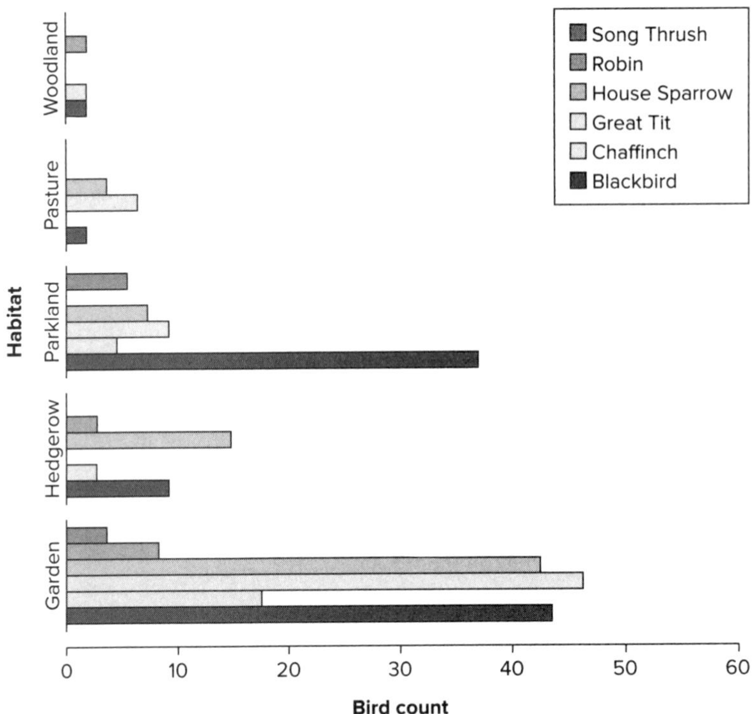

FIGURE 7-38

When you have a data frame containing multiple samples, you may want to present a bar chart of their means. The following example shows a data frame composed of several columns of numeric data; the columns are samples (that is, repeated observations). You want to summarize each one using a mean and create a bar plot of those means:

```
> head(mf)
  Length Speed Algae  NO3 BOD
1     20    12    40 2.25 200
2     21    14    45 2.15 180
3     22    12    45 1.75 135
4     23    16    80 1.95 120
5     21    20    75 1.95 110
6     20    21    65 2.75 120
```

You can make your bar plot in one of two ways. You can use the `colMeans()` command to extract the mean values, which you then plot:

```
> barplot(colMeans(mf), ylab = 'Measurement')
```

You can also use the `apply()` command to extract the mean values:

```
> barplot(apply(mf, 2, mean, na.rm = T), ylab = 'Measurement')
```

The `apply()` command is a little more complex than `colMeans()` but is also more powerful; you could chart the median values, for example:

```
> barplot(apply(mf, 2, median, na.rm = T), ylab = 'Median Measurement')
```

This produces a simple plot (see Figure 7-39).

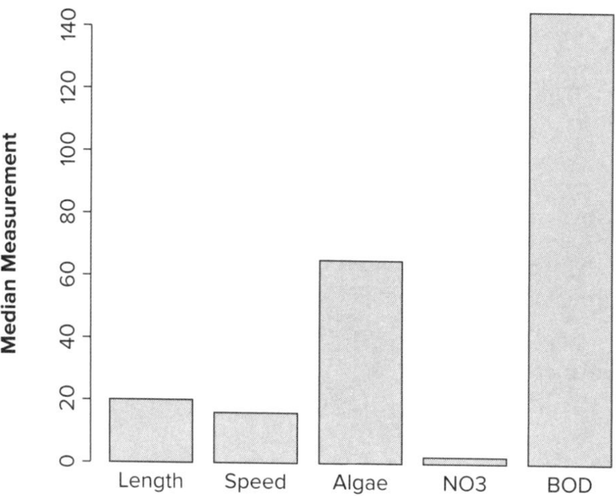

FIGURE 7-39

You can alter additional parameters to customize your `barplot()`; you return to some of these in Chapter 11. For the time being you can try the following activity to help familiarize yourself with the basics.

TRY IT OUT Creating Some Bar Charts

Available for download on Wrox.com

Use the `hoglouse`, `bf`, and `bfs` data objects from the `Beginning.RData` file for this activity, which you will use to create some bar charts. The other data you will need, `VADeaths` is built in to R.

1. Look at the `hoglouse` data, which are part of the `Beginning.RData` file. The data are in a data frame, which has two columns: `fast` and `slow`. Each row is also named with the sampling site. Create a bar chart of the `fast` data as follows:

```
> barplot(hoglouse$fast, names = rownames(hoglouse), cex.names = 0.8,
col = 'slategray')
> abline(h=0)
> title(ylab = 'Hoglouse count', xlab = 'Sampling site')
```

2. Now look at the `VADeaths` data; these come built into R, and you can view them simply by typing the name. Create a bar chart of these data. Because you have five rows you can also create five colors to help pick out the categories. Add a legend to the plot:

```
> cols = c('brown', 'tan', 'sienna', 'thistle', 'yellowgreen')
> barplot(VADeaths, legend = TRUE, col = cols)
> title(ylab = 'Death rates per 1000 per year')
```

3. Re-plot the `VADeaths` data, but this time use grouped bars:

```
> barplot(VADeaths, legend = T, beside = TRUE, col = cols)
> title(ylab = 'Death rates per 1000 per year')
```

4. Now plot the `VADeaths` data again, but this time make the bars horizontal:

```
> barplot(VADeaths, legend = T, beside = TRUE, col = cols, horiz = TRUE)
> title(xlab = 'Death rates per 1000 per year')
```

5. Look at the `bf` data object. You have three columns representing three samples. Draw a bar chart of the medians for the three samples:

```
> barplot(apply(bf, 2, median, na.rm=T), col = 'lightblue')
> abline(h=0)
> title(ylab = 'Butterfly Count', xlab = 'Site')
```

6. Look now at the `bfs` data object. These data are in a two-column format with a response variable and a predictor variable. Create a new bar chart using the median values:

```
> barplot(tapply(bfs$count, bfs$site, FUN = median), col = 'lightblue',
xlab = 'Site', ylab = 'Butterfly abundance')
> abline(h=0)
```

How It Works

When you plot a single column from a data object, you need to use the `$` syntax to enable R to read the column. You could also use the `apply()` or `with()` commands, but in any event you need to specify the names of the data explicitly.

You can specify colors as a vector of names, which are referred to by the `col =` instruction. By default, multiple categories are represented as stacked bars; to display them as grouped bars you use `beside = TRUE` as an instruction.

If horizontal bars are required, you can use the `horizontal = TRUE` instruction. However, the left axis is still the y-axis and the bottom axis is still the x-axis.

When you have data that require summarizing before plotting, you can embed the summary command within the `barplot()` command. Where data are in multiple-column format, the `apply()` command is a flexible option, but when you have data in a `response ~ predictor` layout you use the `tapply()` command.

Bar charts are a useful and flexible tool, as you have seen. The options covered in this section enable you to produce bar charts for a wide range of uses. You can add other instructions to the `barplot()` command, which you learn about in Chapter 11.

COPY GRAPHICS TO OTHER APPLICATIONS

Being able to create a graphic is a useful start, but generally you need to transfer the graphs you have made to another application. You may need to make a report and want to include a graph in a word processor or presentation. You may also want to save a graph as a file on disk for later use. In this section you learn how to take the graphs you create and use them in other programs, and also how to save them as graphics files on disk.

Use Copy/Paste to Copy Graphs

When you make a graph using R, it opens in a separate window. If your graphic is not required to be of publication quality, you can use `copy` to transfer the graphic to the clipboard and then use `paste` to place it in another program. This method works for all operating systems, and the image you get depends on the size of the graphics window and the resolution of your screen.

If you need a higher quality image, or if you simply need the graphic to be saved as a graphic file to disk, the method you need to employ depends upon the operating system you are using.

Save a Graphic to Disk

You can save a graphics window to a file in a variety of formats, including PNG, JPEG, TIFF, BMP, and PDF. The way you save your graphics depends on the operating system you are using. In Windows and Mac the GUI has options to save graphics. In Linux you can save graphics only via direct commands, which you can also use in the other operating systems too, of course.

Windows

The Windows GUI allows you to save graphics in various file formats. Once you have created your graphic, click the graphics window and select Save As from the File menu. You have several options to choose from (see Figure 7-40).

The JPEG option gives you the opportunity to select from one of several compressions. The TIFF option produces the largest files because no compression is used. The PNG option is useful because the PNG file format is widely used and file sizes are quite small.

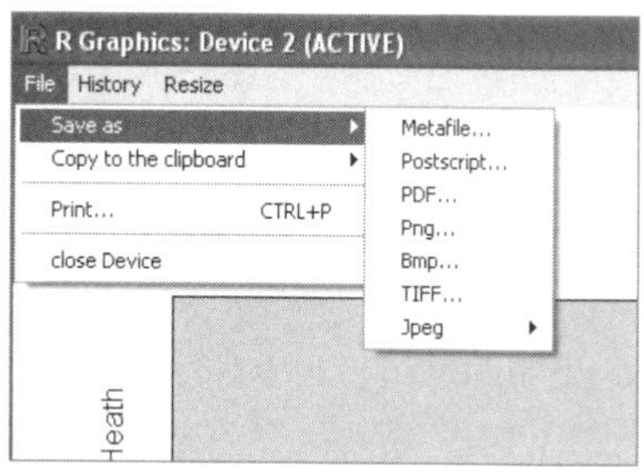

FIGURE 7-40

You can also use commands typed from the keyboard to save graphics files to disk, and you can go about this in several ways. The simplest is via the `dev.copy()` command. This command copies the contents of the graphics window to a file; you designate the type of file and the filename. To finish the process you type the `dev.off()` command. In the following example the graphics window is saved using the `png` option:

```
> dev.copy(png, file = 'R graphic test.eps')
png:R graphic test.eps
                     3
> dev.off()
windows
      2
```

When you use this command the filename has to be specified in quotes and the file extension needs to be given. By default the file is saved in your working directory. You can see what the current working directory is using the `getwd()` command that you met in Chapter 2, "Starting Out: becoming Familiar With R."

Macintosh

The Macintosh GUI allows graphics to be saved as PDF files. PDF is handled easily by Mac and is seen as a good option because PDF graphics can be easily rescaled. To save the graphics window, click the window to select it and then choose Save or Save As from the File menu.

If you want to save your graphic in another format, you need to use the `dev.copy()` and `dev.off()` commands, much like you saw in the preceding section regarding the Windows operating system.

In the following example, the graphics window is saved as a PDF file. The filename must be specified explicitly—the default location for saved files is the current working directory.

```
> dev.copy(pdf, file = 'Rplot eg.pdf')
pdf
  3
> dev.off()
quartz
     2
```

You can save a file to another location by specifying the full path as part of the filename.

Linux

In Linux, R is run via the terminal and you cannot save a graphics file using "point and click" options. To save a graphics file you need to use commands typed from the keyboard.

The `dev.copy()` and `dev.off()` commands are used in the same way as described for Windows or Mac operating systems. You start by creating the graphic you require and then use the `dev.copy()` command to write the file to disk in the format you want. The process is completed by typing the `dev.off()` command.

In the following example, the graphics window is saved as a PNG file. The file is saved to the default working directory—if you want it to go somewhere else, you need to specify the path in full as part of the filename.

```
> dev.copy(png, file = 'R graphic test.eps')
png
  3
> dev.off()
X11cairo
       2
```

The `dev.copy()` command requires you to specify the type of graphic file you require and the filename. You can specify other options to alter the size of the final image. The most basic options are summarized in Table 7-4.

TABLE 7-4: Additional Graphics Instructions for the dev.copy() Command

INSTRUCTION	EXPLANATION
`width = 480`	The width of the plot in pixels; defaults to 480.
`height = 480`	The height of the plot in pixels; defaults to 480.
`res = NA`	The resolution in pixels per inch. Effectively, the default works out to be 72.
`quality = 75`	The compression to use for JPEG.

The additional instructions shown in Table 7-4 enable you to alter the size of the final graphic. The `dev.copy()` command enables you to make a graphics file quickly, but the final results are not always exactly the same as you may see on the screen. If you use a high resolution and large size, the text labels may appear as a different size from your graphics window. You find out more about graphics and the finer control of various elements of your plots in Chapter 11.

NOTE *The* `res =` *instruction alters the resolution of the image, but this information is not stored in the resulting file! If you open the file later in a graphics program, you may see the resolution recorded as 72 dpi simply because most programs assume this resolution if none is given.*

SUMMARY

- R has extensive graphical capabilities. The basic graphs that can be produced can be customized extensively.
- The box-whisker plot is produced using the `boxplot()` command. This kind of graph is especially useful for comparing samples.
- The scatter plot is created using the `plot()` command and is used to compare two continuous variables. The `plot()` command also enables you to do this for multiple pairs of variables.
- The `plot()` command can produce line plots and the `axis()` command can create customized axes from categorical variables.
- Pie charts are used to display proportional data via the `pie()` command.
- The Cleveland dot chart is a recommended alternative to a pie chart and is created using the `dotchart()` command.
- Bar charts are used to display values across a range of categories. The `barplot()` command can produce simple bar charts, or multiple category charts using stacked columns or grouped columns.
- Graphics can be copied to the clipboard, or saved directly to disk as a graphics file.

EXERCISES

Available for download on Wrox.com

You can find the answers to the exercises in Appendix A.

Use the `bfs` data object from the `Beginning.RData` file for Exercise 5. The other data objects are all built into R.

1. Look at the `warpbreaks` data that comes built into R. Create a box-whisker plot of the number of `breaks` for the different `tension`. Make the plot using horizontal bars and display the whiskers to the extreme range of the data. How can you draw this graph to display only a single type of wool?

2. The `trees` data come as part of R. The data is composed of three columns: the `Girth` of black cherry trees (in inches), the `Height` (in feet), and the `Volume` of wood (in cubic feet). How can you make a scatter plot of girth versus volume and display a line of best-fit? Modify the axes so that the intercept is shown clearly. Use an appropriate plotting symbol and colors to help make the chart more “interesting.”

3. The `HairEyeColor` data are built into R. These data are in the form of a table, which has three dimensions. As well as the usual rows and columns, the table is split in two: `Male` and `Female`. Use the “males” table to create a Cleveland dot chart of the data. Use the mean values for the columns as an additional grouping summary result.

4. Look at the `HairEyeColor` data again. This time make a bar chart of the “female” data. Add a legend and make the colors reflect the different hair colors.

5. The `bfs` data object is part of the example data used in this book (you can download the entire data set from the companion website). Here you have two columns, butterfly abundance (`count`) and habitat (`site`). How can you draw a bar chart of the median butterfly abundance from the three sites?

▶ WHAT YOU LEARNED IN THIS CHAPTER

TOPIC	KEY POINTS
Box-whisker plots: `boxplot()`	The box-whisker plot is useful because it presents a lot of information in a compact manner. The data can be specified as separate vectors, an entire data frame (or matrix), or using the formula syntax. You can present bars vertically (the default) or horizontally.
Scatter plots: `plot()`	The basic `plot()` command is used to make scatter plots. You can specify the data in several ways, as two vectors or as a formula. If you specify an entire data frame (or matrix), a multiple correlation plot may result (see next item).
Multiple correlation plots: `pairs()`	The `pairs()` command is used to create multiple correlation plots, which also result when the `plot()` command is used on a multiple column data object.
Line plots and custom axes: `axis()`	The `plot()` command produces points by default, but you can force the points to "join up" or create a line-only plot using the `type =` instruction. The `axis()` command is used to create customized axes, especially useful when your x-axis is categorical rather than a continuous variable.
Pie charts: `pie()`	Pie charts are used to display proportional data. The `pie()` command can produce pie charts, which can be customized to display data counter-clockwise, for example.
Cleveland dot charts: `dotchart()`	The Cleveland dot chart is an alternative to the pie chart. It is more flexible because you can present multiple categories in one plot and can also display group summary results (for example, mean).
Bar charts: `barplot()`	The bar chart is used to display data over various categories. The `barplot()` command can produce simple bar charts and can make stacked charts from multiple category data. These data can also be displayed with bars grouped rather than stacked. A legend can be added.
Graphical instructions: `xlab` `ylab` `main` `xlim` `ylim` `pch` `cex` `lty` `lwd`	Many graphical instructions can be applied to plots. Axis labels can be specified and the scales altered. The plotting symbols and colors can be changed as well as the size of the symbols and labels.
Colors: `colors()`	Many colors are available to customize graphics. The `colors()` command shows the names of the colors available and the `col` instruction is most commonly used to apply these to the graphic.

continues

▶ WHAT YOU LEARNED IN THIS CHAPTER *(continued)*

TOPIC	KEY POINTS
Axis titles: `title()`	The `title()` command can add titles to axes as well as to the main plot. This is an alternative to specifying the titles from the main graphical command, which can be helpful to make commands shorter.
Lines on charts: `abline()`	The `abline()` command can be used to add lines to charts. Horizontal or vertical lines can be added. The other use is to take results from linear models to determine slope and intercept, thus adding a line of best-fit. The lines can be customized to have different styles, colors, and weights.
Marginal text: `mtext()`	The `mtext()` command can add extra text to the margins of plots. Text can be added to any axis and placed left, right, or centered.

Moving and saving graphics:
`dev.copy()`
`dev.off()`
	Graphics windows can be copied to the clipboard and transferred to most other programs. The Windows and Mac GUI also permit the saving of graphics via a menu. Graphics can be saved to a file on disk using the `dev.copy()` command. This can create a range of graphics formats (for example: PNG, JPEG, TIFF, PDF) and you can also alter the size and resolution of the files. The process is finalized using the `dev.off()` command.

8

Formula Notation and Complex Statistics

WHAT YOU WILL LEARN IN THIS CHAPTER:

- How to use formula notation for simple hypothesis tests
- How to use formula notation in graphics
- How to carry out analysis of variance (ANOVA)
- How to conduct post-hoc tests
- How the formula syntax can be used to define complex analytical models
- How to carry out complex ANOVA
- How to draw summary graphs of ANOVA
- How to create interaction plots

The R program has great analytical power, but so far most of the situations you have seen are fairly simple. In the real world things are usually more complicated, and you need a way to describe these more complex situations to enable R to carry out the appropriate analytical routines. R uses a special syntax to enable you to define and describe more complex situations. You have already met the ~ symbol; you used this as an alternative way to describe your data when using simple hypothesis testing (see Chapter 6, "Simple Hypothesis Testing") and also when visualizing the results graphically (see Chapter 7, "Introduction to Graphical Analysis"). This formula syntax permits more complex models to be defined, which is useful because much of the data you need to analyze is itself more complex than simply a comparison of two samples. In essence, you put the response variables on the left of the ~ and the predictor variable(s) on the right, like so:

```
response ~ predictor.1 + predictor.2
```

In this syntax you simply link the predictor variables using a + sign, but you are able to specify more complicated arrangements, as you will see. This chapter begins with a quick review of the formula syntax in relation to those two-sample tests and graphs you met before. After that you move on to look at analysis of variance, which is one of the most widely used of all statistical methods.

EXAMPLES OF USING FORMULA SYNTAX FOR BASIC TESTS

Some commands enable you to specify your data in one of two forms. When you carry out a `t.test()` command, for example, you can specify your data as two separate vectors or you can use the formula notation described in the introduction:

```
t.test(sample.1, sample.2)
t.test(response ~ predictor, data = data.name)
```

In the first example you specify two numeric vectors. If these vectors are contained in a data frame, you must "extract" them in some fashion using the $ syntax or the `attach()` or `with()` commands. The options are shown in the following example:

```
> grass2
  mow unmow
1  12     8
2  15     9
3  17     7
4  11     9
5  15    NA

> t.test(grass2$mow, grass2$unmow)

> with(grass2, t.test(mow, unmow))

> attach(grass2)
> t.test(mow, unmow)
> detach(grass2)
```

In this case you have a simple data frame with two sample columns. If you have your data in a different form, you can use the formula notation:

```
> grass
  rich graze
1   12   mow
2   15   mow
3   17   mow
4   11   mow
5   15   mow
6    8 unmow
7    9 unmow
8    7 unmow
9    9 unmow

> t.test(rich ~ graze, data = grass)
```

This time the following data frame contains two columns, but now the first is the response variable and the second is a grouping variable (the predictor factor) which contains exactly two levels (`mow` and unmow). Where you have more than two levels, you can use the subset = instruction to pick out the two you want to compare:

```
> summary(bfs)
     count             site   
 Min.   : 3.000   Arable: 9  
 1st Qu.: 5.000   Grass :12  
 Median : 8.000   Heath : 8  
 Mean   : 8.414              
 3rd Qu.:11.000              
 Max.   :21.000              

> t.test(count ~ site, data = bfs, subset = site %in% c('Grass', 'Heath'))
```

In this example you see that you have a data frame with two columns; the first is numeric and is the response variable. The second column contains three different levels of the grouping variable.

When you are looking at correlations you can use a similar approach. This time, however, you are not making a prediction about which variable is the predictor and which is the response, but merely looking at the correlation between the two:

```
cor.test(vector.1, vector.2)
cor.test(~ vector.1 + vector.2, data = data.name)
```

In the first case you specify the two numeric vectors you want to correlate as individuals. In the second case you use the formula notation, but now you leave the left of the ~ blank and put the two vectors of interest on the right joined by + sign.

In the following activity you can practice using the formula notation by carrying out some basic statistical tests.

TRY IT OUT Use Formula Notation for Some Basic Stats Tests

Available for download on Wrox.com

Use the grass and hog data objects from the Beginning.RData file for this activity; you also use the trees code which is built-into R. You will use these data to practice the use of the formula notation in some basic statistical tests.

1. Look at the grass data object. The grass data comprises two columns: the first is called rich and is numeric. The second is called graze and is a factor comprised of two levels. Use the str() and summary() commands to examine the data like so:

```
> str(grass)
> summary(grass)
```

2. Carry out a Student's t-test to see if there is a difference in species richness between the two grazing treatments:

```
> t.test(rich ~ graze, data = grass)
```

3. Now look at the hog data. Use the str() and summary() commands to see that this data frame has two columns; one is numeric and the other is a factor with two levels:

```
> str(hog)
> summary(hog)
```

4. Use a U-test to see if there is a difference in the abundance of hoglouse between the `fast` and `slow` samples:

```
> wilcox.test(count ~ site, data = hog, exact = FALSE)
```

5. Now look at the `trees` data. Use the `names()` command to see the column names as well as the `summary()` and `str()` commands to look at the data structure:

```
> names(trees)
> str(trees)
> summary(trees)
```

These data comprise three columns of numerical data: `Girth`, `Height`, and `Volume`.

6. Use the Pearson product moment method to see if there is a correlation between `Girth` and `Height`:

```
> cor.test(~ Girth + Height, data = trees, method = 'pearson')
```

How It Works

The `str()` command enables you to see the structure of the data object, confirming in the first two data examples that you have a factor variable and a numerical variable. The `summary()` command is an alternative that enables you to see, for example, that there are unequal numbers of observations for the two levels of the factor variable.

The formula syntax enables you to describe the situation and carry out the analysis without having to use the `attach()` or `with()` commands. In most cases, you place the response variable to the left of the ~ and predictor variables to the right. In the correlation case, nothing goes before the ~ and the two variables to correlate go after. This reinforces the notion that you are conducting a simple correlation between two numeric variables and not making any assumptions about cause and effect.

FORMULA NOTATION IN GRAPHICS

When you need to present a graph of your results, you can use the formula syntax as an alternative to the basic notation. This makes the link between the analysis and graphical presentation a little clearer, and can also save you some typing.

You met the formula notation in regard to some graphs in Chapter 7, "Introduction to Graphical Analysis." For example, if you want to create a box-whisker plot of your `t.test()` result, you could specify the elements to plot using exactly the same notation as for running the test. Your options are as follows:

```
boxplot(vector.1, vector.2)
```

or

```
boxplot(response ~ predictor.1 + predictor.2, data = data.name)
```

In these examples the first case shows that you can specify multiple vectors to plot simply by listing them separately in the `boxplot()` command. The second example shows the formula notation where you specify the response variable to the left of the ~ and put the predictor variables to the right. In this example, the predictor variables are simply joined using the + sign, but you have a range of options as you see shortly.

In the case of a simple x, y, scatter plot you also have two options for creating a plot:

```
plot(x.variable, y.variable)
```

or

```
plot(y.variable ~ x.variable, data = data.name)
```

Notice how the x variable is specified first in the first example, but in the second case it is, of course, the predictor variable, so it goes to the right of the ~.

Whenever you carry out a statistical test, it is important that you also produce a graphical summary. In the following activity you will produce some graphs based on the statistical tests you carried out in the previous activity.

TRY IT OUT Use Formula Notation to Create Graphical Summaries of Stats Tests

Available for download on Wrox.com

Use the grass and hog data objects from the Beginning.RData file for this activity; you also use the trees code which is built-into R. You will use these data to practice use of the formula notation in producing summary graphs.

1. Earlier you looked at the grass data and carried out a t-test on these data. Now create a boxplot to illustrate the result:

   ```
   > boxplot(rich ~ graze, data = grass, col = 'lightgreen')
   ```

2. Your graph needs some titles for the axes and perhaps a main title, so use the title() command to add them:

   ```
   > title(ylab = 'Species Richness', xlab = 'Grazing Treatment',
   main = 'Species richness and grazing')
   ```

3. Now look at the hog data. Earlier you conducted a U-test on these data. Create a boxplot to illustrate the result, and make the bars run horizontally:

   ```
   > boxplot(count ~ site, data = hog, col = 'tan', horizontal = TRUE)
   ```

4. This graph needs labeling so use the title() command to add titles to the axes as well as a main title:

   ```
   > title(ylab = 'Water speed', xlab = 'Hoglouse abundance',
    main = 'Hoglouse and water speed')
   ```

5. The trees data comprise three columns of numerical data. Use the formula notation to produce a pairs plot showing the relationship between all the variables:

   ```
   > pairs(~Girth + Height + Volume, data = trees)
   ```

6. The formula syntax can produce a scatter plot of two variables, so use it to compare Girth and Height from the trees data:

   ```
   > plot(~ Girth + Height, data = trees)
   ```

7. Now use a more conventional formula to create the scatter plot. This time add custom titles to the axes and alter the plotting characters:

   ```
   > plot(Girth ~ Height, data = trees, col = 'blue', cex = 1.2,
   xlab = 'Height (ft.)', ylab = 'Girth (in.)')
   ```

8. Add a main title to the scatter plot using the `title()` command:

```
> title(main = 'Girth and Height in Black Cherry')
```

How It Works

The formula notation enables you to specify the layout of the graph, meaning that you do not need to use the `attach()` or `with()` commands, nor use the `$` symbol. All the regular graphics commands can be used. When plotting a chart with bars/boxes horizontally, the `ylim` and `xlim` instructions refer to the left and bottom axes, respectively.

The scatter plot can handle the syntax in two ways. In the first case you used `~ predictor1 + predictor2`, and so on. This made a pairs plot in the first case showing all the predictors plotted against one another. When only two predictors are used you get a regular scatter plot, but notice that the first predictor becomes the x-axis and the second becomes the y-axis. The arrangement is different when you use the `response ~ predictor` syntax, when the response becomes the y-axis and the predictor becomes the x-axis. Note also that the `plot()` command takes the names of the columns and uses them to make axis titles, so you need to specify them explicitly as part of the command if you want something different.

ANALYSIS OF VARIANCE (ANOVA)

Analysis of variance is an analytical method that allows for comparison of multiple samples. It is probably the most widely used of all statistical methods and can be very powerful. As the name suggests, the method looks at variance, comparing the variability between samples to the variability within samples. This is not a book about statistics, but the analysis of variance is such an important topic that it is important that you can carry out ANOVA.

The formula notation comes in handy especially when you want to carry out analysis of variance or linear regression, see Chapter 10, "Regression (Linear Modeling)." You are able to specify quite complex models that describe your data and carry out the analyses you require. You can think of analysis of variance as a way of linear modeling. R has an `lm()` command that carries out linear modeling, including ANOVA (see Chapter 10). However, you also have a "convenience" command, `aov()`, that gives you an extra option or two that are useful for ANOVA.

One-Way ANOVA

You can use the `aov()` command to carry out analysis of variance. In its simplest form you would have several samples to compare. The following example shows a simple data frame that comprises three columns of numerical data:

```
> head(bf)
  Grass Heath Arable
1     3     6     19
2     4     7      3
3     3     8      8
4     5     8      8
5     6     9      9
6    12    11     11
```

To run the aov() command you must have your data in a different layout from the one in the preceding example, which has a column for each numerical sample. With aov () you require one response variable (the numerical data) and one predictor variable that contains several levels of a factor (character labels). To achieve this required layout you need to convert your data using the stack() command.

Stacking the Data before Running Analysis of Variance

The stack() command can be used in several ways, but all produce the same result; a two-column data frame. If your original data have multiple numeric vectors, you can create a stacked data frame simply by giving the name of the original data like so:

```
> stack(bf)
  values   ind
1      3 Grass
2      4 Grass
3      3 Grass
4      5 Grass
5      6 Grass
6     12 Grass
...
```

This produces two columns, one called values and the other called ind. If you give your new stacked data frame a name, you can then apply new names to these columns using the names() command:

```
> bfs = stack(bf)
> names(bfs) = c('count', 'site')
```

However, there is a potential problem because the original data may contain NA items. You do not really want to keep these, so you can use the na.omit() command to eliminate them like so:

```
> bfs = na.omit(stack(bf))
> names(bfs) = c('count', 'site')
```

This eliminates any NA items and is stacked in the appropriate manner. In most cases like this you want to keep all the samples, but you can select some of them and create a subset using the select = instruction as part of the stack() command like so:

```
> names(bf)
[1] "Grass"  "Heath"  "Arable"
> tmp = stack(bf, select = c('Grass', 'Arable'))
> summary(tmp)
     values           ind
 Min.   : 3.00   Arable:12
 1st Qu.: 4.00   Grass :12
 Median : 8.00
 Mean   : 8.19
 3rd Qu.:11.00
 Max.   :21.00
 NA's   : 3.00
```

In this case you create a new item for your stacked data; you require only two of the samples and so you use the select = instruction to name the columns required in the stacked data (note that the selected samples must be in quotes). Here you can see from the summary that you have transferred some NA items to the new data frame, so you should re-run the commands again but use na.omit() like so:

```
> tmp = na.omit(stack(bf, select = c('Grass', 'Arable')))
> summary(tmp)
     values            ind    
 Min.   : 3.00   Arable: 9  
 1st Qu.: 4.00   Grass :12  
 Median : 8.00              
 Mean   : 8.19              
 3rd Qu.:11.00              
 Max.   :21.00              
```

Now you can see that the NA items have been stripped out. Notice, too, that the headings are values and ind, which is not necessarily what you want (although they are logical and informative). You instead need to use the names() command to alter the headings, giving the names you require like so:

```
> names(tmp) = c('count', 'site')
```

Note that the names are given in quotes (single or double, as long as they match). Once your data are in the right format, you are ready to move on to carrying out the analysis.

Running aov() Commands

Once you have your data in the appropriate layout, you can proceed with the analysis of variance using the aov() command. You use the formula notation to indicate which is the response variable and which is the predictor variable, like so:

```
> summary(bfs)
     count             site   
 Min.   : 3.000   Arable: 9  
 1st Qu.: 5.000   Grass :12  
 Median : 8.000   Heath : 8  
 Mean   : 8.414              
 3rd Qu.:11.000              
 Max.   :21.000              

> bfs.aov = aov(count ~ site, data = bfs)
```

In this example, you can see that you have a numeric vector as the response variable (count) and a predictor variable (site) comprising three levels (Arable, Grass, Heath). This kind of analysis, where you have a single predictor variable, is called one-way ANOVA. To see the result you simply type the name of the result object you created:

```
> bfs.aov
Call:
   aov(formula = count ~ site, data = bfs)

Terms:
                   site Residuals
Sum of Squares  55.3678  467.6667
Deg. of Freedom       2        26

Residual standard error: 4.241130
Estimated effects may be unbalanced
```

This gives you some information, but to see the classic ANOVA table of results you need to use the `summary()` command like so:

```
> summary(bfs.aov)
            Df Sum Sq Mean Sq F value Pr(>F)
site         2  55.37  27.684  1.5391 0.2335
Residuals   26 467.67  17.987
```

Here you can now see the calculated F value and the overall significance.

Simple Post-hoc Testing

You can carry out a simple post-hoc test using the Tukey Honest Significant Difference test via the `TukeyHSD()` command, as shown in the following example:

```
> TukeyHSD(bfs.aov)
  Tukey multiple comparisons of means
    95% family-wise confidence level

Fit: aov(formula = count ~ site, data = bfs)

$site
                  diff       lwr      upr     p adj
Grass-Arable -3.166667 -7.813821 1.480488 0.2267599
Heath-Arable -1.000000 -6.120915 4.120915 0.8788816
Heath-Grass   2.166667 -2.643596 6.976929 0.5110917
```

In this case you have a simple one-way ANOVA and the result of the post-hoc test shows the pair-by-pair comparisons. The result shows the difference in the means, the lower and upper 95 percent confidence intervals, and the p-value for the pairwise comparison.

Extracting Means from aov() Models

Once you have conducted your analysis of variance and the post-hoc test, you may want to see what the mean values are for the various levels of the predictor variable. One way to do this is to use the `model.tables()` command; this shows you the means or effects for your ANOVA:

```
> model.tables(bfs.aov, type = 'effects')
Tables of effects

 site
    Arable  Grass  Heath
     1.586 -1.580 0.5862
rep  9.000 12.000 8.0000

> model.tables(bfs.aov, type = 'means')
Tables of means
Grand mean

8.413793

 site
    Arable  Grass Heath
        10  6.833     9
rep      9 12.000     8
```

The default is to display the effects, so if you do not specify `type = 'means'`, you get the effects. You can also compute the standard errors of the contrasts by using the `se = TRUE` instruction. However, this works only with a balanced design, which the current example lacks. Chapter 9 looks at other ways to examine the means and other components of a complex analysis.

In the following activity you use analysis of variance to examine some data; you will need to rearrange the data into an appropriate layout before carrying out ANOVA, a post-hoc test and a graphical summary.

TRY IT OUT Carry Out a One-Way Analysis of Variance

Available for download on Wrox.com

Use the `cw` data object from the `Beginning.RData` file for this activity, which you will be analyzing using ANOVA.

1. Look at the `cw` data; they are modified from an example that you can find in R. These data are weights of chicks (in grams) that have been fed different diets. Each column shows a different diet with the weight of each chick at the end of the experiment.
2. To carry out analysis of variance you need to rearrange the data into a two-column format with a response column and a predictor column. Do this using the `stack()` command, but because the data contain `NA` items, they will need to be removed first:

```
> cws = na.omit(stack(cw))
```

3. The resulting data frame has plain headings, so use the `names()` command to rename them to something more descriptive:

```
> names(cws) = c('weight', 'diet')
```

4. Now use the `str()` and `summary()` commands to see what the data comprise:

```
> str(cws)
> summary(cws)
```

This shows that you have a numerical response variable and a multi-level predictor variable.

5. Create a graphical summary of the data to help visualize the situation:

```
> boxplot(weight ~ diet, data = cws)
```

6. Conduct a one-way ANOVA on the data:

```
> cws.aov = aov(weight ~ diet, data = cws)
> summary(cws.aov)
```

7. There is a significant effect of diet on the weight, but not all diets are the same. A post-hoc analysis will reveal where the important differences lie:

```
> TukeyHSD(cws.aov)
```

How It Works

The `aov()` command needs the data to be in a format with a response column and a predictor column. The `stack()` command reassembles the data into the correct layout. You need to use the `na.omit()` command to strip out `NA` items.

Now you can use the formula syntax to draw a boxplot of the data. The ANOVA is run using similar syntax with the aov() command. The post-hoc test shows that only the diets D1 and D3 are significantly different.

Two-Way ANOVA

In a basic one-way ANOVA you have one response variable and one predictor variable, but you may come across a situation in which you have more than one predictor variable, as in the following example:

```
> pw
   height    plant water
1       9 vulgaris    lo
2      11 vulgaris    lo
3       6 vulgaris    lo
4      14 vulgaris   mid
5      17 vulgaris   mid
6      19 vulgaris   mid
7      28 vulgaris    hi
8      31 vulgaris    hi
9      32 vulgaris    hi
10      7   sativa    lo
11      6   sativa    lo
12      5   sativa    lo
13     14   sativa   mid
14     17   sativa   mid
15     15   sativa   mid
16     44   sativa    hi
17     38   sativa    hi
18     37   sativa    hi
```

In this case you have a data frame with three columns; the first column is the response variable called height, and the next two columns are predictor variables called plant and water. This is a fairly simple example, but if you had more species and more treatments it becomes increasingly harder to present the data as separate samples. It is much more sensible, then, to use the layout as you see here with each column representing a certain variable. If you use the summary() command it appears that you have a balanced experimental design like so:

```
> summary(pw)
     height              plant    water
 Min.   : 5.00   sativa  :9    hi :6
 1st Qu.: 9.50   vulgaris:9    lo :6
 Median :16.00                 mid:6
 Mean   :19.44
 3rd Qu.:30.25
 Max.   :44.00
```

The summary() command shows you that each of the predictor variables is split into equal numbers of observations (replicates). You now have to take into account two predictor variables, so your

ANOVA model becomes a little more complicated. You can use one of the two following commands to carry out an analysis of variance for these data:

```
> pw.aov = aov(height ~ plant + water, data = pw)
> pw.aov = aov(height ~ plant * water, data = pw)
```

In the first command you specify the response variable to the left of the ~ and put the predictor variables to the right, separated by a + sign. This takes into account the variability due to each factor separately. In the second command the predictor variables are separated with a * sign, and this indicates that you also want to take into account interactions between the predictor variables. You could also have written this command in the following manner:

```
> pw.aov = aov(height ~ plant + water + plant:water, data = pw)
```

The third term in the ANOVA model is `plant:water`, which indicates the interaction between these two predictor variables. If you run the `aov()` command with the interaction included, you get the following result:

```
> pw.aov = aov(height ~ plant * water, data = pw)
> summary(pw.aov)
            Df  Sum Sq Mean Sq  F value    Pr(>F)
plant        1   14.22   14.22   2.4615  0.142644
water        2 2403.11 1201.56 207.9615 4.863e-10 ***
plant:water  2  129.78   64.89  11.2308  0.001783 **
Residuals   12   69.33    5.78
~DH-
Signif. codes:  0 '***' 0.001 '**' 0.01 '*' 0.05 '.' 0.1 ' ' 1
```

Again you see the "classic" ANOVA table, but now you have rows for each of the predictor variables as well as the interaction.

COMPARING ANOVA RESULTS WITH ANOVA()

If you have more than one `aov()` result (based on the same data) you can use the `anova()` command to compare them. For example:

```
> pw.aov1 = aov(height ~ plant + water, data = pw)
> pw.aov2 = aov(height ~ plant * water, data = pw)
> anova(pw.aov1, pw.aov2)
Analysis of Variance Table

Model 1: height ~ plant + water
Model 2: height ~ plant * water
  Res.Df     RSS Df Sum of Sq      F   Pr(>F)
1     14 199.111
2     12  69.333  2    129.78 11.231 0.001783 **
```

You can see that the second result (with the interaction) is significantly different from the first result (without the interaction).

More about Post-hoc Testing

You can run the Tukey post-hoc test on a two-way ANOVA as you did before, using the `TukeyHSD()` command like so:

```
> TukeyHSD(pw.aov)
  Tukey multiple comparisons of means
    95% family-wise confidence level

Fit: aov(formula = height ~ plant * water, data = pw)

$plant
                      diff       lwr       upr    p adj
vulgaris-sativa -1.777778 -4.246624 0.6910687 0.142644

$water
             diff        lwr       upr     p adj
lo-hi  -27.666667 -31.369067 -23.96427 0.0000000
mid-hi -19.000000 -22.702401 -15.29760 0.0000000
mid-lo   8.666667   4.964266  12.36907 0.0001175

$`plant:water`
                                diff         lwr        upr     p adj
vulgaris:hi-sativa:hi      -9.333333 -15.92559686  -2.741070 0.0048138
sativa:lo-sativa:hi       -33.666667 -40.25893019 -27.074403 0.0000000
vulgaris:lo-sativa:hi     -31.000000 -37.59226353 -24.407736 0.0000000
sativa:mid-sativa:hi      -24.333333 -30.92559686 -17.741070 0.0000004
vulgaris:mid-sativa:hi    -23.000000 -29.59226353 -16.407736 0.0000007
sativa:lo-vulgaris:hi     -24.333333 -30.92559686 -17.741070 0.0000004
vulgaris:lo-vulgaris:hi   -21.666667 -28.25893019 -15.074403 0.0000014
sativa:mid-vulgaris:hi    -15.000000 -21.59226353  -8.407736 0.0000684
vulgaris:mid-vulgaris:hi  -13.666667 -20.25893019  -7.074403 0.0001702
vulgaris:lo-sativa:lo       2.666667  -3.92559686   9.258930 0.7490956
sativa:mid-sativa:lo        9.333333   2.74106981  15.925597 0.0048138
vulgaris:mid-sativa:lo     10.666667   4.07440314  17.258930 0.0016201
sativa:mid-vulgaris:lo      6.666667   0.07440314  13.258930 0.0469217
vulgaris:mid-vulgaris:lo    8.000000   1.40773647  14.592264 0.0149115
vulgaris:mid-sativa:mid     1.333333  -5.25893019   7.925597 0.9810084
```

You get a more lengthy output here compared to a one-way ANOVA because you are now looking at a lot more pairwise comparisons. You can reduce the output slightly by specifying which of the terms in your model you want to compare. You use the `which` instruction to give (in quotes) the name of the model term (or terms) you are interested in, as shown in the following example:

```
> TukeyHSD(pw.aov, which = 'water')
> TukeyHSD(pw.aov, which = c('plant', 'water'))
> TukeyHSD(pw.aov, which = 'plant:water')
```

In the first case you look for pairwise comparisons for the `water` treatment only. In the second case you look at both the `water` and `plant` factors independently. In the final case you look at the interaction term only. The results show you the difference in means and also the lower and upper confidence intervals at the 95 percent level. You can alter the confidence level using the `conf.level =` instruction like so:

```
> TukeyHSD(pw.aov, which = 'plant:water', conf.level = 0.99)
  Tukey multiple comparisons of means
    99% family-wise confidence level

Fit: aov(formula = height ~ plant * water, data = pw)

$`plant:water`
                              diff         lwr         upr     p adj
vulgaris:hi-sativa:hi    -9.333333 -17.8003408  -0.8663259 0.0048138
sativa:lo-sativa:hi     -33.666667 -42.1336741 -25.1996592 0.0000000
vulgaris:lo-sativa:hi   -31.000000 -39.4670075 -22.5329925 0.0000000
...
```

Now you can see the lower and upper confidence intervals displayed at the 99 percent level.

You can also alter the way that the output is displayed; if you look at the first column you see it is called `diff`, because it is the difference in means. You can force this to assume a positive value and to take into account the increasing average in the sample by using the `ordered = TRUE` instruction. The upshot is that the results are reordered in a subtly different way. Also, the significant differences are those for which the lower end point is positive:

```
> TukeyHSD(pw.aov, which = 'plant:water', ordered = TRUE)
  Tukey multiple comparisons of means
    95% family-wise confidence level
    factor levels have been ordered

Fit: aov(formula = height ~ plant * water, data = pw)

$`plant:water`
                              diff         lwr       upr     p adj
vulgaris:lo-sativa:lo     2.666667 -3.92559686  9.258930 0.7490956
sativa:mid-sativa:lo      9.333333  2.74106981 15.925597 0.0048138
vulgaris:mid-sativa:lo   10.666667  4.07440314 17.258930 0.0016201
vulgaris:hi-sativa:lo    24.333333 17.74106981 30.925597 0.0000004
sativa:hi-sativa:lo      33.666667 27.07440314 40.258930 0.0000000
sativa:mid-vulgaris:lo    6.666667  0.07440314 13.258930 0.0469217
vulgaris:mid-vulgaris:lo  8.000000  1.40773647 14.592264 0.0149115
vulgaris:hi-vulgaris:lo  21.666667 15.07440314 28.258930 0.0000014
sativa:hi-vulgaris:lo    31.000000 24.40773647 37.592264 0.0000000
vulgaris:mid-sativa:mid   1.333333 -5.25893019  7.925597 0.9810084
vulgaris:hi-sativa:mid   15.000000  8.40773647 21.592264 0.0000684
sativa:hi-sativa:mid     24.333333 17.74106981 30.925597 0.0000004
vulgaris:hi-vulgaris:mid 13.666667  7.07440314 20.258930 0.0001702
sativa:hi-vulgaris:mid   23.000000 16.40773647 29.592264 0.0000007
sativa:hi-vulgaris:hi     9.333333  2.74106981 15.925597 0.0048138
```

In this case, you see that the differences in the means are all positive. The lower confidence intervals that are positive produce significant p-values and the negative ones do not.

Graphical Summary of ANOVA

You should always produce a graphical summary of your analyses; a suitable graph for an ANOVA is the box-whisker plot, which you can produce using the `boxplot()` command. The instructions you give to this command to produce the plot mirror those you used to carry out the `aov()` as you can see in the following example:

```
> pw.aov = aov(height ~ plant * water, data = pw)
> boxplot(height ~ plant * water, data = pw, cex.axis = 0.9)
> title(xlab = 'Interaction', ylab = 'Height')
```

In this case an extra instruction, `cex.axis = 0.9`, is added to the `boxplot()` command. This makes the axis labels a bit smaller so they fit and display better (recall that values greater than 1 make the labels bigger and values less than 1 make them smaller). The `title()` command has also been used to add some meaningful labels to the plot, which looks like Figure 8-1.

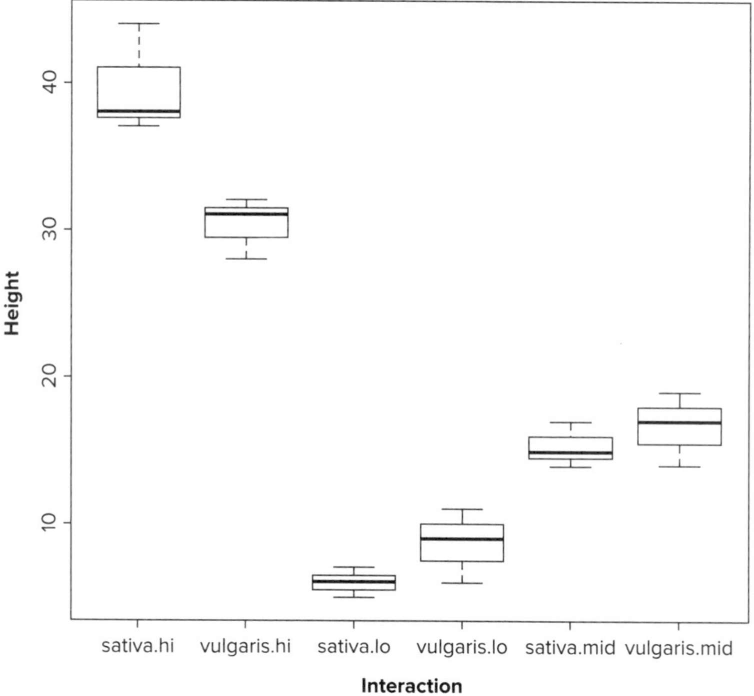

FIGURE 8-1

If you compare the boxes to the results of the `TukeyHSD()` command, you can see that the first result listed for the interactions is `vulgaris.lo - sativa.lo`, which corresponds to the two lowest means (presented with the smaller taken away from the larger to give a positive difference in means). If you look at the second item in each pairing, you see that it corresponds to higher and higher means until the final pairing represents the comparison between the boxes with the two highest means (in this example, this is `sativa:hi - vugaris.hi`).

Graphical Summary of Post-hoc Testing

The `TukeyHSD()` command has its own dedicated plotting routine via the `plot()` command:

```
> plot(TukeyHSD(pw.aov))

> pw.ph = TukeyHDS(pw.aov)
> plot(pw.ph)
```

In the first case the `TukeyHSD()` command is called from within the `plot()` command, and in the second case the post-hoc test was given a name and the `plot()` command is called on the result object. Both give the same result (see Figure 8-2).

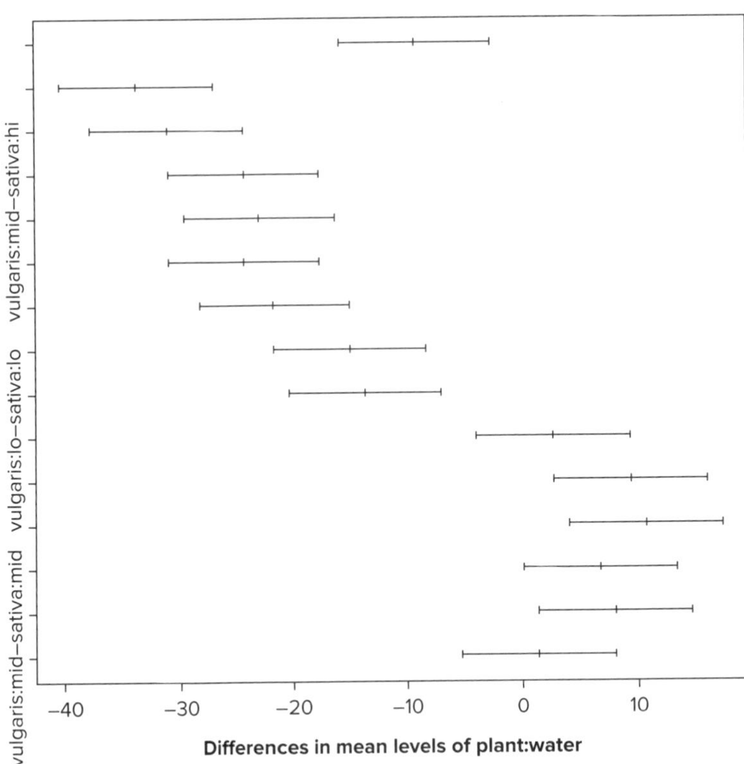

FIGURE 8-2

The main title and x-axis labels are defaults; you cannot easily alter these. You can, however, make the plot a bit more readable. At present the y-axis labels are incompletely displayed because they evidently overlap one another. You can rotate them using the `las =` instruction so that they are horizontal. You must give a numeric value to the instruction; Table 8-1 shows the results for various values.

TABLE 8-1: Options for the las Instruction for Axis Labels

COMMAND	EXPLANATION
`las = 0`	Labels always parallel to the axis (the default)
`las = 1`	All labels horizontal
`las = 2`	Labels perpendicular to the axes
`las = 3`	All labels vertical

You can also adjust the size of the axis labels using the `cex.axis =` instruction, where you specify the expansion factor for the labels. In this case the labels will still not fit because the margin of the plot is simply too small. You can alter this, but you need to do some juggling. The commands you need to produce a finished plot are as follows:

```
> op = par(mar = c(5, 8, 4, 2))
> plot(TukeyHSD(pw.aov, ordered = TRUE), cex.axis = 0.7, las = 1)
> abline(v = 0, lty = 2, col = 'gray40')
> par(op)
```

You cannot set the margins from within the `plot()` command directly and must use the `par()` command to set the options/parameters you require. The `par()` command is used to set many graphical parameters, and the options set remain in force for all plots. Following are the steps you need to perform to complete the plot using the preceding commands:

1. Begin by using the `par()` command to set the margins in "lines of text"; specify bottom, left, top, and right margins, respectively, and specify them all in the command. The default settings are `(5, 4, 4, 2) + 0.1`. In this case, set the left margin to 8 to give room for the labels. Note how you give a name to your setting; this enables you to return to the original values after you are done. You may need to do a bit of juggling to get the right settings for your graphs.
2. Now use the `plot()` command and create your post-hoc plot using the ordered values. The labels are set to be a little smaller than standard (`cex = 0.7`) and are set to horizontal (`las = 1`).
3. Next, add a vertical line using the `abline()` command. Previously you used this to create horizontal lines as well as fitting a line of best fit. Here you make a vertical line and make it dashed (`lty = 2`) and a gray color (`col = 'gray40'`).
4. The last command resets the graphical parameters to whatever they were before you altered the margin command. This perhaps seems a trifle counter-intuitive, but that is the way it is; the call to the `par()` command effectively sets the current settings and saves them to the object you named. Then it resets the graphical parameters you specified while holding the original settings in the new named object. The resulting post-hoc plot appears in Figure 8-3.

By using the `order =` instruction you have ensured that all the significant pairwise comparisons have the lower end of the confidence interval > 0. This enables you to spot the significant interactions at a glance.

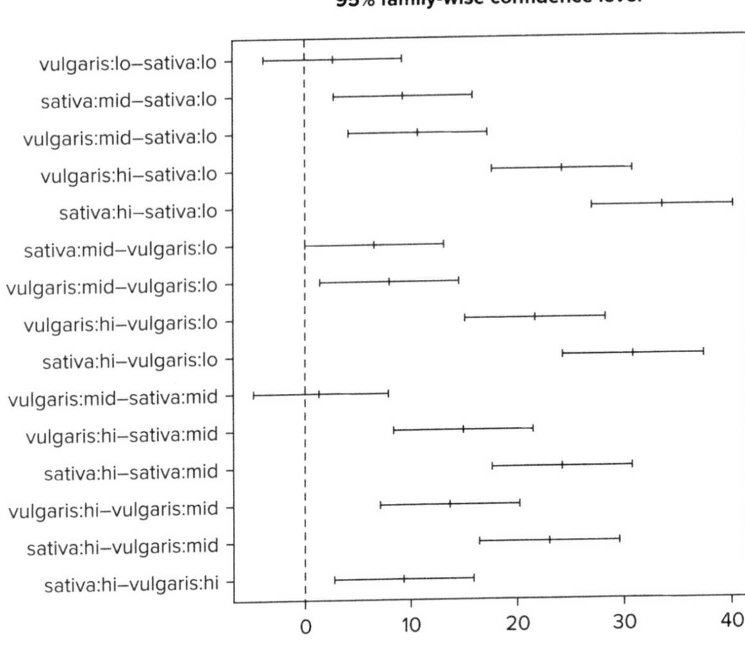

FIGURE 8-3

In the following activity you will carry out a two-way analysis of variance using some sample data that are built-into R.

TRY IT OUT Carry Out a Two-Way Analysis of Variance

In this activity you will explore the `warpbreaks` data, which come built-into R, using two-way ANOVA. You will also visualize the data as well as carrying out a post-hoc test.

1. Look at the `warpbreaks` data that come as part of R. You can use a variety of commands to explore the data:

```
> head(warpbreaks)
> names(warpbreaks)
> str(warpbreaks)
> summary(warpbreaks)
```

2. The data contain a response variable, `breaks`, and two predictor variables, `wool` and `tension`. Create a visual summary of these data using a boxplot:

```
> boxplot(breaks ~ wool * tension, data = warpbreaks)
```

3. It looks as though some differences exist, so now carry out a two-way analysis of variance:

```
> wb.aov = aov(breaks ~ wool * tension, data = warpbreaks)
> summary(wb.aov)
```

4. It appears that there is a significant interaction effect. To explore the data further, carry out a Tukey post-hoc test:

```
> TukeyHSD(wb.aov)
```

5. It may be easier to see the significant differences by re-ordering the factors, so use the `order = TRUE` instruction as part of the post-hoc command:

```
> TukeyHSD(wb.aov, order = TRUE)
```

6. Visualize the post-hoc test more clearly by creating a graphical summary of the Tukey test:

```
> plot(TukeyHSD(wb.aov, order = T), las = 1, cex.axis = 0.8)
> abline(v = 0, lty = 'dotted', col = 'gray60')
```

How It Works

The `boxplot()` command can use the formula syntax to split the data into the same chunks as you will use in the analysis of variance. The same syntax can be applied to the `aov()` command to carry out a two-way ANOVA. The summary of the analysis shows significant effects of `tension` as well as the interaction between `wool` and `tension`. The `TukeyHSD()` command shows the various pairwise comparisons.

The pairwise comparisons are easier to see if the factors are reordered, because any values > 0 in the `lwr` column register as significantly different. Plotting the `TukeyHSD()` result makes the task of spotting differences easier, too. Additional instructions tweak the plot to make it even easier to read. The `las = 1` instruction forces both axis labels to be horizontal, whereas the `cex.axis = 0.8` instruction makes the labels a little smaller and enables the y-axis labels to fit without the need to modify the plot margins.

Extracting Means and Summary Statistics

Once you have carried out a two-way ANOVA and done a post-hoc test you will probably want to view the mean values for the various components of your ANOVA model. You can use a variety of commands, all discussed in the following sections.

Model Tables

You can use the `model.tables()` command to extract means or effects like so:

```
> model.tables(pw.aov, type = 'means', se = TRUE)
Tables of means
Grand mean

19.44444

 plant
plant
  sativa vulgaris
  20.333   18.556
```

```
 water
water
   hi    lo   mid
35.00  7.33 16.00

 plant:water
          water
plant      hi    lo    mid
  sativa   39.67  6.00 15.33
  vulgaris 30.33  8.67 16.67

Standard errors for differences of means
        plant water plant:water
        1.133 1.388       1.963
replic.     9     6           3
```

In this case, the mean values are examined and the standard errors of the differences in the means are shown, much as you did when looking at the one-way ANOVA. In this case, because you have a balanced design, the `se = TRUE` instruction produce the standard errors. You see that you are shown means for the individual predictor variable as well as the interaction. If you want to see only some of the means, you can use the `cterms =` instruction to state what you want:

```
> model.tables(pw.aov, type = 'means', se = TRUE, cterms = c('plant:water'))
```

In this case you produce only means for the interactions and the grand mean (which you always get). If you create an object to hold the result of the `model.tables()` command, you can see that it is comprised of several elements:

```
> pw.mt = model.tables(pw.aov, type = 'means', se = TRUE)
> names(pw.mt)
[1] "tables" "n"      "se"
```

Some of these elements are themselves further subdivided:

```
> names(pw.mt$tables)
[1] "Grand mean"  "plant"       "water"       "plant:water"
```

You can therefore access any part of the result that you require using the `$` syntax to slice up the result object; in the following example you extract the interaction means:

```
> pw.mt$tables$'plant:water'
          water
plant      hi       lo       mid
  sativa   39.66667  6.00000 15.33333
  vulgaris 30.33333  8.66667 16.66667
```

Notice that some of the elements are in quotes for the final part; you can see this more clearly if you look at the `tables` part:

```
> pw.mt$tables
$`Grand mean`
[1] 19.44444

$plant
plant
  sativa vulgaris
20.33333 18.55556
```

```
$water
water
      hi       lo      mid
35.00000  7.33333 16.00000

$`plant:water`
         water
plant      hi       lo       mid
  sativa   39.66667  6.00000 15.33333
  vulgaris 30.33333  8.66667 16.66667
```

The `'Grand mean'` and `'plant:water'` parts are in quotes. This is essentially because they are composite items—the first contains a space and the second contains a `:` character.

Table Commands

You can also extract components of your ANOVA model by using the `tapply()` command, which you met previously, albeit briefly (in Chapter 5). The `tapply()` command enables you to take a data frame and apply a function to various components. The basic form of the command is as follows:

```
tapply(X, INDEX, FUN = NULL, ...)
```

In the command, `X` is the variable that you want to have the function applied to; usually this is your response variable. You use the `INDEX` part to describe how you want the `X` variable split up. In the current example you would use the following:

```
> attach(pw)
> tapply(height, list(plant, water), FUN = mean)
               hi       lo      mid
sativa   39.66667 6.000000 15.33333
vulgaris 30.33333 8.666667 16.66667
> detach(pw)
```

Here you use the `list()` command to state the variables that you require as the index (if you have only a single variable, the `list()` part is not needed). Note that you have to use the `attach()` command to enable the columns of your data frame to be readable by the command. You might also use the `with()` command or specify the vectors using the `$` syntax; the following examples give the same result:

```
> with(pw, tapply(height, list(plant, water), FUN = mean))
> tapply(pw$height, list(pw$plant, pw$water), FUN = mean)
```

Once you have the command working you can easily modify it to use a different function; you can obtain the number of replicates, for example, by using `FUN = length`:

```
> with(pw, tapply(height, list(plant, water), FUN = length))
         hi lo mid
sativa    3  3   3
vulgaris  3  3   3
```

Interaction Plots

It can often be useful to visualize the potential two-way interactions in an ANOVA, and indeed you probably ought to do this before actually running the analysis. You can visualize the situation using an interaction plot via the `interaction.plot()` command. The basic form of the command is as follows:

```
interaction.plot(x.factor, trace.factor, response, ...)
```

To obtain a basic plot, you need to specify three items:

1. The first is the `x.factor`, which determines how the interaction is split.
2. Then you specify the `trace.factor`, which is how the categories in the `x.factor` are split. In other words, the `x.factor` and the `trace.factor` combine to display the interaction.
3. Finally, you specify the `response` variable; this is plotted on the y-axis. You can thus alter the appearance of the plot by swapping the order in which you specify the `x.factor` and `trace.factor` variables. This is best illustrated by showing two alternatives using the current example:

```
> interaction.plot(water, plant, height)
> interaction.plot(plant, water, height)
```

In the first case you split the x-axis by the `water` treatment, whereas in the second case you split the x-axis according to the `plant` variable. The plots that result look like Figure 8-4.

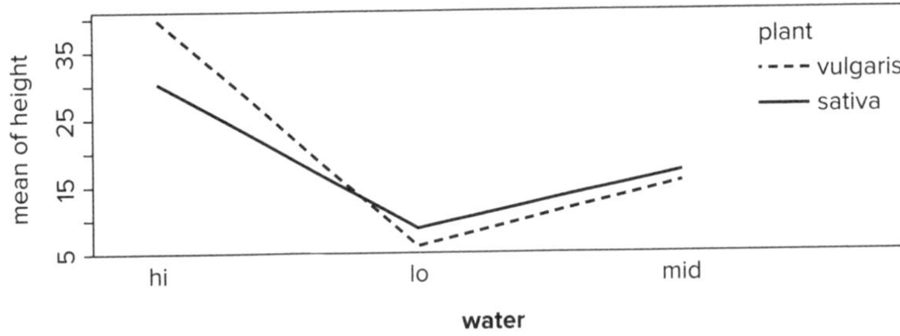

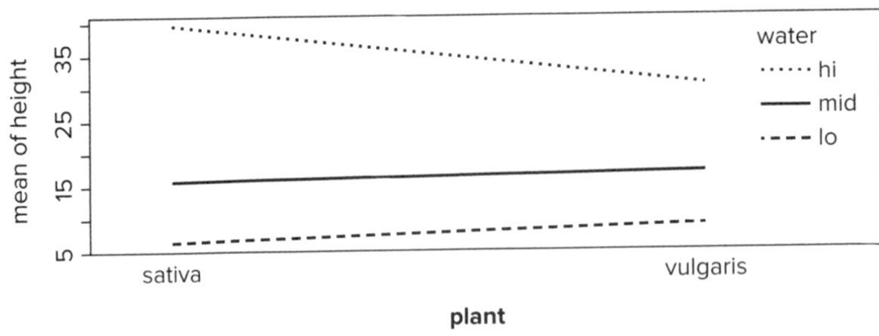

FIGURE 8-4

The top plot shows the x-axis split by the `water` treatment and the bottom plot shows the axis split by the other predictor variable (`plant`). You see how to split your plot window into sections in Chapter 11, "More About Graphs."

You can give a variety of additional instructions to the `interaction.plot()` command. To start with, you may want to see points on the plot in addition to (or instead of) the lines; you use the `type =` instruction to do this. You have several options: `type = 'l'`, the default, produces lines only; `type = 'b'` produces lines and points; and `type = 'p'` shows points only. In the following example you produce an interaction plot using both lines and points:

```
> attach(pw)
> interaction.plot(plant, water, height, type = 'b')
> detach(pw)
```

Notice how the `attach()` command is used to read the variables in this case. The plot that results looks like Figure 8-5.

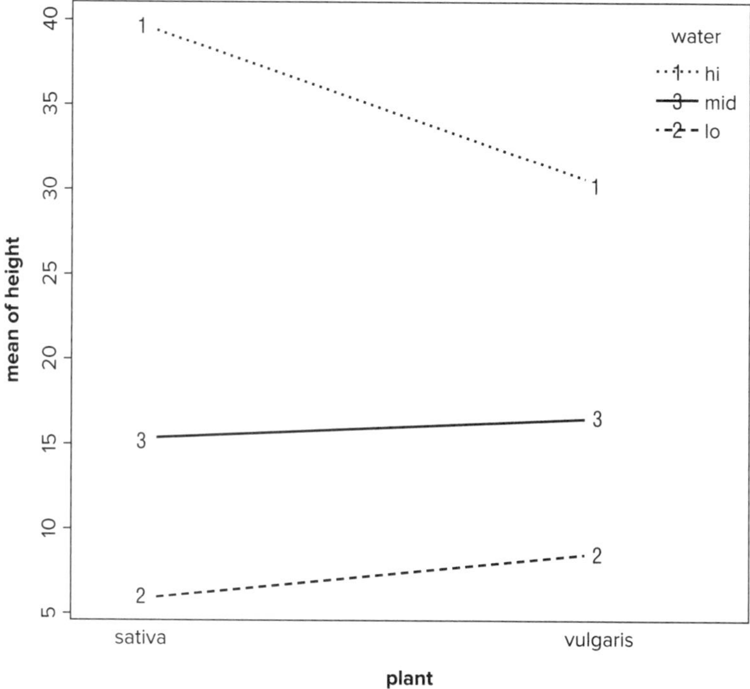

FIGURE 8-5

When you add points, the plotting characters are by default simple numbers, but you can alter them using the `pch =` instruction. You can specify the `pch` characters in several ways, but the simplest is to use the number of levels in the `trace.factor` down to 1. In this example, this would equate to `pch = 3:1`:

```
> interaction.plot(plant, water, height, type = 'b', pch = 3:1)
```

You can also alter the style of line using the `lty =` instruction. The default is to use the number of levels in the `trace.factor` down to 1, and in the example this equates to `lty = 3:1`:

```
> interaction.plot(plant, water, height, type = 'b', pch = 3:1, lty = 3:1)
```

You can use colors as well as line styles to aid differentiation by using the `col =` instruction. By default the color is set to black, that is, `col = 1`, but you can specify others by giving their names or numerical values. For example:

```
> interaction.plot(plant, water, height, type = 'b', pch = 3:1, lty = 3:1,
col = c('red', 'blue', 'darkgreen'))
```

You can also use a different summary function to the mean (which is the default) by using the `fun =` instruction (note that this is in lowercase); in the following example the median is used rather than the mean:

```
> interaction.plot(plant, water, height, type = 'b', pch = 3:1, fun = median)
```

You can specify new axis titles as well as an overall title by using the `xlab =`, `ylab =`, and `main =` instructions like you have seen previously. The following example plots lines and points using specified plotting characters and customized titles:

```
> interaction.plot(plant, water, height, type = 'b', pch = 3:1,
xlab = 'Plant treatment', ylab  = 'Mean plant height cm',
main = 'Interaction plot')
```

The final plot looks like Figure 8-6.

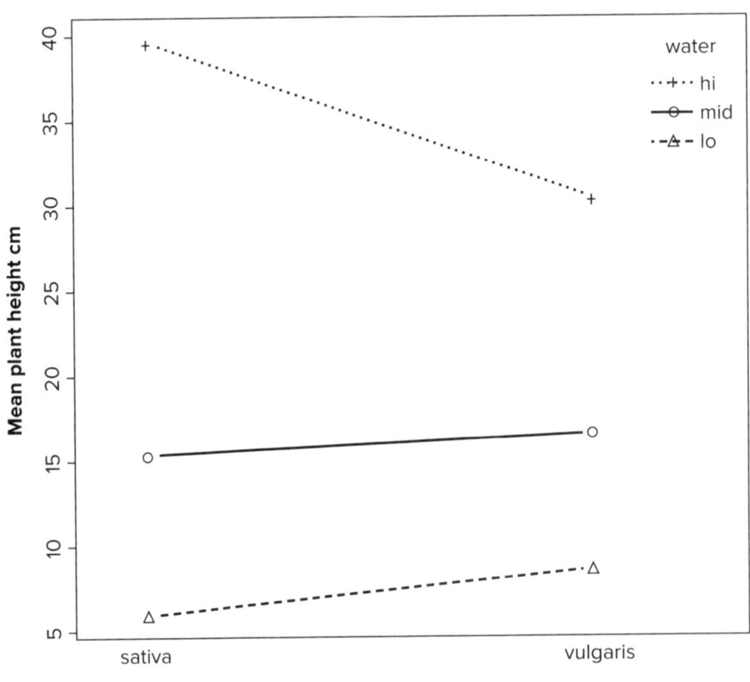

FIGURE 8-6

Table 8-2 shows a summary of the main instructions for the `intreraction.plot()` command.

TABLE 8-2: Instructions to be Used for the interaction.plot() Command

INSTRUCTION	EXPLANATION
`x.factor`	The factor whose levels form the x-axis.
`trace.factor`	Another factor representing the interaction with the x-axis.
`response`	The main response factor, which is plotted on the y-axis.
`fun = mean`	The summary function used; defaults to the *mean*.

`type = 'l'`
`type = 'b'`
`type = 'p'`
	The type of plot produced: `'l'` for lines only, `'b'` for both lines and points, `'p'` for points only.

`pch = as.character(1:n)`
`pch = letters/LETTERS`
`pch = 1:n`
	The plotting characters. The default uses numerical labels, but symbols can be used by specifying numeric value(s). So, `pch = 1:3` produces the symbols corresponding to values 1 to 3. `pch = letters` uses standard lowercase letters, and `pch = LETTERS` uses uppercase letters.

`lty = nc:1`	Sets the line type. Line types can either be specified as an integer (0 = blank, 1 = solid [default], 2 = dashed, 3 = dotted, 4 = dotdash, 5 = longdash, 6 = twodash) or as one of the character strings `"blank"`, `"solid"`, `"dashed"`, `"dotted"`, `"dotdash"`, `"long-dash"`, or `"twodash"`, where `"blank"` uses "invisible lines" (that is, does not draw them).
`lwd = 1`	The line widths. 1 is the standard width; larger values make it wider and smaller values make is narrower.
`col = 1`	The color of the lines. Defaults to `"black"` (that is, 1).
`xlab = 'x axis title'`	The x-axis title.
`ylab = 'y axis title'`	The y-axis title.
`main = 'main plot title'`	A main graph title.
`legend = TRUE`	Should the legend be shown? (Defaults to `TRUE`.)

In the following activity you will explore a two-way ANOVA using the `interaction.plot()` command.

TRY IT OUT Make an Interaction Plot of a Two-Way ANOVA

In this activity you will revisit the `warpbreaks` data, which come built-into R, using the `interaction.plot()` command to help visualize the relationship between the variables.

1. Earlier you carried out a two-way ANOVA on the `warpbreaks` data. Look again at the data to remind yourself of the situation:

```
> names(warpbreaks)
> boxplot(breaks ~ wool * tension, data = warpbreaks)
```

2. An interaction plot would be helpful to explore the relationship between `tension` and `wool`. Create a basic plot:

```
> with(warpbreaks, interaction.plot(tension, wool, breaks))
```

3. Make the plot clearer by adding data points in addition to the lines:

```
> with(warpbreaks, interaction.plot(tension, wool, breaks, type = 'b'))
```

4. Now modify the plot by altering the plotting characters, colors, and line styles:

```
> with(warpbreaks, interaction.plot(tension, wool, breaks, type = 'b',
pch = 1:2, col = 1:2, lty = 1:2))
```

5. Alter the way the axis labels are displayed and force them to be horizontal:

```
> with(warpbreaks, interaction.plot(tension, wool, breaks, type = 'b',
pch = 1:2, col = 1:2, lty = 1:2, las = 1))
```

6. Now switch the data around to display the `wool` variable on the x-axis. Use the median as the value plotted on the y-axis.

```
> with(warpbreaks, interaction.plot(wool, tension, breaks, fun = median,
type = 'b', pch = 1:3, col = 1:3, lty = 1:3, las = 1))
```

How It Works

The `interaction.plot()` command requires at least three pieces of information. The first is the variable to show on the x-axis, the second is the variable to display as the trace factor (that is, the lines/points), and the third is the value to plot on the y-axis. The default plot shows lines only and uses the mean as the function to apply to the y-axis data.

You can display both lines and points using `type = 'b'`, which presents the points as numbers. You can alter the plotting character using `pch =`. In this case you used `1:2` to display symbols relating to those values, but you could specify them in a different manner. `c(16, 23)`, for example, would display symbols 16 and 23. The colors are altered using the `col = 1:2` instruction, but you could specify them by name. The `lty = 1:2` instruction altered the line styles. The `las = 1` instruction forced the axis labels to display horizontally rather than parallel to the axis (`las = 0` is the default).

The mean is the default and you altered this in the final plot by specifying `fun = median`. There are now three trace items (that is, three levels of the `tension` variable).

***NOTE** Many command instructions require you to provide several values, for example you might require three colors and plotting symbols in an `interaction.plot()` command. If you specify too many values then the extra ones are ignored. If you do not specify enough values then the ones you do provide are recycled as necessary.*

More Complex ANOVA Models

So far you have looked at fairly simple analyses of variance, one-way and two-way. You can use the formula notation to create more complex models as occasions demand. In all cases, you place your response variable to the left of the ~ and put your predictor variables to the right. In Table 8-3 a range of formulae are shown that illustrate the possibilities for representing complex ANOVA models. In these examples, `y` is used to represent the response variable (a continuous variable) and `x` represents a predictor in the form of a continuous variable. Uppercase `A`, `B`, and `C` represent factors with discrete levels (that is, predictor variables).

TABLE 8-3: Formula Syntax for Complex Models

FORMULA	EXPLANATION
`y ~ A`	One-way analysis of variance.
`y ~ A + x`	Single classification analysis of covariance model of `y`, with classes determined by `A` and covariate `x`.
`y ~ A * B` `y ~ A + B + A:B`	Two-factor non-additive analysis of variance of `y` on factors `A` and `B`, that is, with interactions.
`y ~ B %in% A` `y ~ A/B`	Nested analysis of variance with `B` nested in `A`.
`y ~ A + B %in% A` `y ~ A + A:B`	Nested analysis of variance with factor `A` plus `B` nested in `A`.
`y ~ A * B * C` `y ~ A + B + C + A:B + A:C + B:C + A:B:C`	Three-factor experiment with complete interactions between factors `A`, `B`, and `C`.

`y ~ (A + B + C)^2`
`y ~ (A + B + C) * (A + B + C)`
`y ~ A * B * C - A:B:C`
`y ~ A + B + C + A:B + A:C + B:C`
	Three-factor experiment with model containing main effects and two-factor interactions only.

continues

TABLE 8-3 *(continued)*

FORMULA	EXPLANATION
`y ~ A * B + Error(C)`	An experiment with two treatment factors, `A` and `B`, and error strata determined by factor `C`. For example, a split plot experiment, with whole plots (and hence also subplots), determined by factor `C`.
`y ~ A + I(A + B)` `y ~ A + I(A^2)`	The `I()` insulates the contents from the formula meaning and allows mathematical operations. In the first example, you have an additive two-way analysis of variance with `A` and the sum of `A` and `B`. In the second example you have a polynomial analysis of variance with `A` and the square of `A`.

You can see that when you have more complex models, you often have more than one way to write the model formula. The operators +, *, -, :, and ^ have explicit meanings in the formula syntax; the + simply adds new variables to the model. The * is used to imply interactions and the - removes items from the model. The : is used to show interactions explicitly, and the ^ is used to specify the level of interactions in a more general manner.

If you want to use a mathematical function in your model, you can use the `I()` command to "insulate" the part you are applying the math to. Thus `y ~ A + I(B + C)` is a two-way ANOVA with `A` as one predictor variable; the other predictor is made by adding `B` and `C`. That is not a very sensible model, but the point is that the `I()` part differentiates between parts of the model syntax and regular math syntax.

You can specify an explicit error term by using the `Error()` command. Inside the brackets you specify terms that define the error structure of your model (for example, in repeated measures analyses).

You can use transformations and other mathematical manipulations on the data through the model itself, as long as the syntax is not interpreted as model syntax, so `log(y) ~ A + log(B)` is perfectly acceptable. If there is any ambiguity you can simply use the `I()` command to separate out the math part(s).

Other Options for aov()

A few additional commands can be useful when carrying out analysis of variance. Here you see just two, but you look at others when you come to look at linear modeling and the `lm()` command in Chapter 10, "Regression (Linear Modeling)."

Replications and Balance

You can check the balance in your model by using the `replications()` command. If you run the command on the original data, you get something like the following:

```
> summary(pw)
     height           plant    water
 Min.   : 5.00   sativa  :9   hi :6
 1st Qu.: 9.50   vulgaris:9   lo :6
```

```
 Median :16.00                 mid:6
 Mean   :19.44
 3rd Qu.:30.25
 Max.   :44.00

> replications(pw)
plant water
    9     6
Warning message:
In replications(pw) : non-factors ignored: height
```

In this case you have a data frame with three columns; the first is the response variable (which is numeric) and this is ignored. The next two columns are factors (character vectors) and are counted toward your replicates. In the previous example you used a two-way ANOVA, but a better way to use the command is to give the formula for the `aov()` model. You can do this in two ways: you can specify the complete formula or you can give the result object of your analysis. This latter option only works if you have actually run the `aov()` command. If you have run the `aov()` command, the formula is taken from the result, although you still need to state where the original data are. The following example shows the `replications()` command applied to the two-way ANOVA result that was calculated earlier:

```
> replications(pw.aov, data = pw)
      plant       water plant:water
          9           6           3

> replications(height ~ plant * water, data = pw)
      plant       water plant:water
          9           6           3
```

If your `aov()` model is unbalanced, you get a slightly different result. In the following example, a slight imbalance is caused by deleting the final row and saving the result to a new data frame called `pw2`:

```
> pw2 = pw[1:17, ]
> replications(height ~ plant * water, data = pw2)
$plant
plant
  sativa vulgaris
       8        9

$water
water
 hi  lo mid
  5   6   6

$`plant:water`
          water
plant       hi lo mid
  sativa     2  3   3
  vulgaris   3  3   3
```

There were 18 rows in the original data frame; the new data is made up of the first 17 of them. You now get a more complex result showing you that you have one fewer replicate; you can see where the imbalance lies. The result is shown as a list; you can tell this because it is split into several blocks, each named and starting with a `$`. In the previous example you had a balanced model, and the result of the `replications()` command was a simple vector (it looks more complicated because it also has names). You can use this feature to make a test for imbalance because you can test to see if your result is a list or not:

```
!is.list(replications(formula,data))
```

In short, you add `!is.list()` to your `replications()` command. This looks to see if the result is *not* a list. If it is not a list, the balance must be okay so you get `TRUE` as a result. If it *is* a list, there is not balance and you should get `FALSE`. If you run this command on the two examples, you get the following:

```
> !is.list(replications(height ~ plant * water, data = pw))
[1] TRUE
> !is.list(replications(height ~ plant * water, data = pw2))
[1] FALSE
```

The first case is the original data and you have balance. In the second case the last row of data is deleted, and, of course, the balance is lost.

Balance is always important in ANOVA designs. There are other ways to check for the balance and view the number of replicates in an `aov()` model; you look at these in the next chapter.

SUMMARY

- The formula syntax enables you to describe your data in a logical manner, that is, with a response variable and a series of predictor variables.
- The formula syntax can be used to carry out many simple stats tests because most of the commands will accept either formula notation or separate variables.
- The formula syntax can be applied to graphics, which enables you to plot more complex arrangements.
- The `aov()` command carries out analysis of variance (ANOVA). The formula syntax is used to describe the analysis you require, so the data must be in the appropriate layout with columns for response and predictor variables.
- The `stack()` command can rearrange multiple samples into a response ~ predictor arrangement. If there are `NA` items, the `na.omit()` command can be used to remove them.
- After the ANOVA you can run post-hoc tests to separate the effects of the individual samples. The `TukeyHSD()` command carries out a common version, the Tukey Honest Significant Difference.
- The results of the `TukeyHSD()` command can be plotted graphically to help visualize the pairwise comparisons.
- The `model.tables()` command can be used to extract means from the data after the ANOVA has been carried out. Alternatively, you can use the `tapply()` command to view the means or use another function (for example, standard deviation).
- The `interaction.plot()` command enables you to visualize the interaction between two predictor variables in a two-way ANOVA.
- The replications and model balance of your data can be examined by using the `replications()` command.

EXERCISES

Available for download on Wrox.com

You can find the answers to these exercises in Appendix A.

Use the `chick` and `bats` data objects from the `Beginning.RData` file for these exercises.

1. What are the main advantages of the formula syntax?

2. Look at the `chick` data object. These data represent weights of chicks fed a variety of diets. How can you prepare these data for analysis of variance? Carry out the one-way ANOVA; is there a significant difference in chick weights due to diet?

3. Now that you have an ANOVA result for the `chick` data, carry out a post-hoc test and also visualize the data and results using graphics. What steps do you need to carry out to do this?

4. Look at the `bats` data file. There are three bat species and two methods of counting them. The `Box` method involves looking in bat nest-boxes during the day, and the `Det` method involves using a sonic detector during the previous evening. What steps will you need to carry out to conduct an ANOVA?

5. The `bats` data yielded a significant interaction term in the two-way ANOVA. Look at this further. Make a graphic of the data and then follow up with a post-hoc analysis. Draw a graph of the interaction.

▶ WHAT YOU LEARNED IN THIS CHAPTER

TOPIC	KEY POINTS
Formula syntax response ~ predictor	The formula syntax enables you to specify complex statistical models. Usually the response variables go on the left and predictor variables go on the right. The syntax can also be used in more simple situations and for graphics.
Stacking samples `stack()`	In more complex analyses, the data need to be in a layout where each column is a separate item; that is, a column for the response variable and a column for each predictor variable. The `stack()` command can rearrange data into this layout.
Analysis of variance (ANOVA) `aov()`	The `aov()` command carries out ANOVA. You can specify your model using the formula syntax and can carry out one-way, two-way, and more complicated ANOVA.
`TukeyHSD()`	The Tukey Honest Significant Difference is the most commonly used post-hoc test and is used to carry out pairwise comparisons after the main ANOVA. You can `plot()` the result of the `TukeyHSD()` command to help visualize the pairwise comparisons.
Interaction plots `interaction.plot()`	The interaction plot is a graphical means of visualizing the difference in response in a two-way ANOVA. The lines show different levels of a predictor variable (compared to the other predictor) and non-parallel lines indicate an interaction.

Extracting elements of an ANOVA
`model.tables()`
`tapply()`
	The elements of an ANOVA can be extracted in several ways. The `model.tables()` command is able to show means or effects from an `aov()` result. The `tapply()` command is more general, but is useful in being able to use any function on the data; thus, you can extract means, standard deviation, and number of replicates from the data.

Replications and balance `replications()`	The `replications()` command is a convenient command that enables you to check the balance in an ANOVA model design.

Manipulating Data and Extracting Components

WHAT YOU WILL LEARN IN THIS CHAPTER:

- How to create data frames and matrix objects ready for complex analyses
- How to create or set factor data
- How to add rows and columns to data objects
- How to use simple summary commands to extract column or row information
- How to extract summary statistics from complex data objects

The world can be a complicated place, and the data you have can also be correspondingly complicated. You saw in the previous chapter how to use analysis of variance (ANOVA) via the `aov()` command to help make sense of complicated data. This chapter builds on this knowledge by walking you through the process of creating data objects prior to carrying out a complicated analysis.

This chapter has two main themes. To start, you look at ways to create and manipulate data to produce the objects you require to carry out these complex analyses. Later in the chapter you look at methods to extract the various components of a complicated data object. You have seen some of these commands before and others are new.

CREATING DATA FOR COMPLEX ANALYSIS

To begin with, you need to have some data to work on. You can construct your data in a spreadsheet and have it ready for analysis in R, or you may have to construct the data from various separate elements. This section covers the latter scenario.

When you need to carry out a complex analysis, the likelihood is that you will have to make a complex data object. The more complicated the situation you are examining, the more important it is that your data are arranged in a sensible fashion. In general, this means that you should have a column for each variable that you are dealing with—usually this means a column containing the response variable and additional columns each containing a predictor variable.

You have already seen various ways to create data items:

- Using the `c()` command to create simple vectors
- Using the `scan()` command to create vectors from the keyboard, clipboard, or a file from disk
- Using the `read.table()` command to read data previously prepared in a spreadsheet or some other program

If you read data from another application, like a spreadsheet, it is likely that your data are already in the layout you require. If you have individual vectors of data, you need to construct data frames and matrix objects before you can carry out the business of complex analysis.

Data Frames

The data frame is probably the most useful kind of data object for complex analyses because you can have columns containing a variety of data types. For example, you can have columns containing numeric data and other columns containing factor data. This is unlike a matrix where all the data must be of one type (for example, all numeric or all text).

To make a data frame you simply use the `data.frame()` command, and type the names of the objects that will form the columns into the parentheses. However, you need to ensure that all the objects are of the same length. The following example contains two simple vectors of numerical data that you want to make into a data frame. They have different lengths, so you need to alter the shorter one and add `NA` items to pad it out:

```
> mow ; unmow
[1] 12 15 17 11 15
[1] 8 9 7 9
> length(unmow) = length(mow)
> unmow
[1]  8  9  7  9 NA
> grassy = data.frame(mow, unmow)
> grassy
  mow unmow
1  12     8
2  15     9
3  17     7
4  11     9
5  15    NA
```

The `length()` command is usually used to query the length of an object, but here you use it to alter the original data by setting its length to be the same as the longer item. If you use a value that turns out to be shorter than the current length, your object is truncated and the extra data are removed.

You can use a variety of other commands to set the names of the columns, and also add names for the individual rows. The following example looks at the main column names using the `names()` command:

```
> names(grassy)
[1] "mow"    "unmow"
> names(grassy) = c('mown', 'unmown')
> names(grassy)
[1] "mown"    "unmown"
```

Here, you query the column names and then set them to new values. You can do something similar with row names. In the following example you create a vector of names first and then set them using the `row.names()` command:

```
> grn = c('Top', 'Middle', 'Lower', 'Set aside', 'Verge')
> row.names(grassy)
[1] "1" "2" "3" "4" "5"
> row.names(grassy) = grn
> row.names(grassy)
[1] "Top"         "Middle"     "Lower"      "Set aside" "Verge"
```

Notice that the original row names are a simple index and appear as characters when you query them. The newly renamed data frame appears like this:

```
> grassy
          mown unmown
Top         12      8
Middle      15      9
Lower       17      7
Set aside   11      9
Verge       15     NA
```

You may prefer to have your data frame in a different layout, with one column for the response variable and one for the predictor (in most cases this is preferable). In the current example you would have one column for the numerical values, and one to hold the treatment names (`mown` or `unmown`). You can do this in several ways, depending on where you start.

In this case you already have a data frame and can convert it using the `stack()` command:

```
> stack(grassy)
   values    ind
1      12   mown
2      15   mown
3      17   mown
4      11   mown
5      15   mown
6       8 unmown
7       9 unmown
8       7 unmown
9       9 unmown
10     NA unmown
```

Now you have the result you want, but you have an NA item that you do not really need. You can use na.omit() to strip out the NA items that may occur:

```
> na.omit(stack(grassy))
  values     ind
1     12    mown
2     15    mown
3     17    mown
4     11    mown
5     15    mown
6      8 unmown
7      9 unmown
8      7 unmown
9      9 unmown
```

The column names are set to the defaults of values and ind. You can use the names() command to alter them afterward. The stack() command really only works when you have a simple situation with all samples being related to a single predictor variable. When you need multiple columns with several predictor variables, you need a different approach.

When you need to create vectors of treatment names you are repeating the same names over and over according to how many replicates you have. You can use the rep() command to generate repeating items and take some of the tedium out of the process. In the following example and subsequent steps, you use the rep() command to make labels to match up with the two samples you have (mow and unmow):

```
> mow ; unmow
[1] 12 15 17 11 15
[1] 8 9 7 9

> trt = c(rep('mow', length(mow)), rep('unmow', length(unmow)))
> trt
[1] "mow"   "mow"   "mow"   "mow"   "mow"   "unmow" "unmow" "unmow" "unmow"

> rich = c(mow, unmow)
> data.frame(rich, trt)
  rich   trt
1   12   mow
2   15   mow
3   17   mow
4   11   mow
5   15   mow
6    8 unmow
7    9 unmow
8    7 unmow
9    9 unmow
```

1. To begin, create a new object to hold your predictor variable, and use the rep() command to repeat the names for the two treatments as many times as is necessary to match the number of observations. The basic form of the rep() command is:

   ```
   rep(what, times)
   ```

2. In this case you want a character name, so enclose the name in quotation marks. You could also use a numerical value for the number of repeats, but here you use the length() command to work out how many times to repeat the labels for each of the two samples.

3. Create the final data object by joining together the response vectors as one column and the new vector of names representing the treatments (the predictor variable). The `data.frame()` command does the actual joining. Notice that in this example a name is not specified for the final data frame; if you want to use the data frame for some analysis (quite likely), you should give the new frame a name like so:

```
> grass.dat = data.frame(rich, trt)
```

The `rep()` command is useful to help you create repeating elements (like factors) and you will see it again shortly. Before then, you look at creating matrix objects.

Matrix Objects

A matrix can be thought of as a single vector of data that is conveniently split up into rows and columns. You can make a matrix object in several ways:

- If you have vectors of data you can assemble them in rows or columns using the `rbind()` or `cbind()` commands.
- If you have a single vector of values you can use the `matrix()` command.

The following examples and subsequent steps illustrate the two methods:

```
> mow ; unmow
[1] 12 15 17 11 15
[1] 8 9 7 9
> length(unmow) = length(mow)
> cbind(mow, unmow)
     mow unmow
[1,]  12     8
[2,]  15     9
[3,]  17     7
[4,]  11     9
[5,]  15    NA
```

1. Begin with two vectors of numeric values, and because they are of unequal length, use the `length()` command to extend the shorter one.
2. Next use the `cbind()` command to bind together the vectors as columns in a matrix. If you want your vectors to be the rows, you use the `rbind()` command like so:

```
> rbind(mow,unmow)
      [,1] [,2] [,3] [,4] [,5]
mow     12   15   17   11   15
unmow    8    9    7    9   NA
```

3. Notice that you end up with names for one margin in your matrix but not the other; in the first example the row names are not set, and in the second example the column names are not set. You can set the row names or column names using the `rownames()` or `colnames()` commands.

If you have your data as one single vector, you can use an alternative method to make a matrix using the `matrix()` command. This command takes a single vector and splits it into a matrix with the number of rows or columns that you specify. This means that your vector of data must be divisible by the number of rows or columns that you require. In the following example and subsequent steps you have a single vector of values that you use to create a matrix:

```
> rich
[1] 12 15 17 11 15  8  9  7  9
> length(rich) = 10
> rich
 [1] 12 15 17 11 15  8  9  7  9 NA

> matrix(rich, ncol = 2)
     [,1] [,2]
[1,]   12    8
[2,]   15    9
[3,]   17    7
[4,]   11    9
[5,]   15   NA
```

1. Start by making sure your original data are the correct length for your matrix and, as before, use the `length()` command to extend it.
2. Next use the `matrix()` command to create a matrix with two columns. The command reads along the vector and splits it at intervals appropriate to create the columns you asked for. This has consequences for how the data finally appear; if you use the `nrow =` instruction to specify how many rows you require (rather than `ncol`), the data will not end up in their original samples because the matrix is populated column by column:

   ```
   > mow ; unmow
   [1] 12 15 17 11 15
   [1]  8  9  7  9 NA
   > matrix(rich, nrow = 2)
        [,1] [,2] [,3] [,4] [,5]
   [1,]   12   17   15    9    9
   [2,]   15   11    8    7   NA
   ```

3. If you wish to create a matrix in rows, use the `byrow = TRUE` instruction:

   ```
   > matrix(rich, nrow = 2, byrow = TRUE)
        [,1] [,2] [,3] [,4] [,5]
   [1,]   12   15   17   11   15
   [2,]    8    9    7    9   NA
   ```

Like before with the first method, when you use the `matrix()` command none of the margin names are set; you need to use the `rownames()` or `colnames()` commands to set them.

Creating and Setting Factor Data

When you create data for complex analysis, like analysis of variance, you create vectors for both the response variables and the predictor variables. The response variables are generally numeric, but the predictor variables may well be characters and refer to names of treatments. Alternatively, they may be simple numeric values with each number representing a separate treatment. When you create a data frame that contains numeric and character vectors, the character vectors are regarded as being factors. In the following example you can see a simple data frame created from a numeric vector and a character vector:

```
> rich ; graze
[1] 12 15 17 11 15  8  9  7  9
[1] "mow"    "mow"    "mow"    "mow"    "mow"    "unmow" "unmow" "unmow" "unmow"
> grass.df = data.frame(rich, graze)
> str(grass.df)
'data.frame': 9 obs. of  2 variables:
 $ rich : int  12 15 17 11 15 8 9 7 9
 $ graze: Factor w/ 2 levels "mow","unmow": 1 1 1 1 1 2 2 2 2
```

When you use the `str()` command to examine the structure of the data frame that was created, you see that the character vector has been converted into a factor. If you add a character vector to an existing data frame, it will remain as a character vector unless you use the `data.frame()` command as your means of adding the new vector; you see this in a moment.

You can force a numeric or character vector to be a factor by using the `factor()` command:

```
> graze
[1] "mow"    "mow"    "mow"    "mow"    "mow"    "unmow" "unmow" "unmow" "unmow"
> graze.f = factor(graze)
> graze.f
[1] mow   mow   mow   mow   mow   unmow unmow unmow unmow
Levels: mow unmow
```

Here you see that the original characters are made into factors, and you see the list of levels when you look at the object (note that the data are not in quotes as they were when they were a character object). If you want to add a character vector to an existing data frame and require the new vector to be a factor, you can use the `as.factor()` command to convert the vector to a factor. In the following example you see the result of adding a vector of characters without using `as.factor()` and then with the `as.factor()` command:

```
> grass.df$graze2 = graze
> grass.df
  rich graze graze2
1   12   mow    mow
2   15   mow    mow
3   17   mow    mow
4   11   mow    mow
5   15   mow    mow
6    8 unmow  unmow
7    9 unmow  unmow
8    7 unmow  unmow
9    9 unmow  unmow
> str(grass.df)
'data.frame': 9 obs. of  3 variables:
 $ rich  : int  12 15 17 11 15 8 9 7 9
 $ graze : Factor w/ 2 levels "mow","unmow": 1 1 1 1 1 2 2 2 2
 $ graze2: chr  "mow" "mow" "mow" "mow" ...

> grass.df$graze2 = as.factor(graze)
> str(grass.df)
'data.frame': 9 obs. of  3 variables:
```

```
 $ rich  : int  12 15 17 11 15 8 9 7 9
 $ graze : Factor w/ 2 levels "mow","unmow": 1 1 1 1 1 2 2 2 2
 $ graze2: Factor w/ 2 levels "mow","unmow": 1 1 1 1 1 2 2 2 2
```

In the first instance you see that the character vector appears in the data frame without quotes, but the `str()` command reveals it is still comprised of characters. In the second case you use the `as.factor()` command, and the new column is successfully transferred as a factor variable. You can, of course, set a column to be a factor afterward, as you can see in the following example:

```
> grass.df$graze2 = factor(grass.df$graze2)
```

In this case you convert the `graze2` column of the data frame into a factor using the `factor()` command. If you use the `data.frame()` command then any character vectors are converted to factors as the following example shows:

```
> grass.df = data.frame(grass.df, graze2 = graze)
```

Notice how the name of the column created is set as part of the command; the `graze2` object is created on the fly and added to the data frame as a factor.

You may want to analyze how your factor vector is split up at some point because the factor vector represents the predictor variable, and shows you how many treatments are applied. You can use the `levels()` command to see how your factor vector is split up. You can use the command in two ways; you can use it to query an object and find out what levels it possesses, or you can use it to set the levels. Following are examples of two character vectors:

```
> graze
[1] "mow"    "mow"    "mow"    "mow"    "mow"    "unmow" "unmow" "unmow" "unmow"
> levels(graze)
NULL
```

Here the data are plain characters and no levels are set; when you examine the data with the `levels()` command you get `NULL` as a result.

```
> graze.f
[1] mow   mow   mow   mow   mow   unmow unmow unmow unmow
Levels: mow unmow
> levels(graze.f)
[1] "mow"    "unmow"
```

Here you see the names of the levels that you created earlier. If you have a numeric variable that represents codes for treatments, you can make the variable into a factor using the `factor()` command as you have already seen, but you can also assign names to the levels. In the following example you create a simple numeric vector to represent two treatments:

```
> graze.nf = c(1,1,1,1,1,2,2,2,2)
```

You can now assign names to each of the levels in the vector like so:

```
> levels(graze.nf)[1] = 'mown'
> levels(graze.nf)[2] = 'unmown'

> levels(graze.nf)
[1] "mown"   "unmown"
```

```
> graze.nf
[1] 1 1 1 1 1 2 2 2 2
attr(,"levels")
[1] "mown"   "unmown"

> class(graze.nf)
[1] "numeric"
```

You can set each level to have a name; now your plain numeric values have a more meaningful label. However, the vector still remains a numeric variable rather than a factor. You can set all the labels in one command with a slight variation, as the following example shows:

```
> graze.nf = factor(c(1,1,1,1,1,2,2,2,2))
> graze.nf
[1] 1 1 1 1 1 2 2 2 2
Levels: 1 2

> levels(graze.nf) = list(mown = '1', unmown = '2')
> graze.nf
[1] mown   mown   mown   mown   mown   unmown unmown unmown unmown
Levels: mown unmown
```

In this case you create your factor object directly using numeric values but wrap these in a `factor()` command; you can see that you get your two levels, corresponding to the two values. This time you use the `levels()` command to set the names by listing how you want the numbers to be replaced.

You can also apply level names to a vector as you convert it to a factor via the `factor()` command:

```
> graze.nf = c(1,1,1,1,1,2,2,2,2)
> graze.nf
[1] 1 1 1 1 1 2 2 2 2

> factor(graze.nf, labels = c('mown', 'unmown'))
[1] mown   mown   mown   mown   mown   unmown unmown unmown unmown
Levels: mown unmown
```

In this instance you have a simple numeric vector and use the `labels =` instruction to apply labels to the levels as you make your factor object.

You can use the `nlevels()` command to give you a numeric result for the number of levels in a vector:

```
> graze
[1] "mow"    "mow"    "mow"    "mow"    "mow"    "unmow"  "unmow"  "unmow"  "unmow"
> nlevels(graze)
[1] 0
> graze.f
[1] mow   mow   mow   mow   mow   unmow unmow unmow unmow
Levels: mow unmow
> nlevels(graze.f)
[1] 2
```

You can also use the `class()` command to check what sort of object you are dealing with like so:

```
> class(graze)
[1] "character"
> class(graze.f)
[1] "factor"
```

In the first case you can see clearly that the data are characters, whereas in the second case you see that you have a factor object. The `class()` command is useful because, as you have seen, it is possible to apply levels to vectors of data without making them into factor objects. Take the following for example:

```
> nlevels(graze.nf)
[1] 2
> class(graze.nf)
[1] "numeric"
```

In the preceding example you have set two levels to your vector, but it remains a numeric object.

If you want to examine a factor variable but only want to view the levels as numeric values rather than as characters (assuming they have been set), you can use the `as.numeric()` command like so:

```
> as.numeric(graze.nf)
[1] 1 1 1 1 1 2 2 2 2
```

Now you can switch between character, factor, and numeric quite easily.

Making Replicate Treatment Factors

You have already seen how to create vectors of levels using the `rep()` command. The basic form of the command is:

```
rep(what, times)
```

You can use this command to create repeating labels that you can use to create a vector of characters that will become a factor object.

```
> trt = factor(c(rep('mown', 5), rep('unmown', 4)))
> trt
[1] mown   mown   mown   mown   mown   unmown unmown unmown unmown
Levels: mown unmown
```

In this instance you make a factor object directly from five lots of `mown` and four lots of `unmown`, which correspond to the two treatments you require.

When you have a balanced design with an equal number of replications, you can use the `each` instruction like so:

```
> factor(rep(c('mown', 'unmown'), each = 5))
 [1] mown   mown   mown   mown   mown   unmown unmown unmown unmown unmown
Levels: mown unmown
```

The `each` instruction repeats the elements the specified number of times. You can use the `times` and `each` instructions together to create more complicated repeated patterns.

You can also create factor objects using the `gl()` command. The general form of the command is:

```
gl(n, k, length = n*k, labels = 1:n)
```

In this command, `n` is the number of levels you require and `k` is the number of replications for each of these levels. You can also set the overall length of the vector you create and add specific text labels to your treatments. For example:

```
> gl(2, 5, labels = c('mown', 'unmown'))
 [1] mown   mown   mown   mown   mown   unmown unmown unmown unmown unmown
Levels: mown unmown
```

```
> gl(2, 1, 10, labels = c('mown', 'unmown'))
 [1] mown   unmown mown   unmown mown   unmown mown   unmown mown   unmown
Levels: mown unmown

> gl(2, 2, 10, labels = c('mown', 'unmown'))
 [1] mown   mown   unmown unmown mown   mown   unmown unmown mown   mown
Levels: mown unmown
```

In the first case you set two levels and require five replicates; you get five of one level and then five of the other. In the second case you set the number of replicates to 1, but also set the overall length to 10; the result is alternation between the levels until you reach the length required. In the third case you set the number of replicates to be two, and now you get two of each treatment until you reach the required length.

When you have a lot of data you will generally find it more convenient to create it in a spreadsheet and save it as a CSV file. However, for data with relatively few replicates it is useful to be able to make up data objects directly in R. In the following activity, you practice making a fairly simple data object comprising a numeric response variable and two predictor variables.

TRY IT OUT Make a Complex Data Frame

In this activity you will make a data frame that represents some numerical sample data and character predictor variables. This is the kind of thing that you might analyze using the `aov()` command.

1. Start by creating some numerical response data. These relate to the abundance of a plant at three sites:

```
> higher = c(12, 15, 17, 11, 15)
> lower = c(8, 9, 7, 9)
> middle = c(12, 14, 17, 21, 17)
```

2. Now join the separate vectors to make one variable:

```
> daisy = c(higher, lower, middle)
```

3. Make a predictor variable (the cutting regime) by creating a character vector:

```
> cutting = c(rep('mow', 5), rep('unmow', 4), rep('sheep', 5))
```

4. Create a second predictor variable (time of cutting):

```
> time = rep(gl(2, 1, length = 5, labels = c('early', 'late')), 3)[-10]
```

5. Assemble the data frame:

```
> flwr = data.frame(daisy, cutting, time)
```

6. Tidy up:

```
>rm(higher, lower, middle, daisy, cutting, time)
```

7. View the final data:

```
> flwr
```

How It Works

You start by making the numerical response variable. In this case you have three sites and you create three vectors using the `c()` command; you could have used the `scan()` command instead. Next, you join the three vectors together. You could have done this right at the start, but this way you can see more easily that the three are different lengths.

The first predictor value (how the meadows were cut) is created as a simple character vector. You can see that you need five replicates for the first and third, but only four for the second. You use the `rep()` command to generate the required number of replicates.

The next predictor variable (time of year) is more difficult because each site was monitored early and late alternately. The solution is to create the alternating variable and remove the "extra." The `gl()` command creates the variable and is wrapped in a `rep()` command to make an alternating variable with length of five repeated three times. The tenth item is not required and is removed using the `[-10]` instruction.

Now the final data frame can be assembled using the `data.frame()` command, and the unwanted preliminary variables can be tidied away using the `rm()` command. You can view the final result by typing its name:

```
> flwr
   daisy cutting  time
1     12     mow early
2     15     mow  late
3     17     mow early
4     11     mow  late
5     15     mow early
6      8   unmow early
7      9   unmow  late
8      7   unmow early
9      9   unmow  late
10    12   sheep early
11    14   sheep  late
12    17   sheep early
13    21   sheep  late
14    17   sheep early
```

Adding Rows or Columns

When it comes to adding data to an existing data frame or matrix, you have various options. The following examples illustrate some of the ways you can add data:

```
> grassy
           mown unmown
Top          12      8
Middle       15      9
Lower        17      7
Set aside    11      9
Verge        15     NA

> grazed
[1] 11 14 17 10  8
```

```
> grassy$grazed = grazed
> grassy
           mown unmown grazed
Top          12      8     11
Middle       15      9     14
Lower        17      7     17
Set aside    11      9     10
Verge        15     NA      8
```

In the preceding example you have a new sample and want to add this as a column to your data frame. The sample is the same length as the others so you can add it simply by using the `$`. In the next example you use the `data.frame()` command, but this time you are combining an existing data frame with a vector; this works fine as long as the new vector is the same length as the existing columns:

```
> grassy
           mown unmown
Top          12      8
Middle       15      9
Lower        17      7
Set aside    11      9
Verge        15     NA

> grassy = data.frame(grassy, grazed)
> grassy
           mown unmown grazed
Top          12      8     11
Middle       15      9     14
Lower        17      7     17
Set aside    11      9     10
Verge        15     NA      8
```

You add a row to a data frame using the [row, column] syntax. In the following example you have a new vector of values that you want to add as a row in your data frame:

```
> Midstrip
[1] 10 10 12

> grassy['Midstrip',] = Midstrip
> grassy
           mown unmown grazed
Top          12      8     11
Middle       15      9     14
Lower        17      7     17
Set aside    11      9     10
Verge        15     NA      8
Midstrip     10     10     12
```

You have now assigned the appropriate row of the data frame to your new vector of values; note that you give the name in the brackets using quotes.

If the new data are longer than the original data frame, you must expand the data frame to "make room" for the new items; you can do this by assigning `NA` to new rows as required. In the following example you have a simple data frame and want to add a new column, but this is longer than the original data:

```
> grassy
           mown unmown
Top          12      8
Middle       15      9
Lower        17      7
Set aside    11      9
Verge        15     NA
> grazed
[1] 11 14 17 10  8  9

> grassy$grazed = grazed
Error in `$<-.data.frame`(`*tmp*`, "grazed", value = c(11, 14, 17, 10,  :
  replacement has 6 rows, data has 5
```

When you try to add the new data, you get an error message; there are not enough existing rows to accommodate the new column. In this instance the data frame has named rows; you require only one extra row so you can name the row as you create it:

```
> grassy['Midstrip',] = NA
> grassy
           mown unmown
Top          12      8
Middle       15      9
Lower        17      7
Set aside    11      9
Verge        15     NA
Midstrip     NA     NA

> grassy$grazed = grazed
> grassy
           mown unmown grazed
Top          12      8     11
Middle       15      9     14
Lower        17      7     17
Set aside    11      9     10
Verge        15     NA      8
Midstrip     NA     NA      9
```

Once you have the additional row you can add the new column as before. In this case you added a column that required only a single additional row, but if you needed more you could do this easily:

```
> grassy[6:10,] = NA
> grassy
           mown unmown
Top          12      8
Middle       15      9
Lower        17      7
Set aside    11      9
Verge        15     NA
6            NA     NA
7            NA     NA
8            NA     NA
9            NA     NA
10           NA     NA
```

You added rows six to ten and set all the values to be `NA`. Notice, however, that the row names of the additional rows are unset and have a plain numerical index value. You have to reset the names of the rows using the `row.names()` command:

```
> row.names(grassy) = c(row.names(grassy)[1:6], "A", "B", "C", "D")
```

In this case you take the names from the first six rows and add to them the new names you require (in this case, uppercase letters).

When you have a matrix you can add additional rows or columns using the `rbind()` or `cbind()` commands as appropriate:

```
> grassy.m
      top upper mid lower bottom
mow    12    15  17    11     15
unmow   8     9   7     9     NA
> grazed
[1] 11 14 17 10  8

> grassy.m = rbind(grassy.m, grazed)
> grassy.m
       top upper mid lower bottom
mow     12    15  17    11     15
unmow    8     9   7     9     NA
grazed  11    14  17    10      8

> grassy.m
     mow unmow
[1,]  12     8
[2,]  15     9
[3,]  17     7
[4,]  11     9
[5,]  15    NA

> grassy.m = cbind(grassy.m, grazed)
> grassy.m
     mow unmow grazed
[1,]  12     8     11
[2,]  15     9     14
[3,]  17     7     17
[4,]  11     9     10
[5,]  15    NA      8
```

In the first case you use `rbind()` to add the extra row to the matrix, and in the second case you use `cbind()` to add an extra column.

You cannot use the `$` syntax or square brackets to add columns or rows like you did for the data frame. If you try to add a row, for example, you get an error:

```
> grassy.m
     mown unmown
[1,]   12      8
[2,]   15      9
[3,]   17      7
[4,]   11      9
[5,]   15     NA
```

```
> grassy.m[6,] = NA
Error in grassy.m[6, ] = NA : subscript out of bounds
```

You have to use the `rbind()` or `cbind()` commands to add to a matrix. You can, however, create a *blank* matrix and fill in the blanks later, as the following example shows:

```
> extra = matrix(nrow = 2, ncol = 2)
> extra
     [,1] [,2]
[1,]   NA   NA
[2,]   NA   NA

> rbind(grassy.m, extra)
      mown unmown
 [1,]   12      8
 [2,]   15      9
 [3,]   17      7
 [4,]   11      9
 [5,]   15     NA
 [6,]   NA     NA
 [7,]   NA     NA
```

Here you create a blank matrix by omitting the data, which is filled in with `NA` items. You give the dimensions, as rows and columns, for the matrix and then use the `rbind()` command to add this to your existing matrix.

You can also specify the data explicitly like so:

```
matrix(data = NA, ncol = 2, nrow = 2)
matrix(NA, ncol = 2, nrow = 2)
matrix(data = 0, ncol = 2, nrow = 2)
matrix(data = 'X', ncol = 2, nrow = 2)
```

In the first two cases you use `NA` as your data, in the second case you fill the new matrix with the number zero, and in the final case you use an uppercase character `X`.

Adding rows and columns of data to existing objects is useful, especially when you are dealing with fairly small data sets. You do not always want to resort to your spreadsheet for minor alterations. In the following activity you get a bit of extra practice by adding a column and then a row to a data frame you created in the previous activity.

TRY IT OUT Add Rows and Columns to Existing Data

In this activity you will add some rows and columns to an existing data frame (the one you created in an earlier activity).

1. Look at the `flwr` data frame that you created earlier:

   ```
   > flwr
   ```

2. Now create a new numerical vector:

   ```
   > poa = c(8, 9, 11, 12, 10, 15, 17, 16, 16, 7, 8, 8, 5, 9)
   ```

3. Add the new response variable to the previous data frame:

   ```
   > flwr$poa = poa
   ```

4. Rearrange the columns so that the two response variables are on the left:

```
> flwr = flwr[c(1,4,2,3)]
```

5. Create data that will form a new row (the missing replicate from the `unmow` cutting regime):

```
> row15 = data.frame(10,18,'mow','early')
```

6. Add the extra row to the existing data:

```
> flwr[15,] = row15
```

7. Tidy up:

```
> rm(poa, row15)
```

8. View the final result:

```
> flwr
```

How It Works

Any new column of data must be the same length as the existing data frame; pad out with `NA` items if necessary. In this case the new vector is the same length and is created using the `c()` command (although `scan()` would be more efficient). Because the target data frame exists, you can add the new variable using the `$`. The alternative would have been to use the `data.frame()` command, which is fine but requires more typing.

It is always useful to have the response variables on the left and predictors on the right, so the data are rearranged simply by specifying the column order in square brackets.

Adding a row is more complex because you need a combination of numeric and character values. The easiest way is to make a simple data frame containing the row data you require; this enables you to mix numbers and characters. The new row is added to the bottom of the existing data using the square brackets; row 15 does not exist so you create it, and assign the new data to this row.

You remove the *working data* to tidy up the workspace and view the final result simply by typing the name of the data:

```
> flwr
   daisy poa cutting  time
1     12   8     mow early
2     15   9     mow  late
3     17  11     mow early
4     11  12     mow  late
5     15  10     mow early
6      8  15   unmow early
7      9  17   unmow  late
8      7  16   unmow early
9      9  16   unmow  late
10    12   7   sheep early
11    14   8   sheep  late
12    17   8   sheep early
13    21   5   sheep  late
14    17   9   sheep early
15    10  18     mow early
```

SUMMARIZING DATA

Summarizing data is an important element of any statistical or analytical process. However complex the statistical process is, you always need to summarize your data in terms of means or medians, and generally break up the data into more manageable chunks. In the simplest of cases you merely need to summarize rows or columns of data, but as the situation becomes more complex, you need to prepare summary information based on combinations of factors.

The summary statistics that you extract can be used to help visualize the situation or to check replication and experimental design. The statistics can also be used as the basis for graphical summaries of the data.

You have various commands at your disposal, and this section starts with simple row/column summaries and builds toward more complex commands.

Simple Column and Row Summaries

When you only require a really simple column sum or mean, you can use the `colSums()` and `colMeans()` commands. Equivalent commands exist for the rows, too. These are all used in the following example:

```
> fw
         count speed
Taw          9     2
Torridge    25     3
Ouse        15     5
Exe          2     9
Lyn         14    14
Brook       25    24
Ditch       24    29
Fal         47    34

> colMeans(fw)
 count  speed
20.125 15.000

> colSums(fw)
count speed
  161   120

> rowMeans(fw)
     Taw Torridge     Ouse      Exe      Lyn    Brook    Ditch      Fal
     5.5     14.0     10.0      5.5     14.0     24.5     26.5     40.5

> rowSums(fw)
     Taw Torridge     Ouse      Exe      Lyn    Brook    Ditch      Fal
      11       28       20       11       28       49       53       81
```

In the example, the data frame has row names set so the `rowMeans()` and `rowSums()` commands show you the means and sums for the named rows. When row names are not set, you end up with a simple numeric vector as such:

```
> rowSums(mf)
 [1] 274.25 262.15 215.75 240.95 227.95 228.75 197.85 264.75 247.95 262.35 267.35
```

```
[12] 264.35 259.05 245.85 229.75 247.45 275.35 253.05 201.25 295.05 275.55 176.85
[23] 204.95 218.85 208.75
```

If you have NA items, you end up with NA as a result; to avoid this you can use the na.rm = TRUE instruction to ignore NA items in the sum or mean calculation like so:

```
> colSums(bf)
 Grass  Heath Arable
    82     NA     NA

> colSums(bf, na.rm = TRUE)
 Grass  Heath Arable
    82     72     90
```

If some of your data are not numeric, you must specify either the rows (or columns) you want to include or what you want to exclude; the following examples all produce the same result:

```
> str(mf)
'data.frame': 25 obs. of  6 variables:
 $ Length: int  20 21 22 23 21 20 19 16 15 14 ...
 $ Speed : int  12 14 12 16 20 21 17 14 16 21 ...
 $ Algae : int  40 45 45 80 75 65 65 65 35 30 ...
 $ NO3   : num  2.25 2.15 1.75 1.95 1.95 2.75 1.85 1.75 1.95 2.35 ...
 $ BOD   : int  200 180 135 120 110 120 95 168 180 195 ...
 $ site  : Factor w/ 5 levels "Exe","Lyn","Ouse",..: 4 4 4 4 4 5 5 5 5 5 ...

> colMeans(mf[-6])
> colMeans(mf[1:5])
> colMeans(mf[c(1,2,3,4,5)])
 Length   Speed   Algae     NO3     BOD
 19.640  15.800  58.400   2.046 145.960
```

At the beginning you see that the data frame has five columns of numeric data and one character vector (actually, it is a factor). In the first case you exclude the factor column using [-6]; in the second case you specify columns one to five using [1:5]. In the last case you list all five columns you require explicitly.

Although these commands are useful, they are somewhat limited and are intended as *convenience* commands. They are also only useful when your data are all numeric, and you may very well have data comprising numeric predictor variables and factor response variables. In these cases you can call upon a range of other summary commands, as you see shortly.

Complex Summary Functions

When you have complicated data you often have a mixture of numeric and factor variables. The simple colMeans() and colSums() commands are not sufficient enough to extract information from these data. Fortunately, you have a variety of commands that you can use to summarize your data, and you have seen some of these before. Here you see an overview of some of these methods.

To help illustrate the options, start by taking a numeric data frame and adding a factor: a simple vector of site names:

```
> mfnames = c(rep('Taw',5), rep('Torridge',5), rep('Ouse',5), rep('Exe',5),
rep('Lyn',5))
```

```
> mf$site = factor(mfnames)

> str(mf)
'data.frame': 25 obs. of  6 variables:
 $ Length: int  20 21 22 23 21 20 19 16 15 14 ...
 $ Speed : int  12 14 12 16 20 21 17 14 16 21 ...
 $ Algae : int  40 45 45 80 75 65 65 65 35 30 ...
 $ NO3   : num  2.25 2.15 1.75 1.95 1.95 2.75 1.85 1.75 1.95 2.35 ...
 $ BOD   : int  200 180 135 120 110 120 95 168 180 195 ...
 $ site  : Factor w/ 5 levels "Exe","Lyn","Ouse",..: 4 4 4 4 4 5 5 5 5 5 ...
```

Now that you have a suitable practice sample, it is time to look at some of the complex summary functions that you can use.

The rowsum() Command

You can calculate the sums of rows in a data frame or matrix and group the sums according to some factor or grouping variable. In the following example, you use the `rowsum()` command to determine the sums for each of the sites that are listed in the `site` column:

```
> rowsum(mf[1:5], group = mf$site)
         Length Speed Algae   NO3 BOD
Exe          88    83   235  7.15 859
Lyn         110    73   355 12.95 534
Ouse        102    76   325 10.35 753
Taw         107    74   285 10.05 745
Torridge     84    89   260 10.65 758
```

The result shows all the sites listed, and for each numeric variable you have the sum. Note that you specified the columns in the data using `[1:5]`; these are the numeric columns. You could also eliminate the non-numeric column like so:

```
> rowsum(mf[-6], mf$site)
```

In this case the sixth column contained the grouping variable. You can also specify a single column using its name (in quotes):

```
> rowsum(mf['Length'], mf$site)
         Length
Exe          88
Lyn         110
Ouse        102
Taw         107
Torridge     84
```

When you have a matrix, your grouping variable must be separate because a matrix is comprised of data of all the same type. In the following example, you create a simple vector specifying the groupings:

```
> bird
              Garden Hedgerow Parkland Pasture Woodland
Blackbird         47       10       40       2        2
Chaffinch         19        3        5       0        2
Great Tit         50        0       10       7        0
House Sparrow     46       16        8       4        0
Robin              9        3        0       0        2
Song Thrush        4        0        6       0        0
```

```
> grp = c(1,1,1,2,2,3)

> rowsum(bird, grp)
  Garden Hedgerow Parkland Pasture Woodland
1    116       13       55       9        4
2     55       19        8       4        2
3      4        0        6       0        0
```

The group vector must be the same length as the number of rows in your matrix; in this case, six rows of data. You might also create a character vector as in the following example:

```
> grp = c('black', 'color', 'color', rep('brown', 3))

> grp
[1] "black" "color" "color" "brown" "brown" "brown"

> rowsum(bird, grp)
      Garden Hedgerow Parkland Pasture Woodland
black     47       10       40       2        2
brown     59       19       14       4        2
color     69        3       15       7        2
```

It is also possible to specify part of the matrix using a grouping contained within the original matrix:

```
> rowsum(bird[,1:4], bird[,5])
  Garden Hedgerow Parkland Pasture
0    100       16       24      11
2     75       16       45       2
```

Here you use the last column as the grouping, and the result shows the group labels (as numbers). However, you can use only a numeric grouping variable, of course, because the matrix can contain only data of a single type.

The apply() Command

You can use the `apply()` command to apply a function over all the rows or columns of a data frame (or matrix). To use it, you specify the rows or columns that you require, whether you want to apply the function to the rows or columns, and finally, the actual function you want, like so:

```
apply(X, MARGIN, FUN, ...)
```

You replace the `MARGIN` part with a numeric value: 1 = rows and 2 = columns. You can also add other instructions if they are related to the function you are going to use; for example, you can exclude `NA` items, using `na.rm = TRUE`. In the following case you use the `apply()` command to apply the median to the first five columns of your data frame:

```
> apply(mf[1:5], 2, median)
Length  Speed  Algae    NO3    BOD
 20.00  16.00  65.00   1.95 145.00
```

You put the columns you require in the square brackets; in this case you used `[1:5]`. Because your object is a data frame, you can simply list the column names; more properly you should use [row, col] syntax:

```
> apply(mf[,1:5], 2, median)
```

. added the comma, saying in effect that you want all the rows but only columns one through .e. If you want to apply your function to the rows, you simply switch the numeric value in the MARGIN part:

```
> apply(mf[,1:5], 1, median)
 [1] 20 21 22 23 21 21 19 16 16 21 21 26 21 20 19 18 17 19 21 21 22 25 24 23 22
```

Notice that you have not specified MARGIN or FUN in the command, but have used a shortcut. R commands have a default order for instructions; so as long as you put the arguments in the default order you do not need to name them. If you do name them then the instructions can appear in any order. The full version for the preceding example would be written like so:

```
> apply(X = mf[,1:5], MARGIN = 1, FUN = median)
```

The apply() command enables you to use a wider variety of commands on rows and columns than the rowSums() or colMeans() commands, which obviously are limited to sum() and mean(). However, you can use apply() only on entire rows or columns that are discrete samples. When you have grouping variables, you need a different approach.

Using tapply() to Summarize Using a Grouping Variable

The summary commands you have looked at so far have enabled you to look at entire rows or columns; only the rowsum() command lets you take into account a grouping variable. When you have grouping variables in the form of predictor variables, for example, you can use the tapply() command to take into account one or more factors as grouping variables.

The following illustrates a fairly simple example where you have a data frame comprising several numeric columns, and a single column that is a grouping variable (a factor):

```
> tapply(mf$Length, mf$site, FUN = sum)
     Exe       Lyn      Ouse       Taw Torridge
      88       110       102       107       84
```

The tapply() command works only on a single vector at a time; in this instance you choose the Length column using the $ syntax. Next you specify the INDEX that you want to use; in other words, the grouping variable. Finally, you select the function that you want to apply; here you choose the sum. The general form of the command is as follows:

```
tapply(X, INDEX, FUN = NULL, ...)
```

If you omit the FUN part, or set it to NULL, you get a vector that relates to the INDEX. This is easiest to see in an example:

```
> tapply(mf$Length, mf$site, FUN = NULL)
 [1] 4 4 4 4 4 5 5 5 5 5 3 3 3 3 3 1 1 1 1 1 2 2 2 2 2
```

If you refer to the original data you will see that the fourth site is the Exe factor, and because this is alphabetically the first, it is returned first. The vector result shows the rows of the original data that relate to the grouping factor.

When you have more than one grouping variable, you can list several factors to be your INDEX. In the following example you have a data frame comprising a column of numeric data and two factor columns:

```
> str(pw)
'data.frame': 18 obs. of  3 variables:
```

```
 $ height: int  9 11 6 14 17 19 28 31 32 7 ...
 $ plant : Factor w/ 2 levels "sativa","vulgaris": 2 2 2 2 2 2 2 2 2 1 ...
 $ water : Factor w/ 3 levels "hi","lo","mid": 2 2 2 3 3 3 1 1 1 2 ...

> tapply(pw$height, list(pw$plant, pw$water), mean)
               hi       lo      mid
sativa   39.66667 6.000000 15.33333
vulgaris 30.33333 8.666667 16.66667
```

This time you specify the columns you want to use as grouping variables in a `list()` command; there are only two variables here and the first one becomes the rows of the result and the second becomes the columns.

If you have more than two grouping variables, the result is subdivided into more tables as required. In the following example you have an extra factor column and use all three factors as grouping variables:

```
> str(pw)
'data.frame': 18 obs. of  4 variables:
 $ height: int  9 11 6 14 17 19 28 31 32 7 ...
 $ plant : Factor w/ 2 levels "sativa","vulgaris": 2 2 2 2 2 2 2 2 2 1 ...
 $ water : Factor w/ 3 levels "hi","lo","mid": 2 2 2 3 3 3 1 1 1 2 ...
 $ season: Factor w/ 2 levels "spring","summer": 1 2 2 1 2 2 1 2 2 1 ...

> pw.tap = tapply(pw$height, list(pw$plant, pw$water, pw$season), mean)
, , spring

         hi lo mid
sativa   44  7  14
vulgaris 28  9  14

, , summer

           hi  lo mid
sativa   37.5 5.5  16
vulgaris 31.5 8.5  18
```

In this case the third grouping variable has two levels, which results in two tables, one for `spring` and one for `summer`. The result is presented as a kind of R object called an array; this can have any number of dimensions, but in this case you have three. If you look at the structure of the result using the `str()` command, you can see how the dimensions are set:

```
> pw.tap = tapply(pw$height, list(pw$plant, pw$water, pw$season), mean)
> str(pw.tap)
 num [1:2, 1:3, 1:2] 44 28 7 9 14 14 37.5 31.5 5.5 8.5 ...
 - attr(*, "dimnames")=List of 3
  ..$ : chr [1:2] "sativa" "vulgaris"
  ..$ : chr [1:3] "hi" "lo" "mid"
  ..$ : chr [1:2] "spring" "summer"
```

You can see that the first dimension is related to the `plant` variable, the second is related to the `water` variable, and the third is related to the `season` variable; in other words, the dimensions are in the same order as you specified in the `tapply()` command.

You can use the square brackets to extract parts of your result object, but now you have the extra dimension to take into account. To extract part of the result object you need to specify three values in the square brackets (corresponding to each of the three dimensions, plant, water, and season). In the following example you select a single item from the pw.tap result object by specifying a single value for each of the three dimensions.

```
> pw.tap[1,1,1]
[1] 44
```

The item you selected corresponds to the first plant (sativa), the first water treatment (hi), and the first season (spring), and you see the result, 44. If you want to see several items you can specify multiple values for any dimension. In the following example you select two values for the plant dimension (1:2), which will display a result for both sativa and vulgaris.

```
> pw.tap[1:2,1,1]
  sativa vulgaris
      44       28
```

The two result values (44 and 28) correspond to the first water treatment (hi) and the first season (spring). In the following example you select multiple values for the first two dimensions (plant and water) but only a single value for the third (season).

```
> pw.tap[1:2,1:3,1]
          hi lo mid
sativa    44  7  14
vulgaris 28  9  14
```

Now you can see that you have selected all of the plant and water treatments but only a single season (spring).

The result is an array object, and as you have seen, it can have multiple dimensions. You can use the class() command to determine that the result is indeed an array object:

```
> class(pw.tap)
[1] "array"
```

Summarizing data using grouping variables is an important task that you will need to undertake often. Most often you will need to check means or medians for the groups, but many other functions can be useful. In the following activity you practice using the mean, but you could try out some other functions (for example, median, sum, sd, or length).

TRY IT OUT Use Grouping Variables to Summarize Complex Data

In this activity you will examine the data object you created in an earlier activity by using some grouping variables to split the data in various ways and summarize using the mean.

1. Look back at the flwr data object that you created earlier:

```
> flwr
```

2. You have two response variables (daisy and poa) and two predictor variables (cutting and time). Summarize the daisy variable by obtaining the mean for the grouping variable cutting:

```
> tapply(flwr$daisy, flwr$cutting, mean)
     mow    sheep    unmow
13.33333 16.20000  8.25000
```

3. Now add the second grouping variable:

```
> tapply(flwr$daisy, list(flwr$cutting, flwr$time), mean)
          early late
mow   13.50000 13.0
sheep 15.33333 17.5
unmow  7.50000  9.0
```

4. Alter the result by changing the order of the grouping variables:

```
> tapply(flwr$daisy, list(flwr$time, flwr$cutting), mean)
       mow    sheep unmow
early 13.5 15.33333   7.5
late  13.0 17.50000   9.0
```

5. Look at the other predictor variable:

```
> with(flwr, tapply(poa, list(cutting, time), mean))
      early late
mow   11.75 10.5
sheep  8.00  6.5
unmow 15.50 16.5
```

6. Alter the order of the result:

```
> with(flwr, tapply(poa, list(time, cutting), mean))
        mow sheep unmow
early 11.75   8.0  15.5
late  10.50   6.5  16.5
```

How It Works

The `tapply()` command requires three instructions: the data to summarize, a grouping variable (which can be a list of several), and the summary function to apply. If the data are not separate vectors, you need to use `$`, `attach()`, or `with()` to "read" the variables. Here you start by using `$`.

When you have two grouping variables, use the `list()` command to specify them. The first grouping variable listed forms the rows of the result and the second forms the columns. Any additional variables result in separate tables and an array object.

The `tapply()` command is very useful, but you may only want to have a simple table/matrix as your result rather than a complicated array. It is possible to summarize a data object using multiple grouping factors using other commands, as you see next.

The aggregate() Command

The `aggregate()` command enables you to compute summary statistics for subsets of a data frame or matrix; the result comes out as a single matrix rather than an array item, even with multiple grouping factors. The general form of the command is as follows:

```
aggregate(x, by, FUN, ...)
```

You specify the data you want followed by a `list()` of the grouping variables and the function you want to use. In the following example you use a single grouping variable and the `sum()` function:

```
> aggregate(mf[1:5], by = list(mf$site), FUN = sum)
   Group.1 Length Speed Algae   NO3 BOD
1      Exe     88    83   235  7.15 859
2      Lyn    110    73   355 12.95 534
3     Ouse    102    76   325 10.35 753
4      Taw    107    74   285 10.05 745
5 Torridge     84    89   260 10.65 758
```

In this case you specify all the numeric columns in the data frame, and the result shows the sum of each of the groups represented by the grouping variable (`site`).

You can also use the `aggregate()` command with a formula syntax; in this case you specify the response variable to the left of the ~ and the predictor variables to the right, like so:

```
> aggregate(Length ~ site, data = mf, FUN = mean)
      site Length
1      Exe   17.6
2      Lyn   22.0
3     Ouse   20.4
4      Taw   21.4
5 Torridge   16.8
```

This allows a slightly simpler command because you do not need the `$` signs as long as you specify where the data are to be found. In this case you chose a single response variable (`Length`) and the `mean()` as your summary function. You can select several response variables at once by wrapping them in a `cbind()` command:

```
> aggregate(cbind(Length, BOD) ~ site, data = mf, FUN = mean)
      site Length   BOD
1      Exe   17.6 171.8
2      Lyn   22.0 106.8
3     Ouse   20.4 150.6
4      Taw   21.4 149.0
5 Torridge   16.8 151.6
```

Here you chose two response variables (`Length` and `BOD`), which are given in the `cbind()` command (thus making a temporary matrix). You can select all the variables by using a period instead of any names to the left of the ~:

```
> aggregate(. ~ site, data = mf, FUN = mean)
      site Length Speed Algae  NO3   BOD
1      Exe   17.6  16.6    47 1.43 171.8
2      Lyn   22.0  14.6    71 2.59 106.8
3     Ouse   20.4  15.2    65 2.07 150.6
4      Taw   21.4  14.8    57 2.01 149.0
5 Torridge   16.8  17.8    52 2.13 151.6
```

Here you use all the variables in the data frame. This works only if the remaining variables are all numeric; if you have other character variables, you need to specify the columns you want explicitly.

Because of the nature of the output/result, some people may find the `aggregate()` command more useful in presenting summary statistics than the `tapply()` command discussed earlier. In the following example, you have a data frame with one response variable and three predictor variables:

```
> str(pw)
'data.frame': 18 obs. of  4 variables:
 $ height: int  9 11 6 14 17 19 28 31 32 7 ...
 $ plant : Factor w/ 2 levels "sativa","vulgaris": 2 2 2 2 2 2 2 2 2 1 ...
 $ water : Factor w/ 3 levels "hi","lo","mid": 2 2 2 3 3 3 1 1 1 2 ...
 $ season: Factor w/ 2 levels "spring","summer": 1 2 2 1 2 2 1 2 2 1 ...

> pw.agg = aggregate(height ~ plant * water * season, data = pw, FUN = mean)
      plant water season height
1    sativa    hi spring   44.0
2  vulgaris    hi spring   28.0
3    sativa    lo spring    7.0
4  vulgaris    lo spring    9.0
5    sativa   mid spring   14.0
6  vulgaris   mid spring   14.0
7    sativa    hi summer   37.5
8  vulgaris    hi summer   31.5
9    sativa    lo summer    5.5
10 vulgaris    lo summer    8.5
11   sativa   mid summer   16.0
12 vulgaris   mid summer   18.0
```

The result is a simple data frame, and this can make it easier to extract the components than for the array result you had previously with the `tapply()` command.

You could have achieved the same result by using the period instead of the grouping variable names like so:

```
>aggregate(height ~ . , data = pw, FUN = mean)
```

So, like the previous example, the period means, "everything else not already named." If you replace the period with a number 1, you get quite a different result:

```
>aggregate(height ~ 1 , data = pw, FUN = mean)
    height
1 19.44444
```

You get the overall mean value here; essentially you have said, "don't use any grouping variables."

The `aggregate()` command is very powerful, partly because you can use the formula syntax and partly because of the output, which is a single data frame. In the following activity you practice using the command using the mean as the summary function, but you could try some others (for example, `median`, `sum`, `sd`, or `length`).

TRY IT OUT Use the aggregate() Command to Make Summary Results

In this activity you look at a data object you created in an earlier activity. You use the `aggregate()` command to explore the means of various groupings.

1. Look again at the `flwr` data object that you created earlier:

```
>flwr
```

2. You have two response variables (daisy and poa) and two predictor variables (cutting and time). Begin by summarizing the mean of the daisy variable grouped by cutting:

```
> aggregate(flwr$daisy, by = list(flwr$cutting), FUN = mean)
  Group.1        x
1     mow 13.33333
2   sheep 16.20000
3   unmow  8.25000
```

3. Now add the time variable and group using both predictors:

```
> aggregate(flwr$daisy, by = list(flwr$cutting, flwr$time), FUN = mean)
  Group.1 Group.2        x
1     mow   early 13.50000
2   sheep   early 15.33333
3   unmow   early  7.50000
4     mow    late 13.00000
5   sheep    late 17.50000
6   unmow    late  9.00000
```

4. Summarize both response variables using both the predictors as grouping variables:

```
> aggregate(flwr[1:2], by = list(flwr$cutting, flwr$time), FUN = mean)
  Group.1 Group.2    daisy   poa
1     mow   early 13.50000 11.75
2   sheep   early 15.33333  8.00
3   unmow   early  7.50000 15.50
4     mow    late 13.00000 10.50
5   sheep    late 17.50000  6.50
6   unmow    late  9.00000 16.50
```

5. Now use the formula syntax to summarize the poa response variable by using both grouping variables:

```
> aggregate(poa ~ cutting + time, data = flwr, FUN = mean)
  cutting  time   poa
1     mow early 11.75
2   sheep early  8.00
3   unmow early 15.50
4     mow  late 10.50
5   sheep  late  6.50
6   unmow  late 16.50
```

6. Summarize both response variables using both predictor variables:

```
> aggregate(. ~ cutting + time, data = flwr, FUN = mean)
  cutting  time    daisy   poa
1     mow early 13.50000 11.75
2   sheep early 15.33333  8.00
3   unmow early  7.50000 15.50
4     mow  late 13.00000 10.50
5   sheep  late 17.50000  6.50
6   unmow  late  9.00000 16.50
```

7. Obtain the same result by specifying the response variables explicitly:

```
> aggregate(cbind(poa, daisy) ~ cutting + time, data = flwr, FUN = mean)
```

8. This time use all the variables, but save some typing and specify the grouping variables with a period:

```
> aggregate(cbind(poa, daisy) ~ ., data = flwr, FUN = mean)
```

9. Ignore all the grouping variables and obtain an overall mean for the two response variables:

```
> aggregate(cbind(poa, daisy) ~ 1, data = flwr, FUN = mean)
       poa    daisy
1 11.26667 12.93333
```

How It Works

Using the `aggregate()` command without the formula syntax requires a `list()` even if you are summarizing using a single grouping variable. The result is a single data frame with the first columns ordered in the same order in which you specify the grouping variables, with the final column containing the response. You can specify multiple response variables from a data frame by using the square brackets.

The formula syntax enables you to specify the data in a logical manner, and the result also contains more appropriate column headings. Multiple response variables can be given by using the `cbind()` command to name them explicitly. You can use a period to state that you require all variables not already named in the command. That works here because you do not have any other variables. You can use the period to specify the predictor variables, too.

Using a 1 instead of any grouping variables gives an overall value, essentially ignoring the groupings.

SUMMARY

- Vector objects need to be of equal length before they can be made into a data frame or matrix.
- You can use the `rep()` command to create replicate labels as factors. You can also use the `gl()` command to generate factor levels.
- The levels of a factor can be examined using the `levels()` and `nlevels()` commands.
- A character vector can be converted to a factor using the `as.factor()` and `factor()` commands.
- Data frames can be constructed using the `data.frame()` command. Matrix objects can be constructed using `matrix()`, `cbind()`, or `rbind()` commands.
- Simple summary commands can be applied to rows or columns using `rowSums()` and `colMeans` commands.
- The `apply()` command can apply a function to rows or columns.
- The `rowsum()` command can use a grouping variable to sum data across rows. Grouping variables can be used in the `tapply()` and `aggregate()` commands along with any function.
- If more than two grouping variables are used with the `tapply()` command, a multi-dimensional array object is the result. In contrast, the `aggregate()` command always produces a single data frame as the result and can use the formula syntax.

Available for download on Wrox.com

You can find answers to these exercises in Appendix A.

1. Look at the `bees` data object from the `Beginning.RData` file for this exercise. The data are a matrix, and the columns relate to individual bee species and the rows to different flowers. The numerical data are the number of bees observed visiting each flower. Create a new factor variable that could be used as a grouping variable. Here you require the general color type to be represented; you can think of the first two as being equivalent (blue) and the last three as equivalent (yellow).

2. Take the `bees` matrix and add the grouping variable you just created to it to form a new matrix.

3. Use the `flcol` grouping variable you just created to summarize the `Buff.tail` column in the `bees` data; use any sensible summarizing command. Can you produce a summary for all the bee species in one go?

4. Look at the `ChickWeight` data item, which comes built into R. The data comprise a data frame (although it also has other attributes) with a single response variable and some predictor variables. Look at median values for `weight` broken down by `Diet`. Now add the `Time` variable as a second grouping factor.

5. Access the `mtcars` data, which are built in to R. The data are in a data frame with several columns. Summarize the miles-per-gallon variable (`mpg`) as a mean for the three grouping variables `cyl`, `gear`, and `carb`.

▶ WHAT YOU LEARNED IN THIS CHAPTER

TOPIC	KEY POINTS
Making data items: `length()`	Vectors need to be the same length if they are to be added to a data frame or matrix. The `length()` command can query the current length or alter it. Setting the length to shorter than current truncates the item and making it longer adds `NA` items to the end.

Making data items:
`names()`
`row.names()`
`rownames()` `colnames()`
	You can use several commands to query and alter names of columns or rows. The `rownames()` and `colnames()` commands are used for matrix objects, whereas the `names()` and `row.names()` commands work on data frames.

Stacking separate vectors: `stack()`	You can use the `stack()` command to combine vectors and so form a data frame suitable for complex analysis. This really only works when you have a single response variable and a single predictor.
Removing NA items: `na.omit()`	The `na.omit()` command strips out unwanted `NA` items from vectors and data frames.

Repeated elements:
`rep()`
`gl()`
	You can generate repeated elements, such as character labels that will form a predictor variable, by using the `rep()` or `gl()` commands. Both commands enable you to generate multiple levels of a variable based on a repeating pattern.

Factor elements:
`factor()` `as.factor()`
`levels()` `nlevels()`
`as.numeric()`
	A factor is a special sort of character variable. You can force a vector to be treated as a factor by using the `factor()` or `as.factor()` commands. The `levels()` command shows the different levels of a factor variable, and the `nlevels()` command returns the number of discrete levels of a factor variable. A factor can be returned as a list of numbers by using the `as.numeric()` command.

Constructing a data frame: `data.frame()`	Several objects can be combined to form a data frame using the `data.frame()` command.

Constructing a matrix:
`matrix()`
`cbind()` `rbind()`
	You can create a matrix in two main ways: by assembling a vector into rows and columns using the `matrix()` command or by combining other elements. You can combine elements by column using the `cbind()` command or by row using the `rbind()` command.

Simple row or column sums or means:
`rowSums()` `colSums()`
`rowMeans()` `colMeans()`
	Numerical objects (data frames and matrix objects) can be examined using simple row/column sums or means using `rowSums()`, `colSums()`, `rowMeans()`, or `colMeans()` commands as appropriate. These cannot take into account any grouping variable.

continues

WHAT YOU LEARNED IN THIS CHAPTER *(continued)*

TOPIC	KEY POINTS
Simple sum using a grouping variable: `rowsum()`	The `rowsum()` command enables you to add up columns based on a grouping variable. The result is a series of rows of sums (hence the command name).
Apply a command to rows or columns: `apply()`	The `apply()` command enables you to give a command across rows or columns of a data frame or matrix.
Use a grouping variable with any command: `tapply()`	The `tapply()` command enables the use of grouping variables and can utilize any command (for example, `mean`, `median`, `sd`), which is applied to a single vector (or element of a data frame or matrix).
Array objects: `object[x, y, z , ...]`	An array object has more than two dimensions; that is, it cannot be described simply by rows and columns. An array is typically generated by using the `tapply()` command with more than two grouping variables. The resulting array has several dimensions, each one relating to a grouping variable. The array itself can be subdivided using the square brackets and identifying the appropriate dimensions.
Summarize using a grouping variable: `aggregate()`	The `aggregate()` command can utilize any command and number of grouping variables. The result is a two-dimensional data frame; regardless of how many grouping variables are used.

10

Regression (Linear Modeling)

WHAT YOU WILL LEARN IN THIS CHAPTER:

- How to carry out linear regression (including multiple regression)
- How to carry out curvilinear regression using logarithmic and polynomials as examples
- How to build a regression model using both forward and backward stepwise processes
- How to plot regression models
- How to add lines of best-fit to regression plots
- How to determine confidence intervals for regression models
- How to plot confidence intervals
- How to draw diagnostic plots

Linear modeling is a widely used analytical method. In a general sense, it involves a response variable and one or more predictor variables. The technique uses a mathematical relationship between the response and predictor variables. You might, for example, have data on the abundance of an organism (the response variable) and details about various habitat variables (predictor variables). Linear modeling, or multiple regression as it is also known, can show you which of the habitat variables are most important, and also which are statistically significant. Linear regression is quite similar to the analysis of variance (ANOVA) that you learned about earlier. The main difference is that in ANOVA, the predictor variables are discrete (that is, they have different levels), whereas in regression they are continuous.

Although this is not a book about statistical analysis, the techniques of regression are so important that you should know how to carry them out. The `lm()` command is used to carry out linear modeling in R. To use it, you use the formula syntax. Undertaking regression involves a range of other R skills that are generally useful; this will become evident as you work through the examples in the text.

SIMPLE LINEAR REGRESSION

The simplest form of regression is akin to a correlation where you have two variables—a response variable and a predictor. In the following example you see a simple data frame with two columns, which you can correlate:

```
> fw
         count speed
Taw          9     2
Torridge    25     3
Ouse        15     5
Exe          2     9
Lyn         14    14
Brook       25    24
Ditch       24    29
Fal         47    34

> cor.test(~ count + speed, data = fw)

       Pearson's product-moment correlation

data:  count and speed
t = 2.5689, df = 6, p-value = 0.0424
alternative hypothesis: true correlation is not equal to 0
95 percent confidence interval:
 0.03887166 0.94596455
sample estimates:
      cor
0.7237206
```

Note that in this simple correlation you do not have a response term to the left of the ~ in the formula. You can run the same analysis using the `lm()` command; this time, though, you place the predictor on the left of the ~ and the response on the right:

```
> lm(count ~ speed, data = fw)

Call:
lm(formula = count ~ speed, data = fw)

Coefficients:
(Intercept)        speed
     8.2546       0.7914
```

NOTE *Correlation and simple regression are similar in that you are looking to compare one variable with another. In the Pearson correlation you are assuming that the data are normally distributed and are looking to see how close the relationship is between the variables. In regression you are taking the analysis further and assuming a mathematical, and therefore predictable, relationship between the variables. The results of regression analysis show the slope and intercept values that describe this relationship. The R squared value that you obtain from the regression is the square of the correlation coefficient from the Pearson correlation, which demonstrates the similarities between the methods.*

The result shows you the coefficients for the regression, that is, the intercept and the slope. To see more details you should save your regression as a named object; then you can use the `summary()` command like so:

```
> fw.lm = lm(count ~ speed, data = fw)
> summary(fw.lm)

Call:
lm(formula = count ~ speed, data = fw)

Residuals:
    Min      1Q  Median      3Q     Max
-13.377  -5.801  -1.542   5.051  14.371

Coefficients:
            Estimate Std. Error t value Pr(>|t|)
(Intercept)   8.2546     5.8531   1.410   0.2081
speed         0.7914     0.3081   2.569   0.0424 *
---
Signif. codes:  0 '***' 0.001 '**' 0.01 '*' 0.05 '.' 0.1 ' ' 1

Residual standard error: 10.16 on 6 degrees of freedom
Multiple R-squared: 0.5238,     Adjusted R-squared: 0.4444
F-statistic: 6.599 on 1 and 6 DF,  p-value: 0.0424
```

Now you see a more detailed result; for example, the p-value for the linear model is exactly the same as for the standard Pearson correlation that you ran earlier. The result object contains more information, and you can see what is available by using the `names()` command like so:

```
> names(fw.lm)
 [1] "coefficients"  "residuals"     "effects"       "rank"
 [5] "fitted.values" "assign"        "qr"            "df.residual"
 [9] "xlevels"       "call"          "terms"         "model"
```

You can extract these components using the `$` syntax; for example, to get the coefficients you use the following:

```
> fw.lm$coefficients
(Intercept)       speed
  8.2545956   0.7913603

> fw.lm$coef
(Intercept)       speed
  8.2545956   0.7913603
```

In the first case you type the name in full, but in the second case you see that you can abbreviate the latter part as long as it is unambiguous.

Many of these results objects can be extracted using specific commands, as you see next.

Linear Model Results Objects

When you have a result from a linear model, you end up with an object that contains a variety of results; the basic `summary()` command shows you some of these. You can extract the components using the `$` syntax, but some of these components are important enough to have specific commands. The following sections discuss these components and their commands in detail.

Coefficients

You can extract the coefficients using the `coef()` command. To use the command, you simply give the name of the linear modeling result like so:

```
> coef(fw.lm)
(Intercept)       speed
  8.2545956   0.7913603
```

You can obtain confidence intervals on these coefficients using the `confint()` command. The default settings produce 95-percent confidence intervals; that is, at 2.5 percent and 97.5 percent, like so:

```
> confint(fw.lm)
                  2.5 %    97.5 %
(Intercept) -6.06752547 22.576717
speed        0.03756445  1.545156
```

You can alter the interval using the `level =` instruction, specifying the interval as a proportion. You can also choose which confidence variables to display (the default is all of them) by using the `parm =` instruction and placing the names of the variables in quotes as done in the following example:

```
> confint(fw.lm, parm = c('(Intercept)', 'speed'), level = 0.9)
                   5 %      95 %
(Intercept) -3.1191134 19.628305
speed        0.1927440  1.389977
```

Note that the intercept term is given with surrounding parentheses like so, `(Intercept)`, which is exactly as it appears in the `summary()` command.

Fitted Values

You can use the `fitted()` command to extract values fitted to the linear model; in other words, you can use the equation of the model to predict `y` values for each `x` value like so:

```
> fitted(fw.lm)
      Taw  Torridge      Ouse       Exe       Lyn     Brook     Ditch       Fal
 9.837316 10.628676 12.211397 15.376838 19.333640 27.247243 31.204044 35.160846
```

In this case the rows of data are named, so the result of the `fitted()` command also produces names.

Residuals

You can view the residuals using the `residuals()` command; the `resid()` command is an alias for the same thing and produces the same result:

```
> residuals(fw.lm)
        Taw    Torridge        Ouse         Exe         Lyn       Brook
 -0.8373162  14.3713235   2.7886029 -13.3768382  -5.3336397  -2.2472426
      Ditch         Fal
 -7.2040441  11.8391544
```

Once again, you see that the residuals are named because the original data had row names.

Formula

You can access the formula used in the linear model using the `formula()` command like so:

```
> formula(fw.lm)
count ~ speed
```

This is not quite the same as the complete call to the `lm()` command which looks like this:

```
> fw.lm$call
lm(formula = count ~ speed, data = fw)
```

Best-Fit Line

You can use these linear modeling commands to help you visualize a simple linear model in graphical form. The following commands all produce essentially the same graph:

```
> plot(fw$speed, fw$count)
> plot(~ speed + count, data = fw)
> plot(count ~ speed, data = fw)
> plot(formula(fw), data = fw)
```

The graph looks like Figure 10-1.

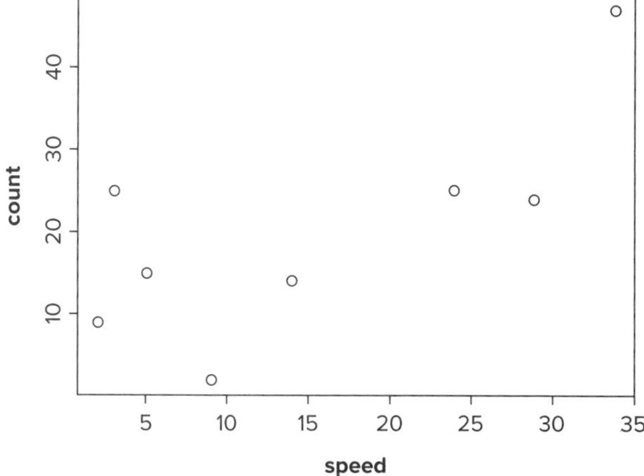

FIGURE 10-1

To add a line of best-fit, you need the intercept and the slope. You can use the `abline()` command to add the line once you have these values. Any of the following commands would produce the required line of best-fit:

```
> abline(lm(count ~ speed, data = fw))
> abline(a = coef(fw.lm[1], b = coef(fw.lm[2])))
> abline(coef(fw.lm))
```

The first is intuitive in that you can see the call to the linear model clearly. The second is quite clumsy, but shows where the values come from. The last is the most simple to type and makes best use of the `lm()` result object. The basic plot with a line of best-fit looks like Figure 10-2.

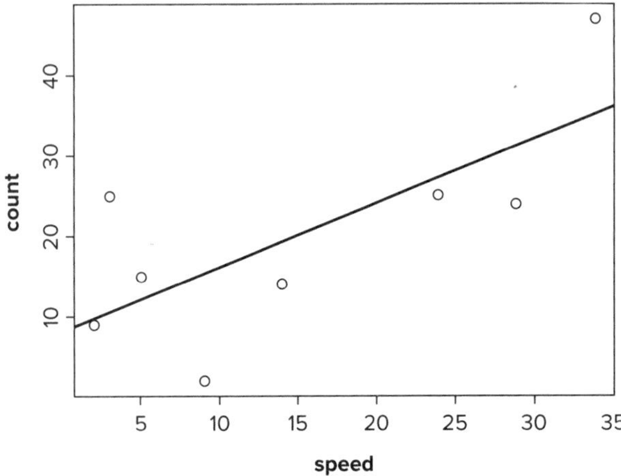

FIGURE 10-2

You can draw your best-fit line in different styles, widths, and colors using options you met previously (`lty`, `lwd`, and `col`). Table 10-1 acts as a reminder and summary of their use.

TABLE 10-1: Summary of Commands used in Drawing Lines of Best-Fit

COMMAND	EXPLANATION
`lty = n`	Sets the line type. Line types can be specified as an integer (0 = blank, 1 = solid (default), 2 = dashed, 3 = dotted, 4 = dotdash, 5 = longdash, 6 = twodash) or as one of the character strings `"blank"`, `"solid"`, `"dashed"`, `"dotted"`, `"dotdash"`, `"longdash"`, or `"twodash"`, where `"blank"` uses invisible lines (that is, does not draw them).
`lwd = n`	Sets the line width using an numerical value where 1 is standard width, 2 is double width, and so on. Defaults to 1.
`col = color`	Sets the line color using a named color (in quotes) or an integer value. Defaults to `"black"` (that is, 1). You can see the list of colors by using `colors()`.

You look at fitting curves to linear models in a later section.

Simple regression, that is, involving one response variable and one predictor variable, is an important stepping stone to the more complicated multiple regression that you will meet shortly (where you have one response variable but several predictor variables). To put into practice some of the skills, you can try out regression for yourself in the following activity.

TRY IT OUT Carry Out Linear Regression

In this activity you will carry out a simple regression and look at the results, as well as produce a graph with a line of best-fit.

1. Look at the `cars` data; these come as part of R and you can access them simply by typing the name. You have two variables, `speed` and `distance`:

```
> str(cars)
'data.frame':     50 obs. of  2 variables:
 $ speed: num  4 4 7 7 8 9 10 10 10 11 ...
 $ dist : num  2 10 4 22 16 10 18 26 34 17 ...
```

2. Create a simple regression of stopping distance and car speed:

```
> cars.lm = lm(dist ~ speed, data = cars)
> summary(cars.lm)
```

3. Now look at the result object:

```
> names(cars.lm)
```

4. Get the coefficients; you can do this in two ways:

```
> cars.lm$coeff
> coef(cars.lm)
```

5. Now obtain the confidence intervals of the coefficients:

```
> confint(cars.lm)
```

6. Get the fitted values for the regression model; once again, you can use two methods:

```
> cars.lm$fitted
> fitted(cars.lm)
```

7. Look at the residuals from the regression model:

```
> cars.lm$resid
> resid(cars.lm)
```

8. Remind yourself of the formula used in the analysis:

```
> cars.lm$call
lm(formula = dist ~ speed, data = cars)
> formula(cars.lm)
dist ~ speed
```

9. Draw a scatter plot of the relationship:

```
> plot(dist ~ speed, data = cars)
```

10. Add a line of best-fit to the scatter plot:

```
> abline(cars.lm)
```

How It Works

The `cars` data are available from within R and the `str()` command enables you to see what you are dealing with. You can bring up more information if you type:

```
> help(cars)
```

The regression is a simple one carried out using the `lm()` command, and by using the `names()` command you can see that the result is comprised of several parts. Some of these are available using dedicated commands.

The `plot()` command draws a scatter plot of the two variables. You could try altering the axis titles or the plotting character by including some extra instructions (recall Chapter 7 on graphs). Finally, you add the line of best-fit with the `abline()` command. The command is able to extract the coefficients from the result you created, and uses these to place the line. You might try looking at Table 10-1 and making the line appear slightly differently.

Similarity between lm() and aov()

You can think of the `aov()` command as a special case of linear modeling, with the command being a "wrapper" for the `lm()` command. Indeed you can use the `lm()` command to carry out analysis of variance. In the following example, you see how to use the `aov()` and `lm()` commands with the same formula on the same data:

```
> str(pw)
'data.frame': 18 obs. of  4 variables:
 $ height: int  9 11 6 14 17 19 28 31 32 7 ...
 $ plant : Factor w/ 2 levels "sativa","vulgaris": 2 2 2 2 2 2 2 2 2 1 ...
 $ water : Factor w/ 3 levels "hi","lo","mid": 2 2 2 3 3 3 1 1 1 2 ...
 $ season: Factor w/ 2 levels "spring","summer": 1 2 2 1 2 2 1 2 2 1 ...

> pw.aov = aov(height ~ water, data = pw)
> pw.lm = lm(height ~ water, data = pw)
```

You can use the `summary()` command to get the result in a sensible layout like so:

```
> summary(pw.aov)
            Df  Sum Sq Mean Sq F value    Pr(>F)
water        2 2403.11 1201.56  84.484 6.841e-09 ***
Residuals   15  213.33   14.22
---
Signif. codes:  0 '***' 0.001 '**' 0.01 '*' 0.05 '.' 0.1 ' ' 1

> summary(pw.lm)

Call:
lm(formula = height ~ water, data = pw)

Residuals:
    Min      1Q  Median      3Q     Max
-7.0000 -2.0000 -0.6667  1.9167  9.0000

Coefficients:
            Estimate Std. Error t value Pr(>|t|)
(Intercept)   35.000      1.540  22.733 4.89e-13 ***
waterlo      -27.667      2.177 -12.707 1.97e-09 ***
watermid     -19.000      2.177  -8.726 2.91e-07 ***
---
```

```
Signif. codes:  0 '***' 0.001 '**' 0.01 '*' 0.05 '.' 0.1 ' ' 1

Residual standard error: 3.771 on 15 degrees of freedom
Multiple R-squared: 0.9185,     Adjusted R-squared: 0.9076
F-statistic: 84.48 on 2 and 15 DF,  p-value: 6.841e-09
```

In the first case you see the "classic" ANOVA table, but the second summary looks a bit different. You can make the result of the `lm()` command look more like the usual ANOVA table by using the `anova()` command like so:

```
> anova(pw.lm)
Analysis of Variance Table

Response: height
          Df  Sum Sq Mean Sq F value    Pr(>F)
water      2 2403.11 1201.56  84.484 6.841e-09 ***
Residuals 15  213.33   14.22
---
Signif. codes:  0 '***' 0.001 '**' 0.01 '*' 0.05 '.' 0.1 ' ' 1
```

ANOVA is essentially a special form of linear regression and the `aov()` command produces a result that mirrors the look and feel of the classic ANOVA. For most purposes you will use the `aov()` command for ANOVA and the `lm()` command for linear modeling.

MULTIPLE REGRESSION

In the previous examples you used a simple formula of the form response ~ predictor. You saw earlier in the section on the `aov()` command that you can specify much more complex models; this enables you to create complex linear models. The formulae that you can use are essentially the same as you met previously, as you will see shortly. In multiple regression you generally have one response variable and several predictor variables. The main point of the regression is to determine which of the predictor variables is statistically important (significant), and the relative effects that these have on the response variable.

Formulae and Linear Models

When you looked at the `aov()` command to carry out analysis of variance, you saw how to use the formula syntax to describe your ANOVA model. You can do the same with the `lm()` command, but in this case you should note that the `Error()` instruction is not valid for the `lm()` command and will work only in conjunction with the `aov()` command.

The syntax in other respects is identical to that used for the `aov()` command, and you can see some examples in Table 10-2. Note that you can specify intercept terms in your models. You can do this in `aov()` models as well but it makes less sense.

NOTE *In Table 10-2 lowercase `x` and `y` refer to continuous variables, uppercase `X` refers to a numeric matrix, and uppercase `A`, `B`, and `C` are factor variables with two or more levels.*

-2: Formula Syntax and Regression Modeling

FORMULA	EXPLANATION
`y ~ x`	Linear regression of `y` on `x`. Implicit intercept.
`y ~ 1 + x`	Explicit intercept.

`y ~ 0 + x`
`y ~ -1 + x`
`y ~ x -1`
	Linear regression of `y` on `x` through origin, that is, without intercept.

`log(y) ~ x1 + x2`	Multiple regression of transformed variable `y` on `x1` and `x2` with implicit intercept.
`y ~ poly(x, 2)` `y ~ 1 + x + I(x^2)`	Polynomial regression of `y` on `x` of degree 2. First form uses orthogonal polynomials. Second form uses explicit powers.
`y ~ X + poly(x, 2)`	Multiple regression `y` with model matrix consisting of matrix `X` as well as orthogonal polynomial terms in `x` to degree 2.
`y ~ A`	One-way analysis of variance.
`y ~ A + x`	Single classification analysis of covariance model of `y`, with classes determined by `A` and covariate `x`.
`y ~ A * B` `y ~ A + B + A:B`	Two-factor non-additive analysis of variance of `y` on factors `A` and `B`, that is, with interactions.
`y ~ B %in% A` `y ~ A/B`	Nested analysis of variance with `B` nested in `A`.
`y ~ (A + B + C)^2` `y ~ A * B * C - A:B:C`	Three-factor experiment with model containing main effects and two-factor interactions only.

`y ~ A * x`
`y ~ A/x`
`y ~ A/(1 + x) -1`
	Separate linear regression models of `y` on `x` within levels of `A`, with different coding.
	Last form produces explicit estimates of as many intercepts and slopes as there are levels in `A`.

You can see from this table that you are able to construct quite complex models using the formula syntax. The standard symbols -, +, * , /, and ^ have specific meanings in this syntax; if you want to use the symbols in their regular mathematical sense, you use the `I()` instruction to “insulate” the terms from their formula meaning. So, the following examples are quite different in meaning:

```
y ~ x1 + x2
y ~ I(x1 + x2)
```

In the first case you indicate a multiple regression of `y` against `x1` and `x2`. The second case indicates a simple regression of `y` against the sum of `x1` and `x2`. You see an example of this in action shortly in the section, “Curvilinear Regression.”

Model Building

When you have several or many predictor variables, you usually want to create the most statistically significant model from the data. You have two main choices: *forward stepwise regression* and *backward deletion*.

- **Forward stepwise regression:** Start off with the single best variable and add more variables to build your model into a more complex form
- **Backward deletion:** Put all the variables in and reduce the model by removing variables until you are left with only significant terms.

You can use the `add1()` and `drop1()` commands to take either approach.

Adding Terms with Forward Stepwise Regression

When you have many variables, finding a starting point is a key step. One option is to look for the predictor variable with the largest correlation with the response variable. You can use the `cor()` command to carry out a simple correlation. In the following example you create a correlation matrix and, therefore, get to see all the pairwise correlations; you simply select the largest:

```
> cor(mf)
           Length       Speed      Algae         NO3        BOD
Length  1.0000000 -0.34322968  0.7650757  0.45476093 -0.8055507
Speed  -0.3432297  1.00000000 -0.1134416  0.02257931  0.1983412
Algae   0.7650757 -0.11344163  1.0000000  0.37706463 -0.8365705
NO3     0.4547609  0.02257931  0.3770646  1.00000000 -0.3751308
BOD    -0.8055507  0.19834122 -0.8365705 -0.37513077  1.0000000
```

The response variable is `Length` in this example, but the `cor()` command has shown you all the possible correlations. You can see fairly easily that the correlation between `Length` and `BOD` is the best place to begin. You could begin your regression model like so:

```
> mf.lm = lm(Length ~ BOD, data = mf)
```

In this example you have only four predictor variables, so the matrix is not too large; but if you have more variables, the matrix would become quite large and hard to read. In the following example you have a data frame with a lot more predictor variables:

```
> names(pb)
 [1] "count"      "sward.may"  "mv.may"     "dv.may"     "sphag.may"  "bare.may"
 [7] "grass.may"  "nectar.may" "sward.jul"  "mv.jul"     "brmbl.jul"  "sphag.jul"
[13] "bare.jul"   "grass.jul"  "nectar.jul" "sward.sep"  "mv.sep"     "brmbl.sep"
[19] "sphag.sep"  "bare.sep"   "grass.sep"  "nectar.sep"

> cor(pb$count, pb)
     count sward.may   mv.may     dv.may sphag.may   bare.may  grass.may
[1,]     1 0.3173114 0.386234 0.06245646 0.4609559 -0.3380889 -0.2345140
     nectar.may sward.jul    mv.jul  brmbl.jul sphag.jul   bare.jul  grass.jul
[1,]   0.781714 0.1899664 0.1656897 -0.2090726 0.2877822 -0.2283124 -0.1625899
     nectar.jul sward.sep   mv.sep  brmbl.sep sphag.sep   bare.sep  grass.sep
[1,]   0.259654 0.6476513 0.877378 -0.2098358 0.7011718 -0.4196179 -0.6777093
     nectar.sep
[1,]  0.7400115
```

If you had used the plain form of the cor() command, you would have a lot of searching to do, but here you limit your results to correlations between the response variable and the rest of the data frame. You can see here that the largest correlation is between count and mv.sep, and this would make the best starting point for the regression model:

```
> pb.lm = lm(count ~ mv.sep, data = pb)
```

It so happens that you can start from an even simpler model by including no predictor variables at all, but simply an explicit intercept. You replace the name of the predictor variable with the number 1 like so:

```
> mf.lm = lm(Length ~ 1, data = mf)
> pb.lm = lm(count ~ 1, data = pb)
```

In both cases you produce a "blank" model that contains only an intercept term. You can now use the add1() command to see which of the predictor variables is the best one to add next. The basic form of the command is as follows:

```
add1(object, scope)
```

The object is the linear model you are building, and the scope is the data that form the candidates for inclusion in your new model. The result (shown here) is a list of terms and the "effect" they would have if added to your model:

```
> add1(mf.lm, scope = mf)
Single term additions

Model:
Length ~ 1
       Df Sum of Sq     RSS    AIC
<none>              227.760 57.235
Speed   1    26.832 200.928 56.102
Algae   1   133.317  94.443 37.228
NO3     1    47.102 180.658 53.443
BOD     1   147.796  79.964 33.067
```

In this case you are primarily interested in the AIC column. You should look to add the variable with the lowest AIC value to the model; in this instance you see that BOD has the lowest AIC and so you should add that. This ties in with the correlation that you ran earlier. The new model then becomes:

```
> mf.lm = lm(Length ~ BOD, data = mf)
```

You can now run the add1() command again and repeat the process like so:

```
> add1(mf.lm, scope = mf)
Single term additions

Model:
Length ~ BOD
       Df Sum of Sq    RSS    AIC
<none>              79.964 33.067
Speed   1    7.9794 71.984 32.439
Algae   1    6.3081 73.656 33.013
NO3     1    6.1703 73.794 33.060
```

You can see now that Speed is the variable with the lowest AIC, so this is the next variable to include. Note that terms that appear in the model are not included in the list. If you now add the new term to the model, you get the following result:

```
> mf.lm = lm(Length ~ BOD + Speed, data = mf)
> summary(mf.lm)

Call:
lm(formula = Length ~ BOD + Speed, data = mf)

Residuals:
    Min      1Q  Median      3Q     Max
-3.1700 -0.5450 -0.1598  0.8095  2.9245

Coefficients:
            Estimate Std. Error t value Pr(>|t|)
(Intercept) 29.30393    1.62068  18.081 1.08e-14 ***
BOD         -0.05261    0.00838  -6.278 2.56e-06 ***
Speed       -0.12566    0.08047  -1.562    0.133
---
Signif. codes:  0 '***' 0.001 '**' 0.01 '*' 0.05 '.' 0.1 ' ' 1

Residual standard error: 1.809 on 22 degrees of freedom
Multiple R-squared: 0.6839,     Adjusted R-squared: 0.6552
F-statistic:  23.8 on 2 and 22 DF,  p-value: 3.143e-06
```

You can see that the Speed variable is not a statistically significant one and probably should not to be included in the final model. It would be useful to see the level of significance before you include the new term. You can use an extra instruction in the add1() command to do this; you can use test = 'F' to show the significance of each variable if it were added to your model. Note that the 'F' is not short for FALSE, but is for an F-test. If you run the add1() command again, you see something like this:

```
> mf.lm = lm(Length ~ BOD, data = mf)

> add1(mf.lm, scope = mf, test = 'F')
Single term additions

Model:
Length ~ BOD
       Df Sum of Sq    RSS    AIC F value  Pr(F)
<none>              79.964 33.067
Speed   1    7.9794 71.984 32.439  2.4387 0.1326
Algae   1    6.3081 73.656 33.013  1.8841 0.1837
NO3     1    6.1703 73.794 33.060  1.8395 0.1888
```

Now you can see that none of the variables in the list would give statistical significance if added to the current regression model.

In this example the model was quite simple, but the process is the same regardless of how many predictor variables are present.

Removing Terms with Backwards Deletion

You can choose a different approach by creating a regression model containing all the predictor variables you have and then trim away the terms that are not statistically significant. In other words,

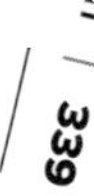

ırt with a big model and trim it down until you get to the best (most statistically significant). this you can use the `drop1()` command; this examines a linear model and determines the effect of removing each one from the existing model. Complete the following steps to perform a backwards deletion.

1. To start, create a "full" model. You could type in all the variables at once, but this would be somewhat tedious so you can use a shortcut:

```
> mf.lm = lm(Length ~ ., data = mf)
```

2. In this instance you use `Length` as the response variable, but on the right of the ~ you use a period to represent "everything else." Check what the actual formula has become using the `formula()` command:

```
> formula(mf.lm)
Length ~ Speed + Algae + NO3 + BOD
```

3. Now use the `drop1()` command and see which of the terms you should delete:

```
> drop1(mf.lm, test = 'F')
Single term deletions

Model:
Length ~ Speed + Algae + NO3 + BOD
       Df Sum of Sq    RSS    AIC F value   Pr(F)
<none>              57.912 31.001
Speed   1   10.9550 68.867 33.333  3.7833 0.06596 .
Algae   1    6.2236 64.136 31.553  2.1493 0.15818
NO3     1    6.2261 64.138 31.554  2.1502 0.15810
BOD     1   12.3960 70.308 33.850  4.2810 0.05171 .
---
Signif. codes:  0 '***' 0.001 '**' 0.01 '*' 0.05 '.' 0.1 ' ' 1
```

4. Look to remove the term with the lowest `AIC` value; in this case the `Algae` variable has the lowest `AIC`. Re-form the model without this variable. The simplest way to do this is to copy the model formula to the clipboard, paste it into a new command, and edit out the term you do not want:

```
> mf.lm = lm(Length ~ Speed + NO3 + BOD, data = mf)
```

5. Examine the effect of dropping another term by running the `drop1()` command once more:

```
> drop1(mf.lm, test = 'F')
Single term deletions

Model:
Length ~ Speed + NO3 + BOD
       Df Sum of Sq     RSS    AIC F value     Pr(F)
<none>               64.136 31.553
Speed   1     9.658  73.794 33.060  3.1622   0.08984 .
NO3     1     7.849  71.984 32.439  2.5699   0.12385
BOD     1    88.046 152.182 51.155 28.8290 2.520e-05 ***
---
Signif. codes:  0 '***' 0.001 '**' 0.01 '*' 0.05 '.' 0.1 ' ' 1
```

You can see now that the `NO3` variable has the lowest `AIC` and can be removed. You can carry out this process repeatedly until you have a model that you are happy with.

Comparing Models

It is often useful to compare models that are built from the same data set. This allows you to see if there is a statistically significant difference between a complicated model and a simpler one, for example. This is useful because you always try to create a model that most adequately describes the data with the minimum number of terms. You can compare two linear models using the `anova()` command. You used this earlier to present the result of the `lm()` command as a classic ANOVA table like so:

```
> mf.lm = lm(Length ~ BOD, data = mf)

> anova(mf.lm)
Analysis of Variance Table

Response: Length
          Df  Sum Sq Mean Sq F value    Pr(>F)
BOD        1 147.796 147.796  42.511 1.185e-06 ***
Residuals 23  79.964   3.477
---
Signif. codes:  0 '***' 0.001 '**' 0.01 '*' 0.05 '.' 0.1 ' ' 1
```

You can also use the `anova()` command to compare two linear models (based on the same data set) by specifying both in the command like so:

```
> mf.lm1 = lm(Length ~ BOD, data = mf)
> mf.lm2 = lm(Length ~ ., data = mf)

> anova(mf.lm1, mf.lm2)
Analysis of Variance Table

Model 1: Length ~ BOD
Model 2: Length ~ Speed + Algae + NO3 + BOD
  Res.Df    RSS Df Sum of Sq      F  Pr(>F)
1     23 79.964
2     20 57.912  3    22.052 2.5385 0.08555 .
---
Signif. codes:  0 '***' 0.001 '**' 0.01 '*' 0.05 '.' 0.1 ' ' 1
```

In this case you create two models; the first contains only a single term (the most statistically significant one) and the second model contains all the terms. The `anova()` command shows you that there is no statistically significant difference between them; in other words, it is not worth adding anything to the original model!

You do not need to restrict yourself to a comparison of two models; you can include more in the `anova()` command like so:

```
> anova(mf.lm1, mf.lm2, mf.lm3)
Analysis of Variance Table

Model 1: Length ~ BOD
Model 2: Length ~ BOD + Speed
Model 3: Length ~ BOD + Speed + NO3
  Res.Df    RSS Df Sum of Sq      F Pr(>F)
1     23 79.964
2     22 71.984  1    7.9794 2.6127 0.1209
3     21 64.136  1    7.8486 2.5699 0.1239
```

Here you see a comparison of three models. The conclusion is that the first is the minimum adequate model and the other two do not improve matters.

Building the best regression model is a common task, and it is a useful skill to employ; in the following activity you practice by creating a regression model with the forward stepwise process.

TRY IT OUT Build a Regression Model

In this activity you will build a regression model using the forward stepwise procedure.

1. Look at the `mtcars` data item. This is built into R.

```
> str(mtcars)
```

2. Start by creating a blank model using `mpg` as the response variable:

```
> mtcars.lm = lm(mpg ~ 1, data = mtcars)
```

3. Determine which predictor variable is the best starting candidate:

```
> add1(mtcars.lm, mtcars, test = 'F')
```

4. Add the best predictor variable to the blank model:

```
> mtcars.lm = lm(mpg ~ wt, data = mtcars)
```

5. Do a quick check of the model summary:

```
> summary(mtcars.lm)
```

6. Now look again at the remaining candidate predictor variables:

```
> add1(mtcars.lm, mtcars, test = 'F')
```

7. Add the next best predictor variable to your regression model:

```
> mtcars.lm = lm(mpg ~ wt + cyl, data = mtcars)
```

8. Now check the model summary once more:

```
> summary(mtcars.lm)
```

9. Check the remaining variables to see if there are any other candidate predictors to add:

```
> add1(mtcars.lm, mtcars, test = 'F')
```

10. The current model remains the most adequate.

How It Works

The `mtcars` data is part of R and you can examine it simply by typing its name. The `str()` command shows you that the variables are all continuous numeric data. If you want to find out more, use the help entry for these data:

```
> help(mtcars)
```

In this activity you dive right in and create a regression model, but you could explore the data more fully using a pairs plot, for example, and look at the correlations between the `mpg` variable (the response) and the others:

```
> pairs(mtcars)
> cor(mtcars$mpg, mtcars)
```

The blank model contains the response variable and the number 1, which is essentially a simple intercept. The `add1()` command now gets to work by looking at the influence of each predictor variable if you were to add it to the basic model. You want to select the variable with the lowest `AIC` value. This will also have the highest F-value. Once you have identified a variable, you can edit the original `lm()` command to add the new term in place of the 1. The first variable added is `wt`, and after this the `add1()` command reveals that the `cyl` variable is the next candidate.

Once the model includes `wt` and `cyl` variables, the `add1()` command shows that none of the remaining predictor variables would be statistically significant if added. The `hp` variable has the lowest `AIC` value, but the F-value is too low to be statistically significant.

This means that the minimum adequate descriptive model includes only two predictor variables. You could add the `hp` variable and use the `summary()` command to convince yourself that the new model is no better.

NOTE *A regression model contains explanatory variables (called terms). Each of these terms may be statistically significant. The model also has an overall statistical significance. In general, you aim to produce a model that is minimally adequate. In other words you only add terms if they significantly improve the model.*

CURVILINEAR REGRESSION

Your linear regression models do not have to be in the form of a straight line; as long as you can describe the mathematical relationships, you can carry out linear regression. When your mathematical relationship is not in straight-line form then it is described as curvilinear). The basic relationship for a linear regression is:

$$y = mx + c$$

In this classic formula, `y` represents the response variable and `x` is the predictor variable; this relationship forms a straight line. The `m` and `c` terms represent the slope and intercept, respectively. When you have multiple regression, you simply add more predictor variables and slopes, like so:

$$y = m_1x_1 + m_2x_2 + m_3x_3 + m_nx_n + c$$

The equation still has the same general form and you are dealing with straight lines. However, the world is not always working in straight lines and other mathematical relationships are probable. In the following example you see two cases by way of illustration; the first case is a logarithmic relationship and the second is a polynomial.

In the logarithmic case the relationship can be described as follows:

$$y = m \log(x) + c$$

In the polynomial case the relationship is:

$$y = m_1x + m_2x^2 + m_3x^3 + m_nx^n + c$$

The logarithmic example is more akin to a simple regression, whereas the polynomial example is a multiple regression. Dealing with these non-straight regressions involves a slight deviation from the methods you have already seen.

Logarithmic Regression

Logarithmic relationships are common in the natural world; you may encounter them in many circumstances. Drawing the relationships between response and predictor variables as scatter plots is generally a good starting point. This can help you to determine the best approach to take.

The following example shows some data that are related in a curvilinear fashion:

```
> pg
   growth nutrient
1       2        2
2       9        4
3      11        6
4      12        8
5      13       10
6      14       16
7      17       22
8      19       28
9      17       30
10     18       36
11     20       48
```

Here you have a simple data frame containing two variables: the first is the response variable and the second is the predictor. You can see the relationship more clearly if you plot the data as a scatter plot using the `plot()` command like so:

```
> plot(growth ~ nutrient, data = pg)
```

This produces a basic scatter graph that looks like Figure 10-3.

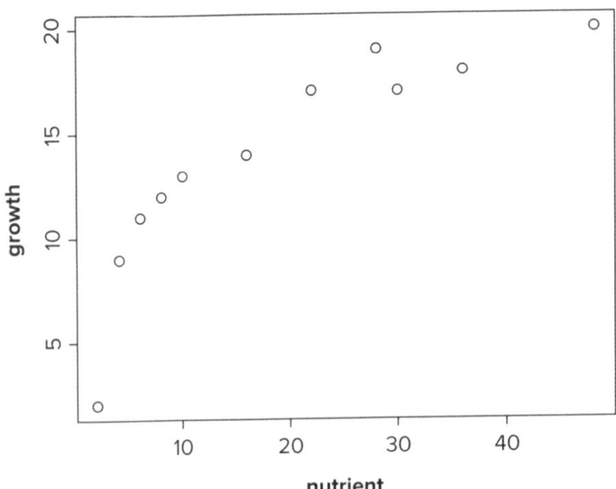

FIGURE 10-3

You can see that the relationship appears to be a logarithmic one. You can carry out a linear regression using the log of the predictor variable rather than the basic variable itself by using the `lm()` command directly like so:

```
> pg.lm = lm(growth ~ log(nutrient), data = pg)
> summary(pg.lm)

Call:
lm(formula = growth ~ log(nutrient), data = pg)

Residuals:
    Min      1Q  Median      3Q     Max 
-2.2274 -0.9039  0.5400  0.9344  1.3097 

Coefficients:
              Estimate Std. Error t value Pr(>|t|)    
(Intercept)     0.6914     1.0596   0.652     0.53    
log(nutrient)   5.1014     0.3858  13.223 3.36e-07 ***
---
Signif. codes:  0 '***' 0.001 '**' 0.01 '*' 0.05 '.' 0.1 ' ' 1

Residual standard error: 1.229 on 9 degrees of freedom
Multiple R-squared: 0.951, Adjusted R-squared: 0.9456
F-statistic: 174.8 on 1 and 9 DF,  p-value: 3.356e-07
```

Here you specify that you want to use `log(nutrient)` in the formula; note that you do not need to use the `I(log(nutrient))` instruction because `log` has no formula meaning.

You could now add the line of best-fit to the plot. You cannot do this using the `abline()` command though because you do not have a straight line, but a curved one. You see how to add a curved line of best-fit shortly in the section "Plotting Linear Models and Curve Fitting"; before that, you look at a polynomial example.

Polynomial Regression

A polynomial regression involves one response variable and one predictor variable, but the predictor variable is encountered more than once. In the simplest polynomial, the equation can be written like so:

$$y = m_1x + m_2x^2 + c$$

You see that the predictor is shown twice, once with a slope `m1` and once raised to the power of 2, with a separate slope `m2`. Each time you add an `x` to a new power, the curve bends. In the simplest example here, you have one bend and the curve forms a U shape (which might be upside down).

Polynomial relationships can occur in the natural world; examples typically include the abundance of a species in response to some environmental factor. The following example shows a typical situation. Here you have a data frame with two columns; the first is the response variable and the second is the predictor:

```
> bbel
  abund light
1     2     2
2     3     4
3     8     6
4    13     8
```

```
5      16    10
6      23    16
7      26    22
8      25    28
9      20    30
10     17    36
11      6    48
```

It appears that the response variable increases and then decreases again. If you plot the data (see Figure 10-4), you can see the situation more clearly:

```
> plot(abund ~ light, data = bbel)
```

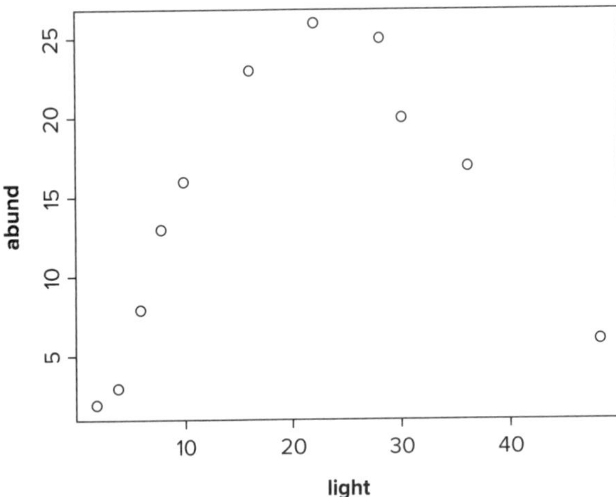

FIGURE 10-4

The relationship in Figure 10-4 looks suitable to fit a polynomial model—that is, $y = x + x^2 + c$—and you can therefore specify this in the `lm()` model like so:

```
> bbel.lm = lm(abund ~ light + I(light^2), data = bbel)
```

Notice now that you place the `light^2` part inside the `I()` instruction; this ensures that the mathematical meaning is used. You can use the `summary()` command to see the final result:

```
> summary(bbel.lm)

Call:
lm(formula = abund ~ light + I(light^2), data = bbel)

Residuals:
   Min     1Q Median     3Q    Max
-3.538 -1.748  0.909  1.690  2.357

Coefficients:
             Estimate Std. Error t value Pr(>|t|)
(Intercept) -2.004846   1.735268  -1.155    0.281
light        2.060100   0.187506  10.987 4.19e-06 ***
I(light^2)  -0.040290   0.003893 -10.348 6.57e-06 ***
---
Signif. codes:  0 '***' 0.001 '**' 0.01 '*' 0.05 '.' 0.1 ' ' 1
```

```
Residual standard error: 2.422 on 8 degrees of freedom
Multiple R-squared: 0.9382,     Adjusted R-squared: 0.9227
F-statistic: 60.68 on 2 and 8 DF,  p-value: 1.463e-05
```

The next step in the modeling process would probably be to add the line representing the fit of your model to the existing graph. This is the subject of the following section.

PLOTTING LINEAR MODELS AND CURVE FITTING

When you carry out a regression, you will naturally want to plot the results as some sort of graph. In fact, it would be good practice to plot the relationship between the variables before conducting the analysis. The `pairs()` command that you saw in Chapter 7 makes a good start, although if you have a lot of predictor variables, the individual plots can be quite small.

You can use the `plot()` command to make a scatter plot of the response variable against a single predictor variable. For instance, earlier you created a linear model like so:

```
> mf.lm = lm(Length ~ BOD, data = mf)
```

You can make a basic scatter graph of these data using the `plot()` command:

```
> plot(Length ~ BOD, data = mf)
```

The graph that results looks like Figure 10-5.

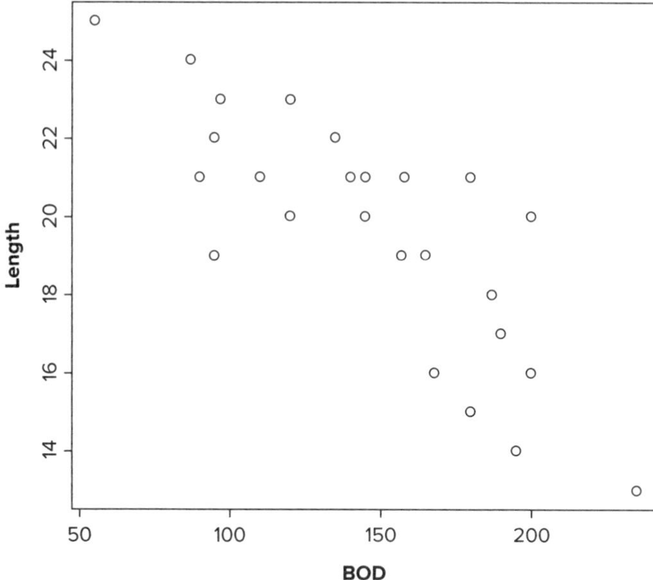

FIGURE 10-5

If you have only one predictor variable, you can also add a line of best-fit, that is, one that matches the equation of the linear model.

Best-Fit Lines

If you want to add a best-fit line, you have two main ways to do this:

- The `abline()` command produces straight lines.
- The `lines()` command can produce straight or curved lines.

You have already met the `abline()` command, which can only draw straight lines, so this will only be mentioned briefly. To create the best-fit line you need to determine the coordinates to draw; you will see how to calculate the appropriate coordinates using the `fitted()` command. The `lines()` command is able to draw straight or curved lines, and later you will see how to use the `spline()` command to smooth out curved lines of best-fit.

Adding Line of Best-Fit with abline()

To add a straight line of best-fit, you need to use the `abline()` command. This requires the intercept and slope, but the command can get them directly from the result of an `lm()` command. So, you could create a best-fit line like so:

```
> abline(mf.lm)
```

This does the job. You can modify the line by altering its type, width, color, and so on using commands you have seen before (`lty`, `lwd`, and `col`).

Calculating Lines with fitted()

You can use the `fitted()` command to extract the fitted values from the linear model. These fitted values are determined from the x values (that is, the predictor) using the equation of the linear model. You can add lines to an existing plot using the `lines()` command; in this case you can use the original x values and the fitted y values to create your line of best-fit like so:

```
> lines(mf$BOD, fitted(mf.lm))
```

The final graph looks like Figure 10-6.

You can do something similar even when you have a curvilinear fit line. Earlier you created two linear models with curvilinear fits; the first was a logarithmic model and the second was a polynomial:

```
> pg.lm = lm(growth ~ log(nutrient), data = pg)
> bbel.lm = lm(abund ~ light + I(light^2), data = bbel)
```

When you come to plot these relationships, you start by plotting the response against the predictor, as shown in the following two examples:

```
> plot(growth ~ nutrient, data = pg)
> plot(abund ~ light, data = bbel)
```

The first example plots the logarithmic model and the second plots the polynomial model. You can now add the fitted curve to these plots in exactly the same way as you did to produce Figure 10-6 by using the original x values and the fitted values from the linear model:

```
> lines(pg$nutrient, fitted(pg.lm))
> lines(bbel$light, fitted(bbel.lm))
```

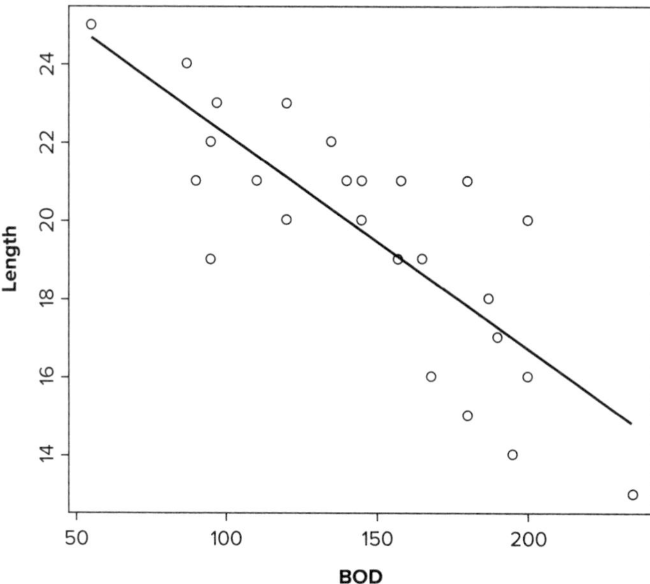

FIGURE 10-6

This produces a line of best-fit, although if you look at the polynomial graph as an example (Figure 10-7), you see that the curve is really a series of straight lines.

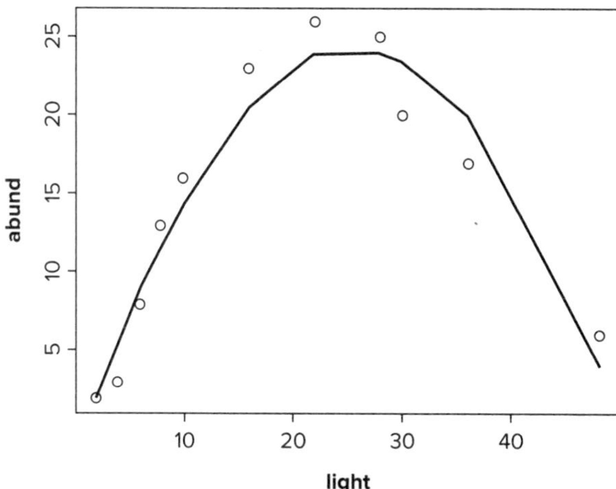

FIGURE 10-7

What you really need is a way to smooth out the sections to produce a shapelier curve. You can do this using the `spline()` command, as you see next.

Producing Smooth Curves using spline()

You can use spline curve smoothing to make your curved best-fit lines look better; the `spline()` command achieves this. Essentially, the `spline()` command requires a series of `x`, `y` coordinates that make up a curve. Because you already have your curve formed from the `x` values and fitted `y` values, you simply enclose the coordinates of your `line()` in a `spline()` command like so:

```
> lines(spline(bbel$light, fitted(bbel.lm)))
```

This adds a curved fit line to the polynomial regression you carried out earlier. The complete set of instructions to produce the polynomial model and graph are shown here:

```
> bbel.lm = lm(abund ~ light + I(light^2), data = bbel)
> plot(abund ~ light, data = bbel)
> lines(spline(bbel$light, fitted(bbel.lm)), lwd = 2)
```

The final graph appears like Figure 10-8.

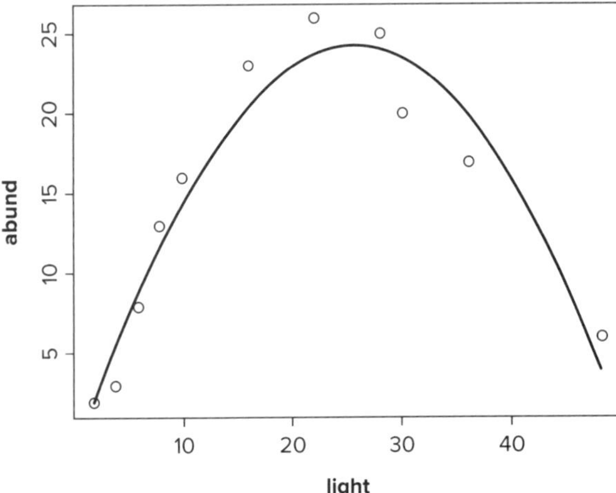

FIGURE 10-8

In this case you have made your smooth line a trifle wider than the standard using the `lwd =` instruction that you saw previously.

In the following activity you will carry out a logarithmic regression and create a plot that includes a curved line of best-fit.

TRY IT OUT Carry out Logarithmic Regression and Add a Line of Best-Fit

Available for download on Wrox.com

Use the `pg` data from the `Beginning.RData` file for this activity, which you use here to carry out a logarithmic regression. You will draw the relationship between the variables and add a curved line of best-fit.

1. Use the logarithmic example data `pg` that you saw earlier to create a logarithmic regression:

```
> pg.lm = lm(growth ~ log(nutrient), data = pg
```

2. Look at the model summary:

```
> summary(pg.lm)
```

3. Draw the basic graph to show the relationship:

```
> plot(growth ~ nutrient, data = pg, ylab = 'Plant growth',
 xlab = 'Nutrient concentration')
```

4. Add the line of best-fit:

```
> lines(spline(pg$nutrient, fitted(pg.lm)), lwd = 1.5)
```

5. Redraw the graph using the logarithm of the predictor variable:

```
> plot(growth ~ log(nutrient), data = pg, ylab = 'Plant growth', xlab = 'log(Nutrient)')
```

6. Now add a line of best-fit:

```
> abline(coef(pg.lm))
```

How It Works

The regular `lm()` command carries out a simple regression where you specify the predictor variable in terms of its logarithm. When the basic graph is plotted, the curved nature of the relationship becomes clear. The line of best-fit is curved and the `lines()` command adds it to the existing plot. The `spline()` command curves the line and makes it smooth. The `y` values for the line are taken from the fitted values (via the `fitted()` command).

If you plot the graph using the same formula as the linear regression, you see that the points are more nearly in a straight line. In this case you can use the `abline()` command to draw the line of best-fit. This time you use the coefficients from the regression to form the coordinates for the line.

Confidence Intervals on Fitted Lines

After you have drawn your fitted line to your regression model, you may want to add confidence intervals. You can use the `predict()` command to help you do this. If you run the `predict()` command using only the name of your linear model result, you get a list of values that are identical to the fitted values; in other words, the two following commands are identical:

```
>fitted(mf.lm)
>predict(mf.lm)
       1        2        3        4        5        6        7        8        9
16.65687 17.76092 20.24502 21.07305 21.62507 21.07305 22.45310 18.42334 17.76092
      10       11       12       13       14       15       16       17       18
16.93288 18.97537 19.69299 19.96901 19.69299 18.58895 17.37450 17.20889 19.03057
      19       20       21       22       23       24       25
22.72912 14.72480 16.65687 24.66119 22.89472 22.34270 22.45310
```

However, you can make the command produce confidence intervals for each of the predicted values by adding the `interval = "confidence"` instruction like so:

```
> predict(mf.lm, interval = 'confidence')
```

```
        fit      lwr      upr
1  16.65687 15.43583 17.87791
2  17.76092 16.78595 18.73588
3  20.24502 19.45005 21.03998
4  21.07305 20.17759 21.96851
5  21.62507 20.62918 22.62096
6  21.07305 20.17759 21.96851
7  22.45310 21.27338 23.63282
8  18.42334 17.56071 19.28597
9  17.76092 16.78595 18.73588
10 16.93288 15.77840 18.08737
11 18.97537 18.17562 19.77511
12 19.69299 18.92137 20.46462
13 19.96901 19.19054 20.74747
14 19.69299 18.92137 20.46462
15 18.58895 17.74852 19.42938
16 17.37450 16.32009 18.42891
17 17.20889 16.11799 18.29980
18 19.03057 18.23527 19.82587
19 22.72912 21.48183 23.97640
20 14.72480 12.98494 16.46466
21 16.65687 15.43583 17.87791
22 24.66119 22.89113 26.43126
23 22.89472 21.60574 24.18371
24 22.34270 21.18925 23.49615
25 22.45310 21.27338 23.63282
```

The result is a matrix with three columns; the first shows the fitted values, the second shows the lower confidence level, and the third shows the upper confidence level. By default, `level = 0.95` (that is both upper and lower confidence levels are set to 95 percent), but you can alter this by changing the value in the `level =` instruction.

Now that you have values for the confidence intervals and the fitted values, you have the data you need to construct the model line as well as draw the confidence bands around it. To do so, perform the following steps:

1. Begin by using the `predict()` command to produce the confidence intervals, which you make into a named object:

   ```
   >prd = predict(mf.lm, interval = 'confidence', level = 0.95)
   ```

2. Next add your x data to the result object. You do it in this way because you want to make sure that the values are sorted in order of increasing x value. Your result object is a matrix, but convert it to a data frame as you add the x data like so:

   ```
   > attach(mf)
   > prd = data.frame(prd, BOD)
   > detach(mf)
   ```

   Notice that you used the `attach()` and `detach()` commands to get the `BOD` data. You could have used `mf$BOD`, but then the column would be named `mf.BOD`. You could, of course, rename the columns in the new data frame, but in the end it is easier to keep the name of your x variable as it was originally written. You cannot use the `with()` command in this case; if you try it you get an error:

   ```
   > with(mf, prd = data.frame(prd, BOD))
   Error in eval(expr, envir, enclos) : argument is missing, with no default
   ```

Instead, make the result matrix into a data frame first and then add the original x values (BOD) like so:

```
> prd = data.frame(prd)
> prd$BOD = mf$BOD
```

You now have a data frame containing the original x values, as well as the fitted values and lower and upper confidence intervals:

```
> head(prd)
       fit      lwr      upr BOD
1 16.65687 15.43583 17.87791 200
2 17.76092 16.78595 18.73588 180
3 20.24502 19.45005 21.03998 135
4 21.07305 20.17759 21.96851 120
5 21.62507 20.62918 22.62096 110
6 21.07305 20.17759 21.96851 120
```

3. The only remaining problem is that the x values (that is, BOD) are not in numerical order, and if you try to make a line it will not come out looking right; to counteract this, re-sort the data frame using the ascending numerical values of the y data. Use the order() command to alter the sort order of your data frame:

```
> prd = prd[order(prd$BOD),]
> head(prd)
        fit      lwr      upr BOD
22 24.66119 22.89113 26.43126  55
23 22.89472 21.60574 24.18371  87
19 22.72912 21.48183 23.97640  90
7  22.45310 21.27338 23.63282  95
25 22.45310 21.27338 23.63282  95
24 22.34270 21.18925 23.49615  97
```

4. Now at last you have the data you need sorted in the correct order; you can build your plot starting with the original data:

```
> plot(Length ~ BOD, data = mf)
```

5. Now add your lines using the data frame you created:

```
> lines(prd$BOD, prd$fit)
```

6. This makes the line of best-fit and gives the same result as using the abline() command. Follow up by adding the lower and upper confidence bands like so:

```
> lines(prd$BOD, prd$lwr, lty = 2)
> lines(prd$BOD, prd$upr, lty = 2)
```

7. In this case, make the confidence lines dashed using the lty = 2 instruction. The full process is shown in the following command lines:

```
> prd = predict(mf.lm, interval = 'confidence', level = 0.95) # make CI
> attach(mf)
> prd = data.frame(prd, BOD) # add y-data
> detach(mf)
> prd = prd[order(prd$BOD),] # re-sort in order of y-data
> plot(Length ~ BOD, data = mf) # basic plot
```

```
> lines(prd$BOD, prd$fit) # also best fit
> lines(prd$BOD, prd$lwr, lty = 2) # lower CI
> lines(prd$BOD, prd$upr, lty = 2) # upper CI
```

This produces a plot that looks like Figure 10-9.

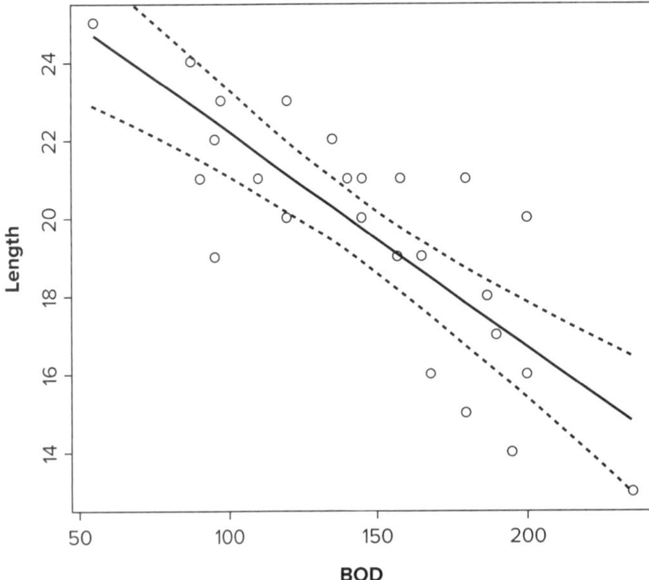

FIGURE 10-9

NOTE *At first these lines of commands are a bit daunting, but you have to type them in full only once. You can easily copy and paste them for future use; you simply alter the names of the variables.*

If you use these commands on a curvilinear regression, your lines will be a little angular so you can use the `spline()` command to smooth out the lines as you saw earlier:

```
>lines(spline(x.values, y.values))
```

If you were looking at the logarithmic regression you conducted earlier, for example, you would use the following:

```
> plot(growth ~ nutrient, data = pg)
> prd = predict(pg.lm, interval = 'confidence', level = 0.95)
> prd = data.frame(prd)
> prd$nutrient = pg$nutrient
> prd = prd[order(prd$nutrient),]
> lines(spline(prd$nutrient, prd$fit))
> lines(spline(prd$nutrient, prd$upr), lty = 2)
> lines(spline(prd$nutrient, prd$lwr), lty = 2)
```

Confidence intervals are an important addition to a regression plot. To practice the skills required to use them you can carry out the following activity.

TRY IT OUT Add Confidence Intervals to a Regression Plot

In this activity you will plot a logarithmic regression and add a curved line of best-fit and confidence intervals.

1. Look again at the logarithmic regression you made earlier:

```
> pg.lm = lm(growth ~ log(nutrient), data = pg
```

2. Redraw the plot:

```
> plot(growth ~ nutrient, data = pg, ylab = 'Plant growth',
 xlab = 'Nutrient concentration')
```

3. Create an object that contains the fitted values and 95-percent confidence intervals:

```
> prd = predict(pg.lm, interval = 'confidence')
```

4. Convert these data from a matrix into a data frame:

```
> prd = as.data.frame(prd)
```

5. Now add the original predictor data to the predicted values and confidence intervals:

```
> prd$nutrient = pg$nutrient
```

6. Reorder the values in ascending order of the predictor variable:

```
> prd = prd[order(prd$nutrient),]
```

7. Add the line of best-fit:

```
> lines(spline(prd$nutrient, prd$fit))
```

8. Add the upper confidence band:

```
> lines(spline(prd$nutrient, prd$upr), lty = 2)
```

9. Add the lower confidence band:

```
> lines(spline(prd$nutrient, prd$lwr), lty = 2)
```

How It Works

The logarithmic regression uses the `lm()` command and the regular `plot()` produces a curve, as you have already seen. The `predict()` command produces a matrix containing the predicted (that is, fitted) values, and the `interval = 'confidence'` instruction makes columns for 95-percent confidence values (upper and lower). You need to convert these data into a data frame, and add the original predictor values to the frame.

In this case the values are already in ascending order, but it is a good habit to make sure by using the `order()` command. Now the `prd` object contains the original predictor variable, the fitted values, as well as values for upper and lower confidence intervals. The `lines()` commands add the lines to the plot, and the `spline()` commands make the lines curved (rather than segments of straight lines).

SUMMARIZING REGRESSION MODELS

Once you have created your regression model you will need to summarize it. This will help remind you what you have done, as well as being the foundation for presenting your results to others. The simplest way to summarize your regression model is using the `summary()` command, as you have seen before. Graphical summaries are also useful and can often help readers visualize the situation more clearly than the numerical summary.

In addition to producing graphs of the regression model (which you see later), you should check the appropriateness of your analysis; you can do this using diagnostic plots. This is the subject of the next section.

Diagnostic Plots

Once you have carried out your regression analysis, you should look at a few diagnostics. The methods of regression have some underlying assumptions, and you should check that these are met before presenting your results to the world at large.

You can produce several diagnostic plots quite simply by using the `plot()` command like so:

```
plot(my.lm)
```

Once you type the command, R opens a blank graphics window and gives you a message. This message should be self-explanatory:

```
Hit <Return> to see next plot:
```

Each time you press the Enter key, a plot is produced; you have four in total and you can stop at any time by pressing the ESC key. The first plot shows residuals against fitted values, the second plot shows a normal QQ plot, the third shows (square root) standardized residuals against fitted values, and the fourth shows the standardized residuals against the leverage. In the following example, you can see a simple regression model and the start of the diagnostic process:

```
> mf.lm = lm(Length ~ BOD + Speed, data = mf)
> plot(mf.lm)
Hit <Return> to see next plot:
```

In Figure 10-10 the graphics window has been set to display four graphs so the diagnostic plots all appear together.

You see how to split the graphics window in Chapter 11 "More About Graphs." If you do not want all the plots, you can select one (or more) by adding a simple numeric instruction to the `plot()` command like so:

```
> plot(my.lm, 1)
> plot(my.lm, c(1,3))
> plot(my.lm, 1:3)
```

In the first case you get only the first plot. In the second case you get plots one and three, and in the final example you get plots one through three.

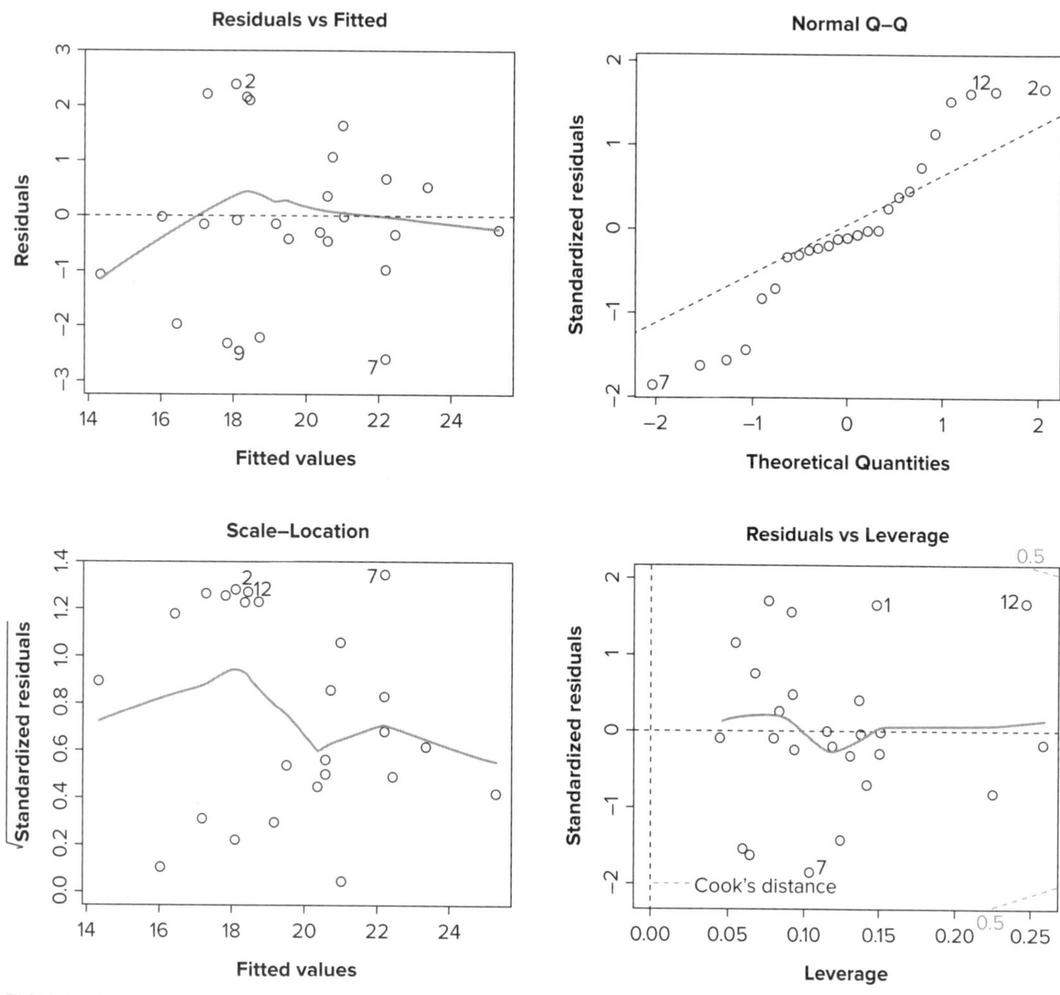

FIGURE 10-10

Summary of Fit

If your regression model has a single predictor variable, you can plot the response against the predictor and see the regression in its entirety. If you have two predictor variables, you might attempt a 3-D graphic, but if you have more variables you cannot make any sensible plot. The diagnostic plots that you saw previously are useful, but are aimed more at checking the assumptions of the method than showing how "good" your model is.

You could decide to present a plot of the response variable against the most significant of the predictor variables. Using the methods you have seen previously you could produce the plot and add a line of best-fit as well as confidence intervals. However, this plot would tell only part of the story because you would be ignoring other variables.

One option to summarize a regression model is to plot the response variable against the fitted values. The fitted values are effectively a combination of the predictors. If you add a line of best-fit, you have a visual impression of how good the model is at predicting changes in the response variable; a better model will have the points nearer to the line than a poor model. The approach you need to take is similar to that you used when fitting lines to curvilinear models. In the following activity you try it out for yourself and produce a summary model of a multiple regression with two predictor variables.

TRY IT OUT Produce a Summary Plot of a Multiple Regression

In this activity you will create a multiple regression model and then make a summary plot of the result.

1. Start by making a regression model. Use the `mf` data that you used earlier to make a two-factor model with `BOD` and `Speed` as the predictor variables:

```
> mf.lm = lm(Length ~ BOD + Speed, data = mf)
```

2. Now make a result object to hold the predicted values:

```
> prd = predict(mf.lm, interval = 'confidence')
```

3. Convert the predicted values result from a matrix to a data frame:

```
> prd = as.data.frame(prd)
```

4. Add the response variable to the predicted values data frame:

```
> prd$Length = mf$Length
```

5. Reorder the predicted values in ascending order of the response variable:

```
> prd = prd[order(prd$Length),]
```

6. Make a scatter plot of the response variable against the predicted/fitted values:

```
> plot(Length ~ fit, prd, xlab = 'Fitted Values')
```

7. Add a line of best-fit:

```
> abline(lm(Length ~ fit, prd))
```

How It Works

The basic `lm()` command makes the regression, and the `predict()` command uses the model to create fitted values (that is, values of the response variable predicted by the model) as well as confidence intervals. The result object is a matrix, so you need to convert it to a data frame before adding new columns. The response variable is added to the predicted variables simply using the `$` syntax; you need this because the data need to be reordered so that they are in ascending order (of the response variable).

The `order()` command reorders the data according to the variable you specify, in this case the `Length` variable, which is the response factor. The `plot()` command can now produce a scatter plot showing the original response data against the values predicted by the model. The `abline()` command draws the line of best-fit. Note that you need to use another `lm()` command to do this. The final graph should look like Figure 10-11.

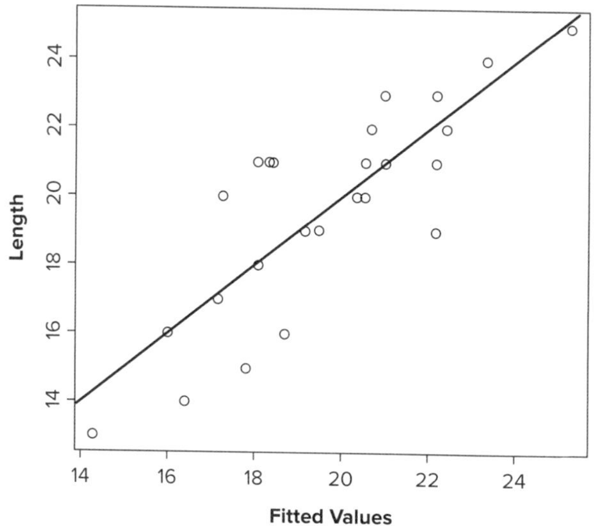

FIGURE 10-11

It would be possible to draw the confidence intervals on the plot, but you need to reorder the predicted values again (in order of *fit*). The commands would be as follows.

```
> prd = prd[order(prd$fit),]
> lines(prd$fit, prd$upr)
> lines(prd$fit, prd$lwr)
```

You will see that the lines are not smooth; this is because the confidence intervals are based on several predictor variables, so even using the `spline()` command would not make nice, smooth curves.

SUMMARY

- You use the `lm()` command for linear modeling and regression.
- The regression does not have to be in the form of a straight line; logarithmic and polynomial regressions are possible, for example.
- Use the formula syntax to specify the regression model.
- Results objects that arise from the `lm()` command include coefficients, fitted values, and residuals. You can access these via separate commands.
- You can build regression models using forward or backward stepwise processes.
- You can add lines of best-fit using the `abline()` command if they are straight.
- You can add curved best-fit lines to plots using the `spline()` and `lines()` commands.
- Confidence intervals can be calculated and plotted onto regression plots.
- You can produce diagnostic plots easily using the `plot()` command.

EXERCISES

You can find the answers to these exercises in Appendix A.

1. Look at the `mtcars` data that are built into R. You saw these data earlier when you used the `mpg` variable as the response and built a regression model. Compare three linear models: use the `wt` and `cyl` variables by themselves and together.

2. Earlier you looked at the `mtcars` data and built a regression model; the `wt` variable was the best single predictor variable in the regression. How can you plot the relationship between `mpg` and `wt` and include a line of best-fit and 99-percent confidence intervals?

3. The regression model you created earlier was a forward, additive model; that is, you added terms one after another. Take the `mtcars` data again and create a backward deletion model. How does this compare to the earlier (forward) model?

4. How can you compare the forward and backward regression models for the `mtcars` data?

5. Now you have created a range of regression models for the `mtcars` data. How can you produce an overall model plot that shows the line of best-fit and confidence bands?

▶ WHAT YOU LEARNED IN THIS CHAPTER

TOPIC	KEY POINTS
Simple regression: `cor.test()` `lm()`	Simple linear regression that could be carried out using the `cor.test()` command can also be carried out using the `lm()` command. The `lm()` command is more powerful and flexible.
Regression results: `coef()` `fitted()` `resid()` `confint()`	Results objects created using the `lm()` command contain information that can be extracted using the `$` syntax, but also using dedicated commands. You can also obtain the confidence intervals of the coefficients using the `confint()` command.
Best-fit lines: `abline()`	You can add lines of best-fit using the `abline()` command if they are straight lines. The command can determine the slope and intercept from the result of an `lm()` command.
ANOVA and `lm()`: `anova()`	Analysis and linear modeling are very similar, and in many cases you can carry out an ANOVA using the `lm()` command. The `anova()` command produces the classic ANOVA table from the result of an `lm()` command.
Linear modeling: formula syntax	The basis of the `lm()` command is the formula syntax (also known as model syntax). This takes the form of response ~ predictor(s). Complex models can be specified using this syntax.
Model building: `add1()` `drop1()`	You can build regression models in a forward stepwise manner or by using backward deletion. Moving forward, terms are added using the `add1()` command. Backward deletion uses the `drop1()` command.
Comparing regression models: `anova()`	You can compare regression models using the `anova()` command.
Curvilinear regression `lm()`	Regression models do not have to be in the form of a straight line, and as long as the relationship can be described mathematically, the regression can be described using the model syntax and carried out with the `lm()` command.
Adding best-fit lines: `abline()` `fitted()` `spline()`	Lines of best-fit can be added using the `abline()` command if they are straight. If they are curvilinear, the `lines()` command is used. The lines can be curved using the `spline()` command. The `fitted()` command extracts values from the `lm()` result that can be used to determine the best-fit.

continues

▶ WHAT YOU LEARNED IN THIS CHAPTER *(continued)*

TOPIC	KEY POINTS

Confidence intervals:
`predict()`
`lines()` `spline()`
	Confidence intervals can be determined on the fit of an `lm()` model using the `predict()` command. These can then be plotted on a regression graph using the `lines()` command; use the `spline()` command to produce a smooth curve if necessary.

Diagnostic plots: `plot()`	You can use the `plot()` command on an `lm()` result object to produce diagnostic plots.

11

More About Graphs

WHAT YOU WILL LEARN IN THIS CHAPTER:

- How to add error bars to existing graphs
- How to add legends to plots
- How to add text to graphs, including superscripts and subscripts
- How to add mathematical symbols to text on graphs
- How to add additional points to existing graphs
- How to add lines to graphs, including mathematical expressions
- How to plot multiple series on a graph
- How to draw multiple graphs in one window
- How to export graphs to graphics files and other programs

Previously, you saw how to make a variety of graphs. These graphs were used to illustrate various results (for example, scatter plots and box-whisker plots) and also to visualize data (for example, histograms and density plots). It is important to be able to create effective graphs because they help you to summarize results for others to see, as well as being useful diagnostic tools. The methods you learned previously will enable you to create many types of useful graphs, but there are many additional commands that can elevate your graphs above the merely adequate.

In this chapter you look at fine-tuning your plots, adding new elements, and generally increasing your graphical capabilities. You start by looking at adding various elements to existing plots, like error bars, legends, and marginal text. Later you see how to create a new type of graph, enabling you to plot multiple series on one chart.

ADDING ELEMENTS TO EXISTING PLOTS

Once you have a basic graph of some sort, you will often want to add extra things to it to help the reader understand the situation better. These extra things may be simple axis labels or more complex error bars and legends. Generally speaking, the graphical commands you have seen so far produce adequate graphs, but the addition of a few tweaks can render them more effective at communicating the situation to the reader.

Error Bars

Error bars are an important element in many statistical plots. If you create a box-whisker plot using the `boxplot()` command, you do not need to add any additional information regarding the variability of the samples because the plot itself contains the information. However, bar charts created using the `barplot()` command will not show sample variability because each bar is a single value—for example, mean. You can add error bars to show standard deviation, standard error, or indeed any information you like by using the `segments()` command.

Using the segments() Command for Error Bars

The `segments()` command enables you to add short sections of a straight line to an existing graph. The basic form of the command is as follows:

```
segments(x_start, y_start, x_end, y_end)
```

The command uses four coordinates to make a section of line; you have `x`, `y` coordinates for the starting point and `x`, `y` coordinates for the ending point. To see the use of the `segments()` command in a bar chart perform the following steps.

1. You first need some data. Use the following a data frame with three sample columns:

```
> bf
   Grass Heath Arable
1      3     6     19
2      4     7      3
3      3     8      8
4      5     8      8
5      6     9      9
6     12    11     11
7     21    12     12
8      4    11     11
9      5    NA      9
10     4    NA     NA
11     7    NA     NA
12     8    NA     NA
```

2. Plot the means of these three samples, and for error bars use standard error. Start by creating an object containing the mean values; you can use the `apply()` command in this case:

```
> bf.m = apply(bf, 2, mean, na.rm = TRUE)
> bf.m
    Grass     Heath    Arable
 6.833333  9.000000 10.000000
```

3. Notice that you had to use the `na.rm = TRUE` instruction to ensure that you removed the `NA` items.

4. You now need to get the standard error so you can determine the length of each error bar. There is no command for standard error directly, so you need to calculate using *standard deviation ÷ sqrt(n)*. Start by getting the standard deviations like so:

```
> bf.sd = apply(bf, 2, sd, na.rm = TRUE)
> bf.sd
   Grass    Heath   Arable
5.131601 2.138090 4.272002
```

5. When you have `NA` items, you need a slightly different approach to get the number of observations because the `length()` command does not use `na.rm` as an instruction. The easiest way is to calculate the column sums and divide by the column means because *xbar = sum(x) / n:*

```
> bf.s = apply(bf, 2, sum, na.rm = TRUE)
> bf.s
 Grass  Heath Arable
    82     72     90
> bf.l = bf.s / bf.m
> bf.l
 Grass  Heath Arable
    12      8      9
```

6. Now that you have the number of replicates, carry on and determine the standard errors:

```
> bf.se = bf.sd / sqrt(bf.l)
> bf.se
   Grass    Heath   Arable
1.481366 0.755929 1.424001
```

7. You now have all the elements you require to create your plot; you have the mean values to make the main bars and the size of the standard errors to create the error bars. However, when you draw your plot you create it from the mean values; the error bars are added afterward. This means that the y-axis may not be tall enough to accommodate both the height of the bars and the additional error bars. You should check the maximum value you need, and then use the `ylim` instruction to ensure the axis is long enough:

```
> bf.m + bf.se
    Grass     Heath    Arable
 8.314699  9.755929 11.424001
```

8. You can see that the largest value is 11.42; this knowledge now enables you to scale the y-axis accordingly. If you want to set the scale "automatically," you can determine the single value like so:

```
> max(bf.m + bf.se)
[1] 11.424
```

9. To make this even better, round this value up to the nearest higher integer:

```
> bf.max = round(max(bf.m + bf.se) + 0.5, 0)
> bf.max
[1] 12
```

10. You can now make your bar chart and scale the y-axis accordingly:

```
> bp = barplot(bf.m, ylim = c(0, bf.max))
```

The graph that results looks like Figure 11-1.

You can add axis labels later using the `title()` command. Notice that you gave your plot a name—you will use this to determine the coordinates for the error bars. If you look at the object you created, you see that it is a matrix with three values that correspond to the positions of the bars on the x-axis like so:

```
> bp
     [,1]
[1,]  0.7
[2,]  1.9
[3,]  3.1
```

In other words, you can use these as your x-values in the `segments()` command. You are going to draw lines from top to bottom, starting from a value that is the mean plus the standard error, and finishing at a value that is the mean minus the standard error. You add the error bars like this:

```
> segments(bp, bf.m + bf.se, bp, bf.m - bf.se)
```

The plot now has simple lines representing the error bars (see Figure 11-2).

The `segments()` command can also accept additional instructions that are relevant to lines. For example, you can alter the color, width, and style using instructions you have seen before (that is, `col`, `lwd`, and `lty`).

You can add cross-bars to your error bars using the `segments()` command like so:

```
> segments(bp - 0.1, bf.m + bf.se, bp + 0.1, bf.m + bf.se)
> segments(bp - 0.1, bf.m - bf.se, bp + 0.1, bf.m - bf.se)
```

The first line of command added the top cross-bars by starting a bit to the left of each error bar and drawing across to end up a bit to the right of each bar. Here you used a value of ±0.1; this seems to work well with most bar charts. The second line of command added the bottom cross-bars; you can see that the command is very similar and you have altered the + sign to a – sign to subtract the standard error from the mean.

You can now tidy up the plot by adding axis labels and "grounding" the bars; the full set of commands is as follows:

```
> bp = barplot(bf.m, ylim = c(0, bf.max))
> segments(bp, bf.m + bf.se, bp, bf.m - bf.se)
> segments(bp - 0.1, bf.m + bf.se, bp + 0.1, bf.m + bf.se)
> segments(bp - 0.1, bf.m - bf.se, bp + 0.1, bf.m - bf.se)
> box()
> title(xlab = 'Site - Habitat', ylab = 'Butterfly abundance')
> abline(h = seq(2, 10, 2), lty = 2, col = 'gray85')
```

The `box()` command simply adds a bounding box to the plot; you could have made a simple "grounding" line using the following:

```
abline(h = 0)
```

You add simple axis titles using the `title()` command, and finally, use `abline()` to make some gridlines. The finished plot looks like Figure 11-3.

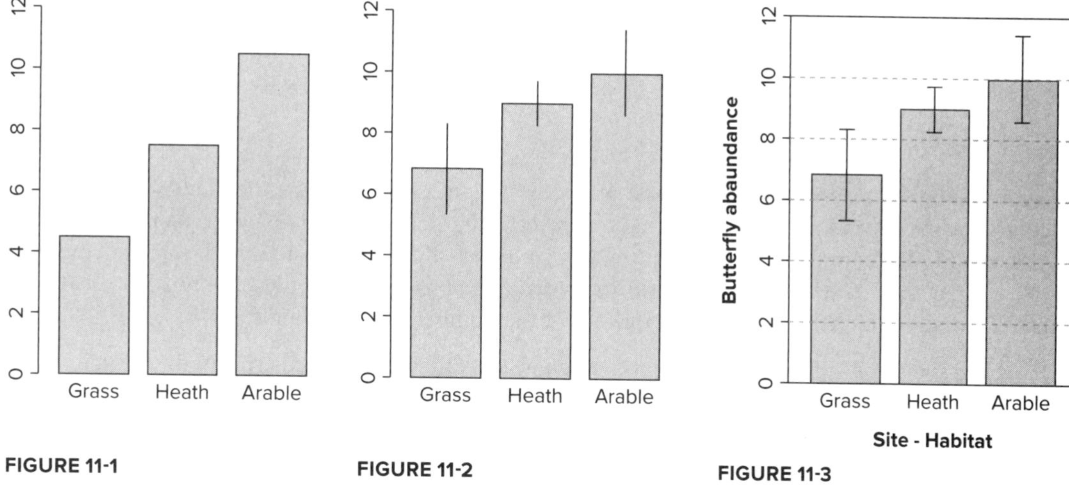

FIGURE 11-1 FIGURE 11-2 FIGURE 11-3

You can add additional instructions to your `segments()` command when drawing the error bars. You might, for example, make the lines wider using the `lwd =` instruction or alter the color using the `col =` instruction. Most of the other graphical instructions that you have seen will work on the `segments()` lines.

In the following activity you add some error bars for yourself.

TRY IT OUT Create and Add Error Bars to a Bar Chart

Available for download on Wrox.com

Use the `grass` data object from the `Beginning.RData` file for this activity. It has two columns of data: `rich` is the response variable and `graze` is the predictor.

1. Make a result object that contains mean values for the two levels of the response variable:

```
> grass.m = tapply(grass$rich, grass$graze, FUN = mean)
```

2. Now determine the standard error:

```
> grass.sd = tapply(grass$rich, grass$graze, FUN = sd)
> grass.l = tapply(grass$rich, grass$graze, FUN = length)
> grass.se = grass.sd / sqrt(grass.l)
```

3. Work out the maximum height that the bar plus error bar will reach:

```
> grass.max = round(max(grass.m + grass.se)+0.5, 0)
```

4. Create the basic bar chart and add axis labels:

```
> bp = barplot(grass.m, ylim = c(0, grass.max))
> title(xlab = 'Treatment', ylab = 'Species Richness')
```

5. Draw in the basic error bars:

```
> segments(bp, grass.m + grass.se, bp, grass.m - grass.se, lwd = 2)
```

6. Add hats to the error bars:

```
> segments(bp - 0.1, grass.m + grass.se, bp + 0.1, grass.m + grass.se, lwd = 2)
> segments(bp - 0.1, grass.m - grass.se, bp + 0.1, grass.m - grass.se, lwd = 2)
```

How It Works

Because you have a response variable and a predictor variable, you must use the `tapply()` command to calculate the means and the values required for the error bars. Because you have no `NA` items, you do not need to modify the command. You can extract the number of replicates using the `length()` command as the `FUN` instruction. You need the mean values to make the basic plot and the standard error, calculated from the standard deviation and the square root of the number in each sample.

The error bars may be "too tall" for the axis, so you need to add the standard error to the mean to work out the limit of the y-axis. You can now use the `barplot()` command along with the `ylim` instruction to make the plot and ensure that the y-axis is the right length. The plot is given a name so that you can determine the x-coordinate of the bars. The `segments()` command draws the error bars from a point that lies one standard error above the mean to a point one standard error below. You use the `lwd` instruction to make the error bars a bit wider. Finally, you add the hats in two similar commands, first the top and then the bottom.

Using the arrows() Command to Add Error Bars

You can also use the `arrows()` command to add your error bars; you look at this command a little later in the section on adding various sorts of line to graphs. The main difference from the `segments()` command is that you can add the "hats" to the error bars in one single command rather than separately afterward.

Adding Legends to Graphs

If you have more than one series of data to plot as a bar chart, you may need to create a legend to add to your plot. There is a `legend()` command to create legends and add them to existing plots. You can also use `legend` as an instruction in some plot types, including the `barplot()` command. In the following example you see a data matrix; the `barplot()` command is used to create a bar chart and include a legend:

```
> bird
              Garden Hedgerow Parkland Pasture Woodland
Blackbird         47       10       40       2        2
Chaffinch         19        3        5       0        2
Great Tit         50        0       10       7        0
House Sparrow     46       16        8       4        0
Robin              9        3        0       0        2
Song Thrush        4        0        6       0        0

> barplot(bird, beside = TRUE, legend = TRUE)
```

This produces a graph that looks like Figure 11-4.

This is simple enough, and you created something similar in Chapter 7. However, you are able to customize the legend with a variety of additional instructions. The `legend()` command itself allows quite a few parameters to be set, and you can pass these directly via the `barplot()` command using the `args.legend()` instruction. In the following example, you alter the position of the legend from its `"topright"` default position, and also turn off the border to the legend like so:

```
> barplot(bird, beside = TRUE, legend = TRUE, args.legend = list(x = 'right', bty = 'n'))
```

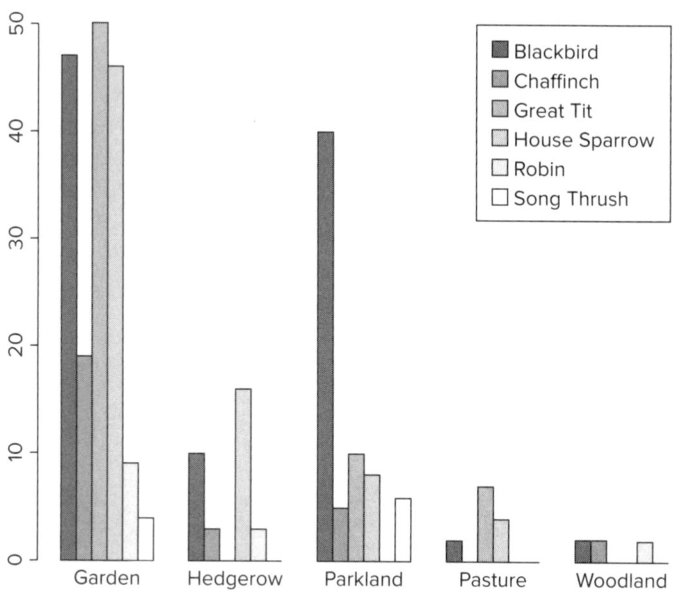

FIGURE 11-4

The new graph looks like Figure 11-5.

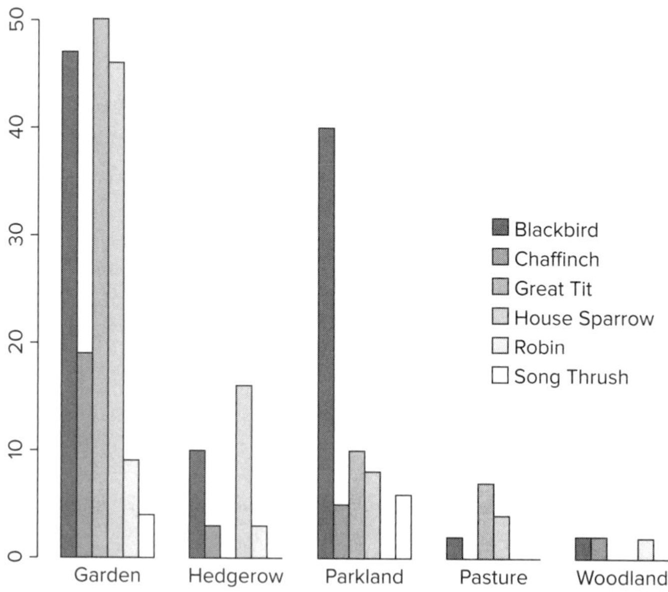

FIGURE 11-5

You include all the instructions for the `legend()` part inside a `list()` command. These instructions can alter the colors displayed, the plotting characters, the text, and other items. You see some of these instructions shortly.

Color Palettes

The `barplot()` example (refer to Figure 11-5) used default colors (gamma-corrected gray colors, in this case), but you can alter the colors of the bars by specifying them explicitly or via the `palette()` command. If you use the `palette()` command without any instructions, you see the current settings:

```
> palette()
[1] "black"   "red"     "green3"  "blue"    "cyan"    "magenta" "yellow"
[8] "gray"
```

These colors will be used for plots that do not have any special settings (many do). It is useful to be able to set the colors so that you can match up the colors of the bars of a `barplot()` to the colors in a `legend()`.

In the current `barplot()` example you have six series of data (corresponding to the six rows), so you require your customized palette to have six colors. You have various options; in the following example you create six gray colors:

```
> palette(gray(seq(0.5, 1, len = 6)))
> palette()
[1] "#808080" "gray60"  "gray70"  "gray80"  "#E6E6E6" "white"
```

In this case you start with a 50 percent gray (0.5) and end up with white (1); you split the sequence into six parts (`len = 6`). You can reset to the default palette at any time using the following:

```
> palette('default')
```

Now, whenever you need your sequence of colors you can use `palette()` to utilize them like so:

```
> palette(gray(seq(0.5, 1, len = 6)))
> barplot(bird, beside = TRUE, col = palette(), legend = TRUE,
args.legend = list(bty = 'n'))
```

You do not need to specify the colors of the legend in this case because you have specified the `palette()` colors for the plot. However, if you use the `legend()` command separately, you do need to specify the fill colors for the legend boxes like so:

```
> barplot(bird, beside = T, col = palette())
> legend(x = 'topright', legend = rownames(bird), fill = palette())
```

You see more about legends in the next section. Table 11-1 lists some other color palette commands you can use.

TABLE 11-1: Color Palettes

COLOR PALETTE COMMAND	EXPLANATION
`rainbow(n, alpha = 1, start = 0, end = max(1,n - 1)/n)`	Sets rainbow colors (red, orange, yellow, and so on); `n` = the number of colors required; `alpha` = the transparency (1 is solid); `start` = beginning color (1 = red, 1/6 = yellow, and so on); `end` = end color.

COLOR PALETTE COMMAND	EXPLANATION
`heat.colors(n, alpha = 1)`	Sets reds and oranges as the colors.
`terrain.colors(n, alpha = 1)`	Uses a range of colors starting with greens, then yellow and tan.
`topo.colors(n, alpha = 1)`	Uses "topographic" colors, starting with blues, then greens and yellows.
`cm.colors(n, alpha = 1)`	Uses blues and pinks.
`gray(levels)`	Sets grays where 0 = black and 1 = white. Usually a vector of levels is given. For example, `seq(0.5, 1, len = 6)` producing six gray colors from 50 percent to white.

You can also specify the `palette()` colors explicitly like so:

```
> palette(c('blue', 'green', 'yellow', 'pink', 'tan', 'cornsilk'))
> palette()
[1] "blue"     "green"    "yellow"   "pink"     "tan"      "cornsilk"
```

Placing a Legend on an Existing Plot

As you saw previously, you can create a legend as part of a `barplot()` command. However, with most graphs the legend must be added separately after the main plot has been drawn. The `legend()` command is what you need to do this.

When placing a legend on an existing plot you need to control the colors used so that you can match up the plot colors with the legend colors. In the following example, you create a gray palette using six shades of gray to match the number of bars you will get in each category using the following commands:

```
> palette(gray(seq(0.5, 1, len = 6)))
> barplot(bird, beside = TRUE, col = palette())
```

You see in the second command the instructions to plot the bar chart using the `palette()` colors. Now you can use the `legend()` command to add a legend. The general form of the `legend()` command is as follows:

```
legend(x, y = NULL, legend, fill = NULL, col = par('col')
```

The first part defines the `x` and `y` coordinates of the top-left part of the legend, You can specify a single value as text, for example, `"topright"`. The `legend =` part is a vector containing the names to appear in the legend. The `fill =` part is used when you have a bar or pie chart and want to show the bar or slice color by the names; it creates a simple block of color. The `col =` part is used when you have plots with points and/or lines.

In the current example, you place the legend at the top-right corner of the graph like so:

```
> legend(x = 'topright', legend = rownames(bird), fill = palette(), bty = 'n')
```

You set the names of the rows to appear as your legend text and use the `palette()` colors to become the colored boxes beside each name. Finally, you use the `bty = 'n'` instruction to set the border type to "none" (the default is "o", presumably for "on").

In this case the graph looks exactly the same as the one you drew earlier (refer to Figure 11-4) except that the legend has no border. You can use all the `legend()` instructions as part of a `barplot()` by setting `legend = TRUE` and then using `args.legend = list(...)`. You replace the contents of the brackets with the instructions as required; the instructions are summarized in Table 11-2.

TABLE 11-2: Legend Instructions/Parameters

INSTRUCTION	EXPLANATION
`legend(...)`	
`x =`	The `x` coordinate for the top-left of the legend box. If `y` is not specified, you can use one of the following text strings: `'topright'`, `'topleft'`, `'left'`, `'right'`, `'top'`, `'bottom'`, `'bottomright'`, `'bottomleft'`, `'center'`. These may be abbreviated.
`y = NULL`	The `y` coordinate for the top left of the legend box.
`legend`	A vector of names to be used as the text for the legend.
`fill = NULL`	If specified, this causes blocks to appear beside the legend names filled in the color(s) specified.
`col`	Used to set colors for lines or points if specified.
`bty`	The box/border type for the legend; `bty = 'n'` sets the box/border to "none" and `bty = 'o'` sets the box/border to "on."
`pch`	The plotting character to use in the legend beside the names; these will be set to the color specified in the `col =` instruction.
`lty`	Sets the line type if appropriate.
`lwd`	Sets the line width if appropriate.

A host of additional instructions can be used with the `legend()` command; look at the help entry via the `help(legend)` command. You see a few more examples later when you look at the `matplot()` command.

Adding Text to Graphs

Adding text to a graph can improve its readability enormously, and generally turn it into an altogether more useful object. You have already seen a few examples of how to add text to an existing plot; the most obvious one being the axis labels (using `xlab` and `ylab`). Text can also be used within the plot area, to show statistical results, for example.

Here you look at ways to add text to the main plotting area, as well as means to customize your axis labels in various useful ways.

Making Superscript and Subscript Axis Titles

So far the axis titles that you have used have all been plaintext, but you may want to use superscript or subscript. The key to achieving this is the `expression()` command; this takes plaintext and converts it into a more complex form. You can use the `expression()` command to create mathematical symbols too, which you see later.

You can use the `expression()` command directly as part of your `plot()` command or you can create your text label separately; in any event you use rules similar to "regular expressions" to generate the output you require. In the following example you create a simple scatter plot and then add titles to the axes using the `title()` command; this makes it easier to see:

```
> plot(count ~ speed, data = fw, xlab = "", ylab = "")
> title(xlab = expression('Speed ms'^-1))
> title(ylab = expression('Count '['per net']))
> title(main = 'Superscript\nand\nSubscript')
```

The `plot()` command simply draws a scatter plot; you suppress the axis titles by using double quotes. In `expression()` syntax a caret symbol (`^`) means "create superscript," so the first part of your label is in regular quotes and the `^-1` part that follows creates a superscript $^{-1}$. To create subscript you enclose the part you want in square brackets; note that you have two sets of quoted text, one outside the `[]` and the other inside the `[]`.

Although not strictly an axis label, the example included a main title to illustrate that you can create newlines using `\n`; in this example, the `\n` is ignored as text and the text following it appears on a fresh line. The graph that results from this looks like Figure 11-6.

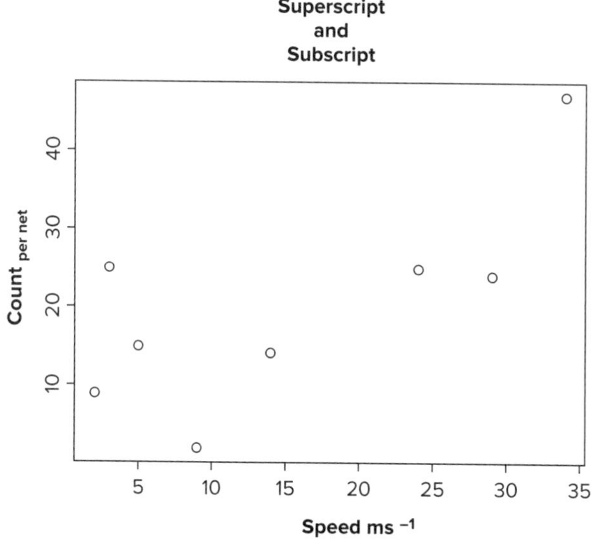

FIGURE 11-6

You do not always need to put your text in quotes like regular axis labels because the `expression()` command converts what you want into a text string. However, the command does not like spaces, and in this case you required `Speed ms`$^{-1}$ as a label. You can use the `*` to link the items together; the following example would have produced the same text as before:

```
> title(xlab = expression(Speed*' '*ms^-1))
```

This time you use a pair of quotes with a single space to split the two elements. You also used quotes for the subscripted label; you cannot avoid them in the `['per net']` part, because the space needs to be present. You could, however, drop the quotes from the first part; the following would give you the same result as before (`Count`$_{\texttt{per net}}$):

```
> title(ylab = expression(Count['per net']))
```

Better still would be to avoid quotes altogether and use the tilde (~) symbol. This takes the place of spaces in the `expression()` command. In the current example, therefore, you would use the following commands:

```
> title(xlab = expression(Speed ~ ms^-1))
> title(ylab = expression(Count[per ~ net]))
```

So, the spaces you see in the commands are actually ignored and it is the ~ symbols that produce the spaces in the final text labels.

If you require your labels to be in another typeface, such as italic, you need to alter the `expression()` text itself by adding an extra part. You have several options, as shown in Table 11-3.

TABLE 11-3: Modifying the Font in a Text expression()

COMMAND	EXPLANATION
`plain(text)`	The text in the brackets is plaintext.
`italic(text)`	Makes the text in the brackets italic font.
`bold(text)`	Creates bold font.
`bolditalic(text)`	Sets the font for the following text to bold and italic.

For the example you have here, your x- and y-axis labels could be set to italics in the following manner:

```
> title(ylab = expression(italic(Count['per net'])))
> title(xlab = expression(italic(Speed*' '*ms^-1)))
```

It is possible to build up quite complex labels in this manner, but it is also easy to make a mistake! For this reason it can be helpful to create objects to hold the `expression()` labels:

```
> xl = expression(italic(Speed ~ ms^-1))
> yl = expression(italic(Count[per ~ net]))
> plot(count ~ speed, data = fw, xlab = xl, ylab = yl)
```

You can also use the `expression()` command to create mathematical symbols and expressions; you return to these shortly.

Orienting the Axis Labels

For the most part you have used labels on your plots that were oriented in a single direction: horizontal to the axis. You can alter this using the `las =` instruction. Recall that you used this when looking at the results of a Tukey HSD test. The instruction is useful in helping to fit in labels that would otherwise overlap. Table 11-4 summarizes the options for the `las` instruction.

TABLE 11-4: Options for the las() Command for Axis Label Orientation

COMMAND	EXPLANATION
`las = 0`	Labels always parallel to the axis (the default).
`las = 1`	All labels horizontal.
`las = 2`	Labels perpendicular to the axes.
`las = 3`	All labels vertical.

If you rotate the axis labels, it is possible that they may not fit into the plot margin, and you may need to alter this to make room. This is the subject of the following section.

Making Extra Space in the Margin for Labels

You can alter the margins of a plot with a call to the `mar =` instruction. You cannot set the margins "on the fly" while you are creating a plot so you must use the `par()` command before you start. The general form of the `mar()` instruction is as follows:

```
mar = c(bottom, left, top, right)
```

You use numeric values to set the size of the margins (as lines of text). The default values are:

```
mar = c(5, 4, 4, 2) + 0.1)
```

It is a good idea to save the original values so that you can recall/reset them later. The easiest way is to create an object to hold the old values:

```
> opt = par(mar = c(8, 6, 4, 2))
various graphical commands here...
> par(opt)
```

In this example you create an object called `opt` and set the margins to new values. Then you carry out various graphical commands before resetting. It can take some trial and error to get the correct values for an individual plot, but the up arrow can recall an earlier command, so this process it not too hard.

Setting Text and Label Sizes

You can set the sizes of text and labels using the `cex =` instruction. You can use several subsettings, as summarized in Table 11-5.

TABLE 11-5: Options for Setting Character Expansion

COMMAND	EXPLANATION
`cex = n`	Sets the magnification factor for the plotting characters (or text). If n = 1, "normal" size is used. Values > 1 make items larger and values < 1 make them smaller.
`cex.axis = n`	The magnification factor for axis labels; for example, units on y-axis.
`cex.lab = n`	Magnification factor for main axis labels.
`cex.names = n`	Sets the magnification factor for names labels; for example, bar category labels.
`cex.main = n`	The magnification factor for the main plot title.

Adding Text to the Plot Area

Adding text to an existing graph can be useful for many reasons; you may need to label various points or state a statistical result, for example. You can add text to an existing graph by using the `text()` command. You specify the `x` and `y` coordinates for your text and then give the text that you require; this can be in the form of text in quotes or an `expression()`. The general form of the command is as follows:

```
text(x, y, labels = , ...)
```

The text you create is effectively centered on the `x`, `y` coordinates that you supply; you can alter this by using the `pos =` instruction. The following example shows the range of options:

```
> plot(1:10, 1:10, pch = 3, cex = 1.5)
> text(4, 4, 'Centered on point')
> text(3, 3, 'Under point (pos = 1)', pos = 1)
> text(5, 5, 'Left of point (pos = 2)', pos = 2)
> text(6, 6, 'Above point (pos = 3)', pos = 3)
> text(7, 7, 'Right of point (pos = 4)', pos = 4)
```

The simple `plot()` command creates a scatter plot with points (as +) so you can see the effects of altering the text position. The graph that results looks like Figure 11-7.

You can add a variety of other instructions to modify the text; changing its size, color, and so on. Table 11-6 shows a few of the options.

TABLE 11-6: Options for Altering Text Appearance when Added to a Graph

INSTRUCTION	EXPLANATION
`col`	Sets the text color, usually with a simple name. For example, `'gray50'`.
`cex = n`	The character expansion factor >1 makes text larger and <1 makes it smaller.
`font = n`	Sets the font type; 1 = plain (default), 2 = bold, 3 = italic, 4 = bold italic.

INSTRUCTION	EXPLANATION
`pos = n`	The position of the text relative to the coordinates; 1 = below, 2 = to the left, 3 = above, 4 = to the right. If missing, the text is centered on the coordinates.
`offset = 0.5`	An additional offset in character widths (default = 0.5).
`srt = n`	The rotation of the text in degrees, thus `srt = 180` produces upside down text.

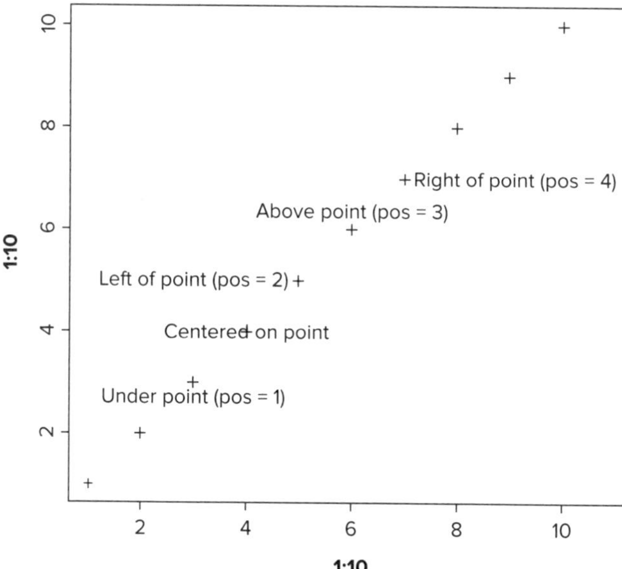

FIGURE 11-7

Knowing exactly where to place the text can be a bit hit-or-miss and involves some trial and error. However, it is also possible to determine the appropriate coordinates by using the `locator()` command. You have two possibilities. You can simply use the `locator()` command to find coordinates by clicking on a plot:

```
locator(1)
```

You now select the graph window, and when you left-click in the plot area you get the `x` and `y` coordinates of the position you clicked; you can then use these in your `text()` command. Alternatively, you can use `locator(1)` as part of the `text()` command:

```
> text(locator(1), 'Text appears at the point you click')
```

After you press Enter the program waits for you to click in the plot window; then the text appears. In this example the text would be centered on the point you click, but you can add the `pos =` instruction to alter this (refer Table 11-6).

NOTE *The* `locator()` *command enables you to set the location of items you add to your plots by clicking with the mouse. The default position for text is centered on the point you click, but for a legend the point you click sets the top left of the legend.*

Adding Text in the Plot Margins

You have already seen how to label the main axes using `xlim` and `ylim` instructions, but sometimes you need to add text into the marginal area of a graph. You can add text to the plot margins using the `mtext()` command. The general form of this command is as follows:

```
mtext(text, side = 3, line = 0, font = 1, adj = 0.5, ...)
```

You can use regular text (in quotes) or an `expression()`, or indeed any object that produces text. The `side =` instruction sets which margin you want (1 = bottom, 2 = left, 3 = top, 4 = right); the default is the top (side = 3). You can also offset the text by specifying the line you require; 0 (the default) is at the outer part of the plot area nearest the plot. Positive values move the text outward and negative values move it inward. You can also set the font, color, and other attributes. The following example produces a simple plot to demonstrate:

```
> plot(1:10, 1:10)
> mtext('mtext(side = 1, line = -1)', side = 1, line = -1)
> mtext('mtext(side = 2, line = -1, font = 3)', side = 2, line = -1, font = 3)
> mtext('mtext(side = 3, font = 2)', side = 3, font = 2)
> mtext('mtext(side = 3, line = 1, font = 2)', line = 1, side = 3, font = 2)
> mtext('mtext(side = 3, line = 2, font = 2, cex = 1.2)', cex = 1.2, line = 2,
side = 3, font = 2)
> mtext('mtext(side = 3, line = -2, font = 4, cex = 0.8)', cex = 0.8, font = 4,
line = -2)
> mtext('mtext(side = 4, line = 0)', side = 4, line = 0)
```

This produces a graph that looks like Figure 11-8.

You can adjust how far along each margin the text appears using the `adj =` instruction; a value of 0 equates to the bottom or left of the margin, and a value of 1 equates to the top or right of the margin. The default equates to 0.5, the middle of the side. Table 11-7 shows the main options.

TABLE 11-7: Options for using the mtext() Command

OPTION	EXPLANATION
`side = 3`	Sets the side of the plot window to add the text; 1 = bottom, 2 = left, 3 = top (default), 4 = right.
`line = 0`	Which line of the margin to use; 0 (the default) is nearest to the plot window. Larger values move outward and lower (`-ve`) values move into the plot area.
`adj = n`	How far along the axis/margin to place text: 0 equates to left or bottom alignment and 1 equates to right or top alignment.

OPTION	EXPLANATION
`cex = n`	The character expansion factor; values > 1 make text larger and values < 1 make it smaller.
`col = color`	The color to use; generally a text value. For example, `"gray40"`.
`font = 1`	Sets the font; 1 = plain (default), 2 = bold, 3 = italic, 4 = bold italic.
`las = 0`	The orientation of the text relative to the axis/margin: 0 = parallel to axis (default), 1 = horizontal, 2 = perpendicular to axis/margin, 3 = vertical.

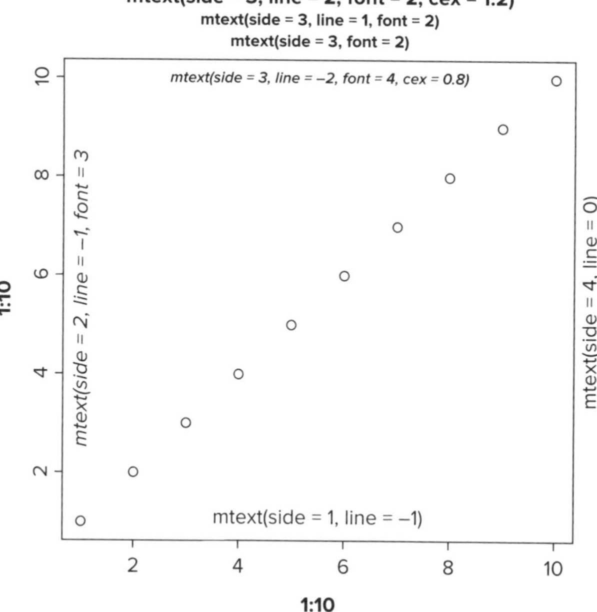

FIGURE 11-8

Creating Mathematical Expressions

Earlier you saw how to use the `expression()` command to make superscript and subscript text. The command also enables you to specify complex mathematical expressions in a similar manner. You have lots of options, but the following examples illustrate the most useful ones:

```
> plot(1:10, 1:10, type = 'n')
> opt = par(cex = 1.5)

> text(1, 1, expression(hat(x)))
> text(2, 2, expression(alpha==x))
> text(3, 3, expression(beta==y))
```

```
> text(4, 4, expression(frac(x, y)))
> text(5, 5, expression(sum(x)))
> text(6, 6, expression(sum(x^2)))
> text(7, 7, expression(bar(x) == sum(frac(x[i], n), i==1, n)))
> text(8, 8, expression(sqrt(x)))
> text(9, 9, expression(sqrt(x, 3)))

par(opt)
```

This produces something like Figure 11-9.

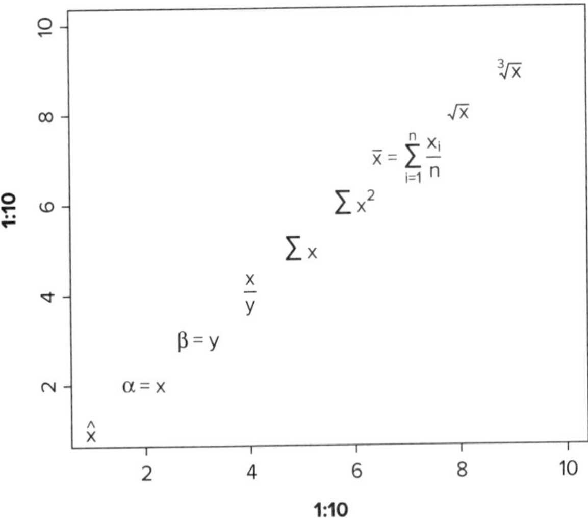

FIGURE 11-9

You begin by creating a blank plot and then reset the `cex` instruction to produce text 1.5 times larger than normal. The `cex` instruction could, of course, be used for each `text()` command, but this way is more efficient.

The first command produces a simple letter x with a hat: $\hat{x}$. The second command produces a Greek character. You use two equal signs to get your final text: $\alpha = x$. The next example uses the Greek letter beta and you end up with $\beta = y$.

The fourth command creates a fraction; you specify the top and the bottom parts of the fraction separated with a comma. The fifth command creates a Σ character, and you make this more complex in the sixth command by adding a superscript.

The seventh command is quite complicated and uses several elements including a subscript. The final two commands use the square root symbol.

You can alter the character size directly using the `cex =` instruction and can also control the color via the `col =` instruction. The typeface must be set from within the expression itself. For example:

```
expression(italic(x^2))
```

This command produces x^2, with the whole lot being in an italic typeface. The `expression()` syntax enables you to produce more or less any text you require; for full details look at `help(plotmath)`. Table 11-8 outlines a few of the options for producing math inside text expressions.

TABLE 11-8: Producing Math Inside Text Expressions

EXPRESSION	RESULT
`x + y`	Produces x plus y. For example, x + y.
`x - y`	Produces x minus y. For example, x – y.
`x == y`	Creates x equals y. For example, x = y.
`x %+-% y`	Creates x plus or minus y. For example, x ± y.
`x %/% y`	Produces x divided by y. For example, x ÷ y.
`bar(x)`	Produces x with an over-bar.
`frac(x, y)`	A fraction with x on the top and y on the bottom.
`x %up% y`	Makes x up-arrow y. For example, x y.
`infinity`	An infinity symbol.
`italic(test)`	Sets italic text.
`plain(text)`	Sets plaintext.
`alpha - omega`	Lowercase Greek symbols.
`Alpha - Omega`	Uppercase Greek symbols.
`180*degree`	Adds the degree symbol. For example, 180°.
`x ~ y`	Leave a space between x and y. For example, x y.

Recall the bar chart you created earlier when you created and added error bars using the `segments()` command. In the following activity you will recreate the graph and add a variety of text items to it.

TRY IT OUT Add Text Items to a Graph

In this activity you will redraw the bar chart you made earlier and add text items to the graph.

1. Make the y-axis labels horizontal and the names of the bars larger than standard:

```
> bp = barplot(grass.m, ylim = c(0, grass.max), las = 1, cex.names = 2)
> segments(bp, grass.m + grass.se, bp, grass.m, lwd = 2)
> segments(bp - 0.1, grass.m + grass.se, bp + 0.1, grass.m + grass.se, lwd = 2)
```

2. Now add a title to the y-axis using a superscript:

```
> title(ylab = expression(Richness~per~m^2))
```

3. Now add a title to the x-axis using a subscript:

```
> title(xlab = expression(Treatment[cutting]))
```

4. Add the mean values for each bar to the top part of each bar:

```
> text(bp, grass.m - 0.5, as.character(grass.m))
```

5. Now make a text object that contains the result of a t-test:

```
> result = 't = 4.8098\ndf = 5.411\np = 0.0039'
```

6. Add the result of the t-test to the area above the right bar and make it italic. Click on a point a little way above the top of the error bar to leave room for the three lines of text:

```
> text(locator(1), result, font = 3)
```

7. Now add a note in the right margin reminding you that the values on the bars represent means:

```
> mtext('Mean values', side = 4)
```

8. Finally, add a bounding box around the plot area:

```
> box()
```

How It Works

The first command creates a names bar chart. You set the axis labels to horizontal using the `las = 1` instruction. The `cex.names = 2` part makes the names larger than normal. The `segments()` commands add the error bars and their top hats. The `titles()` commands use the `expression()` to create the superscript and subscripts.

The mean values are taken from the earlier result (`grass.m`) and made into text using the `as.character()` command. The `text()` command places them just below the top of each bar.

Using `\n` creates newlines in text strings, so you can create a multiline text object by including these. The `\n` is used here to separate the parts of the t-test result. The `locator(1)` command waits for a single click of the mouse and places the text centered on that point. Setting `font = 3` makes the resulting text italic. The `mtext()` command adds a note to the margin; the right margin in this case.

Adding Points to an Existing Graph

You may need to add points to an existing graph, for example, if you need to create a scatter plot containing more than one sample. You can add points to an existing plot window by using the `points()` command. This works more or less like the `plot()` command, except that you do not create a new graph. The general form of the `points()` command is as follows:

```
points(x, y = NULL, type = "p", ...)
```

You specify the `x` and `y` coordinates for your points like you would with any other `plot()`; this means that you can use a formula, in which case you do not need the `y =` instruction because the `x` and `y` coordinates are taken from the formula. You can also add other graphical instructions that affect the plotting characters; you can alter the size, color, and type for example. You cannot, however, alter the y-axis size or the axis labels because these will only work when you make a new plot.

Instead, you use the `title()` command to make axis titles or the `mtext()` command. The following example shows the creation of a simple two-series scatter plot. The data are a simple data frame with three columns:

```
> fwi
  speed sfly mfly
1     9    2   22
2     6    3   15
3     7    4   10
4     5    6    9
5     4   23    5
6     3   26    4
7     4   33   12
8     7   20    8
```

The first column contains the predictor variable (the x-axis) and the next two columns are response variables (two lots of y-axis). You can create a simple scatter plot using the `plot()` command like so:

```
> plot(sfly ~ speed, data = fwi, pch = 21, ylab = 'Abundance', xlab = 'Speed')
```

Notice that you have specified the plotting character and axis titles explicitly. The graph now shows one series of data in the plot window. You can add the second series by using the `points()` command:

```
> points(mfly ~ speed, data = fwi, pch = 19)
```

To differentiate between the two series of data, you use a different plotting character (`pch = 19`); you can also use a different color or size via the `col =` and `cex =` instructions. To add a legend to help the reader see the different series, you can use the `legend()` command in the following way:

```
> legend(x = 'topright', legend = c('Stonefly', 'Mayfly'), pch = c(21,19), bty =
'n')
```

In this case you place the legend at the top right of the plot window and set the legend text explicitly. You also set the plotting characters that appear in the legend to match those used in the plots; if you had used different colors you could set the colors to match in a similar fashion. The commands are repeated in the following code:

```
> plot(sfly ~ speed, data = fwi, pch = 21, ylab = 'Abundance', xlab = 'Speed')
> points(mfly ~ speed, data = fwi, pch = 19)
> legend(x = 'topright', legend = c('Stonefly', 'Mayfly'), pch = c(21,19), bty =
'n')
```

The final graph looks like Figure 11-10.

In the current example it does not make a lot of sense to join the dots, but it is possible to create points that are joined for use in more appropriate circumstances.

You can use the `points()` command very much like the `plot()` command and create a series of joined-up points. When you create a scatter plot that uses only points, you do not need to be concerned about the order in which the items are plotted. In the current example, however, the x-data are unsorted, and if you tried to plot them with connecting lines, you would end up with a mess! You need to sort them in ascending order of the x-variable. Once your data are in the right order, you can proceed with the line-plot.

In the following activity, you reorder the data that you have seen here to produce a line-plot with two series of data.

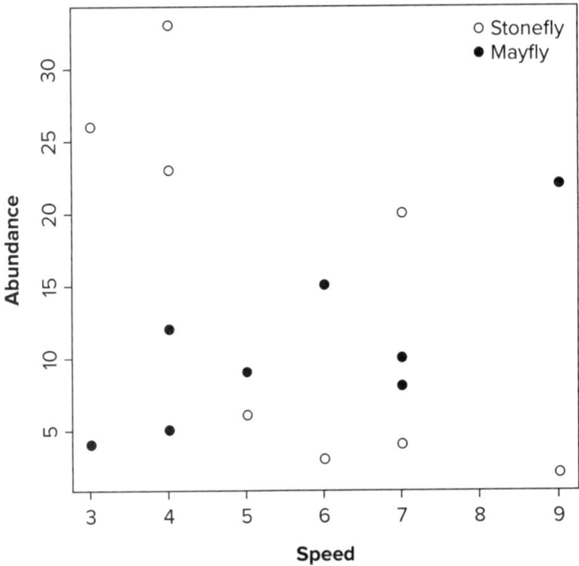

FIGURE 11-10

TRY IT OUT Make a Two-Series Scatter/Line Plot with Legend

Available for download on Wrox.com

Use the `fwi` data object from the `Beginning.RData` file for this activity. You will use the data to make a line-plot.

1. Reorder the data in ascending x-values, that is, by the `speed` variable, for the line-plot to work. You can take two approaches:
   - ➤ Sort the data "on the fly"
   - ➤ Sort the data before you start
2. To sort the data on the fly, make the line-plot using the `sfly` variable and specify the sort order directly:

```
> plot(sfly[order(speed)] ~ sort(speed), data = fwi, pch = 21, ylab = 'Abundance',
 xlab = 'Speed', type = 'b', lty = 2, cex = 1.5, lwd = 2)
```

3. Add the second series (the `mfly` variable) and similarly specify the sort order:

```
> points(mfly[order(speed)] ~ sort(speed), data = fwi, pch = 19, type = 'b', lty = 3,
 cex = 1.5, lwd = 2)
```

4. Now add the legend:

```
> legend(x = 'topr', legend = c('Stonefly', 'Mayfly'), pch = c(21, 19), bty = 'n',
lty = c(2, 3), pt.cex = 1.5, lwd = 2)
```

5. To sort the data before plotting, create a copy of the data sorted in the correct order:

```
> fwi = fwi[order(fwi$speed),]
```

6. Now make the first plot using the `sfly` variable:

```
> plot(sfly ~ speed, data = fwi, type = 'b', pch = 21, lty = 2, ylab = 'Aundance',
 xlab = 'Speed', cex = 1.5, lwd = 2)
```

7. Add the second series (the `mfly` variable) to the graph:

```
> points(mfly ~ speed, data = fwi, type = 'b', pch = 19, lty = 3, cex = 1.5, lwd = 2)
```

8. Now add the legend:

```
> legend(x = 'topr', legend = c('Stonefly', 'Mayfly'), pch = c(21, 19), bty = 'n',
 lty = c(2, 3), pt.cex = 1.5, lwd = 2)
```

How It Works

The data need to be sorted in order of the predictor variable so that the line that joins the points connects them in the right order. You can do this as you go along by specifying the response variable using the `order()` command. The predictor variable uses the `sort()` command. The plotting character and line style are given explicitly using `pch` and `lty` instructions so that you can match them later with the legend. The `points()` command adds the second series to the graph; once again, the data are rearranged using `order()` and `sort()`.

The second approach is to rearrange the data before you start; here you use the predictor variable as the index to order the data. The `plot()` and `points()` commands are now a little simpler.

In either approach, the final step is the legend itself. This is added to the top right of the plot, and the plotting symbols and line styles are set to match those of the series you plotted. Note that you use the `pt.cex` instruction, which alters the size of the symbols in the legend but does not alter the text size as `cex` would. The final plot appears like Figure 11-11.

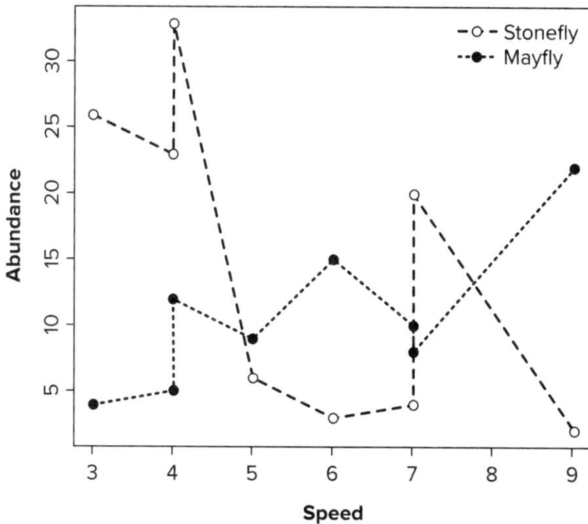

FIGURE 11-11

If you want to alter the color of the points, you can easily do so using the `col =` instruction. The color of the points displayed in the `legend()` is also set via the `col =` instruction. If you want to alter the color of the legend text itself, you need to use the `text.col =` instruction.

Adding Various Sorts of Lines to Graphs

You have seen some examples of adding lines to existing plots already; you saw how to add straight lines using the `abline()` command. You also saw how to create lines fitted to results of linear regressions using `lines()` and the `spline()` command to make them curved. You also saw how to use the `segments()` command to add sections of straight line; you used these to create error bars. In this section you review some of these methods and add a few extra ways to draw straight and curved lines onto existing graphs.

Adding Straight Lines as Gridlines or Best-Fit Lines

You can use the `abline()` command to add straight lines to an existing plot. The command will accept instructions in several ways; you can use a slope and intercept as explicit values:

```
abline(a = slope, b = intercept, ...)
```

The command thus works using the equation of a straight line, that is, $y = a + bx$. You can also specify the equation directly from the result of a linear model:

```
abline(lm(response ~ predictor, data = data), ...)
```

You may already have a linear model and can use the result directly if you have saved it as a named object. Finally, you can specify that you want a horizontal or vertical line:

```
abline(h = value, ...)
abline(v = value, ...)
```

You can alter the display of your line using other instructions; for example, you can change the color, width, style, or thickness. The following activity gives you a chance to explore some of the possibilities.

TRY IT OUT Add Various Lines to a Graph

Available for download on Wrox.com

Use the `fwi` data object from the `Beginning.RData` file for this activity. You will use the data to make a scatter plot.

1. Make a scatter plot and be sure to include the origin:

```
> plot(sfly ~ speed, data = fwi, ylim = c(0,30), xlim = c(0,10))
```

2. Use the result of a linear regression to add a line of best-fit to the graph:

```
> abline(lm(sfly ~ speed, data = fwi))
```

3. Now make a series of horizontal gridlines:

```
> abline(h = seq(5, 30, 5), lty = 2, col = 'gray50')
```

4. Make a series of vertical gridlines:

```
> abline(v = 1:9, lty = 2, col = 'gray50')
```

5. Add a line using a fixed equation:

```
> abline(a = 0, b = 1, lty = 3, lwd = 1.8)
```

How It Works

The `plot()` command draws a basic scatter plot (in this case) using simple data you saw earlier. You specify the x- and y-axis limits explicitly because you want to see the origin of the plot (that is, the 0, 0 coordinate). The first `abline()` command produces a line of best-fit from the linear model between the two variables; this line is unmodified.

The next command creates horizontal lines as gridlines; you use the `h =` instruction and a sequence of values using `seq()`. You also make these horizontal lines dashed (`lty = 2`) and colored. The next line creates vertical lines; this time you use a simple sequence from one to nine. The final command creates a line using explicit intercept and slope values. The final graph looks like Figure 11-12.

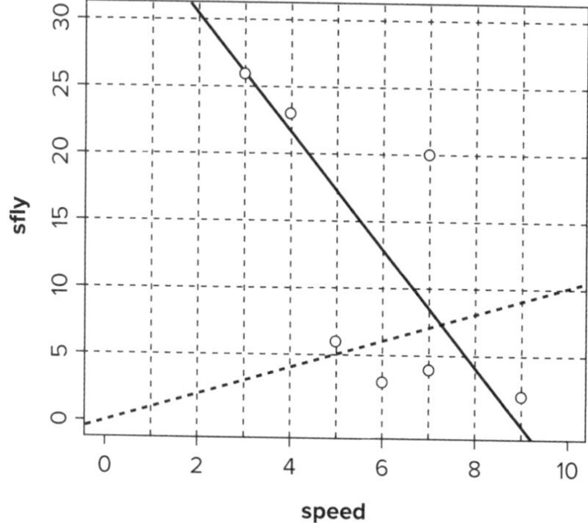

FIGURE 11-12

The `abline()` command is pretty flexible, but it can draw only straight lines; you see how to create curved lines shortly. The command options/instructions for the `abline()` command are summarized in Table 11-9.

TABLE 11-9: The abline() Command and its Options

COMMAND/INSTRUCTION	EXPLANATION
`abline(a = intercept, b = slope)`	Draws a straight line with intercept = a and slope = b.
`abline(coef = lm_object)`	Uses a linear model result to create intercept and slope. Alternatively, any vector containing two values may be interpreted as the intercept and slope.
`abline(h = value)`	Draws horizontal lines at the `y` coordinates specified in the value.

continues

TABLE 11-9 *(continued)*

COMMAND/INSTRUCTION	EXPLANATION
`abline(v = value)`	Draws vertical lines at the x coordinates specified in the value.
`lty = n`	Sets the line type. Line types can either be specified as an integer (0 = blank, 1 = solid (default), 2 = dashed, 3 = dotted, 4 = dotdash, 5 = longdash, 6 = twodash) or as one of the character strings `"blank"`, `"solid"`, `"dashed"`, `"dotted"`, `"dotdash"`, `"longdash"`, or `"twodash"`, where `"blank"` uses "invisible lines" (that is, does not draw them).
`col = color`	Sets the line color; usually as a text value. For example, `"gray50"`.
`lwd = n`	Sets the line width as a proportion; > 1 makes line wider and < 1 makes the line narrower.

Making Curved Lines to Add to Graphs

You can add curved lines to plots in a variety of ways. The `lines()` command is especially flexible and allows you to add to existing plots. In a general way, the command takes `x` and `y` coordinates and joins them together on your plot. The general form of the command is:

```
lines(x, y = NULL, ...)
```

You can specify the coordinates in many ways. Earlier you used the results of linear modeling to create curved lines of best-fit to both logarithmic and polynomial regressions; you used the original x-values and took the y-values from the `fitted()` command like so:

```
> bbel.lm

Call:
lm(formula = abund ~ light + I(light^2), data = bbel)

Coefficients:
(Intercept)        light   I(light^2)
   -2.00485      2.06010     -0.04029

> plot(abund ~ light, data = bbel)
> lines(bbel$light, fitted(bbel.lm))
```

In this case you specify both `x` and `y` coordinates individually, but you could have used a formula instead:

```
> lines(fitted(bbel.lm) ~ light, data = bbel)
```

This produced a slightly angular line because the `x`, `y` coordinates are joined by short sections of straight lines, so you used the `spline()` command to bend the line and produce a better curve as shown in the following:

```
> lines(spline(bbel$light, fitted(bbel.lm)))
```

You can alter the appearance of the line in many ways. You might change the line style, color, or width, for example, using graphical instructions that you have used before. You can also use the `type =` instruction to create a line with points along it. The following example demonstrates some of the possibilities:

```
> plot(abund ~ light, data = bbel, type = 'n')
> lines(spline(bbel$light, fitted(bbel.lm)), type = 'b', pch = 16, lty = 3,
col = 'gray50')
> title(main = 'Fitted polynomial regression')
```

In this case you use the data from a polynomial regression, but do not actually plot the data (you use `type = 'n'` to suppress the points). Next you use the `fitted()` command to get the y-values for the polynomial model. The `spline()` part of the command smooths out the curve to produce a better bend. As part of the `lines()` command, you set the `type = 'b'` to create a line and points along it; you also alter the plotting character, the line style, and the color. Finally, you add an overall title to the plot. The final plot looks like Figure 11-13.

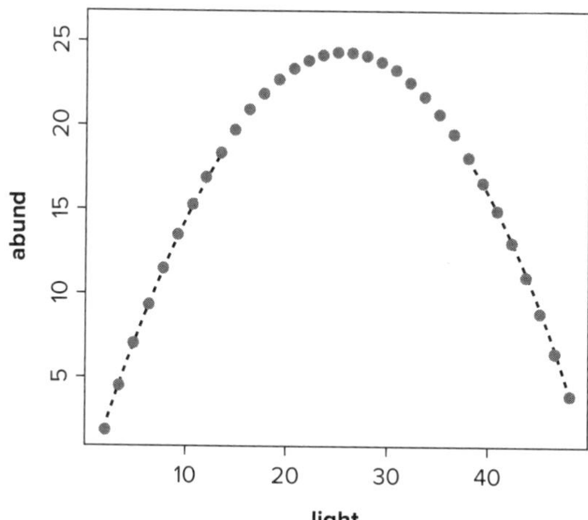

FIGURE 11-13

Some of the additional graphical instructions you can apply are summarized in Table 11-10.

TABLE 11-10: Graphical Instructions that Can be Applied to Lines on Graphs

INSTRUCTION	EXPLANATION
`type = 'type'`	Sets the kind of line drawn. `type = 'l'` (the default) produces a line only, `'b'` produces a line split by points, `'o'` produces a line overlain with points, `'n'` suppresses the line.

continues

TABLE 11-10 *(continued)*

INSTRUCTION	EXPLANATION
`lty = n`	Sets the line type. Line types can either be specified as an integer (0 = blank, 1 = solid (default), 2 = dashed, 3 = dotted, 4 = dotdash, 5 = longdash, 6 = twodash) or as one of the character strings `"blank"`, `"solid"`, `"dashed"`, `"dotted"`, `"dotdash"`, `"longdash"`, or `"twodash"`, where `"blank"` uses "invisible lines" (that is, does not draw them).
`lwd = n`	Sets line width where n = 1 is "normal" width. Values > 1 make line wider and values < 1 make it narrower.
`col = 'color'`	Sets line color, usually as a text names. For example, `'gray50'`.
`pch = n`	Sets plotting character (used if `type = 'b'` or `'o'`); usually specified as a numerical value but a quoted character may be used. For example, `"+"`.

Plotting Mathematical Expressions

You can draw mathematical functions, either as a new plot or to add to an existing one. The `plot()` command can be pressed into service here and you can also use the `curve()` command. The general form of both these commands is similar. Following is the `curve()` command:

```
curve(expr, from = NULL, to = NULL, n = 101, add = FALSE, type = 'l', log = NULL,
...)
```

You start by creating an expression to plot. This can be a simple math function (for example, `log`, `sin`) or a more complex function that you define. You also need to determine the limits of the plot, that is, the starting and ending values for your x-axis. The command works out the mathematical expression for *n* times, spread across the range of values you specify; *n* is set at 101 by default but you can add extra points to produce a smoother curve. You can add a mathematical curve to an existing plot using the `add = TRUE` instruction. By default, a line is drawn but you can specify other types, for example, `type = 'b'`, to produce points joined by sections of line. You can also specify a log scale for one or both axes. Finally, you can alter the line type, color, and other parameters much like the other plotting commands you have seen.

Here are some simple examples:

```
> plot(log)
> plot(log, from = 1, to = 1e3)
> curve(log10, from = 1, to = 1e3, add = TRUE, lty = 3)
```

In the first line you plot a simple logarithm (natural log); the limits of the x-axis are set from 0 to 1 by default. In the second line, you specify that you want to use 1 and 1000 as the x-axis limits. In the third line you add a curve to the existing plot; you specify log to the base 10 and also set the line type to dotted (that is, `lty = 3`).

If you want a logarithmic axis you can specify this via the `log =` instruction like so:

```
> curve(log, from = 1, to = 1e3, log = 'x')
```

You use a simple text label to say which axis you require to be on the log scale: "" for neither (the default), "x" for just the x-axis, "xy" for both, and "y" for the y-axis only.

The axis titles are created using default values, and if you plot more than one mathematical function you may want to alter these. In the following example you change the y-axis title:

```
> curve(sin, -pi*2, pi*2, lty = 2, lwd = 1.5, ylab = 'Function', ylim = c(-1,1.5))
> curve(cos, -pi*2, pi*2, lty = 3, lwd = 1, add = TRUE)
> legend(x = 'topright', legend = c('Sine', 'Cosine'), lty = c(2, 3),
lwd = c(1.5, 1), bty = 'n')
> title(main = 'Sine and Cosine functions')
```

In this case you alter the y-axis title, and also the limits of the axis to accommodate the legend. You make the first curve in one style (`lty = 2`) and a bit wider than "normal" (`lwd = 1.5`). The second curve is set to a different style (`lty = 3`) and, of course, set to the same axis limits as the sine curve (from $-\pi * 2$ to $\pi * 2$). Next, you add a legend to differentiate between the two curves; note that you specify the legend text and the line styles and thicknesses explicitly. The final graph looks like Figure 11-14.

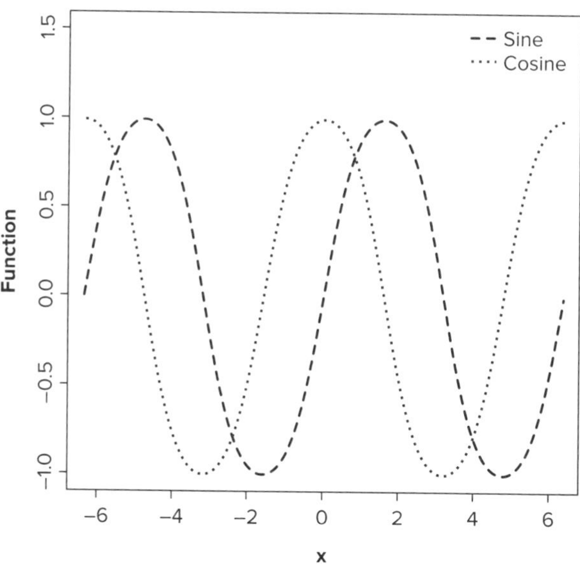

FIGURE 11-14

If you require a more complex mathematical function, you must specify it separately using the `function()` command; then you can refer to your function in the `curve()` command. In the following example you create a simple mathematical function:

```
> pn = function(x) x + x^2
> pn
function(x) x + x^2
```

The `function()` command has two parts: the first part is a list of arguments and the second part is the list of commands that use these arguments. In this case, the single argument is in the parentheses, x; the value of x is added to $x2$ and this is what the function does, creates $x + x2$ values. You can see how it works by using the new function on some values directly like so:

```
> pn(1)
[1] 2
> pn(2)
[1] 6
> pn(1:4)
[1]  2  6 12 20
```

When you use the new function as part of a `curve()` command, you therefore plot the following equation:

$$y = x + x^2$$

Recall the polynomial model you had before:

```
> bbel.lm

Call:
lm(formula = abund ~ light + I(light^2), data = bbel)

Coefficients:
(Intercept)        light   I(light^2)
   -2.00485      2.06010     -0.04029
```

You could set a function to mimic this formula and then plot that like so:

```
> pn = function(x) (2.06*x)+(-0.04 * x^2)-2
> curve(pn, from = 0, to = 50, lwd = 2, lty = 3, ylab = 'Function')
> title(main = expression(2.06*x~-0.04*x^2*~-2))
```

The first line sets the polynomial function; for every value of x you type, the function will evaluate $y = 2.06x - 0.04x^2 - 2$. Now you use the `curve()` command to draw this function; you set the line type to dashed and make it a little wider than normal. In the last line you set an `expression()` to create the formula as the title. The graph that results looks like Figure 11-15.

Table 11-11 summarizes the instructions that can be used with the `curve()` command. You see the `function()` command again in the next chapter when you look at creating simple scripts to help you automate your work.

TABLE 11-11: Instructions Used with the curve() Command

INSTRUCTION	EXPLANATION
`expr`	A mathematical expression to evaluate; for example, `log`, `sin`, `cos`. A predefined `function()` can be used.
`from =`	The starting value for the x-axis and expression to be evaluated.
`to =`	The ending value for the x-axis and expression to be evaluated.

INSTRUCTION	EXPLANATION
`n = 101`	The number of points to evaluate.
`lty = n`	The line type; for example, 2 = dashed, 3 = dotted.
`lwd = n`	The line width. 1 = "normal", > 1 makes line wider, < 1 makes it thinner.
`col = 'color'`	The line color, usually as a text string. For example, `"gray50"`.
`type = 'l'`	The type of plot used. `'l'` is the default and draws a line only, `'b'` produces sections of line with points between.
`pch = n`	The plotting character, usually as a numeric value but can be a text string. For example, "+" (the same as `pch = 3`). Used only if `lty = 'b'`, `'p'`, or `'o'`.
`add = FALSE`	If set to `TRUE`, the curve is added to an existing plot.

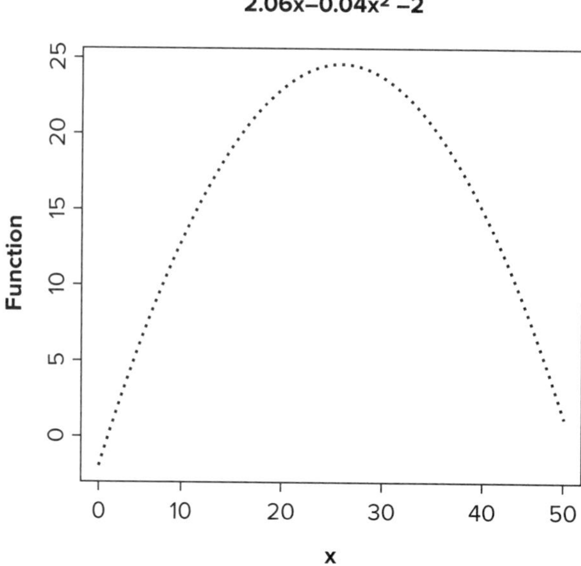

FIGURE 11-15

Adding Short Segments of Line to an Existing Plot

You can add short segments of line to an existing plot using the `segments()` command; you saw this before when adding error bars to a bar chart. The basic form of the command is as follows:

```
segments(x0, y0, x1, y1, ...)
```

You provide the starting coordinates and the ending coordinates. You can also use a host of other graphical instructions to alter the appearance of these segments; for example, `lty`, `col`, and `lwd` to alter line type, color, and width, respectively.

If you have a series of coordinates you can use these to draw shapes onto existing plots.

Adding Arrows to an Existing Graph

You can use the `arrows()` command in much the same way as the `segments()` command. The `arrows()` command draws sections of line from one point to another and adds arrowheads as specified in the command instructions. The basic form of the command is as follows:

```
arrows(x0, y0, x1, y1, length = 0.25, angle = 30, code = 2, ...)
```

The command requires the `x` and `y` coordinates of the starting and ending points. The `length =` instruction specifies the length of the arrowhead (if appropriate) and the `angle =` instruction is the angle of the head to the line; this defaults to 30°. The `code =` instruction specifies on which end(s) the arrowheads should be drawn; 1 = the back end (that is, *x0*, *y0*), 2 = the front end (that is, *x1*, *y1*), and 3 = both ends.

One use for the `arrows()` command is to create error bars with hats. Previously you used the `segments()` command to add error bars but you used three separate commands, one for the bars and one for each of the hats. You can use the `arrows()` command to add the hats at either end:

```
> arrows(bp, bf.m+bf.se, bp, bf.m-bf.se, length = 0.1, angle = 90, code = 3)
```

In this case you use a length of 0.1 to give a short hat and set the angle at 90°. The `code = 3` instruction sets heads at both ends. The values for the coordinates are determined from the data; look back at the previous section on error bars for a reminder on how to do this.

You can specify other graphical instructions to alter line style, color, and width, for example. In the following example you see some of these instructions applied:

```
> fw
         count speed
Taw          9     2
Torridge    25     3
Ouse        15     5
Exe          2     9
Lyn         14    14
Brook       25    24
Ditch       24    29
Fal         47    34

> plot(count ~ speed, data = fw, pch = '.')
> s = seq(length(fw$speed)-1)
> s
[1] 1 2 3 4 5 6 7

> arrows(fw$speed[s], fw$count[s], fw$speed[s+1], fw$count[s+1], length = 0.15,
angle = 20, lwd = 2, col = 'gray50')
```

You complete the following steps to achieve the preceding example:

1. You have a simple data frame and use the `plot()` command to create a scatter graph, setting the plotting character to a period (`.`).
2. Next, you create a simple sequence that is one shorter than the length of your data; you had eight rows so you need to end up with seven values.
3. Next, you use the `arrows()` command to add arrows that go from point to point; you set the head length to 0.15 and the angle to 20°. In this case the default is for the arrowheads to appear at the far end, so you do not need to specify `code = 2`.
4. Finally, you set the arrows to be a bit wider than normal and to a mid-gray color. The final graph appears like Figure 11-16.

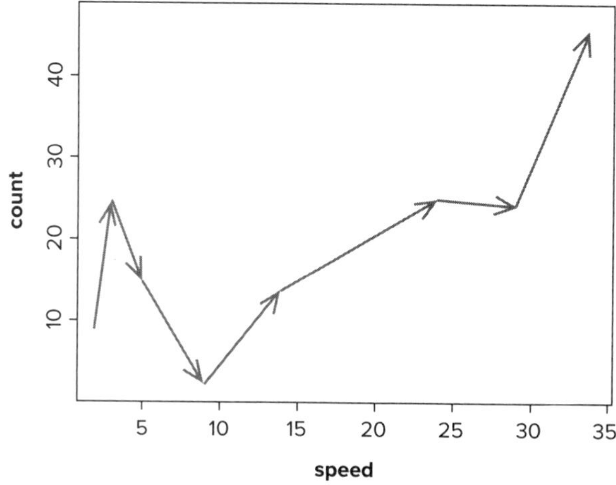

FIGURE 11-16

In this case the data were already sorted in ascending order of x-value (*speed*), but if they were not, you would need to reorder the data in some fashion. The following example reverses the order of the data:

```
> fws = fw[order(fw$speed, decreasing = TRUE),]
```

If you now plotted the data and the arrows using the `fws` data (which is sorted in reverse), your arrows would run in the opposite direction. Table 11-12 summarizes the `arrows()` command instructions.

TABLE 11-12: Instructions for the arrows() Command

INSTRUCTION	EXPLANATION
`x0, y0`	The starting coordinates for the arrow.
`x1, y1`	The ending coordinates for the arrow.

continues

TABLE 11-12 *(continued)*

INSTRUCTION	EXPLANATION
`length = 0.25`	The length of any arrowhead.
`angle = 30`	The angle of the head to the main arrow in degrees.
`code = 2`	Which arrowheads are to be drawn; 0 = neither, 1 = the beginning point, 2 = the ending point, 3 = both ends.
`lty =`	The line type/style. For example, 1 = plain, 2 = dashed, 3 = dotted.
`lwd = n`	Line width. 1 = default, > 1 makes line wider, < 1 makes line thinner.
`col = 'color'`	Line color, usually as a text string. For example, `"gray50"`.

MATRIX PLOTS (MULTIPLE SERIES ON ONE GRAPH)

Sometimes you need to produce a plot that contains several series of data. If your data are categorical, the `barplot()` command is the natural choice (although the `dotchart()` command is a good alternative). If your data are continuous variables, a scatter plot of some kind is required. You saw previously how to add extra points or lines to a scatter plot. However, the `matplot()` command makes a useful and powerful alternative.

In Chapter 8, "Formula Notation and Complex Statistics" you looked at interaction plots using the `interaction.plot()` command. You can produce a similar graph using the `matplot()` command, which plots the columns of one matrix against the columns of another. This command is particularly useful for plotting multiple series of data on the same chart. The general form of the command is as follows:

```
matplot(x, y, type = 'p', lty = 1:5, pch = NULL, col = 1:6)
```

The `x` refers to the matrix containing the columns to be used as the x-data. The `y` refers to the matrix containing the columns to be plotted as the y-data. The two matrix objects do not have to contain the same number of columns, but they do need to have the same number of rows. By default, only points are plotted, but if you select `type = 'b'`, for example, the style of line differs for each column in your y-matrix; the `lty =` instruction uses values from one to five and recycles these values as required. If you require different line types, you can specify them yourself. The plotting characters are set by default to use numbers from one to nine, then zero, then lowercase letters, and finally the uppercase letters. You can, of course, set the symbols you require using the `pch =` instruction explicitly. You can also set the colors of the plotted lines/characters by altering the `col =` instruction; by default this uses colors one through six (black, red, green, blue, cyan, violet).

The following example shows two data matrices. The first contains two columns and these relate to two response variables. The second matrix is a single column representing a predictor variable:

```
> ivert
     sfly mfly
[1,]   26    4
```

```
[2,]   23    5
[3,]   33   12
[4,]    6    9
[5,]    3   15
[6,]    4   10
[7,]   20    8
[8,]    2   22
> spd
     speed
[1,]     3
[2,]     4
[3,]     4
[4,]     5
[5,]     6
[6,]     7
[7,]     7
[8,]     9
```

To create a basic plot, you can try the following:

```
> matplot(spd, ivert)
```

In this case you have a single *x*-variable (`spd`), and the two columns in your y-data are plotted against this. Using all the defaults, you end up with a plot that shows two sets of points, with the plotting characters being black `"1"` and red `"2"`.

In the following example you add some additional instructions to produce a more customized plot and follow this up with a legend:

```
> matplot(spd, ivert, type = 'b', pch = 1:2, col = 1, lty = 2:3, xlab = 'Speed',
ylab = 'Invertebrate count')
> legend(x = 'topright', legend = c('Stonefly', 'Mayfly'), pch = 1:2, col = 1,
bty = 'n', lty = 2:3)
```

Your `matplot()` command produces a plot with both lines and points using the `type = 'b'` instruction. This time you specify the plotting characters explicitly using `pch = 1:2` (an open circle and an open triangle). You set both lines to black using `col = 1`, but vary the line type using `lty = 2:3` (producing a dashed line and a dotted line). Finally, you add explicit axis titles using the `xlab =` and `ylab =` instructions.

When you add your legend using the `legend()` command, you can copy some of the instructions because you need to match the line type, color, and plotting characters. To do so perform the following steps:

1. Begin by setting the legend position at the top right of the plot window.
2. Next, specify the text for the legend explicitly. The rest of the instructions match the `matplot()` ones except for `bty = 'n'`, which suppresses the border around the legend.
3. The final plot looks like Figure 11-17.

If you were to have two columns in your x-values matrix, the first column of the x-matrix would match up to the first column of the y-matrix, and so on. If you have more columns in the y-matrix than in the x-matrix, the columns of the x-matrix are recycled as necessary. In this way, you can arrange your data so that you produce the multi-series plot you need.

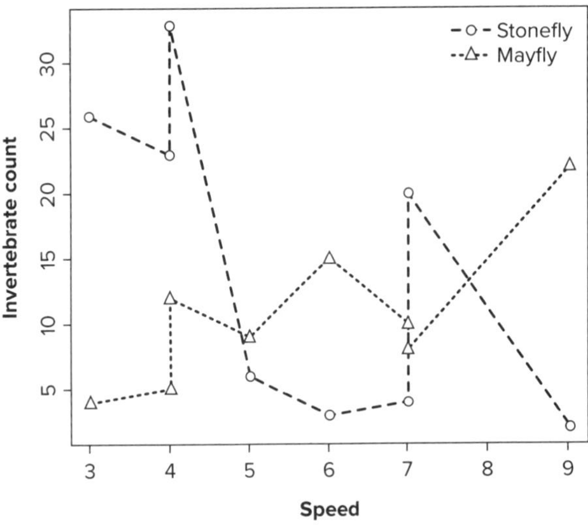

FIGURE 11-17

In addition to the `matplot()` command, you can add points and lines to an existing graph using `matpoints()` and `matlines()` commands. These use the same kinds of additional instructions as before to alter plotting character, color, and so on. Table 11-13 summarizes the commands associated with matrix plots.

TABLE 11-13: Options for Matrix Plots

INSTRUCTION	EXPLANATION
`x`	A matrix of numerical data, the columns of which will form the x-axis of the plot.
`y`	A matrix of numerical data, the columns of which will form the y-axis of the plot. If only one matrix is specified, this will become the y-axis data and a simple index will be used for the x-axis.
`type =`	The type of plot. Defaults to 'p' for `matplot()` and `matpoints()`; defaults to `'l'` for `matlines()`. Allowable types are `'n'`, `'p'`, `'b'`, and `'o'` for no plot, points, both, and overplot (similar to both except points overlie the line).
`lty = 1:5`	Line type. 1 = plain, 2 = dashed, 3 = dotted. The default values are 1:5, and if more are required the values are recycled.
`lwd = 1`	Line width. 1 = normal, > 1 makes line wider, < 1 makes line narrower.
`pch = null`	The plotting symbols used; by default numbers 1–9 are used, followed by 0, then lowercase and uppercase letters. Explicit symbols may be specified by numerical value or as a text string. For example, `"+"`.

INSTRUCTION	EXPLANATION
`col = 1:6`	Color of the plotted line and/or points. The default values are 1:6 (black, red, green, blue, cyan, or violet), which are recycled if required. Colors may be specified as a numerical value but are more often given as a text string. For example, `'gray50'`.
`...`	Other graphical instructions. For example, `ylim`, `xlab`, or `cex`.

MULTIPLE PLOTS IN ONE WINDOW

It is sometimes useful to create several graphs in one window. This could be because they are closely related and you want to display them together. You could make separate plots and then later position them together using a graphics program or your word processor. However, it is more efficient to split a graphical window into sections and draw your graphs into the sections directly from R. You are able to achieve this in a couple of ways, as you see in the following sections.

Splitting the Plot Window into Equal Sections

You can split the graphical window into several parts using the graphical instructions `mfrow()` and `mfcol()`; you can access these instructions only via the `par()` command. Usually, it is a good idea to store the current `par()` instructions so that they can be recalled/reset later. The `mfrow()` and `mfcol()` instructions both require two values, the number of rows and the number of columns, like so:

```
mfrow = c(nrows, ncols)
mfcol = c(nrows, ncols)
```

Once set, the split plot window remains in force until altered or reset to its original values. In the following example you split the window into four; that is, two rows and two columns:

```
> opt = par(mfrow = c(2,2))
> plot(Length ~ BOD, data = mf, main = 'plot 1')
> plot(Length ~ Algae, data = mf, main = 'plot 2')
> plot(Length ~ Speed, data = mf, main = 'plot 3')
> plot(Length ~ NO3, data = mf, main = 'plot 4')
> par(opt)
```

The first command sets the number of rows and columns for the plot window; note that you create an object to hold the current settings. The next four lines produce simple scatter plots; this is where the difference between `mfrow()` and `mfcol()` becomes evident. In the case of `mfrow()` the plots are created row by row, whereas if you had set `mfcol()` the plots would fill up column by column. At the end you reset the window by calling up the object you created earlier. The final plot looks like Figure 11-18.

You can skip a plot by using the `plot.new()` command. The result of issuing a `plot.new()` command is that the current plot is finished; if you have a split window, you skip over the next position in the sequence. You must remember that the current plot is not the one that you just drew, but the one that is ready to draw into! In the following example you set the window to four sections again, but draw plots by column:

```
> opt = par(mfcol = c(2,2))
> plot(Length ~ BOD, data = mf, main = 'plot 1')
> plot.new()
> plot.new()
> plot(Length ~ NO3, data = mf, main = 'plot 4')
> par(opt)
```

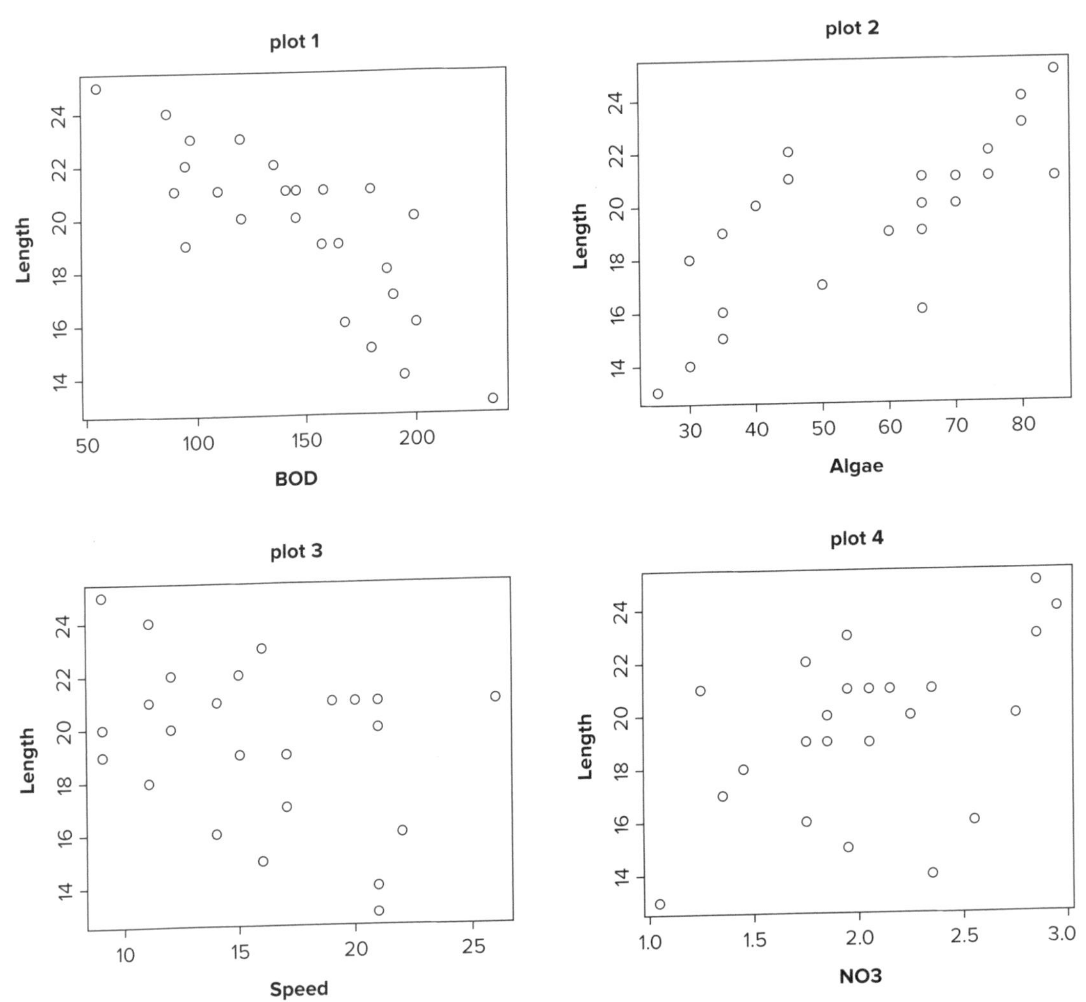

FIGURE 11-18

After you issue the `mfcol()` instruction the plot is ready (although you cannot see it), and so the first plot will go into the top-left position. The next plot is ready to go into the bottom left, but you use `plot.new()` to skip it and get the next ready instead. However, you decide to skip this too and so the next plot goes into the bottom section of the window. The final graph appears like Figure 11-19. The blank areas might be useful to add text, for example, or perhaps some other graphic.

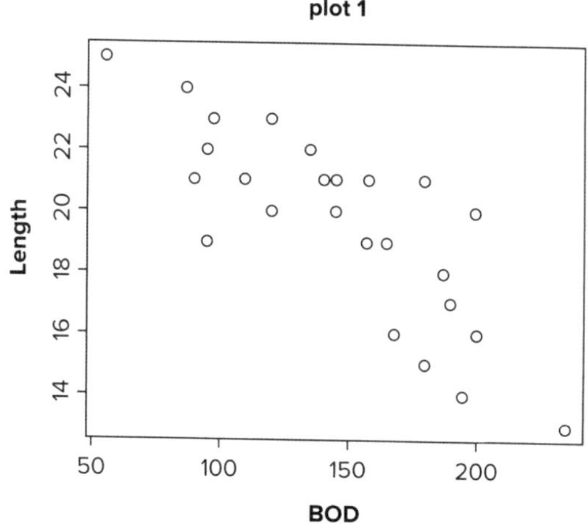

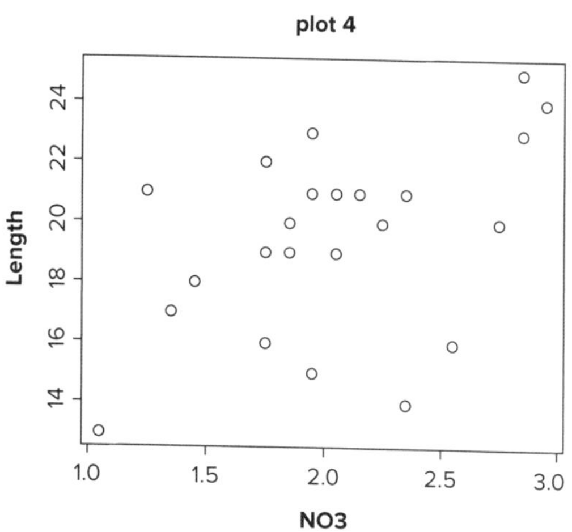

FIGURE 11-19

NOTE *You can draw directly into a portion of the plot window by using the* `mfg` *instruction with the* `par()` *command. The plot window must already have been set via the* `mfrow` *or* `mfcol` *instruction. You specify* `par(mfg = c(i, j))` *where* `i` *and* `j` *are the row and column coordinates to be used.*

Splitting the Plot Window into Unequal Sections

You can control the sections of the plotting window more exactly using the `split.screen()` command. This command provides finer control of the splitting process and you can also place a plot in exactly the section you require. The basic form of the command is as follows:

```
split.screen(figs = c(rows, cols))
```

This is similar to the `mfrow()` instruction you saw in the previous section, but you can go further; you can subdivide each of the sections you just created as well. The following example is a good way to illustrate the possibilities:

```
> split.screen(figs = c(2, 1))
[1] 1 2
> screen()
[1] 1
```

In this case you divide the graphics window into two rows and one column; the command gives you a message showing that you now have two areas available. The second command, `screen()`, checks to see which is the current window; you get a 1 in this instance, which indicates that you are at the top. You switch to the bottom row (screen two) because you want to subdivide it:

```
> screen(2)
> split.screen(figs = c(1, 2))
[1] 3 4
```

You start by simply switching to screen number two using `screen(2)`, then you split this into more parts; in this case you decide to make a single row and two columns. Your graphics window is now split into four parts; this is not immediately obvious! You have the original split, which was the top half and the bottom half. You have the bottom half also split into two parts; this makes four altogether. You can see how many parts you have by using the `close.screen()` command like so:

```
> close.screen()
[1] 1 2 3 4
```

When you use this command without any instructions, you get a list of the available screens. You can plot into any of the screens by selecting one and then using the `plot()` command (or any other command that produces a graph). In the following example you make a scatter plot in screens two and one:

```
> screen(2)
> plot(Length ~ Algae, data = mf, main = 'plot 2')
> screen(1)
> plot(Length ~ BOD, data = mf, main = 'plot 1')
```

The graph that results looks like Figure 11-20.

You still have split the bottom part into two sections (that is, one row and two columns), so you could create a more complex plot. You begin by erasing the bottom plot (screen two) using the `erase.screen()` command like so:

```
> opt = par(bg = 'white')
> erase.screen(n = 2)
> par(opt)
```

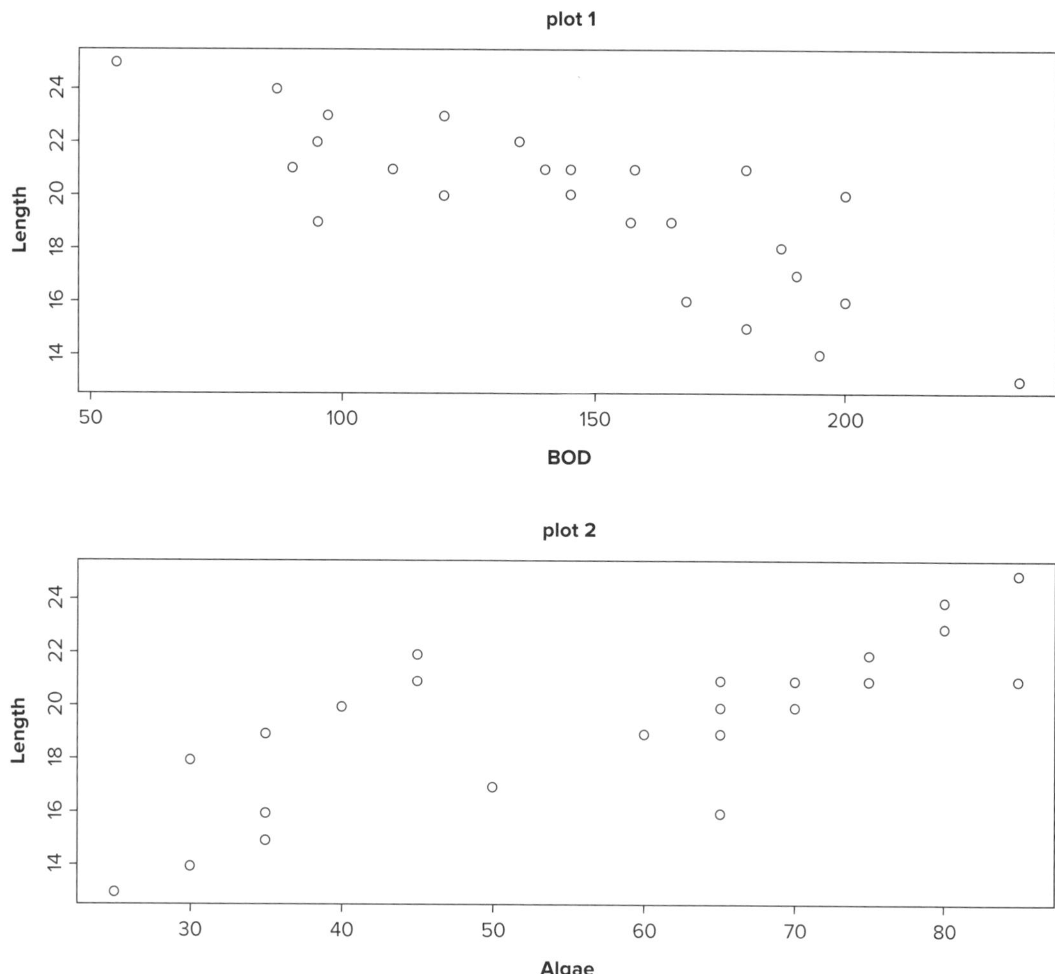

FIGURE 11-20

The default for this command is to use the currently selected screen, so you must be careful to specify which screen you want to erase. By default, the background color of the plot is used to erase the drawing; in many cases this is transparent, so you set it to white in this case to ensure that you wipe out the current plot. You can now draw into the cleared area at the bottom of the plot window:

```
> screen(3)
> plot(Length ~ Speed, data = mf, main = 'plot 3')
> screen(4)
> plot(Length ~ NO3, data = mf, main = 'plot 4')
```

Recall that you split the window into four parts with screens three and four making up the bottom half. You start by selecting `screen(3)` and plotting a scatter plot; you then select `screen(4)` and make another plot. The result is shown in Figure 11-21.

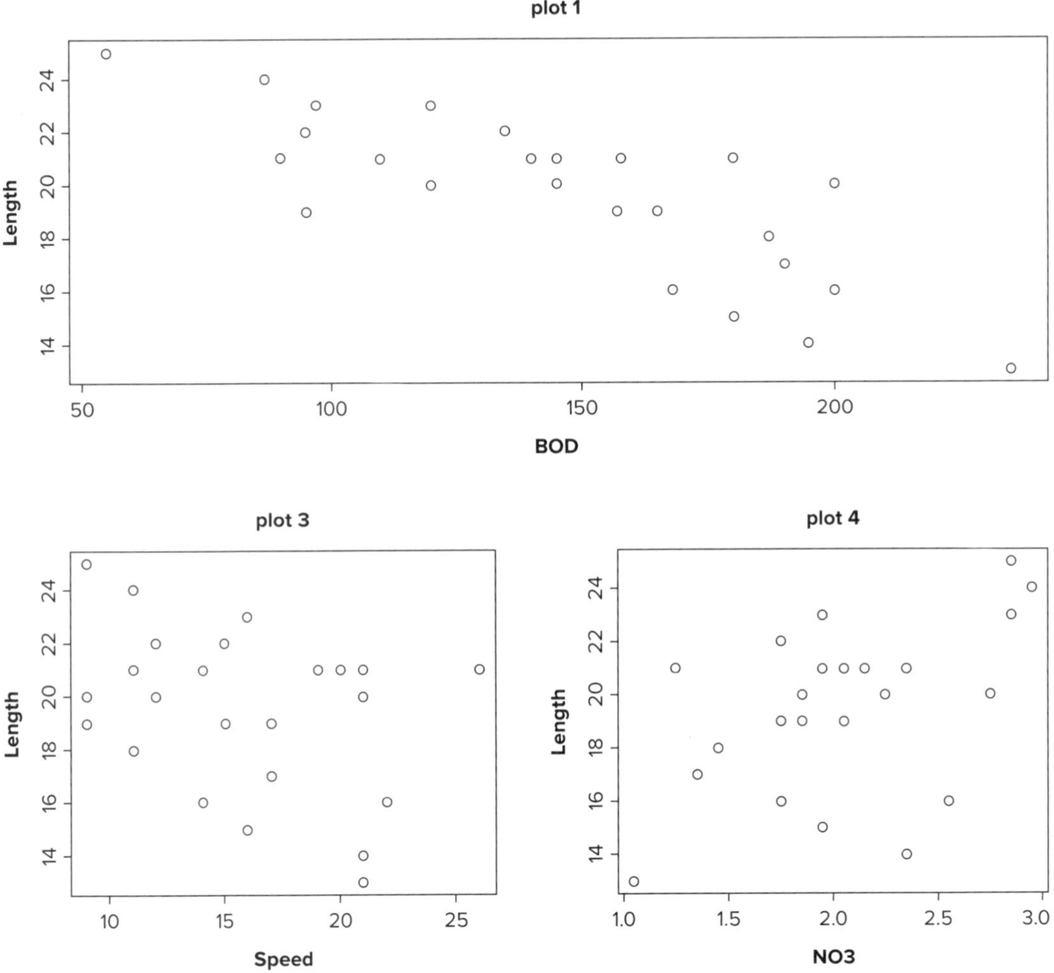

FIGURE 11-21

You can use the `close.screen()` command to remove splits:

```
> close.screen(n = 3:4)
[1] 1 2
```

Here you see that you retain screens one and two. If you want to close all the screens, you can specify this as an instruction in the `close.screen()` command like so:

```
> close.screen(all.screens = TRUE)
> close.screen()
[1] FALSE
```

When you use the `close.screen()` command without any instructions, you now see `FALSE` as a result, indicating that you have no screens remaining (that is, no splits, only the basic graphical window).

When you use split screens it is advisable to complete an entire plot before switching to a new screen; so complete the addition of titles, extra text, lines, and points before moving to the next. Table 11-14 shows a summary of splitting screens.

TABLE 11-14: Summary of Screen (Graphics Window) Splitting Commands and Options

COMMAND/INSTRUCTION	EXPLANATION
`split.screen(figs, screen)`	Splits the graphical window into subsections.
`figs`	The number of rows and columns required. For example, `c(2,2)` sets two rows and two columns.
`screen`	A numerical value specifying which screen is to be split; only works if the graphical window is already split.
`screen(n = )`	Switches to the screen specified by `n`. If `n` is missing, the current screen number is given.
`erase.screen(n = )`	Erases the selected screen by drawing over it in the current background color; this may be translucent and not appear to have any effect.
`opt = par(bg = 'white')` `par(opt)`	Sets the background color to white, which enables a screen to be erased. The command also stores all graphical parameters, so all can be reset using `par(opt)`.
`close.screen()`	Returns the numbers of the available screens remaining.
`n`	Selects the screen to be closed; the numbers of the remaining available screens is returned.
`all.screens = TRUE`	If set to `TRUE`, all screens are closed and the single graphical window remains.

EXPORTING GRAPHS

Once you have made a graph, you will have it on your computer screen. This may well be extremely useful as a diagnostic tool, but to reach a wider audience you will need to transfer your graph to another location. If you are going to use the graph in a report or presentation, you will need to place it into an appropriate program. Previously (in Chapter 7) you saw how to use copy and paste to transfer graphs directly into other programs and how to save the graphic window as a file on disk. Here you see a brief review of these processes before looking at ways to fine-tune your graphics via the device driver, which can produce high-quality graphics files.

Using Copy and Paste to Move a Graph

For many purposes, using the clipboard is simple and produces acceptable quality graphics for your word processor or presentation. You can resize the graphic window using your mouse like you would for any other program window and your graph will be resized accordingly.

If you want more control over the size of the graphics window, you can create a blank window with the dimensions you require using one of the following commands:

```
windows(height, width, bg)
quartz(height, width, bg)
X11(height, width, bg)
```

Which command you need depends on the operating system you are using at the time.

- For Windows users, the `windows()` command creates a new graphic window.
- For Macintosh users, the `quartz()` command opens a graphic window. The `X11()` command also opens a graphic window, but in the X11 application.
- For Linux users, the `X11()` command opens a graphic window.

You set the height and width in inches; the defaults depend on your system. You can also specify the background color using the `bg` instruction; the default is `bg = "transparent"`.

The default size for the graphics window can be set in the options for the GUI in Windows and Macintosh. In Linux you have to set a default in a profile file to run each time R loads. For most users the defaults are acceptable (7 inches), and for special uses it is quite simple to use the `X11()` command to produce a custom-sized window.

Saving a Graph to a File

Saving to a file generally makes a better quality graphic than using the clipboard. As you saw in Chapter 7, you have a variety of options for saving graphics files according to your operating system.

Windows

When you have a graphics window you will see that it contains a menu bar. The File menu enables you to save the contents of the window to a disk file. You have several choices of format, including PNG, JPEG, BMP, TIFF, and PDF. The JPEG option also allows you to specify the compression.

Macintosh

The Mac does not present you with a menu as part of the graphics window. Once the graph is selected, the File menu enables you to save your graph as a file. The default is to use PDF format. It is not trivial to alter the default. If you need a file in a different format, you can use the device driver, as you see shortly.

Linux

In Linux there is no GUI, and R runs via the Terminal application. This means that you cannot save the graphics window in this fashion; you must use the device driver in some manner.

Using the Device Driver to Save a Graph to Disk

The device driver allows more subtle control of your graphics and the quality of the finished article. If you are a Linux user, you have to use the device driver in some way unless a simple copy-and-paste operation will suffice. In Chapter 5 you saw how to use the device driver briefly. Here you see a few more of the options available to you.

You can think of the device driver as a way to send your graphics to an appropriate location; this may be the screen, a PNG file, or a PDF file. You can use the device driver in two main ways:

- Send an existing screen graphic to a file.
- Create a graphic file directly on disk.

The device driver can accept a variety of instructions, including the size of the graphic as well as the color of the background and the resolution (DPI). Here you see the device driver in action for saving PNG and PDF files.

PNG Device Driver

You access the PNG device via the `png()` command, which has the following general form:

```
png(filename = "Rplot%03d.tif", width = 480, height = 480, units = "px",
bg = "white",  res = NA)
```

You must specify a filename in quotes; the default will be used if you do not. This file will be written to your default directory. To alter the location you must either alter the default or specify the location explicitly as part of the filename. The height and width are specified in pixels by default, and the `units` instruction controls which units are used; you can specify `"in"`, `"cm"`, or `"mm"` as alternatives to the `"px"` default. The `bg` instruction sets the background color, and the `res` instruction controls the resolution.

The resolution is not recorded in the file unless you specify it explicitly. Many graphics programs will assume that 72 dpi has been used, so in practice it is a good idea to specify one—72 dpi is the standard for screen use, and with the 480 pixels size this comes out to 6.67 inches. You can use the `png()` command to create a file directly, or to copy a screen graphic to disk.

PDF Device Driver

The PDF device driver is accessed via the `pdf()` command and has similar options to the `png()` command.

```
pdf(file = "Rplot%03d.pdf", width, height, bg, colormodel)
```

The filename must be given in quotes and are saved to your default directory unless you alter it or specify the location explicitly as part of the filename. The height and width are measured in inches and use the default of 7 inches. The background color is set to `"transparent"` by default.

The `colormodel` instruction enables you to specify the general color of the plot; the default is `"rgb"`, which produces colored graphics. You can also specify `"gray"` to produce a grayscale plot.

Copying a Graph from Screen to Disk File

If you have created a graph on the screen and want to save it as a disk file, you can use device driver to copy the file. In effect, you are copying the graphic from one device to another. You can use two commands to achieve this:

```
dev.copy(device)
dev.print(device)
```

These are very similar, and you can treat them the same for most purposes. The `device` instruction is essentially the `png()` or `pdf()` command that you saw previously (you can also use `tiff()`, `jpeg()`, and `bmp()` commands).

The difference between the two `dev` commands is that `dev.print()` writes the graphic file immediately, whereas the `dev.copy()` command opens the graphic file and sends a copy but does not finish. This means that you can add additional commands to the graphic on disk without altering the one on the screen! Once you are finished with the graphic, you must close the device to finish writing the file and complete the operation. You do this using a new command:

```
dev.off()
```

No additional instructions are required. The graphics file created is closed and becomes available as soon as the `dev.off()` command is executed. The `dev.print()` command does not need you to do this because the file is written and closed in one go.

Making a New Graph Directly to a Disk File

The device driver enables you to create a graphic directly as a disk file, bypassing the screen entirely. This can be particularly useful if you need to create an especially large graphic that might not fit on the screen. You can also control the resolution and produce high-quality graphics suitable for publication.

The starting point is the device itself. Earlier you saw the `png()` and `pdf()` devices, which are likely to be the most useful. The steps you require to do create a graphics file on disk are as follows:

1. Create the device using the appropriate driver. You need to specify the filename and the size, as well as the resolution and any special background color.
2. Issue the graphics commands that you need to produce the basic graphic. This involves the `plot()` command or something similar (for example, `boxplot()`, `barplot()`, or `dotchart()` commands).
3. Add additional graphics commands to embellish your graph such as `title()` to add axis titles or `abline()` to add a line of best-fit.
4. Finish the plot by closing the graphics device using the `dev.off()` command.

Your computer will be set up to create graphics windows of a certain size. When you make a graph directly on disk, it is important to match the resolution you require to the appropriate size (in pixels); otherwise, the text, plotting characters, and so on will either be far too small or far too large. In the following activity you create a graph and explore the effects of altering the resolution.

TRY IT OUT Save a Graph to Disk and Explore the Effects of Resolution

Available for download on Wrox.com

For best results you should make a trial plot on the screen. Start by making a graphics window of a set size using the `windows()`, `quartz()`, or `X11()` commands as appropriate. Then create your graph. Once you have a graph that you are happy with, you can match the size and resolution by specifying the dimensions as *width * dpi* and *height * dpi*. So, if you get a good result with a 7 inch x 7 inch window and require a dpi of 300, you can specify 7 * 300 as the size. You can recall the graphics commands that you used to create your graph simply using the up arrow.

Use the `fwi` data object from the `Beginning.RData` file for this activity.

1. Make a graphic on the screen to check the layout using your default settings:

```
> plot(sfly ~ speed, data = fwi, main = 'Scatter plot', pch = 16, cex = 2, las = 1)
> abline(h = mean(fwi$sfly), lty = 3, lwd = 2)
> abline(v = mean(fwi$speed), lty = 3, lwd = 2)
> abline(lm(sfly ~ speed, data = fwi), lty = 2, col = 'blue')
> text(max(fwi$speed), mean(fwi$sfly)+ 0.5, 'Mean sfly', pos = 2, font = 3)
> text(mean(fwi$speed), max(fwi$sfly), pos = 4, srt = 270, 'Mean speed', font = 3)
```

2. Now create a new graphics window at a fixed size using the appropriate command for your OS:

```
> windows(width = 7, height = 7)
> quartz(width = 7, height = 7)
> X11(width = 7, height = 7)
```

3. Redraw the graph in the new window.

4. Now create a PNG file using the device driver. Set the resolution to 300 dpi:

```
> png(file = '7in 300dpi.tif', height = 2100, width = 2100, res = 300, bg = 'white')
```

5. Send the graphics commands once again, and then finish by closing the device driver:

```
> Graphics commands here..
> def.off()
```

6. Create a new PNG file and set the resolution to 150 dpi:

```
> png(file = '7in 150dpi.tif', height = 2100, width = 2100, res = 150, bg = 'white')
```

7. Send the graphics commands once again, and then finish by closing the device driver:

```
> Graphics commands here..
> def.off()
```

8. Create a new PNG file and set the resolution to 600 dpi:

```
> png(file = '7in 600dpi.tif', height = 2100, width = 2100, res = 600, bg = 'white')
```

9. Send the graphics commands once again, and then finish by closing the device driver:

```
> Graphics commands here..
> def.off()
```

10. Go to your working directory and look at the differences in the graphics (using your OS).

How It Works

The basic graphics commands make the plot using some embellishments that you have already seen in the text. The appearance of the graph will be slightly different depending on the default size of your graphics window. Therefore, to make sure you can visualize the final output, you create a new window using a set size; here you used seven inches for both width and height.

The device driver requires size and resolution information. In the first case you used 2100 pixels and 300 dpi. In other words, you used $7 \times 300 = 2100$ pixels as the size to match the onscreen graphic. Once the device is ready, you send the graphics commands to actually draw the plot and close using the `dev.off()` command.

The next two graphs you produce keep the same number of pixels but alter the resolution. In Figure 11-22 you can see the effect this has on the way the graphic appears. Low resolution and large size make everything very small; as you increase the resolution, everything becomes larger.

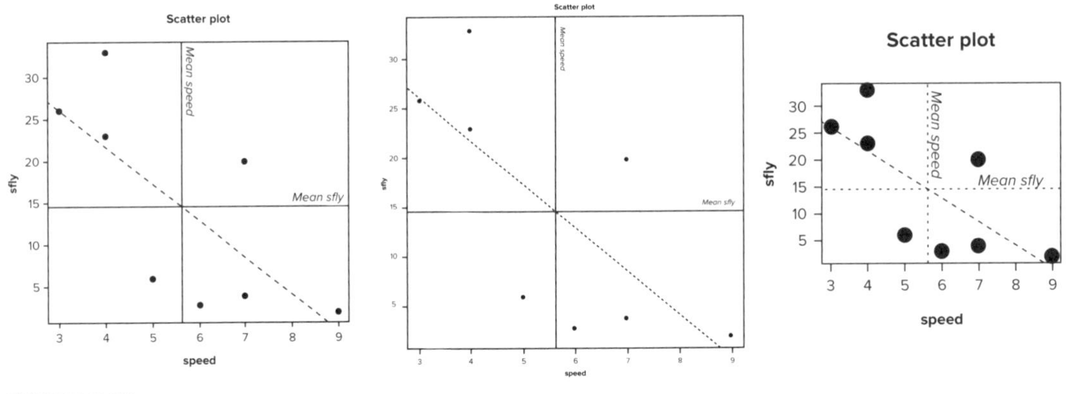

FIGURE 11-22

It is therefore important to match up the final size of the graphic with an appropriate resolution.

SUMMARY

- You can add error bars to graphs using `segments()` or `arrows()` commands.
- You can add legends using the `legend` instruction from some graph commands; for example, `barplot()` or separately using the `legend()` command.
- You can define color palettes using the `palette()` command.
- Use the `expression()` command to create complex text including superscripted and subscripted typeface. It can also create mathematical text.

- You can alter the plot margins to accommodate text by using the `mar` instruction within the `par()` command.
- Text labels on axes can be altered in various ways; for example, altering the orientation, color, size, and font.
- You can add text and points to existing graphs using the `text()` and `points()` commands.
- Various commands can add lines to graphs, including `abline()`, `lines()`, and `curve()`. The `spline()` command can bend sections of straight line to create a smooth curve.
- The `matplot()` command can plot multiple series on one chart. The `matpoints()` and `matlines()` can add to an existing plot.
- The graphical window can be split into sections to allow multiple graphs to be produced in one window. The sections do not have to be the same size.
- The device driver can create a blank graphics window as well as copy an existing graphic to a disk file. You can also create a graphic directly as a disk file.

EXERCISES

Available for download on Wrox.com

You can find answers to these exercises in Appendix A.

1. Use the `hogl` data object from the `Beginning.RData` file for this activity. Create a bar chart of the mean values for the two samples. Alter the aspect ratio of the plot to produce a graph 4 inches wide and 7 inches tall. Now add error bars to show the standard error using the `arrows()` command.

2. Use the `hoglouse` data object from the `Beginning.RData` file for this activity. Make a bar chart of these data. Use blocks of bars for each sample (that is, not stacked) and use a palette of rainbow colors. Include a legend; there will be room at the top left of the plot.

3. Examine the `hoglouse` data again. This time make a horizontal bar chart using stacked bars to highlight differences between *fast* and *slow*. You will find that there is no room for the category labels, so make the margin a bit wider. Add a legend to your plot separately and use a mouse-click to position it in an appropriate location.

4. Look at the `mf` data, which you've seen previously. Make a scatter plot using the `matplot()` command that shows the `Length` against both `Speed` and `Algae` variables. You should be able to use different colors and plotting symbols for each series, and add a legend (it will fit nicely at the bottom right of the plot). Add appropriate axis titles and include a subscript to indicate that `Length` was measured in mm.

▸ WHAT YOU LEARNED IN THIS CHAPTER

TOPIC	KEY POINTS
Error bars: `segments()` `arrows()`	Error bars can be added using `segments()` or `arrows()` commands.
Legends: `legend()`	The `legend()` command can be used to add a legend to an existing plot. The `barplot()` command can use a `legend` instruction to add a legend directly.
Colors: `palette()`	The `palette()` command can be used to create a palette of colors that can be used on plots where multiple series are drawn. Colors can also be specified explicitly.

Text:
`expression()` `text()`
`srt` `col` `cex` `font`
	The `expression()` command can produce text that is superscripted or subscripted. It can also produce mathematical symbols. The `text()` command can add text to an existing plot. This text can be modified; by typeface, orientation, color, and size, for example.

Axis labels:
`las` `cex.axis` `col.axis`
`par(mar)`
	You can modify axis labels by altering their color, size, and orientation. The margins of the plot window can also be altered using the `par()` command and the `mar` instruction.

Marginal text: `mtext()`	Text can be placed in the margins of the plot (inside or out) using the `mtext()` command. You can control the size, color, and position of the text.

Math:
`expression()`
`curve()`
	Mathematical symbols can be created using the `expression()` command. Mathematical functions can be drawn using the `curve()` command. Non-standard functions can be drawn using the `function()` and `curve()` commands together.

Lines:
`abline()` `curve()` `lines()`
Gridlines:
`segments()` `arrows()`
	Lines can be added to graphs in several ways. Straight lines can be added using the `abline()` command (for example, for lines of best-fit and gridlines). Fitted lines (for example, to regression models) can be added using the `lines()` command and these can be curved and smoothed using `splines()`. The `segments()` and `arrows()` commands can also add sections of straight line to graphs.

TOPIC	KEY POINTS
Multiple series graphs: points() lines() matplot() matpoints() matlines()	The points() and lines() commands can be used to add extra series of data to an existing plot. The matplot() command plots one matrix against another and so achieves a similar result.
Splitting the graphics window: par(mfrow) par(mfcol) plot.new() split.screen() screen() close.screen() erase.screen()	The graphics window can be split into equal sections using the mfrow and mfcol instructions as part of the par() command. The split.screen() command can produce unequally sized windows (as well as equal ones).
Exporting graphs: windows() quartz() X11() png() pdf() dev.copy() dev.print() dev.off()	You can transfer a graph to another program using copy and paste. The device driver allows a finer control of graphic quality and can produce files in several formats including PNG, PDF, and TIFF. You can copy an existing (screen) graphic to a file or create one directly.

12

Writing Your Own Scripts: Beginning to Program

WHAT YOU WILL LEARN IN THIS CHAPTER:

- How to store series of commands as snippets to be used with copy/paste
- How to make your own help file
- How to create simple customized functions
- How to edit, store, and recall customized functions
- How to add notes/annotations to your scripts
- How to create complex program code

Because R is a programming language, you have great flexibility in the approach you can take to running it. When you first begin to use R you will probably type commands directly from the keyboard. Later, as you become more confident, you will likely use snippets of commands stored in other areas, like a text file. The next step is to create simple functions that carry out something useful; you can call up these functions time and time again, and can save a lot of typing and effort. As your confidence and ability grow you will move on to creating larger *scripts*, that is, sets of R commands stored in a file that you can execute at any time.

Scripts can be especially useful because they enable you to prepare complex or repetitive tasks, which you can bring into operation at any time. Indeed, R is built along these lines, and you can think of the program as a bundle of scripts; by making your own you are simply increasing the usefulness of R and bending it to meet your own specific requirements.

Programming R is a wide subject in its own right. This chapter introduces you to the basic ideas so that you can set off on your own journey of discovery. Of course, you have gained a lot of experience at using R up to this point, so the step up to creating your own programs is only a small one.

COPY AND PASTE SCRIPTS

R is very flexible, and because it accepts plain text to drive the commands, you can store useful snippets to use at a later date. You can copy and paste the text from a word processor (or other program) into R and either run the command "as is" or edit the command before you press Enter.

WARNING *Word processors often use smart quotes and special characters. These are not always understood by R. If you use a word processor it is best to save the file as plain text to ensure that these special characters are removed.*

Make Your Own Help File as Plain Text

As you learn how to use R it is a good idea to keep a plain text file as a "notepad" (on Windows computers the `Notepad.exe` program is a good choice for this task). You can use this text file to keep notes and examples of R commands. However, a plain list of commands without explanation is not helpful. You can, of course, add explanatory notes in some way as you go along; the following example might be part of your notes file:

```
Code to work out means of columns in a data frame:
---------------------------------
apply(data, 2, mean, na.rm = TRUE)
---------------------------------
data = name of data frame
2 = columns (1 for rows)
mean = the mean command (can use others)
na.rm = TRUE = remove NA items if appropriate
```

To use this you can simply copy the text to the clipboard and paste it into the R console window; in the example here you want the line of text that is between the dashed lines. You can edit the name of the data and add a name for the result as you like. This is a good way to build up a library of commands that you can use and become familiar with.

When you copy command lines from R, you inevitably copy the > character that forms the "command entry point" as well. This book has used this approach so that you can see which lines were typed from the keyboard and which lines are results (that is, generated by R itself). So, if you copy commands into a text file it is a good idea to edit out the > characters at the beginning of command lines; keeping them in will give errors as you can see in the following example:

```
> > apply(data, 2, mean, na.rm = TRUE)
Error: unexpected '>' in ">"
```

NOTE *Make a text entry by copying all the commands you want from R, including the > characters, as one block. Then edit the characters out of the text file. This is a lot faster than copying each R command individually.*

NOTE *If you use Windows, you can use the script editor to run commands directly. Open a new or existing script (from the File menu) and you can run lines or selected text using Ctrl+R.*

Using Annotations with the # Character

As you look through R help entries, you will see lines of explanation in the examples (not always very clear, perhaps) that are associated with the # character, also known as the hash or pound character. R essentially ignores anything that follows a # character so the best use of this character is to keep notes. For instance, in your text file you can use the # character to create annotations that help you remember what is going on. The following example shows some commands that you might use to make yourself a basic bar chart with error bars (using standard error) and used the # character to organize the information:

```
# Barplot with se error bars.
# make copy of data called dat.
mn=apply(dat,2,mean,na.rm = TRUE) # set the mean values.
stdev=apply(dat,2,sd,na.rm = TRUE) # make the std deviation.
tot=apply(dat,2,sum,na.rm = TRUE) # get the sum for each column.
n=mn/tot # work out the no. observations (length does not accept na.rm=T).
se=stdev/sqrt(n) # calculate std err.
mx=round(max(mn+se)+0.5,0) # largest value to set y-axis.
bp=barplot(mn, ylim = c(0,mx)) # make plot and set y-axis to max value.
arrows(bp,mn+se,bp,mn-se,length=0.1,angle=90,code=3) # add error bars.
# If y-axis still too short change mx value to a larger one.
# END
```

NOTE *When you create snippets of code to use as copy/paste scripts, make data names standard—for example,* `my.data`*. Then before you use the script, make a copy of your current data called* `my.data`*. This saves you having to edit the script each time you want to use it.*

CREATING SIMPLE FUNCTIONS

When you use R, you'll realize that there are a lot of commands that you can use! In spite of this, on some occasions it would be useful to have others, especially to carry out some tasks that you might require reasonably often. You can use the `function()` command to create new commands that you can then store and use again later. The general form of the command is like so:

```
function(args) expr
```

Inside the parentheses you type the arguments that you require for the function to work; after the parentheses you type the expression you require using the arguments you have provided.

One-Line Functions

The following example shows a simple one-line function that you can create yourself:

```
> log2 = function(x) log(x, base = 2)
```

Here you create an object called `log2`; the function has only one simple argument, which you call `x`. After the `function()` part you type the actual expression you want to evaluate; in this case you use the `log()` command using base 2. When you use your function, you type its name and give appropriate instructions inside the parentheses. In this case you require numeric input, and you see the result of the function when you type a value into the new command:

```
> log2(64)
[1] 6
> log2(seq(2,8,2))
[1] 1.000000 2.000000 2.584963 3.000000
> log2(c(2,4,8,16))
[1] 1 2 3 4
```

The object you created as part of your new function resides in the computer memory and can be listed like other objects. You can also save your function along with the workspace when you quit R or as part of a `save.image()` command. Your function object is bundled and encoded along with the other objects, but this is no problem because you can retrieve the function object at any time and edit it as you require. When you use `save()` to save individual R objects, they require a filename with a file extension. Data items usually have an `.Rdata` extension and functions that you create usually get a simple `.R` file extension. This enables you to differentiate between the two types of objects because `.Rdata` items are encoded and can be opened only by R, whereas `.R` items are usually plain text and can be read, and perhaps edited, by other programs.

Using Default Values in Functions

When you create a function with the `function()`, command you give the various arguments as part of the command; you can also specify default values using = and the default value. The following example uses a fairly simple mathematical equation to determine the flow of water in a stream (the Manning equation); you have three arguments and one of them has a default:

```
manning = function(radius, gradient, coef=0.1125) (radius^(2/3)*gradient^0.5/coef)
```

The three arguments are `radius`, `gradient`, and `coef` (the Manning coefficient). You set the `coef` argument to have a default value of 0.1125. If you do not specify a `coef` when you run the function, the following value will be used:

```
> manning(radius = 1, gradient = 1/500)
[1] 0.3975232
```

You can use abbreviations when you run your new command as long as they are unambiguous (here the arguments have completely different names):

```
> manning(gra = 1/500, ra = 1)
[1] 0.3975232
```

You can even omit the names completely, but in that case you must specify the values for the arguments in exactly the correct order:

```
> manning(1, 1/500)
[1] 0.3975232
```

Of course, you can override the default values for any of the set arguments like so:

```
> manning(radius = 1, gradient = 1/500, coef = c(0.08, 0.11, 0.2))
[1] 0.5590170 0.4065578 0.2236068
```

Here you give three values for your `coef` argument and obtain three results.

Simple Customized Functions with Multiple Lines

A one-line script is very useful, but most of the time you will need longer and potentially more complex functions, which require several lines of commands. In that case you need a way to stop R from evaluating the function before you have finished typing it. One option would be to type the commands into a text editor and then copy and paste them into R. Another solution is to use curly brackets (`{}`). You use these brackets to create subsections of commands so you can use them to define the lines that form your function. The following example shows a simple function that determines the running median of a numeric vector:

```
> cummedian = function(x) {
+ tmp = seq_along(x)
+ for(i in 1:length(tmp)) tmp[i] = median(x[1:i])
+ print(tmp)
+ }
```

The first line starts the function by assigning it a name and listing the arguments; here there is only one argument, `x`. Rather than use any expressions at this point, you simply type a `{` and press the Enter key.

WARNING *If you are using a Macintosh, you may have to delete the closing* `}` *that appears (the program adds closing brackets and quotes automatically on a Mac, but not for Windows or Linux).*

Now R is expecting something after the `{` and you see the insertion symbol change to a `+` rather than the usual `>` character. R will keep expecting something and allow you to enter multiple lines until you enter a closing `}`.

Notice that the penultimate line is `print(tmp)`; this displays your result to the screen (you could also have used `return(tmp)` to get the same output). You look at methods of displaying results shortly when you look at longer and more complex scripts.

If you type the name of your newly created `function()`, you see the lines of command that make up the `function()` like so:

```
> cummedian
function(x) {
tmp = seq_along(x)
for(i in 1:length(tmp)) tmp[i] = median(x[1:i])
print(tmp)
}
```

NOTE *If you included any comment lines before the* `function()` *line, they will not be visible and will not be saved as part of the function. If you include comments at any point between the curly brackets, they will be retained.*

You can also use the `args()` command to view the required arguments for your `function()`:

```
> args(manning)
function (radius, gradient, coef = 0.1125)
NULL
> args(cummedian)
function (x)
NULL
```

Storing Customized Functions

If you create a simple function from the command line and have created a name for it, the object will appear along with other objects when you use the `ls()` command. You can save your customized functions along with all the data by saving the workspace when you use `quit()` to quit the program. You can also save one or several function objects using the `save()` command like so:

```
> save(manning, cummedian, file = 'My Functions.R')
```

In this example you save two custom functions to a file called `My Functions.R`; note that you give the file an `.R` extension to differentiate the file from data. The filename must be in quotes. However, when you use the `save()` command, R converts the object into a special binary form and you no longer have a plain text file!

If you have used `save()` to keep your customized function object on disk, you must use `load()` to get it back again like so:

```
> load('My Functions.R')
```

Ideally you would save your function as a plain text script so that you can edit it. You can make your function objects save to disk as plain text by using the `dump()` command like so:

```
> dump(c('cummedian', 'manning'), file = 'My Functions.R')
```

In this example you use `c()` to create a list of objects that you want to dump to disk; note that the names of the objects must be in quotes. You might also have created a separate character vector of names, or you could use an `ls()` command to make your list:

```
> dump(ls(pattern = 'cummedian|manning'), file = 'My Functions.R')
```

If you use `dump()` to save your function objects, they appear as plain text and you could open and edit them with a text editor.

```
> manning
function(radius, gradient, coeff) {
    (radius^(2/3) * gradient^0.5 / coeff)

## Enter: radius, gradient and Manning coeffficient to return estimated speed

} # end function code
>
```

Compare this to the `manning` function you saw earlier.

In most cases it is not practical to make complicated functions from the command line of R itself; it is better and easier to use a text editor. In Windows and Macintosh versions of R, editors are built-in to R and open when you make or open a script from the File menu. In Linux you must use a separate editor of your choice from the OS. If you use a text editor, you can call up the resulting plain text file from R using the `source()` command:

```
source(file.choose())
```

In this version of the command, you get to choose your file from a browser-like window. This option is not available in Linux OS; you must type the filename explicitly. For example:

```
> source(file = 'My Functions.R')
```

NOTE *Your scripts and custom functions can be saved on disk as either plain text or as R-encoded files (that is, binary). Remember to match up the saving and loading to the correct file type like so:*

- **Disk file as text:** `dump()` to save, `source()` to load
- **Disk file binary:** `save()` to save, `load()` to load

MAKING SOURCE CODE

In addition to the usual commands that you have seen before, a few extra ones are especially useful for use with your customized functions and scripts.

Displaying the Results of Customized Functions and Scripts

When you create a custom function you may use several arguments and create new variables as part of any calculations. In the following example, which you saw earlier, you create a new variable called `tmp`:

```
> cummedian
function(x) {
       tmp = seq_along(x) # a temp variable
       for(i in 1:length(tmp)) tmp[i] = median(x[1:i])
       print(tmp) # the result
       }
```

This variable exists only while the function is being evaluated. It does not remain afterwards, as the following example shows:

```
> cummedian(mf$BOD)
 [1] 200.0 190.0 180.0 157.5 135.0 127.5 120.0 127.5 135.0 151.5 158.0 151.5 145.0
[14] 145.0 145.0 151.5 158.0 157.5 157.0 157.5 158.0 157.5 157.0 151.0 145.0
> tmp
Error: object 'tmp' not found
```

As part of the function, therefore, you must present the result before the end of the series of commands; you can use the `print()` command to do this, which is what the function in the previous example uses. You might also create a "container" to hold the result of your function, in which case the final result is suppressed and saved to the result object instead like so:

```
> tmp = cummedian(mf$BOD)
> tmp
 [1] 200.0 190.0 180.0 157.5 135.0 127.5 120.0 127.5 135.0 151.5 158.0 151.5 145.0
[14] 145.0 145.0 151.5 158.0 157.5 157.0 157.5 158.0 157.5 157.0 151.0 145.0
```

In this case you call your result object `tmp`, which, although it has the same name as the temporary variable, is in fact different!

Displaying Messages as Part of Script Output

You may want to produce text output as part of your script; for example, to embellish the result and make it clearer for the user. Often you will create summary statistics as part of your custom functions, and you can create text to set out the results in various forms to present them to the user more clearly. At other times you may want to pause and wait for an input from the user.

Simple Screen Text

You can produce text on the screen to present results, or to remind the user of what was done. A simple way to do this is to use the `cat()` command, which enables you to present text on the screen. Your text must be in quotes, or be an object that is a character object. See the following example:

```
> msg = 'My work is far from done.'
> cat(msg)
My work is far from done.

> cat('Any text to be used must be in quotes')
Any text to be used must be in quotes
```

If you want to create new lines, you add `\n` to your command like so:

```
> cat('This is line 1\nThis is line 2\nThis is line 3')
This is line 1
This is line 2
This is line 3
```

You can have several parts to your `cat()` command, separated by commas. For example:

```
> cat('Am I done?\n', msg, '\n')
Am I done?
 My work is far from done.
```

In the following simple script you create a data frame using some simple numeric data:

```
## Test script
       dat1 = c(1,2,4,6,7,8)
         dat2 = c(4,5,8,7,6,5)
           dat3 = data.frame(dat1, dat2)

rm(dat1, dat2)
```

```
msg = 'My work is done.'
        cat('\nOur result data is dat3:\n\n')
          print(dat3)
            cat('\n', msg, '\n')
## END
```

The preceding script works in the following manner:

1. Two numeric vectors are created and then joined to make a separate data frame.
2. The two individual vectors are removed to leave the data frame, called `dat3`, intact.
3. A simple character vector is created called `msg`.
4. Now some output is presented using the first `cat()` command, which consists of a single text string that starts with a new line and ends with two new lines.
5. A `print()` command is used to display the data frame object you created.
6. Finally, the `msg` character vector is used as part of another `cat()` command. The text was saved to a plain text file, and to run the lines of command you use the `source()` command. The result is as follows:

```
> source('test script.R')

Our result data is: dat3

  dat1 dat2
1    1    4
2    2    5
3    4    8
4    6    7
5    7    6
6    8    5

 My work is done.
>
```

NOTE *Spaces are ignored in R commands; additional blank lines are ignored as well. Therefore you can use extra spaces and blank lines to make your scripts more readable.*

Now take a look at the following script; in it you create a customized function; this creates cumulative results for a numeric vector. Previously you used a similar script to create a running or cumulative median; here you can specify any mathematical function, although you set the default to the median in this instance:

```
## Cumulative functions
## Mark Gardener 2011

cum.fun = function(x, fun = median, ...) {
  tmp = seq_along(x)
    for(i in 1:length(tmp)) tmp[i] = fun(x[1:i], ...)
```

```
    cat('\n', deparse(substitute(fun)),'of', deparse(substitute(x)),'\n')
      print(tmp)
}

## END
```

In this preceding example you require two arguments, `x` and `fun`; `x` is the vector of numeric values and `fun` is the mathematical function you want to apply. You also include an ellipsis (`...`), which is a way of saying "allow other instructions that might be relevant." You might, for example, want to add `na.rm = TRUE` as an instruction to take care of any `NA` items.

When you get the result it would be helpful to have a reminder of which function you requested when you typed the command. It would also be helpful to take the name of an object and display it as text so you can have a reminder of the data name that was used. This can be tricky though; you cannot include the data or function name here as `x` or `fun` because R will try to coerce the contents of these items as objects rather than as text (R assumes that you want to display the object itself and gives you the contents rather than the name). Additionally, you cannot put the names in quotes because they will become "fixed" and you simply get what was in the quotes. What you actually do, as you can see, is use `deparse(substitute())`. This looks at what you typed in the command as arguments and converts these arguments to text objects.

The result of the `deparse(substitute())` command in the preceding script is as follows:

```
> cum.fun(mf$BOD, mean)

 mean of mf$BOD
 [1] 200.0000 190.0000 171.6667 158.7500 149.0000 144.1667 137.1429 141.0000
 [9] 145.3333 150.3000 151.0000 150.5000 149.6923 149.3571 150.4000 152.6875
[17] 154.8824 155.0000 151.5789 155.7500 157.8571 153.1818 150.3043 148.0833
[25] 145.9600
```

Display a Message and Wait for User Intervention

There are times when you will want to pause the running of a script: this may be to give the user time to see an intermediate result (for example, a graphic) before moving on, or to provide options for the user to select: Pressing one key performs one operation and another key does something else.

You can use the `readline()` command to accept a key press from the user; the script will wait until a key is pressed. As part of the command, you can include a message to be displayed on the screen. For example:

```
> readline(prompt = 'Press <enter> to continue:')
```

The text that follows the `prompt =` instruction is displayed and the script pauses until a key is pressed. Although the text in this case implies that the Enter key should be pressed, any key will do.

You can give the user options by setting an object using the `readline()` command. The following example could be included in a larger script:

```
yorn <- readline(prompt = "Do you want to carry on? (Y or N) :")
   if (yorn == 'Y' || yorn =='y'){
   cat('Thank goodness')
}
```

If the user presses the Y key (uppercase or lowercase), the message is displayed. If the user presses anything else, nothing happens.

You can also create user prompts that provide multiple options. Each option must have its own code within a pair of curly brackets as in the following example:

```
# Explicit options

mopts = function(){
 yorn <- readline(prompt = "Do you want to carry on? (Y or N) : ")

  if(yorn == 'Y' || yorn == 'y') {
    cat('Thank goodness')
     }

  if(yorn == 'N' || yorn =='n') {
    cat('Oh dear')
     }
}
## END
```

This preceding code creates a new function called `mopts`. When this function is run the user is presented with the text prompt. If she types one of the specified options then the appropriate message is displayed. In this case you can see that there are two options and if the user types something other than these two options then nothing will happen. You can create a catch all option by using the `else` command as the following example shows:

```
# Single positive option

sopt = function(){
 yorn <- readline(prompt = "Do you want to carry on? (Y or N) : ")

  if(yorn == 'Y' || yorn == 'y') cat('Thank goodness') else cat('Oh dear')
}
## END
```

The preceding code created a new function called `sopt`. When this function is run the user will see the same prompt as in the `mopts` code. If the user presses the Y key then the `"Thank goodness"` message is displayed. If any other key is pressed then the alternative `"Oh dear"` message is shown.

In the following activity you create a new customized function, which you then save to disk for future use. The script creates a bar chart of mean values and adds standard error bars. The data need to be in column format with one column for the numerical data (the response data) and one column for the grouping (predictor) variable.

TRY IT OUT Create a Complex Script and Save It for Future Use

In this activity you will create a complicated script that creates a function that will draw a bar plot and add error bars.

1. Start by opening a text editor or use the built-in editor from the File menu. The option you choose depends on your OS:
    - **Windows:** New Script
    - **Macintosh:** New Document
    - **Linux:** N/A; you must use an external editor

2. Type a couple of comment lines. These are useful to remind you of when you wrote the script and what it does.

```
## Bar Plot with Error Bars
## Mark Gardener 2011
```

3. Now start the main function command by giving a name and outlining the required arguments/instructions:

```
barplot.eb = function(y, x, data, ...)
```

4. Type a curly bracket and start to enter the steps of the function. Begin by adding comment lines to remind you of what is required.

```
{   # start function code
    # Parameters (data frame must be stacked)
    # y      = y variable
    # x      = x variable
    # data   = data.name
```

5. Now enter some command lines that will read the data, and create some new variables to be used in the plot:

```
attach(data) # start by attaching data to read variables

    mean = tapply(y, x, mean)          # get mean values
    sdev = tapply(y, x, sd)        # get std. dev.
    len = tapply(y, x, length)     # get no. observations
    se = sdev/sqrt(len)            # determine std. err.

detach(data) # detach data file for tidiness
```

6. Enter a command to make a matrix object to hold the results and determine the limits of the y-axis:

```
mat = rbind(mean, se, len) # make matrix of values
upper = round(max(mat[1,]+mat[2,]+0.5),0) # the upper limit to fit e-bars on y-axis
```

7. Now enter the commands that will draw the plot and add the error bars:

```
bp = barplot(mean, ylim = c(0, upper), beside = T, ...)
          # make barplot, fix y-limit to fit largest error bar

segments(bp, mean+se, bp, mean-se) # error bars up/down
  segments(bp-0.1, mean+se, bp+0.1, mean+se) # top hats
  segments(bp-0.1, mean-se, bp+0.1, mean-se) # bottom hats
```

8. Enter the commands that will produce some screen text as information for the user:

```
cat('\nSummary stats for ', deparse(substitute(data)), '\n') # summary message
  print(mat) # show the data summary
    cat('\n') # newline for tidiness
```

9. Now type the final closing curly bracket to signal the end of the function and any final comments:

```
} # end function code

## END
```

10. Save the script file to disk. Make sure you give it an `.R` extension.

11. Now load the code from disk and make it ready for use:

```
> source(file.choose())
```

How It Works

The main `function()` command requires you to state the inputs needed; if you want any to have defaults, include them after an equals sign. The main commands that "drive" the function are placed between curly brackets. Use comments immediately after the first curly bracket as a reminder of the inputs required.

The first part of the script creates summary statistics from the data. The data object is first attached and then detached once the summary statistics are created. The next part makes a matrix object to hold the results; this is used to draw the bar chart, as well as to display a summary for the user.

Finally, the script produces the graph and writes a summary to the screen. The final lines close the curly brackets, ending the actual function, and show a comment (this simply helps you to spot the end of blocks of code; here it is not really necessary).

The final completed script appears like so:

```
## Bar Plot with Error Bars
## Mark Gardener 2011

barplot.eb = function(y, x, data, ...)

    # Parameters
    # y     = y variable
    # x     = x variable
    # data  = data.name

{   # start function code

    attach(data)  # start by attaching data to read variables

    mean = tapply(y, x, mean)    # get mean values
    sdev = tapply(y, x, sd)      # get std. dev.
    len = tapply(y, x, length)  # get no. observations
    se = sdev/sqrt(len)          # determine std. err.

detach(data) # detach data file for tidiness

mat = rbind(mean, se, len) # make matrix of values
upper = round(max(mat[1,]+mat[2,]+0.5),0) # the upper limit to fit error bars on
y-axis

bp = barplot(mean, ylim = c(0, upper), beside = T, ...) # make barplot, fix y-limit to
fit largest error bar

segments(bp, mean+se, bp, mean-se) # error bars up/down
    segments(bp-0.1, mean+se, bp+0.1, mean+se) # top hats
    segments(bp-0.1, mean-se, bp+0.1, mean-se) # bottom hats
```

```
    cat('\nSummary stats for ', deparse(substitute(data)), '\n') # summary message
    print(mat) # show the data summary
    cat('\n') # newline for tidiness

} # end function code

## END
```

The resulting output produces a bar chart with error bars as well as the following text output:

```
> barplot.eb(count, site, data = bfs)

Summary stats for  bfs
        Arable     Grass    Heath
mean 10.000000  6.833333 9.000000
se    1.424001  1.481366 0.755929
len   9.000000 12.000000 8.000000
```

NOTE *When you read a script from disk you do not need to give it a name; simply use the* `source()` *command and select the file from disk.*

There is, of course, a lot more to programming in R and many additional commands that you could employ. However, what you have seen here will take you a long way. By understanding more about how R works you will be able to see more and more how to customize it to carry out those tasks that are important to you.

SUMMARY

- You can make simple scripts in a text editor and use them by simply copying and pasting.
- You can annotate scripts using the # character.
- The `function()` command is the key to creating customized commands.
- You can set default values in custom functions by giving the default value in the command.
- Use curly brackets to define blocks of commands; you can also use them as a way to enter multiple lines of code from the keyboard.
- You can create scripts using a text editor. You can load scripts saved as text using the `source()` command.
- The `dump()` command saves a text representation of a custom function to disk, which can be loaded later using the `source()` command.
- The `save()` command writes a binary file to disk, which can be loaded later using the `load()` command.

- Named objects created by custom functions are temporary.
- The results of custom functions can be displayed using the `print()` command as part of the script.
- The `cat()` command can be used to display a message on screen as part of a script.
- The `readline()` command can pause and display a message, prompting user input, for example.

EXERCISES

You can find answers to these exercises in Appendix A.

1. Make a simple function that raises a number to any power (that is, x^y). Call your function `pwr` (there is already a command called `power`). Make the default raise the input number(s) to the power of 2.
2. How can you save your new `pwr` function/command to disk for later recall?
3. Retype your custom `pwr` function/command but this time incorporate some annotations.
4. Alter your `pwr` function/command so that the user must type the required power from the keyboard separately.
5. How can you modify the `pwr` function/command that you made to present the user with a summary of what was done?

▶ WHAT YOU LEARNED IN THIS CHAPTER

TOPIC	KEY POINTS
Copy and Paste	You can copy and paste text from another application into R. This enables you to create help files and snippets of code for future use.
Customized functions: `function(args) expr`	Create customized functions using the `function()` command; `args` = arguments to pass to `expr` (the actual function). Args may provide default values.

Multiple lines of text
`{ various commands }`
`function(args) {`
`various commands }`
	Curly brackets can be used to separate subroutines. This allows multiple lines to be entered into console.

Annotations: # comment	Anything following the # is ignored and so it can be used for comments.
Function arguments/instructions: `args(function_name)`	The `args()` command returns the arguments/instructions required by the named function.
Looking at function code: `function_name`	Supplying the function name without `()` and instructions displays the text of the script.

Read text files as scripts:
`source('filename')`
`source(file.choose())`
	Reads a text file and executes the lines of text as R commands.

Saving to disk: `save(object, 'filename')`	Saves a binary version of an object (including a function) to disk.
Loading from disk: `load('filename')`	Loads a binary object from disk.
Save objects as text: `dump('names_list', file = 'filename')`	Attempts to write a text version of an object to disk.

Text messages on screen:
`cat('text1', 'text2')`
`cat(chr_object)`
`"\n"`
`"\'"`
	Produces a message in the console; requires plain text strings, explicitly or from character objects. Items may be separated by commas. A newline is produced using `"\n"`. A quote character (single or double) is produced by preceding it with a backslash (\).

TOPIC	KEY POINTS
Displaying results: `print(object)`	Prints the named object to the console (that is, the screen).
Wait for user input: `readline(prompt = "text")`	Pauses and waits for input from the user. A message can be displayed using the `prompt =` instruction.
Convert user input to text: `deparse(substitute(x))`	Takes a named object and converts its name to text, which can then be displayed via `cat()`.

APPENDIX

Answers to Exercises

This appendix provides the solutions for the end-of-chapter exercises located in Chapters 1–12.

CHAPTER 1

Exercise 1 Solution

To install the coin library/package you need to type the following command:

```
>install.package('coin')
```

Note that the name must be in quotes. Then you select the closest mirror site and the package is downloaded and installed for you.

Exercise 2 Solution

To load the coin library and make it ready to use you type the following:

```
>library(coin)
```

Once the library is active its commands are available for you to use. You can try to bring up the help entry for the package using the following:

```
>help(coin)
```

This does not work for all packages; a better alternative is to use the HTML help system by typing:

```
>help.start()
```

This opens the main R help files in your default browser. You can now follow the links to the packages and then find coin from the list.

Exercise 3 Solution

The `MASS` package is already loaded as part of the R installation but is not ready to use until you type:

```
>library(MASS)
```

Once you have the library available you can open the help entry using:

```
>help(bcv)
```

Exercise 4 Solution

You can use the `search()` command to get a list of objects that are available for use.

Exercise 5 Solution

To clear the coin package from memory (and remove it from the `search()` path), type the following:

```
>detach(package:coin)
```

CHAPTER 2

Exercise 1 Solution

You can use either the `c()` command or the `scan()` command to enter these data. The problem is that the bee names contain spaces, which are not allowed. You must alter the names to remove the spaces; the period is the simplest solution.

If you decided to use the `c()` command then the first vector would be created like so:

```
> Buff.tail = c(10, 1, 37, 5, 12)
```

If you decided to use the `scan()` command then the process is in two parts. The first part is to initiate the data entry like so:

```
> Buff.tail = scan()
```

The second part is to enter the data:

```
> 10 1 37 5 12
```

To finish the data entry process you must enter a blank line.

If you decide to use the `c()` command, the entire data entry process would look like the following:

```
> Buff.tail = c(10, 1, 37, 5, 12)
> Garden.bee = c(8, 3, 19, 6, 4)
> Red.tail = c(18, 9, 1, 2, 4)
> Honey.bee = c(12, 13, 16, 9, 10)
> Carder.bee = c(8, 27, 6, 32, 23)
```

Exercise 2 Solution

You can use the `ls()` command to list all the objects currently in memory. However, there will often be quite a few other objects so you can narrow your display by using a regular expression like so:

```
> ls(pattern = 'tail|bee')
```

Note that you must not include a space on either side of the | pipe character. This listing shows all objects that contain "tail" or "bee". You could also list objects that ended with "tail" or "bee" by adding the dollar sign as a suffix like so:

```
> ls(pattern = '.tail$|.bee$')
```

To save the data objects you can use the `save()` command. The names of the objects could be typed into the command to make a long listing, but this is tedious. The regular expression you typed earlier can be used to produce the list of objects to be saved like so:

```
> save(list = ls(pattern = 'tail|bee'), file = 'bee data all.RData')
```

To remove the unwanted individual vectors you need to use the `rm()` command. The names of the objects could be typed into the command as a list or the regular expression could be used once again. This time you must ensure that you do not remove the `bees` data frame so type the `ls()` command first to check:

```
> ls(pat = 'tail$|bee$')
```

Now the `$` suffix ensures that you only selected those objects that ended with the text. You can use the up arrow to recall the command and edit it to form the `rm()` command like so:

```
> rm(list = ls(pat = 'tail$|bee$'))
```

Note that you must use the `list =` instruction to ensure that the result of the `ls()` part is treated like a list.

Now quit R using the `q()` command and select "No" when asked of you want to save the workspace. Restart R and use the `ls()` command once again. All the bee data are gone. To retrieve the data you use the `load()` command.

```
> load('bee data all.RData')
```

This command retrieves the data that you saved earlier; the individual vectors that you made are all included in the one file. If you are using Windows or Macintosh you can also use the `file.choose()` instruction rather than the explicit filename like so:

```
> load(file.choose())
```

You can also load the data by double clicking on the appropriate file from a Windows Explorer or Mac Finder window.

CHAPTER 3

Exercise 1 Solution

You can use either the `c()` command or the `scan()` command to enter these data. The problem is that the bee names contain spaces, which are not allowed. You must alter the names to remove the spaces; the period is the simplest solution.

If you decided to use the `c()` command then the first vector would be created like so:

```
> Buff.tail = c(10, 1, 37, 5, 12)
```

If you decided to use the `scan()` command then the process is in two parts. The first part is to initiate the data entry like so:

```
> Buff.tail = scan()
```

The second part is to enter the data:

```
> 10 1 37 5 12
```

To finish the data entry process you must enter a blank line.

If you decide to use the `c()` command the entire data entry process would look like the following:

```
> Buff.tail = c(10, 1, 37, 5, 12)
> Garden.bee = c(8, 3, 19, 6, 4)
> Red.tail = c(18, 9, 1, 2, 4)
> Honey.bee = c(12, 13, 16, 9, 10)
> Carder.bee = c(8, 27, 6, 32, 23)
```

To create a data frame you must decide on a name for the object and then use the `data.frame()` command like so:

```
> bees = data.frame(Buff.tail, Garden.bee, Red.tail, Honey.bee, Carder.bee)
```

To create row names you can use either the `row.names()` or `rownames()` command. The plant names also contain spaces, which need to be dealt with as before by replacing with a full stop. The shortest method is to assign the names as a simple list of data like so:

```
> row.names(bees) = c('Thistle', 'Vipers.bugloss', 'Golden.rain',
'Yellow.alfalfa', 'Blackberry')
```

You might also decide to create a vector to hold the plant names as a separate object:

```
> plant.names = c('Thistle', 'Vipers.bugloss', 'Golden.rain',
'Yellow.alfalfa', 'Blackberry')
> row.names(bees) = plant.names
```

This last method is slightly longer but the vector of plant names can be useful for other purposes.

Exercise 2 Solution

To make a matrix you need the data as separate columns (or rows) or as a single vector of values. You already have the separate vectors for the different bees so begin by using the `cbind()` command to join them column by column into a new matrix:

```
> beematrix = cbind(Buff.tail, Garden.bee, Red.tail, Honey.bee, Carder.bee)
```

Your new matrix will not contain any row names so to include them you need to use the `rownames()` command:

```
> plant.names = c('Thistle', 'Vipers.bugloss', 'Golden.rain',
'Yellow.alfalfa', 'Blackberry')
> rownames(beematrix) = plant.names
```

The second way to create a matrix is to use a single vector of values and use the `matrix()` command. To create a single vector you could combine the individual bee vectors:

```
> bee.data = c(Buff.tail, Garden.bee, Red.tail, Honey.bee, Carder.bee)
```

Now you can create a new matrix; you will need five columns (one for each bee species):

```
> beematrix2 = matrix(bee.data, ncol = 5)
```

The new matrix does not contain row or column names. You already created a vector of plant names, which can be used with the `rownames()` command:

```
> rownames(beematrix2) = plant.names
```

In order to make column names you must either type the names directly into the `colnames()` command or create a vector of bee names to use:

```
> bee.data = c(Buff.tail, Garden.bee, Red.tail, Honey.bee, Carder.bee)
```

Now you can use the `colnames()` command (remember that the `names()` command does not work with a matrix):

```
> colnames(beematrix2) = bee.names
```

To convert a matrix to a data frame you can use the `as.data.frame()` command:

```
> mat.to.frame = as.data.frame(beematrix2)
```

To convert a data frame into a matrix you can use the `as.matrix()` command:

```
> frame.to.mat = as.matrix(bees)
```

To make a list you can use the `list()` command:

```
> bee.list = list(bees, plant.names, bee.names)
```

If you look at the new list you see that the elements are not named so you must add names using the `names()` command.

```
> names(bee.list) = c('bees', 'plant.names', 'bee.names')
```

Now you have a single item that contains the data as well as separate items with the row and column names.

Exercise 3 Solution

To tidy up you will need to use the `rm()` command. You can type the names into the command individually or you can use the `ls()` command along with a regular expression to remove several items at once.

```
> rm(list = ls(pat = 'bee$|tail|^beem'))
```

The preceding command creates a list of objects ending with "bee" as well as those containing "tail". It also lists the two matrix objects as they begin with "beem". The command removes all the individual bee vectors as well as the two matrix objects. You can use a separate command to remove the two vectors of names:

```
> rm(bee.names, plant.names)
```

To display the data for the Blackberry only you need to determine which row you need and then use the [row, column] syntax; there are two options:

```
> bees[5,]
> bees['Blackberry',]
```

In the first case the number of the row was used whilst in the second example the name of the row was used.

To display the data for Golden rain and Yellow alfalfa requires a bit more thought. You could simply determine the appropriate rows and use these values like so:

```
> bees[3:4, ]
> bees[c(3, 4), ]
```

You might have thought about creating an index to work out the appropriate rows:

```
> ii = which(rownames(bees)=='Golden.rain'|rownames(bees)=='Yellow.alfalfa')
> bees[ii, ]
```

To display the data for the Red tail bee only you can use the `$` syntax like so:

```
> bees$Red.tail
```

However, all you see are the plain values; the plant names are not shown alongside the values. You could achieve the same result using the [row, column] syntax too:

```
> bees[, 3]
> bees[, 'Red.tail']
```

Once again the numerical values are shown without any labels. With a slight modification you can display the appropriate column along with the labels by omitting the row designation like so:

```
> bees[3]
> bees['Red.tail']
```

In either case, you will see the data for the Red tail bee as well as the appropriate row names as labels.

Exercise 4 Solution

The first step is to create an index to re-order the rows. You can use the `order()` command to achieve this using the Buff tail column like so:

```
> ii = order(bees$Buff.tail, bees$Red.tail, decreasing = TRUE)
```

Remember that you need to specify `decreasing = TRUE` as the default is for ascending (that is, `decreasing = FALSE`). The index can now be used to create a new data frame with the new row order:

```
> bees.r = bees[ii, ]
```

Now you have re-ordered the rows (Golden rain should be the top row) you can create an index to re-order the columns. You can use the `order()` command again to alter the order of the first row:

```
> ii = order(bees.r[1,], decreasing = TRUE)
```

Once again you need to specify `decreasing = TRUE` as an instruction. Now you can apply the new index to the data to alter the order of the columns:

```
> bees.rc = bees.r[, ii ]
```

You can tidy up by removing any unwanted data frames using the `rm()` command.

CHAPTER 4

Exercise 1 Solution

If you type its name you see the `mf` data. At first glance this appears to be a data frame because it is a two-dimensional object with rows and columns. However, the object might be a matrix or even a table object. To examine the structure and type more closely you can use the `str()` and `class()` commands:

```
> str(mf)
'data.frame': 25 obs. of  5 variables:
 $ Length: int  20 21 22 23 21 20 19 16 15 14 ...
 $ Speed : int  12 14 12 16 20 21 17 14 16 21 ...
 $ Algae : int  40 45 45 80 75 65 65 65 35 30 ...
 $ NO3   : num  2.25 2.15 1.75 1.95 1.95 2.75 1.85 1.75 1.95 2.35 ...
 $ BOD   : int  200 180 135 120 110 120 95 168 180 195 ...
> class(mf)
[1] "data.frame"
```

You can now see that this is a data frame. You can get a basic summary of the entire data frame using the `summary()` command:

```
> summary(mf)
     Length          Speed           Algae            NO3             BOD       
 Min.   :13.00   Min.   : 9.0   Min.   :25.0   Min.   :1.050   Min.   : 55.0  
 1st Qu.:18.00   1st Qu.:12.0   1st Qu.:40.0   1st Qu.:1.750   1st Qu.:110.0  
 Median :20.00   Median :16.0   Median :65.0   Median :1.950   Median :145.0  
 Mean   :19.64   Mean   :15.8   Mean   :58.4   Mean   :2.046   Mean   :146.0  
 3rd Qu.:21.00   3rd Qu.:20.0   3rd Qu.:75.0   3rd Qu.:2.350   3rd Qu.:180.0  
 Max.   :25.00   Max.   :26.0   Max.   :85.0   Max.   :2.950   Max.   :235.0  
```

Because all the columns are numerical, you see a numerical summary for each one. You can select a single column and summarize it by using the `$` syntax or include the `with()` command to allow R to read the columns inside the data frame:

```
> mean(mf$Speed)
[1] 15.8
> with(mf, median(Algae))
[1] 65
```

You can summarize all the columns at once using the `colMeans()` command or apply any summary function using the `apply()` command:

```
> colMeans(mf)
 Length   Speed   Algae      NO3     BOD
 19.640  15.800  58.400    2.046 145.960
> apply(mf, 2, sd)
   Length      Speed      Algae        NO3        BOD
 3.080584   4.681524 19.457218   0.504546  44.954125
```

Exercise 2 Solution

The `bfs` object is a data frame. You can determine this by using the `str()` or `class()` commands. These data comprise only two columns: a response variable (`count`) and a predictor variable (`site`). The basic `table()` command produces a contingency table:

```
> table(bfs)
      site
count Arable Grass Heath
   3       1     2     0
   4       0     3     0
   5       0     2     0
   6       0     1     1
   7       0     1     1
   8       2     1     2
   9       2     0     1
   11      2     0     2
   12      1     1     1
   19      1     0     0
   21      0     1     0
```

You can produce an identical table by specifying the columns explicitly:

```
> with(bfs, table(count, site))
```

The `ftable()` command can also produce the same result like so:

```
> ftable(bfs)
> ftable(site ~ count, data = bfs)
```

Either command produces the same result. The table can be produced in a different configuration by specifying the columns in a different order:

```
> with(bfs, table(site, count))
        count
site     3 4 5 6 7 8 9 11 12 19 21
  Arable 1 0 0 0 0 2 2  2  1  1  0
  Grass  2 3 2 1 1 1 0  0  1  0  1
  Heath  0 0 0 1 1 2 1  2  1  0  0
```

The `ftable()` command can also produce this result:

```
> ftable(count ~ site, data = bfs)
```

The difference between the two commands is that the result of the `table()` command has a class of "table", whereas the `ftable()` command produces a result with class of "ftable".

Exercise 3 Solution

The invert object is a simple data frame. To create a cross-tabulated contingency table you need to use the xtabs() command like so:

```
> invert.tab = xtabs(Qty ~ Taxa + Habitat, data = invert)
> invert.tab
        Habitat
Taxa      Upper Lower Stem
  Aphid     230   175  321
  Bug        34    31   35
  Beetle     72    23  101
  Spider     11     3    5
  Ant        12     9   15
```

The resulting object holds two classes, as you can see when using the class() command:

```
> class(invert.tab)
[1] "xtabs" "table"
```

To reconstruct the original data you need to use the as.data.frame() command. Because the object holds a table class this will work adequately:

```
> as.data.frame(invert.tab)
     Taxa Habitat Freq
1   Aphid   Upper  230
2     Bug   Upper   34
3  Beetle   Upper   72
4  Spider   Upper   11
5     Ant   Upper   12
6   Aphid   Lower  175
7     Bug   Lower   31
8  Beetle   Lower   23
9  Spider   Lower    3
10    Ant   Lower    9
11  Aphid    Stem  321
12    Bug    Stem   35
13 Beetle    Stem  101
14 Spider    Stem    5
15    Ant    Stem   15
```

CHAPTER 5

Exercise 1 Solution

The predictor column of the orchis data frame is comprised of three different sites (that is, levels), as you can see if you use the summary() command. To produce a histogram of the data for just the sprayed site, you need to extract the data from the main data frame. One way to do this is to use the $ syntax:

```
> orchis$flower[which(orchis$site=='sprayed')]
 [1] 1 2 5 4 7 6 4 3 4 5
```

The histogram can be drawn using these data but you need to remember to set `freq = FALSE` so that the y-axis displays the density:

```
> hist(orchis$flower[which(orchis$site=='sprayed')], freq = FALSE)
```

Now the x-axis is set to density you can use the `lines()` command to add the density plot over the existing histogram. The `density()` command itself will calculate where the lines will be plotted and the `lines()` command actually draws them. You can alter the appearance of the density line; in this case the line is drawn slightly wider than standard using the `lwd = 2` instruction:

```
> lines(density(orchis$flower[which(orchis$site=='sprayed')]), lwd = 2)
```

You might also have used the `unstack()` command to create the data; in this case the third column represents the `sprayed` sample. The following commands would all have created the same result, a new vector of numeric values:

```
> sprayed = unstack(orchis)[,3]
> sprayed = unstack(orchis)[,'sprayed']
```

You could then have used the `hist()` and `density()` commands on the new vector.

Exercise 2 Solution

The Wilcoxon statistic is examined via the `pwilcox()`, `dwilcox()`, `rwilcox()`, and `qwilcox()` commands. You might have to examine the help files to find out more. The following help commands would get you to the right place:

```
help(Distributions)
help(dwilcox)
help(Wilcoxon)
```

To obtain a critical value you need to use the `qwilcox()` command. The first instruction should be the level of significance (as a probability) and this needs to be halved, because the test is two-tailed. The command also requires the number of replicates in the two samples:

```
> qwilcox(c(0.975, 0.995), 8, 8)
[1] 50 56
```

You now know that if you get a value of 50 or greater the result would be significant at $p < 0.05$. If you obtained a value of 56 or greater, then $p < 0.01$.

Assuming your result of 77 represents the larger of the two calculated U values, you can determine the significance using the `pwilcox()` command like so:

```
> 2*(1-pwilcox(77, 10, 10))
[1] 0.03546299
```

The test is two-tailed so the result must be multiplied by two. You can also use the "other end" of the distribution in the command to avoid having to use the `1-` part:

```
> pwilcox(77, 10, 10, lower.tail = FALSE)*2
[1] 0.03546299
```

CHAPTER 6

Exercise 1 Solution

You can view the InsectSprays data by simply typing its name. It will not appear if you use ls(), although you can make the item visible using data(InsectSprays). Start with a summary() command to see what you are dealing with:

```
> summary(InsectSprays)
     count           spray
 Min.   : 0.00   A:12
 1st Qu.: 3.00   B:12
 Median : 7.00   C:12
 Mean   : 9.50   D:12
 3rd Qu.:14.25   E:12
 Max.   :26.00   F:12
```

To run a t-test you will need to use the subset instruction to select the A and B samples from the spray variable.

```
> t.test(count ~ spray, data = InsectSprays, subset = spray %in% c('A', 'B'))

       Welch Two Sample t-test

data:  count by spray
t = -0.4535, df = 21.784, p-value = 0.6547
alternative hypothesis: true difference in means is not equal to 0
95 percent confidence interval:
 -4.646182  2.979515
sample estimates:
mean in group A mean in group B
       14.50000        15.33333
```

Exercise 2 Solution

The data frame contains two separate samples, therefore you must use the vector syntax; a formula is not appropriate. You can use the attach() command to allow the individual vectors to be "read" from the data frame, or the with() command to achieve the same result. The wilcox.test() command can be used like so:

```
> with(hogl, wilcox.test(fast, slow))

       Wilcoxon rank sum test with continuity correction

data:  fast and slow
W = 12.5, p-value = 0.02651
alternative hypothesis: true location shift is not equal to 0

Warning message:
In wilcox.test.default(fast, slow) : cannot compute exact p-value with ties
```

The $ syntax can also be used to pick out the separate vectors. Because there are tied ranks you might turn off the attempt to use an exact p-value:

```
> wilcox.test(hogl$fast, hogl$slow, exact = FALSE)

        Wilcoxon rank sum test with continuity correction

data:  hogl$fast and hogl$slow
W = 12.5, p-value = 0.02651
alternative hypothesis: true location shift is not equal to 0
```

Now you do not see the warning message.

Exercise 3 Solution

The `sleep` data can be examined simply by typing its name. Because the variables are inside a data frame, the `with()` command is useful to allow R to "read" them. Because you have a grouping variable (called `group`) you need to split the data into two parts. You can do this using a conditional statement and the t-test can be run like so:

```
> with(sleep, t.test(extra[group==1], extra[group==2], paired = TRUE))

        Paired t-test

data:  extra[group == 1] and extra[group == 2]
t = -4.0621, df = 9, p-value = 0.002833
alternative hypothesis: true difference in means is not equal to 0
95 percent confidence interval:
 -2.4598858 -0.7001142
sample estimates:
mean of the differences
                  -1.58
```

The `[group==1]` part extracts the data relating to group 1. A more long-winded way would be to `unstack()` the data into a new form and then run the test:

```
> sleep2 = unstack(sleep, form = extra ~ group)
> names(sleep2) = c('Grp1', 'Grp2')
> t.test(sleep2$Grp1, sleep2$Grp2, paired = T)
```

Exercise 4 Solution

You can view the `mtcars` data simply by typing its name. A complete correlation matrix can be created by using the `cor()` command and giving the data name in the parentheses:

```
cor(mtcars)
```

To narrow the focus you can type the name of a single variable in addition to the overall data. This is analogous to `cor(x, y)`. For the `mpg` variable you would type:

```
cor(mtcars$mpg, mtcars)
```

Note that you need the `$` so that the variable can be "read." To conduct a correlation test you can use either the vector or the formula syntax. The `$` sign can be used like so:

```
> cor.test(mtcars$mpg, mtcars$qsec)

       Pearson's product-moment correlation

data:  mtcars$mpg and mtcars$qsec
t = 2.5252, df = 30, p-value = 0.01708
alternative hypothesis: true correlation is not equal to 0
95 percent confidence interval:
 0.08195487 0.66961864
sample estimates:
     cor
0.418684
```

The formula syntax can also be used and gives the same result:

```
> cor.test(~ mpg + qsec, data = mtcars)
```

Exercise 5 Solution

You can use the `chisq.test()` command to carry out a goodness-of-fit test. In this case you need to use the `visit` column as the main data and the `ratio` variable as the data to form the foundation for the test:

```
> chisq.test(bv$visit, p = bv$ratio, rescale = TRUE)

       Chi-squared test for given probabilities

data:  bv$visit
X-squared = 191.9482, df = 7, p-value < 2.2e-16
```

You might also have considered using the Kolmogorov-Smirnov test that you met in the previous chapter:

```
> ks.test(bv$visit, bv$ratio)
```

CHAPTER 7

Exercise 1 Solution

The simplest way to create the box-whisker plot is to use the formula syntax to state how the graph should be constructed. You can use the `range = 0` instruction to force the whiskers to extend to the max and min. The `horizontal = TRUE` instruction forces the plot to be displayed horizontally. To select a single wool type you need to use the `subset` instruction that you met earlier. The full command is shown here:

```
> boxplot(breaks ~ tension, data = warpbreaks, horizontal = TRUE,
range = 0, subset = wool %in% 'A', col = 'cornsilk')
> title(xlab = 'Number of breaks', ylab = 'Tension', main = 'Wool type "A"')
```

The `title()` command has been used to add titles to the plot, but you could have specified the text as part of the main `boxplot()` command.

Exercise 2 Solution

The `plot()` command is best used in this case. The formula notation is the simplest way to specify the data to plot. The axes are scaled to fit the points into the plot area, and this will not show the origin of the graph. The line of best-fit will not cross the y-axis unless you modify the scales of the axes. The following command shows how to rescale and draw the axes to show the line to its best advantage. You may have to experiment to get the best values. The `xaxs = 'i'` and `yaxs = 'i'` instructions have been used to remove extra space at the ends of the axes.

```
> plot(Girth ~ Volume, trees, ylim = c(5, 20), xlim = c(0,70), pch = 17,
col = 'darkgreen', xaxs = 'i', yaxs = 'i', cex = 1.5,
xlab = 'Volume (cubic ft.)', ylab = 'Girth (inches)')
> abline(lm(Girth ~ Volume, trees), lty = 2, lwd = 2, col = 'green')
```

The `abline()` command is used to add a trend line using the `lm()` command to determine slope and intercept from a linear model.

Exercise 3 Solution

These data are in a 3D table, so you need the `table[row, col, group]` syntax to get the parts you require. The dot chart is produced using the following command lines:

```
> dotchart(HairEyeColor[,,1], gdata = colMeans(HairEyeColor[,,1]),
gpch = 16, gcolor = 'blue')
> title(xlab = 'Number of individuals', main = 'Males Hair and Eye color')
> mtext('Grouping = mean', side =3, adj = 1)
```

You get the main table using `HairEyeColor[,,1]`, which selects all rows and columns of the first group (`male`). To get the column means you use the `colMeans()` command on the same data. The other instructions set the plotting character and color for the group results. The `mtext()` command is optional because you could have given this information in a caption. In this case, the reader is informed that the mean is the grouping summary used, and the title is placed at the top (`side = 3`) and right justified (`adj = 1`).

Exercise 4 Solution

The table is a 3D table with rows, columns, and a grouping (`male`, `female`). The following command makes a grouped bar chart with appropriate colors for the bars:

```
> barplot(HairEyeColor[,,2], legend =TRUE, col = c('black', 'tan',
'tomato','cornsilk'), beside = TRUE)
> title(xlab = 'Hair Color', ylab = 'Frequency')
```

The main command uses `[, , 2]` to select all rows and all columns from the second group (`female`), which is the part that contains the data required.

You could have specified the colors as a separate object and simply referred to them. The colors are specified in row order; look at the data to see the colors required. You have to use the `colors()` command to determine what colors are available; some experimentation might be required to get the best colors from those at your disposal.

Exercise 5 Solution

To get the summary data you need to use the `tapply()` command. The bar chart is then simply drawn using the `barplot()` command like so:

```
> barplot(tapply(bfs$count, bfs$site, FUN = median))
> abline(h=0)
> title(xlab = 'Habitat', ylab = 'Butterfly abundance')
```

The `$` syntax is used in the preceding code, but you can also use the `with()` command to achieve the same result. Alternatively, you might create a new data object to hold the result of the `tapply()` command and then create the bar chart from that:

```
> with(bfs, barplot(tapply(count, site, FUN = median)))
```

In any event, the final commands draw a line under the bars to "ground" them and add some axis labels.

CHAPTER 8

Exercise 1 Solution

The formula syntax enables you to specify complex models. You do not need to use the `attach()` or `with()` commands or use the `$` syntax because the `data =` instruction points to the data. In addition, it is easy to create graphs because you can copy the majority of the command for the graph from the command used for the analysis.

Exercise 2 Solution

The `chick` data comprises six columns, and `NA` items need to be removed. The first stage is to stack the data into two columns with a response variable and a predictor variable (make this into a new object). These columns will need sensible names.

```
> chicks = na.omit(stack(chick))
> names(chicks) = c("weight", "feed")
```

The ANOVA is carried out using the `aov()` command fairly simply:

```
> chicks.aov = aov(weight ~ feed, data = chicks)
> summary(chicks.aov)
```

The result is highly significant; feed does have an effect on the weights of the chicks.

Exercise 3 Solution

The first step is to draw a boxplot of the data. It is fairly easy to use the up arrow to recall the `aov()` command and edit it to make the graphic.

```
> boxplot(weight ~ feed, data = chicks)
```

It looks like there are differences in feeds, but a post-hoc test will show you the significance of the pairwise comparisons:

```
> TukeyHSD(chicks.aov)
> TukeyHSD(chicks.aov, ordered = TRUE)
```

The first command is perhaps easier to compare to the boxplot, but the second version will be more useful when you plot the differences in means:

```
> plot(TukeyHSD(chicks.aov, ordered = TRUE))
```

You can see where the significant differences lie, but the labels do not fit very well, so you need to modify the margins of the plot and redraw it with different settings:

```
> oldpar = par(mar = c(5,8,4,2)+0.1)
> plot(TukeyHSD(chicks.aov, ordered = TRUE), las = 1, cex.axis = 0.85)
> abline(v = 0, lty = 3, col = 'gray50')
> par(oldpar)
```

The first command alters the margins (the second value relates to the left margin), making more room for the labels on the left. The previous `plot()` command can be edited to rotate the labels (`las = 1`) and make the axis labels smaller (`cex.axis = 0.85`). Your computer may have different graphics settings, so you may require slightly different values than these. The `abline()` command draws a vertical line, which shows where the significant differences lie (any bars that do not cross this line are significant). The final command resets the margins back to the previous settings.

Exercise 4 Solution

To begin with you should look at the data itself and see what you are dealing with. The `summary()` and `str()` commands are useful and using the `names()` command helps to remind you of the column headings. You might have used the `tapply()` command to check for a balanced design like so:

```
> tapply(bats$count, list(bats$spp, bats$method), FUN = length)
```

Because you have two predictor variables, a two-way ANOVA is indicated. This can be carried out using the `aov()` command:

```
> bats.aov = aov(count ~ spp * method, data = bats)
> summary(bats.aov)
```

Neither main effect is significant, but there is a highly significant interaction term.

Exercise 5 Solution

The interaction is highly significant. A good first step is to draw a boxplot of the data. The `aov()` command can be recalled and edited to save some typing:

```
> boxplot(count ~ spp * method, data = bats, cex.axis = 0.8, las = 1)
```

The axis labels need to be made smaller to fit using the `cex.axis = 0.8` instruction. The `las = 1` instruction makes all labels horizontal.

The TukeyHSD() command will run the post-hoc test. The basic command is useful to compare to the boxplot, but reordering the factors is more helpful when plotting the pairwise comparisons:

```
> TukeyHSD(bats.aov)
> TukeyHSD(bats.aov, ordered = TRUE)
```

If you try plotting the post-hoc result, you will see that the labels do not fit, so you will need to modify the margins to make room:

```
> oldpar = par(mar = c(5,8,4,2)+0.1)
> plot(TukeyHSD(bats.aov, ordered = TRUE), las = 1, cex.axis = 0.75)
> abline(v = 0, lty = 3, col = 'gray50')
> par(oldpar)
```

The las = 1 instruction forces axis labels to be horizontal and the cex.axis = 0.75 instruction makes the labels smaller. You may need slightly different values to get the best fit.

To create an interaction plot you will need to use the interaction.plot() command. You can make a simple plot tracing the method or the species like so:

```
> with(bats, interaction.plot(spp, method, count))
> with(bats, interaction.plot(method, spp, count))
```

Note that you need to use the with() command here unless you use attach() first (remember to use detach() afterwards). Alternatively, you can use the $ syntax instead. Which one you use is up to you. The first plot shows two lines, one for each method; the second plot shows three lines, one for each species. The plot can be jazzed up and made more "interesting" with a few additional instructions:

```
> with(bats, interaction.plot(spp, method, count, type = 'b', pch = 1:3,
col = 1:3))
```

Note that three colors and plotting symbols were used even though there are only two lines. The third is ignored. You could edit this and switch the spp and method variables to trace the species.

CHAPTER 9

Exercise 1 Solution

First look at the data:

```
> bees
                Buff.tail Garden.bee Red.tail Honey.bee Carder.bee
Thistle                10          8       18        12          8
Vipers.bugloss          1          3        9        13         27
Golden.rain            37         19        1        16          6
Yellow.alfalfa          5          6        2         9         32
Blackberry             12          4        4        10         23
```

Treat the Thistle and Vipers.bugloss rows as being the same color and the others as another color. You can make a simple character variable like so:

```
> flcol = c(rep('blue',2), rep('yellow', 3))
```

This is not a factor as is. You can still use it as a grouping variable, but to force it to be a factor you need to re-do the command or convert the result. Either of the following will do:

```
> flcol = as.factor(flcol)
> flcol = factor(c(rep('blue',2), rep('yellow', 3)))
```

A third way you can achieve the result is to use the factor command with a vector and set the levels like so:

```
> flcol = factor(c(1,1,2,2,2), labels = c('blue', 'yellow'))
```

Exercise 2 Solution

A matrix can contain data only of a single type, either numeric or character. If you need to add something to an existing matrix, the data type must match. Here you have a numeric matrix and a factor (as a vector). The simplest way to achieve the result is to convert the `flcol` factor variable into a numeric vector; then it can be added to the matrix. You can do this with separate commands or in one go:

```
> bees2 = cbind(bees, flcolor = as.numeric(flcol))
```

In this case the `flcolor` object is created as a temporary object from the original factor variable. The `cbind()` command adds this to the original matrix.

It is useful to add the new data as a named object, because then the column will take on the name of the data. This saves you having to use the `colnames()` command afterward.

Exercise 3 Solution

Because the `bees` object is a matrix, you need to specify the column using square brackets. You can obtain a mean for the grouping variable using either of the following commands:

```
> tapply(bees[,1], flcol, FUN = mean)
> tapply(bees[,'Buff.tail'], flcol, FUN = mean)
  blue yellow
   5.5   18.0
```

If you specify all the columns, you can get a summary for all the bee species. You can name the columns explicitly or simply omit the square brackets entirely (thus specifying the entire data):

```
> tapply(bees[1:5], flcol, FUN = mean)
> tapply(bees, flcol, FUN = mean)
$blue
 Buff.tail Garden.bee   Red.tail  Honey.bee Carder.bee
       5.5        5.5       13.5       12.5       17.5

$yellow
 Buff.tail Garden.bee   Red.tail  Honey.bee Carder.bee
 18.000000   9.666667   2.333333  11.666667  20.333333
```

Notice that the result is split into two parts, one for each level of the grouping variable. The result is, in fact, an array, but it has only one dimension! You can extract the elements using the dollar sign and square brackets appropriately:

```
> bee.sum$blue
 Buff.tail Garden.bee   Red.tail  Honey.bee Carder.bee
```

```
      5.5        5.5       13.5       12.5       17.5
> bee.sum[2]
$yellow
 Buff.tail Garden.bee   Red.tail  Honey.bee Carder.bee
 18.000000   9.666667   2.333333  11.666667  20.333333

> bee.sum$blue[1]
Buff.tail
      5.5
```

Exercise 4 Solution

The `ChickWeight` data are built in to R and you can access them simply by typing the name. You can see what data are available by using the `data()` command:

```
> data()
```

The `weight` variable can be summarized by `Diet` using the `tapply()` or `aggregate()` commands:

```
> tapply(ChickWeight$weight, ChickWeight$Diet, FUN = median)
> with(ChickWeight, tapply(weight, Diet, median))
    1     2     3     4
 88.0 104.5 125.5 129.5

> aggregate(ChickWeight$weight, by = list(ChickWeight$Diet), FUN = median)
> aggregate(weight ~ Diet, data = ChickWeight, FUN = median)
  Diet weight
1    1   88.0
2    2  104.5
3    3  125.5
4    4  129.5
```

Notice that you get a slightly different output as the result, although the values are the same. If you add a second grouping variable, you have similar options:

```
> tapply(ChickWeight$weight, list(ChickWeight$Diet, ChickWeight$Time), median)
     0    2    4    6   8    10    12    14    16    18    20    21
1 41.0 49.0 56.0 67.0  79  93.0 106.0 120.5 149.0 160.0 160.0 166.0
2 40.5 48.5 59.0 74.0  90 104.5 130.5 141.0 157.0 184.0 198.5 212.5
3 41.0 49.5 62.5 77.5  98 113.5 141.0 160.0 195.0 229.5 265.0 281.0
4 41.0 51.5 64.5 84.0 103 123.5 153.0 161.5 179.5 200.5 231.0 237.0

> aggregate(ChickWeight$weight, by = list(ChickWeight$Diet,
ChickWeight$Time), FUN = median)

> aggregate(weight ~ Diet + Time, data = ChickWeight, FUN = median)
   Diet Time weight
1     1    0   41.0
2     2    0   40.5
3     3    0   41.0
4     4    0   41.0
5     1    2   49.0
6     2    2   48.5
7     3    2   49.5
8     4    2   51.5
9     1    4   56.0
```

```
10    2    4   59.0
11    3    4   62.5
12    4    4   64.5
...
```

The `aggregate()` command produces a longer output (the display has been shortened in this example), but the values are the same.

The order in which you specify the grouping variables will affect the order of the result, but the values remain the same.

Exercise 5 Solution

The data are built into R and you can access them simply by typing the name `mtcars`. You can see all the available data by using the `data()` command like so:

```
> data()
```

You can gain further information by looking at the help for the data item:

```
> help(mtcars)
```

The best way to create a summary here is to use the `aggregate()` command. Because you will be using three grouping variables, the output will be more easily dealt with:

```
> aggregate(mpg ~ cyl + gear + carb, data = mtcars, FUN = mean)
   cyl gear carb   mpg
1    4    3    1 21.50
2    6    3    1 19.75
3    4    4    1 29.10
4    8    3    2 17.15
5    4    4    2 24.75
6    4    5    2 28.20
7    8    3    3 16.30
8    8    3    4 12.62
9    6    4    4 19.75
10   8    5    4 15.80
11   6    5    6 19.70
12   8    5    8 15.00
```

Here the formula syntax is used, which makes a nicer display and is easier to type than the alternative:

```
> with(mtcars, aggregate(mpg, by = list(cyl, gear, carb), FUN = mean))
```

The `tapply()` command is less useful here because the results are not so comprehensible and come out as an array object:

```
> tapply(mtcars$mpg, list(mtcars$cyl, mtcars$gear, mtcars$carb), FUN = mean)
, , 1

      3    4  5
4 21.50 29.1 NA
6 19.75   NA NA
8    NA   NA NA
```

```
, , 2

      3     4    5
4    NA 24.75 28.2
6    NA    NA   NA
8 17.15    NA   NA
...
```

Notice, too, that you get `NA` items where the combination of grouping variables does not contain a result.

CHAPTER 10

Exercise 1 Solution

Creating the three models involves using the `lm()` command and specifying the predictor variables as appropriate. Give each model a name like so:

```
> mtcars.lm1 = lm(mpg ~ wt, data = mtcars)
> mtcars.lm2 = lm(mpg ~ cyl, data = mtcars)
> mtcars.lm3 = lm(mpg ~ wt + cyl, data = mtcars)
```

You can compare models using the `anova()` command by specifying the models to compare:

```
> anova(mtcars.lm1, mtcars.lm2, mtcars.lm3)
Analysis of Variance Table

Model 1: mpg ~ wt
Model 2: mpg ~ cyl
Model 3: mpg ~ wt + cyl
  Res.Df    RSS Df Sum of Sq      F   Pr(>F)
1     30 278.32
2     30 308.33  0   -30.012
3     29 191.17  1   117.162 17.773 0.000222 ***
---
Signif. codes:  0 '***' 0.001 '**' 0.01 '*' 0.05 '.' 0.1 ' ' 1
```

If you specify the models in a different order, you get results in a different order, but the conclusions are the same. There is no appreciable difference between the single-response models, but adding the second response variable does make a significant difference.

Exercise 2 Solution

The regression is determined easily enough and you have already created a model for this, like so:

```
> mtcars.lm1 = lm(mpg ~ wt, data = mtcars)
```

Draw the relationship using the `plot()` command. You can add the line of best-fit using the `abline()` command and taking the instructions from the linear model like so:

```
> plot(mpg ~ wt, data = mtcars)
> abline(mtcars.lm1)
```

Here, the axis titles are kept to their defaults and the line of best-fit is also kept at its default, but you could use standard instructions to alter the appearance. To get the values for the confidence intervals, you need to use the `predict()` command. Here you want 99-percent confidence intervals so you have to specify the level explicitly (the default is 0.95, that is, 95 percent). Once you have the fitted values and their confidence intervals as a result object, you must convert it to a data frame and add the predictor variable. Then you sort the data in order of the predictor variable:

```
> prd = predict(mtcars.lm1, interval = 'confidence', level = 0.99)
> prd = as.data.frame(prd)
> prd$wt = mtcars$wt
> prd = prd[order(prd$wt),]
```

The final task is to add the confidence interval bands. The `lines()` command will do this, and the `spline()` command will make the lines smooth:

```
> lines(spline(prd$wt, prd$upr))
> lines(spline(prd$wt, prd$lwr))
```

The lines here are kept to their defaults, but you could make them appear differently using some simple instructions (for example, `lty`, `lwd`, and `col`).

Exercise 3 Solution

The starting point for a backward deletion model is all the terms. You can do this by using a period in the model formula like so:

```
> mtcars.lm = lm(mpg ~ ., data = mtcars)
```

Now you need to use the `drop1()` command to examine the terms of the regression model and decide which can be dropped. The first time you run the command you see a result that looks like this:

```
> drop1(mtcars.lm, mtcars.lm, test = 'F')
Single term deletions

Model:
mpg ~ cyl + disp + hp + drat + wt + qsec + vs + am + gear + carb
       Df Sum of Sq    RSS    AIC F value   Pr(F)
<none>              147.49 70.898
cyl     1    0.0799 147.57 68.915  0.0114 0.91609
disp    1    3.9167 151.41 69.736  0.5576 0.46349
hp      1    6.8399 154.33 70.348  0.9739 0.33496
drat    1    1.6270 149.12 69.249  0.2317 0.63528
wt      1   27.0144 174.51 74.280  3.8463 0.06325 .
qsec    1    8.8641 156.36 70.765  1.2621 0.27394
vs      1    0.1601 147.66 68.932  0.0228 0.88142
am      1   10.5467 158.04 71.108  1.5016 0.23399
gear    1    1.3531 148.85 69.190  0.1926 0.66521
carb    1    0.4067 147.90 68.986  0.0579 0.81218
```

You need to select the term (that is, predictor variable) with the lowest `AIC` value; it will also have the smallest F-value (and largest p-value). In this first run you can see that the `cyl` variable meets these criteria (even though it was previously in your model), and therefore you must remove the term from the model. The simplest way to do this is to copy the formula from the `drop1()` result and paste it into the previous `lm()` command (use the up arrow to recall it). You can then edit out the `cyl` term.

You repeat the process, selecting the predictor with the lowest `AIC` value each time and removing it from the model. Eventually you will get to a point where all the remaining terms are statistically significant.

```
> mtcars.lm = lm(mpg ~ wt + qsec + am, data = mtcars)
Single term deletions

Model:
mpg ~ wt + qsec + am
       Df Sum of Sq    RSS    AIC F value      Pr(F)
<none>              169.29 61.307
wt      1   183.347 352.63 82.790 30.3258 6.953e-06 ***
qsec    1   109.034 278.32 75.217 18.0343 0.0002162 ***
am      1    26.178 195.46 63.908  4.3298 0.0467155 *
```

This is the point where you stop. You have now whittled away the non-significant terms.

Exercise 4 Solution

To compare the forward and backward models you need to make sure you know what they are called. Here are the model definitions:

```
> mtcars.lm3 = lm(mpg ~ wt + cyl, data = mtcars)
> mtcars.lm4 = lm(mpg ~ wt + qsec + am, data = mtcars)
```

The first one is the forward model and the second is the backward model. To compare them you need the `anova()` command once again:

```
> anova(mtcars.lm3, mtcars.lm4, test = 'F')
Analysis of Variance Table

Model 1: mpg ~ wt + cyl
Model 2: mpg ~ wt + qsec + am
  Res.Df    RSS Df Sum of Sq    F  Pr(>F)
1     29 191.17
2     28 169.29  1    21.886 3.62 0.06742 .
---
Signif. codes:  0 '***' 0.001 '**' 0.01 '*' 0.05 '.' 0.1 ' ' 1
```

You can see that there is little to choose between them and the difference is not statistically significant. If you use the `summary()` command on each model you will see that the variance explained by both models is similar (that is, the Adjusted R Squared values are similar).

Exercise 5 Solution

The regression model with the fewest terms in it should be the "best" model to select. You generally aim to produce regression models that are as simple as possible.

```
> mtcars.lm3 = lm(mpg ~ wt + cyl, data = mtcars)
```

You are going to end up with a scatter plot that shows the response variable against the fitted values. You need to start by making a result object containing the fitted values and confidence intervals; the `predict()` command will do this:

```
> predict(mtcars.lm3, interval = 'confidence')
```

Now you need to make the data into a data frame, add the response data, and reorder the values in ascending order (of fitted value):

```
> prd = as.data.frame(prd)
> prd$mpg = mtcars$mpg
> prd = prd[order(prd$fit),]
```

Now you have all the data you need to make the plot and add the lines of best-fit and confidence intervals:

```
> plot(mpg ~ fit, data = prd)
> abline(lm(mpg ~ fit, data = prd))
> lines(prd$fit, prd$upr)
> lines(prd$fit, prd$lwr)
```

Here the commands are using all the default settings, but you could add customized axis titles and make the added lines appear differently by using some of the instructions you saw earlier (for example, `lwd`, `col`, and `lty`). Note that the confidence intervals are not completely smooth!

CHAPTER 11

Exercise 1 Solution

Because the data contain `NA` items, you need to take them into account using the `na.rm` instruction. Here you must use the `apply()` command to get the mean values. The `length()` command does not use `na.rm`, so you need to find a different way to get the number of replicates in each sample. The `round()` command is used in conjunction with `max()` to work out the size of the y-axis:

```
> hogl.m = apply(hogl, 2, FUN = mean, na.rm = T)
> hogl.s = apply(hogl, 2, FUN = sum, na.rm = T)
> hogl.sd = apply(hogl, 2, FUN = sd, na.rm = T)
> hogl.l = hogl.s / hogl.m
> hogl.se = hogl.sd / sqrt(hogl.l)
> hogl.y = round(max(hogl.m + hogl.se) + 0.5, 0)
```

To make a graphics window of a fixed size, you use the `windows()` command (on a Mac use `quartz()` and on Linux use `X11()` instead). The bar chart itself is given a name so that you can use it as coordinates for the `arrows()`:

```
> windows(width = 4, height = 7)
> bp = barplot(hogl.m, ylim = c(0, hogl.y))
> arrows(bp, hogl.m + hogl.se, bp, hogl.m - hogl.se, length = 0.1,
angle = 90, code = 3)
```

The `arrows()` command is used to make the error bars; here the line style, width, and color are kept as standard but you might like to experiment!

Exercise 2 Solution

The data are in a data frame and must be a matrix to be dealt with by the `barplot()` command. You could convert the data into a matrix, but it is just as easy here to do it as part of the `barplot()`

command. The legend can be produced easily here as part of the command, rather than separately. The colors of the plot (and also legend) are set using the `col` instruction; the `palette()` command sets up nine rainbow colors:

```
> barplot(as.matrix(hoglouse), beside = TRUE, legend = TRUE,
col = palette(rainbow(9)),
args.legend = list(x = 'topleft', bty = 'n'))
```

The colors are rather lurid; experiment with some others (see the help entry for *palette*). You can also add axis titles with the `title()` command.

Exercise 3 Solution

This could take some experimentation on your system. The illustration here is based on a 7 inch default graphic size. Start by making the plot and see how much extra room you need. The `hoglouse` data are a data frame, so you need to make them into a matrix. However, you are required to differentiate between the *fast* and the *slow*. This means that you have to transpose the data. The result of `t(hoglouse)` will be a matrix, so you can simply plot that.

Once you have estimated how much to alter the margin, you can use the `par()` command and the `mar` instruction to alter the values; note that you have to specify all the margins (the defaults are `c(5, 4, 4, 2) + 0.1`). Now you can issue the `barplot()` command again. You will need to specify the colors explicitly so that you can match them in the separate `legend()` command:

```
> oldpar = par(mar = c(5,5,4,2) + 0.1)
> barplot(t(hoglouse), horiz = TRUE, las = 1, cex.name = 1, legend = FALSE,
col = c('gray30', 'gray80'))
```

The legend can be placed with a call to the `locator()` command. The colors are set to match the previous command. Using your mouse, click the top-left corner of the legend. The final commands simply add a neat line to "ground" the bars and to reset the margins:

```
> legend(locator(1), legend = c('Fast', 'Slow'), bty = 'n',
fill = c('gray30', 'gray80'))
> abline(v=0)
> par(oldpar)
```

You might also want to add axis titles.

Exercise 4 Solution

You have two ways to tackle this. You could create a separate matrix for the `Length` variable and another to hold the two series (that is, `Speed` and `Algae`), or you could create these matrix data "on the fly." Here you see the former approach, which is easier to follow. The `x` and `y` data are prepared first from the original data frame. Now the `matplot()` command is used to draw the series using two explicit plotting characters and named colors. This is so that you can match them in the legend. Note that the `expression()` command is used to make the subscript. Finally, the legend is added using the same plotting characters and colors as the original plot:

```
> mf.x = as.matrix(mf[,2:3])
> mf.y = as.matrix(mf[,1])
> matplot(mf.x, mf.y, type = 'p', pch = 16:17, col = c('black', 'darkgreen'),
ylab = expression(Length[mm]), xlab = 'Speed/Algae', las = 1)
```

```
> legend(x = 'bottomright', legend = c('Speed', 'Algae'),
col = c('black', 'darkgreen'), pch = 16:17, bty = 'n')
```

You might also have used a basic `plot()` command to draw one series and then added the other using the `points()` command.

CHAPTER 12

Exercise 1 Solution

You can use a simple one-line `function()` command to do this:

```
> pwr = function(x, power = 2) (x^power)
```

Now if you run the new `pwr()` command and do not specify the `power =` instruction, the value of 2 will be the default (that is, the square).

Exercise 2 Solution

You have two ways to save the simple customized function to disk:

```
> dump('pwr', file = 'power function dump.R')
> save(pwr, file = 'power function save.R')
```

If you use the `dump()` command the file is written as text, which you can edit in a text editor and load once more using the `source()` command.

If you use the `save()` command, the file is written as binary data, which you cannot edit in a text editor. You can reload this file using the `load()` command.

In either case, the filename must be in quotes, and is written to the working directory unless you specify otherwise.

Exercise 3 Solution

To incorporate some annotations (using the # symbol) you will need multiple lines. This means you need curly brackets. You could type the following lines directly into R or write them with a text editor:

```
pwr = function(x, power = 2) {

    #     x = a number of some kind
    # power = the power to raise x by, defaults to 2

  (x^power)
 }
```

Exercise 4 Solution

You will need the `readline()` command to prompt the user to enter a value:

```
pwr = function(x, power) {

      #     x = a number of some kind
      # power = user will input a value to raise x by

  power = readline(prompt = 'Enter the required power: ')

   (x^as.numeric(power))
 }
```

There is no point in specifying a default here because the user will have to give the required power. Note that you must force the input to be numeric using the `as.numeric()` command.

Exercise 5 Solution

Take the values input by the user and present them as a text summary at the end. You must use the `deparse(substitute())` command(s) here:

```
pwr = function(x, power) {

      #     x = a number of some kind
      # power = user will input a value to raise x by

 power = readline(prompt = 'Enter the required power: ') # wait for user
  power = as.numeric(power) # make sure this is numeric

 result = (x^power)
  cat(deparse(substitute(x)), '^', power, '=', result)
 }
```

Note that this time you modified the `power` value that was input by the user on a separate line; this forced the input to be numeric. The previous method is perfectly acceptable; this merely illustrates an alternative.

INDEX

Symbols

A

B

D

E

F

G

H

Q

R

S

T

U

V